# THE NEW
# AMERICAN
# COMMENTARY

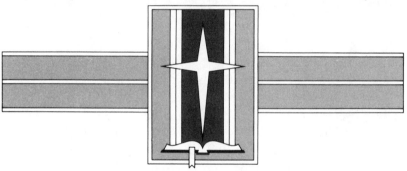

An Exegetical and Theological
Exposition of Holy Scripture

# THE NEW AMERICAN COMMENTARY

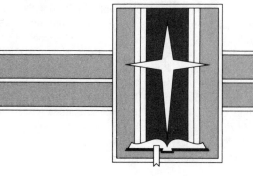

Volume
3B

## NUMBERS

R. Dennis Cole

BROADMAN
&HOLMAN
PUBLISHERS

Nashville, Tennessee

© 2000 • Broadman & Holman Publishers
All rights reserved
ISBN: 978-08054-9503-4
Dewey Decimal Classification: 227
Subject Heading: BIBLE. O.T. NUMBERS
Printed in the United States of America
15 14 13 12 11 10 09 08    10 9 8 7 6 5 4 3 2

---

*To* Ralph Alexander and Ronald Allen
Who introduced me to שִׂמְחַת תּוֹרָה

and

In Memory of John Olen Strange and Billy K. Smith

Who inspired me along this pilgrimage of awe and wonder

# Editors' Preface

God's Word does not change. God's world, however, changes in every generation. These changes, in addition to new findings by scholars and a new variety of challenges to the gospel message, call for the church in each generation to interpret and apply God's Word for God's people. Thus, THE NEW AMERICAN COMMENTARY is introduced to bridge the twentieth and twenty-first centuries. This new series has been designed primarily to enable pastors, teachers, and students to read the Bible with clarity and proclaim it with power.

In one sense THE NEW AMERICAN COMMENTARY is not new, for it represents the continuation of a heritage rich in biblical and theological exposition. The title of this forty-volume set points to the continuity of this series with an important commentary project published at the end of the nineteenth century called AN AMERICAN COMMENTARY, edited by Alvah Hovey. The older series included, among other significant contributions, the outstanding volume on Matthew by John A. Broadus, from whom the publisher of the new series, Broadman Press, partly derives its name. The former series was authored and edited by scholars committed to the infallibility of Scripture, making it a solid foundation for the present project. In line with this heritage, all NAC authors affirm the divine inspiration, inerrancy, complete truthfulness, and full authority of the Bible. The perspective of the NAC is unapologetically confessional and rooted in the evangelical tradition.

Since a commentary is a fundamental tool for the expositor or teacher who seeks to interpret and apply Scripture in the church or classroom, the NAC focuses on communicating the theological structure and content of each biblical book. The writers seek to illuminate both the historical meaning and contemporary significance of Holy Scripture.

In its attempt to make a unique contribution to the Christian community, the NAC focuses on two concerns. First, the commentary emphasizes how each section of a book fits together so that the reader becomes aware of the theological unity of each book and of Scripture as a whole. The writers, however, remain aware of the Bible's inherently rich variety. Second, the NAC is produced with the conviction that the Bible primarily belongs to the church. We believe that scholarship and the academy provide an indispensable foundation for biblical understanding and the service of Christ, but the editors and authors of this series have attempted to communicate the findings of their research in a manner that will build up the whole body of Christ. Thus, the commentary concentrates on theological exegesis while providing practical, applicable exposition.

THE NEW AMERICAN COMMENTARY's theological focus enables

the reader to see the parts as well as the whole of Scripture. The biblical books vary in content, context, literary type, and style. In addition to this rich variety, the editors and authors recognize that the doctrinal emphasis and use of the biblical books differs in various places, contexts, and cultures among God's people. These factors, as well as other concerns, have led the editors to give freedom to the writers to wrestle with the issues raised by the scholarly community surrounding each book and to determine the appropriate shape and length of the introductory materials. Moreover, each writer has developed the structure of the commentary in a way best suited for expounding the basic structure and the meaning of the biblical books for our day. Generally, discussions relating to contemporary scholarship and technical points of grammar and syntax appear in the footnotes and not in the text of the commentary. This format allows pastors and interested laypersons, scholars and teachers, and serious college and seminary students to profit from the commentary at various levels. This approach has been employed because we believe that all Christians have the privilege and responsibility to read and seek to understand the Bible for themselves.

Consistent with the desire to produce a readable, up-to-date commentary, the editors selected the *New International Version* as the standard translation for the commentary series. The selection was made primarily because of the NIV's faithfulness to the original languages and its beautiful and readable style. The authors, however, have been given the liberty to differ at places from the NIV as they develop their own translations from the Greek and Hebrew texts.

The NAC reflects the vision and leadership of those who provide oversight for Broadman Press, who in 1987 called for a new commentary series that would evidence a commitment to the inerrancy of Scripture and a faithfulness to the classic Christian tradition. While the commentary adopts an "American" name, it should be noted some writers represent countries outside the United States, giving the commentary an international perspective. The diverse group of writers includes scholars, teachers, and administrators from almost twenty different colleges and seminaries, as well as pastors, missionaries, and a layperson.

The editors and writers hope that THE NEW AMERICAN COMMENTARY will be helpful and instructive for pastors and teachers, scholars and students, for men and women in the churches who study and teach God's Word in various settings. We trust that for editors, authors, and readers alike, the commentary will be used to build up the church, encourage obedience, and bring renewal to God's people. Above all, we pray that the NAC will bring glory and honor to our Lord who has graciously redeemed us and faithfully revealed himself to us in his Holy Word.

SOLI DEO GLORIA

The Editors

# Author's Preface

Unknown to many readers and interpreters, the often-neglected Book of Numbers presents a marvelous picture of God's grace and faithfulness in relationship to his people Israel. The transitional period in the life of the nation is portrayed in such a way that highlights the eternal principles of unity of organization and purpose for the community of faith, of the richness of God's blessing upon his chosen people, of the necessity of purity and holiness in living the life of faith before God, of the need for obedience to God's Word in order to experience the fullness of his promised blessings, and of the key role of quality leadership in helping to direct the people of God to fulfill their divinely ordained purpose. On the other side of life, the Book of Numbers paints a dark picture of judgment for those who would rebel against the revealed will of God and yield to their own fears, desires, and lusts. Yes, God's grace is evident throughout the Pentateuch. This commentary is written with an aim toward helping pastors, teachers, and studious laypersons experience anew the richness of this unique book of the Bible, and that they would begin to understand the foundational vitality of the Pentateuch in the whole revelation of God in Scripture. My prayer is that the commentary conveys the wonder of the Hebrew Scriptures, and that it helps to guide men and women in their pilgrimage of faith, that their *Simchat Torah* ("Joy of the Law") would grow ever deeper.

This project could not have been completed without the prayers, pressures, encouragement, and sacrifices of a number of people. First and foremost I would like to express by deepest appreciation to my wife, Pam, for her support and patience throughout this project, and our daughters Jennifer, Jessica, and Elizabeth, who sacrificed a lot of time with Dad to allow him to complete this long process.

A special word of thanks is offered to my former Hebrew professors, Drs. Ralph Alexander and Ronald Allen, whose love for the Hebrew Bible helped inspire me to begin a lifelong journey to discover and experience the awe, wonder, and joy of the Scriptures. My interest in the Book of Numbers began with a class entitled "Theology of the Pentateuch" under Dr. Ronald Allen at Western Conservative Baptist Seminary. That passion was rekindled when David Dockery extended the invitation to me to write this commentary for Broadman & Holman just prior to my sabbatical leave from teaching responsibilities at New Orleans Baptist Theological Seminary in the Fall of 1992. At the Albright Institute of Archaeological Research, under the direction of Sy Gitin, this project began while doing research on viniculture and viticulture in the biblical world. Thanks to the expanded vision of E. Ray Clendenen and the series editors, this work was allowed to evolve into a more extensive work than originally planned. By this freedom I could focus upon the literary structure of the book and the tremendous benefits to be gained through this methodology of ferreting out the gems of meaning from the text. Ray encouraged, challenged, and prodded me toward the completion of this project, and his critical insights along with those of the other series editors helped hone my thinking in many areas. I would like to express my appreciation to Trent Butler of Broadman & Holman for his friendship, encouragement, and insights shared along this sometime arduous journey. Gratitude also goes out to Linda Scott, the Manuscript Editor, for her patience, perseverance, and exacting diligence in seeing this project through to its completion.

—Dennis Cole
New Orleans, Louisiana

# Abbreviations

## Bible Books

| | | |
|---|---|---|
| Gen | Isa | Luke |
| Exod | Jer | John |
| Lev | Lam | Acts |
| Num | Ezek | Rom |
| Deut | Dan | 1, 2 Cor |
| Josh | Hos | Gal |
| Judg | Joel | Eph |
| Ruth | Amos | Phil |
| 1, 2 Sam | Obad | Col |
| 1, 2 Kgs | Jonah | 1, 2 Thess |
| 1, 2 Chr | Mic | 1, 2 Tim |
| Ezra | Nah | Titus |
| Neh | Hab | Phlm |
| Esth | Zeph | Heb |
| Job | Hag | Jas |
| Ps (pl. Pss) | Zech | 1, 2 Pet |
| Prov | Mal | 1, 2, 3 John |
| Eccl | Matt | Jude |
| Song | Mark | Rev |

## Apocrypha

| | |
|---|---|
| *Add Esth* | *The Additions to the Book of Esther* |
| *Bar* | *Baruch* |
| *Bel* | *Bel and the Dragon* |
| *1,2 Esdr* | *1, 2 Esdras* |
| *4 Ezra* | *4 Ezra* |
| *Jdt* | *Judith* |
| *Ep Jer* | *Epistle of Jeremiah* |
| *1,2,3,4 Mac* | *1, 2, 3, 4 Maccabees* |
| *Pr Azar* | *Prayer of Azariah and the Song of the Three Jews* |
| *Pr Man* | *Prayer of Manasseh* |
| *Sir* | *Sirach, Ecclesiasticus* |
| *Sus* | *Susanna* |
| *Tob* | *Tobit* |
| *Wis* | *The Wisdom of Solomon* |

# Commonly Used Sources

| | |
|---|---|
| AASOR | Annual of the American Schools of Oriental Research |
| AB | Anchor Bible |
| *ABR* | *Australian Biblical Review* |
| *ABD* | *Anchor Bible Dictionary*, ed. D. N Freedman |
| *ABW* | *Archaeology and the Biblical World* |
| AC | An American Commentary, ed. A. Hovey |
| *AcOr* | *Acta orientalia* |
| *AEL* | M. Lichtheim, *Ancient Egyptian Literature* |
| *AHW* | W. von Soden, *Akkadisches Handwörterbuch* |
| *AJBI* | *Annual of the Japanese Biblical Institute* |
| *AJSL* | *American Journal of Semitic Languages and Literature* |
| Akk. | Akkadian |
| AnBib | Analecta Biblica |
| *ANET* | *Ancient Near Eastern Texts*, ed. J. B. Pritchard |
| *ANETS* | *Ancient Near Eastern Texts and Studies* |
| *ANEP* | *Ancient Near Eastern Pictures*, ed. J. B. Pritchard |
| *Ant.* | *Antiquities* |
| AOAT | Alter Orient und Altes Testament |
| AOS | American Oriental Society |
| *AOTS* | *Archaeology and Old Testament Study*, ed. D. W. Thomas |
| ARM | Archives royales de Mari |
| ArOr | Archiv orientální |
| AS | Assyriological Studies |
| ATD | Das Alte Testament Deutsch |
| *ATR* | *Anglican Theological Review* |
| *AusBR* | *Australian Biblical Review* |
| *AUSS* | *Andrews University Seminary Studies* |
| AV | Authorized Version |
| *BA* | *Biblical Archaeologist* |
| BAGD | W. Bauer, W. F. Arndt, F. W. Gingrich, and F. W. Danker, *Greek-English Lexicon of the New Testament* |
| BALS | Bible and Literature Series |
| *BARev* | *Biblical Archaeology Review* |
| *BASOR* | *Bulletin of the American Schools of Oriental Research* |
| *B. Bat* | *Baba Batra* |
| *BBR* | *Bulletin for Biblical Research* |
| BDB | F. Brown, S. R. Driver, and C. A. Briggs, *Hebrew and English Lexicon of the Old Testament* |
| BETL | Bibliotheca ephemeridum theologicarum lovaniensium |
| BFT | Biblical Foundations in Theology |
| *BHS* | *Biblia hebraica stuttgartensia* |
| *Bib* | *Biblica* |
| BibOr | Biblica et orientalia |
| *BibRev* | *Bible Review* |
| *BJRL* | *Bulletin of the Johns Rylands University Library* |
| BJS | Brown Judaic Studies |

| | |
|---|---|
| BKAT | Biblischer Kommentar: Altes Testament |
| *BN* | *Biblische Notizen* |
| *BO* | *Bibliotheca orientalis* |
| *BR* | *Biblical Research* |
| *BSac* | *Bibliotheca Sacra* |
| BSC | Bible Student Commentary |
| BST | Bible Speaks Today |
| *BT* | *The Bible Translator* |
| *BTB* | *Biblical Theology Bulletin* |
| *BurH* | *Buried History* |
| *BZ* | *Biblische Zeitschrift* |
| BZAW | Beihefte zur ZAW |
| *CAD* | *The Assyrian Dictionary of the Oriental Institute of the University of Chicago* |
| *CAH* | *Cambridge Ancient History* |
| CB | Century Bible |
| CBSC | Cambridge Bible for Schools and Colleges |
| CBC | Cambridge Bible Commentary |
| *CBQ* | *Catholic Biblical Quarterly* |
| CBQMS | Catholic Biblical Quarterly Monograph Series |
| CC | The Communicator's Commentary |
| *CCK* | *Chronicles of Chaldean Kings*, D. J. Wiseman |
| CD | Cairo *Damascus Document* |
| CGTC | Cambridge Greek Testament Commentaries |
| *CHAL* | *Concise Hebrew and Aramic Lexicon*, ed. W. L. Holladay |
| Comm. | J. Calvin, *Commentary on the First Book of Moses Called Genesis*, trans., rev. J. King |
| ConB | Coniectanea biblica |
| ConBOT | Coniectanea biblica, Old Testament |
| *COT* | *Commentary on the Old Testament, C. F. Keil and F. Delitzsch* |
| *CR:BS* | *Currents in Research: Biblical Studies* |
| *CSR* | *Christian Scholar's Review* |
| *CT* | *Christianity Today* |
| *CTM* | *Concordia Theological Monthly* |
| *CTR* | *Criswell Theological Review* |
| *CurTM* | *Currents in Theology and Mission* |
| *DCH* | *Dictionary of Classical Hebrew*, ed. D. J. A. Clines |
| *DISO* | C.-F. Jean and J. Hoftijzer, *Dictionnaire des inscriptions sémitiques de l'ouest* |
| DJD | Discoveries in the Judaean Desert |
| *DNWSI* | *Dictionary of Northwest Semitic Inscriptions* |
| *DOTT* | *Documents from Old Testament Times*, ed. D. W. Thomas |
| DSBS | Daily Study Bible Series |
| DSS | Dead Sea Scrolls |
| *EAEHL* | *Encyclopedia of Archaeological Excavations in the Holy Land*, ed. M. Avi-Yonah |
| EBC | Expositor's Bible Commentary |

| | |
|---|---|
| Ebib | Etudes bibliques |
| *EDBT* | *Evangelical Dictionary of Biblical Theology*, W. A. Elwell, ed. |
| *EE* | *Enuma Elish* |
| *EDNT* | *Exegetical Dictionary of the New Testament* |
| *EGT* | *The Expositor's Greek Testament* |
| *EM* | *Ensiqlopedia Miqra'it* |
| *EncJud* | *Encyclopaedia Judaica* (1971) |
| *ErIsr* | *Eretz Israel* |
| *ETL* | *Ephermerides theologicae lovanienses* |
| EvBC | Everyman's Bible Commentary |
| EV(s) | English Version(s) |
| *EvQ* | *Evangelical Quarterly* |
| *ExpTim* | *Expository Times* |
| FB | Forschung zur Bibel |
| FOTL | Forms of Old Testament Literature |
| Gk. | Greek |
| *GBH* | P. Joüon, *A Grammar of Biblical Hebrew*, 2 vols., trans. and rev. T. Muraoka |
| GKC | Gesenius's Hebrew Grammar, ed. E. Kautzsch, trans. A. E. Cowley |
| *GTJ* | *Grace Theological Journal* |
| *GTTOT* | *The Geographical and Topographical Texts of the Old Testament*, ed. J. Simons |
| *HALOT* | L. Koehler and W. Baumgartner, *The Hebrew and Aramaic Lexicon of the Old Testament* |
| *HAR* | *Hebrew Annual Review* |
| HAT | Handbuch zum Alten Testament |
| *HBD* | *Harper's Bible Dictionary*, ed. P. Achtemeier |
| *HBT* | *Horizons in Biblical Theology* |
| HDR | Harvard Dissertations in Religion |
| Her | Hermeneia |
| HKAT | Handkommentar zum Alten Testament |
| *HS* | *Hebrew Studies* |
| HSM | Harvard Semitic Monographs |
| HT | Helps for Translators |
| *HTR* | *Harvard Theological Review* |
| *HUCA* | *Hebrew Union College Annual* |
| *IB* | *Interpreter's Bible* |
| IBC | International Bible Commentary, ed. F. F. Bruce |
| *IBD* | *Illustrated Bible Dictionary*, ed. J. D. Douglas and N. Hillyer |
| ICC | International Critical Commentary |
| *IBHS* | B. K. Waltke and M. O'Connor, *Introduction to Biblical Hebrew Syntax* |
| *IBS* | *Irish Biblical Studies* |
| *IDB* | *Interpreter's Dictionary of the Bible*, ed. G. A. Buttrick et al. |
| *IDBSup* | Supplementary volume to *IDB* |
| *IEJ* | *Israel Exploration Journal* |

| | |
|---|---|
| IES | Israel Exploration Society |
| *IJT* | *Indian Journal of Theology* |
| *Int* | *Interpretation* |
| INT | Interpretation: A Bible Commentary for Teaching and Preaching |
| *IOS* | *Israel Oriental Studies* |
| *ISBE* | *International Standard Bible Encyclopedia*, rev. ed., G. W. Bromiley |
| ITC | International Theological Commentary |
| *ITQ* | *Irish Theological Quarterly* |
| *JAAR* | *Journal of the American Academy of Religion* |
| *JAARSup* | *Journal of the American Academy of Religion*, Supplement |
| *JANES* | *Journal of Ancient Near Eastern Society* |
| *JAOS* | *Journal of the American Oriental Society* |
| *JBL* | *Journal of Biblical Literature* |
| *JBR* | *Journal of Bible and Religion* |
| *JCS* | *Journal of Cuneiform Studies* |
| *JEA* | *Journal of Egyptian Archaeology* |
| *JETS* | *Journal of the Evangelical Theological Society* |
| *JJS* | *Journal of Jewish Studies* |
| *JNES* | *Journal of Near Eastern Studies* |
| *JNSL* | *Journal of Northwest Semitic Languages* |
| *JOTT* | *Journal of Translation and Textlinguistics* |
| *JPOS* | *Journal of Palestine Oriental Society* |
| JPS | Jewish Publication Society |
| JPSV | Jewish Publication Society Version |
| JPST | Jewish Publication Society Torah |
| *JRT* | *Journal of Religious Thought* |
| *JSJ* | *Journal for the Study of Judaism in the Persian, Hellenistic, and Roman Period* |
| *JSOR* | *Journal of the Society for Oriental Research* |
| *JSOT* | *Journal for the Study of the Old Testament* |
| JSOTSup | JSOT—Supplement Series |
| *JSS* | *Journal of Semitic Studies* |
| *JTS* | *Journal of Theological Studies* |
| *JTSNS* | *Journal of Theological Studies, New Series* |
| *JTT* | *Journal of Translation and Textlinguistics* |
| KAT | Kommentar zum Alten Testament |
| KB | L. Koehler and W. Baumgartner, *Lexicon in Veteris Testamenti libros* |
| *KD* | *Kerygma und Dogma* |
| LBBC | Layman's Bible Book Commentary |
| LBH | Late Biblical Hebrew |
| LBI | Library of Biblical Interpretation |
| LCC | Library of Christian Classics |
| *LLAVT* | E. Vogt, *Lexicon Linguae Aramaicae Veteris Testamenti* |
| LSJ | Liddell-Scott-Jones, *Greek-English Lexicon* |
| *LTQ* | *Lexington Theological Quarterly* |

| | |
|---|---|
| *LW* | *Luther's Works. Lecture's on Genesis,* ed. J. Pelikan and D. Poellot, trans. G. Schick |
| LXX | Septuagint |
| MT | Masoretic Text |
| MS(S) | Manuscript(s) |
| NAB | New American Bible |
| NASB | New American Standard Bible |
| NAC | New American Commentary, ed. R. Clendenen |
| *NB* | *Nebuchadrezzar and Babylon,* D. J. Wiseman |
| *NBD* | *New Bible Dictionary,* ed. J. D. Douglas |
| NCBC | New Century Bible Commentary |
| *NEAEHL* | *The New Encyclopedia of Archaeological Excavations in the Holy Land,* ed. E. Stern |
| NEB | New English Bible |
| NIB | The New Interpreter's Bible |
| NICNT | New International Commentary on the New Testament |
| NICOT | New International Commentary on the Old Testament |
| *NIDOTTE* | *The New International Dictionary of Old Testament Theology and Exegesis,* ed. W. A. VanGemeren |
| NJB | New Jerusalem Bible |
| NJPS | New Jewish Publication Society Version |
| *NKZ* | *Neue kirchliche Zeitschrift* |
| *NovT* | *Novum Testamentum* |
| NRSV | New Revised Standard Version |
| *NRT* | *La nouvelle revue the'ologique* |
| *NTS* | *New Testament Studies* |
| NTT | Norsk Teologisk Tidsskrift |
| OBO | Orbis biblicus et orientalis |
| OL | Old Latin |
| *Or* | *Orientalia* |
| OTL | Old Testament Library |
| *OTP* | *The Old Testament Pseudepigrapha,* ed. J. H. Charlesworth |
| *OTS* | *Oudtestamentische Studiën* |
| *OTWSA* | *Ou-Testamentiese Werkgemeenskap in Suid-Afrika* |
| *PCB* | *Peake's Commentary on the Bible,* ed. M. Black and H. H. Rowley |
| *PEQ* | *Palestine Exploration Quarterly* |
| *POTT* | *Peoples of Old Testament Times,* ed. D. J. Wiseman |
| POTW | Peoples of the Old Testament World, ed. A. E. Hoerth, G. L. Mattingly, and E. M. Yamauchi |
| PTMS | Pittsburgh Theological Monograph Series |
| *PTR* | *Princeton Theological Review* |
| *RA* | *Revue d'assyriologie et d'archéologie orientale* |
| *RB* | *Revue biblique* |
| REB | Revised English Bible |
| *ResQ* | *Restoration Quarterly* |
| *RevExp* | *Review and Expositor* |
| *RHPR* | *Revue d'histoire et de philosophie religieuses* |
| RSR | Recherches de science religieuse |

| | |
|---|---|
| *RTR* | *Reformed Theological Review* |
| SANE | Sources from the Ancient Near East |
| SBH | Standard Biblical Hebrew |
| *SBJT* | *Southern Baptist Journal of Theology* |
| SBLDS | Society of Biblical Literature Dissertation Series |
| SBLMS | Society of Biblical Literature Monograph Series |
| SBLSP | Society of Biblical Literature Seminar Papers |
| SBT | Studies in Biblical Theology |
| SHCANE | Studies in the History and Culture of the Ancient Near East |
| *SJT* | *Scottish Journal of Theology* |
| *SJOT* | *Scandinavian Journal of the Old Testament* |
| SJLA | Studies in Judaism in Late Antiquity |
| *SLJA* | *Saint Luke's Journal of Theology* |
| *SOTI* | *A Survey of Old Testament Introduction*, G. L. Archer |
| SP | Samaritan Pentateuch |
| SR | Studies in Religion/Sciences religieuses |
| *SSI* | *Syrian Semitic Inscriptions* |
| *ST* | *Studia theologica* |
| STJD | Studies on the Texts of the Desert of Judah |
| Syr. | Syriac |
| *TBT* | *The Bible Today* |
| *TD* | *Theology Digest* |
| *TDNT* | *Theological Dictionary of the New Testament*, ed. G. Kittel and G. Friedrich |
| *TDOT* | *Theological Dictionary of the Old Testament*, ed. G. J. Botterweck and H. Ringgren |
| TEV | Today's English Version |
| Tg(s). | Targum(s) |
| TJNS | Trinity Journal—New Series |
| *TLOT* | *Theological Lexicon of the Old Testament*, ed. E. Jenni and C. Westermann |
| *TLZ* | *Theologische Literaturzeitung* |
| TNTC | Tyndale New Testament Commentaries |
| TOTC | Tyndale Old Testament Commentaries |
| *TrinJ* | *Trinity Journal* |
| *TS* | *Theological Studies* |
| *TToday* | *Theology Today* |
| *Tur* | *Traditionsgeshichtliche Untersuchungen aum Richterbuch* |
| *TWAT* | *Theologisches Wörterbuch zum Alten Testament*, ed. G. J. Botterweck and H. Ringgren |
| *TWOT* | *Theological Wordbook of the Old Testament* |
| *TynBul* | *Tyndale Bulletin* |
| *UF* | *Ugarit-Forschungen* |
| Ug. | Ugaritic |
| *UT* | C. H. Gordon, *Ugaritic Textbook* |
| Vg | Vulgate |
| *VT* | *Vetus Testamentum* |
| VTSup | Vetus Testamentum, Supplements |
| WBC | Word Biblical Commentaries |

| | |
|---|---|
| WEC | Wycliffe Exegetical Commentary |
| WHJP | *World History of the Jewish People,* ed. B. Mazer |
| WO | *Die Welt des Orients* |
| WTJ | *Westminster Theological Journal* |
| WMANT | Wissenschaftliche Monographien zum Alten und Neuen Testament |
| ZAW | *Zeitschrift für die alttestamentliche Wissenschaft* |
| ZDMG | *Zeitschrift der deutschen morgenländischen Gesellschaft* |
| ZDPV | *Zeitschrift des deutschen Palästina-Vereins* |
| ZPEB | *Zondervan Pictorial Encyclopedia of the Bible* |
| ZTK | *Zeitschrift für katholische Theologie* |

# Contents

# Numbers

Presence of God in Action
God and Revelation
Holiness and Purity of God
Faithfulness of God
Promise and Fulfillment: God, People, and Land
Uniqueness and Exclusivity of God
(2) Anthropological Themes
Population and Demographics
Obedience and Disobedience
Unity or Disunity
Leadership
(3) Land Themes
Promise or Rejection
Celebration
Tribal Allocations
(4) Worship Themes: Sanctification and Purification
Sinai Cycles
Rebellion Cycles
Advent Cycles

## INTRODUCTION

Transitional periods in the life of a nation often serve to define the character and future of that people, for they build upon earlier foundations and yet diverge into new arenas of livelihood, character, and constitution. In the analysis of the broad history of a given people, these intervals are pivotal in assessing major movements that illuminate the particulars of later epochs.

The Book of Numbers serves such a purpose both in the Pentateuch and in the larger presentation of the history of Israel. This focal document contains the recurrent themes of God's revelation to humankind through word, God's work in and through the lives of the patriarchs and their descendants, God's birthing of the nation, and God's blessing through the gift of a productive land. It includes the polar themes of inheritance and disinheritance, obedience and disobedience, and of unity and diversity (or disunity). Numbers anticipates both the inheritance of the land under Joshua's leadership and the internal and external conflicts of Judges, Samuel, and Kings. Prophets such as Hosea and Jeremiah build upon the history and themes of this book, and the Psalmists occasionally refer to incidents contained within its pages.

## 1. Title

The English title "Numbers" is derived from the Greek and Latin nomenclature, dating to no later than the first half of the second century A.D. Tertullian refers to the Balaam stories of the *Book of Arithmi,* so by inference the fourth book of the Pentateuch may have been called by the Greek name *Arithmoi* as early as the first century.[1] In the Vulgate the title was translated as *Numeri,* hence the modern English form.

The early Hebrew nomenclature derived from the first word of the text, *wayedabbēr* ("[YHWH] spoke [to Moses]"), reflecting the mnemonic approach to organizing the contents for memorization and recitation.[2] Later the title was changed to the fifth word of the first verse, *bemidbar* ("in the wilderness [of Sinai]"), apparently as a result of the early haggadic (narrative) commentary *Bemidbar Rabbah.* The latter heading obtains in most modern Hebrew Bibles. Talmudic sources designate the book *ḥomeš happequddîm,* "the fifth of the musterings [=census]." Concerning the relevance of the title "In the Wilderness," G. B. Gray noted:

> As indicative of the contents of the book, the title Numbers is not aptly chosen; for it is only a small part of the book (chap. 1–4, 26) that is concerned with the numbers of the Israelites. Though not chosen for the purpose, the Hebrew title "In the wilderness" would be far more suitable, since the wilderness is the scene of the greater part of the book.[3]

This geographical approach to the book's title is echoed by a majority of commentaries written in the last century.

Thus three descriptive titles have been generated, and each focused on one of the major content issues in the book. One emphasized the census taking, another the geographical setting, and the third the revelatory aspect. Yet the original Hebrew title may better define the content and purpose of Numbers. This is the Word of God, the revelation of the will of God to his people Israel and a challenge to live responsibly the life of faith as that people which are called by his name. For the Book of Numbers, one of the most common phrases in the Hebrew Bible, *wayedabbēr* ("And God spoke") became the

---

[1] Tertullian, *Adversus Marcion* 4.28. Philo does not name the Book of Numbers, as he does the other four volumes of the Books of Moses, but the titles of the four correspond well with later Greek and Latin usage.

[2] See Mishnah, *Yoma* 7.1 and R. Rashi on Exod 38:26. Cf. Jerome, *Pref. in librorum Samuel et Malachi,* ed. J. Migne, xxvii.552. Also referred to by Epiphanius, *Symmicta,* ed. P. Lagarde, ii.178.

[3] G. B. Gray, *Numbers,* ICC (Edinburgh: T & T Clark, 1903), xxii. Similar opinion is shared also by G. Wenham, *Numbers,* TOTC (Downers Grove: InterVarsity Press, 1981), 13; P. Budd, *Numbers,* WBC (Waco: Word, 1984), xvii; and many others.

primary organizational element and theological theme.[4] The question of the preference and appropriateness of the descriptive titles will be examined closely in a later section, "Structure and Outline of the Book of Numbers."

## 2. Textual History, Setting, and Authorship

An analysis of the textual history of any book of the Old Testament is an imposing and arduous endeavor. Traditionally, in conservative evangelical commentaries on individual books of the Pentateuch, authorship and date discussions have begun with the justification and defense of Mosaic authorship and an assessment of the temporal context in relationship to the Exodus from Egypt. On the other hand, modern critical commentaries have focused on the interactive editorial history of the documentary sources in determining the literary development of the book.[5] In this section the sources and history of the text are explored, and then issues of authorship and editorial history are examined.

### (1) Extant Textual Sources

The biblical text has been transmitted through history in many ancient sources, which are represented in modern versions and editions, medieval manuscripts and codices, and those derived from archaeological excavation. Some texts are but several centuries old, as in the numerous manuscripts of the medieval Masoretes, while others from the Qumran corpus of the Dead Sea Scrolls have been in existence for more than two thousand years.[6]

---

[4] Note the uses of וַיְדַבֵּר as a major marker in the text of Numbers in 1:1; 4:1; 5:14,20; 6:1,12,17; 7:22,28; 8:1; 10:8; 11:1; 12:1; 13:1; 14:1,33; 15:1; 16:1; 17:1; 18:1; 19:1; 20:1; 22:1,17, 26; 23:1; 24:1; 25:1; 27:1.

[5] Cp., e.g., R. K. Harrison, *Numbers: An Exegetical Commentary* (Grand Rapids: Baker, 1992), 21–24; with B. A. Levine, *Numbers 1–20, A New Translation with Introduction and Commentary,* AB (New York: Doubleday, 1993), 48–64. Harrison presents an apologetic defense of Mosaic origins against "liberal scholars." Levine sets forth the content of the book in terms of the "Documentary Sources Interacting."

[6] The primary source is the Masoretic text of Codex Leningradensis B 19A, completed in A.D. 1009 and copied from the text of Aaron ben Moses ben Asher. Other sources include the Dead Sea Scroll texts from Cave 4 adjacent to Khirbet Qumran, Mishnaic and Talmudic quotations, and a silver amulet containing a version of the priestly blessing of Num 6:24–26. The Qumran corpus also includes several LXX translations. The entire LXX corpus has been analyzed by J. W. Wevers, *Notes on the Greek Text of Numbers,* SBL Septuagint and Cognate Studies Series 46 (Atlanta: Scholars Press, 1998). Wever edited the critical edition of the LXX text of Numbers in *Numeri, Septuaginta Vetus Testamentum Graecum Auctoritate Academiae Scientiarum Gottingensis,* Gottingen, 1982. Aramaic versions are represented in the Babylonian *Targum Onkelos,* the Jerusalem Targum of *Pseudo-Jonathan* and *Neophyti,* the Samaritan Targum, and the Syriac Peshitta. Qumran fragments include excerpts from twenty-seven of forty-eight columns of the MSS, beginning with 11:31 and continuing in broken fashion through the end of the book (36:13). Though most of the 4QNum texts agree with the MT, N. Jastram demonstrated that many distinctive variants agree with the Samaritan Pentateuch ("4QNum[b] from Qumran" [Ph.D. diss., Harvard University, 1989]).

The primary text for study of the Old Testament since the sixteenth century has been the so-called Masoretic text. The terminology "Masoretic text" (MT) refers to that select group of manuscripts and documents derived from the tradition of Aaron Ben Asher of the Tiberian school of the Masoretes. The Ben Asher codices and exemplars are very similar to each other in text and marginal notations. Other textual traditions exist among the more than six thousand known Masoretic manuscripts, each of which was copied in accordance with the religious scribal instructions called the *halakhot*. Most of the manuscripts date to the two centuries before 1540, yet six codices[7] derive from the tenth century, with eight from the eleventh and more than eighty codices and fragments from the twelfth century.

The Masoretes incorporated many innovative elements into the transmission process to guarantee both the oral and written aspects of the text. These included the counting of letters, words, and phrases and the placement of vowel pointing, accents, and marginal apparatuses. The sanctity of the Name of God, written as the Tetragrammaton YHWH, was preserved in written practice, ceremonial scribal lustration, and vocalization of the substitute *Adonai*. The latest complete critical edition of the MT is the *Biblia Hebraica Stuttgartensia (BHS),* which incorporates some of the Masoretic text's marginal notations and manuscript references, as well as text critical notes of other ancient witnesses to the Hebrew text and suggested editorial emendations.[8]

### (2) *History of the Hebrew Text*

The proposed archetype to the Masoretic Text, commonly referred to as the Proto-Masoretic text, served as the authoritative canon for the Palestinian and Diaspora Jewish communities until the medieval period. E. Tov has delineated three main periods in the historical development of the MT.[9]

EARLY HISTORY (SECOND MILLENNIUM B.C.–A.D. 73). From pre-First Temple era through the destruction of the Second Temple and the fall of Masada. Textual witnesses include the Dead Sea scroll texts dating from the mid-third century B.C. through A.D. 68, Masada manuscripts, several Aramaic translations, and a few brief quotations derived from archaeologi-

---

[7] "Codex" (pl. codices) refers to a book written primarily on double-page parchment sections stitched together in the middle of each section to form a sewn spine. This enabled the reader, copyist, or student to open the manuscript to any point in the text.

[8] *BHS,* ed. A. Alt, O. Eissfeldt, P. Kahle, et al. (Stuttgart: Wurttembergische Bibelanstalt, 1973). The Book of Numbers was edited by W. Rudolph.

[9] E. Tov, *Textual Criticism of the Hebrew Bible* (Minneapolis: Fortress, 1992), 29–39.

cal finds such as the silver scrolls from Jerusalem.[10]

PROTO-MASORETIC ERA (A.D. 74–800). The primary sources are the fragments from around the Bar Kochba period (132–135), unearthed from the caves located in the Wadi Murabaʿat and Naḥal Ḥever,[11] and the Cairo Genizah of the eighth century.[12] The Mishnah, Tiberian and Babylonian Talmuds, Midrashim, and Targums derive from this period, but most of the extant copies date to the third period.[13]

MASORETIC ERA (800–1800). The primary sources are the more than six thousand Masoretic manuscripts and quotations in commentaries and other religious documents.[14]

Recently M. H. Goshen-Gottstein directed the Hebrew University Bible Project (HUBP) in producing a more comprehensive text of the Hebrew Bible. Following his death, E. Tov continues this multivolume work, which will contain most of the variant readings from Qumran, the Masoretic texts, Syriac and Targums, and other important sources.

### (3) Ancient Sources for the Book of Numbers

Representative of the oldest extant texts from period one are the two small silver scrolls found in the excavation of Ketef Hinnom in Jerusalem, containing a version of the priestly blessing of Num 6:24–26. The scrolls, which were probably used in phylacteries or tefillin, date to the Babylonian era, near the end of the First Temple era or soon after its destruction in 586 B.C. These minute samples recount the priestly blessing in a slightly different version from the MT.

The most substantial corpus of textual evidence is the Qumran scroll collection, which includes some eight Numbers fragments. One fragmentary text (4Q paleoLev-Num[a]) is written in the archaizing Hebrew script of the preexilic

---

[10] Textual witnesses from this era are characterized by a modest number of internal differences in matters of content and orthography (spelling), usually limited to single words and phrases. Some scribes and *magihim* ("correctors") of Qumran and the Second Temple era sought to bring texts into conformity, some faithfully copied the text in hand, while others were active in text criticism and emendation for various reasons.

[11] Fragments of the Book of Numbers were found in the Naḥal Ḥever. See DJD II:1–3,88.

[12] See M. C. Davis, *Hebrew Bible Manuscripts in the Cambridge Genizah Collections*, vols. 1–2 (Cambridge: University Press, 1978, 1980). Most of the more than 200,000 fragments remain unpublished, though discovered in the early 1890s. Tens of thousands of these religious documents are reported to be biblical texts.

[13] This period reflects "a relatively large degree of textual consistency" (Tov, *Textual Criticism*, 33) that resulted from a trend toward standardization that began in late Second Temple times. Communities of scribes that fostered the diverse textual traditions of the first period either no longer existed or disassociated themselves from the Judaic community.

[14] Tov describes this period as "characterized by almost complete textual unity." These served as the base text for the BHS (*Textual Criticism*, 34).

era.[15] N. Jastram has analyzed and edited the most complete text of Numbers from Qumran, 4Q Num[b], which he dated to the late Hasmonean or early Herodian period (30 B.C.–A.D. 20) on the basis of paleographic analysis.[16] Jastram describes the scroll as originally containing forty-eight columns, of which all but five from column 17 (Num 11:31–13:5) to column 48 (Num 36:2–13) are represented in varying degrees of completeness. He suggests that though the 4Q Num[b] text does not differ substantially from the MT, the more distinctive variants (nonorthographic and nonmorphological) agree with the Samaritan Pentateuch version, evidencing some antecedent relationship in the text history. Significant textual variations will be discussed at the appropriate place in the commentary. The entire Qumran corpus reflects the yet ongoing activity of orthographic adaptation of the Aramaic script to the Hebrew text of the Old Testament, which had begun in the early postexilic period.

The Samaritan Pentateuch (SamPent) is a recension of the Hebrew text, dated approximately between the fourth and first centuries B.C. and penned in a unique "early" Samaritan-Hebrew script.[17] The SamPent contains more than six thousand variants from the MT, of which some nineteen hundred agree with the LXX.[18] Apart from ideological Samaritan revisions and additions from the Book of Deuteronomy,[19] the SamPent includes unique readings and harmonizations with other Old Testament texts. Notable are the instances where many of the Qumran manuscripts exhibit the same unique readings as the SamPent. These will be discussed at the appropriate point in the commentary.

Wevers has described the LXX version of the Book of Numbers as "the weakest volume in the Greek Pentateuch" in which the translator(s) displays "an active mind engaged in the interpretation of sacred scripture, ready not only to clarify obscure passages, but even to correct what might appear to be factual errors or contradictions within the text."[20] In contrast to Wevers, E. Ulrich suggests that the combined evidence from the Old Greek, 4QLXXNum, the Samaritan Pentateuch, and the biblical texts in Josephus

---

[15] Also referred to as the Syro-Phoenician script. Qumran texts include 1QLev (1:48–50; 36:7–8?); 1Q paleo–Num; 2Q Num[b] (33:47–53); 2Q Num[c] (7:88); 2Q Num[d] (18:8–9); 4Q Num[b] (this text marked new sections with red ink); 4Q 175 (Num 24:15–17); 4Q Lev–Num[a], etc.

[16] N. Jastram, "4Q Num–b from Qumran," Ph.D. diss., Harvard University, 1989.

[17] The critical versions of the SamPent include A. F. von Gall, *Der hebraische Pentateuch der Samaritaner,* 5 vols. (1914–18; reprint, Berlin: W. de Gruyter, 1966); A. and R. Sadaqa, *Jewish and Samaritan Version of the Pentateuch, With Particular Stress on the Difference between Both Texts* (Tel Aviv: University, 1961–65, Hb.); and L. F. Giron Blanc, *Pentateuco Hebreo-Samaritano: Genesis* (Madrid: Biblioteca Universidad Complutense, 1975). The Sadaqa text includes the Abisha` scroll of Deuteronomy.

[18] These figures are now somewhat dated, compiled on the basis of extant sources in the nineteenth century by B. Walton, E. Castellus, and J. Lightfoot.

[19] E.g., Deut 1:20–23a is inserted after Num 12:16.

[20] Wevers, *Notes on the Greek Text of Numbers,* ix.

"demonstrate bountifully that there were variant literary editions of the books of Scripture in the late Second Temple period."[21]

As a whole the text of the Book of Numbers is relatively free from corruption, in comparison to such books as Samuel, Jeremiah, and Hosea. Even in settings like the large census numbers of chaps. 1, 2, and 26, where one might anticipate some history of textual emendation, the MT and other versions are almost totally free from variants. The Balaam oracles contain the most significant numbers of variants, probably due to the antiquity of those accounts, yet the number of differences are not unusual in comparison with other poetic literature. Gray succinctly states that "the text of Numbers appears to have suffered comparatively little from simple errors of transmission."[22] "Taken as a whole, the variants exhibited by the Qumran scroll cannot be said to undermine the Masoretic Text of Numbers, and they seldom indicate that the Qumran scribes had before them, to start with, texts different from those underlying the Masoretic version."[23] Yet, as with other Pentateuchal books, "compositional history" and not the text-critical history of Numbers has been the subject of the most critical analysis and debate through the centuries in biblical scholarship.

### (4) Early Textual History and Authorship

The present form of the Book of Numbers dates at least to the second century B.C., as inferred from the close parallels with the text of the Septuagint, and the fragmentary evidence dates to as much as five centuries earlier. The surviving Qumran copies echo the previous generations of scribal transmission, through which the text had arrived at a status of limited fluidity[24] by the mid-second century B.C. when the community was founded.[25] By inference the text of the Book of Numbers was essentially the same as the later Proto-MT by no later than the early postexilic era. Thus the text of the Book of Numbers suffered little scribal emendation after the fifth century B.C. The debate between modern critical schools of Torah interpretation and traditional approaches is over the means by which the text was transmitted down to the

---

[21] E. Ulrich, *The Dead Sea Scrolls and the Origins of the Bible*, Studies in the Dead Sea Scrolls and Related Literature (Grand Rapids: Eerdmans, 1999), 11.

[22] Gray, *Numbers*, xxxix.

[23] Levine, *Numbers 1–20*, 86.

[24] Regarding the relative fluidity of the Hb. text of Numbers, Levine has stated: "All of these processes indicate a fluid attitude regarding the received text of the Torah in the last pre-Christian centuries, one that permitted considerable editorial license" (*Numbers 1–20*, AB, 87). Yet earlier in the same section, Levine reflects upon Jastram's analysis that "most of the 4Q Num[b] variants represent conscious adaptations of one primary text instead of reflecting dependence on different base texts, although instances of this process can also be detected" (p. 86).

[25] Recent publications of Qumran texts by S. Ben-Wacholder have heightened the probability that the advent of the community and the circumstances of its origins date to the reign of Jonathan son of Mattathias, who reigned over the semiautonomous state of Israel from 161–142 B.C.

fifth century B.C. and the extent to which editors have formed and transformed
the text since the days of Moses.

## (5) Mosaic Authorship: Historical Setting

The traditional approach to the formation of the original text has focused
on the role of Moses as writer and editor of Torah. Recently R. K. Harrison has
renewed the defense of the "probability that Moses wrote a significant amount
of Numbers and supervised the editorial processes by which the bulk of the
composition took shape."[26] Internal and external data have been proffered in
support of this view. First, the writing activity of Moses is recounted in Num
33:1–2 as well as in several other Pentateuchal passages.[27] As will be
addressed below in "Structure and Outline of the Book of Numbers" and
"Structural Theology of the Book of Numbers," the introductory divine revelatory phrase "The LORD spoke to Moses" is one of the book's key theological
statements and organizing elements in the book. As Ashley states the case,
"Hence, when the text claims that, for example, Moses wrote something or
received a communication from God, it is not just literary convention but a
description of historical fact."[28] In the New Testament, Jesus, Stephen, and
Paul refer to Moses' role in the development of Pentateuchal law (John 5:45–
47; Acts 26:22; Rom 10:5). Second, as the key leader, he trained under the auspices of the royal pharaonic educational system (Acts 7:22–42). Hence, Moses
is the natural human figure to be assigned the recording of the revelatory acts
and words of God.

Third, the Pentateuch as a whole possesses an essential unity, which evidences the activity of a single author. Harrison suggests that the šōṭerîm, "the
literate administrators among the Israelite tribes" who worked closely with
Moses during the wilderness journey, may have recorded historical events and
edited portions of the Mosaic legislation in compiling what is essentially the
Book of Numbers.[29] Thus the extant text may have been completed with all
but minor additions and glosses by Samuel's day (eleventh century B.C.). The
primary role of the later Hebrew scribes and šōṭerîm would have been as copy-
ists, not wholesale composers and editors, in order "to preserve those sacred
writings ... and to make their significance clear by updating phraseology,
topography, names, and any other archaic or obscure matters."[30]

---

[26] Harrison, *Numbers*, 21. Harrison suggests that the finished form of the book dates to "the
time of Samuel at the latest" (p. 24).

[27] Exod 17:14; 24:4; 34:27–28; Deut 28:61; 31:9, 22; etc.

[28] T. Ashley, *The Book of Numbers*, NICOT (Grand Rapids: Eerdmans, 1993), 4.

[29] These were first appointed by Moses (with God's direction) in 1:5–18 to conduct the census
and its recording. These men had become a literary guild by the time of Josh 1:10. See Harrison,
*Numbers*, 15–21; E. E. Carpenter and E. B. Smick, "Numbers," *ISBE*, 3:562.

[30] Harrison, *Numbers*, 23.

Fourth, the historical data within the book are said to reflect the cultural and political conditions of either the Late Bronze or early Iron Age I, rather than the Iron IIB (722–538 B.C.) as source-critical scholars would propose. The sociopolitical conditions in the Transjordan as reflected in the narratives of Numbers 20–25 are not those of the nationalism of Moab and Ammon of the time of Mesha (ninth century B.C.) or even Naḥash the Ammonite of the late eleventh or early tenth century B.C. The fluid relationship between the emerging nation of Moab and the tribal based Midianites was more reflective of the period of the Judges than that of the era of the later Israelite Divided Kingdom.

The two most widely accepted dates for the Exodus are 1440 and 1290–1270 B.C., placing the parameters of the historical events in Numbers at 1440–1400 B.C. or 1290–1250 B.C.[31] The Early Date position would set the Sinai to Moab experience of the Israelites in the eighteenth dynasty of Egyptian pharaonic history, during the reign of either Amenhotpe II or Thutmose IV. The Late Date position would place the biblical events in the political world of the nineteenth dynasty of Ramses II at the end of the Late Bronze Age. The archaeological *terminus ad quem* for the existence of Israel in Canaan is the stele of Ramses II's successor Merneptah dated to ca. 1220 B.C. Upon the walls of the temple of Medinet Habu, Merneptah recorded his exploits in Canaan in seeking to restore the Egyptian hegemony over the coastal and Shephelah regions. In the somewhat punitive raids, Merneptah recounts that he had encountered and defeated several rebellious cities, and of Israel he claims to have destroyed Israel's grain fields.[32] Ashley simply states that "much of the material in the Book of Numbers makes good sense in the Mosaic age, indeed, better sense than in the postexilic age,"[33] in which most source critics would place the composition of the book. He notes several reasons: (1) The laws and institutions discussed in the priestly legislation and narrative simply do not fit in the postexilic age. (2) Many and basic unifying features of the book are anchored in the person of Moses rather than the personages of postexilic Jerusalem.

---

[31] The suggested Late Date of the Exodus, which lacks the biblical specificity of the Early Date (1 Kgs 6:1), may be dated to as early as 1290 or perhaps as late as 1260. These dates depend somewhat upon the dating of the nineteenth dynasty in Egypt, the Ramesside Kingdom, for which Early, Middle, and Late chronologies are proposed by various Egyptologists. By the time of the Merneptah stele, the differentiation between the three chronologies narrows to less than twenty years, generally dated between 1225 and 1205 B.C. The Early Date proponents place the Exodus between 1460 and 1436 B.C., hence the wilderness journeys would be dated to 1420/1396 B.C.

[32] Note that the text portion that reads, "I attacked Israel, his seed is not," is to be understood as a typical vaunting self-justifying speech form of ANE victory stele. The term translated "seed" has an agricultural determinative, hence "grain" is the proper translation rather than the implication that the people of Israel have been annihilated.

[33] Ashley, *Numbers*, 3.

## (6) Modern Source Critical Theory

The modern critical scholars, typified by Gray and Levine, envision the editing as a more complex process over a period of four to five centuries. Levine succinctly states: "It is source analysis that holds the key to literary development."[34] According to this view the JE source, said to have been compiled during the ninth to eighth centuries B.C., set forth a systematic presentation of the presettlement period described in Deuteronomy 1–4, retrojecting materials and events of the settlement and early kingdom periods into that formative era of Israelite history. Critical scholars project that the purpose of the JE writers was to provide their Israelite contemporaries a historical and theological foundation for their present reality. Kadesh Barnea and Edomite traditions are said to be exemplars of this reading back into the national prehistory the beginnings of Judahite defensive fortification of its southern frontier and the origins of the animosity against the Edomites.[35] Kingdom era conflicts with the Midianites, Canaanites, and Amalekites are all traced back to this early period to sanction and exculpate Israelite political policies and to justify its sovereignty over the land being attacked and usurped.

Source critical scholars have discerned relatively few Deuteronomistic elements in Numbers because of the perceived agreement with the JE source's conquest and settlement ideology. Levine suggests that the "Deuteronomist voices a different policy with respect to Israelite relationships with the Canaanites and Transjordanian peoples."[36] For example, the Edomites for the Deuteronomist are rightful divine heirs to their inhabited territory, and yet the archetypal enemy of Israel for JE and P.[37] Numbers, however, does contain proposed Deuteronomic elements concerning Moses,

---

[34] Levine, *Numbers 1–20*, 48. The first major proponent of this approach was J. Wellhausen in his *Prolegomena to the History of Ancient Israel*, in which he posited four literary sources, namely J (Jahwist/Yahwist), E (Elohist), D (Deuteronomist), and P (Priestly). He suggested these sources emerged through the evolution of Israelite religion from the tenth–eighth centuries B.C. monarchial period (J and E), to the Josianic reforms of the seventh century (D), and finally the postexilic priestly community (P). The Pentateuch was believed to have been brought into its present form in postexilic Judah by primarily priestly redaction in the fifth–fourth centuries B.C.

[35] Cf. Numbers commentaries of Budd (*Numbers*, 113–16), Gray (*Numbers*, 99–100), and Levine (*Numbers 1–20*, 327–28) on 11:3; 13:26 (Budd, *Numbers*, 142; Gray, *Numbers*, 144; Levine, *Numbers 1–20*, 369); on 20:1,14–22 (Budd, *Numbers*, 216–17; Gray, *Numbers*, 256–58; Levine, *Numbers 1–20*, 483–85); etc.

[36] Levine, *Numbers 1–20*, 100.

[37] These scholars suppose that the suggested priestly focus of Num 20:14–21 (cf. Amos 1:11), which describes the Edomite refusal to allow the Israelites to pass through Edomite land, is in agreement with the JE narrative source, though the focus of Deut 2:1–8 is upon the territorial rights of the descendants of Esau with no mention of conflict between the two ethnic entities. See Budd, *Numbers*, 91–92, 98–101. Yet, in fact, Deut 2:1–8 gives additional background to the Edomite decision recounted in Num 20:14–21 (fear over possible loss of divinely granted territory).

as M. Weinfeld notes, such as in the use of the term "servant *('ebed)* of God."[38] This designation is typical of the Deuteronomistic school and anticipatory of the Davidic role in the United Monarchy. Yet the present study will demonstrate that the Book of Numbers has a considerable Deuteronomic cast in its structure and theology, due not to the formulation of a Deuteronomistic school in the late preexilic or postexilic prophetic community, but to the circumstances Israel faced in the Sinai desert and on their way to the Promised Land. The Deuteronomic character of the text is evidenced in the broad structure of the book: the faithfulness of the people at Sinai and the resultant blessing, their unfaithfulness in the wilderness resulting in divine retribution, and the challenge to faithfulness in the conquest of the Promised Land. In the larger context of the Pentateuch, the Book of Numbers functions as a transitional book between the more halakhic Book of Leviticus and that of the Book of Deuteronomy. It shares a number of priestly themes with the Book of Leviticus[39] and the details of the historical prologue of the Book of Deuteronomy.

Recent source critics claim the Priestly source (P)[40] contains early settlement and monarchial materials, but it is primarily postexilic. The Priestly authors-editors-compilers are presumed responsible for the form, structure, and content of the canonical Book of Numbers. The concern of P is historiography, priestly guidance for the leadership, Temple and ritual activity, and preservation of tribal genealogical materials. Budd delineates the exclusively P material, which is acknowledged widely by critical scholars as: chaps. 1–9; 15; 17–19; 26–31; 33–36; with 10; 13–14; 16; 20; 25; and 32.[41] Another school of literary source criticism, exemplified by Y. Kaufmann and M. Weinfeld,[42] asserts a P priority over D and hence a preexilic foundation. Against such a counterproposal, Levine asserts that "the traditional alignment of the Torah sources in the order J, E, D, P, ... seems most persuasive for other reasons, most notably because of internal evidence, aug-

---

[38] Moses is referred to as God's servant in Num 11:11; 12:7,8. But Caleb is also YHWH's faithful servant in 14:24. In 31:49; 32:4,5,25,27,31 the Reubenites and Gadites are described as servants of Moses ("we your servants") in the typical ANE suzerain-vassal vernacular. See M. Weinfeld's analysis of the phraseology of the Deuteronomic school in *Deuteronomy and the Deuteronomistic School* (Oxford: Clarendon, 1978).

[39] Such as the consecrational provisions for the priests (Lev 8; 21; 22; Num 8; 18).

[40] By *Priestly* I mean the supposed Priestly literary source proffered by critical scholars for priestly material in the Pentateuch. By *priestly* I refer to the material in the Book of Numbers, and in the Old Testament in general, that describes the roles, function or special interest of the priests in Israelite religion.

[41] Budd, *Numbers,* xviii–xix.

[42] Y. Kaufmann, *The Religion of Israel* (London: Allen & Unwin, 1961); Weinfeld, *Deuteronomy and the Deuteronomic School.* Weinfeld set forth extensive criteria for determining Deuteronomistic material throughout the OT.

mented by comparative considerations."[43] Though its origins may date to the preexilic era, most source critical scholars point to a renewed priestly literary creativity in early postexilic Judah (late sixth century B.C.) lasting well into the Second Temple times, perhaps as late as the early fourth century. No doubt Ezra, a priest and scribe, played a key role in the religious developments of the postexilic Jerusalem community, especially in the teaching of the Torah (Ezra 7:10). But to assign him and the priestly community with the responsibility for composing and editing the priestly material and fashioning the Pentateuch belies the internal and external evidence for a much earlier text origin and composition.

In a more recent defense of the antiquity of the priestly material in the Pentateuch, J. Milgrom has delineated eleven priestly terms and fifteen priestly institutions mentioned in Numbers that disappeared by the postexilic period. He also cites thirteen priestly terms and ten priestly institutions that originated "in the earliest period of (or prior to) Israel's national existence."[44] Included among the ancient terms are *ʿēda* (assembly), *môʿēd* (national assembly), *maṭṭeh* (tribe), *ʾelep* (clan), *naśiʾ* (chieftain), *ʿăvōda* (physical work), *mišmeret* (guardianship), *ʾāšam* (feel guilt), *ḥallâ* (loaf), *lehem tāmîd* and *lehem pānîm* (shewbread), which is later called *maʿăreket*, and *ʾummâ* (tribe). Among the ancient institutions of Israel were the square shape of the Israelite camp, the early roles of the Levites, the purification rites for the Nazirite, the boiled shoulder of the Nazirite lamb, the Late Bronze Age shape of the tabernacle menorah, details from the campaign against the Midianites, the boundaries of the Promised Land, the census which has parallel in second millennium B.C. Mari, the Temple and Levitical tithes, and the bronze serpent.

Another argument contra the postexilic date of the priestly material is ancient morphology of the names of the sons of Jacob and the leaders of the tribes in Numbers 1–2.[45] These typically date to the second millennium B.C. Finally, the territorial allocations among the tribes, beginning in Numbers 32 and completed in Joshua 14–22, are radically different from the concerns of the postexilic community, which were confined to only a small portion of that which was formerly Judah and Benjamin. The matter of territorial provision for the daughters of Zelophehad, which frames the material of chaps. 27–36, is rendered meaningless outside of an early preexilic setting. In the postexilic era, land grant opportunities in northern Transjordan would have been meaningless.

---

[43] Levine, *Numbers 1–20*, 103.

[44] Milgrom, *Numbers*, JPS Torah Commentary (Philadelphia: Jewish Publication Society, 1990), xxxii–xxxv.

[45] See discussion in K. Kitchen, "The Patriarchal Age: Myth or History," *BAR* 21.2 (1995): 48–57, 88–95.

## (7) Synthesis and Conclusions

As is the case with Exodus, Leviticus, and Deuteronomy, the internal evidence of the Book of Numbers suggests a Mosaic origin for much of the material. Indeed the text reveals that Moses recorded certain materials, as noted earlier. Yet the Book of Numbers does not identify its author in the modern sense. The eminent prophet with whom God is said to have communicated in an undefinable manner[46] must be reckoned as the central character in the book and the indispensable human figure in the composition of the Book of Numbers. Whether the Mosaic material was recorded by Moses, his attendant officials (the šoṭerîm), as posited by Harrison, and/or later scribes through a history of oral and written transmission, the internal evidence does not afford a definitive conclusion regarding the final form of the canonical Book of Numbers. Even the more traditional evangelical scholars[47] acknowledge a textual history that includes a limited amount of history of interpolation, editing, and updating of materials. Yet in accepting later emendations, one need acknowledge the perpetual work of the Holy Spirit in and through faithful servants to finalize and preserve his revelation. As described earlier in this section concerning the evidence from extant textual sources, this textual editorial process continued well into the Second Temple period.

The majority of recent source-critical scholars, such as Gray, Budd, and Levine, have all but dismissed the role of Moses from even the earliest materials in the book. If Moses were such a revered legendary and bigger-than-life figure as the source and tradition critics would suggest, then why would Moses be present as such a human personage in the Book of Numbers? In this book he expresses doubt and self-pity (11:11–15 and even rebels against God as did the majority of the Israelite population (20:10–12). Even with these lapses of personal demeanor and character, he remained a great leader and spokesman for God. Milgrom calls Moses a "giant" who in Numbers "attains unprecedented moral stature."[48] He exemplifies humility, quality leadership, administrative acumen, and great wisdom and grace. Gray poignantly asserts that even the statement in 33:2 that Moses recorded the stages in the Israelite journey is debatable, because "that passage is closely related to others (P) which are clearly of far later origin than the age of Moses. Consequently the Mosaic authorship even of

---

[46] See below the section "Structure and Outline." Yahweh is said to have "spoken," "said," or "commanded" something to Moses sixty-three times. The exact nature of this descriptive revelatory terminology remains both a mystery and a wondrous reality.

[47] Harrison, *Numbers*, 15–24; Ashley, *Numbers*, 5–7.

[48] Milgrom, *Numbers*, xli–xlii.

this particular passage cannot be seriously considered."[49] For many the personality of Moses belongs to the realm of religious saga or heroic legend, created by the source authors to provide foundational credibility to the Torah. The fact that later Judaism created Mosaic legends, however, does not mean the biblical accounts are legendary.

The tradition critical approach of Noth resulted in his describing the Book of Numbers as confused and lacking order in its content and presenting "factually contradictory concepts."[50] He states: "Numbers participates only marginally in the great themes of the Pentateuchal tradition."[51] The first ten chapters are said to reflect the "Theophany at Sinai" motif, prominent in the latter half of Exodus, though describing various aspects of the content of the book as consisting of "numerous individual units, having no connection with one another and in whose sequence no factual arrangement can be discerned."[52] The literary structure outline approach of the present commentary stands in sharp contradistinction to Noth's approach. The Book of Numbers is both cohesive structurally and theologically, as I have sought to demonstrate throughout the commentary sections. Milgrom has likewise demonstrated the role of the Book of Numbers in the Pentateuch, in an introductory section entitled "Inner Cohesion and Links with Other Texts in the Hexateuch."[53]

The tacit assumption of critical scholars is that material in the Pentateuch, which reflects the priestly concerns of the postexilic community, demands later compositional origin. They posit the belief that such elements as the organization of the priests and Levites, lists of leaders and genealogical references, internal chronology, purification rites for the Israelite existence in Canaan, and international relations with the Edomites, Midianites, Ammonites, and Amalekites are supposedly the composition of the Priestly school and should be dated no earlier than the sixth to fifth centuries B.C. Such assumptions are countered by observation of the content and character of literature of the ancient Near East that predates even the earliest of dates for Moses and the Israelite wilderness experience. The literatures of Sumer, Middle Babylonia and Assyria, Early Ugarit, Anatolia, and Egypt reflect priestly systems more complex than Israelite, with detailed guild structures and numerous sacrificial rites. Dynastic lists and court histories, each with its own method of chronological reckoning, abound in the extant materials. Ancient Near Eastern legal texts reflect varying

---

[49] Gray, *Numbers*, xxx. Budd associates the content of this verse with the knowledge of the Yahwist or JE source about the geography of the region, based on commercial trade routes rather than pilgrim itineraries (*Numbers*, 353). Gray suggests that the "compiler must ... have had before him an ancient written source which he believed to have been written by Moses" (*Numbers*, 444).

[50] Noth, *Numbers*, 4.

[51] Ibid., 5.

[52] Ibid., 6.

[53] Milgrom, *Numbers*, xii–xvii.

complexity of structure, and their contents reveal a world of domestic and international relations paralleled by Israel, some chronologically antecedent and some subsequent. The Book of Numbers has an editorial and textual history that continued for more than a thousand years, yet in retrospect the process of discovery and understanding of the text and its history has endured for more than two millennia.

## 3. Structure and Outline of the Book of Numbers

Comprehension of the composition and framework of any literary document is essential to its interpretation, appreciation, and integration into the mind and life of the reader. Lengthy biblical books such as those of the Pentateuch, the Former and Latter Prophets, and some of the Writings, demand at least some understanding of structural factors in order to attain an acceptable and trustworthy exegesis. Collections such as the Pentateuch require one to address the issues of macrostructure, on the group and individual book levels, as well as the subtleties of the paragraph and pericope microstructures in interpretive endeavors.

The Book of Numbers perhaps has been neglected in evangelical circles because of a seeming lack of coherence and overall meaning and purpose. Seminary curricula seldom provide more than a brief overview of the book in survey courses. Complete courses dedicated to Numbers are almost nonexistent. Preaching from this text is relegated to the Balaam stories and oracles, the rebellious spy account, and an occasional reference to the Nazirite material to support a sermon on alcoholism. A closer examination of the internal factors in discerning the framework of Numbers will afford its readers, interpreters, and homileticians the handles and keys for opening up a new realm of Pentateuchal studies.

### (8) History of Analysis

The structure of the Book of Numbers furnishes several keys to understanding its content and theology. A perusal of outlines among commentaries of the past century, however, yields multifarious approaches, each organized around either a perceived central theme or a grammatical or artificial framework. For some the book appears to be a collection of somewhat unrelated fragments from legal, priestly, historical, and census materials, arranged under the three geographical markers in the text. The following examples reflect the majority three-part approach built upon this framework.

G. B. Gray divides the book as follows:[54]

---

[54] G. B. Gray, *A Critical and Exegetical Commentary on Numbers,* ICC (1903).

| I.   | Scene: The Wilderness of Sinai                | 1:1–10:10    |
|------|-----------------------------------------------|--------------|
| II.  | Scene: North of Sinai, West of the Arabah     | 10:11–21:9   |
| III. | Scene: East of the Arabah                     | 21:10–36:13  |

P. J. Budd structures his study as:[55]

| I.   | Constituting the Community at Sinai           | 1:1–9:14     |
|------|-----------------------------------------------|--------------|
| II.  | Journey—Setbacks and Success                  | 9:15–25:18   |
| III. | Final Preparations for Settlement             | 26:1–35:34   |
|      | (chap. 36 appendix, supp for chap. 27:1–11)   | 36:1–13      |

J. de Vaulx offers the following outline:[56]

| I.   | Organization of the People of God Before Its Departure | 1:1–10:10 |
|------|--------------------------------------------------------|-----------|
| II.  | Journey in the Desert from Sinai to the Plains of Moab | 10:11–22:1 |
| III. | In the Plains of Moab, Preparations for Entrance into the Promise Land | 22:1–36:13 |

One of the difficulties in the geographical framework approach to outlining the Book of Numbers is the placement of the division between the second and third sections. D. T. Olson, in his survey of Numbers commentaries, has noted: "In fact, among the 33 commentators who based their suggested outlines of Numbers on its geographical notations, 18 significantly different proposals were presented."[57] Other attempts based upon source critical theory, internal chronology, or traditions history have proved equally inadequate. In general, most of these outline variants reflect an arbitrary and artificial approach that does not give adequate attention to the book's internal grammatical and thematic elements.

The most recent investigation of the structural problems in Numbers is that of Olson, in the revision of his Yale dissertation entitled *The Death of the Old and the Birth of the New: The Framework of the Book of Numbers and the Pentateuch.* Olson proposed that the two censuses in chaps. 1 and 26 serve as the major indicators of outline and theme.

I. The End of the Old: First Generation of God's People (1:1–25:18)
    A. The Preparation and Inauguration of the March of the Holy People Israel (1:1–10:36)

---

[55] Budd, *Numbers.*

[56] J. de Vaulx, *Les Nombres, Sources Bibliques* (1972).

[57] D. T. Olson, *The Death of the Old and the Birth of the New: The Framework of the Book of Numbers and the Pentateuch,* BJS 71 (Chico, Cal.: Scholars Press, 1985), 35; cf. id., *Numbers,* IBC (Louisville: John Knox, 1996), 3–7.

1. Preparation and Ritual Organization of the March (1:1–10:10)
2. The Inauguration of the March (10:11–36)

B. The Cycle of Rebellion, Death, and Deliverance of the Holy People of Israel with Elements of Hope but Ultimate Failure (11:1–25:18)

1. Repeated Incidents of Rebellion and Atonement (11:1–20:29)
2. The End of the First Generation: Signs of Hope Coupled with Ultimate Failure (21:1–25:18)

II. The Birth of the New: The Second Generation of God's People Prepare to Enter the Promised Land (26:1–36:13)

A. Preparation and Organization of the New Holy People of God

1. The Second Census of the Twelve Tribes and the Levites (26:1–65)
2. The Daughters of Zelophehad (27:1–11)
3. The Commissioning of Joshua by Moses (27:12–23)
4. Further Cultic and Legal Regulations for the New Generation (28:1–30:16)
5. Moses' Last Act of Military Leadership: Revenge versus Midianites (31:1–54)
6. The Request of Reuben and Gad for the Allotment of Land in Transjordan (32:1–33:56)
7. Law as Promise: Divine Commands concerning the Anticipated Residence of the People in the Promised Land (34:1–36:13)

B. Will This Second Generation Be Faithful and Enter the Promised Land (Promise) or Rebel and Fail as the First Generation (Warning)?

The Book of Numbers serves as a pivotal transition document in the Pentateuch between the sojourning first generations *(tôlĕdōt)* of Genesis and Exodus and the Promised Land inheritants under Joshua. Support for Olson's approach is derived from other internal factors, such as the additional elements in the second census and the theme of death and rebirth. His innovative and insightful study invites further inquiry into the substructures of the text of Numbers.

### (9) Structural Analysis

Structural analysis of the canonical text of a biblical book must take into consideration the following elements: (1) grammatical indicators; (2) thematic repetition and development; (3) chiastic, convergent, and divergent structures and substructures; (4) mnemonic devices; (5) rhetorical devices; and (6) form variants. Grammatical forms may serve as indicators by which the author(s) and editor(s) marked divisions, developed arguments, and drew attention to certain factors. Repetition of themes and integral elements may signal key theological issues or provide structural cohesiveness. Chiastic, convergent, and divergent structures function as vehicles for conveying important theological points. Mnemonic devices facilitated oral recitation, memorization, and transmission. Literary skill and artistry of the author-editor are demonstrated in the use of rhetorical devices and variations of form for the purpose of highlighting internal components.

A close examination of the Book of Numbers yields several of these essential elements for determining the outline, infrastructure, and principal themes.

1. Repetitious grammatical structures.  (a) The first word in the Hebrew text, the preterite form, *wayĕdabbēr* (lit., "and he spoke"), which as noted above served as the title or heading of the early Hebrew text, occurs numerous times in the Book of Numbers; but in several cases it stands as a major marker in the text.[58] (b) A second preterite form, *wayyōʾmer,* functions similarly.[59] (c) The temporal preterite form *wayĕhî* (lit., "and it was") serves both conjunctive and disjunctive functions.[60]

2. Thematic repetition.  The following themes are recurrent throughout the Book of Numbers: (a) census and tribal lists; (b) historical references, ranging from geographical notes to incident introductions and summaries; (c) laws related to purification, offerings, inheritance, et cetera; (d) the roles and functions of the priests and Levites; and (e) rebellions of the Israelites and their leaders.

3. Convergent and divergent themes.  Some of the above themes find convergence and divergence, developing chiastic movements in the various structural cycles. These provide additional thematic development and broad emphases in the book, and they anticipate further expansion in later books.

The following structural outline results from this assemblage, with other

---

[58] The form וַיְדַבֵּר occurs in 1:1; 2:1; 3:1,5,11,14,44; 4:1,17,21; 5:1,5,11; 6:1,22; 8:1,5,23; 9:1,9; 10:1; 12:1 (וַתְּדַבֵּר); 13:1; 14:26, 39; 15:1, 17; 16:20, 23, 26; 17:1, 9, 16, 21; 18:8, 25; 19:1; 20:7; 21:5; 25:10, 16; [26:1; 27:6, 12 (Sam Pent)]; 27:15; 28:1; 30:2; 31:1, 3; 33:50; 34:1, 16; 35:1, 9. The complete formula וַיְדַבֵּר יְהוָה אֶל־ PN לֵאמֹר occurs in 1:1; 2:1; 3:5,11,14,44; 4:1,17, 21; 5:1,5,11; 6:1,22; 8:1,5, 23; 9:1, 9; 10:1; 13:1; 14:26; 15:1,17; 16:20,23,26; 17:1,9,16; 18:25; 19:1; 20:7; 25:10, 16; 26:1*; 27:6*,15; 28:1; 30:2; 31:1,3; 33:50; 34:1, 16; 35:1,9. Occurrences of extended formula with the added imperative of דַּבֵּר ("speak") 5:5–6, 11–12; 6:1–2, 22–23; 8:1–2; 9:9–10; 15:1–2,17–18; 37–38; 16:23–24; 17:16–17; 18:25–26 (variant); 33:50–51; צַו ("command") 5:1–2; 28:1–2; 34:1–2; 35:1–2, 9–10; שָׂא ("lift up, take up") 1:1–2; 4:1–2,21–22; 26:1–2; קַח ("take") 3:44–45; 8:5–6; 20:7–8; אֱמֹר ("say") 17:1–2; others 3:5–6,14–15; 10:1–2; 13:1–2; 16:20–21,26; 17:9–10; 25:16–17; 31:1–2,3; negative injunction 4:17–18.

[59] The וַיֹּאמֶר forms occur numerously throughout the book. Those of significant placement on primary and secondary division levels include 3:40; 7:11; 10:29,31,35; 11:11,16,23; 12:4,6,14; 14:11,13,14,20; 15:35,37; 16:8,16; 17:25; 18:1,20; 20:12; 21:8,34; 22:12,29,34,35; 23:1,3,11,13, 25,27; 25:4; 26:1; 27:6,12; 30:1; 31:21,25; 32:5,6,20,25; 36:2. Of these, the complete formula וַיֹּאמֶר ... לֵאמֹר occurs only in 7:4; 15:37; 26:1 (וַיְדַבֵּר in SamPent); 27:6 (like 26:1, the MS evidence for וַיְדַבֵּר is strong—SamPent and several Gk. MSS); 31:25; 32:25.

[60] Disjunctive function (marking a new section) of וַיְדַבֵּר in 7:1; 10:11; 11:1; 25:19 and conjunctive in 15:32; 16:31; 17:7; 26:20; 31:32.

structural elements to be discussed with the exegesis of various subsections:

1. Historical setting
2. Twelve tribe listing
3. Matters related to the priests and/or Levites
4. Laws defining the nature of the faithful community

These elements vary in content, length, and order depending upon the nature and intent of the given cycle. For example, the tribal lists of the census in chaps. 1 and 2 reflect the fullness of God's blessing and order and unity in the community; whereas, in chaps. 32 and 34 discord enters the picture of the nation at the doorstep of the Promised Land. In chaps. 3 and 4 the orderly responsibilities of the Levites and priests are delineated for the faithful community; whereas, in chap. 16 the Levite Korah instigates a rebellion, and in the third climactic rebellion cycle, a Mesopotamian prophet-diviner carries out the only priestly duties where all others have failed seditiously.

### *(10) Structural Outline*

Book One: The End of the First Generation in the Wilderness (1:1–25:18)
  I. Faithfulness of Israel at Sinai (1:1–10:10)
    1. Sinai Cycle A: Census and Consecration (1:1–6:27)
      (1) Historical Prologue: In the Wilderness (1:1)
      (2) Military Conscription Census of the Twelve Tribes of Israel (1:2–46)
        EXCURSUS: THE LARGE NUMBERS IN NUMBERS
      (3) Holy Arrangement of the Israelite Camps (2:1–34)
      (4) Responsibilities and Census of the Levite Clans (3:1–4:49)
      (5) Purification Laws for the Faithful Community (5:1–31)
      (6) The Sacred Nazirite Vow (6:1–21)
      (7) The Priestly Blessing (6:22–27)
    2. Sinai Cycle B: Tabernacle and Celebration (7:1–10:10)
      (1) Offerings of the Leaders of the Israelite Tribes (7:1–89)
      (2) Menorah Lamp Arrangement (8:1–4)
      (3) Installation of the Levites (8:5–26)
      (4) The Second Passover: With New Delineations (9:1–14)
      (5) Pattern of the Journey: The Lord and the Cloud (9:15–23)
      (6) The Silver Trumpets (10:1–10)
  II. THE REBELLIOUS GENERATION IN THE WILDERNESS (10:11–25:18)
    1. Rebellion Cycle A: From Sinai to Zin—Decline of the Old Generation (10:11–15:41)
      (1) Historical Reference: The Movement from Sinai to the Desert of Paran (10:11–13)
      (2) The Departure from Sinai (10:14–36)

      (4) Boundaries of land and Cisjordan Tribal (9 1/2) Leaders
          (34:1–29)
      (5) Levitical Cities and the Cities of Refuge (35:1–34)
      (6) Inheritance Laws: Zelophehad Clarifications (Laws and Land)
          (36:1–12)
   3. Conclusion to the Book of Numbers (36:13)

### (11) Derived Themes

Analysis of this outline offers several significant themes and subthemes developed variously throughout the book. Some modern critical source theory approaches, because of presuppositions concerning the history of the text and the role of the priestly editors, have overlooked the nature and purpose of the book. The central and unifying theme of the Book of Numbers is the faithfulness of God to fulfill his promise to his people, even when they rebel against him. Moses and not Aaron is the central human figure, even in the setting forth of the primacy of the Levitical priesthood (Num 17:1–13). The key motifs are as follows:

1. God at Work in Israel—God is at work in history via his presence and providential purpose.

2. Tribal Community—Unity and disunity are the polar structures of the tribal coalition: unity is evident when they are obedient to Yahweh; disunity, when in rebellion. This differentiation anticipates future discontent and disharmony.

3. Journey of Faith—The journey theology of Genesis, which keeps Israel in pursuit of the dream by faith.[61] Identification is made with the patriarchal ancestors.

4. Rebellion—Rebellion among God's people will be judged. The past and present examples anticipate a future history of contention with God.

5. Land and People—They pursue the promise, but they reject it and then later prepare for entry into the Land. "The promise of land proleptically fulfilled for each generation."[62]

6. Promise and Fulfillment—God will work on behalf of his people to fulfill his promises, even among a rebellious generation.

7. Priests and Levites—The priests and Levites serve a key cultic role on behalf of God for the community of faith.

8. Purification Rites—Purification ritual delineation is needed to prevent and atone for defilement.

9. Wilderness Motif—The wilderness motif provides Israelite history with a model of purification in the wilderness setting.

---

[61] W. Brueggemann, *Genesis,* IBC (Philadelphia: John Knox, 1982), 121–22.
[62] Olson, *Death of the Old,* 187.

10. Numerous Descendants—The blessing of progeny extends throughout the generations. Twice the census taking evidences God's richest blessing upon the people, fulfilling the promise of numerous descendants.

11. God's Leaders—Leadership is needed among God's people to carry out his work in an orderly manner. The motif of leadership in matters of administration and cult obtain in Moses succeeded by Joshua and Aaron followed by Eleazar. But even God's chosen leaders may fall.

## 4. Structural Theology of the Book of Numbers

The overarching theme of the Book of Numbers is that Yahweh reveals himself to his people as the faithful God of Israel through word and deed. In word and deed he demonstrates his loyalty and faithfulness to his people, challenging them to be faithful to the special covenant relationship he has revealed to and established with them. The resultant analysis of the structure of the book has yielded seven cycles of material in three movements, with each cycle consisting of the following basic elements:

1. Historical setting
2. Twelve tribe listing
3. Cycle development
4. Matters related to the priests and/or Levites
5. Laws defining the nature of the faithful community

The seven cycles evidence a literary symmetry within the three movements in a 2–3–2 pattern, collectively reflecting the three stages in the life of the people in the wilderness. The three stages of faithfulness (2 cycles), rebellion (3 cycles), and resolution (2 cycles) forecast the remaining history of the nation in its cyclical pattern of devotion, rejection, and renewal found in the Former Prophets. Hence the Deuteronomic pattern provides an overarching umbrella to the entire book. Individual elements in the above pattern may be orchestrated within the given cycle by means of expansion, reduction, reordering, or deletion so as to emphasize the message within.

The geographical movement of the nation parallels the threefold pattern of the response-relationship the people had with God. (1) In the setting of Mount Sinai, two cycles of material emphasize God's faithfulness to his people, the fullness of his blessing, and the purity and unity of the people in their devotion. (2) In the wilderness regions and the Plains of Moab the rebelliousness of the people is outlined in three cycles, each including individual, small group, and national responses. This movement climaxes with the defiance of the great prophet Moses followed by the unwilling faithful response of the pagan prophet Balaam. (3) The final chapter consisting of two cycles is situated in the Plains of Moab on the doorstep of the land of promise, with full anticipation of the inheritance of the promise and God's richest blessing through the fruitfulness of the land.

TYPES OF MATERIAL

| | | | | | |
|---|---|---|---|---|---|
| Historical Setting | HS | Priests/Levites | PL | Leadership | LD |
| Promised Land | LA | Tribal Listing | TL | Celebration | CE |
| Sacrifices / Offerings | SO | Rebellion | RB | Military Victory | MV |
| Journey Narrative | JN | Community Laws | CL | Balaam Oracles | BO |

CYCLE DEVELOPMENT

I    HS - TL - PL - CL - PL

II   HS - TL/CE - PL - HS - CL/CE - PL

III  HS - TL - JN - RB - JN - LA - TL - RB - <MV> - CL

IV   HS - RB - PL - TL - PL - CL

V    HS/JN - TL - RB - JN - PL - MV - RB - JN/ - MV - HS - BO/PL - HS - RB/PL /

VI   HS - TL - PL - CL - LD - CL/CE - CL

VII  HS - TL - MV - LA/TL - JN - LA/TL - PL -CL - HS

**Parallel**

**Parallel**

**Parallel**

**Parallels**

**Inclusio (Zelophehad's Daughters)**

### (1) Sinai Cycle A: The Community in Faithfulness and Purity (1:1–6:27)

The first movement consists of two cycles reflecting the blessing of God upon the descendants of Abraham, Isaac, and Jacob (Gen 12:1–3; 13:14–17; 15:4–21; 17:1–8; 22:16–18; 26:2–5; 28:11–15). When the Lord speaks, the faithful community responds to his leading. The historical setting is Mount Sinai, the mount of blessing and revelation, in the first day of the first month of the second year after the Exodus (1:1). In the first cycle the census of the male descendants of the sons of Jacob demonstrates God's faithfulness in fulfilling the promise to Abraham of a great nation and numerous descendants. The people were organized in an orderly manner in their encampment around the sacred worship center, the Tent of Meeting, where Moses or the high priest encountered the presence of God. God's symbolic presence in the ark of the covenant was the epicenter of the community, followed in concentric circles by the tabernacle courts, then the clans of the priests and Levites (enumerated in chaps. 3 and 4), and then by three tribes on each of the four sides of the tent structure. The faithful Israelites responded in doing "everything the LORD commanded Moses."[63]

The focus in the cycle development is on the duties and responsibilities of the priests and Levites who attend and maintain the sacred sphere. The Levites substituted for and functioned as the firstborn of the Israelites in this service before God. The cultic issues of purity and dedication of the people who are to be holy before an absolutely holy God ensue (5:1–31). Uncleanness of all kinds, whether as a result of disease, personal sin or guilt, or marriage defilement, must be removed from the camp. Chapter 6 completes the cycle with two dedicatory elements: personal commitment of one's life before the Lord in the vow of the Nazirite and the Aaronic priestly benediction. A life of holiness before God is a life of peace and grace and blessing.

### (2) Sinai Cycle B: The Tabernacle and the Community of Faith (7:1–10:10)

The second Sinai cycle has as its implied historical setting the completion of the tabernacle under the direction of Moses, thereby tying Num 7:1 directly to Exod 40:17–33.[64] After Moses sets up the tabernacle on the first day of the first month of the second year (hence chronologically before the setting of Sinai cycle one), each of the twelve tribes daily in sequence brings dedicatory utensils and offerings to the tabernacle, each presenting like gifts (7:2–88). At the conclusion of this unified effort of faithful donation of sacrifices to Yahweh, Moses enters the Tent of Meeting and God communicates with his servant

---

[63] 1:54; 2:34; 3:39,51; 4:37,49; 5:4.
[64] Parallel phraseology: לְהָקִים אֶת־הַמִּשְׁכָּן and הוּקַם הַמִּשְׁכָּן respectively.

prophet. When the community of faith has one mind and one spirit, God reveals himself to them.

After appropriately setting the oil lamps in the lampstand (8:1–3), symbols of the light of God's presence, the Levites are set apart in the presence of the people through proper purification rites so that they may serve the Lord and perform their required duties in regard to the tabernacle. Cleansing from sin and physical impurity is prerequisite to faithful service (8:4–14). The historical setting advances to the fourteenth of the first month to deal with several issues regarding the celebration of Passover: impurity of those who have touched the dead, delay of celebration for those who have been in another country and missed the required pilgrimage, and admission of resident aliens who desire to join in the festival activities (9:1–14). This section serves retrospectively to call to remembrance God's great act of salvation in the Exodus and prospectively to anticipate God's great blessing in the productivity of the Promised Land.

The setting then returns to the beginning of the month when the tabernacle construction had been completed and the symbols of God's presence and leadership—the cloud over the tent by day and the pillar of fire by night[65]—had descended upon this mobile desert sanctuary (9:15–23). As the cloud-pillar would migrate through the wilderness regions, the sacred enclosure and the faithful community would follow.[66] The God of Israel is not confined by space and time, and he is there constantly to provide direction, sustenance, and protection.

The cycle concludes with the preparation of the two silver trumpets that served numerous functions in providing direction to the people (10:1–10). The use of one or both of the trumpets, sounded in varying fashion, allowed the priests to convey important instructions to the congregation, such as: (1) the calling of a full assembly, (2) the gathering of the tribal heads, (3) the orderly departing of the camps, (4) alarming the people for warfare, and (5) celebrating the festivals with sacrifices and offerings. The final words of Moses from the Lord, "they will be a memorial for you before your God. I am the LORD your God," resound with the message of the entire Pentateuch: Yahweh, God of Israel, exists, and he desires to relate directly and intimately with his people.

### (3) Rebellion Cycle A: People and Leaders (10:11–15:41)

The third cycle begins as the first has ended, with the people faithfully responding to God's direction through Moses. The initial section (10:11–36)

---

[65] Exod 13:21–22 and 40:34–38 serve as an inclusio focused upon God's presence with his people and his leadership from the day of the Exodus to the completion of the sanctuary, in and around which his presence symbolically abides.

[66] Note the repetition of the phrase עַל־פִּי יְהוָה (lit., "by the mouth of Yahweh") here as throughout the lyrical account of Yahweh's cloud (9:16–23).

functions transitionally between the cycles of faithfulness and rebellion. The historical setting is the twentieth of the second month (Iyyar) of the second year after the Exodus (10:11). They set out from the Sinai Wilderness in orderly fashion by tribal camps aligned behind the ark of the covenant. Each of the twelve and the divisions of the priests and Levites advance three days across the Sinai peninsula, with Moses echoing the words of praise and thanksgiving for God's victories and blessings. But suddenly the picture is altered—the people are no longer the faithful, orderly, responsive, and thankful children of God. God had meant *good (tov)* for his people (10:29), but they would respond by grumbling *evil (raᶜ)* before him (11:1).

The cycle development is extensive, showing the levels of rebellion that unfold in the life of this formerly faithful assembly. The incident of fire, a common symbol of God's judgment, following the peoples' complaints about the severity of the desert, serves as an exemplar of the rebellions to come (11:1–3). The pattern is portrayed in six steps: the people rebel, God's displeasure is described, a form of judgment is meted out, Moses intercedes on behalf of the people, the judgment subsides, and often the incident locale is given an appropriate name for remembrance. The second complaint is concerning food supply, rebelling against God's faithful provision for their needs (11:4–35). Next the family of Moses revolts against his God-given authority (12:1–16). The fourth rebellion is the rejection of the land of promise (13:1–14:45). Here a faithful remnant is embodied in Joshua and Caleb. The tribal listing is repeated at the beginning of this incident to contrast with the previous tribal listings, which picture the people in a state of blessing and devotion. The description of the offerings in chap. 15 commences with the phrase "After you enter the land I am giving you as a home," which is in sharp contradistinction to Israel's renunciation of its territorial heritage. God will bring abundant blessing to his children when they respond in faithfulness to his words of instruction and hope. The second group of offerings set forth the sacrificial requirements for one who has transgressed the Law unintentionally out of ignorance or accident, but the section closes with severe judgment for anyone who deliberately and willfully rejects God and his word (15:22–31). An example of this form of judgment ensues: stoning for the breaking of the Sabbath. The cycle concludes on a dedicatory note: Israelites will wear special garment attachments as symbols of their faithfulness and their desire to know Yahweh as their Saving God. The last phrase of the cycle (15:41) repeats that of the conclusion to the first two cycles (10:10), "I am the LORD your God [ʾănî YHWH ʾĕlōhêkem]."

### (4) Rebellion Cycle B: Priests and Levites (16:1–19:22)

The history of Israel's rebellion against God and his anointed leaders continues through the actions of the Levites of Korah, the members of the tribe of the eldest son of Jacob, and the members of the council of elders. The focus is pri-

marily on the degeneration of the Levites, who remained unmentioned in the
first rebellion cycle. The formerly loyal Levites, faithful defenders of Yahweh in
the golden calf incident after the Exodus, are challenging the authority of Moses
and Aaron. Eventually the rebellion spreads throughout the community, and God
threatens annihilation. Moses and Aaron intercede for the people. Some 14,700
die in a plague, but the larger population is spared (16:16–50).

The tribal list portion of the cycle pattern is truncated in 17:1–3 and absent
in the last rebellion cycle; representative staffs from the leaders of the twelve
tribes are collected, and a test of priestly priority ensues. The productivity of
Aaron's staff over against the others demonstrates the Lord's selection of
Moses' brother in priestly responsibility (17:4–13). Priestly duties are reiterated and expanded and are parallel to those outlined in chaps. 3 and 4 (18:1–
32). Purification offerings provide a context of sacerdotal cleansing, beginning
with the red heifer ash offering for one who has been polluted by touching a
dead body, providing purification for those who had come in contact with the
14,700 killed in the plague (16:49). The context is expanded in 19:9 to include
purification from sin.

### (5) *Rebellion Cycle C: From Moses to Balaam and Back to the People (20:1–25:18)*

The third rebellion cycle is the most enigmatic, containing the episodes and
oracles of the divination prophet Balaam. Here the rebellion cycles climax and
conclude. The historical setting is a series of movements from the Wilderness
of Zin to the borders of Edom and into the Plains of Moab. Two key individuals
fall into the seditious pattern of the nation: Moses and Balaam. Moses' defiance in striking the rock represents the final collapse of the seditious nation,
for the greatest of the prophets has joined in the rejection of God's sovereignty
over the lives of the people (20:2–13).

Following Moses' profaning act, passage through Edom is denied (20:14–
21), and Aaron dies, one of the few remaining from the generation of Israel
that experienced God's dramatic saving activity in the Exodus (20:22–29).
After a brief victory at Arad (21:1–3), the community repeats its pattern of
rebellion (21:4–9). But the journey quickly resumes through the Plains of
Moab, in which God gives victories over Sihon and Og of the Amorites in
Heshbon and Bashan respectively. After these victories the scene changes dramatically (21:10–35).

Balaam, a pagan sorcerer of Mesopotamian origin, whom one might expect
to rebel against the God of Israel (and he does), now becomes an unexpected
spokesman for God (22:1–20). Moses is silent in the narrative. Yet even if the
most faithful, devoted leader of the people of God should fall into sin, God will
use whatever resource is necessary to communicate with and for his people.
Jesus said in response to the Pharisees who requested that his disciples be

rebuked, "I tell you if they keep quiet, the stones will cry out."[67] That a donkey should be the most spiritually observant character in this section stands in sharp contradistinction to the nations and the individual leaders, a literary slap-in-the-face toward any humanly originated means of conceiving of God and his ways (22:21–35). God will ultimately accomplish his will by whatever means and agency necessary. What echo from the mouth of this most unusual servant of God are some of the most extraordinary words of praise for God and his purpose for his people. Reversal of fortunes reverberates through several episodes of the story: a persistent pagan prophet learns from a donkey, a Moabite king's desires are thwarted by God, and Balaam's intent to curse and bring condemnation upon Israel is turned by God into an opportunity to bring blessing beyond compare for the near and distant future (23:1–24:25). God reveals his character and his intent to bring abundant hope and beneficence to all of humanity, indeed to the Jews and to the Gentiles.

The third rebellion cycle concludes with another collapse of Israel's character, in spite of the wondrous revelation through the prophet Balaam (25:1–19). Idolatry at the doorstep of the land of promise accomplishes the punishment of the earlier generation and warns future generations of the consequences of rejecting God's law: judgment, plague, disease, and finally death. Temptations toward idolatry would plague Israel throughout their future in the land. Lest one think that the Balaam of chaps. 22–24 turned toward this God who had used him, we find that the illustrious prophet is the instigator of the means by which Israel would fall. The first generation ends in tragic judgment, and the new generation is faced with the issue of faithfulness to God, which will determine the course of their future.

### (6) Advent Cycle A: The Birth of the New Generation Who Will Inherit the Land (26:1–30:16)

The cycles of rebellion are concluded, seemingly, and now the new generation must face the challenges of their ancestors who died in the wilderness as God had spoken. Only Moses, Eleazar, Joshua, and Caleb remain from the rebellious generation; and Eleazar has succeeded his father Aaron as high priest. The historical setting is stated briefly, "After the plague" (of Beth Peor, 25:19). A second census is prescribed by God through Moses according to the tribal list, the results of which evidence that God faithfully has worked to continue the blessing of producing through the seed of Abraham a large nation, in spite of her continuous rebellion against him. God's promise is not nullified by the people's disobedience (26:1–65). A reminder of the past judgment upon Korah and his followers is issued in the Reuben tribal census (26:8–11). Their number has decreased due to their unfaithfulness, but they remain a sizable

---

[67] Luke 19:39–40.

tribe. God is longsuffering and will continue to bring blessing. Focus in the passage turns to the setting in the land of promise, that the coming land allocations should be based upon the size of population in each tribe. Another emphasis in the tribal census comes at the conclusion, none of the previously censused generation survived to be counted with the new.

The cycle development of the land theme is given a special casuistic context regarding the rights of women to inherit land portions. The daughters of Zelophehad are granted property rights in accordance with laws related to family inheritance, ensuring that all of Israel would receive God's provisions in the new land (27:1–11). The theme is expanded in an inclusio with the final chapter of Numbers. A second development is the transfer of leadership to Joshua, a new leader for a new generation. Moses had rebelled against God and his holiness, even as the people had. Thus he would not enter the land of promise[68] (27:12–23). (See Cycle Development Chart on p. 62.)

God will not only multiply the people, but he also will provide for them abundantly, so that they may bring special offerings of consecration and thanksgiving in celebration of God's goodness and faithfulness. Daily, weekly, monthly, and yearly offerings from the produce of the land are set forth, entailing a continuous life of devoted celebration of God. Special emphasis is placed upon the Feast of tabernacles, with great abundance of sacrifices being rendered unto God, an intentional reflection upon the earlier rejection of the abundance of the land after the report of the spies. The reference to "vows" in 29:39 provides the link between the offerings of chaps. 28–29 and the special "vows" of chap. 30. Special considerations are given to relief for women who take vows within or outside the context of a father's or husband's knowledge and approval.

### (7) Advent Cycle B: Preparation for War and Entry into the Promised Land (31:1–36:13)

The final cycle draws the reader's attention to the hope for assuming inheritance of the land of promise and blessing, but it also warns against falling into the same rebellious traps of their ancestral generation. The historical reference, victories over the Midianites, will prepare them for the wars to come in the conquest. The tribal listing comes via inference, whereby one thousand from each of the twelve tribes are called to battle against five Midianite kings and Balaam (31:1–12). The conclusion to the Midianite battle account raises issues of purification and conquest methodology. Questions regarding the survival of the Midianite women suggest that sources of idolatry and immorality must be purged, and purification from touching the dead is necessary for participation in the holy

---

[68] Deut 34:1–12. Under Joshua's leadership, the people would follow faithfully even as they had followed God's leadership through Moses in the Exodus and wilderness journey. Cf. Num 1:54; 2:34; 3:39,51; 4:37,49; 5:4.

community. Reference to Balaam's instigation of the Baal Peor incident reminds the readers of the hazards of straying from singular devotion to Yahweh their God and that God will eventually punish those who rebel against him (31:13–24). Portions of the spoils of war are given in tribute to the priests and Levites, whose responsibilities relate to the tabernacle rather than to warfare.

But soon the tribal unity of chaps. 1–10 and 26 begins to dissipate, especially in regard to matters of the land. Reubenites and Gadites request territorial allotments in the Transjordanian highlands between the Moabite plateau and Bashan, areas not included in the boundaries of the land of their inheritance (32:1–42). This tribal disunity portends future issues of discord such as the near annihilation of the Benjaminite tribe over the incident of the Levite concubine and the division of the kingdoms in the days of Rehoboam and Jeroboam II. Unity of focus and faith, as reflected in the initial Sinai cycles, is prerequisite for the people of God to fulfill the goals he has for them.

The stages of Israel's journey highlight God's leadership throughout the desert experience, from the dramatic departure from Egypt to the doorstep of Canaan and Jericho (33:1–49). Now if they are to fulfill God's plan in inheriting the land, several steps must be taken: drive out the present inhabitants, remove the sources of idolatry, take possession of the region, and divide the land according to tribal population. Attention is drawn to the key issue of idolatry, providing a portentous deuteronomic warning about failure to follow through in this fundamental matter. The first two commandments of Exod 20:1–17 express the foundational structure of the covenantal relationship between God and Israel: no other gods and no images of deity. If the people refuse to address this matter, however, then God will deal with his people in the manner he planned to deal with the idolatrous inhabitants. Israel could be driven from the land by foreigners (33:50–56).

The territorial boundaries evidence God's plan in fulfilling the promise to Abraham, Isaac, and Jacob. From the southern Negev to Lebanon, and from the Mediterranean to the Jordan River and rift valley, God's abundant blessing awaits those who will by faith proceed at his command (34:1–12). Yet again the Cisjordan tribes are nine and one-half, not the twelve plus the Levites, and the Transjordanian highlands are not included within the boundaries of the inheritance (34:13–15).

Provisions for the Levites are presented throughout the land (cf. Josh 21), and territorial rights are delineated. The faithful Levites (Exod 32:28–29) will receive property in forty-eight towns, with six of them serving as cities of refuge for anyone causing the accidental death of another (35:1–5). Other laws relating to murder and manslaughter complete this section devoted to the well being of the tribal community in the Promised Land (35:6–34). Homicide renders the land unclean, and God cannot coexist with the profane. Isaiah declared that the hands of the people were full of blood (Isa 1:15), and Jeremiah noted that the preservation of the innocents was prerequisite for living in the land (Jer 7:5–7). The community of faith must preserve the sanctity of life in order to maintain the righteousness and purity of the people before God and the nations.

In the final chapter additional stipulations regarding property possession among women, based upon the earlier case of Zelophehad's daughters, are delineated. The women are to marry within their tribal lineage in order to maintain territorial dominion of the tribal units. Again the gift of land and its proper distribution is in focus, with the integrity of each individual tribe maintained (36:1–12).

The Book of Numbers concludes with a summary statement concerning the role of Moses in disseminating God's revelation to the people (36:13). The crossing of the Jordan and the subsequent conquest of Jericho are anticipated when the story of the journey resumes.

## 5. Theology of the Book of Numbers

The major theological themes in the Book of Numbers derive from the infrastructure and content as demonstrated in the above "Structure and Outline of the Book of Numbers." The cyclical structure of the contents evidence the contrasting themes of God's revelation and humanity's response, God's unending faithfulness and humanity's propensity toward disobedience. The census enumerations and tribal lists bespeak God's fulfillment of the promise to Abraham to make of him a great nation. The recurring priestly purification texts evidence the holiness of God and outline the need for the people of God likewise to be holy, so as to be distinctively his. Together these themes highlight the necessity of wholeness, the unity of God, priests, and people working toward the realization and accomplishment of God's design for the world.

### (1) Nature and Work of God

The principal character in the Book of Numbers is unequivocally God. That God exists and proactively works in and through the lives of his special creation, humanity, male and female, is a quintessential theme of the Book of Numbers. The book is composed such that several aspects of God's nature are disclosed: (1) Presence—God exists and extends himself so as to abide with his people. (2) Revelation—God relates and reveals himself to humanity. (3) Faithfulness—God is for his people and fulfills his promises. (4) Holiness—God is holy and unchanging, and he demands the sanctity of his followers. (5) Uniqueness and Exclusivity—God is singular and will not endure the worship of other forms of deity.

PRESENCE OF GOD IN ACTION. The existence of God and the relational character of God exude from the pages of Scripture. The symbols of God's presence in the Book of Numbers are several. The tabernacle ("tabernacle of the Testimony" in 9:15; 10:11), especially the ark of the covenant (Exod 25:10–22; 37:1–9; Num 10:34), represent his relational presence. No anthropomorphic, zoomorphic, or botanical iconography was to be formed representing God (Exod 20:3–4). Instead a mobile sanctuary was constructed containing evidences of God's relational nature. The tabernacle defined a sacred space that has no temporal or geographical boundaries, containing a transportable wooden box with gold overlay in which were placed several of the visible evidences of his relationship to Israel: (1) the covenant tablets, representing the formal relationship between God and his people (Deut 10:1–5); (2) manna, God's provision in the wilderness (Exod 16:1–5,31–36; Num 11:7–9); and (3) later the golden symbols of the plague brought upon the Philistines while the ark circulated among their cities. Aaron's staff, a sign of the priesthood and the rebelliousness of the people, was to be placed in front of the Testimony (Num 17:1–11). The ark also served to represent God as their guide through the wilderness and commander in times of warfare (10:35–36).

In continuity with the Book of Exodus, God's presence was evidenced by the cloud that led the people by day as they journeyed from Sinai through the wilderness (Exod 13:21; Num 9:15–23; 10:12,34). A revelatory cloud pillar appeared when Miriam and Aaron opposed Moses (Num 12:5). God manifested himself through fire (11:1) and through a messenger-angel who appeared to Balaam and his donkey (22:22–35).

GOD AND REVELATION.    The revelation of the word and will of God for his people comes through several means. The often-repeated formula "YHWH spoke to *X* ... saying" provides the basic framework for the book as a whole. The agent of the revelatory process is usually Moses, though God may use a woman (Miriam, 12:4), a priest (Aaron, 12:4), a messenger-angel (22:22–35), a prophet-diviner (Balaam, 22:9–12), or even an animal (Balaam's donkey, 22:28–30).

Though the precise mechanism by or through which God disclosed himself to Moses and others remains a mystery, the introductory formulae of other prophetic literature provide insight into the nature and character of the process. For Isaiah, Ezekiel, and Daniel visionary insight afforded knowledge and understanding of God's word (Isa 1:1; 2:1; 29:11; Ezek 1:1; Dan 2:19). In Jeremiah and Ezekiel the phrase "The word of the LORD came to me" (lit., "was to me") characterizes the means by which the word of God became an overwhelming realization in his life (Jer 1:4; 2:1; Ezek 6:1; 7:1). The special relationship the prophet Moses had with God is evidenced in the phraseology of Num 12:6–8a.

> When a prophet of the Lord is among you
>> I reveal myself to him in visions
>>> I speak to him in dreams.
>> But this is not true of My servant Moses
>>> He is faithful in all my house.
>> With him I speak face to face (lit. "mouth to mouth")

> clearly and not in riddles
> he sees the form of the Lord.

The words of the apostle in 2 Pet 1:20–21 echo a parallel understanding of the nature of special revelation.

> Above all, you must understand that no prophecy came about by the prophet's own interpretation. For prophecy never had its origin in the will of man, but men spoke from God as they were carried along by the Holy Spirit.

God reveals himself through various acts of intervention into the human saga, via fruitful blessing, harsh judgment, or through dynamic reversal of the course of human events. Provision of manna for sustenance in the desert, water for drinking, and huts for dwelling are but a few of the means by which God reveals his beneficent nature. On the other hand, judgment via scorching fire, tragic loss in battle, or fatal disease may evidence his demand for holiness and faithfulness. The Balaam cycles are replete with examples of God thwarting human efforts to obstruct his revelatory acts. And if human agents fail in the process, he may use even a simple animal.

HOLINESS AND PURITY OF GOD. The Book of Leviticus delineates in detail the legislative criteria for Israel's holiness, and their fidelity would evidence to the nations the holiness of God. The Book of Numbers emphasizes certain demands for obedience to standards and statutes that would demonstrate Israel's acceptance or rejection of God's requirement that Israel be holy even as he is holy (Lev 19:2). God cannot and will not tolerate sin, uncleanness, injustice, or rebellion; hence purification and atonement rituals are presented, along with features that identify the people and evidence their sanctification (e.g., linen tassels).

M. Douglas has delineated a new approach to the analysis of the Book of Numbers in her recent volume.[69] Defilement is defined as "taboo" and is parallel to the Mesopotamian complex of forces that evoke responses such as oaths, vows, blessings, and cursings. The contents of these responses grow out of the people's understanding of the intrinsic character of being in deity.[70] Defilement is brought about by the abrogation of purity stipulations. The priests are the teachers, interpreters, and guarantors of purification. Israelite purity stands contra the dominant ideologies of the ancient Near Eastern world, in which impurity derives from contact with foreigners or lower classes, for the Book of Leviticus encourages the people to love the foreigner and the depressed constituents of society (Lev 19:14,15,34). The Book of Numbers is consequently divided into revolving cycles of story (Israel's sojourn in the wil-

---

[69] M. Douglas, *In the Wilderness*, JSOTSup 158 (Sheffield: JSOT Press, 1993).

[70] Douglas (ibid., 22–25) is following M. Geller's approach to purity and defilement, outlined in "The Šurpu Incantations and Lev. V.1–5," *JSS* 25.2 (1980): 183.

derness) and laws defining Israel's distinctive religion of holiness. Douglas's overall approach is somewhat artificial and simplistic and does not deal with the literary structure of the book. She also does not give due consideration to the moral and ethical character of the revelation of God.

In the Sinai cycles physical infirmities, personal liability, and familial discord are addressed (5:1–31). The Levites are set aside and ceremonially cleansed to ensure the sanctity of the tabernacle and its furnishings (3:1–4:49; 8:5–26). In the rebellion cycles judgment or death or plague is meted upon those who rebel and reject God's law. Identifying garment tassels are prescribed to aid the Israelites in remembering and obeying God's instructions. The red heifer sacrifice and subsequent use of the ashes in producing ritual purification waters provide for ceremonial expurgation of impurity due to the touching of the dead or sin. The rebellion cycle concludes with a plague judgment upon those Israelites who have succumbed to idolatry (25:1–18). God certainly cannot countenance the worship of other deities from the nations that surrounded Israel in the wilderness or in the land when they should arrive and settle.

FAITHFULNESS OF GOD. J. Milgrom describes God's word as "this unimpeachable reliability," for the Lord will fulfill his promises to his people in spite of their rebelliousness. He cannot endure disobedience, nor can he allow defilement to continue unattended. Hence, the cycles of purification ritual testify to God's demand for holiness and purity. God's faithfulness is demonstrated in a variety of forms: (1) deliverance from Egypt, (2) provisions in the wilderness—food, water, and shelter, (3) leadership—Moses, the pillar, priests and Levites, (4) land—though initially rejected by the people through the counsel of the majority of the spies, he repeatedly promises to provide this inheritance, and (5) victory over their enemies. The words of the prophet-diviner Balaam exemplify this element of God's character:

> God is not man, that he should lie,
>> nor a son of man, that he should change his mind.
> Does he speak and then not act?
>> Does he promise and not fulfill?
> I have received a command to bless.
>> He has blessed, and I cannot change it.

> No misfortune is seen in Jacob,
>> no misery observed in Israel.
> The LORD their God is with them,
>> the shout of the King is among them. (23:19–20)

God is at work in history and on behalf of his people.

PROMISE AND FULFILLMENT: GOD, PEOPLE, AND LAND. God promised to make Abraham into a great nation (Gen 12:2) and give his descendants the land of the Canaanites and the Amorites (Gen 15:18–21; 17:8). The two censuses evidence the magnitude of God's fulfillment of the promise of abundant descendants. The fulfillment of the promise of land for an inheritance remains elusive. The people reject the land based upon the majority opinion of the spies sent to reconnoiter the region, thus rebelling against God and his leadership from Egypt to the southern border of the territory. Hence, an unresponsive generation must pass away before the realization of this portion of the promise.

The Book of Numbers contains numerous anticipatory elements about the land when the promise would be brought to culmination. In Num 15:1–21 instructions are outlined concerning offerings that would be presented to God in celebration of his abundant blessing upon the harvest of herds and crops. Balaam's third oracle portends God's blessing upon the land (24:5–7). The provision of land for the daughters of Zelophehad assume territorial tribal allocations within the land of promise (27:1–23; 36:1–12). The bounteous offerings delineated for each of the holy days in chaps. 28–29 also indicate God's future blessing in the produce of the land. God even provides for those tribes seeking land allocation on the east side of the Jordan River. The boundaries delineated in chap. 34 echo an inheritance described generally in Gen 15:18–21. Provisions for the Levites and the protection afforded by the cities of refuge in both Cisjordan and Transjordan complete the anticipated fulfillment of blessing.

Warnings, however, abound for those who would reject God's blessing of land or abuse the privilege via murder, bloodshed, or idolatry. Severe judgment awaits any generation that rebels against God. Famine, drought, invasion, and eventually exile would be the resultant portion for the unfaithful generation of Israelites. Opportunities for blessing are wide open before the people, but the future remains in their hands.

UNIQUENESS AND EXCLUSIVITY OF GOD. The God of Israel is one, uniquely God, and therefore worthy of humanity's exclusive devotion. He cannot endure unrestrained the worship of other elements of his creation, whether nature, humanity, or alternate perceptions of deity. He is beyond human reason to comprehend and incomparable to human character (23:19).

Iconography of deity, aberrant cultic locations, cultic instruments, and worshipers of any alternative deity were to be removed from the land of promise (32:51–56). Failure to carry out this instruction would result in judgment. The consequences of the worship of Baal Peor in the plains of Moab served as an example for the people to remember (25:6–9).

### (2) Anthropological Themes

God's instruction to Adam to multiply and have dominion over the earth was a responsibility that lay within the realm of possibility for man through his adherence to God's direction. The Lord in his ever-creative manner had called out from a world of idolatry in Mesopotamia an individual whom he would bless personally and through whom he would bring great blessing to the world.

POPULATION AND DEMOGRAPHICS.   The large census numbers in the Book of Numbers, from which the biblical book derived its Greek, Latin, and English name, have puzzled scholars for centuries. A population of fighting men totaling 603,550 would yield an aggregate population of two million or more. From the original seventy persons who went down to Egypt (Gen 46:27; Exod 1:5) developed an enormous population of the descendants of Jacob. These passages serve to magnify the power of the promise to make of Abraham a great nation. His seed was to be as numerous as the stars in the heavens and the grains of sand on the seashore, and God had fulfilled his promise.[71]

OBEDIENCE OR DISOBEDIENCE.   A prominent programmatic theme in the Book of Numbers, based upon the broad structure of the canonical text, is that of obedience—disobedience—challenge to faithfulness. The language of the first two cycles geographically centered at Sinai is one of faithful obedience of the people to God's commands. The three wilderness cycles emphasize the rebellious nature of a people who are dissatisfied with God's provisions and blessings and have rejected the very gift of the promise, the land of the Cisjordan. These rebellions take the form of murmuring and complaining against God, challenging God's establishment of human authority in prophet and priest, spurning his gracious gifts, and breaking the commands of Torah. Such transgressions will not continue unaddressed. Only two of the original generation who experienced the wonder of God's great salvation act in the Exodus would see the fullness of God's benefaction by entering the land of promise. All others would die by fire, disease, plague, snake bite, or simply aging.

UNITY OR DISUNITY.   The challenge for the new generation outlined in the final two cycles would be to learn from their ancestors so as to experience God's blessing through faithful obedience to his revealed will. Otherwise they may suffer the same consequences of the first generation: loss of land and punishment from God. The later history of Joshua to Kings evidences the reality of this pivotal issue for the future of the nation. The two Sinai cycles depict the tribes in harmony and devotion to Yahweh their God, yet the rebellion cycles present a people in disarray, challenging their leaders. A variant report of the spies (a majority error), the rebellion of Korah and some of the Reubenites against Moses' authority, and a question of the future faithfulness of the Transjordan tribes in aiding the rest of the nation in its quest for the Promised Land all present challenges to the people of God. The history, with examples as early as the Book of Joshua, bear out the seriousness of this issue. Will they work together to fulfill the dream of inheritance and blessing or contend with one another to the detriment of the whole nation?

LEADERSHIP.   Foundational to Israel's existence, whether in Egypt, the

---

[71] For an assessment of the large numbers in the two censuses of Num 1–2 and 26, see "Excursus One: The Large Numbers in Numbers" in the commentary on chaps. 1–2.

wilderness of Zin, or in the land of Canaan, was God's guiding presence. Moses was the human instrument for conveying the will of God to the people. His authority was supplemented by the foundational support of the elders, the network of group direction through the tribal heads, and the cultic contributions of the priests and Levites. Together these provided the nation with an orderliness in administration, thus fulfilling the purpose of the nation. Moses and his successor Joshua were men of faith and vision, confident in God's promises, and able to see beyond the world's temporary challenges.

Moses and Aaron function also as royal and priestly leaders, providing a model for the generations to come, as in the administration of David and Zadok in the tenth century. When challenged as the appointed leaders, God's displeasure or choice is evidenced, as in the rebellions of Miriam and Aaron, the Korah uprising, and the contest of tribal staffs.

Even the most noble of the chosen leaders, however, must maintain a quality relationship with God manifested through continual devotion to his instruction and dominion. The rebellion cycles of 10:11–25:18 depict the deteriorating confidence of the people in their leaders and the degenerative deeds of the leaders themselves. The climax in this section is the unholy defiance of Moses against God in the striking of the rock. Thus he is prohibited from entering the land, and only Joshua and Caleb, the visionary spies from chaps. 13 and 14, would remain from the former generation to experience God's fullest blessing in the fulfillment of the promise of land.

The mentor-student relationship between Moses and Joshua is evidenced throughout the book. Joshua was there to witness the Spirit of God resting upon the elders (11:28–29), and he was a faithful spy along with Caleb among the majority who were unfaithful. After the second generation census, the Spirit-endowed Joshua was ordained by God before the new high priest Eleazar ben Aaron to succeed Moses in leading the people to the Promised Land (27:12–23).

### (3) Land Themes

The Books of Numbers and Deuteronomy provide transitional connective elements between the Patriarchal and Exodus narratives and the Joshua-led entry into the land of promise. In M. Noth's reconstruction of Israel's narrative history, the promises of innumerable descendants, the land of Canaan, and abundant blessing are lesser factors in the content and theology of Numbers.[72] In the above "Structural Theology," however, the theme of the promise of land was shown to figure prominently in the rebellion and future hope sections of the book.

PROMISE OR REJECTION. The land that had been promised to Abraham's

---

[72] M. Noth, *A History of Pentateuchal Traditions*, trans. B. Anderson (Chico, Cal.: Scholars Press, 1981), 79**.

descendants was rejected by the vast majority of the Exodus generation. As Davies noted, "their behaviour was characterized by a blatant ingratitude and contempt for Yahweh's purpose ... a blatant repudiation of the beneficent acts of Yahweh in redeeming them from bondage."[73] In the wilderness the Israelites longed for their former status of safe enslavement rather than yearning for the fulfillment of God's promise in the temporary uncertainty of their freedom. The wilderness, Brueggemann has pointed out, presents two sharply antithetical views: "The wilderness is the route of promise on the way to land, or the wilderness is unbearable abandonment to be avoided by return to slavery."[74] The land and its produce were to be the crowning evidence of God's goodness and faithfulness, yet an unfaithful and rebellious generation would rather die in the barrenness of the desert than inherit God's richest blessing.

God had demonstrated his love and provision for the people in the miraculous manifestation of his power in the Exodus sequence, defeating the pharaoh of Egypt who was for much of the Late Bronze Age in control of the land of Canaan promised to Israel. Yet the majority of the spies who searched out the land from south to north viewed the people who were in subjectivity to the imperialistic pharaohs of the eighteenth and nineteenth dynasties as insurmountable foes and unconquerable giants. Thus the book presents a challenge to the second generation of Abraham's descendants to launch out across the Jordan in faith, drive out the idolatrous inhabitants, and inherit the fruitful land, a land flowing with milk and honey (13:21–33; 33:51–54).

CELEBRATION.   The bountiful agricultural produce of the land of promise, exemplified in the grapes, pomegranates, and figs brought forth by the spies, would be a blessing to the next generation of the descendants of Jacob. Despite the unfaithfulness of the former generation, God would remain faithful to his promise to Abraham, Isaac, and Jacob and lead them into a land that would yield such abundance that they would bring its fruits to worship their beneficent provider. In Num 15:1–21, juxtaposed against the preceding two chapters citing Israel's rejection of the land, the sacrifices before Yahweh of the harvest of field and flock of the land are outlined. The blessings are promised, but the people must by faith advance obediently into the land and inherit its fullness. Resident aliens are enjoined to celebrate God's goodness together with the native Israelites. The agricultural elements for the various sacrifices and festival offerings presuppose the continuous provisions by God in the land (Num 28–29).

TRIBAL ALLOCATIONS.   The land is to be apportioned among the tribal units according to their relative populations, an orderly process to be overseen by appointed leaders from each of the tribes. The boundaries of the land for

---

[73] E. W. Davies, *Numbers,* NCB (Grand Rapids: Eerdmans, 1995), lviii.

[74] W. Brueggemann, *The Land: Place as Gift, Promise, and Challenge in Biblical Faith,* Overtures to Biblical Theology (Philadelphia: Fortress, 1977), 37.

inheritance are summarized in 34:1–12. Yet striking is the fact that the Transjordan regions requested for allotment by the tribes of Reuben, Gad, and a portion of Manasseh are positioned outside the perimeter. This section portends coming jealousy and disagreements among the tribes of the Book of Judges and the later Divided Monarchy history.

Special provisions of land and produce are made for the priests and Levites who had been assigned responsibilities relative to the transportation and maintenance of the tent of meeting and its cultic paraphernalia. The priests were assigned the responsibility of delineating between the clean and the unclean, teaching the Israelites to distinguish the clean from the unclean and the sacred from the profane, and instructing them in all the commandments of the Lord (Lev 10:11). These duties could best be administered by living in proximity to the people distributed throughout the land.

*(4) Worship Themes: Sanctification and Purification*

Ritual worship practices through sacrificial offerings were common to all cultures of the ancient Near East. Examples of the rendering of animal, grain, vegetable, liquid, and incense unto deity, by individual or group, through total or partial forfeiture or destruction in the context of sacred space (temple, altar, cultic stand, etc.) are attested from the Neolithic period (8000–4000 B.C.) onward. These cultic acts served several key functions within local societies: (1) to engage in some form of relationship with deity, (2) to maintain or celebrate the relationship, or (3) to restore an abrogated relationship. Wenham observes that ritual "is a means of communication between God and man, a drama on a stage watched by human and divine spectators. Old Testament rituals express religious truths visually as opposed to verbally."[75]

Burnt offerings for consecration (Lev 1:1–17) exemplify this concept. A person presents an animal before God, makes some form of identification with the offering by placing the hand upon its head, slaughters and sections the animal in the presence of the priest, and gives the pieces to the priest for preparation for cremation upon the altar. The offering is totally consumed by the fire, rendering it fully (with the exception of ash residue) unto the realm of the invisible God. The blood, the source of life, is sprinkled and poured out by the priest on and around the altar, presenting it back to God, the ultimate source of all life. God's holy presence necessitates perfect sacrifices, proper ritual acts, and purified personnel.

SINAI CYCLES. In the cycles of the Book of Numbers, the kinds of purification activity and personnel are correlated with the historical context. Hence, in the first Sinai cycle, in which the bountiful community of blessing is described in orderly array, the responsibilities of the priests and Levites are

---

[75] Wenham, *Numbers,* 29.

detailed. The subsequent purification rituals focus upon certain taboos that may effect the defilement of the community constituency, namely physical contamination, interpersonal injustice, or marital infidelity. The section concludes on a positive note, the delineation of the Nazirite vow ritual, whereby nonpriestly individuals may voluntarily consecrate themselves to the Lord for some special purpose (unidentified in the text). A reminder of priestly preeminence is included at the conclusion of the chapter.

In the second Sinai cycle, offerings of cultic implements, sacrificial animals, and incense are integrated with the listing of the twelve tribes, thereby presenting a unified and balanced picture of community life in proper relationship to God. The process of purification in the consecration of the Levites, assisting agents to Aaron and his sons the priests, follows in the context. Passover restrictions, pillar of fire and cloud instructions, and signal trumpet directives complete this cycle that is replete with cultic material.

REBELLION CYCLES. The positioning of the offerings delineated in 15:1–21 is intentional, contrasting the content of the rebellions of 11:1–14:45. God's will is to bless his people, even though they may at times defy him by rejecting his beneficence. A people living in holy communion with God will render back to God a symbolic portion of that with which he has blessed them and sustained them: animals, grains, oil, and wine. Several "commands from the LORD" complete the purifications section: (1) atonement offerings for inadvertent wrongs of the individual or community, done out of ignorance or negligence, (2) community cleansing via the stoning execution of one who has broken the Sabbath, the sign of the covenant, and (3) blue-corded tassels for identity and reminder of the covenant commands of their saving God.

The Korah and Reubenite insurrection of the second rebellion cycle provides the background for two levels of purifications delineated in 18:8–19:22. First, priests and Levites who consume offerings and tithes presented to the Lord must be ritually clean, unlike the seditious Korahites. Second, ashes derived from the ritual slaughtering of a red cow are to be stocked in the sanctuary for purification from corpse contamination. Korah's encroachment of the tabernacle resulted in its defilement, hence the sprinkling of blood at the entry (19:4), and nearly fifteen thousand died in connection with the rebellion, necessitating a massive purification process. God will not permit sin to permeate his presence, and any such defilement demands immediate cleansing.

In the final rebellion cycle, Aaron dies and Moses disregards God's holiness, for which he is prohibited from entering the Promised Land. Ritual activity is performed instead by a reluctant and antagonistic sorcerer. Yet as Balaam states in the second oracle, God will not allow his people to be cursed by such an individual.

> For indeed there is no sorcery against Jacob,
>     no divination against Israel.

Now it will be said of Jacob,
  indeed of Israel, what God has performed! (23:23)

Three times Balaam has seven altars built with seven sets of bull and ram sacrifices. He then offers a pronouncement of blessing upon Israel. A fourth oracle of ultimate blessing, the promise of a glorious messianic ruler, ensues without a concomitant ritual act as the Spirit of God comes upon him. The Balaam oracles stand as a testimony of God's faithfulness to Israel and his commitment to work on behalf of his people, even though they rebel against him. He will eventually bring them back to himself.

ADVENT CYCLES. The first advent cycle contains extensive ritual delineation with two subjects at hand, offerings for the various holy days and vows relating to women. The offerings anticipate God's rich blessings upon fields and flocks in the Promised Land, and envision a nation in faithful devotion to God as they celebrate their relationship to God through the offerings of consecration, communion, and atonement. Special emphasis is given to the Feast of tabernacles, during which the priests sacrifice abundant animal offerings—decreasing the number of bulls from thirteen on the first day to seven on the seventh day along with two rams and fourteen lambs—and their accompanying grain and wine gifts.

The final cycle of the Book of Numbers contains several ritual applications. The disposition of the plunder from the defeat of the Midianites includes fire and water purification of metallic objects, water purification for those items unable to withstand fire, and portions of people and animals captured as gifts for the Lord in provision for the priests and Levites. In addition, those soldiers and captives contaminated by touching the dead were required to go through the process of ritual purification as delineated in Numbers 19. This becomes the model for ritual cleansing for future battles when they entered the land of promise.

The final chapters describe special applications of casuistic law that define the holy and undefiled community. Pastoral provisions are made for the Levites in towns throughout the land so they might care for the gifts presented to them and carry out their appointed duties among the larger populace.[76] Six cities of refuge are prescribed for protection of individuals in cases of accidental death. Deaths caused by the intentional use of weapons are deemed murder and are punishable by death. The context of the cases of death concludes with a summary cultic statement. Bloodshed defiles the land in which the people dwell and in which Yahweh's presence is manifest. The land is to be holy, consecrated for the people of God whom God had commanded to be holy (Exod 19:6; Lev 11:44–45; 20:7).

---

[76] The Levitical cities around which they have designated pasture lands are identified in Josh 21:1–42.

The first section of the Book of Numbers contains five cycles of material, two devoted to the sanctification of the people before leaving Mount Sinai (chaps. 1–6,7–10a), and three devoted to the rebellion and judgment of the nation after leaving Mount Sinai (chaps. 10b–15; 16–19; 20–25). Each cycle is composed of the following elements: (1) historical setting, (2) twelve tribal listings or census references, (3) cycle development, (4) Levitical and priestly matters, and (5) sacrifices, offerings, and legal stipulations which define the nature of the community of faith. Variations from this general pattern serve to highlight particular aspects under consideration within the cycle.

——— **I. FAITHFULNESS OF ISRAEL AT SINAI (1:1–10:10)** ———

The setting for the initial two cycles of material in the Book of Numbers is the Sinai Desert, with particular focus on the tabernacle, the epicenter of Israelite religious life.

## 1. Sinai Cycle A: Census and Consecration of the Tribes of Israel (1:1–6:27)

The first cycle introduces several key themes in the Book of Numbers: the twelve-tribe confederation of the descendants of the sons of Jacob, the special status of the priests and Levites, and the consecration of the nation via sacrifices, offerings, and vows. Numbers picks up where Exodus leaves off, in the region of Sinai desert and specifically at Mount Sinai, the paramount place of revelation. Numbers also continues the important theme of the Word of Yahweh, which dominates the Pentateuch.

### (1) Historical Setting: Prologue (1:1)

**[1]The LORD spoke to Moses in the Tent of Meeting in the Desert of Sinai on the first day of the second month of the second year after the Israelites came out of Egypt. He said:**

**1:1** The Book of Numbers commences with one of the key phrases of the Pentateuch, *wayĕdabbēr YHWH el-Mōšeh … lēʾmōr,* "[Then] Yahweh spoke to Moses … saying."[1] On the use of this verse to provide a Hebrew title to the book, see "Introduction: Title."

The term *wayĕdabbēr* occurs at least sixty-one times in the book, of which fifty have Yahweh as the speaker.[2] Of the other eleven occurrences, Moses is the speaker in nine, Miriam and Aaron in one, and on one occasion (21:5) the people speak against God in a passage that completes the cycles of rebellion. Seven times *wayĕdabbēr* functions as a major sectional divider, plus ten times as a minor division marker. Allen noted that divine speech is recorded "over 150 times and in more than twenty ways."[3] When Yahweh spoke, the words were always of paramount importance.

---

[1] See "Introduction: Structure and Outline" for a detailed analysis of the use of this phrase in the Pentateuch and throughout the Book of Numbers.

[2] The quotation introductory term לֵאמֹר ("saying") completes the divine speech formula forty-four times, and these most often are followed by imperative verbs of speech or action. The alternative וַיֹּאמֶר occurs four times, all with לֵאמֹר.

[3] R. B. Allen, "Numbers," EBC, vol. 2 (Grand Rapids: Zondervan, 1986), 702.

Divine speech commences in Scripture with the creative activity of God in Genesis 1. Creation of the cosmos serves as the basis for communication and the establishment of a relationship between God and man in Genesis 3. Though other ancient Near Eastern religions aspired to convey the communicative capabilities of their gods,[4] in resounding polemics the former and latter prophets decried the foreign deities as speechless, motionless, and incapable of action.[5] Precisely how this divine disclosure between the eternal God and his servant Moses transpired remains a mystery. Biblical writers such as Jeremiah (*wayĕhî dĕbar-YHWH ʾēlî lēʾmōr,* "the word of the LORD was to me," or "the word of the LORD became a realization to me," 1:4) utilized varied expressions for the process. Theologians have probed this enigma for millennia, giving rise to varied theories of inspiration. But however this communication was accomplished, whether by audible human speech form, mental and spiritual impression and compulsion, or by intellectual impregnation of ideas, the prophet Moses became the instrument for divine illumination of humankind of the will and word of God. Communication is an essential element of any relationship and is paramount in the realm of divine-human intercourse. Of the essential tenets of Judaism set forth by Maimonides in the twelfth century A.D., the essence of divine communication and the preeminence of Moses among the prophets are fundamental. The wondrous miracle of revelation is that God could reveal himself to and through his chosen spokesmen in such a way that human language could express precisely that which God intended (2 Pet 1:19–21; 2 Tim 3:16–17).

The NIV and many other versions translate the Hebrew Tetragrammaton YHWH as LORD. This revealed name of God (Exod 3:12–18; 6:1–8) describes his eternal existence and causative essence. Many modern scholars transcribe the name as Yahweh, though Jewish people long have considered the Name too sacred to pronounce or attempt to transliterate. Instead they substitute Adonai (*ʾădōnāy*) in all recitations so as to avoid the remotest possibility of profaning the Name. Some earlier translations of the Old Testament, such as KJV, ASV, and NEB, employ the hybrid form Jehovah, derived from the consonants of the Tetragrammaton and the vowels of Adonai. Christian evangelical scholarship has used two divergent approaches in referring to YHWH. Some, such as K. L. Barker and R. B. Allen, prefer to use the transcribed Yahweh as the personal name of God in Scripture translation and recitation as well as in biblical research.[6] Others,

---

[4] Compare, e.g., the Egyptian creation myth of Memphis, whereby "all the divine order really came into being through what the heart thought and the tongue commanded" ("The Theology of Memphis," *ANET,* 5.

[5] 1 Sam 5:1–12; 1 Kgs 18:25–38; Isa 44:6–20; Jer 10:1–16; Ps 135:15–18.

[6] K. L. Barker, *The NIV: The Making of a Contemporary Translation* (Grand Rapids: Zondervan, 1986), 106–9. R. B. Allen, "Numbers," EBC (Grand Rapids: Zondervan, 1990).

such as R. K. Harrison, hold that YHWH is not a personal name of God but a descriptive title of which the precise pronunciation is unproven.[7] The former approach is preferred by the present author, though the translation LORD will be employed frequently.

The "Tent of Meeting" (ʾōhel mô'ēd) was the location of divine disclosure to Moses, where God and man met in revelatory communion and where Aaron made atonement for the nation on Yom Kippur.[8] Several alternative expressions designate this movable worship center: "the tent of the testimony" (ʾōhel ha'ēdût), "the tabernacle of the testimony" (miškan ha'ēdût), and "the tabernacle" (hammiškān). The concept of a portable sanctuary or shrine is known from Egyptian sources, dating to as early as the Old Kingdom period (2700–2200 B.C.). Tent shrines with wooden pillars were depicted in ritual purification scenes on tomb murals.[9]

Portable shrines were transported on conquest campaigns in Mesopotamia as early as the third millennium B.C. Several accounts of the capture of representative statues of deities are well known from Babylonian and Hittite records. Marduk, the patron deity of the city of Babylon, was taken captive by the Hittites under Mursilis II ca. 1590 B.C. and later in history abducted to Susa by the Elamites. Such tabernacles served as places of counsel and refuge for kings and military leaders, with protection afforded by the troops or peoples that surrounded the tent upon encampment. An additional parallel in biblical history is the account of the use of the ark at the battle of Ebenezer (1 Sam 4:1–11).

The phrase "Desert of Sinai" locates the census taking in the rugged regions of the Sinai Peninsula. The precise location of the encampment of Israelites near Mount Sinai (Mount Horeb), the mountain of God, has been debated since at least as early as the fourth century A.D. The question of the identification of Mount Sinai is integrally related to the study of the location of (a) the specific area of the Sinai wilderness referenced, (b) Moses' earlier encounters with God, and (c) the route of the Exodus journey. Early Christian historians generally believed that Mount Sinai was located in the south-

---

[7] R. K. Harrison, *Numbers: An Exegetical Commentary* (Grand Rapids: Baker, 1992), 31.

[8] Note that some scholars posit a priestly "Tent of Meeting" at the center of the camp (2:17; 3:38), whereas epic tradition is said to suggest a tent outside the camp (Num 11:24–27; 12:4–5; Exod 17:15; 24:3–8). R. de Vaux suggested the two were the same tent ("Ark of Covenant-Tent of Reunion," in *The Bible and the Ancient Near East* (New York: Doubleday, 1971), 136–51. Contrast the view of M. Haran, *Temples and Temple Service in Ancient Israel* (Oxford: Clarendon, 1978), 262–73.

[9] K. A. Kitchen, "Some Egyptian Background to the Old Testament," *TynBul* 5–6 (1960): 7–13. B. S. Childs, *The Book of Exodus*, OTL (Philadelphia: Westminster, 1974): 529–52. A. M. Blackman, *The Rock Tombs of Meir* (Oxford: University Press, 1977), vol. V, plates 42,43. K. Lange and M. Hirmer, *Egypt: Architecture, Sculpture, Painting in Three Thousand Years* (London: Phaedon, 1956): plates 137–39.

ern region of the Sinai peninsula, pointing to such grand peaks as Jebel Musa, Jebel Serbal, Jebel Katarina, or Ras es-Safsafeh, which dominate the regional terrain. Jebel Musa was the choice of Eusebius, according to his geographical *Onomasticon*.[10] Aesthetics played as much a part in the decision making as detailed analysis of biblical and regional geography.[11]

In modern research, several other identifications have been suggested by historians and geographers. M. Noth, basing his decision on the location of the Midianite territory in which Moses sojourned for some forty years, placed the mountain on the East side of the Gulf of Aqaba (Eilat). This locale was followed generally by Abib Koury of the American University of Beirut and others. Profs. Menahem Har-El and George L. Kelm, proposing an Exodus journey through the central Sinai peninsula from the Bitter Lakes region to Ezion-geber and then to Kadesh-barnea, advance an identification of Mount Sinai with Jebel Sin-Bisher.[12] Other suggestions include Har Karkom, Khirbet el- Qom, Jebel Helal, and Jebel Feiran.[13] Ancient and modern Christian tradition has adhered to the location decided by the early church, where the Monastery of St. Catherine has endured for centuries.

Chronologically, the scene of the census is set "on the first day of the second month of the second year" after the Exodus, eleven months after Moses first ascended the mountain of revelation. An absolute chronological reckoning of this statement of relative chronology has long been debated by biblical scholars.[14] Those who grant at least some historical credence to the Exodus in history have generally proffered dates ranging from 1570 B.C. to

---

[10] Eusebius, *Onomasticon* 14.5.9.

[11] The peak of Jebel Musa stands at 7,365 ft., Jebel Serbal at 7,265 ft., and Ras es-Safsafeh 6,540 ft. Compared to the less elevated peaks of Jebel Sin-Bisher (2,755 ft.) and Kh. el-Qom (2,345 ft.), the southern peaks of Sinai offered early geographers more aesthetic and grandiose options.

[12] G. L. Kelm, "The Route of the Exodus," *Biblical Illustrator* 7 (1979): 11–32. M. Harel, "The Route of the Exodus of the Israelites from Egypt" (Ph.D. diss., New York University, 1964).

[13] For a detailed discussion of the location of Mount Sinai, compare the following articles: G. I. Davies, *The Way of the Wilderness: A Geographical Study of the Wilderness Itineraries in the Old Testament* (Cambridge: Cambridge University Press, 1979), 23–24, 27–33, 37–41, 63–69; M. Harel, "Sinai," *Encyclopaedia Miqraith,* V:1021–22; "The Route of the Exodus of the Israelites from Egypt"; W. M. F. Petrie and C. T. Currelly, *Researches in Sinai* (London: John Murray, 1906), 247–50; A. E. Lucas, *The Route of the Exodus of the Israelites from Egypt* (London: Arnold, 1938), 4–45; G. E. Wright, "Sinai," *IDB* 4:376–78; Y. Aharoni, *The Land of the Bible,* rev. ed. (Philadelphia: Westminster, 1979), 197–99; J. Hoffmeier, *Israel in Egypt: The Evidence for the Authenticity of the Exodus Tradition* (New York: Oxford University Press, 1996), 187, 197 n. 114.

[14] The phrase "absolute chronology" denotes the common means of establishing a precise year for a given event in history in terms of $X$ number of years B.C. or A.D. (B.C.E. = Before the Common Era in circles other than Christian, or C.E. = the Common Era). "Relative chronology" describes the dating method given in most ANE texts as well as the Bible, using expressions such as "In the third year of Asa king of Judah, Baasha son of Ahijah became king in Tirzah, and he reigned twenty-four years" (1 Kgs 15:33). Dating of one event is given relative to that of another event.

1250 B.C., with ca. 1440 and ca. 1290 B.C. most commonly supported.[15] The earlier dates would place the Exodus at the advent of or mid-eighteenth New Kingdom (Empire) in Egyptian history, the latter during the Ramesside nineteenth dynasty. The issue remains one of intense debate among evangelical scholars, needing further study in biblical, historical, literary, and archaeological research.

### (2) Military Conscription Census of the Twelve Tribes of Israel (1:2–46)

[2]"Take a census of the whole Israelite community by their clans and families, listing every man by name, one by one. [3]You and Aaron are to number by their divisions all the men in Israel twenty years old or more who are able to serve in the army. [4]One man from each tribe, each the head of his family, is to help you.

CENSUS INSTRUCTIONS.  **1:2–4**  Directions for taking the census are given in an imperatival phrase, which translates the Hebrew "lift up the head" *(śĕʾû ʾet-rōʾš)* and echoes the phraseology of Exod 30:12. In the Exodus passage, census taking is anticipated as a means of assessing a tariff for sanctuary (tabernacle) maintenance in the amount of one-half shekel per person. The method and boundaries of numbering all the congregation of Israel is "by clans and families," literally "by families and their fathers' households." The term "tribe" *(maṭṭeh)* is used in v. 4 with reference to those who would assist Moses and Aaron in making the assessment. Listing in the subsequent text is by tribal summary, with the figure given reflecting the total of clans and families within each tribe.

In typical Hebrew fashion, the directions become more specific as the narrative progresses. The ultimate purpose of the census is to enumerate the male members who are at least twenty years of age and eligible for military service. The "divisions" *(lĕṣibʾōtām,* lit., "by their armed divisions") are classified for the future need of mustering militia for the entry and conquest of the land of promise, a kind of draft enlistment process. The term *ṣābāʾ* is generally used in the context of military forces and in the divine appellation

---

[15] The earliest date of 1570 B.C. has been suggested by J. Bimson in his innovative analysis of Egyptian chronology and Mycenaean III B–C pottery, *Redating the Exodus* (Winona Lake: Eisenbrauns, 1980). The date of 1440 B.C. has the support of 1 Kgs 6:1, which places beginning of the construction of the Solomonic temple in Jerusalem (accepted widely as 965–960 B.C.) 480 years after the Exodus. Limited archaeological evidence has been afforded in support of this "early date" theory, and that material is highly debated. The so-called "late date" theory (1290 B.C.) derives from Exod 1:11, where the pharaonic name Ramses is mentioned as the name of one of the store cities built by the enslaved Israelites. This date was once preferred on the basis of archaeological evidence from such sites as Hazor, Bethel, and Lachish, but many Syro-Palestinian archaeologists have abandoned this view and despair the possibility that archaeology can answer the question of the date of the Exodus or even substantiate its historicity. Present discussion focuses more upon the nature, manner, extent, and time frame of the Israelite emergence as the dominant ethnic element in the region.

*YHWH ṣĕbāʾôt*, often translated "Yahweh of hosts" or "Yahweh of armies." No upper age limit is given, and several notable Israelite leaders served valiantly in their elder years (e.g., Moses).[16] The work was to be accomplished under the direction of Moses and Aaron, with the assistance of one patriarchal leader (*rōʾš lĕbêt ʾăbōtâw*, "head of the household of his father") from each of the twelve tribes.

⁵These are the names of the men who are to assist you:

> from Reuben, Elizur son of Shedeur;
> ⁶from Simeon, Shelumiel son of Zurishaddai;
> ⁷from Judah, Nahshon son of Amminadab;
> ⁸from Issachar, Nethanel son of Zuar;
> ⁹from Zebulun, Eliab son of Helon;
> ¹⁰from the sons of Joseph:
> from Ephraim, Elishama son of Ammihud;
> from Manasseh, Gamaliel son of Pedahzur;
> ¹¹from Benjamin, Abidan son of Gideoni;
> ¹²from Dan, Ahiezer son of Ammishaddai;
> ¹³from Asher, Pagiel son of Ocran;
> ¹⁴from Gad, Eliasaph son of Deuel;
> ¹⁵from Naphtali, Ahira son of Enan."

¹⁶These were the men appointed from the community, the leaders of their ancestral tribes. They were the heads of the clans of Israel.

CENSUS ASSISTANTS ENLISTED (1:5–16). **1:5–16** Verses 5a and 16 provide an inclusio for framing the enlisted aides in the assessment of the able militia for the nation of Israel. The word for "assist" in the Hebrew is *ʿāmad* ("to stand"), for the elder statesman for each tribe was to stand as a spokesman in the registration of community members. The twelve names recorded here recur in 2:3–31 (tribal camp arrangements), 7:12–83 (tribal offerings for the sanctuary), and 10:14–27 (tribal divisions depart from Sinai), though in varying order. These men functioned as representatives for their ancestral tribes in matters of military conscription, worship leadership, and general administration. The Levites and their tribal leaders (Aaron and Moses) are not cataloged here, due to their nonmilitary function on behalf of the nation, but are added subsequently at the conclusion of the census. The

---

[16] For an extensive analysis of ANE warfare, see Y. Yadin, *The Art of Warfare in Biblical Lands* (New York: McGraw-Hill, 1963). Cf. the broader treatment of issues of war in M. C. Lind, *Yahweh Is a Warrior: The Theology of Warfare in Ancient Israel* (Scottsdale: Herald, 1980), P. D. Miller, *The Divine Warrior in Early Israel* (Cambridge: Harvard University Press, 1973), P. C. Craigie, *The Problem of War in the Old Testament* (Grand Rapids: Zondervan, 1978), and T. Longman III and D. E. Reid, *God Is Warrior* (Grand Rapids: Zondervan, 1995).

order of the tribal patriarchs generally follows the birth order according to their mothers, as is true in Gen 29–30; 41; 46: (1) the sons of Jacob through Leah—Reuben, Simeon, [Levi], Judah, Issachar, Zebulun, [Dinah] (Gen 29:31–35; 30:17–21); (2) the sons of Jacob through Rachel—Joseph = Ephraim and Manasseh in reverse order and Benjamin, the youngest of all (Gen 30:22–24; 35:16–18; 41:50–52); (3) the sons of Jacob through Leah's handmaid Zilpah—Gad and Asher (Gen 30:9–13); and (4) the sons of Jacob through Rachel's handmaid Bilhah—Dan and Naphtali (Gen 30:4–8). In (3) and (4) Gad and Dan are reversed for some undetermined reason. Levi and Dinah are excluded from the list. Levi is considered separately for temple service, and Dinah was a woman / daughter and thus of unequal status with her brothers.

The following are the appointed tribal leaders, with a suggested meaning of each name supplied. Caution should be taken against reading the derived meaning of a name into the character of the individual since these were given prior to any demonstration of personality trait. Appellations came by family tradition, birth circumstances, and special designation.

| Tribe | Name | Derived Meaning(s) |
|---|---|---|
| Reuben | Elizur | (My) God Is a Rock, Is Strong (God of Strength) |
| | ben Shedeur | Shaddai Is a Flame (Fire, Light) |
| Simeon | Shelumiel | (My) Peace Is God |
| | ben Zerishaddai | (My) Strength Is Shaddai, (My) Rock Is Shaddai |
| Judah | Nahshon | Serpent |
| | ben Amminadab | (My) People Are Noble |
| Issachar | Nathanel | Gift of God |
| | ben Zuar | Little One |
| Zebulun | Eliab | (My) God Is Father |
| | ben Helon | Rampart?? |
| Joseph | | |
| Ephraim | Elishama | (My) God Hears, Has Heard |
| | ben Ammihud | (My) People Are Majestic |
| Manasseh | Gamaliel | Reward of God |
| | ben Pedahzur | Ransomed Rock, Strength |
| Benjamin | Abidan | (My) Father Is Judge |
| | ben Gideoni | (My) Hewer |
| Dan | Ahiezer | (My) Brother Is a Helper |
| | ben Ammishaddai | (My) People of Shaddai |
| Asher | Pagiel | Encountered by God, Met by God |
| | ben Ocran | Troubled |
| Gad | Eliasaph | (My) God Has Added, Multiplied, Enriched |
| | ben Deuel | Knowing God |
| Naphtali | Ahira | (My) Brother Is Evil |
| | ben Enan | One Who Sees |

The antiquity of the names of the tribal patriarchs and the leaders in the census taking has been acknowledged by many scholars. J. Milgrom has noted that sixteen of the twenty-four names never recur in biblical literature, and none contain the abbreviated theophoric element YH (for Yahweh), as is the case throughout the Book of Genesis.[17] The theophoric elements El (ʾel, "God"), Ab (ʾab, "father"), Shaddai (Šhadday, "Almighty"), Zur (tsûr, "rock"), and Ezer (ʿezer, "strength") all date at least to the second millennium B.C., lending further credence to the antiquity of the list of names. Some of these recur through Israelite history, including the postexilic period, which led M. Noth to suggest that the so-called priestly source (P) cited "an old list of the nesiʾîm of the twelve Israelite tribes." Noth believed these men were pre-Davidic officials and not simply those chosen for the occasion of a census.[18] Gray, convinced that this text was a P-souce creation, proffered the opinion that though some of the names were "unquestionably ancient, the list is certainly unhistorical." He further betrays his bias against the actual antiquity of the historical text by absurdly suggesting that "a late compiler might select only ancient names in composing a fictitious list."[19] Both views of Noth and Gray are based on the idea of a self-justifying postexilic priesthood, but the tribal differentiation in the list would have little practical value in the limited territory of Jerusalem in the postexilic era. The historical, literary, and theological value of the lists in the present context and throughout the Pentateuch are more fitting in the patriarchal and premonarchial periods of Israelite history. Further credence to the historical antiquity of this list is found in the parallels cited in the Late Bronze Age (1550–1200 B.C.) texts from Mari, which contain the theophoric elements Shaddai and Zur.[20]

Only the leaders from the tribes of Judah and Ephraim figure significantly in the later history of Israel. Through the Judahite line of Amminadab and Nahshon came Boaz, who married Ruth and fathered the Davidic ancestry (Ruth 4:20–22) and consequently the Messianic line of Jesus Christ (Matt 1:4–16; Luke 3:23–33). Elishama ben Ammihud, through his son Nun, was the grandfather of Joshua (1 Chr 7:26–27), who succeeded Moses as the leader of Israel as the nation entered the land of promise.

---

[17] J. Milgrom, *Numbers,* JPS Torah Commentary (Philadelphia: Jewish Publication Society, 1990).

[18] M. Noth, *Numbers,* OTL (Philadelphia: Westminster, 1968), 17–19.

[19] Gray, *Numbers,* 6. Cp. the views of Budd, *Numbers,* 4–6, and D. T. Olson, *The Death of the Old and the Birth of the New: The Framework of the Book of Numbers and the Pentateuch,* BJS (Chico, Cal.: Scholars Press, 1985), 68–80. Olson compares the tribal lists and genealogies of Numbers to the תוֹלְדוֹת formula of Gen 2:4a; 5:1–32; 11:10–27.

[20] W. F. Albright, "The Names Shaddai and Abram," *JBL* 54 (1935): 180–87.

[17]Moses and Aaron took these men whose names had been given, [18]and they called the whole community together on the first day of the second month. The people indicated their ancestry by their clans and families, and the men twenty years old or more were listed by name, one by one, [19]as the LORD commanded Moses. And so he counted them in the Desert of Sinai:

CENSUS DIRECTED BY MOSES (1:17–19). **1:17–19** Moses and Aaron faithfully heed the direction of the Lord to enlist the tribal leaders in accomplishing the task of gathering the "whole community" together on the first day of the second month (1:1) for the purpose of assessing the number of men twenty years of age and older, those responsible and capable of serving in the armies of Israel. Families and clans were identified, and the men were enlisted one at a time by name until the entire assembly had been registered. The phrase "in the Desert of Sinai" acts as an inclusio for the section of vv. 1–19. Verse 19 serves as a summary statement, for which the details of the poll ensue. The resulting reiterative material renders a dramatic conclusion to this introduction, designed to show the tremendous growth of the nation under God's magnificent blessing. This text resonates with the Book of Exodus, which commences with a concise description of the plenteous multiplication of the descendants of Jacob—Israel.

[20]From the descendants of Reuben the firstborn son of Israel:
All the men twenty years old or more who were able to serve in the army were listed by name, one by one, according to the records of their clans and families. [21]The number from the tribe of Reuben was 46,500.

[22]From the descendants of Simeon:
All the men twenty years old or more who were able to serve in the army were counted and listed by name, one by one, according to the records of their clans and families. [23]The number from the tribe of Simeon was 59,300.

[24]From the descendants of Gad:
All the men twenty years old or more who were able to serve in the army were listed by name, according to the records of their clans and families. [25]The number from the tribe of Gad was 45,650.

[26]From the descendants of Judah:
All the men twenty years old or more who were able to serve in the army were listed by name, according to the records of their clans and families. [27]The number from the tribe of Judah was 74,600.

[28]From the descendants of Issachar:
All the men twenty years old or more who were able to serve in the army were listed by name, according to the records of their clans and families. [29]The number from the tribe of Issachar was 54,400.

[30]From the descendants of Zebulun:

All the men twenty years old or more who were able to serve in the army were listed by name, according to the records of their clans and families. [31]The number from the tribe of Zebulun was 57,400.

[32]From the sons of Joseph:

From the descendants of Ephraim:

All the men twenty years old or more who were able to serve in the army were listed by name, according to the records of their clans and families. [33]The number from the tribe of Ephraim was 40,500.

[34]From the descendants of Manasseh:

All the men twenty years old or more who were able to serve in the army were listed by name, according to the records of their clans and families. [35]The number from the tribe of Manasseh was 32,200.

[36]From the descendants of Benjamin:

All the men twenty years old or more who were able to serve in the army were listed by name, according to the records of their clans and families. [37]The number from the tribe of Benjamin was 35,400.

[38]From the descendants of Dan:

All the men twenty years old or more who were able to serve in the army were listed by name, according to the records of their clans and families. [39]The number from the tribe of Dan was 62,700.

[40]From the descendants of Asher:

All the men twenty years old or more who were able to serve in the army were listed by name, according to the records of their clans and families. [41]The number from the tribe of Asher was 41,500.

[42]From the descendants of Naphtali:

All the men twenty years old or more who were able to serve in the army were listed by name, according to the records of their clans and families. [43]The number from the tribe of Naphtali was 53,400.

CENSUS RESULTS BY TRIBAL HOUSEHOLDS (1:20–43). **1:20–43** All the men twenty years old or more who were able to serve in the army were listed by name, according to the records of their clans and families. The list of tribes does not adhere to the order given in 1:5–15, and in fact diversity occurs throughout the Book of Numbers. Note the following chart of variants.

**Tribal Lists in the Book of Numbers**

| Num 1:5–15 | Num 1:20–43 | Num 2:3–31 | Num 7:12–83 =Num 10:14–28 |
|---|---|---|---|
| Reuben | Reuben | Judah – EAST | Judah |

### Tribal Lists in the Book of Numbers

| Num 1:5–15 | Num 1:20–43 | Num 2:3–31 | Num 7:12–83 =Num 10:14–28 |
|---|---|---|---|
| Simeon | Simeon | Issachar – EAST | Issachar |
| Judah | Gad | Zebulun – EAST | Zebulun |
| Issachar | Judah | Reuben – SOUTH | Reuben |
| Zebulun | Issachar | Simeon – SOUTH | Simeon |
| Joseph-Ephraim | Zebulun | Gad – SOUTH | Gad |
| Jospeh-Manasseh | Joseph-Ephraim | Ephraim – WEST | Ephraim |
| Benjamin | Joseph-Manasseh | Manasseh – WEST | Manasseh |
| Dan | Benjamin | Benjamin – WEST | Benjamin |
| Asher | Dan | Dan – NORTH | Dan |
| Gad | Asher | Asher – NORTH | Asher |
| Naphtali | Naphtali | Naphtali – NORTH | Naphtali |
| Levi= Moses + Aaron | Levi 1:47–53 not counted | Levi 3:1–4:49 counted (2x) | Levi 8:5–26 |

### Tribal Lists in the Book of Numbers

| Num 10:14–28 | Num 13:4–15 | Num 26:5–51 | Num 34:16–29 |
|---|---|---|---|
| Judah | Reuben | Reuben | Judah |
| Issachar | Simeon | Simeon | Simeon |
| Zebulun | Judah | Gad | Benjamin |
| Reuben | Issachar | Judah | Dan |
| Simeon | Ephraim | Issachar | Manasseh(1/2) |
| Gad | Benjamin | Zebulun | Ephraim |
| Ephraim | Zebulun | Manasseh | Zebulun |

**Tribal Lists in the Book of Numbers**

| Num 10:14–28 | Num 13:4–15 | Num 26:5–51 | Num 34:16–29 |
|---|---|---|---|
| Manasseh | Manasseh | Ephraim | Issachar |
| Benjamin | Dan | Benjamin | Asher |
| Dan | Asher | Dan | Naphtali |
| Asher | Naphtali | Asher | Reuben (TJ) |
| Naphtali | Gad | Naphtali | Gad (TJ) Manasseh (1/2TJ) |
| Levi=Moses | (no Levi) | Levi (26:57–62) | Levite Towns & Refuge Cities |

Each list serves a specific purpose within the book, though the reasons for the variants in the listing order may not always be clear. The function of each tribal listing is as follows: (1) 1:5–15—listing of tribal leaders for the census-taking process, (2) 1:20–43—census taking by tribe, (3) 2:3–31—tribal organization around the tabernacle, (4) 7:12–83—tribal presentations of offerings, (5) 10:14–28—tribal order of departure from Sinai, (6) 13:4–15—tribal representatives for the survey of the land, (7) 26:5–51—second census taken according to tribes, with clans listed for future land allotment, (8) 34:16–29—tribal leaders registered for land inheritance. In 17:1–8 the tribal names are not listed, but representatives from each tribe, this time including Levi, present their staffs before the Lord in the Tent of the Testimony for the purpose of establishing the priority of the Aaronic priesthood. In 31:3–6 one thousand men from each tribe are mustered for exacting vengeance against the Midianites.

As to the variations from the tribal lists in the Book of Genesis, D. Olson suggests:

> Although the lists in Numbers display a somewhat altered form from the genealogies and tribal lists of the book of Genesis, they perform similar literary and theological functions. They mark major structural divisions. They make a theological claim about the *continuity* of the covenantal promises and laws given to the patriarchs for each succeeding generation. They make a theological claim for the *inclusiveness* of the covenant promises and laws for all Israel. Furthermore, the expanded segmented genealogies of Numbers 26 suggest a *partial fulfillment* of the promise of an abundance of descendants which was given to the patriarchs in the Genesis narrative.[21]

The results are presented according to a repetitive formula composed of the

---

[21] Olson, *The Death of the Old and the Birth of the New.*

following elements: (1) tribal nomenclature, (2) military conditions of enlistment, (3) clan and familial basis, (4) tribal name reiterated, (5) tribal total. The recurrent pattern has been noted by numerous commentators and is often taken as indicative of the formulaic tendencies of the priestly editors of the text of the Pentateuch. Such repetitiveness can be observed in ancient texts, long predating even the time of Moses, and in and of itself is not an indicator of early or late antiquity. The totals for the twelve tribes counted in the two military conscription censuses, which exclude the Levites, are as follows:

| Tribe | First Census | Second Census |
|---|---|---|
| Reuben | 46,500 | 43,730 |
| Simeon | 59,300 | 22,200 |
| Gad | 45,650 | 40,500 |
| Judah | 74,600 | 76,500 |
| Issachar | 54,400 | 64,300 |
| Zebulun | 57,400 | 60,500 |
| Ephraim | 40,500 | 32,500 |
| Manasseh | 32,200 | 52,700 |
| Benjamin | 35,400 | 45,600 |
| Dan | 62,700 | 64,400 |
| Asher | 41,500 | 53,400 |
| Naphtali | 53,400 | 45,400 |
| TOTAL | 603,550 | 601,730 |

All tribal totals are rounded off to the hundreds, with the exception of Gad's fifty. Interesting is the fact that there are no textual variants for the given numbers in the MT (BHS), LXX, and other major texts, which is also true for the equivalent numbers given in 2:1–32. The LXX places Gad after Benjamin, grouping together the four sons of Jacob's concubines Zilpah and Bilhah (cf. 1:5–15).

**⁴⁴These were the men counted by Moses and Aaron and the twelve leaders of Israel, each one representing his family. ⁴⁵All the Israelites twenty years old or more who were able to serve in Israel's army were counted according to their families. ⁴⁶The total number was 603,550.**

CENSUS SUMMARY AND TOTAL (1:44–46). **1:44–46** The summary and total of the able fighting men of age among the tribes of Israel is set forth in formulaic structure and repeats several of the same phrases as the census instructions and individual listings. Verses 44–45 echo the wording of 17–18, and v. 46 presents the grand total of 603,550. This tremendous number, as well as the sizable figures tendered for each individual tribe, has posed the greatest dilemma for biblical interpreters since the Middle Ages. Many modern commentators summarily dismiss these numbers as hyperbolic or fictitious, while others provide a brief history of interpretation.

Numerous suggestions have been proffered for comprehending these unbe-
lievable sums, which would rival the greatest of the kingdoms of the ancient
Near East. A summary of approaches is in order.

## Excursus: The Large Numbers in Numbers

Biblical scholars of all theological and denominational backgrounds have
observed problems in the interpretation of the large census numbers of chaps. 1–
2 and 26 (cf. Exod 38:26) for centuries. The total population estimate that would
result from applying the census totals of 603,550 (1:46) and 601,730 (26:51)
seem astronomically large. The issue is not whether the population of Israelites
could not have mathematically risen to such a figure during the four hundred plus
year of Egyptian sojourn, or that God could or could not have provided ample
food resources in the Sinai region in which only a few thousand people reside
today. But internal and external problems with a simple literal reading of the
extant text necessitate careful analysis in order to resolve seeming incongruity
within the book and in relation to other Pentateuchal sources.[22]

### Internal and External Difficulties

Several problems need to be resolved before coming to a conclusion regarding the population of the Israelite company that hastily exited Egypt. The first is
the sheer magnitude of the resultant population surviving in the rocky and mountainous desert and later occupying portions of the land of Canaan. If one takes the
figure of 603,550 males conscripted for the Israelite army, which was probably
only about 70 percent of the adult male population, and add equal numbers
(probably more) of females, and then reckon another 25 percent for children, the
total population could have been in the range of 2.0 to 2.5 million. The physical
logistical problems resulting from having so many people symmetrically camped
around the central shrine would have been immense, since they occupied mini-
mally three to five square miles in extremely crowded conditions. Waste and gar-
bage disposal and burial necessities would have been considerable. For Moses to
have communicated with the entire assembly of Israel (Exod 16:6; Num 17:6)
would have been a logistical nightmare. Ashley further notes that only two midwives are listed (Exod 1:15) as serving the Hebrew population in Goshen.[23]
Many hundreds would have been needed to attend to a population of two million
or more, though these two women may have been listed simply as exemplars
serving the Israelite population.

A second dilemma arises from the internal comparison of the male military
totals with the census of the firstborn (22,273) and enumeration of the Levites
(22,000) for the redemption of the firstborn (1:39–51). If we take the total male
population over one month old (perhaps 700,000) and divide by the 22,273 total

---

[22] Note the summaries in Milgrom, *Numbers*, 336–39; G. Wenham, *Numbers*, 60–66; T. Ashley, *The Book of Numbers*, NICOT (Grand Rapids: Eerdmans, 1993), 60–66; Gray, *Numbers*, ICC,
10–15; E. W. Davies, *Numbers*, NCBC, 14–18, and elsewhere.

[23] Ashley, *Numbers*, 60–61.

firstborn, there would have had to have been more than thirty males per family. Wenham remarks: "The average mother must then have had more than 50 children."[24] Even bigamy could not account for this inconsistency, and this figure is far beyond imagination and inconsistent with the average number of males per family listed in the various genealogical records in the Bible in which the average is approximately 2.5 males per household.

The third difficulty concerns the relationship between the census total and the biblical statements regarding Israel's potential inability to fully occupy the land (Exod 23:25–30; Deut 7:7–22). Until recent decades of extensive immigration of Jews into Israel from around the globe, the population was only slightly more than one million. In addition, because of their inability to drive out the Canaanites, the early Israelites subsisted in less than half of what is modern Israel and Palestine, occupying perhaps slightly more than the region of the West Bank. In addition the sizes of the armies utilized in the attacks on the cities in the Book of Joshua are much smaller than the 603,550 suggested. In the second attack on Ai and Bethel, the initial company sent at night is 30,000 followed by the second battalion of Joshua and the others, perhaps a total of 60,000 to 70,000 of "all the fighting men" (8:3). The seemingly disastrous effects of the death of 36 men in the first attack on Ai by 3,000 Israelites implies the army was considerably smaller than 600,000. In the period of the judges of Israel, the military forces of the Danite tribe, which moved North and subdued Laish, numbered only 600 (Judg 18:11–17), compared to 64,400 in Num 26:42–43. An army of 603,550 would not likely have had any difficulty subduing the Canaanite population of perhaps 200,000 males (high end figure) or the Egyptian army, which they greatly feared (estimated at less than 20,000).

### Suggested Solutions

1. The census figures may be literal and precise. God could have miraculously provided manna and quail for all of the attendant needs of the community of faith, whether it be 2,000 or 2,000,000. Keil interprets the census of the firstborn as reference to those males one month old or more who were born in the thirteen months after the Exodus.[25] Shiphrah and Puah were just two of the many Hebrew midwives who shared Pharaoh's counsel with others. Likewise, the Israelites may have only sent representative forces into battle in the conflicts mentioned in Exodus through Joshua. Yet the combined problematic evidence above seems to argue against this kind of solution.

2. Some have considered the census figures to be literal and precise but to represent a later population total, such as during the Davidic kingdom, that have been retrojected into the Exodus era.[26] This solution was offered by A. Dillman and W. F. Albright, but no evidence of these particular figures is afforded by the

---

[24] Wenham, *Numbers,* 61.

[25] Keil, *Numbers,* 5–6.

[26] Cf. 2 Sam 24:9, in which Joab's military census yields 800,000 in Israel and 500,000 in Judah. Note also Joab's eagerness in seeing the full blessing of God in multiplying David's troops "by a hundred times over" (24:3).

texts of Samuel or Kings.[27] By the time of the monarchy, the distinctiveness of the Simeon tribe and its cities has been eclipsed, for they seem to have been assimilated into the more prominent Judah. Hence they would have been difficult to census in this obscurity.

3. The numbers have been interpreted as forms of gematria. Several scholars have offered solutions along the line of gematria, that is, mathematical calculation based on the Hebrew use of letters for numbers in calculations. This practice is common from the latter part of the Hasmonean period (167–63 B.C.) and became popular among certain groups of Medieval Jews such as the Karaites (eighth–ninth century A.D.) and the early forms of Kabbalah in Hassidic Jewry (seventeenth century to present). G. Fohrer thus derived 603,551 from the phrase "sons of Israel" (*bny ysr'l* = 603) and "every head" (*kl r's* —551, rounded to 550). But gematria cannot explain the individual tribal censuses, nor is there conclusive evidence of the use of gematria in the Old Testament era.

4. Some have offered as a solution variations on the meaning of *'elep*, translated "thousands" in most English and European translations.[28] Additionally, most numbers after the summation of "thousands" are rounded off to the hundreds between 200 and 700, with the exception of Gad at 650. None are rounded off to a low end 100 or a high end of 800 or 900. A couple of alternative solutions have been set forth based on the suggested meanings of the Hebrew term generally translated "thousands" or "myriads." One is to translate the term as "clan," hence the census of Judah would be 74 clans numbering 600 (avg. 8 per clan) and the tribe of Dan having 62 clans totaling 700 men (avg. 11), and the totals for Numbers 1 would be 598 clans with 5,550 fighting men, and similarly 5,730 men from 596 clans in Numbers 26.[29] The census totals of 603,550 and 601,730 would have then had to be later summations than the original tribal delineations, and there is no textual evidence in history to support such a variation. If Mendenhall's suggestion that the armies of Egypt numbered 20 to 25,000, then an Israelite military contingent of less than 6,000, with a total population of 20 to 25,000, would not have been perceived as such a threat as would a group considerably larger.[30]

---

[27] A. Dillman, *Das Bücheri Numeri, Deuteronomium und Joshua* (Leipzig: Hirzel, 1886), 7; W. F. Albright, *From Stone Age to Christianity,* 2nd ed. (New York: Doubleday, 1957), 253, 290–91; "The Administrative Divisions of Israel and Judah," *JPOS* 5 (1925): 17–25.

[28] The basic meaning of the Semitic root *'lp,* vocalized as *'eleph,* is attested as "thousands" in Aramaic, Arabic, Sabean, and others. The alternative vocalization *'alluph* is generally translated "chief" as in Exod 15:15 or "clan" in Gen 36:15; Zech 12:5,6. This interpretation is supported by the LB Mari usage of *'lp* as "clan" (ARM 1.23.42;6.33.65); A Malamat, "A Recently Discovered Word for 'Clan' in Mari and Its Hebrew Cognate," in *Solving Riddles and Untying Knots: Biblical, Epigraphic, and Semitic Studies in Honor of Jonas C. Greenfield,* ed. Z. Zevit, S. Gitin, M. Sokoloff (Winona Lake: Eisenbrauns, 1995), 177–79.

[29] This suggestion was proffered by Sir W. M. F. Petrie, the noted Egyptian and Palestinian archaeologist, in his *Researches in Sinai* (London: Murray, 1906), 208–21, and followed by G. Mendenhall, "The Census Lists of Numbers 1 and 26," *JBL* 77 (1958): 52–66, among others.

[30] Note in Exod 1:7–10 the pharaoh's fear of Hebrew population growth.

M. Noth suggested a variation of this method whereby the meaning of *ʾelep* was applied figuratively to the size of military units (approximately ten in Numbers) and suggested that "thousands" would have been applicable during the Davidic monarchy as the population of Israel and its armies multiplied.[31] Milgrom notes that the major difficulty with this interpretation "aside from the minuscule and variable size of *ʾelef*, is that in the early texts *ʾelef* stands for the entire clan and not just the fighting force (e.g., 1 Sam 23:23; Mic 5:1)."[32] Likewise, J. W. Wenham's suggestion that *ʾlp* be vocalized as *ʾallûp* ("tribal chieftain") faces a difficulty in the Levite census of Num 3:14–39 numbering all males who were at least one month old. Neither twenty-two groups of no persons, nor infant chieftains are tenable interpretations.

5. Some have argued that the numbers are symbolic. M. Barnouin advanced the theory that the numbers reflect the application of Mesopotamian mathematics and astronomy, whereby the tribal numbers are related to astronomical calculations of lunar years and planetary cycles.[33] The number of the host of heaven, which are the armies of Yahweh, are equivalent to the magnitude of Israel's army, in a manner parallel to the earthly tabernacle being a reflection of God's heavenly abode (Exod 25:9,22,40). God told Abraham that his descendants would be as numerous as the stars in the heavens (Gen 22:17). Joseph had a dream concerning his brothers, the tribal ancestors delineated in Numbers 1 and 26, in the metaphor of the sun, moon, and stars (Gen 37:9). Barnouin's suggestion regarding a theological symbolism in the numbers has credence potentially, yet Ashley is perhaps correct in assessing that his system "seems more clever than convincing."[34] Would the Israelites have been familiar enough with this methodology to have constructed a census of the nation by tribal ancestry based on astronomical observations? Furthermore, the question remains regarding the census of the Levites, whose total is at odds with the system.

6. The numbers could be deliberate and purposeful hyperbole. The suggestion proposed by R. B. Allen was that "the large numbers in the census lists in the Book of Numbers are deliberately and purposefully exaggerated as a rhetorical device to bring glory to God, derision to enemies, and point forward to the fulfillment of God's promise to the fathers that their descendants will be innumerable as the stars." He hypothesizes that the military census figures in Exodus and Numbers have been magnified rhetorically by a factor of ten, yielding armies of 60,355 and 60,137 (total population approx. 250,000) that would best fit the social and demographic issues of the late second millennium B.C., "without diminishing at all the sense of the miraculous and providential care of God."[35] This number would have been a threat to cities the size of Jericho and Pi-Ramses,

---

[31] M. Noth, *Numbers*, trans. J. Martin (London: SCM Press, 1968), 21–22. See also Mendenhall, "The Census Lists of Numbers 1 and 26," 52–66. A more recent proponent of this theory is G. Kelm, *Escape from Conflict*, (Ft. Worth: IAR Publications, 1991), 98–105.

[32] Milgrom, *Numbers*, 339.

[33] M. Barnouin, "Les recensements de Livre des Nombres et l'astronomie babylonienne," *VT* 27 (1977): 280–303. His system utilizes multiples of one hundred, the days of the lunar and solar years, the days for the orbits of Mercury, Venus, Mars, Jupiter, and Saturn.

[34] Ashley, *Numbers*, 63.

[35] Allen, "Numbers," 688–89.

but not so large that they could not have ransacked the land of Canaan merely by physical rampage. The "least of the nations," compared to the Hittites, Egyptians, or even the city-state of Ugarit, would have been necessarily dependent upon their God in the process of inheriting the land God had promised to them. Allen notes that this smaller number does not lessen the miraculous but amplifies it.

> The supernatural increase of the people in Egypt, the crossing of the Red Sea in one night, the gathering of the people at Mount Sinai, their daily provision in the desert, their entry into the Promised Land—all was miracle! ... But we can now envision a series of miracles that fits the geography, the topography, and the times.[36]

This total also fits the numbering of the firstborn, in that 22,000 firstborn among 60,355 males over twenty years old, an appropriate number considering the average of 2.5 to 3.0 males per household in the Old Testament.[37] More recently D. Fouts has suggested that the hyperbolic use of numbers in the Book of Numbers presents a parallel to ancient Near Eastern texts from Mesopotamia that utilize large hyperbolic numbers in military conscription texts and other population counts.[38]

Israel's power was not in the size of their armies or their enormous population but in their God. He would send angels before them to fight their battles and confuse their enemies. The hyperbolic use of numbers was not for misrepresentation but for powerful demonstration of Yahweh's continuing blessing upon Israel in the past, multiplying seventy persons into more than sixty thousand or six hundred thousand or three million, and the numbers were a statement of confidence in a God who would continue to multiply his people like the stars of the heaven.[39]

**[47]The families of the tribe of Levi, however, were not counted along with the others. [48]The LORD had said to Moses: [49]"You must not count the tribe of Levi or include them in the census of the other Israelites. [50]Instead, appoint the Levites to be in charge of the tabernacle of the Testimony—over all its furnishings and everything belonging to it. They are to carry the tabernacle and all its furnishings; they are to take care of it and encamp around it. [51]Whenever the tabernacle is to move, the Levites are to take it down, and whenever the tabernacle is to be**

---

[36] Ibid., 689.

[37] 22,273 (+15 percent males under twenty yrs.) = 25,614 x 2.5 = 64,035, approximating Allen's 60,355 figure. Note, however, that in figuring this aspect, the inconsistency in applying the 10x multiplication to the census of the Levites, hence yielding 2,200 Levites substituted for 22,273 firstborn males. Cf. also the Exod 38:25–28 weight of silver used to make the bases, hooks, caps, and bands for the post that held the sanctuary curtains, which is based on the census of 603,550. Allen concludes that the hyperbolic aspect of the census of Num 1–2 must take priority over the numbers in Exodus in estimating the actual population.

[38] D. Fouts, "The Use of Large Numbers in the Old Testament" (Ann Arbor: University Microfilms, 1991), 27–38; id. "A Defense of the Hyperbolic Interpretation of Large Numbers in the Old Testament," *JETS* 40/4 (1997): 377–87.

[39] Note that the number of stars visible to the naked human eye on a clear night is approximately seventeen thousand, and thus even sixty thousand far exceeds that expectation.

set up, the Levites shall do it. Anyone else who goes near it shall be put to death. [52]The Israelites are to set up their tents by divisions, each man in his own camp under his own standard. [53]The Levites, however, are to set up their tents around the tabernacle of the Testimony so that wrath will not fall on the Israelite community. The Levites are to be responsible for the care of the tabernacle of the Testimony."

RESPONSIBILITIES OF UNCOUNTED LEVITES (1:47–53). **1:47–53** Based upon the zealous actions of the Levites at Mount Sinai subsequent to the making of the golden calf (Exod 32:26–29), the tribe of Moses, Aaron, and Miriam was set apart for special service in the Tent of Meeting. No longer would they be required to serve in a military capacity, but they would function as guardians, maintenance personnel, transporters, and intermediary cultic servants for the nation. Thus they were not to be counted among the potential military personnel of 1:17–46.

The general description of being "in charge of the tabernacle of the Testimony"[40] is set forth here, with further elucidation in chaps. 3 and 4 in which the various clans of Levites are given specific responsibilities. The descriptive phrase "tabernacle of the Testimony" (*miškan haᶜēdūt*, "dwelling place of the testimony) refers to the covenant nature of the relationship of Israel to Yahweh, following its usage in Exod 38:21. The term "Testimony" (*ᶜēdūt*) denotes the Ten Words inscribed on stone tablets (Exod 31:18; 32:15; 34:27–28), which were kept in the "ark of the Testimony" (Exod 25:16–22; 26:33–34; 40:3,20).[41] The Ten Commandments served as the foundational elements from which all Israelite law was derived by interpretation. Hence later the term "testimony" alluded to the Torah in general.

The general responsibilities are delineated: (1) "carry," transporting of tent and furnishings until the sanctuary reaches its final destination; (2) "take care of" (*šārēt*), keeping and guarding of all tabernacle furnishings and vessels; (3) "encamp around" (*śābîb lamiškān yaḥănû*, "surrounding ... the tabernacle they shall camp"), protection from outside defilement and proximity for service; (4) "take down," dismantle for transport;[42] and (5) "set up," erect after transport. For anyone else even to approach the tabernacle or its furnishings, usurping the holy duties of the Levites or violating the holiness of the tabernacle, was a grave and heinous act of defilement, punishable by death. As Aaron's sons Nadab and Abihu experienced, improper service by assigned personnel was an equally abominable act (Lev 10:1–5; Num 3:2–4). The threat of death for anyone who would violate the tabernacle or its furnishings and equipment for service reflects the absolute holiness

---

[40] Note that some scholars differentiate between the "Tent of Meeting" and the "Tabernacle of the Testimony." See n. 9.

[41] Cf. W. J. Harrelson, "Testimony," *IDB*, IV:579.

[42] *Targum Onkelos* 7.3.

of the Divine Presence. Only those set apart by God for the tabernacle service could participate in the performance of duties required for transportation, maintenance, guardianship, and service.

The Levite clans were to encamp in formation surrounding the tabernacle, effectively establishing an outer perimeter of sacred space around the central holy place. The responsibilities of the Levites regarding their tabernacle service is presented in four stages in 1:47–53 and 3:1–4:33 with increasing specificity in Levite responsibility. These sections are followed by a concluding summary in 4:34–49, reflecting a typical Pentateuchal pattern of moving from the general to the particular in somewhat cyclical fashion. Each stage also contains a stern warning regarding violation of the sanctity of the tabernacle at its various levels. First (1:47–53), the general duties of the Levites as a whole are described. In the second passage (3:1–10), the first level of division among the Levites is highlighted, in the separation of the sons of Aaron as priests in the sanctuary service. Third (3:21–38), the positioning of each of the three clans plus the priests on the four sides of the tabernacle is outlined, with the Gershonites on the west, the Kohathites on the south, the Merarites on the north, and the priests on the favored east side. Under the discussion of each of the clans is the census of all males age one month or more for the purpose of the tabulation of the firstborn for Levite redemption, and a further delineation of each clan's duties. Fourth (4:1–49), the duties of each of the three Levite clans are detailed regarding that portion of the tabernacle over which each has responsibility. Each of these final sections also contains a census of those males age thirty to fifty. These individuals of aged maturity would carry out the actual duties delineated previously.

The Israelite tribes were to camp around the tabernacle, equally distributed on each of the four sides according to the troop alignments delineated in 2:1–31, with each person lining up according to the tribal division or flag (degel). Rabbi Rashi suggested a colored flag according to the color of stone in the high priest's breastplate (Exod 28:17–21). Gray proposed simply "company" based upon a parallel Aramaic usage in the Septuagint, Elephantine papyri, Peshitta, Targums, and the War Scroll of Qumran. The Septuagint translates the term as *dunamei,* referring to military troop strength. In the postbiblical era the term came to mean a garrison of one thousand troops who lived in the encampment with their wives and children. Most of these translations derive from late first millennium B.C. usage, whereas in the bronze ages of the second millennium B.C. the Akkadian cognate verb *dagalu* refers to something "seen" such as a flag, emblem, or banner. The context could allow for either interpretation, with the *degel* referring either to the tribal unit or some identifying visible marker.

⁵⁴**The Israelites did all this just as the LORD commanded Moses.**

CENSUS CONCLUSION: FAITHFUL OBEDIENCE (1:54). **1:54** The statement of Israel's obedience to Yahweh's commands through Moses is one of the keys to understanding the theological structure of the Book of Numbers. In the two Sinai cycles of 1:1–10:10, obedience is a hallmark of the community of faith and its leadership, whereas in the three cycles that ensue rebelliousness is the central organizing theme, affecting almost everyone in the community—even Moses. The theological-geographical context is that of the departure from Sinai, the mountain of God and the locale of the receiving of the Commandments of God in revelation.[43]

*(3) Holy Arrangement of the Israelite Camps (2:1–34)*

¹**The LORD said to Moses and Aaron:** ²**"The Israelites are to camp around the Tent of Meeting some distance from it, each man under his standard with the banners of his family."**

³**On the east, toward the sunrise, the divisions of the camp of Judah are to encamp under their standard. The leader of the people of Judah is Nahshon son of Amminadab.** ⁴**His division numbers 74,600.**
⁵**The tribe of Issachar will camp next to them. The leader of the people of Issachar is Nethanel son of Zuar.** ⁶**His division numbers 54,400.**
⁷**The tribe of Zebulun will be next. The leader of the people of Zebulun is Eliab son of Helon.** ⁸**His division numbers 57,400.**
⁹**All the men assigned to the camp of Judah, according to their divisions, number 186,400. They will set out first.**

¹⁰**On the south will be the divisions of the camp of Reuben under their standard. The leader of the people of Reuben is Elizur son of Shedeur.** ¹¹**His division numbers 46,500.**
¹²**The tribe of Simeon will camp next to them. The leader of the people of Simeon is Shelumiel son of Zurishaddai.** ¹³**His division numbers 59,300.**
¹⁴**The tribe of Gad will be next. The leader of the people of Gad is Eliasaph son of Deuel.** ¹⁵**His division numbers 45,650.**

¹⁶**All the men assigned to the camp of Reuben, according to their divisions, number 151,450. They will set out second.**

¹⁷**Then the Tent of Meeting and the camp of the Levites will set out in the middle of the camps. They will set out in the same order as they encamp, each in his own place under his standard.**

---

[43] Note the recurrence of the phraseology that Moses, Aaron, the priests, the patriarchal leaders, and the people performed their tasks dutifully according to that which God commanded: 1:19,54; 2:33–34; 3:16,39,42,51; 4:37,41,45,49(2x); 5:4; 8:3–4,20–22; 9:5,8,18,20,23. Only in 10:13; 17:11 (MT 17:26); and 20:9,27 does this phraseology occur in the three rebellion cycles. Then in the advent cycles the theme recurs in 26:4; 27:11,22–23; 31:7,31,41,47; 32:25; 36:5,10.

¹⁸On the west will be the divisions of the camp of Ephraim under their standard. The leader of the people of Ephraim is Elishama son of Ammihud. ¹⁹His division numbers 40,500.

²⁰The tribe of Manasseh will be next to them. The leader of the people of Manasseh is Gamaliel son of Pedahzur. ²¹His division numbers 32,200. ²²The tribe of Benjamin will be next. The leader of the people of Benjamin is Abidan son of Gideoni. ²³His division numbers 35,400.

²⁴All the men assigned to the camp of Ephraim, according to their divisions, number 108,100. They will set out third.

²⁵On the north will be the divisions of the camp of Dan, under their standard. The leader of the people of Dan is Ahiezer son of Ammishaddai. ²⁶His division numbers 62,700.

²⁷The tribe of Asher will camp next to them. The leader of the people of Asher is Pagiel son of Ocran. ²⁸His division numbers 41,500.

²⁹The tribe of Naphtali will be next. The leader of the people of Naphtali is Ahira son of Enan. ³⁰His division numbers 53,400.

³¹All the men assigned to the camp of Dan number 157,600. They will set out last, under their standards.

³²These are the Israelites, counted according to their families. All those in the camps, by their divisions, number 603,550. ³³The Levites, however, were not counted along with the other Israelites, as the LORD commanded Moses.

³⁴So the Israelites did everything the LORD commanded Moses; that is the way they encamped under their standards, and that is the way they set out, each with his clan and family.

INTRODUCTION (2:1–2). **2:1–2** With the military census of the twelve tribes complete and the Levite responsibility introduced, the orderly arrangement of the children of Israel is introduced by the standard revelatory formula of the Book of Numbers.[44] Here Aaron is included with Moses as the receptor of the instruction, a construction often found in priestly contexts.[45]

The arrangement of the twelve tribes in symmetrical fashion around the central sanctuary reflects the orderliness of a unified community that is faithfully following the commands of the Lord. Allen describes this setting as expressing "the joy of the writer in knowing the relation of each tribe to the whole, each individual to the tribe, and the nation to the central shrine—and to the Lord Yahweh."[46] As wonder and beauty are reflected in the order

---

[44] See commentary on 1:1 above and "Introduction: Outline" for the role of the formula וַיְדַבֵּר יְהוָה אֶל־ PN ... לֵאמֹר.

[45] See Moses + Aaron in priestly contexts of 4:1,17; 16:20; 19:1; as well as 14:26 in the judgment against Israel because of their rejection of the land. The two names also occur in priestly contexts where וַיֹּאמֶר is used, including 20:12,23, plus 26:1, in which Eleazar replaces Aaron after his father's death. The formula with Aaron only occurs in 18:1,20 (וַיֹּאמֶר) and 18:8 (with וַיְדַבֵּר).

[46] Allen, "Numbers," 712.

of creation, so the unity and symmetry of the chosen people of his creation evoke splendor and awe. The wondrous sentiment is echoed in the words of Balaam's third oracle, recounted as the spirit of God came over him as he observed "Israel encamped tribe by tribe" in the plains of Moab:

> How beautiful are your tents, O Jacob,
>     your dwelling places, O Israel!
> Like valleys they spread out,
>     like gardens beside a river;
>     like aloes planted by the LORD,
>     like cedars beside the waters. (24:5–6)

Each man is to camp according to the standard which signifies his ancestral house, around and out and away from the tabernacle.[47] The terms *degel* ("standard") and *'ōtōt* ("signs") refer to some kind of banner or flag that has some identifiable insignia or color that specifies the given tribal unit (see above 1:52). In the War Scroll from the Qumran caves, distinguishable standards were to be carried by each division within the ancestral tribe.[48] The structure of v. 2 emphasizes the individual in relationship to the larger Israelite community of faith.[49] Allen notes: "The people of Israel were a community that had their essential meaning in relationship to God and to one another. But ever in the community was the continuing stress on the individual to know where he belonged in the larger grouping. Corporate solidarity in ancient Israel was a reality of daily life; but the individual was also very important."[50]

The general instructions are provided in 2:2, followed by the more specific delineation of the tribal encampments. The census figures of chap. 1 are utilized in the setting forth of the grouping of three tribes on each of the four sides of the tabernacle, with each group of three having a leading tribe in the coming march from Mount Sinai. The listing of the chieftains from each of the tribes is also repeated. The symmetrical pattern of the four encampments, with mention of the Levites between the second and third groups, is as follows:

Direction from Tabernacle
    Tribe—Leader w/Standard—Military Census
    Tribe—Leader—Military Census
    Tribe—Leader—Military Census
Summation of Census

---

[47] Lit., "Each man according to his standard with the signs of the house of their fathers, the children of Israel shall camp; outwardly surrounding the Tent of Meeting they shall camp." See Milgrom, *Numbers,* 12.

[48] *1 Q M* 3:27–43.

[49] The distributive use of אִישׁ, placed first in the Hb. word order of v. 2, highlights the role of the individual within his family and ancestral tribal units.

[50] Allen, "Numbers," 713.

EAST SIDE, SOUTH SIDE, WEST SIDE, AND NORTH SIDE ENCAMP-
MENTS (2:3–31). **2:3–31** The outline of the four three-tribal encampments begins with the east side, the direction of sunrise and toward which
the door-curtains of the tabernacle opened. The order then rotates clockwise
around the tabernacle. Led by the tribe of Judah, whose ancestral head had
supplanted both the firstborn Reuben and the favored Joseph in importance,
the group of Judah, Issachar, and Zebulun is listed first through third rather
than in fourth through sixth positions in 1:20–43. Reuben, Simeon, and Gad
move from first through third to fourth through sixth. Otherwise the order
of the tribes remains the same as the previous military census. The role of
Judah in the coming history of the nation is augmented by the fact that
through the fourth son of Jacob and Leah and the eighth son of Jesse the
royal line would be established (Gen 29:31–35; 1 Sam 16:6–13; 2 Sam
7:12–17). The supplanting of the firstborn according to God's sovereign
choosing is a prominent theme in the Hebrew Bible, with such examples as
Isaac and Ishmael, Jacob and Esau, Ephraim and Manasseh highlighting the
divine direction for transcending the common tradition of the ancient Near
East.

The structure of the tribal encampments and the order of their marching
through the wilderness is as follows:[51]

### THE TRIBAL ENCAMPMENTS OF ISRAEL

EAST

| | | |
|---|---|---|
| JUDAH | Nahshon ben Amminadab | 74,600 |
| Issachar | Nethanel ben Zuar | 54,400 |
| Zebulun | Eliab ben Helon | 57,400 |
| CAMP OF JUDAH | | 186,400 |

SOUTH

| | | |
|---|---|---|
| REUBEN | Elizur ben Shedeur | 46,500 |
| Simeon | Shelumiel ben Zurishaddai | 59,300 |
| Gad | Eliasaph ben Reuel[52] | 46,650 |
| CAMP OF REUBEN | | 151,450 |

---

[51] Several chiastic constructions frame the broad structure of vv. 3–31, amplifying the symmetry of the pericope. Note the following outline of the directive vv. 3,10,18, and 25:

| 3 | Direction | Camp | Troops |
|---|---|---|---|
| 10 | Camp | Direction | Troops |
| 18 | Camp | Troops | Direction |
| 25 | Camp | Direction | Troops |

Verses 10 and 25 are parallel, but chiastic constructions exist between vv. 3 and 10, 18 and 25, as
well as more broadly between vv. 3 and 25.

[52] Written as "Deuel" in 1:14 and 7:42, "Reuel" in 2:14 may be a later transcription error when
the rēš and dālet were more easily confused. SamPent and Vg. read Deuel.

## TABERNACLE AND LEVITES

WEST

| | | |
|---|---|---|
| EPHRAIM | Elishama ben Ammihud | 40,500 |
| Manasseh | Gamaliel ben Pedahzur | 32,200 |
| Benjamin | Abidan ben Gideoni | 35,400 |
| CAMP OF EPHRAIM | | 108,100 |

NORTH

| | | |
|---|---|---|
| DAN | Ahiezer ben Ammishaddai | 62,700 |
| Asher | Pagiel ben Ochran | 41,500 |
| Naphtali | Ahira ben Enan | 53,400 |
| CAMP OF DAN | | 157,600 |
| GRAND TOTAL | | 603,550 |

The total of all of the encampments, not including the Levites, is equivalent to the total given in 1:46. As in chap. 1, the Levites are exempt from military conscription and are reserved for special service of the tabernacle. The organization of the tribes according to their units and standards was accomplished according to God's commands, as were all the acts of Moses, Aaron, the priests, and the people through the first cycle of events in Numbers.[53] In the marching forth from Mount Sinai, the tribes dutifully and faithfully adhere to these instructions for orderly encampment, assembly and disassembly of the tabernacle, and disembarkment on the journey through the wilderness.

## TRIBAL ENCAMPMENTS AROUND THE TABERNACLE

| | | | | |
|---|---|---|---|---|
| | | Asher  DAN  Naphtali | | |
| | | Merari–Levites | | |
| Benjamin | | | | Issachar |
| EPHRAIM | Gershon–Levites | **TENT OF MEETING** | Aaronic Priests | JUDAH |
| Manasseh | | | | Zebulun |
| | | Kohath Levites | | |
| | Gad | REUBEN  Simeon | | |

CONCLUSION: FAITHFUL OBEDIENCE (2:32–34). **2:32–34** The concluding phraseology recounts the theme of the Sinai cycles, that Israel under Moses's leadership is following faithfully the instruction of Yahweh their God. Harmony, symmetry, and purity highlight this responsive relationship between God and people.

The conclusion and complement to the census of the Israelite tribes and the structural delineation of the faithful community is the census of the Levites and the delineation of the roles of their clans within that community. Structurally the cycle development and Levitical elements merge to heighten the emphasis on the priestly tribe. In content chaps. 3–4 parallel chaps. 1–2,

---

[53] See comments on 1:54 and 3:16,51.

which set forth the census of the other twelve tribes and the structural organization of the larger community. The section divides into seven parts in the following structural pattern:

A Genealogical Listing: Aaronic Line (3:1–4)
  B Responsibilities of the Levites (3:5–10)
    C Dedication of the Levites for the Firstborn (3:11–13)
A′ Genealogical Listing: Levitical Clans (3:14–20)
  B′ Responsibilities and Census of the Levite Clans (3:21–39)
    C′ Dedication of the Levites for the Firstborn (3:40–51)
  B″ Responsibilities and Census of the Levite Clans: Age 30–50 (4:1–49)

This pattern of repetition with expansion is paralleled several times in Leviticus, such as in the delineation of the purification rituals of Yom Kippur (16:1–34).

## (4) Responsibilities and Census of the Levite Clans (3:1–4:49)

**[1]This is the account of the family of Aaron and Moses at the time the LORD talked with Moses on Mount Sinai.**

**[2]The names of the sons of Aaron were Nadab the firstborn and Abihu, Eleazar and Ithamar. [3]Those were the names of Aaron's sons, the anointed priests, who were ordained to serve as priests. [4]Nadab and Abihu, however, fell dead before the LORD when they made an offering with unauthorized fire before him in the Desert of Sinai. They had no sons; so only Eleazar and Ithamar served as priests during the lifetime of their father Aaron.**

INTRODUCTION: GENEALOGY OF AARON AND MOSES (3:1–4). **3:1–4** The introduction to chaps. 3 and 4 contains the standard genealogical introductory formulae, "This is the account of the family of" and "the names of … were," more literally "these are the generations *[toledot]*[54] of X," and "these are the names," paralleled by the genealogies of Genesis.[55] In chap. 1 the census process is organized around the *toledoth* of each of the tribal patriarchs. The recitation of one's ancestral genealogy remains an important part of family tradition in the Middle East.

Within the cultural framework of the ancient Near East, genealogical records served several purposes: (1) to provide historical connection and

---

[54] The תּוֹלְדֹת are the family genealogical records, variously translated as "the account of the family" (NIV), "the line" (Milgrom, JPS), "family histories" (Ashley, *Numbers*), "family records" (Harrison), et al. See also the Genesis תּוֹלְדֹת of Adam (5:1), Noah (6:9), the sons of Noah (10:1), Shem (11:10), Terah (11:27), Ishmael (25:12), Isaac (25:19), Esau (36:1,9), and Jacob 37:2). Outside of Genesis, Exodus (6:16,19; 28:10), and Numbers, תּוֹלְדֹת are found only in Ruth 4:18 and 1 Chr 1:29; 5:7; 7:2,4,9; 8:28; 9:9.34; 26:31.

[55] The dual usage of genealogical introductory formulae is also found in Gen 25:12–13 and 36:9–10.

foundation of one's existence in the present in relation to the past, (2) to preserve familial community and organization within the larger societal structure, (3) to justify one's position within the present structure, and (4) to provide future generations with a source of pride and presence. The larger literary structures in the Bible that contain genealogies often have two parts. First is the recounting of the names of the ancestors, and second is an account of the role of the ancestors in the family history.

The positioning of the account of the Aaronic line in the introduction of this section emphasizes the centrality of the priesthood within this ancestral tribe.[56] The family lineage of Levi was delineated previously in Exod 6:16–25, recounting the role of Moses and Aaron in leading the children of Israel out of Egypt. Moses is included because of his position as brother of Aaron and his station next to Aaron in the Israelite camp.[57] More often Moses appears first in the pair in contexts of revelation or leadership narratives.[58] But here the Aaronic priesthood is in focus in relation to the larger Levitical tribe, and Aaron was the firstborn of Amram. The setting of the genealogical recitation is in the context of the second trip of Moses up to Mount Sinai, presumably after the Levites demonstrated their devotion to Yahweh in the incident of the golden calf (Exod 32:1–29).

The names of the sons of Aaron are listed in traditional genealogical form, beginning with the firstborn, Nadab, followed by Abihu, Eleazar, and Ithamar. The repetition of the phrase "these are the names" heightens the role of the sons of Aaron as "the anointed priests" *(hakōhănîm hammĕšuḥîm)* for the Israelite community. The consecration by means of oil and blood anointing is described variously as to the general description (Exod 28:1–29:35) and ritual inauguration (Lev 8:1–9:24). God's blessing upon Aaron and his sons was demonstrated by the fire of his glory, which consumed the sacrificial offerings. Aaron functioned as the first anointed

---

[56] Harrison (*Numbers*, 61–63) has suggested alternately that 3:1 serves as a concluding colophon that began in 2:1. The setting of revelation on Mount Sinai is then in view for the directions regarding the structuring of the Israelite community. Harrison is right in noting that most of the תּוֹלְדֹת of Genesis function as colophons much like their counterparts in Babylonian texts. But as Milgrom notes (JPS, 13), this structure is parallel to Gen 25:12–18, where the double rubric of תּוֹלְדֹת and "these are the names" occurs. Likewise, in the following תּוֹלְדֹת of Isaac in Gen 25:19, the function is to introduce the account of the lineage from Isaac and Rebekah to Esau and Jacob. Additionally, the placement of Aaron before Moses in the verse introduction is appropriate for the introduction to the following context concerning the Aaronic priesthood rather than the instruction to Moses to structure the Israelite encampment.

[57] Milgrom, *Numbers*, 15. Cf. also Exod 6:23; Lev 10:1–2; and Num 26:59–61.

[58] See 1:17,44; 2:1; 4:1,17,34,41,46; 14:26; 16:20; 19:1; 20:12,23. Only in the context of chap. 18 does the Lord speak only to Aaron, a section devoted to the support of the priesthood. After the death of Aaron, God speaks to "Moses and Eleazar" once (26:1). Milgrom (*Numbers*, 15) notes that of the seventy-eight times Moses and Aaron appear together, Aaron precedes Moses only in genealogical texts (Exod 6:20; Num 3:1; 26:59; 1 Chr 5:29; 25:13).

high priest for the desert sanctuary in the ceremony of the Day of Atonement (Lev 16:1–34). Harrison notes that a Middle Bronze (2200–1550 B.C.) Mari text parallel to the phraseology of ordination, which means literally to "fill their hand" *(millē' yādām)*, "probably referred to offerings placed in the priests' hands during the consecration ceremony, which conferred upon them the authority to discharge priestly functions in the Tabernacle."[59]

The consecration of individuals such as kings (1 Sam 16:13; Isa 45:1) and prophets (1 Kgs 19:15,16), via the anointing with purified olive oil in ritual ceremony, set apart these persons as special servants of Yahweh. In the post-exilic era the term began to be used as a more technical designation for God's future leader and deliverer. The usage in the Dead Sea Scrolls reflects the full progression of the term's development, where priestly and royal roles are in focus. Hence the Greek form *Christos* was applied to Jesus by early Christians in recognition of him as Messiah, God's ultimate anointed servant. According to the writer of Hebrews, his high priesthood according to the order of Melchizedek exceeds that of the Aaronic order, and he serves in a "greater and more perfect sanctuary" than the tabernacle in the wilderness and the temples of Solomon, Zerubbabel, and Herod the Great (Heb 7:11–9:15). In Jesus the Messiah the shadowy imperfection of the Israelite sacrificial system was made complete and transcended by Jesus' function as the perfect High Priest, offering himself as the ultimate unblemished sacrifice—once for all eternity, in a perfect heavenly sanctuary before the throne of God. By this he accomplished salvation and sanctification for the community of faith so that they might encourage one another to love and good works (Heb 10:5–25).

Aaron and his four sons had been anointed as priests, but his two oldest sons died (Lev 10:1–2) dramatically by fire that emerged from the presence of the Lord in the sanctuary. Aaron's sons had violated cultic code in offering an unholy censer of incense, perhaps usurping the authority of their father as high priest, whose sole authority it was to offer the incense via censer on the Day of Atonement. Neither improper nor innovative ritual activity was permissible. In the context of the ultimate sanctity of the inner sanctuary, the profaning of God's holiness warranted rapid retribution. The continued context (10:8) of the original account in Leviticus may indicate a further breach of conduct by Nadab and Abihu in rendering tabernacle service while intoxicated, an infraction punishable by death.

The account served as a reminder to future generations of priests that violation of the precise ritual of the sanctuary would result in severe punishment. These special servants were to function as exemplars of holiness to the people of God, who were to be holy because their God was holy. In the

---

[59] Harrison, *Numbers*, 64.

present context of the delineation of duties and the taking of the census of the Levites, the passage serves to inform the priestly reader of the seriousness of their task. Also, not only were Nadab and Abihu terminated, but they left no sons to carry on their lineage. This judgment left the high priestly lineage in the hands of Eleazar and Ithamar, who continued to serve faithfully as priests in the service of their father Aaron and the Lord.

**⁵The LORD said to Moses, ⁶"Bring the tribe of Levi and present them to Aaron the priest to assist him. ⁷They are to perform duties for him and for the whole community at the Tent of Meeting by doing the work of the tabernacle. ⁸They are to take care of all the furnishings of the Tent of Meeting, fulfilling the obligations of the Israelites by doing the work of the tabernacle. ⁹Give the Levites to Aaron and his sons; they are the Israelites who are to be given wholly to him. ¹⁰Appoint Aaron and his sons to serve as priests; anyone else who approaches the sanctuary must be put to death."**

LEVITE CONSECRATION TO SERVICE (3:5–10).  **3:5–10**  This section and the following (vv. 14–39) are introduced by the key structural announcement formula in Numbers, "And the LORD spoke" *(wayĕdabbēr YHWH),* pointing again to the theological focus on the revelatory nature of divine speech. As compared to 3:1, only Moses is the receptor, though Aaron, his sons, and the three clans of Levi are the primary subjects.

Moses is commanded to "bring ... and present"[60] the Levites before Aaron, and both terms carry cultic connotations in this context. In ceremonial fashion the Levites are dedicated to the service of providing assistance to Aaron the high priest, guarding and maintaining the various furnishings of the Tent of Meeting, and serving the cultic needs of the entire community. The term "assist" *(šērtû)* denotes a subservient ministry the Levites have on behalf of the Israelite people. Twice the Hebrew verbal phraseology sequence *wĕšāmrû ... laʿăbōd ʾet-ʿăbōdat* (lit. "and they shall guard ... to serve the service of"), translated "they are to perform duties ... by doing the work" (v. 7) and "they are to take care ... by doing the work" (v. 8), describes the responsibilities of guarding and safekeeping the tabernacle.[61] In 1:50–53 the positioning of the Levites around the Tent of Meeting provided a kind of sacred barrier around the worship center so as to perform the sacred service of the sanctuary and ensure the safety of the laity of the other tribes. Encroachment upon the sacred space by anyone but a priest or Levite was a capital crime. Thus the priests and Levites were to be set aside as (1) special cultic servants of the Aaronic priesthood, the people, and God; (2) transportation and maintenance personnel of all of the physical elements of

---

⁶⁰ The Hb. phrase הַקְרֵב אֶת־מַטֵּה לֵוִי וְהַעֲמַדְתָּ אֹתוֹ לִפְנֵי אַהֲרֹן הַכֹּהֵן, "Bring before [Aaron] ... and have them stand," describes a formal presentation for commissioning to service.

⁶¹ Cf. Adam's caretaking of the garden in Gen 2:15.

the tabernacle; and (3) guardians of the sanctity of the Holy Place.

The Levites are dedicated totally ("Give ... to be given wholly," *nātatâ nětûnim nětûnim*) as the only Israelites who can function in the cultus. A further special appointment *(tipqōd)* of Aaron and his sons as priests over the Tent of Meeting, carries a restrictive aspect in that only the anointed priests may provide the cultic service of the inner sanctum of the sanctuary.[62] Abrogation of this law constitutes a capital offense. The particular responsibilities of the three clans of Levites are delineated later in this chapter.

**[11]The LORD also said to Moses, [12]"I have taken the Levites from among the Israelites in place of the first male offspring of every Israelite woman. The Levites are mine, [13]for all the firstborn are mine. When I struck down all the firstborn in Egypt, I set apart for myself every firstborn in Israel, whether man or animal. They are to be mine. I am the LORD."**

LEVITE REPLACEMENT OF THE FIRSTBORN (3:11–13). **3:11–13** The context describes the substitutionary purpose of the Levites in dedication to God on behalf of the other twelve tribes, which is to serve in place of the firstborn of the people whom might otherwise be appointed to such a task in the patriarchal structure of the community. The background of the replacement by the Levites of the firstborn males of the Israelite women is that of the dedication of the firstborn set forth in Exod 13:2,11–16; 22:29–30; 34:19–20. The first issue of the womb of every female—human and animal—belonged to the Lord. From the flocks and herds, even including the donkey that was redeemed with a lamb, the people were to present the animals to the priests on the eighth day after their birth. The designation of the firstborn male of the Israelite female is paralleled by the account of the firstborn of Abraham through Sarah (Gen 21:1–7), and serves as the precedent for subsequent delineation of the firstborn of Israel and the Jews, as well the tracing of Jewish lineage through history. The explanation for the dedication is found in the context of the Exodus account in which God brought death to the firstborn of Egypt while he delivered the firstborn of Israel. This was to be like a sign on their hand and a symbol on their foreheads, indicative of their status as servants of Yahweh their God who brought them out of Egypt (Exod 13:14–16). Animals were sacrificed and humans were dedicated, hence the consecration of the Levites as special servants of Aaron and the priests of Yahweh.

**[14]The LORD said to Moses in the Desert of Sinai, [15]"Count the Levites by their families and clans. Count every male a month old or more." [16]So Moses counted them, as he was commanded by the word of the LORD. [17]These were the names of**

---

[62] Note the LXX adds "over the Tent of Meeting" here and so emphasizes the exclusive role of the priests in serving within the sacred precinct.

the sons of Levi: Gershon, Kohath and Merari. <sup>18</sup>These were the names of the Gershonite clans: Libni and Shimei. <sup>19</sup>The Kohathite clans: Amram, Izhar, Hebron and Uzziel. <sup>20</sup>The Merarite clans: Mahli and Mushi. These were the Levite clans, according to their families.

GENEALOGICAL DELINEATION OF THE LEVITE CLANS (3:14–20). **3:14–20** Instructions in the Levite census taking are given to Moses in a divine directive, the third occurrence of *wayĕdabbēr YHWH* in this chapter. The setting is that of the Desert of Sinai, in the context of the Israelites in transit, as they were following the cloud pillar by day and the fire pillar by night. Guardianship, transportation, and the process of assemblage and dismantling are in view.

The first Levite census entails all males age one month or more and their positioning on the four directional sides of the tabernacle, whereas the second Levite census (4:1–49) counts only those age thirty to fifty who would be eligible for sacred service. The minimum age of one month also varies from the twenty-year-old minimum of the military conscription census in chap. 1. The lower age was no doubt necessary to procure a number of Levites sufficient to approximate the number of firstborn among the Israelite families. The command to "count the Levites" comes by divine directive to Moses, notes Milgrom, emphasized by the fact that "this reference to the Lord's oracle and command occurs seven times in chapters 3 and 4."[63] The census of the Levites is therefore carried out with divine assistance. Moses faithfully would complete the task according to the Lord's instruction, which exemplifies the loyal devotion of the Israelites in the Sinai context as depicted in the two cycles of material in Num 1:1–10:10.

In a highly structured genealogical pattern, the family groups in the lineage of the three sons of Levi are listed in the same order as in Exod 6:16–19. The genealogical formula "these are the names" (*ʾēleh šĕmôt*) introduces "the sons of Levi" in Exod 6:16, whereas the formula introduces in a collective distributive construction the sons of Gershon (v. 18), the sons of Kohath (v. 19), and the sons of Merari (v. 20). The passage concludes with a formula variation, "these are the clans of the Levites by their ancestral house[s]."

<sup>21</sup>To Gershon belonged the clans of the Libnites and Shimeites; these were the Gershonite clans. <sup>22</sup>The number of all the males a month old or more who were counted was 7,500. <sup>23</sup>The Gershonite clans were to camp on the west, behind the tabernacle. <sup>24</sup>The leader of the families of the Gershonites was Eliasaph son of Lael. <sup>25</sup>At the Tent of Meeting the Gershonites were responsible for the care of the tabernacle and tent, its coverings, the curtain at the entrance to the Tent of Meeting, <sup>26</sup>the curtains of the courtyard, the curtain at the entrance to the court-

---

[63] Milgrom, *Numbers*, 19. The Hb. עַל־פִּי יְהוָה denotes a form of divine oracle, repeated in 3:39,51; 4:37,49. The divine command formula צִוָּה יְהוָה אֹתוֹ in 3:42 and 4:49.

yard surrounding the tabernacle and altar, and the ropes—and everything related to their use.

²⁷To Kohath belonged the clans of the Amramites, Izharites, Hebronites and Uzzielites; these were the Kohathite clans. ²⁸The number of all the males a month old or more was 8,600. The Kohathites were responsible for the care of the sanctuary. ²⁹The Kohathite clans were to camp on the south side of the tabernacle. ³⁰The leader of the families of the Kohathite clans was Elizaphan son of Uzziel. ³¹They were responsible for the care of the ark, the table, the lampstand, the altars, the articles of the sanctuary used in ministering, the curtain, and everything related to their use. ³²The chief leader of the Levites was Eleazar son of Aaron, the priest. He was appointed over those who were responsible for the care of the sanctuary.

³³To Merari belonged the clans of the Mahlites and the Mushites; these were the Merarite clans. ³⁴The number of all the males a month old or more who were counted was 6,200. ³⁵The leader of the families of the Merarite clans was Zuriel son of Abihail; they were to camp on the north side of the tabernacle. ³⁶The Merarites were appointed to take care of the frames of the tabernacle, its crossbars, posts, bases, all its equipment, and everything related to their use, ³⁷as well as the posts of the surrounding courtyard with their bases, tent pegs and ropes.

³⁸Moses and Aaron and his sons were to camp to the east of the tabernacle, toward the sunrise, in front of the Tent of Meeting. They were responsible for the care of the sanctuary on behalf of the Israelites. Anyone else who approached the sanctuary was to be put to death.

³⁹The total number of Levites counted at the LORD's command by Moses and Aaron according to their clans, including every male a month old or more, was 22,000.

CENSUS AND RESPONSIBILITIES OF THE LEVITE CLANS (3:21–39). **3:21–39** The presentation of the census and duties of each of the Levite clans follows the traditional order. The Gershonite family groups of Libni and Shimei totalled 7,500 males one month old and up, and they were to camp on the west side of the tabernacle, that is on the back side opposite the entryway. The patriarchal leader (*nĕśîʾ bêt-ʾāb*, "prince of the father's household") of the clans of Gershon⁶⁴ was Eliasaph ben Lael, under whom the clans administered the caretaking of the tabernacle and the Tent coverings and curtains. The tabernacle was composed of ten curtains of finely twisted blue, purple and scarlet linen, each twenty-eight by four cubits, with cherubim woven into them. They were attached to the framing by gold clasps attached to blue loops (Exod 26:1–6). The Tent was composed of eleven goat-hair curtains, each thirty by four cubits, with an additional cov-

---

⁶⁴ Spelled Gershom in 1 Chr 6:16,17,20,43,62,71 (Hb. MT 1 Chr 6:1,2,5,28,47,56) in which context the fuller listing of the Gershonite genealogy obtains.

ering made of ram skins dyed red and hides of sea cows (Exod 26:7–14). Assumed under their duties were repairs, refurbishing, and cleansing. Under the Davidic monarchy the Gershonite descendants in the family of Asaph were renowned musicians and treasurers of the Temple.[65]

Milgrom notes that whereas Mesopotamian and Egyptian temples had statues of divine emissaries as guardians for their various temples, Israel knew of no such demonic entities in their prophetic religion. There was but one true power in the universe, the God of Israel, and his sanctuary must be protected and secured from the intrusion or defilement by "the only remaining adversary—man."[66] Samuel guarded the sanctuary as Eli was growing blind. Sources from Mari and Hattusas depict specially assigned temple guardians.

The Kohathite family groups of Amram, Izhar, Hebron, and Uziel numbered 8,600.[67] They were to camp on the south side of the tabernacle and carry out their duties under the leadership of Elizaphan ben Uzziel. The Kohathites were guardians and transporters of the various articles of the tabernacle, including the ark of the covenant, the table for the shewbread, the seven-tiered lampstand, the other tools and articles needed to administer the service of the sanctuary, and the sacred curtain, which was placed over the ark. Their duties commenced only after Eleazar and his brothers the priests covered each of the items properly for transportation as the Lord would lead the people through the wilderness. The Kohathites were not allowed to handle the actual furnishings[68] The expanded delineation of the Kohathite responsibilities is found in 4:24–26. Some Kohathites under the rebellious leadership of Korah would later challenge the authority of Moses and Aaron over the Israelite community (Num 16:1–50). Like the Gershonites, Levites from the clans of Kohath served as musicians during the Davidic monarchy (1 Chr 6:33–38).

The Merarite family groups of Mahli and Mushi numbered 6,200 of age one month or older. They were to camp on the north side of the tabernacle and serve as caretakers and transporters of the support structures for the tabernacle and the Tent.[69] These included bases, posts, frames, and equipment needed to erect and dismantle the structures. Like the Gershonites and Kohathites, Levites from the clans of Merari served later as musicians dur-

---

[65] Cf. the patriarchal name Eliasaph, meaning "God of Asaph." Regarding their role as musicians see 1 Chr 6:31–32,39 (Hb. 6:16–17,24) and as treasurers (see 1 Chr 26:20–22).

[66] Milgrom, Excursus 4, "The Levites: Guardians of the Tabernacle," 341.

[67] The Lucianic recension of the LXX reads 8,300, which when added to the 7,500 of Gershon and the 6,200 of Merari totals the 22,000 of 3:39. This census serves as the basis for the redemption of the firstborn.

[68] The various items are delineated in 4:7–14. Peshitta adds "the [bronze] laver and its base."

[69] Note the apposition in this verse of הַמִּשְׁכָּן ("the Tabernacle") and אֹהֶל־מוֹעֵד ("Tent of Meeting"), suggesting they are viewed as equivalent at this time.

ing the Davidic monarchy (1 Chr 6:44–47).

On the east side of the sanctuary, the preeminent position of entry and the direction of the sunrise, were camped Aaron and his sons the priests. There they guarded the angle that was most vulnerable to intrusion. The Hebrew construction may have dual directions in view, protection *from* the intrusion by a rebellious or unwitting nonpriestly Israelite and protection *for* the people from divine punishment that would result. Encroachment upon or within the Holy Place was punishable by death. Symbolically God's holiness and purity, depicted in the degrees of sacred space descending from the Holy of Holies to the perimeter of the tabernacle, were protected by the positioning of the clans of Levi, the tribe consecrated for divine service.

The total of the census of the three family groups of the Levites was 22,000 of age one month or older. This total agrees with the sum of the individual clans, when one adopts the preferred Septuagint reading of 8,300 as the census of the Kohathites. Otherwise the total comes to 22,300, and the five-shekel redemption of each of the excess firstborn of Israel, who numbered 22,273 (v. 43), would have been unnecessary.

**Comparison of Levite Census Texts**

| Levite Tribal Clan | MT | LXX | Suggested Totals |
|---|---|---|---|
| Gershonites (v. 22) | 7,500 | 7,500 | 7,500 |
| Kohathites (v. 28) | 8,600 | 8,600[70] | 8,300 |
| Merarites (v. 34) | 6,200 | 6,050[71] | 6,200 |
| TOTAL | 22,300[72] | 22,150[73] | 22,000 |

**40**The LORD said to Moses, "Count all the firstborn Israelite males who are a month old or more and make a list of their names. **41**Take the Levites for me in place of all the firstborn of the Israelites, and the livestock of the Levites in place of all the firstborn of the livestock of the Israelites. I am the LORD."

**42**So Moses counted all the firstborn of the Israelites, as the LORD commanded him. **43**The total number of firstborn males a month old or more, listed by name, was 22,273.

**44**The LORD also said to Moses, **45**"Take the Levites in place of all the first-

---

[70] The LXX ἑξακόσιοι (600) was changed to τριακόσιοι in the Lucianic recension. This agrees with a few MSS of the Hb. text, the Peshitta and Vg.

[71] J. W. Wevers says: "The reason for the difference is not known" (*Notes on the Greek Text of Numbers,* SBL Septuagint and Cognate Studies Series, 46 [Atlanta: Scholars Press, 1998], 47). The LXX reads ἑξακισχίλιοι καὶ πεντήκοντα (6,050).

[72] Note this total exceeds the 22,273 total of Israel's firstborn, removing the need for the five-shekel redemption price for the 273 in excess of 22,000, the number given in the summation of v. 39. Preference is to adopt the LXX reading of the Kohathite census (8,300) so that the sum of 22,000 is attained.

[73] The LXX total in v. 39 reads δύο καὶ εἴκοσιχιλιαδες (22,000), which in itself is not an accurate total of the three clan censuses of vv. 22, 28, 34.

born of Israel, and the livestock of the Levites in place of their livestock. The Levites are to be mine. I am the LORD. [46]To redeem the 273 firstborn Israelites who exceed the number of the Levites, [47]collect five shekels for each one, according to the sanctuary shekel, which weighs twenty gerahs. [48]Give the money for the redemption of the additional Israelites to Aaron and his sons."

[49]So Moses collected the redemption money from those who exceeded the number redeemed by the Levites. [50]From the firstborn of the Israelites he collected silver weighing 1,365 shekels, according to the sanctuary shekel. [51]Moses gave the redemption money to Aaron and his sons, as he was commanded by the word of the LORD.

DEDICATION OF THE LEVITES IN FIRSTBORN REDEMPTION (3:40–51). **3:40–51** Following the census of the Levite clans, the Lord instructs Moses to take a census of the firstborn males by listing the names of the Israelites who were one month old and up. The variant form of the introductory formula for divine speech, *wayyōʾmer YHWH ʾel Mōšeh* ("Then Yahweh said to Moses"), occurs here; and the twice-stated refrain, "I am the LORD," in vv. 41 and 45 accentuates their divine ownership in the dedication.[74] The total was 22,273, leaving an excess of 273 unredeemed firstborn males beyond the census of the 22,000 Levites. The instructions in Exod 13:7–22; 22:29–30; 34:19–20; and Num 3:12–13 were to substitute the Levites for the firstborn in service to the Lord. In addition, the livestock of the Levites also would be dedicated to the Lord in place of the firstborn of the livestock belonging to the Israelites.

The term "redemption" (*pĕdûyê*, root *pāda*) has its origins in the Akkadian literature, where in Babylonian legal texts the cognate term *padû* denotes a form of monetary payment equivalent to the market value of an object or person, remitted in order to transfer property from one party to another. Property yielded in payment of debt could be redeemed at an agreed price. Persons who were slaves or indentured servants due to indebtedness could be freed from bondage by payment of the redemption fee.[75] Israel was indebted to God for the deliverance of their firstborn, who were saved from death by the painting of the lamb's blood on the doorposts and lintels of their households when the angel of death passed over. Redemption for the nation was gained via the sacrifice of the paschal lamb, whose blood sig-

---

[74] The formula לֵאמֹר PN אֶל־ יְהוָה וַיְדַבֵּר for divine speech occurs only three times in the two Sinai cycles of 1:1–10:10, but more often (21x) in the rebellion cycles of 10:11–25:19, particularly in the Balaam oracles. The form פְּקֹד אֶל־מֹשֶׁה יְהוָה וַיֹּאמֶר is found in 3:40; 7:4,11; 11:16,23; 12:4,14; 14:11,20; 15:35,37; 17:25; 18:1; 20:12,23; 21:8,34; 22:9,12,20, (+ 32,35 > angel of YHWH). Twice Balaam notes that the Lord has put the word (דָּבָר) in his mouth (23:5,16); once he returns with YHWH's word as spoken (דִּבֶּר 2x in 22:8); and once Balaam says, "What YHWH speaks, I will speak" (דִּבֶּר 2x in 24:13). In the final two Advent cycles, יְהוָה וַיְדַבֵּר in divine speech occurs 3x only in 27:6,12 and 31:25.

[75] Harrison, *Numbers*, 75–78.

naled the angel of death to deliver the faithful Israelite households from his mission of death. Therefore the firstborn males of the children of Israel belonged to God as his servants, but they could now be redeemed by (1) the rendering of the Levites as substitutionary payment or (2) the payment of the redemption fee of five shekels for those unaccounted for in the Levite census. Harrison notes:

> Redemption was always described in terms of some kind of a cost factor. God was obviously not discharging a debt to someone by redeeming His elect at the time of the Exodus. But at that period, and on all subsequent occasions when the firstborn were redeemed, God made it clear that the price of a life was another life. The original cost factor subsisted in the effort that a loving, provident God made to redeem His chosen people by "passing over" the firstborn of Israel when He instituted the final plague upon Egypt.[76]

Redemption in the New Testament is an expansion on the Old Testament theme, whereby Jesus Christ became our Paschal Lamb, whose blood in his death has brought deliverance from death due to our sin. In the context of Peter's exhortation for Christians to live in holiness and obedience and not to conform to the ways of this world, he reminded them: "For you know that it was not with perishable things such as silver or gold that you were redeemed from the empty way of life handed down to you from your forefathers, but with the precious blood of Christ, a lamb without blemish or defect" (1 Pet 1:18–19).[77]

The price for the redemption of the excess firstborn of the Israelites was five shekels, or about 2.1 ounces of silver per person according to the twenty-gerah sanctuary shekel. The sanctuary shekel was mentioned previously in Exod 30:11–16 in the context of the half-shekel *(beqaᶜ)* atonement price for each of the Israelites delivered from Egyptian bondage. Five shekels was the standard price of a slave in the Late Bronze Age in Egypt and Mesopotamia and amounted to six months' wages for the average day laborer.[78]

The repeated statement in vv. 42 and 51 that Moses was obedient in faithfully carrying out the commands of the Lord is one of the keys to understanding the theological structure of the Book of Numbers. In the two Sinai cycles of 1:1–10:10, obedience is a hallmark of the community of faith and

---

[76] Ibid., 77.

[77] *TWOT* 2:716–17.

[78] G. J. Wenham, "Leviticus 27:2–8 and the Price of Slaves," *ZAW* 90 (1978): 254–65. Harrison notes that the fee was a nominal one in light of Lev 27, because five shekels was considered the value of a small male child, whereas a mature adult male was valued at fifty shekels. Hence the redemption price was minimal in light of the fact that the excess firstborn likely would have been from all age groups. Again the price reflects consistency within the context of the last half of the second millennium B.C. rather than the first millennium as some scholars would have it (cf. Budd, *Numbers*, 41).

its leadership, whereas in the three cycles that ensue, rebelliousness is the central organizing theme, affecting almost everyone in the community— even Moses. The theological-geographical context is that of the departure from Sinai, the mountain of God and the locale of the receiving of the commandments of God in revelation.

FURTHER RESPONSIBILITIES AND CENSUS OF LEVITES FOR SERVICE (4:1–49). In moving from the general to the specific, observable in the structural outline of chaps. 3 and 4 above, details concerning the specific responsibilities of each of the three clans of the Levites are delineated herein. An additional census is taken of the males of each of the clans who are of such maturity (ages thirty–fifty) so as to assume and discharge the sacred tasks as outlined. The order of the tribes shifts from Gershonite priority to that of the Kohathites, and the second-born son is elevated to a preferred position over his older brother in the handling of the holy things. Patriarchal parallels include the exalting Isaac over Ishmael, Jacob over Esau, and Joseph over Reuben. R. Allen states that such texts evidence "the grace of God that reaches out in sovereign selection, bringing blessing to whom he chooses to bring blessing, elevating whom he desires to elevate, for reasons of his own will."[79]

Two of the three passages detailing the priestly clan responsibilities commence with the standard revelatory introduction formula, those for the Kohathites and the Gershonites. The Merarite segment simply begins with the command to "Count the Merarites."[80] In the section regarding the Kohathites, the introductory formula is used a second time in the delineation of the actual hands-on care for the holy things. Special instructions were needed since the Kohathites were not permitted to actually touch the holy vessels of the tabernacle, lest they die.

[1]The LORD said to Moses and Aaron: [2]"Take a census of the Kohathite branch of the Levites by their clans and families. [3]Count all the men from thirty to fifty years of age who come to serve in the work in the Tent of Meeting.

[4]"This is the work of the Kohathites in the Tent of Meeting: the care of the most holy things. [5]When the camp is to move, Aaron and his sons are to go in and take down the shielding curtain and cover the ark of the Testimony with it. [6]Then they are to cover this with hides of sea cows, spread a cloth of solid blue over that

---

[79] Allen, "Numbers," 733.

[80] In the Kohathite pericope Aaron's name is included as recipient of the instruction in the standard formula לֵאמֹר אַהֲרֹן וְאֶל־מֹשֶׁה אֶל יְהוָה וַיְדַבֵּר. Aaron's name is not included with that of Moses in the instructions for the Gershonites. With the omission of the introductory formula in the beginning of the Merarite pericope, the structure reflects a typical Hebraism, whereby using a declining distributive formula, the directives move from complex to simple, with the intention that the full form of the instruction be applied to all three pericopes: (1–2) YHWH spoke to Moses & Aaron; (21–22) YHWH spoke to Moses. No introductory phrase cited but assumed.

and put the poles in place.

⁷"Over the table of the Presence they are to spread a blue cloth and put on it the plates, dishes and bowls, and the jars for drink offerings; the bread that is continually there is to remain on it. ⁸Over these they are to spread a scarlet cloth, cover that with hides of sea cows and put its poles in place.

⁹"They are to take a blue cloth and cover the lampstand that is for light, together with its lamps, its wick trimmers and trays, and all its jars for the oil used to supply it. ¹⁰Then they are to wrap it and all its accessories in a covering of hides of sea cows and put it on a carrying frame.

¹¹"Over the gold altar they are to spread a blue cloth and cover that with hides of sea cows and put its poles in place.

¹² "They are to take all the articles used for ministering in the sanctuary, wrap them in a blue cloth, cover that with hides of sea cows and put them on a carrying frame.

¹³"They are to remove the ashes from the bronze altar and spread a purple cloth over it. ¹⁴Then they are to place on it all the utensils used for ministering at the altar, including the firepans, meat forks, shovels and sprinkling bowls. Over it they are to spread a covering of hides of sea cows and put its poles in place.

¹⁵"After Aaron and his sons have finished covering the holy furnishings and all the holy articles, and when the camp is ready to move, the Kohathites are to come to do the carrying. But they must not touch the holy things or they will die. The Kohathites are to carry those things that are in the Tent of Meeting.

¹⁶"Eleazar son of Aaron, the priest, is to have charge of the oil for the light, the fragrant incense, the regular grain offering and the anointing oil. He is to be in charge of the entire tabernacle and everything in it, including its holy furnishings and articles."

¹⁷The LORD said to Moses and Aaron, ¹⁸"See that the Kohathite tribal clans are not cut off from the Levites. ¹⁹So that they may live and not die when they come near the most holy things, do this for them: Aaron and his sons are to go into the sanctuary and assign to each man his work and what he is to carry. ²⁰But the Kohathites must not go in to look at the holy things, even for a moment, or they will die."

*Kohathite Service Detailed (4:1–20).* **4:1–16** The clan of the Kohathites are given priority among the Levites in the care for the most holy things.[81] Aaron is included in the counting of the Kohathites with whom he and his sons the priests would work most closely in guarding the sanctity of the holy items of the tabernacle. The service (*'ăvōda*, physical labor)[82]

---

[81] Hb. קֹדֶשׁ הַקֳּדָשִׁים, "holy of the holy things" in 4:4,19; cf. קֹדֶשׁ הַקֳּדָשִׁים of Exod 26:33, denoting the "holy of holies" or "holiest place" in the tabernacle.

[82] Milgrom (Excursus 6, "'Avodah': The Levites' Work Profile," 343–44) notes that this type of physical service is exclusively assigned to the Levites, never the priests. He also notes that chap. 3 emphasizes the מִשְׁמֶרֶת (guardianship) of the tabernacle; chap. 4 focuses on the physical service of taking down the tabernacle, preparing its elements for journey, and the actual transporting of the objects.

charged exclusively to the sons of Kohath was the physical transport of the
sacred components, but they would handle the items only after the
Aarononic priests had wrapped each separate object in the appropriate coverings. These would be carried on their shoulders, but the objects themselves
were never to be touched.

The first step for Aaron's sons was to take down the shield curtain, or veil,
separating the sanctuary from the holy of holies containing the ark of the
covenant, and then cover the ark with that veil. The veil was made of blue,
purple, and scarlet yarn with figures of cherubim finely woven into it (Exod
26:31–33). Thus the curtain served continuously to preserve the sanctuary of
the ark. Additional coverings were added, including "hides of sea cows" or
"dolphins" that were yellow-orange in color,[83] followed by a solid blue
garment-like *(beged)* covering. The blue color *(tĕkēlet)* was actually a royal
violet, that was also woven into the tassels *(ṣîṣit)* of the undergarments worn
by Israelite males (Num 15:37–40) and the robes worn by the high priest
(Exod 28:6–33). This violet dye was produced from the gland of the varieties
of murex snails found in abundance along the Mediterranean coast from
Greece around the coast of Asia Minor to Phoenicia.[84] After the three coverings have been installed over the ark of the covenant, the gold overlayed
wooden poles made for transporting it were inserted in the gold rings. Once
set in place, the poles were not to be removed (Exod 25:10–16; 37:3–5).

The table of the Presence, made of gold overlaid acacia wood and upon
which were set the twelve loaves of bread—one for each of the tribes, was
to be covered with a fitted garment of violet cloth. The bowls, jars, jugs,
utensils, and bread were set on the cloth. These showbread loaves were
replaced every Sabbath by the priests and were symbolic of God's provision
and presence—he is the nation's bread of life (Exod 24:5–9; 25:30). Other
nations utilized the altar as a table for providing food and drink for the gods,
but in Israel's system the provision of bread and wine were consumed by
Yahweh's intermediaries the priests. Over the cloth, bread, and implements
a scarlet garment-like cloak was placed, followed by a yellow-orange covering of skins similar to the middle of the coverings over the ark of the covenant. Only the ark and the table of the Presence had three layers of covering,
indicating their higher level of sanctity, whereas other sacred objects had
only two. Like the ark, the table was fitted with rings for transportation by
gold overlaid wooden poles.

The seven-tiered golden lampstand, symbolic of God as light to the world

---

[83] The NJPS has "dolphins" for תַּחַשׁ, which Milgrom translates as "yellow-orange." He notes
that this dye was used in preparing animal skins for protective coverings, sealing the given object
from the harsher elements of nature (ibid., 25).

[84] For an extended discussion of the process see Milgrom, Excursus 38, 410–12; L. B. Jensen,
"Royal Purple of Tyre," *JNES* 22 (1963): 104–18.

(Exod 25:31–40), and the golden altar for incense burning (Exod 30:1–10) were covered successively with a violet *(tĕkēlet)* cloth and then a yellow-orange covering of hides. The lampstand, its lamps, and its accompanying implements were set into a carrying frame. The altar was fitted with rings like the ark and the table.

The focus in the dismantling process turns to the large bronze sacrificial altar that was situated in the courtyard of the tabernacle. Ashes of earlier sacrifices were removed and disposed of, and the altar was covered with a purple *(ʾargāmān)* cloth. The previous cultic objects were to be covered with violet *(tĕkēlet)* garments, reserved for the most sacred of components. As with the table of the Presence and the lampstand, the accompanying utensils were placed upon the cloth, followed by a covering of yellow-orange skins.

The Samaritan Pentateuch and the Septuagint add the bronze laver at the conclusion of v. 14 that is missing from the MT (Exod 30:17–21,25–29).[85] Washing the feet and the hands with the basin's waters was essential to purification before fully entering the Tent of Meeting and attending the cultic activity upon the bronze altar.

At the conclusion of the priestly preparation for transporting the tabernacle and its cultic elements, the Kohathites would enter the area and man the carrying poles and frames. The coverings and poles served to preserve the sanctity of the various objects from human contamination or defilement. The warning is issued against contact with the objects themselves by anyone but the ritually pure priests, lest the penalty of death be enacted. The absolute holiness of God is to be maintained symbolically via the maintenance of the sanctity of those things that serve to worship him. The apostle Paul encouraged Christians to present their bodies as living sacrifices, holy and pleasing to God, indeed as implements of holiness that should remain undefiled (Rom 12:1–4). Likewise, the apostle Peter urged Christians to be holy, purified by the obeying of the truth instead of being conformed to the evil desires of this world (1 Pet 1:13–23).

The responsibilities of Eleazar, the son of Aaron, are twofold: oversight of the ingredients utilized with the various sacred objects and oversight of the entire tabernacle complex, with its previously delineated furnishings. Hence Eleazar supervised the priests and the Kohathites in the preparation and porterage of the sacred objects, as well as the Gershonites and Merarites in the fulfillment of their respective duties. The particular sacrifice described as the "regular grain offering" is unspecified, though the daily grain offering that is offered by the priests and burned completely (Lev 6:14–23[Hb. 7–16]) seems the most likely.

---

[85] Wevers probably is right in suggesting that the MT omission is due to homoioteleuton (*Notes on the Greek Text of Numbers*, 63).

**4:17–20** In typical Pentateuchal pattern the last section is an expansion on a previous theme of the profound yet perilous task of the Kohathites in the porterage of the covered sacred objects. The sacrilege of violating the holiness of any of the holy objects, whether furnishings, vessels, or implements, made one culpable of being cut off from the nation by divine wrath. Aaron and his sons the priests were to maintain close oversight of the Kohathites lest they experience death in their service. Hence individual assignments were made by the Aaronic priests for careful and proper performance of duties. The solemnity of the service gives rise to the specification that the census be limited to mature adult males, aged thirty to fifty. Even a casual glimpse at the actual holy objects could bring such an immediate and untimely death. The use of the term "holy things" (*haqqōdeš*, "the holy") in 4:4 and 4:20 forms an inclusio, highlighting the primary theme of this section. As noted above, extensive measures were taken to insure the absolute holiness of the tabernacle and its furnishings, which were symbols of God's presence with and for his people.

[21]The LORD said to Moses, [22]"Take a census also of the Gershonites by their families and clans. [23]Count all the men from thirty to fifty years of age who come to serve in the work at the Tent of Meeting.

[24]"This is the service of the Gershonite clans as they work and carry burdens: [25]They are to carry the curtains of the tabernacle, the Tent of Meeting, its covering and the outer covering of hides of sea cows, the curtains for the entrance to the Tent of Meeting, [26]the curtains of the courtyard surrounding the tabernacle and altar, the curtain for the entrance, the ropes and all the equipment used in its service. The Gershonites are to do all that needs to be done with these things. [27]All their service, whether carrying or doing other work, is to be done under the direction of Aaron and his sons. You shall assign to them as their responsibility all they are to carry. [28]This is the service of the Gershonite clans at the Tent of Meeting. Their duties are to be under the direction of Ithamar son of Aaron, the priest.

*Gershonite Service Detailed (4:21–28).* **4:21–28** The delineation of the service responsibilities of the Gershonites and the Merarites is less extensive though no less important. The census instructions to Moses concerning the Gershonites, to count the mature adult males of ages thirty to fifty, reiterates the basic content of 4:1–3, with minor variations. The introduction to the Merarite service lacks the introductory formula of divine speech. In summary, the Gershonites were responsible for the dismantling and reassembling of various curtains of the tabernacle and tent; and the Merarites, the framing structure and supports. After their service of packing was completed, those elements were then placed on oxcarts for transportation.

The service of the Gershonites involved the taking down and packing of six different sets of tabernacle fabrics. The tabernacle had ten curtains, made in two groups of five and hung with gold clasps through the fabric support loops (Exod 26:1–6). The tent covering consisted of eleven curtains of goat hair, assembled in two groups of five and six, hung with bronze clasps through the fabric support loops. A red-dyed ram skin cloak covered the tent covering, which was in turn followed by a covering of the yellow-red skins (Exod 26:7–14). The woven entrance curtain included finely twisted linen along with violet, purple, and scarlet yarn, supported by gold hooks on five gold-overlayed acacia wood posts (Exod 26:36–37). As with the Kohathite service, the Gershonite work of dismantling these curtains and coverings was supervised by Aaron and his sons the priests, who would make individual assignments to these Levites. In particular, Aaron's fourth son Ithamar had direct charge over the Gershonites.

²⁹"Count the Merarites by their clans and families. ³⁰Count all the men from thirty to fifty years of age who come to serve in the work at the Tent of Meeting. ³¹This is their duty as they perform service at the Tent of Meeting: to carry the frames of the tabernacle, its crossbars, posts and bases, ³²as well as the posts of the surrounding courtyard with their bases, tent pegs, ropes, all their equipment and everything related to their use. Assign to each man the specific things he is to carry. ³³This is the service of the Merarite clans as they work at the Tent of Meeting under the direction of Ithamar son of Aaron, the priest."

*Merarite Service Detailed (4:29–33).* **4:29–33** The service of the Merarites involved the dismantling of the tabernacle and tent framework after the Gershonites had removed the curtains and coverings. Vertical posts, crossmembers, socket bases, and pegs for supporting the posts using cords were labeled and listed so as to assure ease in reassembly. Four oxcarts were needed to transport the numerous objects. As with the Gershonite work, the Merarite service was supervised by Aaron's son Ithamar.

Once more the first Sinai cycle themes of orderliness and holiness are maintained, even through the process of dismantling for transportation as God would lead the nation through the wilderness. Organization through priestly oversight, the order in which the tabernacle elements were disassembled and prepared for transport, priestly covering of the sacred objects that then are carried by the Kohathites, and the labeling of the complex of frames all contribute to this theme.

³⁴Moses, Aaron and the leaders of the community counted the Kohathites by their clans and families. ³⁵All the men from thirty to fifty years of age who came to serve in the work in the Tent of Meeting, ³⁶counted by clans, were 2,750. ³⁷This was the total of all those in the Kohathite clans who served in the Tent of Meeting. Moses and Aaron counted them according to the LORD's command through Moses.

[38]The Gershonites were counted by their clans and families. [39]All the men from thirty to fifty years of age who came to serve in the work at the Tent of Meeting, [40]counted by their clans and families, were 2,630. [41]This was the total of those in the Gershonite clans who served at the Tent of Meeting. Moses and Aaron counted them according to the LORD's command.

[42]The Merarites were counted by their clans and families. [43]All the men from thirty to fifty years of age who came to serve in the work at the Tent of Meeting, [44]counted by their clans, were 3,200. [45]This was the total of those in the Merarite clans. Moses and Aaron counted them according to the LORD's command through Moses.

[46]So Moses, Aaron and the leaders of Israel counted all the Levites by their clans and families. [47]All the men from thirty to fifty years of age who came to do the work of serving and carrying the Tent of Meeting [48]numbered 8,580. [49]At the LORD's command through Moses, each was assigned his work and told what to carry.

Thus they were counted, as the LORD commanded Moses.

SUMMARY CENSUS OF LEVITES (4:34–49). **4:34–49** Each of the clans was counted by Moses, Aaron, and community leaders according to the Lord's instructions. Harrison describes the four elements that characterized the census: "(1) registering of eligible males, (2) statement of age groups enrolled, (3) total number of males counted, and (4) closing formula for each of the three groups stressing the divine source of the census instructions and the human vehicle by which they were implemented."[86]

Of the 22,000 Levites counted in the previous census (3:39), the following totals are derived:

| Levite Clans | Census of Age One Month | Census of Age Thirty to Fifty |
|---|---|---|
| Kohath (S) | 8,300[87] | 2,750 |
| Gershon (W) | 7,500 | 2,630 |
| Merari (N) | 6,200 | 3,200 |
| | | |
| Totals | 22,300 | 8,580 |

The rounding of the numbers is evidenced in the difference between the 22,000 Levites of 3:39, the 22,273 firstborn males of 3:43, and the 22,300 of the sum of 3:22,28,34.

---

[86] Harrison, *Numbers,* 101.

[87] Taking the Gl recension over the 8,600 census of the MT. See chart on p. 98

### (5) Purification Laws for the Faithful Community (5:1–31)

The first four chapters of the Book of Numbers have set forth the collective nation of Israel and established the cultic leadership of this chosen and abundantly blessed people. The camp has been numbered and organized with the Levites constituting the first level of the congregation in service to Yahweh. Chapters 5 and 6 contain treatises on four areas of purification and sanctification, whereby the holiness of the camp is maintained or ensured: (1) separation of unclean persons from the camp of the holy (5:1–4), (2) restitution for wrongdoing against another person (5:5–10), (3) ensuring marital fidelity through the ordeal of jealousy (5:11–31), and (4) individual sanctification through the Nazirite vow (6:1–21). This section concludes with the Priestly Benediction, a blessing confirming the Lord's blessing upon the camp of the holy and faithful.

The holiness of God and the assertion that the collective people of God must maintain standards of purity and holiness are emphasized severally in the Pentateuch, usually in the context of standards of cleanness and uncleanness (the sacred and the profane) with regard to dietary restrictions (Exod 22:31; Lev 11:44; Deut 14:2) and matters of idolatry and immorality (Lev 20:7,26). Though special restrictions are placed upon those holding a priestly office in the community, ultimately the entire community was to function as a kingdom of priests (Exod 19:6) who could function as God's priesthood on behalf of world kingdoms, calling all nations to the One True God and to holiness. Priests had the responsibility of teaching the Torah to the peoples (Lev 10:11). Likewise Peter calls upon the church as the people of God to be a holy priesthood on behalf of the world by living lives free from all forms of impurity and defilement:

> You also, like living stones, are being built into a spiritual house to be a holy priesthood offering spiritual sacrifices acceptable to God through Jesus Christ. … But you are a chosen people, a royal priesthood, a holy nation, a people belonging to God, that you may declare the praises of him who called you out of darkness into his wonderful light. … Dear friends, I urge you as aliens and strangers in the world, to abstain from sinful desires, which war against your soul. Live such good lives among the pagans that, though they accuse you of doing wrong, they may see your good deeds and glorify God on the day he visits us. (1 Pet 2:5,9,11,12)

Concentric circles define the sacred space, from the holiest place surrounding the ark of the covenant *(dĕbîr)*, to the court of the desert sanctuary *(hêkāl)*, and extending to the camp *(mahăneh)*. Restrictions regarding the types of uncleanness set forth in chap. 5 have been addressed previously in Exodus and Leviticus.[88]

---

[88] Skin diseases (Lev 13:1–46), bodily discharges (Lev 15:1–32), contact with dead animals, (Lev 11:24–25), marital and sexual fidelity (Exod 20:14,17; Lev 18:6–20; 19:20).

M. Douglas posits that humans developed social distinctions of conformity and disunity based upon their observations of natural forces. She defines "dirt" or "uncleanness" as that which is "out of place" in society and "holiness" as that which is in harmony with nature, having "wholeness and completeness."[89] With regard to biblical purity she highlights the human understanding of Levitical legislation as denoting an ideal for humanity. But the Hebrew Bible provides even further distinction between the common and the unclean, as well as between the holy and the pure. Douglas sees in Numbers and Leviticus a "paradox in so far as they legislate against impurity without designating any social category as inherently impure ... or liable to contaminate others."[90] But the Torah in fact legislates against any kind of class system, even to the point of giving resident aliens status in worship and purification under the same matrix of law as the Israelite. Ethical and moral distinctions, not class systems, play a significant role in the understanding of these distinctions. Hence Douglas observes: "The Judaism of Leviticus and the book of Numbers is not among the exclusive religions, nor do its commands weigh heavily upon its congregation. Purification is easy, and open to all who wish for it."[91]

**[1]The LORD said to Moses, [2]"Command the Israelites to send away from the camp anyone who has an infectious skin disease or a discharge of any kind, or who is ceremonially unclean because of a dead body. [3]Send away male and female alike; send them outside the camp so they will not defile their camp, where I dwell among them." [4]The Israelites did this; they sent them outside the camp. They did just as the LORD had instructed Moses.**

CULTIC ISOLATION OF VARIOUS DISEASE CARRIERS (5:1–4). **5:1–4** The placement of cultic laws at this point in the structure of the Book of Numbers serves to further define the faithful community in the first cycle of material. The army of Israel has been counted, setting forth the holy host that would be launched by Yahweh into the Promised Land (chap. 1). The tribes have been organized around the central shrine, with its center being the Holy of Holies, the epicenter of God's presence and holiness (chap. 2). The attendants to this holy place have been counted, and their roles and responsibilities have been delineated (chaps. 3–4). Now the holiness of the community is defined in terms of certain restrictions on persons whose lives evidence some unholy state.

The chapter commences with the introductory formula of divine speech,

---

[89] M. T. Douglas, *Purity and Danger* (London: Routledge & Kegan Paul, 1966), 1–55.
[90] Id., *In The Wilderness: The Doctrine of Defilement in the Book of Numbers,* JSOTSup 158 (Sheffield: JSOT Press, 1993), 158.
[91] Ibid.

*wayĕdabbēr YHWH el- Mōšeh lēʾmōr,*[92] providing continuity with the previous revelatory introductions. The repetition of this phrase, carrying with it one of the key themes of the Book of Numbers, is designed to reinforce the serious nature of maintaining the purity of the congregation of the chosen people of God. The first laws address the issue of restricting persons from the inner circles of holiness who have contracted one of three serious physical infirmities: (1) any infectious skin disease (*ṣārûaʿ,* "eruption"),[93] (2) any discharge *(zāb),* or (3) any contamination from a corpse (*tāmêʾ lānāpeš,* "uncleanness from the dead body"). Such persons were to be sent away by the priests, who were charged with the responsibility of maintaining the purity of the camp and its inhabitants (Lev 10:10–11). Likewise, the priests were assigned the task of assessing the purity of an individual who had become unclean by any such means.

Scholars have debated extensively the meaning of *ṣārûaʿ,* often translated "leprosy" in earlier versions. Some have stated that the form of leprosy known today as Hansen's disease was unknown in the ancient world.[94] Harrison and G. Wenham argue for the inclusion of Hansen's disease among the varieties of infectious skin diseases that might render one impure.[95] The extensive description of the disease, its effects, treatment, the purification process after having had the disease, and the adjudication by the priest at the conclusion of the purification rituals all evidence a disease similar to Hansen's. Other serious skin infections, perhaps like psoriasis or eczema, may also be included in this ritual exclusion.

The discharges denoted by the term *zāb* are those emitted by male and female genitalia, such as gonorrhea. This and other such diseases are more extensively addressed in Lev 15:1–33. Isolation from the larger community of persons having contracted such highly infectious sexually transmitted diseases would reduce further contamination, but more importantly this practice preserved the sanctity of the sanctuary of the Most Holy God in the midst of his people. This meaning is derived from the phrase in v. 3, "Send them outside the camp so that they will not defile their camp, where I dwell among them."

Anyone contaminated by contact with dead persons (*tāmêʾ lānāpeš,* defiled by the body/corpse), an issue addressed more extensively in Num 19:1–22, must also be separated from the holy community. Once again,

---

[92] See discussion of this phrase in "Introduction: Title" section, 2.

[93] This form of the term, often translated "leprosy" (Hansen's disease), occurs in Lev 13:44,45; 14:3. The more common form מְצֹרָע occurs in Lev 14:2; 22:4; 2 Sam 3:29; 2 Kgs 5:1,11. The extended treatment of this disease is found in Lev 13:1–14:32.

[94] See J. F. A. Sawyer, "A Note on the Etymology of *tsaraʾat,*" *VT* 26 (1976): 137–38; B. A. Levine, *Numbers 1–20, A New Translation with Introduction and Commentary,* AB (New York: Doubleday, 1993), 184–85.

[95] Harrison, *Numbers,* 100–101; *Leviticus,* 120; Wenham, *Numbers,* 37; *Leviticus,* 120.

though hygienic reasons may have played a part in such legislation, ritual purification and separation from the center of holiness in the community is the focus of this passage. Male and female members of the community are treated alike; separation from the holiness of the community has no gender preferential treatment. Similarly, those who voluntarily take a Nazirite vow (Num 6:1–21) must refrain from touching a corpse, lest they become defiled and go through the specified process of purification. The pericope concludes with one of the focal themes of Num 1:1–10:10, that of the obedience of Moses and the people in following God's commands on this issue.[96] Likewise, the holiness of God, his sanctuary and the community, harmony and order within the community, and ritual purity are recurrent themes in this pericope.

**[5]The LORD said to Moses, [6]"Say to the Israelites: 'When a man or woman wrongs another in any way and so is unfaithful to the LORD, that person is guilty [7]and must confess the sin he has committed. He must make full restitution for his wrong, add one fifth to it and give it all to the person he has wronged. [8]But if that person has no close relative to whom restitution can be made for the wrong, the restitution belongs to the LORD and must be given to the priest, along with the ram with which atonement is made for him. [9]All the sacred contributions the Israelites bring to a priest will belong to him. [10]Each man's sacred gifts are his own, but what he gives to the priest will belong to the priest.'"**

RESTITUTION FOR WRONGS DONE (5:5–10). **5:5–10**  The second of the three camp purification pericopes commences with the introductory formula for divine instruction, emphasizing the revelatory nature of the content. Responsibility for reparation because of wrong done against another individual falls equally upon the human genders; man and woman are equally accountable before God for their sin. Anyone who sins against another person effectively commits a sacrilege against God.[97] The term for sin *(ḥaṭṭāʾt)* is the standard term for "missing" a standard of practice or "breaking" a covenant command,[98] which in this case effects harm to another person or that individual's property. This text clearly states that wrongs committed against another person or that one's property are sins against the Lord of the covenant community. Such a covenant breach incurs culpability for the *ʾāšām*, or guilt offering, which entails full restitution plus a penalty of one-fifth. The setting of such sins is more extensively delineated

---

[96] See comments above on 1:54 and listing of similar phraseology in n. 44.

[97] Milgrom suggests a twofold prerequisite by which a person defrauds his fellow and then commits a sacrilege against God by means of a false oath (*Numbers*, 35).

[98] G. H. Livingston, "חָטָא (ḥāṭāʾ)," *TWOT* 1:277–79; K. Koch, חָטָא, *chāṭāʾ*," *TDOT* 4:309–19. Koch summarizes that the general Semitic usage of *ḥṭʾ* or *ḥṭ* as that which "designates negative conditions and conduct, especially with reference to human agents in a religious context" (p. 310).

in Lev 6:1–7.[99] In addition to the restitution of property to an individual, Leviticus addresses the matter of cultic reparation by which one brings an atonement offering of an unblemished lamb.

Harrison describes the structure of the pericope: (1) protasis of the conditional situation, involving the breach of God's law (5–6); (2) the apodosis, in which the procedure leading to forgiveness is described (7); (3) a special contingency and the provision for it (9–10); and (4) the priest's portion.[100] This passage differs from the Leviticus legislation in that additional casuistic clause is delineated, the community issue of the person wronged being deceased. If the person originally wronged by the transgressor has no relative (*gōʾēl,* "kinsman redeemer")[101] who may receive the restorative payment, then the *ʾāšām* shall be rendered unto the priest along with the atonement offering of the ram. Leviticus and Numbers presume a relative monetary value for personal property, whereby the 20 percent penalty may be applied. Milgrom suggests that this law may refer back to an "older, premonarchial tradition" in that the property does revert to the royal state by "eminent domain," as did Naboth's vineyard in the case of Ahab's expropriation of the land (1 Kgs 21:15).[102]

Consistent with the theme of Num 1:1–10:10, the harmony, wholeness and holiness of the community are of considerable concern. The individual as part of the community has certain responsibilities within the larger context, and sin has a deleterious effect on both. Therefore, the sanctity of the individual, community, and sanctuary must be maintained. Societal consonance for ancient Israel, as well as for all human society, is assured in such cases through repentance, restitution, and (ritual) restoration.

[11]Then the LORD said to Moses, [12]"Speak to the Israelites and say to them: 'If a man's wife goes astray and is unfaithful to him [13]by sleeping with another man, and this is hidden from her husband and her impurity is undetected (since there is no witness against her and she has not been caught in the act), [14]and if feelings of jealousy come over her husband and he suspects his wife and she is impure— or if he is jealous and suspects his wife even though she is not impure— [15]then he is to take his wife to the priest. He must also take an offering of a tenth of an ephah of barley flour on her behalf. He must not pour oil on it or put incense on it, because it is a grain offering for jealousy, a reminder offering to draw attention to guilt.

[16]"'The priest shall bring her and have her stand before the LORD. [17]Then he

---

[99] NIV 6:1–7 = Hb. 5:20–26. Additionally, Lev 5:14–19 addresses other sins that require the אָשָׁם, generally those deriving from unintentional or unknowing circumstances. Exod 22:7–15 contains similar legislation with respect to responsibilities for one's neighbor's property.

[100] Harrison, *Numbers,* 102–3.

[101] For further studies of the role of the *gōʾēl* in the OT, see R. L. Harris, *TWOT,* 1:144–45; H. Ringgren, *TDOT,* 2:350–55.

[102] Milgrom, *Numbers,* 35.

shall take some holy water in a clay jar and put some dust from the tabernacle
floor into the water. [18]After the priest has had the woman stand before the LORD,
he shall loosen her hair and place in her hands the reminder offering, the grain
offering for jealousy, while he himself holds the bitter water that brings a curse.
[19]Then the priest shall put the woman under oath and say to her, "If no other
man has slept with you and you have not gone astray and become impure while
married to your husband, may this bitter water that brings a curse not harm you.
[20]But if you have gone astray while married to your husband and you have defiled
yourself by sleeping with a man other than your husband"— [21]here the priest is
to put the woman under this curse of the oath—"may the LORD cause your people to curse and denounce you when he causes your thigh to waste away and your
abdomen to swell. [22]May this water that brings a curse enter your body so that
your abdomen swells and your thigh wastes away."

" 'Then the woman is to say, "Amen. So be it."

[23]" 'The priest is to write these curses on a scroll and then wash them off into
the bitter water. [24]He shall have the woman drink the bitter water that brings a
curse, and this water will enter her and cause bitter suffering. [25]The priest is to
take from her hands the grain offering for jealousy, wave it before the LORD and
bring it to the altar. [26]The priest is then to take a handful of the grain offering as
a memorial offering and burn it on the altar; after that, he is to have the woman
drink the water. [27]If she has defiled herself and been unfaithful to her husband,
then when she is made to drink the water that brings a curse, it will go into her
and cause bitter suffering; her abdomen will swell and her thigh waste away, and
she will become accursed among her people. [28]If, however, the woman has not
defiled herself and is free from impurity, she will be cleared of guilt and will be
able to have children.

[29]" 'This, then, is the law of jealousy when a woman goes astray and defiles
herself while married to her husband, [30]or when feelings of jealousy come over a
man because he suspects his wife. The priest is to have her stand before the LORD
and is to apply this entire law to her. [31]The husband will be innocent of any
wrongdoing, but the woman will bear the consequences of her sin.' "

THE CASE OF A SUSPECTED ADULTEROUS WIFE (5:11–31).   **5:11–31**
Marital fidelity is foundational to societal wellbeing, and for the community
of faith that is called by Yahweh God of Israel, sanctity in regard to the marriage relationship is essential. The third case for ensuring community purification is that which concerns a woman suspected by her husband of having
an adulterous affair.[103] The pericope begins as the previous two cases with
the introductory formula for divine instruction, highlighting the revelatory
nature of the content.

The case commences with a wife who has had an adulterous affair with

[103] M. Fishbane, "Accusations of Adultery: A Study of Law and Scribal Practice in Numbers
5:11–31," *HUCA* 45 (1974): 25–45; T. Frymer-Kensky, "The Strange Case of the Suspected
Sotah," *VT* (1984): 11–26.

another man that she hides from her husband.[104] There have been no witnesses to this abrogation of marital sanctity, so the two have not been caught.[105] Basic Levitical law prescribed death as a penalty for both partners in an adulterous relationship (Lev 20:10). Men and women are equally accountable before God for sexual relationships outside of marriage. Only later does the husband suspect that his wife has been unfaithful,[106] based upon some observed but here undefined circumstances. The case presumes the guilt of the woman in the initial section, whereas the summary allows for the perceived jealousy of the husband in initiating the procedure. The case assumes that an innocent woman, unjustly accused by her husband, need not be apprehensive of the outcome and will be able to live free of guilt and condemnation. The case law addresses the issue of the adjudication of the other man with whom the woman was involved. On the opposite gender side of the issue, the wife has no reciprocal proviso for bringing charges against a suspected unfaithful husband. Several Pentateuchal passages address issues in which women have legal recourse against men. In Deut 25:5–10 a woman could bring a case against a brother-in-law who failed to fulfill his role in levirate marriage. A violated virgin would be especially provided for by the abusive male (Deut 23:25–29).

The test for the unfaithfulness of the suspected wife involves a trial by ordeal for the woman before a chosen priest of the sanctuary. The following steps are taken in addressing the potential covenant abrogation:

Stage 1
1. Husband Takes Wife to Priest
    (15)        Grain offering for jealousy *(minḥat qĕnāʾōt)*
                + 1/10 ephah of barley flour on her behalf (no oil or incense)
                = REMINDER offering—Draw attention to the guilt
2. Priest Presents Woman to the Lord
    (16–22a) Takes HOLY WATER in clay jar
                Adds DUST from tabernacle floor to water

---

[104] Adultery is of course prohibited in the Ten Commandments (Exod 20:14; Deut 5:18).

[105] The text reads literally שְׁכָבַת־זֶרַע, "effusion of seed [=semen]," hence sexual intercourse. Milgrom notes that the key reason the allegedly guilty woman is not put to death after the ordeal is because she was unapprehended, a fact cited four times in her indictment. "Unapprehended adultery remains punishable only by God, and there is no need for human mediation. The legal term for adultery which is punishable by death, namely נאַף is avoided in this section, with jurisdiction in this kind of case removed from the human judicial system ("A Husband's Pride, A Mob's Prejudice," *BR* 13 [1996]: 21).

[106] Milgrom (ibid., 37) notes that this is the only time the phrase מָעֲלָה בוֹ מָעַל ("break faith with him") is used to describe this covenant abrogation outside of matters related to the sanctuary. The term מָעַל often refers to the straying after other gods in idolatry polemics among the Israelite prophets.

> Loosens woman's hair
> Places REMINDER offering in her hands
> Holds bitter water
> Priest puts woman under oath:
> "If no other man has slept with you and you have not gone
> astray. ... May this water not harm you"
> But, "If you have ... may the water swell / waste ..."
> (curse of a barren and miscarrying womb)

3. Woman responds "Amen, So be it"
   (22b)

Stage 2

1. Priest  Writes the Curse on a Scroll, Then
   (23–26a) Washes off words into the bitter water
            Prepares the water of cursing, bitter suffering
            Takes the reminder offering from her hands
            Waves offering before the Lord,
            Brings to the Altar
            Burns one handful on altar as memorial offering

2. Woman  Drinks WATER w/DUST & WORDS OF CURSE
   (26b–28)
            Results
            If guilty >> Barrenness, miscarriage, accursed
            If not guilty >>Clear from guilt, able to conceive

Summary   Law of Jealousy
Two Circumstances: Adultery of Wife Presumed or Unknown
                   Husband Suspects Wife of Adultery

Milgrom has discerned a chiastic structure in the fuller pericope, where the crux of the case is the "oath imprecation" of vv. 19–24, giving unity to the text as a whole. Many modern scholars such as Levine, Budd, and Gray interpret the repetition in the text representing a conflation of two or more sources.[107] Through recent literary studies, such repetition has been demonstrated to frame the literary structure of the biblical text. This artistry was part of the Hebrew narrative style and not the result of some editorial assemblage of suggested sources.[108]

---

[107] Noth, *Numbers*, 49; Budd, *Numbers*, 62–64; Gray, *Numbers*, 49.

[108] Cf. literary work of R. Alter, The Art of Biblical Narrative (New York: Basic, 1981); J. Sailhamer, *The Pentateuch as Narrative: A Biblical Theological Commentary* (Grand Rapids: Zondervan, 1992), esp. 375–77. On the literary structure of this passage and its meaning, see T. Frymer-Kensky, "The Strange Case of the Suspected *Sotah* (Numbers V 13–31)," *VT* 34 (1984): 11–26; M. Fishbane, "Accusations of Adultery: A Study of Law and Scribal Practice in Numbers 5.11–31," *HUCA* 45 (1974): 25–45; and H. C. Brichto, "The Case Law of the *ŚOTÁ* and a Reconsideration of Biblical Law," *HUCA* 46 (1975): 55–70.

A　The Case [Presented] (vv. 11–14)
B　Preparation of the Ritual Ordeal (vv. 15–18)
C　The Oath-Imprecation (vv. 19–24)
B′　Execution of the Ritual Ordeal (vv. 25–28)
A′　The Case [Summarized] (vv. 29–31)[109]

Hence the central moment comes when the woman takes an oath before the priest and before God, who is the only one who knows the truth of the situation and the one who must ultimately mete out the appropriate justice.

The grain offering brought by the husband on behalf of the wife was similar to the grain offering of consecration in Lev 2:1–3; 6:14–23, except that in the present case cheaper and coarser barley flour is utilized instead of finely ground wheat flour, and the barley flour is not to be mixed with oil or incense. The offering also parallels the sin offering of one-tenth of an ephah of fine flour brought by a poor person, which likewise is not mixed with oil or incense (Lev 5:11–13). The text describes this grain offering as a "reminder offering," which sets the case as a meeting place between God and the individual. The event is consecrated as the woman holds the barley flour in her hands, the priest burns a portion of it on the altar, and then the woman drinks the water-dust mixture. The sacral water was probably taken from the bronze laver in the tabernacle courtyard, used by the priests for ritual purification (Exod 30:17–21). Hence the waters combined with dust from the floor of the holy place, and the sacred words of the curse become either a means for purification and relief from guilt or waters of condemnation and the means of the curse of barrenness.[110] The phrase translated "not harm" in the NIV, namely *hinnāqî,* would better be rendered "innocent," hence "free from the waters of bitterness" and cursing. Harrison notes, "The ritual relied for its efficacy upon the psychological suggestion interacting with a revived memory, as the person stood in Israel's sacred place before God."[111] The mind and heart of the woman would be either vindicated in the presence of God and the priest if she were innocent or terrified to the point of marital disgrace before them, with God being ultimately responsible for her death if she were guilty.

The loosened hair of the woman can signify remorse (Lev 10:6; 21:10; Ezek 24:17) or uncleanness (Lev 13:45), both of which carry a servile status. The dust *(ʿāpār)* from the floor of the sanctuary is presumed to be ritually pure, derived from the inner sacred space. It carried no intrinsic deleterious effect, but such activity has parallels in the literature from Mari and Babylon. Dust from the gate area, which were protected by great deific figures, was consumed with water from the river and used in water ordeals in several judi-

---

[109] Milgrom, *Numbers,* 351.
[110] Cf. J. Sasson, "Nu 5 and the Waters of Judgment," *BZ* 16 (1972): 249–51.
[111] Harrison, *Numbers,* 109.

cial cases. The suspected individual was then thrown into the river or required to swim a given distance from the shore. If the person survived, he was innocent; if he drowned, he was guilty.[112] In the present case the woman stands in a position of servility or contrition, with her personal offering in her hands, echoing an oath recited by the priest, and drinking a potentially potent potion.[113] Her fate lay in God's hands.

The oath notably begins with a statement of nonculpability if she has been faithful, followed by the antithesis, unlike the statement of the case in v. 12. This oath of cursing *(šĕbūᶜat hāʾālāh)* has efficacy if the woman has been unfaithful, for it renders her abdomen swollen and barren. The meaning of the physical effects of the curse has been debated by scholars. The phrase *laṣbôt beten wĕlanpil yārēk* has been rendered "causing the belly to distend and the thigh to sag" (NJPS), "your abdomen enlarges and you suffer miscarriage" (Harrison), "make your abdomen swell and your thigh waste away" (NASB). Milgrom suggests that the "thigh" may be a euphemism for the procreative organs (e.g., Gen 24:2,9) and thus refers to the physical inability to beget children.[114] Furthermore, she would experience societal pressure of denouncement and shame. The woman in her barren state would be physically hindered from experiencing an essential element of the Abrahamic covenant of blessing, that of multitudinous progeny.[115] The woman then takes this potential burden upon herself by confirming the oath with the twofold "Amen, Amen." This is the first occurrence of the term in the Bible, used here to enhance the veritability of the oath taken by the woman.

If the woman is proven innocent through this trial by ordeal, she is rendered ceremonially cleansed and free from accusation and guilt. Her innocence is established by her continued health and ability to bear children (lit. "bear seed"). Childlessness in the societies of the ancient Near East was believed to be a curse from the gods and subjected one to shame and ridicule, embarrassment and reproach from others.

In most cultures of the ancient Near East, adultery was believed to be a "great sin" or "weighty sin" against the gods and goddesses of the cult, as well as a threat to societal stability.[116] Mesopotamian law codes of the Mid-

---

[112] *ANET*, 166; G. Dossin, "L'ordalie a Mari," *CRAIBL* (1958): 387–92.

[113] Harrison suggests: "In the most literal sense she was holding her life in her hands. The water that she would drink was "bitter" in terms of the awful potential consequences that would become actual if she were in fact guilty" (*Numbers*, 110).

[114] Milgrom, *Numbers*, 41.

[115] Gen 12:2; 22:17. Likewise, the original instruction to Adam was to be fruitful, increase, and fill the earth (Gen 1:28).

[116] Milgrom, *Numbers*, 349. Babylonian, Assyrian, Ugaritic, and Egyptian texts all address the seriousness of adultery. The penalty was often death but could be commuted by the husband via monetary or other compensation. The Bible requires the death penalty for adulterers, signifying the severity of this breach of the Mosaic covenant. Cf. also Milgrom, "A Husband's Pride, a Mob's Prejudice," *BR* 13 (1996): 21.

dle Bronze Age have revealed some parallels to this trial by ordeal involving potential adultery. The Code of Hammurabi reads:

> 131. If a man's wife is accused by her husband, but she was not caught while lying with another man, she shall make an oath by the god and return home.
> 132. If a finger has been pointed at a man's wife because of another man, but she has not been caught lying with the other man, she shall leap into the River for the sake of her husband.[117]

Drawing from this parallel, one might assume that in the biblical case the husband's suspicion leading to jealousy has been aroused by a hint of infidelity rising from a third individual, which may or may not be the case in the biblical account.

The summary of the case law (lit. "This the Torah of the jealousies") rehearses the essentials of the judicial process in dealing with marital infidelity of one's wife.[118] Examples of text and law summary abound in the Book of Numbers and throughout the Pentateuch.[119] First, the two circumstances out of which the case arises are delineated, as noted above. The variation from the introduction is that of the man who initiates the judicial process out of his own feelings of jealousy. The man is free from correction or punishment if the wife is proved innocent. If the woman is proved guilty, the punishment lies solely in the hands of God. The second element in the recapitulation is the ritual standing before God and the priest in the procedure. Third, the status of the husband in the adjudication is stated. He is innocent of any iniquity, regardless of the outcome of his wife's case, but his wife will suffer punishment if she is guilty (lit. "she will bear her iniquity"). Though Harrison suggests that the woman found guilty might be subsequently put to death—since the Torah demands that adulterers be cut off from the nation (Lev 18:20,28; 19:20; 20:10–21; Deut 22:22–27)—the text does not demand such judgment. More likely the case is as Milgrom notes:

> Finally, that the suspected adulteress is not put to death either by man or God provides the necessary clue to explaining how an ordeal—with its inherent magical and pagan elements—was allowed to enter the legislation of the Torah, or to answer the paradox as it was phrased by Rambam: This is the only case in biblical law where the outcome depends on a miracle. The answer, I submit, is inherent in the ordeal. It provides the priestly legislator with an accepted practice by which he could remove the jurisdiction over and punishment of the

---

[117] *ANET*, 171.

[118] Milgrom calls this section "A Resumptive Subscript" (*Numbers*, 42).

[119] Previously in Numbers, 1:16–19 summarizes 1:1–15; 1:44 rehearses 1:20–43; 2:34 recapitulates 2:1–33; 4:46–49 summarizes 4:1–45. Lev 7:37 summarizes 1:1–7:36; 11:46–47 reviews 11:1–45; etc. In the present passage the singular הַתּוֹרָה זֹאת is used, as in Lev 7:37; 11:46; 13:59; 14:54; 15:32.

unapprehended adulteress from human hands and thereby guarantee that she would not be put to death.[120]

The purity and sanctity of the community are thereby assured, so that the nation may be prepared to move forth from Sinai to the Promised Land and experience God's fullest blessing. The three purification issues point to key issues in community life: physical purity, right interpersonal relationships, and marital fidelity. Additionally, as the great Rambam (Nachmanides) put it, this is the sole example in biblical legal literature where the adjudication of a case rests upon God's ability to perform a miracle.

### (6) The Sacred Nazirite Vow (6:1–21)

The prescriptions and descriptions of the Nazirite vow complete the first Sinai cycle of preparation of the Israelite people for the adventurous journey to the Promised Land. Following the section on the purification laws for the camp due to individual uncleanness and unfaithfulness, Moses delineates the means for the laity, both male and female, to dedicate themselves totally for service to the Lord. The priestly and Levitical functions have been outlined, and now the general Israelite population is provided a means for voluntary separation and devotion to a life of holiness. Parallel to the holiness portrayed in the distinctive priestly regulations, here the tribes are bestowed the opportunity to become the "kingdom of priests and a holy nation" (Exod 19:6).

The language of the text reflects that Naziritism was an existing institution, in that the concept of a *nāzîr*[121] is assumed as known to the reader, and thus the purpose of this pericope is to delineate the guidelines and regulate the practice. The present text offers no indication of the impetus for entering into the vow other than personal desire for consecration. Yet the biblical and Near Eastern examples evidence an expanded purpose for the Nazirite vow as well as for other classes of vows.

Vows from the context of the culture of the ancient Near East have been examined by T. Cartledge in *Vows in the Hebrew Bible and the Ancient Near East.* Mesopotamian, Hittite, and Ugaritic vows suggest the following pattern: (1) the vow grows out of a situation of need or distress, (2) is made by a human to the gods, (3) generally is conditional in nature, and (4) a respon-

---

[120] Milgrom, *Numbers*, 350.

[121] The term נָזִיר derives from the Hb. נזר, used in the *nifal* and *hifil* to describe the withholding of self or something from a desired usage, a purposeful abstention or restriction (Cf. Lev 15:31, where the term denotes the "separation" from uncleanness.) The term נָזִיר denotes the consecrated stature of Joseph as the "prince" among his brothers (Gen 49:26). The form נֵזֶר describes the sacred "diadem" or "gold plate" that is attached to the turban (head garment) worn by the high priest (Exod 29:6; 39:30; Lev 8:9). The term is related to the Hb. נדר (vow) in NW Semitic through the Ugaritic and Aramaic *d* and *z* shifts.

sive votive offering is offered publicly at a shrine at some point during or at the completion of the vow conditions.[122] Vows in the Hebrew Bible reflect close parallels in form and general content with those of the Old Testament world.

The Nazirite vow contexts of the births of Samson and Samuel demonstrate the needs of barren women, the making and fulfilling of vows, and the offering of sacrifices at the conclusion of the vow period when the conditions have been fulfilled. Though the time span of the vows of the parents was limited, both young men were dedicated to the Lord for their whole lives. Though the only specifically prescribed restriction for the vow taken on behalf of Samson was that his hair remain uncut, Crenshaw has demonstrated that the matters of vineyards and wine consumption and of touching the dead are integral to the account of Samson's digression from the elements of his consecration.[123] The concern of Numbers 6 is with the consecration and maintenance of the vow rather than with the various conditions, settings, or kinds of Nazirite vows that one may enter. Rather than the lifelong type of vows indicated by the Samson and Samuel accounts, Numbers 6 focuses on the restrictions and purification aspects of the vow.

Milgrom has discerned a chiastic structure in the fuller pericope:

A  Introduction (vv. 1–2)
B  Prohibitions (vv. 3–8)
X  Defilement (vv. 9–12)
B'  Completion (vv. 13–20)
A'  Summary (plus voluntary offerings) (vv. 21)[124]

The crux of the chiasm is the matter of potential defilement, whereby a Nazirite rendered unclean due to exposure to a corpse must be made pure in order to continue service in the community of faith. Hence this section is a continuation (with expansion) of the purification legislation of 5:1–31, which is then concluded by the priestly blessing.

**[1]The LORD said to Moses, [2]"Speak to the Israelites and say to them: 'If a man or woman wants to make a special vow, a vow of separation to the LORD as a Nazirite,**

INTRODUCTION (6:1–2).  **6:1–2**  The chapter commences with the familiar introductory formula of divine speech, *wayĕdabbēr YHWH el-*

---

[122] T. Cartledge, *Vows in the Hebrew Bible and the Ancient Near East,* JSOTSup 147 (Sheffield: JSOT Press, 1992), 114.

[123] J. L. Crenshaw, *Samson: A Secret Betrayed, A Vow Ignored* (Atlanta: John Knox, 1978).

[124] Milgrom, *Numbers,* 359.

*Mōšeh lēʾmōr,*[125] which provides continuity with the previous revelatory introductions. The repetition of this phrase, one of the key themes of the Book of Numbers, is designed to reinforce the serious nature of maintaining the sanctity and purity of the congregation of the chosen people of God. Though issues related to women are often subsumed under the heading of man (=humankind), the context explicitly emphasizes the potential of women entering into this consecration service to Yahweh. Women could not serve as priests in the Israelite cultus, but this manner of service was open to them and could fulfill their desire for holiness and special service to the Lord. A special Hebrew term, *yaplīʾ* from the root *pālāʾ*, is used to relate the avowal process, a term most often used in connection with God's wondrous works and miracles.[126]

**³he must abstain from wine and other fermented drink and must not drink vinegar made from wine or from other fermented drink. He must not drink grape juice or eat grapes or raisins. ⁴As long as he is a Nazirite, he must not eat anything that comes from the grapevine, not even the seeds or skins.**
**⁵"'During the entire period of his vow of separation no razor may be used on his head. He must be holy until the period of his separation to the LORD is over; he must let the hair of his head grow long. ⁶Throughout the period of his separation to the LORD he must not go near a dead body. ⁷Even if his own father or mother or brother or sister dies, he must not make himself ceremonially unclean on account of them, because the symbol of his separation to God is on his head. ⁸Throughout the period of his separation he is consecrated to the LORD.**

PROHIBITIONS (6:3–8).   **6:3–8**   Three areas of restriction for one entering into this special period of service are delineated: (1) abstaining from the vineyard and its products, as well as various intoxicating drinks, (2) refraining from cutting one's hair, and (3) avoiding uncleanness that comes through proximity to a dead body. Only the third restriction, which presumably could happen accidentally in one's household, is addressed in

---

[125] See discussion of this phrase in "Introduction: Title" section. The emphasis in chap. 5 is on community and marital purity. The introduction in 6:1 coincides with that of 5:1,5,11 in this section of the structural outline, and the extended introduction exactly duplicates the introduction of 5:11–12a. Note the following chart of introductory formulae:

5:1–2a   *wayĕdabbēr YHWH el-Mōšeh lēmōr — ṣaw ʾet-bnê yiśrāʾēl*
5:5–6a   *wayĕdabbēr YHWH el-Mōšeh lēmōr — dabbēr ʾel bnê yisrāʾēl ʾîš ʾô ʾiššah kî*
5:11–12a  *wayĕdabbēr YHWH el-Mōšeh lēmōr — dabbēr ʾel bnê yisrāʾēl wĕʾāmartā ʾalēhem*
6:1–2a   *wayĕdabbēr YHWH el-Mōšeh lēmōr — dabbēr ʾel bnê yisrāʾēl wĕʾāmartā ʾalēhem*
        *ʾîš ʾô ʾiššah kî*
The introduction in 6:1–2a is an expanded composite of the previous formulae, indicating the climax in the matters of purification for the people of God.

[126] The phrase אִישׁ אוֹ־אִשָּׁה כִּי יַפְלִא לִנְדֹּר נֶדֶר נָזִיר לְהַזִּיר literally means "when [a man or a woman] does extraordinarily to vow a vow of a Nazirite" and describes that which is beyond the normal activity of human life. Cf. *TWOT* 2:723; *KB*:759–60.

terms of purification ritual to rectify the state of uncleanness. The others would involve voluntary abrogation.

All forms of intoxicating beverage are off limits at all times to the Nazirite for the duration of the vow. This restriction is more extensive than the prohibition placed upon priests, who are limited from consumption of such drinks only during the period of tabernacle or temple service (Lev 10:9). Yet not only is a Nazirite restricted from consuming wine *(yayin)* and fermented drink *(šēkār)*,[127] but that individual also cannot partake of wine vinegar *(ḥōmeṣ yayin)*, vinegar from other fermented liquids *(ḥōmeṣ šēkār)*, unfermented grape juice, grapes, raisins, grape seeds, and hulls,[128] or anything else derived from the vineyard. The reference to seeds and hulls is probably hyperbolic, emphasizing the total abstinence from the vineyard. The vineyard restriction is paralleled by the Rechabite tradition that forbade the planting of vineyards, an indication of a sedentary lifestyle.[129] Abstaining from the vineyard and related products was a personal and generally private act of special devotion of one's life and mind to the Lord.

The vineyard and its produce thus can have an antithetical usage in the Bible. On one hand vineyards are evidence of Yahweh's great blessing upon the land (Isa 5:1-2,7a; Jer 2:21). A large cluster of grapes was brought back by the team of spies who explored the land of Canaan prior to Israel's rejection of the land (Num 13:23-24). Wine is combined with various elements in the sacrificial system for worshiping God and making atonement (Num 15:5,7,10; 28:7-10,14). Israelites living far from Jerusalem were even encouraged to purchase wine and strong drink along with sheep and cattle with money from their tithes, and then they would eat and drink these in the presence of the Lord with rejoicing (Deut 14:24-27). However, excessive consumption is condemned categorically (Prov 20:1; 23:30-31; 31:4; Isa 28:7).[130] In the New Testament limitations regarding wine consumption are

---

[127] The יַיִן is the normal term for fermented grape juice and is distinguished from the *tirosh* wine of a more recent vintage. שֵׁכָר is used to describe fermented drink derived from fruits other than grapes, barley beer, and other grain beverages. Other verb and noun forms from שׁכר are associated with drunkenness. See "Wine" and "Drink, Drinking" in *Eerdmans Dictionary of the Bible*, 1078 and 231. Cf. *TWOT*, *šakar*, 926-27; *yayin*, 375-76; *tîrôš*, 969.

[128] Both terms חַרְצַנִּים, translated "seeds," and זָג, "skins," are hapax legomena whose meanings are derived from the context. Derived from חרץ, "cut, sharpen" (as in the tongue), the חַרְצַנִּים may refer to hard and unripened grapes. The זָג (derived from זגג, "to be clear") are probably the transparent grape hulls.

[129] The Rechabite tradition is recounted in Jer 35, which evidences restrictions on wine consumption, planting of vineyards, sowing seeds, and building houses. Obedience to the teaching of their ancestral patriarch Jonadab ben Rekab was set forth as an example of devotion in contrast to the Israelite disobedience to God.

[130] More than fifty OT passages condemn consumption of wine and other fermented drinks that render one unable to perform normal physical activity or carry out sacred service.

listed among the requirements for overseers and deacons, and drunkenness is the antithesis to being filled with the Spirit (Eph 5:18; 1 Cor 6:10).

Refraining from trimming the hair was the most visible evidence of an individual's decision to become a Nazirite. Holiness is associated with the length of the hair, the crowning glory of the Nazirite. Milgrom suggests that this characteristic was more important than the other two, since it is the one reason to avoid corpse contamination.[131] Men would regularly trim or shave the hair on their heads, but women were less likely to do so. Allen suggests that the women, who would not regularly cut their hair, may have left their hair unkempt as a sign of their Nazirite consecration.[132] Special rituals of shaving of the head and the body were performed in pagan cults in contrast to the Nazirite practice.[133] Harrison compares the Nazirite's life to that of the unpruned vine of the jubilee year left undisturbed to allow the full maturity of the fruit.[134]

The avoidance of contact with a dead body parallels a similar restriction put upon the high priest (Lev 21:11). Both are to avoid a dead body, even that of a member of the immediate family. A corpse carried with it ritual uncleanness that would restrict a priest from service or a Nazirite from maintaining his or her vow.[135] Upon entering into the Nazirite vow, one would not know the potential of a member of one's family passing away and the subsequent demand upon one's psyche being unable to go through the grief process. Jesus alludes to this aspect of the dedication of his disciples when he admonished them to "Follow me, and let the dead bury their own dead" (Matt 8:21–22).

**⁹"'If someone dies suddenly in his presence, thus defiling the hair he has dedicated, he must shave his head on the day of his cleansing—the seventh day. ¹⁰Then on the eighth day he must bring two doves or two young pigeons to the priest at the entrance to the Tent of Meeting. ¹¹The priest is to offer one as a sin offering and the other as a burnt offering to make atonement for him because he sinned by being in the presence of the dead body. That same day he is to consecrate his head. ¹²He must dedicate himself to the LORD for the period of his separation and must bring a year-old male lamb as a guilt offering. The previous days do not count, because he became defiled during his separation.**

PURIFICATION FROM CORPSE DEFILEMENT (6:9–12). **6:9–12** A particular case of uncleanness gave rise to special delineation of ritual purification for the Nazirite. Should a Nazirite become ritually contaminated

---

[131] Milgrom, *Numbers*, 45.
[132] Allen, "Numbers," 751.
[133] Cf. the ANE background to Lev 21:5–7.
[134] Harrison, *Numbers*, 125.
[135] Cf. also the comment on 5:2 and 19:1–22.

accidentally by contact or undue proximity to a corpse, such as when an individual dies in the house or even in the arms of the consecrated person, what recourse was there to resume the period of voluntary consecration? Under normal circumstances, touching a dead body rendered one unclean for seven days (Num 19:11), and the ritual purification of the priests lasts seven days (Lev 8:33).

The rededication of the Nazirite involved four steps: (1) shaving the head, (2) offering two small birds as sin and burnt offerings, (3) consecration of the head in rededication, and (4) offering a lamb as a guilt offering. On the seventh day the cleansing process commenced with the shaving of the hair,[136] the final visible evidence of the vow. But whereas the ordinary person could be purified by the pouring of the sacred water mixed with the ashes of the red heifer, the resanctification of the Nazirite was more extensive. The following day two doves or pigeons were presented to the priest for sacrifice, one for a sin offering for the inadvertent abrogation of the vow[137] and a second for a burnt offering in the ritual reconsecration of the person to God's service. The next rite in the ritual purification sequence was the consecration of the head, whereby the individual dedicates himself for the given period of time for which he had originally dedicated himself. Because of the defilement, the original vow has been annulled and must be completely reinstituted. None of the previous period counts toward the fulfillment of the vow. Finally, a year-old male lamb for a guilt offering is presented to the priest.[138] Hence the normal order for expiation outlined in Leviticus is followed, sin offering (expiation), burnt offering (consecration), and the guilt offering (reparation).

[13]"'Now this is the law for the Nazirite when the period of his separation is over. He is to be brought to the entrance to the Tent of Meeting. [14]There he is to present his offerings to the LORD: a year-old male lamb without defect for a burnt offering, a year-old ewe lamb without defect for a sin offering, a ram without defect for a fellowship offering, [15]together with their grain offerings and

---

[136] According to the Mishnah (*Temûrah* vii.4) the hair was buried because of uncleanness derived from the dead body. Cf. also the tractate Mishnah *Nāzîr* for additional derived practices of the late Second Temple period (H. Danby, *The Mishnah* [New York: Oxford University Press, 1933], 280–93).

[137] This is but one example of an inadvertent sin for which the sin offering was intended. Other sin offerings were sacrificed for unknowing or unintentional breach of the covenant stipulations (Num 15:22–31; Lev 13:1–15:33). For deliberate and intentional breaking of the covenant of holiness, there was no sacrifice prescribed, only death or banishment.

[138] This was similar to the normal guilt offering of a ram (Lev 5:14–19), which Milgrom notes was required "to make expiation for the inadvertent desecration of the consecrated head and vow. … he must repay the sanctuary for the desecrated sanctum" (*Numbers*, 47). The lamb was offered as a guilt offering in the case of purification from an infectious disease (Lev 14:12,21).

drink offerings, and a basket of bread made without yeast—cakes made of fine flour mixed with oil, and wafers spread with oil. <sup>16</sup>"'The priest is to present them before the LORD and make the sin offering and the burnt offering. <sup>17</sup>He is to present the basket of unleavened bread and is to sacrifice the ram as a fellowship offering to the LORD, together with its grain offering and drink offering.

<sup>18</sup>"'Then at the entrance to the Tent of Meeting, the Nazirite must shave off the hair that he dedicated. He is to take the hair and put it in the fire that is under the sacrifice of the fellowship offering.

<sup>19</sup>"'After the Nazirite has shaved off the hair of his dedication, the priest is to place in his hands a boiled shoulder of the ram, and a cake and a wafer from the basket, both made without yeast. <sup>20</sup>The priest shall then wave them before the LORD as a wave offering; they are holy and belong to the priest, together with the breast that was waved and the thigh that was presented. After that, the Nazirite may drink wine.

COMPLETION RITUALS OF THE NAZIRITE VOW (6:13–20). **6:13–20** At the conclusion of the self-prescribed period of the Nazirite vow, that individual would bring[139] the following sacrifices for presentation before the Lord at the entrance to the Tent of Meeting:[140] (1) a year-old unblemished male lamb for a burnt offering, (2) a year-old unblemished female lamb for a sin offering, (3) an unblemished ram for a fellowship (peace) offering, (4) a basket of unleavened cakes *(matsôt)* and unleavened wafers.[141] The three animal sacrifices were to be accompanied by the requisite grain and libation offerings, as described in Num 15:1–12.[142]

| Sacrifice | Element | Grain + Oil | Libation |
|---|---|---|---|
| Burnt offering | Male Lamb | 1/10 eph + 1/4 hin | 1/4 hin wine |
| Sin offering | Female Lamb | 1/10 eph + 1/4 hin | 1/4 hin wine |
| Fellowship offering | Ram | 2/10 eph + 1/3 hin | 1/3 hin wine |

The order in which the sacrifices are offered by the priest to Yahweh is slightly different from the restoration sequence outlined in vv. 9–12 and the listing in vv. 14–15. The sin offering (1) is sacrificed, followed by the burnt offering (2), and then the fellowship offering (3). The basket of cakes and wafers (4) are presented to the Lord, probably by setting them in front of the altar. Later the

---

[139] The text reads יָבִיא אֹתוֹ, "he shall bring it (himself)" and may refer to the formal presenting of oneself to the priests at the entrance to the Tent of Meeting, or it may refer to the collective sacrifices brought at the conclusion of the vow period. The *hifil* sequence of vv. 13–14, יָבִיא ... וְהִקְרִיב, would seem to indicate the latter. Numerous rabbinical sources suggest the reflexive translation, including Targ. Onkelos, R. Ishmael, R. Rashi, and Ibn Ezra.

[140] "At the entrance" probably means in the outer courtyard between the actual doorway to the tent and where the large bronze altar was located.

[141] The unleavened cakes made from fine flour and olive oil and thin wafers (רְקִיק) are described in Lev 2:4–10. Cf. also Exod 29:2,23; Lev 8:26.

[142] Cf. also the delineations for the holy days in Num 28:1–29:40.

cakes and wafers are eaten by the priest and the Nazirite.

The Nazirite then shaved off his consecrated hair, the sign of his devotion, and burned it in the fire upon which the fellowship offering had been placed.[143] The hair was burned so as not to defile that which had been consecrated in the vow and hence in the burning was rendered totally unto God, the true source and possessor of holiness. The priest then took the boiled shoulder section (zĕrōaᶜ) of the ram and placed it in the hands of the offerer along with one of the unleavened cakes and one of the wafers. The zĕrōaᶜ as a portion of the fellowship/peace offering belonging to the priests is only mentioned elsewhere in Deut 18:3. Normally the breast and the upper portion of the right hind leg were reserved for priestly consumption.[144] A parallel to this practice has been observed in Egyptian, Mesopotamian, and Hittite texts and murals in which the right thigh was choice portion for presentation to their various deities.[145] The boiling of sacrifices is known from pre-Israelite Lachish[146] and from Shiloh during the premonarchial period (1 Sam 2:13–14).

The Nazirite handed the elements back to the priest, who lifted and waved them before the Lord in symbolic celebration of God's faithful provision and faithfulness in enabling the Nazirite to complete this special period of holy service. The priests[147] then ate their portions in communal fashion, and the former Nazirite (and probably other members of the family) would eat the other portions of the ram in joyous celebration in the presence of God, thus symbolizing union between God, priests, and people. At that joyful and delectable occasion, the former Nazirite also could resume drinking wine, from which he has been abstained for the given period.

**21"'This is the law of the Nazirite who vows his offering to the LORD in accordance with his separation, in addition to whatever else he can afford. He must fulfill the vow he has made, according to the law of the Nazirite.'"**

SUMMARY (6:21).    **6:21** The section concludes with a summary statement parallel to other legislation in the Book of Numbers and elsewhere in

---

[143] Milgrom suggests the burning of the holy hair was in a special pot placed on a hearth by the sacrificial fire, following Targums Onkelos and Jonathan (*Numbers*, 49, 304n).

[144] Lev 7:30–35.

[145] Textual examples of the special significance of the right thigh in ANE ritual include the Mesopotamian "Epic of Gilgamesh," 6.160–67 (*ANET*, 85) and the Hittite "Purification Ritual Engaging the Help of Protective Demons," L 49–50 (*ANET*, 348).

[146] O. Tufnell et al., *Lachish* 2, "The Fosse Temple" (London: Oxford University Press, 1940), 93–94. Tufnell notes that a collection of right thigh bones was found near the Fosse temple and interpreted the findings as an indication that these special portions were provided for the cultic personnel and then cooked and eaten in the proximity of the sanctuary.

[147] And the Levites according to 11 Q Temple in the Dead Sea Scrolls.

the Pentateuch.[148] Because 5:5–6:21 contains more general legislation and does not arise out a particular historical case in the context, the usual Numbers clause, "They did just as the LORD commanded Moses," is not employed. The conclusion does state that the offerings presented by the Nazirite at the conclusion of the vow are the minimal requirements. Additional sacrificial gifts may be made according to that which may have been committed by the individual at the commencement of the vow, as well as those possible with respect to the person's financial capability.

In Acts 21:22–27, which describes Paul's journey back to Jerusalem, Luke describes the vow that Paul and four other men had taken that involved purification rites of shaving the head, seven days of cleansing, and living in obedience to the Torah. Luke also notes that Paul appealed for help for the four men in "paying their expenses," presumably for the sacrifices in completion of the Nazirite vow. The Mishnah describes the practice of wealthy individuals paying for the vow completion requirements for poor persons.[149] Later, when brought before Felix in Caesarea, Paul was accused by Ananias the high priest and others of inciting riots and desecrating the temple. Regarding the matter of the temple, Paul offered in his defense his taking of the vow as proof of his being ceremonially clean when he entered the courts (Acts 24:1–21). To gain an audience with his people the Jews, he wanted to demonstrate his faithfulness to God and the Torah as a means of sharing a more excellent Way in the Law of Christ.

**[22]The LORD said to Moses, [23]"Tell Aaron and his sons, 'This is how you are to bless the Israelites. Say to them:**
**[24]" ' "The LORD bless you**
**and keep you;**
**[25]the LORD make his face shine upon you**
**and be gracious to you;**
**[26]the LORD turn his face toward you**
**and give you peace." '**
**[27]"So they will put my name on the Israelites, and I will bless them."**

THE PRIESTLY BLESSING (6:22–27). **6:22–27** The conclusion to the first cycle of the Book of Numbers, and the purification and priestly section of the cycle, is an anticipatory benediction to be pronounced by Aaron and his sons over the people of Israel. Allen notes that whereas the Nazirite vow is a rite restricted to individuals, the words of the priestly blessing "are expansive and gracious, and they are inclusive of the whole community."[150] The poetic style of the passage facilitated memory and provided an aesthetic

---

[148] Cf. note on 1:16, 2:34; 4:28,33,49; 5:4; etc.
[149] *Nazir* ii.5. Note also Josephus, *Ant.* 19.6.1.
[150] Allen, "Numbers," 754.

dimension to the priestly legislation.

That this blessing was important in the lives of ancient Israelites is attested in the copy of it found in the excavations of Ketef Hinnom to the southwest of Mount Zion and the Old City of Jerusalem. In digging within the compound of the Scottish St. Andrew's Church on the western slope of the Hinnom Valley in 1979, the expedition led by archaeologist G. Barkai unearthed a late seventh to sixth century B.C. burial complex. Among the remains recovered was a phylactery containing two silver scrolls the size of a small cigarette, upon which were written two versions of the priestly blessing.[151] These had been used as amulets during the lives of the individuals interred there or as burial pendants. The text on the larger one is nearly identical to that of the Masoretic text, and an abbreviated version of the second and third blessings was written on the smaller. As such they attest the authenticity and antiquity of the Priestly Benediction. These texts also contain the oldest attestation to the Tetragrammaton found to date in Jerusalem. The text of the blessing had become a standardized liturgical form no later than the end of the preexilic period, with shortened forms in use by the same era. Ancient Near Eastern texts from the second millennium B.C. contain parallels to the themes of divine countenance, the lifting up of the face, and the blessing of well-being *(šalem)*.[152]

The poetic verbal and rhythmic structure of this short benediction has

---

[151] G. Barkai, "Excavations on the Hinnom Slope in Jerusalem" (Heb) *Qadmoniot* 17 (1984): 94–108; also "The Divine Name Found in Jerusalem," *BAR* 9/2 (1983): 14–19. For a general treatment of the excavations and inscriptions see "Ketef Hinnom," in *The Oxford Encyclopedia of Archaeology in the Near East (OEANE)* 3:285–6, by J. P. Dessel.

[152] Contra the opinion of a majority of scholars, Levine argues that the texts from Ketef Hinnom do not support a preexilic dating of priestly material. For him the postexilic priestly author or compiler of the Book of Numbers simply quoted a text known to him from an earlier era. Levine states, "As such, its date even if preexilic, cannot attest to the date of the document in which it is cited" *(Numbers 1–20*, 244). Notably, however, while Levine acknowledges the study of C. Cohen on the theme of the "shining divine countenance and of the lifting of the divine countenance" as having late second and first millennium B.C. parallels in the Middle Babylonian and Late Bronze Ug. texts (p. 236), and the study of A. Rainey on the Akk. and Ug. background of the gods providing protection and peace (well-being), he then states that "it is probable that expressions of blessing drawn from social and official contexts, originally having no bearing on the cult, provided the discrete components of the fixed liturgical benedictions" (p. 237). This conclusion raises several questions regarding nature of the cult: (1) Do the Mesopotamian and Ugaritic texts have no cultic provenance or context? (2) Was the Priestly Benediction used only in cultic settings after having its origin in the social or political context? Or was it used in such "noncultic" settings by the priests (such as in burials)? (3) How does one define the parameters of cult or cultic usage? These can be answered in the affirmative only if one defines cult very narrowly and does not allow the cult to influence the social and political arenas, which is far from attainable in the world of the ANE.

been delineated by several scholars.[153] D. N. Freedman observed the following metric structure:

| 1 | 3 wds | 12 sylls | *yĕbārekĕkā* | *YHWH* | *vĕyišmĕrekā* |
|---|-------|----------|--------------|--------|---------------|
| 2 | 5 wds | 14 sylls | *yā'ēr* | *YHWH* | *pānāyw 'ēlêkā wîḥunnekā* |
| 3 | 7 wds | 16 sylls | *yiśā'* | *YHWH* | *YHWH pānāyw 'ēlêkā wĕyāśēm lĕkā šālôm* |

The conclusion extends the expanding text in outlining the results of the benediction:

| 4 | 8 wds | 18 sylls | *vĕśmû 'et-šĕmî 'al-bĕnê yiśrā'ēl wa'ănî 'ăbārăkēm.* |
|---|-------|----------|------------------------------------------------------|

The thrice-mentioned YHWH, which grammatically need not be repeated, and the final resounding "I will [surely] bless you," serve to heighten the emphasis that the God of Israel is the source of all grace, blessing, hope, and peace. This passage reiterates the great covenant blessing of Gen 12:1–3, thereby providing continuity with that Pentateuchal foundational element. Wenham notes that "as the lines of the blessing lengthen, their content becomes richer, producing a crescendo that culminates in the word *peace* (26). Each line has the LORD as its subject and is followed by two verbs, the second of which expands on the first."[154] P. Miller adds that "the first clause of each line [invokes] God's movement towards his people, the second clause his activity on their behalf."[155] The first and final words of the benediction are both forms of *brk*, forming a beautiful poetic inclusio. M. Fishbane observes that Malachi's diatribe against the priests in 1:6–2:9 provides a "counterexample" of this blessing while utilizing the language of the benediction.[156]

*May YHWH Bless You and Keep You.* Blessing in the Pentateuch and more particularly in the Book of Numbers includes numerous descendants, fruitful land, good health, long life, protection from enemies, and God's abiding presence. The people also lived under the protective umbrella of his mighty hand and outstretched arm. They had experienced his deliverance from the terrible bondage of Egypt, as well as his provision and protection

---

[153] D. N. Freedman, "The Aaronic Blessing," in *No Famine in the Land*, Studies in Honor of J. L. McKenzie, ed. J. L. Flanagan et al. (Atlanta: Scholars Press, 1975), 35–48. Freedman proposed a reconstructed text that he believed to be more symmetrical than the MT. Cf. also Wenham, *Numbers*, 89–90; Allen, "Numbers," 754.

[154] Wenham, *Numbers*, 90.

[155] P. D. Miller, "The Blessing of God: An Interpretation of Numbers 6:22–27," *Int* 29 (1975): 243.

[156] See M. Fishbane, "Form and Reformulation of the Biblical Priestly Blessing," *JAOS* 103/1 (1983): 115–21. Fishbane compares the present content with that of Mal 1:6–2:9, suggesting the priestly blessing provided the form and content for Malachi's exegetical diatribe against the priests during the fifth century B.C.

thus far through the wilderness, and that aspect of his blessing would guard them throughout their lives for generations to come.

Yahweh's blessing upon his faithful people Israel was in turn to be an instrument of blessing upon the nations of the world (Gen 12:3; 22:18). From the children of Abraham, Isaac, and Jacob, to their children's children, and to the ends of the earth, the purpose of Yahweh's blessing of Israel was a worldwide mission of blessing and hope. Psalm 67:1–2 provides an extension of this theme of blessing in the Book of Numbers:

> May God be gracious to us and bless us
>     and make his face shine upon us,
> that your ways may be known on earth,
>     your salvation among all nations.

*May YHWH Shine His Face upon You and Grace You.* The metaphor portraying God's face as light shining upon his people occurs in numerous biblical and extrabiblical texts. In Psalm 80 the phrase "Restore us, O God [Almighty]; / make your face shine upon us, that we may be saved" functions as a refrain in a context of a plea for God to deliver his people from oppression. In Ps 44:3 the psalmist praises God for victory that was accomplished over the enemies of God's children "by your right hand, your arm, and the light of your face, for you loved them."[157] The imagery of the shining of the divine countenance occurs in several Mesopotamian and Ugaritic contexts, in which the gods bestow gifts and extend mercy to individuals or nations.[158]

The shining of Yahweh's face upon his people, by which his good pleasure and good acts will be exerted on behalf of his precious possession, is enhanced by the invoking of his grace (*wîḥunnekā*, "and may he be gracious unto you"). God's grace is an important theme throughout the Old Testament.[159] Ashley notes, "'Grace' describes the attitude that issues in kindly

---

[157] Cf. also Pss 4:6; 31:16; 67:1; 119:135. See also "*'ôr*" by S. Aalen, *TDOT* 1:147–67.

[158] From boundary stones *(kudurru)* of the reign of Nabu-apla-iddina, the king blesses a priest of Sippar with favor and gifts. See L. W. King, *Babylonian Boundary-Stones and Memorial-Tablets in the British Museum* (London: Chatto & Windus, 1912), text #36. E. Dhorme collected numerous examples of Akk. parallels in "L'emploi métaphorique des noms de parties du corps en hébreu et en akkadien," *RevBib* 30 (1921): 383–412. From the sixth century B.C. context of the reign of Nabu-na'id comes a blessing by the goddess Gula, who "turned her countenance toward me (the king), with her shining face she faithfully looked at me and actually caused (him; i.e., Marduk) to show mercy." This translation is from H. Lewy, "The Babylonian Background of the Kay Kâûs Legend," *AnOr* 17/2 (1949): 51–63. For Ugaritic parallels, see A. Rainey, "*iru* and *asru* in Ugaritic and the land of Canaan," *JNES* 26 (1967): 296–301.

[159] More than forty times verb forms of חנן have Yahweh as subject (41x in the *qal*). See Gen 33:5,11; 43:29; Exod 33:19; 1 Sam 12:22; 2 Kgs 13:23; Pss 4:1; 6:2; 9:13; 25:16; 26:11; 27:7; 30:10; 31:9; 41:4,10; 51:1; 56:1; 57:1; 59:5; 67:1; 77:9; 86:3,16; 102:13; 119:29,58,132; 123:2,3; etc. (Many of these verse numbers vary by one verse higher in the MT.) Nominal forms of the terms חן and especially חנון likewise abound in which God is the source of grace, mercy, and favor.

action of a superior party to an inferior one in which the inferior has no claim on the superior."[160] Humanity cannot earn his grace by obedience; that would be a form of compensation. Nor can God's grace be annulled by one's unfaithfulness. God extends his graciousness out of his steadfast covenant love (ḥesed) and self-determined will to bless whom he desires (Exod 33:19).

*May YHWH Lift His Face toward You and Give You Peace.* The third and final colon of the Priestly Benediction invokes in a consummate expression God's grace and beneficence. Yahweh's lifting of his face, observes M. Gruber, is an expression referring "to an appearance of the countenance expressive of pleasure and affection, functionally equivalent to 'smile.'"[161] The majestic smile of God upon the community of faith and each constituent individual will bring abiding and ultimate peace. Harrison notes that "the Lord's presence is radiating divine favor in the midst of His people" and that as a result "they can confidently expect Him to pour out His covenant mercies upon them."[162] This peace can be described variously as completeness, unity, well-being, prosperity, health, security, and wholeness.[163]

The peace that is bestowed upon redeemed humanity by the light of God's countenance surpasses finite human comprehension. The ultimate expression of peace for humanity came through Jesus Christ, who brought us peace with God through his suffering (Isa 53:5). The announcement of the host of angels at the birth of Christ brought a message of peace to those upon whom God's favor rests (Luke 2:14). In the context of the promise of the Holy Spirit, Jesus reminded his disciples of the kind of peace God shines upon his children: "Peace I leave with you; my peace I give to you. I do not give to you as the world gives. Do not let your hearts be troubled and be not afraid" (John 14:27).

*So They Will Put My Name on the Israelites, and I Will Bless Them.* The pronouncement of the prayer by the priests will confer the Name of Yahweh upon the children of Israel. As Allen states, "The prayer is designed to help the people experience the reality of the blessing of the Lord whose delight is

---

[160] Ashley, *Numbers*, 152. This concept was earlier noted by K. W. Neubauer, "Der Stamm ḥnn im Sprachgebrauch des Alten Testamentum" (Ph.D. diss., Berlin, 1964). Cf. also D. N. Freedman, J. R. Lundbom, and H.-J. Fabry, "ḥānan," *TDOT* 5:22–36, and E. Yamauchi, "ḥānan," *TWOT* 1:302–4.

[161] M. I. Gruber, "The Many Faces of nasaʾ panim, 'lift up the face,'" *ZAW* 95 (1983): 253; S. Ahituv, "The Countenance of Yahweh" (Hebrew), in *Tehillah Le-Moshe: Biblical and Judaic Studies in Honor of Moshe Greenberg,* ed. M. Cogan, B. L. Eichler J. H. Tigay (Winona Lake: Eisenbrauns, 1997): 3–12.

[162] Harrison, *Numbers*, 133.

[163] See G. L. Carr, "šālôm," in *TWOT* 2:930–32. Note also the rare combination of פֶן נָשָׂא and שָׁלוֹם in 1 Sam 25:35, in which David pronounces a blessing upon Abigail for the advice she gave him concerning Nabal.

to bring that blessing near; his promise is that he will do just that very thing."[164] The Name Yahweh carries with it the covenantal promise of his divine presence with his people, even through the deserts of Sinai, Paran, and Zin, and into the Promised Land. In the land of his blessing, which Israel will inherit as his possession, the people will experience the fullness of his blessing of security, prosperity, wholeness, and well-being.[165]

Hence the first Sinai cycle concludes with a reminder of the relationship Yahweh has with his people Israel. The coalescing themes of identity and relationship, blessing and abundance through his Name are echoed by the words of Deut 28:8–11, where the blessing turns outward toward the nations:

The LORD will send a blessing on your barns
and on everything you put your hand to.
The LORD your God will bless you
in the land he is giving you.
The LORD will establish you as his holy people,
as he has promised you on oath,
if you keep the commands of the LORD your God
and walk in his ways.
Then all the peoples on earth will see
that you are called by the Name of the LORD,
and they will fear you.
The LORD will grant you abundant prosperity—
in the fruit of your womb,
the young of your livestock
and the crops of your ground—
in the land he swore to your forefathers to give you.

The blessings of Deut 28:1–14 were set in the context of diligent obedience to the covenant stipulations. The benediction of Numbers 6 concludes a cycle of material focused on the faithful, unified community of God's people, with the symbolic presence of God in the tabernacle as center. The fullness of this blessing in the experience of Israel's future history would come as a result of their continued faithfulness, though not always directly dependent in a cause-effect sequence upon their dutiful obedience. God's grace will be manifested numerous times in the rebellion cycles of Numbers as

---

[164] Allen, "Numbers," 755.

[165] In the Book of Deuteronomy the phraseology שׂוּם שֵׁם or שׁכֵּן שֵׁם is used to denote the setting up of a sanctuary at the place where God would choose for his Name to be worshiped (12:5,11; 14:23–24; 16:2,6,11; 26:2). Also in Deuteronomy the concept of God's name carries with it all that God is in his person and deeds. In the covenant relationship with Israel they were to be known to the nations as his people. He had declared them to be his special people and set them high above the nations in praise, in name, and in honor in order to be a holy people to him (Deut 26:19; 28:10). The Levitical priests were to stand before him to serve in his name and to bless the people in his name (Num 6:22–27).

when God promises to bless his people in the land (15:1ff.), in spite of the fact that they had just rejected it (13:28–14:28). Throughout Israel's history God's grace and longsuffering will be evidenced, even in the midst of his people's disobedience.

Ezekiel tells of how Israel went on to profane the Name among the nations by their unfaithfulness, which led to exile in Assyria and Babylon. But the Lord promised to show himself holy to Israel and the nations by restoring the nation, giving the people a new heart and a new spirit and pouring out his blessing again upon the land of his inheritance (Ezek 36:22–30).

In the New Testament, Jesus said that he came in the Father's Name (John 5:43) and performed miracles in his father's name (John 10:25), living out the Name to the fullest. To the apostles the Name of Jesus was the ultimate transcending name (Phil 2:9), the source of salvation (Rom 10:13), and the power of health and healing (Acts 3:6; 4:9).

## 2. Sinai Cycle B: Tabernacle and Celebration (7:1–10:10)

The second of the two Sinai cycles may be outlined as follows:

Sinai Cycle B: Tabernacle Celebration (7:1–10:10)
1. Historical Reference—Tabernacle Completion (7:1)
2. Tabernacle Offerings—Tribal Lists (7:1–89)
3. Menorah Lamp Arrangement—Light (8:1–4)
4. Levites' Installation (8:5–26)
5. The Second Passover: New Delineations (9:1–14)
6. Pattern of the Journey: The Lord in the Cloud (9:15–23)
7. Trumpets for Marching and Celebration (10:1–10)

### (1) Offerings of the Leaders of the Israelite Tribes (7:1–89)

The first cycle focused God's bountiful blessings on the delivered people and on their wholeness and holiness. The priests and Levites were assigned tasks in service of the sanctuary, matters of purification within the community were delineated, and a special form of dedicatory service was defined for the laity. The cycle concluded with the Priestly Benediction, which pronounced God's plan to watch over his people and bless them with grace and peace. Through God's blessing they would demonstrate to the nations all that was represented in his wondrous name.

The theme of the second Sinai cycle is the celebration of God's presence. Note the following outline:

| | |
|---|---|
| 1. Historical Setting | After the completion of the tabernacle (7:1; 9:15) |
| | Passover in the second year (9:1) |
| 2. Twelve Tribe Listing | Representatives of the twelve tribes bring offerings (7:2–89) |
| 3. Cycle Development | Tabernacle Celebration: Offerings, Menorah Lamps, and |
| | Cloud (7:2–89; 8:1–3; 9:15–23; 10:1–10) |
| 4. Priests and Levites | Installation of Levites for tabernacle Service (8:5–26) |
| 5. Law and Purification | Passover Celebration—Second Month Alternative (9:1–14) |

In deviating from the form outline, emphasis on the primary theme of tabernacle celebration in the cycle development is conveyed throughout. Two historical settings are provided: (1) tabernacle offerings at the completion of the tabernacle on the first day of the first month of the first year (7:1; 9:15) and the second Passover celebration beginning on the fourteenth day of the first month (9:1–2).

The twelve-tribe listing is integrated into the offerings for the tabernacle, thus reflecting the unity and harmony of the people of God in worship. The repetitiveness of the offerings provides a continuously resonant reminder of the total tribal support for the worship center (the tabernacle), the worship leadership (the priesthood), the worship process (sacrifice), and the worshiped God (Yahweh, who gives graciously to his special creation). In cycles three through five, this fellowship will be shattered by rebellion against God, Moses, and Aaron and the priesthood, refusal of the gracious gift of the Promised Land, and rejection of the tribal harmony represented in this section.

The Levites are installed via purification ritual for their declared purpose of serving as God's intermediaries in the worship process. Further matters of law are set forth in relation to the necessary purification for the celebration of God's salvation in the Exodus. The law makes provision for persons rendered unclean for various reasons to celebrate the Passover. The section concludes with the instruction for the people to move out from Sinai and into the larger wilderness in harmony with the symbol of God's presence, following the divine cloud as heralded by the priests on the silver trumpets.

**¹When Moses finished setting up the tabernacle, he anointed it and consecrated it and all its furnishings. He also anointed and consecrated the altar and all its utensils. ²Then the leaders of Israel, the heads of families who were the tribal leaders in charge of those who were counted, made offerings. ³They brought as their gifts before the LORD six covered carts and twelve oxen—an ox from each leader and a cart from every two. These they presented before the tabernacle.**

**⁴The LORD said to Moses, ⁵"Accept these from them, that they may be used in the work at the Tent of Meeting. Give them to the Levites as each man's work requires."**

**⁶So Moses took the carts and oxen and gave them to the Levites. ⁷He gave two carts and four oxen to the Gershonites, as their work required, ⁸and he gave four**

carts and eight oxen to the Merarites, as their work required. They were all under the direction of Ithamar son of Aaron, the priest. ⁹But Moses did not give any to the Kohathites, because they were to carry on their shoulders the holy things, for which they were responsible.

¹⁰When the altar was anointed, the leader brought their offerings for its dedication and presented them before the altar. ¹¹For the LORD had said to Moses, "Each day one leader is to bring his offering for the dedication of the altar."

HISTORICAL SETTING AND INTRODUCTION (7:1–11). **7:1–11** The initial historical setting for this section is the conclusion of the construction of the tabernacle in the Sinai Desert at the foot of God's mountain, described in Exod 40:17 as the first day of the first month of the second year.[167] The following synchronous table shows the sequence of events from Exodus, Leviticus and Numbers:[168]

**Chronology of Events in Exodus, Leviticus, and Numbers**

| Date | Scripture | Event |
| --- | --- | --- |
| 1.14.1 | Exod 14:6,31–32 | Exodus from Egypt |
| 3.14.1 | Exod 19:1 | Israelites arrive at Sinai |
| 1.1.2 | Exod 40:2,17 | Tabernacle erected with Tent of Meeting |
|  | Lev 8:1–36 | Priestly sanctification begins |
|  | Lev 1:1–7:38 | Altar offerings commence |
|  | Num 7:1,3 | Tribal offerings begin |
|  | Num 9:15 | Cloud covers tabernacle |
| 1.8.2 | Lev 9:1 | Priestly sanctification concluded |
| 1.12.2 | Num 7:78–83 | Tribal offerings completed |
| 1.14.2 | Num 9:1 | Second Passover |
| 2.1.2 | Num 1:1–2 | First census commences |
| 2.14.2 | Num 9:11 | Second Passover for the Unclean |
| 2.20.2 | Num 10:11 | Cloud moves — Israel departs Sinai |

The first day of the second year after the Exodus was a momentous day that saw the completion of the tabernacle, the commencement of sacrificial offerings, gifts for worship service from the tribe of Judah, provision from the tribes of carts and oxen for tabernacle transport, and the settling of the cloud of the presence of God. A people in communion with God was ready to worship in harmony and experience his abiding presence.

---

[167] In the Mishnah this day was described as the New Year for the reckoning of the regnal years of kings. The "Day of the Sounding of Trumpets" or "Rosh HaShanah — New Year" was/is the first of the seventh month. This New Year marked the beginning of the festival calendar and the penitential season, which concluded with Yom Kippur. Hence the calendar was marked by two notable New Year's celebrations: spring for Kings and Passover, fall for Trumpets, Yom Kippur, and Booths (Shavuoth).

[168] Adapted and supplemented from Wenham, *Numbers,* 91.

The narrative preterite form *wayĕhî* introduces a new narrative section that resets the historical setting in the context of Moses' completion of the tabernacle construction and sanctification. It also introduces the general overview of the chapter in 7:2–11 and marks the division of the chapter in v. 12, where the daily presentation of offerings by each of the tribes commences. An inclusio utilizing the term *yaqrîbû* ("they brought near") brackets the section, thereby emphasizing the process of approaching the altar, the point of mediation with God, with various gifts. Coppes observes that this common technical term in the cult "connotes every step man performs in presenting his offering to God."[169] Nominal and verbal forms of *qārab* occur thirty-five times in this chapter.[170]

At the completion of the tabernacle construction, Moses carries out the ritual purification of the structure and its furnishings via anointing with oil *(mšḥ)* and consecrating *(qdš)* rites, thus setting them apart for special service by the priests and Levites in the center of Yahweh worship. Attention then is turned to the altar toward and upon which the tribal offerings will be brought and sacrificed and the various utensils employed. The same anointing and consecrating rites were exercised in the dedication of the altar.[171] The initial collective gifts of carts and oxen for transportation of the tabernacle and its goods are donated equally by the leaders of the tribes. The two carts and four oxen presented by Moses to the Gershonites were for carrying the various curtains and coverings for the tabernacle (4:21–28), and the four carts and eight oxen presented to the Merarites provided the necessary means for transporting the poles, bases, crossbars, ropes, and other framing structures (4:29–33). Ithamar the priest was appointed as overseer of the activities of these two clans of Levites. None of the carts and oxen were granted to the Kohathites, since they were to transport the ark and other implements of worship on their shoulders with the poles. Moses plays the role of mediator and facilitator in accepting the carts and oxen from the tribal leaders and formally presenting them to the Levites.

Notable is the fact that these gifts, as well as the plenteous vessels and

---

[169] L. J. Coppes, "*qārab*," *TWOT* 2:812.

[170] In 7:2–11 the verbal form is used five times and the nominal twice. In Judah's initial presentation (7:12–17), one verbal and three nominal forms occur, followed by Issachar's presentation (7:18–23) utilizing two verbal (one could be due to dittography) and two nominal forms. Afterward the structure is standardized with the form קָרְבָּנוֹ ("his offering") occurring after the naming of the tribal leader ("the offering of *X*") at the conclusion followed by the repetition of the tribal leader's name.

[171] A stylistic chiastic construction is employed in v. 1 as follows.

A (tabernacle)    - B (Anointed/Sanctified)    - C (All Its Vessels)
A' (Altar)    - C (All Its Vessels)    B (Anointed/Sanctified)

The vessels are highlighted in the construction, drawing attention to the numerous vessels that will be added in the presentation of gifts by the twelve tribal leaders.

offerings that follow in vv. 12–88, were presented by the tribal leaders spontaneously (rather than by divine command) as the people responded to God's graciousness and faithfulness. In harmonious concert the tribal leaders, as representatives of the larger population of Israelites, voluntarily initiated these acts of service of the God who brought them forth from Egypt, constituted them as a nation, and provided them the Torah. The Lord desires all his people to respond to his faithfulness by harmonious service and willful giving of themselves and their abundance. By doing so they offer complete worship.

¹²The one who brought his offering on the first day was Nahshon son of Amminadab of the tribe of Judah. ¹³His offering was one silver plate weighing a hundred and thirty shekels, and one silver sprinkling bowl weighing seventy shekels, both according to the sanctuary shekel, each filled with fine flour mixed with oil as a grain offering; ¹⁴one gold dish weighing ten shekels, filled with incense; ¹⁵one young bull, one ram and one male lamb a year old, for a burnt offering; ¹⁶one male goat for a sin offering; ¹⁷and two oxen, five rams, five male goats and five male lambs a year old, to be sacrificed as a fellowship offering. This was the offering of Nahshon son of Amminadab.

¹⁸On the second day Nethanel son of Zuar, the leader of Issachar, brought his offering. ¹⁹The offering he brought was one silver plate weighing a hundred and thirty shekels, and one silver sprinkling bowl weighing seventy shekels, both according to the sanctuary shekel, each filled with fine flour mixed with oil as a grain offering; ²⁰one gold dish weighing ten shekels, filled with incense; ²¹one young bull, one ram and one male lamb a year old, for a burnt offering; ²²one male goat for a sin offering; ²³and two oxen, five rams, five male goats and five male lambs a year old, to be sacrificed as a fellowship offering. This was the offering of Nethanel son of Zuar.

²⁴On the third day, Eliab son of Helon, the leader of the people of Zebulun, brought his offering. ²⁵His offering was one silver plate weighing a hundred and thirty shekels, and one silver sprinkling bowl weighing seventy shekels, both according to the sanctuary shekel, each filled with fine flour mixed with oil as a grain offering; ²⁶one gold dish weighing ten shekels, filled with incense; ²⁷one young bull, one ram and one male lamb a year old, for a burnt offering; ²⁸one male goat for a sin offering; ²⁹and two oxen, five rams, five male goats and five male lambs a year old, to be sacrificed as a fellowship offering. This was the offering of Eliab son of Helon.

³⁰On the fourth day Elizur son of Shedeur, the leader of the people of Reuben, brought his offering. ³¹His offering was one silver plate weighing a hundred and thirty shekels, and one silver sprinkling bowl weighing seventy shekels, both according to the sanctuary shekel, each filled with fine flour mixed with oil as a grain offering; ³²one gold dish weighing ten shekels, filled with incense; ³³one young bull, one ram and one male lamb a year old, for a burnt offering; ³⁴one male goat for a sin offering; ³⁵and two oxen, five rams, five male goats and five

male lambs a year old, to be sacrificed as a fellowship offering. This was the offering of Elizur son of Shedeur.

[36]On the fifth day Shelumiel son of Zurishaddai, the leader of the people of Simeon, brought his offering. [37]His offering was one silver plate weighing a hundred and thirty shekels, and one silver sprinkling bowl weighing seventy shekels, both according to the sanctuary shekel, each filled with fine flour mixed with oil as a grain offering; [38]one gold dish weighing ten shekels, filled with incense; [39]one young bull, one ram and one male lamb a year old, for a burnt offering; [40]one male goat for a sin offering; [41]and two oxen, five rams, five male goats and five male lambs a year old, to be sacrificed as a fellowship offering. This was the offering of Shelumiel son of Zurishaddai.

[42]On the sixth day Eliasaph son of Deuel, the leader of the people of Gad, brought his offering. [43]His offering was one silver plate weighing a hundred and thirty shekels, and one silver sprinkling bowl weighing seventy shekels, both according to the sanctuary shekel, each filled with fine flour mixed with oil as a grain offering; [44]one gold dish weighing ten shekels, filled with incense; [45]one young bull, one ram and one male lamb a year old, for a burnt offering; [46]one male goat for a sin offering; [47]and two oxen, five rams, five male goats and five male lambs a year old, to be sacrificed as a fellowship offering. This was the offering of Eliasaph son of Deuel.

[48]On the seventh day Elishama son of Ammihud, the leader of the people of Ephraim, brought his offering. [49]His offering was one silver plate weighing a hundred and thirty shekels, and one silver sprinkling bowl weighing seventy shekels, both according to the sanctuary shekel, each filled with fine flour mixed with oil as a grain offering; [50]one gold dish weighing ten shekels, filled with incense; [51]one young bull, one ram and one male lamb a year old, for a burnt offering; [52]one male goat for a sin offering; [53]and two oxen, five rams, five male goats and five male lambs a year old, to be sacrificed as a fellowship offering. This was the offering of Elishama son of Ammihud.

[54]On the eighth day Gamaliel son of Pedahzur, the leader of the people of Manasseh, brought his offering. [55]His offering was one silver plate weighing a hundred and thirty shekels, and one silver sprinkling bowl weighing seventy shekels, both according to the sanctuary shekel, each filled with fine flour mixed with oil as a grain offering; [56]one gold dish weighing ten shekels, filled with incense; [57]one young bull, one ram and one male lamb a year old, for a burnt offering; [58]one male goat for a sin offering; [59]and two oxen, five rams, five male goats and five male lambs a year old, to be sacrificed as a fellowship offering. This was the offering of Gamaliel son of Pedahzur.

[60]On the ninth day Abidan son of Gideoni, the leader of the people of Benjamin, brought his offering. [61]His offering was one silver plate weighing a hundred and thirty shekels, and one silver sprinkling bowl weighing seventy shekels, both according to the sanctuary shekel, each filled with fine flour mixed with oil as a grain offering; [62]one gold dish weighing ten shekels, filled with incense; [63]one

young bull, one ram and one male lamb a year old, for a burnt offering; [64]one male goat for a sin offering; [65]and two oxen, five rams, five male goats and five male lambs a year old, to be sacrificed as a fellowship offering. This was the offering of Abidan son of Gideoni.

[66]On the tenth day Ahiezer son of Ammishaddai, the leader of the people of Dan, brought his offering. [67]His offering was one silver plate weighing a hundred and thirty shekels, and one silver sprinkling bowl weighing seventy shekels, both according to the sanctuary shekel, each filled with fine flour mixed with oil as a grain offering; [68]one gold dish weighing ten shekels, filled with incense; [69]one young bull, one ram and one male lamb a year old, for a burnt offering; [70]one male goat for a sin offering; [71]and two oxen, five rams, five male goats and five male lambs a year old, to be sacrificed as a fellowship offering. This was the offering of Ahiezer son of Ammishaddai.

[72]On the eleventh day Pagiel son of Ocran, the leader of the people of Asher, brought his offering. [73]His offering was one silver plate weighing a hundred and thirty shekels, and one silver sprinkling bowl weighing seventy shekels, both according to the sanctuary shekel, each filled with fine flour mixed with oil as a grain offering; [74]one gold dish weighing ten shekels, filled with incense; [75]one young bull, one ram and one male lamb a year old, for a burnt offering; [76]one male goat for a sin offering; [77]and two oxen, five rams, five male goats and five male lambs a year old, to be sacrificed as a fellowship offering. This was the offering of Pagiel son of Ocran.

[78]On the twelfth day Ahira son of Enan, the leader of the people of Naphtali, brought his offering. [79]His offering was one silver plate weighing a hundred and thirty shekels, and one silver sprinkling bowl weighing seventy shekels, both according to the sanctuary shekel, each filled with fine flour mixed with oil as a grain offering; [80]one gold dish weighing ten shekels, filled with incense; [81]one young bull, one ram and one male lamb a year old, for a burnt offering; [82]one male goat for a sin offering; [83]and two oxen, five rams, five male goats and five male lambs a year old, to be sacrificed as a fellowship offering. This was the offering of Ahira son of Enan.

TRIBAL GIFTS DELINEATED (7:12–83).  **7:12–83**  In resounding fashion each of the twelve tribal leaders brings corresponding contributions of cultic vessels and sacrificial offerings, presented before the altar for the community worship of Yahweh, God of Israel. G. Wenham notes that the presentation offerings by representatives from each of the tribes "set a precedent and demonstrated that the worship was for every tribe and supported by every tribe."[172] For twelve successive days, beginning on the first day of the first month, a tribal head would present his assortment of gifts before Aaron and Moses in the outer court where the altar had been placed. No one tribe superseded another in the type or magnitude of the offerings,

---

[172] Wenham, *Numbers,* 93.

thereby echoing the unity and harmonious effort of the community through its designated leaders.

The pattern of the text for each of the tribal presentations is as follows: (1) day of presentation, (2) identity of the tribal leader, (3) vessel offerings, (4) sacrificial offerings, (5) inclusio of the identity of the tribal leader. Levine describes chap. 7 as "primarily an administrative record" of the priestly cultic tradition.[173] Following the traditional pattern of temple records of the ancient Near East, Levine suggests that the original text was a tabular list, "intended to be read both horizontally and vertically."[174] The textual structure of the first three days reflects a progressive compression of the introductory formula for describing the presentation, after which the pattern is consistent in vv. 24–83.[175] Levine states: "The system of numeration employed in Num 7:12–88 is perhaps the most revealing feature of all, because it directly links biblical records to known methods of ancient Near Eastern accounting. In Num 7:12–88 the sequence of numeration is (a) item, (b) numeral (quantity); for example, *bāqār šĕnayim*, 'oxen–2.'"[176] G. Wenham claims, however, that the repetitive nature of the material is primarily theological. He writes: "It seems likely that a theological purpose underlies his wordiness: to emphasize as strongly as possible that every tribe had an equal stake in the worship of God, and that each was fully committed to the support of the tabernacle and its priesthood."[177] Actually both may have played a part in the form of the text as it now stands. The original accounting by Moses, Aaron, and his sons the priests may have been in tabular form after the manner of ancient Near Eastern accounting. Then fully incorporated into the narrative form of the text. The various vessels in the tabular account are listed in descending order by weight, as are the various animals sacrificed under each category. The list for each of the twelve tribal leaders is as follows:

| Item | Weight | Contents |
|------|--------|----------|
| 1 Silver Plate | 130 shekels | fine flour + oil (grain offering) |
| 1 Silver Bowl | 70 shekels | fine flour + oil (grain offering) |

---

[173] Levine, *Numbers*, 247.

[174] Ibid., 259–60.

[175] This pattern reduction is as follows:

1. 12–17 *wayĕhî hammaqrîb bayyôm #1    et-qorbānô* TL#1   *weqorbānô* list    *zeh qorban* TL#1
2. 18–23   *bayôm #2 hiqrîb* TL#2 *hiqrib et-qorbānô*           list    *zeh qorban* TL#2 TL#2
3. 24–29   *bayôm #3*            *qorbānô*                       list    *zeh qorban* TL#3
4–12   same as #3

[176] Levine (*Numbers*, 259–66) suggests that "in biblical texts quantities are usually registered differently as … (a) numeral (quantity), (b) item"; yet numerous examples suggest otherwise, e.g., 2 Kgs 18:19. In 2 Chr 30:24 both systems are used in chiastic fashion for delineating the quantities of bulls, sheep, and goats sacrificed during the Passover held in the reign of Hezekiah.

[177] Wenham, *Numbers*, 93.

| 1 Gold Dish | 10 shekels | incense |
| --- | --- | --- |

| Offering Type | Animals |
| --- | --- |
| Consecration: Burnt (ʿōlâ) | 1 young bull 1 ram 1 lamb (yr old male) |
| Atonement: Sin offering (ḥaṭṭāʾāt) | goat (male) |
| Communion: Peace/well-being (šĕlômîm) | 2 oxen 5 rams 5 goats 5 lambs (yr old male) |

The craftsmen of the three types of utensils used the sanctuary shekel, a measurement used in the cultic context for weighing gifts and sacrifices or determining their monetary value. The term *shekel* was used throughout the Levant and Mesopotamia as a standard weight measure, generally ranging from ten to thirteen grams.[178] Milgrom and Wenham compute the resultant weights of the objects as approximately three pounds for the large silver plate, two pounds for the silver basin, and four ounces for the small gold ladle for the incense.[179]

The order of the offerings in each of the tribal presentations reflects an administrative setting rather than the normal functional order within the cult. A. F. Rainey noted that the grain and oil offerings are listed within the context of the vessels in which they are administered in the cultic practice rather than in conjunction with the various animal offerings they accompanied in the actual sacrificial procedures.[180] Only the guilt offering (Lev 5:14–6:7; 7:1–10) is not mentioned in this context of consecration and celebration. As Wenham notes, "The guilt offering was not a part of the normal round of official sacrifices. It was reserved for serious sins, such as sacrilege, the abuse of oaths, adultery with a slave girl, or breach of the Nazirite vow."[181] No specific covenant abrogation is outlined in this context of celebration, and the sin offerings presented are those that are necessary for general atonement prior to consecration and fellowship sacrifices. The normal ritual sequence of the sacrifices was atonement/sin—consecration/burnt—communal/peace, as is evidenced in the ordination and inauguration of the Aaronic priesthood (Lev 8:1–9:21).[182] Hence, the order presented is for administra-

---

[178] See J. B. Betlyon, "Coinage," *AB* I:1076–89, esp. 1078–79; *The Coinage and Mints of Phoenicia*, HSM 26 (Chico, Cal.: Scholars Press, 1980); M. Powell, "Weights and Measures," *OEANE* 5:339–42; A. Bivar, "Coins," *OEANE* 2:41–52, esp. 43–44.

[179] Milgrom, *Numbers*, 55; Wenham, *Numbers*, 92–93. Estimates for these articles range from 2.86–3.43 lbs. for the silver plate, 1.54–2.00 lbs. for the silver basin, and 3.5–5.0 oz. for the gold ladle.

[180] A. F. Rainey, "The Order of the Sacrifices in the Old Testament Ritual Texts," *Bib* 51 (1970): 487–98. Cf. the grain offering accompaniment, initially described in Lev 2:1–10, with the animal sacrifices in Num 28:1–29:40.

[181] Wenham, *Numbers*, 203.

[182] In the case of the cleansing of the leper, the sequence is purification offering (two birds)— guilt offering—sin offering—burnt offering (Lev 14:1–32).

tive purposes rather than for setting the prescribed sequence for each of the offerings.[183] The overarching purpose of the text in the Book of Numbers is the setting forth of a theology of worship and celebration that emphasizes the collective unity and harmony of the people of God, the abundant sacrificial giving of the people, the equal status of all offerers, the role of representative leadership, and the responsiveness of God, who provides for and communes with his faithful servants.

**Tribal Order of Presentation**

| | |
|---|---|
| 1. JUDAH | Nahshon ben Amminadab (7:12–17) |
| 2. ISSACHAR | Nathanel ben Zuar (7:18–23) |
| 3. ZEBULUN | Eliab ben Helon (7:24–29) |
| 4. REUBEN | Elizur ben Shedeur (7:30–35) |
| 5. SIMEON | Shelumiel ben Zurishaddai (7:36–41) |
| 6. GAD | Eliasaph ben Deuel (7:42–47) |
| 7. EPHRAIM | Elishama ben Ammihud (7:48–53) |
| 8. MANASSEH | Gamaliel ben Pedahzur (7:54–59) |
| 9. BENJAMIN | Abidan ben Gideoni (7:60–65) |
| 10. DAN | Ahiezer ben Ammishaddai (7:66–71) |
| 11. ASHER | Pagiel ben Ocran (7:72–77) |
| 12. NAPHTALI | Ahira ben Enan (7:78–83) |

The order of the tribes is the same as in 2:2–31, which outlines the organization of the tribes around the central sanctuary and the order of the march through the wilderness. The account in Num 10:14–28 also reflects the tribal order of the first march from Sinai. These same patriarchal princes of the tribes, who led the way in bringing the offerings, would be appointed (in different order) to conduct the first census at the beginning of the second month, or two and one-half weeks after the completion of the offering presentations. Again the unity and harmony of the people of God in worship and service are emphasized in the text.

**[84]These were the offerings of the Israelite leaders for the dedication of the altar when it was anointed: twelve silver plates, twelve silver sprinkling bowls and twelve gold dishes. [85]Each silver plate weighed a hundred and thirty shekels, and each sprinkling bowl seventy shekels. Altogether, the silver dishes weighed two thousand four hundred shekels, according to the sanctuary shekel. [86]The twelve gold dishes filled with incense weighed ten shekels each, according to the sanctuary shekel. Altogether, the gold dishes weighed a hundred and twenty shekels. [87]The total number of animals for the burnt offering came to twelve young**

---

[183] This view stands contra Harrison (*Numbers*, 140), who views the sequence as prescriptive. Cf. also Levine (*Numbers*, 263–64; "The Descriptive Tabernacle Texts of the Pentateuch," *JAOS* 85 [1965]: 307–18) and Rainey, "Sacrifices and Offerings," *ZPEB* 5:194–211.

bulls, twelve rams and twelve male lambs a year old, together with their grain offering. Twelve male goats were used for the sin offering. [88]The total number of animals for the sacrifice of the fellowship offering came to twenty-four oxen, sixty rams, sixty male goats and sixty male lambs a year old. These were the offerings for the dedication of the altar after it was anointed.

SUMMARY OF OFFERINGS PRESENTED (7:84–88). **7:84–88** In the characteristic Pentateuchal pattern, a summary total of all of the offerings is delineated.[184] Again the phrase "dedication of the altar when it was anointed" provides the literary bracketing (inclusio) for the section of the text, connecting the summary with literary symmetry to the introduction in vv. 1 and 11.[185] The repetition of the phrase "dedication of the altar" *(ḥănukat hammizbēaḥ)* in another inclusio likewise provides unity to the literary subunit of vv. 84–88. Totals of the cultic items and offerings are as follows:

| Item | Weight | Total | |
|---|---|---|---|
| 12 Silver Plates | 130 shekels | 1,560 shekels | |
| 12 Silver Bowls | 70 shekels | 840 shekels | Silver total 2,400 shekels |
| 12 Gold Dishes | 10 shekels | 120 shekels | |

| Offering Type | Total Animals |
|---|---|
| Consecration: Burnt *(ʿōlâ)* | 12 young bulls 12 rams 12 lambs (1 yr. male) |
| Atonement: Sin offering *(ḥaṭṭāʾāt)* | 12 goats (male) |
| Communion: Peace/well-being *(šĕlômîm)* | 24 oxen 60 rams 60 goats 60 lambs (1 yr. male) |

Conclusion: Dedication Offerings for the ALTAR after anointed
Cf. to cleansing of the Holy Place on Yom Kippur

[89]**When Moses entered the Tent of Meeting to speak with the LORD, he heard the voice speaking to him from between the two cherubim above the atonement cover on the ark of the Testimony. And he spoke with him.**

YAHWEH SPEAKS WITH MOSES (7:89). **7:89** The conclusion to this concert of celebration in the presentation of gifts and offerings is revelation, which fulfills the promise of Exod 25:22, "There, above the cover [mercy

---

[184]Note above the census total in Num 1:44–47 in summary from 1:20–42. Also Num 2:32 is a summary total of Num 2:3–31.

[185]Terms for consecration (וַיְקַדֵּשׁ) and anointing (וַיִּמְשַׁח) are used twice each in v. 1, and the phrase "dedication of the altar" (חֲנֻכַּת הַמִּזְבֵּחַ) in vv. 10–11, 84, and 88, hence the sequence:

| v. 1 | hammiškān — | wayyimšaḥ – wayĕqadēš |
|---|---|---|
| | hammizbēaḥ — | wayyimšaḥ – wayĕqadēš |
| vv. 10,11 | ḥănukat hammizbēaḥ (2x) | |
| v. 84 | ḥănukat hammizbēaḥ — | bĕyôm himmāšaḥ |
| v. 88 | ḥănukat hammizbēaḥ — | ʾaḥărê himmāšaḥ |

seat] between the two cherubim that are over the ark of the Testimony, I will meet with you and give you all my commands for the Israelites." Earlier Moses is described as meeting with Yahweh in a tent *outside* the camp, and the people worshiped God as they observed the cloud descending upon it.[186] The Tent of Meeting had been set up in the tabernacle on the first day of the first month (Exod 40:2–17), but Moses was not able to enter the Tent at that time when the cloud covered the Tent and the glory of the Lord filled the tabernacle (Exod 40:34–35). But now, with the completion of the tabernacle and the twelve days of consecration, Yahweh meets with Moses *in the midst* of his people, revealing himself in a new setting. The ultimate fulfillment and demonstration of this image is expressed by the apostle John when he declared: "The Word became flesh and made his dwelling ["tabernacled"] among us. We have seen his glory, the glory of the One and Only, who came from the Father, full of grace and truth" (John 1:14).

Many critical scholars take this passage as an unrelated appendage to the story of the tabernacle consecration.[187] Davies succinctly epitomizes this viewpoint: "This verse is clearly an isolated fragment bearing no obvious connection with what precedes or with what follows."[188] From a slightly different vantage point, Levine describes the import of this verse as "phenomenological," designed to bring together two source traditions: (1) to "acknowledge the function of the tabernacle as an oraculum" (Elohist) and (2) cult and sacrificial role of the tent (Priestly)."[189] The sequence of this passage following the tabernacle celebration, however, closely parallels that of Lev 8:1–9:24. After the instructions to offer the same set of sacrifices for priestly ordination—namely sin, burnt, and fellowship—Moses and Aaron entered and exited the Tent of Meeting (9:23); and then the glory of the Lord appeared to the people. Joy and worship ensued. In Num 7:89 divine disclosure followed the bringing of sacrifices. As Harrison summarizes, "The Lord is communicating through Moses to the people and by implication making Himself available to the Israelites when they need an intermediary through whom they can present petitions to him."[190] Additionally, the following chapter may contain a portion of the word received from the Lord in this setting.

---

[186] Exod 33:7–11, in "Tent of Meeting."

[187] Cf. Gray, *Numbers*, 77; Budd, *Numbers*, 85; Davies, *Numbers*, 73; Noth, *Numbers*, 65; J. Sturdy, *Numbers*, CBSC (New York: Cambridge University Press, 1976), 63. Budd subsequently places the passage in juxtaposition with 8:1–4, since "the scene is the same throughout—inside the Tent of Meeting, and the author throughout is drawing on material from Exodus" (*Numbers*, 87).

[188] Davies, *Numbers*, 73–74.

[189] Levine, *Numbers*, 258–59, 264, 266.

[190] Harrison, *Numbers*, 150.

## (1) Menorah Lamp Arrangement (8:1–4)

¹The LORD said to Moses, ²"Speak to Aaron and say to him, 'When you set up the seven lamps, they are to light the area in front of the lampstand.'"

³Aaron did so; he set up the lamps so that they faced forward on the lampstand, just as the LORD commanded Moses. ⁴This is how the lampstand was made: It was made of hammered gold—from its base to its blossoms. The lampstand was made exactly like the pattern the LORD had shown Moses.

**8:1–4** In the continuing celebration focus of the second cycle of the Book of Numbers, this passage provides further clarification of the positioning of the lamps on the tabernacle menorah so as to provide ample light for the altar of incense and the table of the bread of the presence. The placement of this passage in the present cycle sequence serves two purposes. (1) Since in chap. 7 the heads of the twelve tribes bring offerings for the tabernacle celebration, in chap. 8 the head of the tribe of Levi is provided instruction for the proper arrangement of and attendance to the lampstand, which enables the celebration to continue within the tabernacle enclosure.[191] (2) It provides continuity and expansion of previous tabernacle and priestly related material. The lampstand was previously mentioned in 3:31 and 4:9 among the articles covered, placed on a frame, and transported by the Kohathites. The Menorah was necessary to ensure the proper lighting for various cultic activities within the tabernacle. As Milgrom states: "Only when God began to speak to Moses from the Holy of Holies, after the consecration of the tabernacle, did Moses receive the final instructions concerning the operation of the menorah."[192]

The passage commences with the familiar introductory formula of divine speech, *wayĕdabbēr YHWH ʾel mōšeh lēʾmōr*,[193] providing continuity with the previous revelatory sectional introductions and with the tabernacle setting of 7:89. The repetition of this phrase echoes one of the key themes of the Book of Numbers, God revealing himself to his people. Another comple-

---

[191] Wenham, *Numbers*, 94.

[192] Milgrom, *Numbers*, 60.

[193] See discussion of this phrase in "Introduction: Title" section. The emphasis in chap. 5 is on community and marital purity. The introduction in 6:1 coincides with that of 5:1,5,11 in this section of the structural outline, and the extended introduction exactly duplicates the introduction of 5:11-12a. Note the following chart of introductory formulae:

| | | |
|---|---|---|
| 5:1–2a | *wayĕdabbēr YHWH el–Mōšeh lēʾmōr—ṣaw* | *ʾet-bnê yisraʾel* |
| 5:5–6a | *wayĕdabbēr YHWH el-Mōšeh lēʾmōr—dabbēr ʾel bnê yisraʾel* | *ʾîš ô ʾiššah kî* |
| 5:11–12a | *wayĕdabbēr YHWH el-Mōšeh lēʾmōr—dabbēr ʾel bnê yisraʾel* | *wĕʾāmartā ʾălēhem* |
| 6:1–2a | *wayĕdabbēr YHWH el-Mōšeh lēʾmōr—dabbēr ʾel bnê yisraʾel* | *wĕʾāmartā ʾălēhem* |

The introduction of 6:1–2a is an expanded composite of the previous formulae, indicating the climax in the matters of purification for the people of God.

mentary theme evidenced twice here is obedience to the Lord's commands. This theme will recur throughout this cycle and into the beginning of the following section.[194]

Instructions are given through Moses for Aaron to place the seven individual lamps that sat upon the seven tiers of the tabernacle menorah in such a way that they project light "toward the front" (*ʾel-mûl)* of the lampstand. Previously, instructions were given for its construction (Exod 25:31–40), its provision of oil for continuous burning (Exod 27:20–21),[195] and its construction process (Exod 37:17–24). Inasmuch as the menorah was placed near the southern wall of the tabernacle (Exod 26:35), this positioning of the bowl-shaped vessels would cast the light more efficiently northward across the front of the veil separating the holy of holies.

The golden menorah was shaped after the pattern shown Moses on the mountain. It took the form of a seven-branched flowering tree. Emphasis is placed upon the extent to which the menorah was made from hammered gold, for the text reads literally, "Now this is the making of the menorah, hammered gold even from its base and to its blossom[s] hammered it was." Milgrom notes that the term "blossom" *(pirchāh)* "is a collective noun for the 22 floral projections on the central stem and on the six branches of the menorah (see Exod 25:31–36)."[196] This tree of light recalls the tree of life of Gen 2:10; 3:22–24, crafted with seven tiers, symbolic of perfection, and, as Ashley summarizes, "The whole menorah might be said to symbolize God's perfect presence and life illuminating his sanctuary and, through Moses, his people."[197] The writer of Hebrews reminds us that the earthly tabernacle was but a shadowy imitation of the heavenly sanctuary, "an illustration for the present time" (9:9). But the fullness of light dawned "when Christ came as high priest of the good things that are already here, and he went through the greater and more perfect tabernacle that is not man-made, that is to say, not a part of this creation. He did not enter by means of the blood of goats and calves, but he entered the Most Holy place once for all by his own blood, having obtained eternal redemption" (9:11–12).

---

[194] The phraseology in its various forms, expressing that the people did as Yahweh commanded, is found again in 8:20–22 (consecration of the Levites), 9:5 (celebration of Passover), and 9:23 (camp movement according to the Lord's direction through the cloud). The last mention of this theme until after the three rebellion cycles occurs in 10:13 (in accordance with 9:23), the first example of Israelite movement from Mount Sinai. See further note at 1:54.

[195] Cf. also 30:7–8 (tending the lamps while burning incense) and 40:4 (lampstand brought in after ark and shewbread table).

[196] Milgrom, *Numbers,* 60; also "Excursus 17: The Menorah," 367, in which he summarizes the work of C. L. Meyers, *The Tabernacle Menorah* (Winona Lake: Eisenbrauns, 1976).

[197] Ashley, *Numbers,* 166.

## (2) Installation of the Levites (8:5-26)

This passage outlines the purification and ordination of the Levites who assisted the Aaronic priests in guarding and transporting the tabernacle and its furnishings. The conclusion (8:15-26) contains several recurring motifs that were presented in the initial passages outlining the roles and responsibilities of the Levites. In the two Sinai cycles, a progressive expansion of and detailing of matters relating to the Levites is evidenced in the following structural outline.

### The Role of the Levites in the Sinai Cycles

A (1:47-54)   Seminal Instructions to Levites
Appointed in Charge of Tabernacle
Guard—Encamp around It—Transport
Did as YHWH Commanded (1:54)

  B (3:5-10)   Presentation of the Levites to the Aaronic Priesthood
Assist Priests—Guard
Perform the Service (la‘ăbōd ’et-‘ăbōdat, 3:7,8)

    C (3:11-13)   Levites as Firstborn
Belong to Yahweh

      D (3:14-39)   Levite Census (22,000—1 Mo.+)
Duties Expanded—Encampment Order
Gershon—Kohath—Merari

        E (3:40-51)   Israelite Firstborn Census (22,273)
Levites and Firstborn Redemption

      D' (4:1-49)   Levite Census for Service (Thirty–Fifty Yrs.)
Duties Detailed
Kohath—Gershon—Merari

  B' (8:5-14)   Purification and Sanctification of the Levites
Cleanse by Sprinkling w/ Waters of Purification
Sacrificial Offerings—Burnt (Bull) and Sin (Bull)
Presentation to Israel as Wave Offering

A' (8:15-26)   Summary of Levitical Roles
Perform the Service (la‘ăbōd ’et-‘ăbōdat
3:7,8; 4:23,30,47—8:11,19,22)[198]

---

[198] Note that עֲבֹדָה, "service," and its various forms occur additionally 3x in chap. 3, 16x in chap. 4, and verb forms of עבד 6x. See nominal forms in 3:26,31,36; 4:4,19,24,26,27(2),28, 31,32,33(2),35,39,43,47,49. For verb forms see 4:23,24,26,30,37,41,47; 7:5; 8:15,25,26.

Given Wholly to YHWH (3:9—8:14,16)
Firstborn Substitute (3:11–13,41–51—8:16,18–19)
Prevent Death of Israelites (3:10,38—8:19)
Deliverance from Egypt Motif (3:12–13—8:17)
Did as YHWH commanded (1:54; 3:16,39,42,51; 4:37,41,45,49—
    8:20–22)

Priests and Levites 18:1–32
18:1–7      Priests Duties: Responsibility for Offenses versus Sanctuary
            Levites Duties: Assist and Perform Service of Tent of Meeting
18:8–20     Sacrificial Provisions for the Priests (18:8–20)
18:21–24    General Responsibilities of the Levites (18:21–24)
18:25–32    Levite Tithes and Offerings (18:25–32)

At the nexus of this chiastic structure are the dual roles of the Levites as the firstborn substitute for Israel and the organization of the group for service, by census and the delineation of duties in service of Yahweh in the tabernacle. The present pericope recapitulates the major themes of the entire Levitical corpus in the Sinai cycles.

Milgrom has discerned an additional chiastic structure in Num 8:5–22 that has a similar focus:

A  Introduction (8:5–6)
    B  Prescriptive Procedure (8:7–13)
        X  The Rationale (8:14–19)
    B'  Descriptive Procedure (8:20–22a)
A'  Conclusion (8:22b)

In the "Rationale" Milgrom delineates four elements: (1) separates Levites for God, (2) qualify Levites for sanctuary labor, (3) replace firstborn with Levites, and (4) ransom Israelites from sacrilege of encroachment.[199]

**⁵The LORD said to Moses: ⁶"Take the Levites from among the other Israelites and make them ceremonially clean. ⁷To purify them, do this: Sprinkle the water of cleansing on them; then have them shave their whole bodies and wash their clothes, and so purify themselves.**

RITUAL CLEANSING (8:5–7).    **8:5–7**   The ceremonial installation of the Levites involved several ritual acts: (1) purification via sprinkling of the "water of cleansing," (2) shaving of the body,[200] (3) washing of clothes, (4)

---

[199] Milgrom, *Numbers,* 368–69.

[200] Note the comparison with the Nazirite who upon being defiled by touching or being exposed to a corpse shaved his head in the act of reconsecration to resume the vow and again at the conclusion of the period of dedication (6:9,18).

selection of sacrificial animals, (5) presentation of the Levites before the Israelites at the Tent of Meeting, (6) laying on of hands, (7) presentation of Levites to Yahweh as a wave offering, (8) sacrifice of the bull of the sin offering then the bull of the burnt offering for Levite atonement, (9) presentation to Yahweh as a wave offering.

The source of the water is unspecified, though most interpreters have suggested either the water from the bronze laver[201] or the water and ash mixture used in purification of those exposed to the dead. Milgrom relates the "waters of cleansing" in 8:7 (*mê-ḥaṭṭāʾt*, lit. "water of sin") to the "water of cleansing" in 19:1–22 (*mê niddâ - ḥaṭṭāʾt hiwʾ*, lit. "water for impurity, sin [offering] it is" or simply *mê niddâ*, "water for impurity")[202] utilized for the ritual cleansing of an individual after having made contact with a dead person (19:1–22).[203] Levine, on the other hand, suggests that this "identification is improbable."[204] The specific phraseology of 8:7 occurs only here in the Old Testament, suggesting a unique ritual and cleansing element for ceremonial Levitical purification at the point of their installation. Whatever the source, the ritual purification via sprinkling of the water, followed by shaving the body and washing the clothes, symbolically removed any potential ceremonial defilement that might prevent them from fulfilling their roles as gift to Yahweh and the Aaronic priests and service agents for the tabernacle.

The shaving of the body is somewhat parallel to the practice of Egyptian priests, who shaved their bodies every three days as a means of purification.[205] Shaving was part of the purification process for Nazirites (the head, 6:9,18) and for lepers (Lev 14:9). Washing the clothes likewise was performed in the purification ritual for persons having various skin diseases, such as lepers (Lev 13:6–54; 14:9), persons having various bodily discharges (Lev 15:5–27), persons exposed to or eating from a dead human or animal carcass (Lev 11:25; 17:15–16; Num 31:23–24), including those involved in the rituals of the red heifer sacrifice (Num 19:7–21), and persons involved in the Day of Atonement rituals (Lev 16:26–28). Bathing the body

---

[201] Harrison, *Numbers,* 152.

[202] See also Num 19:13,20,21,21; 31:23 also for מֵ. נָדֶּה. The focus in each of these passages is the specific ritual of cleansing of impurity caused by exposure to the dead or to death.

[203] Milgrom, *Numbers,* 61.

[204] Levine, *Numbers 1–20,* 274. Contra Levine, Milgrom states: "These waters cannot be drawn from the tabernacle laver, a sanctum reserved for priestly use only (Exod 30:17–21) and whose waters are called 'holy water' (5:17), an appropriate designation because only those who themselves are holy (priests) are entitled to partake of them. The washing of the priests prior to their consecration was also done with ordinary water (Exod 29:4; Lev 8:6)" (Milgrom, *Numbers,* 61). Other scholars allow uncertainty to remain since no specific ritual of mixing the water with some other element is delineated in the context of 8:5–22. See Ashley, *Numbers,* 170; Wenham, *Numbers,* 96; Gray, *Numbers,* 79; Levine, *Numbers 1–20,* 274–75, 464.

[205] Herodotus, *History,* 11.37.

was also prescribed for the cleansing of lepers (Lev 14:9), persons having or those exposed to those having various bodily discharges (Lev 15:5–27), the priests involved in Day of Atonement rituals (Lev 16:4,26–28), one exposed to the dead (Num 19:19), and one eating from the carcass of a dead animal (17:15–16). The purification ritual sequence of shaving, bathing, and washing (clothes) was practiced among Mesopotamian cultures.[206] The cleansing process ensured ritual purification *(ṭāhēr)*, so that a level of holiness be maintained for those in service for the Lord. A slightly higher level of holiness could be maintained for the priests, for they received new clothes when they were consecrated for service (Lev 8:12–13).

**⁸Have them take a young bull with its grain offering of fine flour mixed with oil; then you are to take a second young bull for a sin offering. ⁹Bring the Levites to the front of the Tent of Meeting and assemble the whole Israelite community.**

**¹⁰You are to bring the Levites before the LORD, and the Israelites are to lay their hands on them. ¹¹Aaron is to present the Levites before the LORD as a wave offering from the Israelites, so that they may be ready to do the work of the LORD.**

PRESENTATION OF LEVITES WITH SACRIFICES (8:8–11). **8:8–11** Instruction concerning the consecration sacrifice of the burnt offering *(ʿōlâ)*, with its accompanying grain and oil elements, is delineated first, followed by the sin offering *(ḥaṭṭāʾt)*. In each case a bull was to be sacrificed, in parallel to the requirement that a bull be sacrificed for the priest (Lev 4:3; 8:2,14; 16:3,6,11). By the laying of their hands upon the Levites, the leaders or elders of the Israelite tribes conveyed identification with them, since the Levites functioned as the substitution for the Israelite firstborn in the service of the sanctuary. Identity for the purpose of sacrificial substitution was accomplished in the Israelite ritual of laying of one's hands upon a sacrificial animal, whereby the rendering of the life of the animal signified the rendering of one's life unto God in consecration, atonement, or celebration (see below).

The presentation of the Levites as a wave offering (8:13) at the entrance to the tabernacle and before the priests and the Israelite congregation fulfills the complement of the three types of sacrifices prescribed in Leviticus: atonement (sin purification), consecration (burnt), and communal (wave). In this setting, instead of the priests offering an animal on behalf of the Levites, the Levites themselves became the wave-fellowship offering in the full display of the community triunity of priests, Levites, and people. The theme of unity and harmony in community is a major emphasis in the two Sinai cycles. As the Levites were servants of God and the priests, so Christians are

---

[206] R. I. Caplice, *The Akkadian Namburbi Texts: An Introduction* (Los Angeles: Undena, 1974). See also Milgrom, *Numbers,* 62.

called to be living sacrifices as servants of Jesus Christ to carry out his will
and purpose (Rom 12:1–2).

<sup></sup>**¹²"After the Levites lay their hands on the heads of the bulls, use the one for a
sin offering to the LORD and the other for a burnt offering, to make atonement
for the Levites. ¹³Have the Levites stand in front of Aaron and his sons and then
present them as a wave offering to the LORD. ¹⁴In this way you are to set the Levites apart from the other Israelites, and the Levites will be mine.**

OFFERING OF SACRIFICES (8:12–14).   **8:12–14**  The instructions outlined in the previous section were carried out faithfully. The laying of the
hands by the Levites upon the heads of bulls symbolized their identification
with the sacrifices offered on their behalf. Hence the rendering of the lives
of the animals before God symbolized the surrendering of the lives of the
Levites for service in the tabernacle. With the Israelite community in wor-
shipful celebration, the two bulls were slaughtered in their proper order on
behalf of the Levites so that they would be able to serve the Lord and the
people in a state of purification and consecration. The bull of the sin offering
was slaughtered first for purification, followed by the burnt offering for consecration, both of which accomplished the atonement *(lĕkappēr)* for the
Levites. The term *kipper* has been translated variously as "ransom," "make
atonement" (KJV, NIV, Harrison, Ashley), "make expiation" (Milgrom),
"serve as redemption" (Levine), and "give protection" (Budd).[207] Milgrom
posits that the sequence of purification rituals in 8:5–22 are designed to
accomplish physical and moral cleansing and that furthermore, "The purification offering is required to purge the sanctuary of the impurities caused by
any of the Levites' moral (and physical) lapses."[208]
Wenham has observed a chiastic pattern within the delineation of the
responsibilities of the Levites in 8:12–19.

A  To Make Atonement for the Levites (8:12)
  B  To Do Service at the Tent of Meeting (8:15)
    C  Given to Me (8:16)
      D  Instead of the Firstborn Male (8:16)
        E  Every Firstborn Mine, Man or Animal
          as in Exodus from Egypt (8:17)
      D'  Instead of the Firstborn of Israel (8:18)
    C'  Given to Aaron and His Sons (8:19)
  B'  To Do Service at the Tent of Meeting (8:19)
A'  To Make Atonement for Israel (8:19)

[207] See Harrison, *Numbers,* 153; Ashley, *Numbers,* 157; Milgrom, *Numbers,* 63; Levine, *Numbers,* 270; Budd, *Numbers,* 89.
[208] Milgrom, *Numbers,* 63. See also Milgrom's "Excursus 19: Levitical 'Kippur' (8:19), *Numbers,* 369–71, and discussion below.

Concerning this structure, Wenham notes: "This chiastic pattern (A B C D E D C B A) helps to underline the points made explicitly in the text ... [and] draws attention to item E at the centre, which recalls the great redemption from Egypt when the firstborn Egyptians died in the last great plague while God passed over the firstborn Israelites (Exod 11–13)."[209] The historical reference to the first Passover in the great salvation event of the Exodus paves the way for the following chapter, which outlines the second Passover in the history of the nation.

[15]"After you have purified the Levites and presented them as a wave offering, they are to come to do their work at the Tent of Meeting. [16]They are the Israelites who are to be given wholly to me. I have taken them as my own in place of the firstborn, the first male offspring from every Israelite woman. [17]Every firstborn male in Israel, whether man or animal, is mine. When I struck down all the first-born in Egypt, I set them apart for myself. [18]And I have taken the Levites in place of all the firstborn sons in Israel. [19]Of all the Israelites, I have given the Levites as gifts to Aaron and his sons to do the work at the Tent of Meeting on behalf of the Israelites and to make atonement for them so that no plague will strike the Israel-ites when they go near the sanctuary."

LEVITE SUBSTITUTIONARY ROLE (8:15–19).  **8:15–19** Clearly the Levites' role in the tabernacle service was multifaceted. For the physical facilities they functioned as guardians, service and maintenance agents, and transporters under the direction of Aaron and the priests. For the community of faith they functioned in the exclusive position as specially dedicated[210] personnel for the sanctuary service, metaphorically the firstborn of the Isra-elites. According to Israelite tradition, the firstborn of animals and plants belonged to the Lord. The Feast of the Harvest (Exod 23:16), also described as the Feast of Weeks (Shavuoth) or Pentecost, was a time for dedication of the firstfruits of the grain harvest. Firstfruits were also offered at Passover (Lev 23:9–14). According to Exod 22:29b–30, God claimed ownership of the firstborn males of the people, as well as cattle and sheep: "You must give me the firstborn of your sons. Do the same with your cattle and your sheep. Let them stay with their mothers for seven days, but give them to me on the eighth day" (Exod 22:29b–30). The firstborn animals were sacrificed, and the firstborn sons were to be redeemed (Exod 13:11–16). The Levites became the substitute redemption price for all Israelite firstborn because of their demonstrated faithfulness to Yahweh during the golden calf incident

---

[209] Wenham, *Numbers*, 95–96.

[210] Emphatic positioning and repetition are utilized in the Hb. text: כִּי נְתֻנִים נְתֻנִים הֵמָּה לִי, "For being given being given [= totally given] they are to me." Levine notes than the "Hebrew *natan* may, in certain contexts, specifically connote compulsory assignment to cultic service" (Levine, *Numbers*, 1–20, 278).

(Exod 32:26–29; Num 3:13). Numbers 18 recounts the notion that the Levites are the redemption price for the firstborn of Israel and states how provision is made for them through the tithes and firstborn gifts of the flock and the field.

The status of dedicatory firstborn was conveyed by the laying on of the hands and the sacrificing of the bulls. As Milgrom has observed, the phraseology of this transference in 8:10,12, and 19 is parallel, with the implication that "the Levites, unlike the priests, do not perform *kippur*, rather *kippur* is performed with them. ... And our text, 8:19, would then imply that the Levites are ransom for Israel, a lightning rod to attract God's wrath upon themselves whenever an Israelite has encroached upon the sancta."[211] The priests guarded the inner sanctum and the holy things of the tabernacle from encroachment by the Levites or the Israelites, and according to Num 18:1–3 they were to bear the responsibility for offenses against the sanctuary and against the priesthood.

**[20]Moses, Aaron and the whole Israelite community did with the Levites just as the LORD commanded Moses. [21]The Levites purified themselves and washed their clothes. Then Aaron presented them as a wave offering before the LORD and made atonement for them to purify them. [22]After that, the Levites came to do their work at the Tent of Meeting under the supervision of Aaron and his sons. They did with the Levites just as the LORD commanded Moses.**

SUMMARY OF THE LEVITE DEDICATION (8:20–22). **8:20–22** A summary of the section contents is presented in the standard structural pattern. Moses (the leader-prophet), Aaron and the Levites (the priests and their assistants), and all Israel (the people) are pictured in harmony as they fulfill God's commands concerning the dedication of the Levites.[212] Ritual purification, washing clothes, wave offering presentation, and atonement sacrifices are carried out in accordance with God's will.[213]

**[23]The LORD said to Moses, [24]"This applies to the Levites: Men twenty-five years old or more shall come to take part in the work at the Tent of Meeting, [25]but at the age of fifty, they must retire from their regular service and work no longer. [26]They may assist their brothers in performing their duties at the Tent of Meeting, but they themselves must not do the work. This, then, is how you are to assign the responsibilities of the Levites."**

---

[211] Milgrom, *Numbers,* 369, 371. See also "Excursus 40: Sacral Responsibility for Encroachment (chap. 18)."

[212] Similar summaries were identified in 1:44–46; 2:34; 3:49–51; 4:46–49; 6:21; 7:48–51. As to the fulfilling of the Lord's commands, see prior notes on 1:19,54; 2:34; 3:3:39,51; 4:37,41,45,49; 5:4; 8:3–4.

[213] The four preterite forms of 8:21 bring added emphasis to this delineation of dedicatory activity.

POSTLUDE: THE LEVITE RETIREMENT (8:23–26). **8:23–26** This section is introduced by the standard introductory divine speech formula, marking it as an additional legislative section.[214] The age of the Levite for service was increased from the earlier thirty to fifty years of age (Num 4:2) to limits of twenty-five to fifty years. A census of Levites thirty to fifty years of age was taken during David's reign, and assignments were outlined for various groups (1 Chr 23:2–5). Yet later in David's reign (1 Chr 23:24–27), during the reign of Hezekiah (1 Chr 31:16–17), and in the early postexilic community, Levites twenty years of age and older were counted and enlisted for Temple service. R. K. Harrison, following A. Noordzij, suggests that the three variants evidence three different historical settings: (1) an age thirty minimum was established for tabernacle transport and service (Num 4:1–49, such as the 38,000 counted for Temple service in 1 Chr 23:2–5), (2) age twenty-five for service in the Tent of Meeting, and (3) the younger age of twenty was after there was no longer a need for transporting the tabernacle.[215]

Ashley suggests the age limit may have been reduced from thirty to twenty-five due to the deaths of Nadab and Abihu. Ashley writes: "This terrible event might well have caused the age limit to be raised more fully to insure against an immature individual assuming the (at least potentially) dangerous role of Levite."[216] A surplus of Levites to carry out the various duties may also have led to the revision. Wenham estimates that this age limit adjustment would have reduced the ranks by about 20 percent.[217] In the LXX the texts in chap. 4 apparently were harmonized to the lower limit.[218]

The focus in the present context is not upon the age of entry into tabernacle service but upon the age of retirement and supplementary service, which came after age fifty. They would no longer dismantle and transport the tabernacle and its furnishing, but they could continue to serve as guards, insuring the sanctity of the holy place.

### (3) The Second Passover: With New Delineations (9:1–14)

**[1]The LORD spoke to Moses in the Desert of Sinai in the first month of the second year after they came out of Egypt. He said, [2]"Have the Israelites celebrate**

---

[214] See above comment on 1:1; also 2:1; 3:5,11,14,40,44; 4:1,17,21; etc, and "Introduction: Outline."

[215] Harrison, *Numbers,* 156–57; A. Noordzij, *Numbers,* BSC (Grand Rapids: Zondervan, 1983), 81. Note also that 1 Chr 23:3 mentions age thirty for the Davidic census, yet 23:24–27 also has a census of those of age twenty and older, in the context of the transporting of the tabernacle to Jerusalem. See also G. Archer, *Encyclopedia of Bible Difficulties* (Grand Rapids: Zondervan, 1982), 134–35.

[216] Ashley, *Numbers,* 176.

[217] Wenham, *Numbers,* 97–98, n. 2.

[218] The LXX readings and DSS readings.

the Passover at the appointed time. ³Celebrate it at the appointed time, at twilight on the fourteenth day of this month, in accordance with all its rules and regulations."

⁴So Moses told the Israelites to celebrate the Passover, ⁵and they did so in the Desert of Sinai at twilight on the fourteenth day of the first month. The Israelites did everything just as the LORD commanded Moses.

⁶But some of them could not celebrate the Passover on that day because they were ceremonially unclean on account of a dead body. So they came to Moses and Aaron that same day ⁷and said to Moses, "We have become unclean because of a dead body, but why should we be kept from presenting the LORD's offering with the other Israelites at the appointed time?"

⁸Moses answered them, "Wait until I find out what the LORD commands concerning you."

⁹Then the LORD said to Moses, ¹⁰"Tell the Israelites: 'When any of you or your descendants are unclean because of a dead body or are away on a journey, they may still celebrate the LORD's Passover. ¹¹They are to celebrate it on the fourteenth day of the second month at twilight. They are to eat the lamb, together with unleavened bread and bitter herbs. ¹²They must not leave any of it till morning or break any of its bones. When they celebrate the Passover, they must follow all the regulations. ¹³But if a man who is ceremonially clean and not on a journey fails to celebrate the Passover, that person must be cut off from his people because he did not present the LORD's offering at the appointed time. That man will bear the consequences of his sin.

¹⁴"'An alien living among you who wants to celebrate the LORD's Passover must do so in accordance with its rules and regulations. You must have the same regulations for the alien and the native-born.'"

**9:1–14** Legislation generally arises out of new circumstances in society or from the need for clarification of an existing law. In this cycle the legislative section is set within the context of the celebration of the second Passover, which was the first Passover celebrated following Yahweh's dramatic redemption of Israel from Egyptian oppression. According to Exod 12:14–20, Passover and the Feast of Unleavened Bread were to be celebrated during the first month throughout their subsequent history.[219] The Passover pilgrimage was a holy assembly necessitating ceremonial purity. But a new circumstance occurred when some of the Israelites were unable to observe the holy day because contact with the dead had rendered them ceremonially unclean.

The passage begins with the standard introductory divine speech formula,[220] and the historical setting is the Sinai desert, a year after the Exodus from Egypt. After the Lord instructs Moses and Moses obeys in instructing the Israelites to celebrate the Passover, the Israelites obey the word of the

---

[219] See also Exod 32:18; Lev 23:4–8; Num 28:16–25; and Deut 16:1–8.

[220] See above comment on 1:1; also 2:1; 3:5,11,14,40,44; 4:1,17,21; etc. and "Introduction: Outline."

Lord through Moses in holding the commemorative celebration. Then the sequence digresses to an issue of ritual purity and the consequent loss of privilege to celebrate the Passover. After seeking counsel from the Lord, Moses returns with the special instructions for those who are in a state of uncleanness on the fourteenth of Abib (Nisan). This word is also introduced with the divine speech formula, marking it as an additional legislative section. In the instruction that follows, two supplementary issues are addressed, the case where one might be on a distant journey on that date and unable to return in time and the case of the resident alien.

The importance of celebration in the national history of God's work on behalf of his people is heightened by the fact that a proviso is made for an alternative celebration for unclean and distant individuals. Passover was the time to remember in every generation the wondrous salvation work of God in the Exodus, especially in the teaching of God's redemption to one's children (Exod 12:14,24–28). Consistent with the response of the people in the first Passover, as "the Israelites did just what the LORD commanded Moses and Aaron" (Exod 12:28), so the second Passover was celebrated in accord with its original instructions, "just as the LORD commanded Moses" (Num 9:5).[221] Harmony among the people of God and obedience to his instructions are key motifs in the Sinai cycles of the Book of Numbers. As these themes are applied to the Passover celebration and the ensuing passage in which the presence of the Lord and his directing of his faithful people through the cloud of smoke by day and fire by night, the passage presents a glorious picture of God and his community in communion together, responding to his commands and ready to move forth into the world to spread his message of redemption and peace.

Extensive instructions were given to Moses regarding the ritual observance of the Passover. The guidelines delineated in Exod 12:1–28 include: (1) the date and timing of the ritual activity (fourteenth of the first month Abib); (2) directions for preparing, sacrificing, cooking, and eating the Paschal lamb; (3) the eating of the accompanying elements of the unleavened bread (to be eaten for seven days) and bitter herbs; (4) removal of yeast from the household; (5) matters related to resident aliens; and (6) instructions for telling the story of God's great redemption to the children throughout their generations. In Lev 23:4–8 matters of the sacred assemblies and the first and seventh day Sabbaths are added. The phraseology of the sacred assembly (*miqrāʾê qōdeš*, "assemblies of holiness" or "of [the] holy") implies a state of ritual purity for the celebrants during the days of the celebration. Hence the concern in the present legislation is that some Israelites found them-

---

[221] See above 8:20–22, in which the phraseology of obedience is utilized as an inclusio; also see commentary on previous examples in 1:54; 2:34; 3:16,39,42,49; 4:49; 5:4; and 8:3–4.

selves unable to celebrate this sacred festival because of uncleanness caused by contact with a corpse, and they knew failure to keep the Passover would be a breach of the covenant instructions.

One key to understanding this quandary the people experienced is the recurrent phrase "presenting the Lord's offering at its appointed time" in vv. 7 and 13. The second citation indicates that failure to carry out the paschal sacrifice at the appointed time and place, unless unavoidably hindered, made one subject to death or banishment from the community.[222] Milgrom notes that the construction of the verse implies that the "penalty applies only to the nonobservance of the fixed Passover" during the first month, but not to the second month alternative. That the Festival of Unleavened Bread was not included as a part of this second month observance is evidenced by the departure of the Israelites from Sinai on the twentieth day of the second month, before the possible completion of a second month Unleavened Bread celebration. Inclusion of the Feast of Unleavened Bread with the second month Passover, however, must have been permissible, as is evidenced by the following example.

Historically, the application of this second month alternative Passover occurred during the reign of Hezekiah (2 Chr 30:1–27). After the reestablishment of service in the Temple, emissaries were sent throughout Judah and the Israelite territories to the North inviting the Israelites of all tribal origins to celebrate the Passover. Matters of purification and distance are both cited in the text as the reason the people were unable to celebrate these festivals in the first month. An adequate number of ritually pure priests was not available to carry out the ritual activity, and many people were so remote when the invitation was sent out that they were yet unable to assemble in Jerusalem. Thousands of celebrants gathered in Jerusalem, and the Levites were enlisted to carry out the obligation for those who were not ritually pure. Hezekiah prayed that the Lord would be merciful to those who ate the Passover in a state of impurity, and God responded positively.

Resident aliens were permitted to commemorate the Passover if they satisfied the essential requirements outlined in Exod 12:43–49. Males had to be circumcised, accepting this as a sign of the covenant relationship to Yahweh and to the Israelite community. This law applied to the native Israelites as well. In the first Passover celebrated in the land after the crossing of the Jordan and establishing the worship center in Gilgal, the men who had been born during the wilderness journey had to be circumcised.

---

[222] Cf. the Lev 19:8 penalty for consumption of any remnant of a fellowship offering on the third day after it was sacrificed. Such remnants were holy to the Lord.

## (4) Pattern of the Journey: The Lord and the Cloud (9:15–23)

[15]On the day the tabernacle, the Tent of the Testimony, was set up, the cloud covered it. From evening till morning the cloud above the tabernacle looked like fire. [16]That is how it continued to be; the cloud covered it, and at night it looked like fire. [17]Whenever the cloud lifted from above the Tent, the Israelites set out; wherever the cloud settled, the Israelites encamped. [18]At the LORD's command the Israelites set out, and at his command they encamped. As long as the cloud stayed over the tabernacle, they remained in camp. [19]When the cloud remained over the tabernacle a long time, the Israelites obeyed the LORD's order and did not set out. [20]Sometimes the cloud was over the tabernacle only a few days; at the LORD's command they would encamp, and then at his command they would set out. [21]Sometimes the cloud stayed only from evening till morning, and when it lifted in the morning, they set out. Whether by day or by night, whenever the cloud lifted, they set out. [22]Whether the cloud stayed over the tabernacle for two days or a month or a year, the Israelites would remain in camp and not set out; but when it lifted, they would set out. [23]At the LORD's command they encamped, and at the LORD's command they set out. They obeyed the LORD's order, in accordance with his command through Moses.

**9:15–23** Following the Passover considerations, which commenced around the fourteenth day of the first month of the second year (9:1–5), the ensuing section reverts back to the time frame of 7:1 and Exod 40:2, the first day of the second month of the second year the sanctuary construction was completed. The present pericope expands upon the description in Exod 40:34–38, but in a rhythmic fashion that hints of an earlier song of praise about the Lord's presence in the cloud and his providing direction through the wilderness. Perhaps this cadence was echoed in song along the stages of the journey when the people joyfully responded to the Lord's leading. As is true throughout this second Sinai cycle, the atmosphere is one of celebration by a community of faith in communion with its incomparable God, by a community following his commands in jubilant obedience.[223]

Wenham has observed the rhythmic character of this passage, particularly in vv. 17–23. He suggests that "the irregularity of the lines show this is not true poetry: rather it is elevated prose, expressing the excitement of the occasion."[224] The pattern of the phraseology, with its occasional cadence and repetition, echoes that of ancient epic poetry of the second millennium B.C., such as that found in the Ugaritic epic of Keret. Harrison notes: "The repetitions in the text, a feature of both Hebrew and Ugaritic literature, give coherence both to the narratives themselves and to the spiritual attitude of the Hebrews that the sources reflected. The people were one in faith, obedience, and action, in a recapitulation of the covenant ratification events at

---

[223] See the earlier comments on 8:1–4 and n. 179.
[224] Wenham, *Numbers,* 100.

Sinai (Exod 24:6–7) that was to become increasingly less frequent as the months passed."[225] Rhythmic overtones are replete within the passage, as the following literal rendering evidences:

| | | |
|---|---|---|
| 15 In the day | it was erected | the tabernacle |
| | it covered the cloud | the tabernacle to the Tent of Testimony |
| and from evening | it was upon the tabernacle | |
| as the appearance of fire until morning. | | |
| 16 Thus it was continually | the cloud covering it | |
| and the appearance of fire at night. | | |

| | | |
|---|---|---|
| 17 So at a word | it went up the cloud | from upon the Tent |
| and after which | they departed | the children of Israel |
| and in the place which | it dwelled there | the cloud |
| there | they encamped | the children of Israel |

REFRAIN
| | |
|---|---|
| 18 At the word of Yahweh | they departed the children of Israel |
| At the word of Yahweh | they encamped |
| All the days which | it was dwelling |
| The cloud upon the tabernacle | they encamped |

| | | |
|---|---|---|
| 19 So when it remained | the cloud | upon the tabernacle many days |
| then they observed | the children of Israel | the watch of Yahweh |
| And so they did not depart | | |

| | |
|---|---|
| 20 So it was that it was | the cloud |
| a few days | upon the tabernacle |

REFRAIN
| | |
|---|---|
| At the word of Yahweh | they encamped |
| At the word of Yahweh | they departed |

| | | |
|---|---|---|
| 21 So it was that it was | the cloud | from evening until morning |
| and it was lifted up | the cloud | in the morning |
| and they departed | | |
| whether day or night | it was lifted | the cloud |
| then they departed | | |
| 22 whether 2 days/month/days | when it remained | the cloud upon tabernacle to dwell upon it |
| they encamped | the children of Israel | then they did not depart |
| But when it rose up | | they departed |

REFRAIN AND CONCLUSION
| | |
|---|---|
| 23 At the word of Yahweh | they encamped |
| At the word of Yahweh | they departed |
| the watch of Yahweh | they observed |
| At the word of Yahweh | by the hand of Moses |

The above structuring of the text highlights the repetitive phraseology and the

---

[225] Harrison, *Numbers,* 164.

parallel developments within the content.[226]

In Exod 40:34–38 the focus is upon the glory of Yahweh filling the tabernacle and Tent of Meeting upon the completion of the tabernacle construction. Clearly the text emphasizes God's presence. Note the following phraseology from Exod 40:34b–35:

| The cloud | covered | the Tent of Meeting |
|---|---|---|
| and the glory of Yahweh | | filled the tabernacle |
| But Moses was not able to enter into | | the Tent of Meeting |
| for the cloud | settled upon | it |
| And the glory of Yahweh | filled | the tabernacle. |

This kind of A B C A′ B′ chiastic structure evidences a mild emphasis on the limitations placed upon entry into the holy of holies in the tabernacle complex. These limitations apply even to Moses. The parallelism of the passage equates the glory of Yahweh with his presence in the cloud covering the tabernacle. Numbers 9:15–23 emphasizes the theme of God's leadership. Journeying and camping are highlighted in Exod 40:36–38 and in Num 33:1–49. The latter passage focuses on the full victory march itinerary that reached from God's demonstrated victories in Egypt to the staging point for the movement across the Jordan River and the commencement of the process of possessing their promised inheritance.

### (5) The Silver Trumpets (10:1–10)

One final step in the preparation for the journey from Sinai was required. Before the momentous departure, two silver trumpets were to be manufactured for calling the people to break camp and line up in their prescribed order to follow the leading of the Lord via the cloud pillar, which symbolized his presence. The movement of the cloud was the divine directive; the sounding of the trumpets was a call for human response.

The text initially lists two purposes for the trumpet sounding: to call an assembly and to announce the departure of the camps. In typical Pentateuchal style, an introductory outline is set forth (10:2), followed by detailed expansion (here twice in 10:3–7 and again 10:8–10). The first set of directions applied to the Israelites in their wilderness setting. The second set of instructions applied to the entrance into the Promised Land and the future celebration of God's blessings therein.

---

[226] The entire passage also could be arranged along the lines of typical Hebrew 3 : 3 (or 4 : 2), 3 : 4, and 4 : 3 metrical phrasing. E.g., the first refrain in v. 18 would be structured as follows:

| ʿal-pî | YHWH | yisʿû běnê-yiśraʾēl |
|---|---|---|
| ʿal-pî | YHWH | yaḥănu |
| kol-yĕmê | ʾăšer | yiškōn |
| heʿānān | ʿal-hamiškān | yaḥănu |

[1]The LORD said to Moses: [2] "Make two trumpets of hammered silver, and use them for calling the community together and for having the camps set out. [3]When both are sounded, the whole community is to assemble before you at the entrance to the Tent of Meeting. [4]If only one is sounded, the leaders—the heads of the clans of Israel—are to assemble before you. [5]When a trumpet blast is sounded, the tribes camping on the east are to set out. [6]At the sounding of a second blast, the camps on the south are to set out. The blast will be the signal for setting out. [7]To gather the assembly, blow the trumpets, but not with the same signal.

GATHERING AND DISEMBARKING THE CAMPS (10:1–7). **10:1–7** This section is introduced by the divine revelatory formula, which once again serves as a major structural and theological marker in the Book of Numbers.[227] References to Yahweh as the revealer of the Law (10:1) and hence the God of Israel (10:10) function as an inclusio for bracketing the section and highlighting the theme of the passage and one of the themes of the two Sinai cycles (1:1–6:27; 7:1–10:10). As the God of the people he is their Instructor in truth and righteousness, their Guide through the wilderness and into the Promised Land, their Savior from all enemies, and their Center of Life in joyous worship.

The silver trumpets' *(haṣōṣĕrôt)* function sometimes is different from the ram's horn *(šôpār)*, yet at other times it is similar. The *šôpār* announced the Day of Atonement throughout the land (Lev 25:9) and later was employed in the march around Jericho (Josh 6:2–21). The bright pitch of the silver trumpet called the people to march through the wilderness, and it was blown by the priest Phinehas in the battle against Midian (Num 31:6). These trumpets likely were styled after those known from Egypt during the Late Bronze Age, examples of which were found among the remains in King Tutankamun's tomb. These instruments were about two feet long with very narrow tubes,[228] and when blown in certain patterns, they emitted a bright and piercing sound that would communicate clearly to the people the desired intent.

The trumpets were blown with varying tones and lengths of blast. The two likely were of slightly different size and produced varying tones, such that when two were sounded for the purpose of calling the whole community together, both could be distinguished. Two lengths of blast were also prescribed, the short blast *(tāqaʿ tĕrûʿa)* for alerting the camps to break camp and disembark on the journey (vv. 5–6) and the long blast *(tāqaʿ)* for calling

---

[227] See discussions of 1:1; 2:1; 3:5,11,14,40,44; 4:1,17,21; etc. and "Introduction: Outline."

[228] The precise dimensions were 22 7/8 in. long, 1/2 in. wide tubes, with the bell flanging to 3 1/4 in. See also H. Hickmann, *La Trompette dans l'Egypte ancienne* (Cairo: Institut francaise d'archaeologie orientale, 1946), 46; F. W. Galpin, *Music of the Sumerians and Their Immediate Successors the Babylonians and Assyrians* (Freeport, N.Y.: Books for Libraries, 1936), 21, and Plate XI, 25; C. C. J. Polin, *Music of the Ancient Near East* (New York: Vantage, 1954), 40–42; I. H. Jones, "Music, Musical Instruments," *ABD* 3:936–37. Silver metallurgy dates to the Early Bronze Age in Mesopotamia (3300–2300 B.C.). A piece of processed silver was hammered into a thin sheet, hammered and molded around a trumpet form, and then heated to temper the metal.

the assemblies together (vv. 3–4).[229] The variant purposes of the two sounds are distinguished clearly in v. 7, in which the assembly is called together by the long blast *(titqĕʿû)*, but not short sounds *(wĕlōʾ tārîʿû)*.

As the cloud pillar would begin to move from the camp location, the priests would sound the short blast of the trumpet, signaling the eastern encampment of the tribes of Judah, Issachar, and Zebulun to disembark on the next stage of the journey. A second short blast alerted the southern tribal camps of Reuben, Simeon, and Gad to follow the Kohathite clan of the Levites. The final two tribal groups would follow: the Gershonites leading the western camps of Ephraim, Manasseh, and Benjamin and the Merarites leading the northern tribes of Dan, Asher, and Naphtali.[230]

**[8]"The sons of Aaron, the priests, are to blow the trumpets. This is to be a lasting ordinance for you and the generations to come. [9]When you go into battle in your own land against an enemy who is oppressing you, sound a blast on the trumpets. Then you will be remembered by the LORD your God and rescued from your enemies. [10]Also at your times of rejoicing—your appointed feasts and New Moon festivals—you are to sound the trumpets over your burnt offerings and fellowship offerings, and they will be a memorial for you before your God. I am the LORD your God."**

RALLYING FOR BATTLE AND REJOICING IN FESTIVAL OFFERINGS (10:8–10). **10:8–10** The blowing of the silver trumpets was limited to the Aaronic priests throughout the history of Israel.[231] In the Dead Sea War Scroll, a major role of the Levites and priests in the great eschatological battle was to sound the trumpets, which were inscribed with such phrases as "God's battle formations for avenging his wrath against all the sons of darkness" and "Peace of God in the camps of his holy one."[232] This section has a future orientation. It describes the time when the people would be in the land, battling against their enemies for occupation and control of the territory God had granted them. There they would celebrate the bounty of God's blessing and the wonder of his salvation activities of the past. Whole burnt offerings for consecrative atonement and peace offerings for community celebration were accompanied by the long blast of the silver trumpets during the pilgrimage festivals of Passover, Pentecost (Shavuoth), and tabernacles (Booths), and during the monthly New Moon rites.

---

[229] The later rabbis defined the long blast (תקע) as three times the length of the short blast (תרועה), Mish. Rosh Hashanah 4.9. Cf. Wenham, *Numbers*, 102; Milgrom, *Numbers*, 74–75, "Excursus 21: Trumpet and Shophar," 372–73.

[230] See the discussion of the encampment arrangements in the commentary on 2:1–3:37.

[231] Hence the phraseology "lasting ordinance [לְחֻקַּת עוֹלָם, *lĕḥūqat ʿôlām*] for you and the generations to come."

[232] See translation of F. Martinez, *The Dead Sea Scrolls Translated*, 97.

In the context of battle, the trumpets served as a prayer by which the covenant relationship between God and Israel was invoked, and thus they reminded soldiers that God remembers and delivers his people.[233] The covenant themes of remembrance, deliverance, and blessing provide continuity with other portions of the Pentateuch. These themes appear from Noah (Gen 8:1; 9:1–17), to Abraham (Gen 19:29), to Rachel (Gen 30:22), to the Israelites in Egypt (Exod 2:24), and even into the realm of exile (Lev 26:40–45). The connection between festival rejoicing and battling against one's enemies echoes the words of the covenant reiteration in Exod 34:22–24.

The concluding phrase of the Sinai cycles, "I am Yahweh your God," sets forth in profoundly plain terms the sovereignty of God over the nation. As Harrison notes, "He is the supreme Lord and ruler of His people Israel. The nation is the visible expression of His existence, personality, and saving power. Without Him they are meaningless, but they have been chosen specifically out of His abundant love to be a witness to the surrounding nations because of their constitution as a kingdom of priests and a holy nation (Exod 19:6)."[234]

---

[233] The battle context is echoed in the war of Abijah vs. Jeroboam I (2 Chr 13:12–18). Victory came as they relied on the Lord for the victory rather than on their military prowess.

[234] Harrison, *Numbers*, 170.

II. THE REBELLIOUS GENERATION IN THE WILDERNESS
   (10:11–25:18)
   1. Rebellion Cycle A: From Sinai to Zin—Decline and Fall of the First
      Generation (10:11–15:41)
      (1) Historical Reference: From Mount Sinai to the Paran Desert
          (10:11–13)
      (2) The Departure from Sinai (10:14–36)
          The Israelite Tribes Depart in Orderly Array (10:14–28)
          Hobab: Departure or Guidance in the Wilderness?
             (10:29–32)
          First Stage of the Journey (10:33–36)
      (3) First Rebellion: General Murmuring (11:1–3)
      (4) Second Rebellion: Complaint about Food (11:4–35)
          The Rabble's Complaint (11:4–6)
          Yahweh's Provision of Manna (11:7–9)
          Moses' Complaint about the People (11:10–15)
          Yahweh Responds: Assemble Seventy Elders (11:16–17)
          Preparation for Provision of Meat: Purification and
             Confession (11:18–20)
          Moses Expresses Disbelief to Yahweh (11:21–22)
          Yahweh Responds to Moses' Disbelief (11:23)
          Preparation for Blessing: Elders Assembled (11:24)
          Yahweh Sends Spirit upon the Seventy Elders (11:25–27)
          Moses Responds to Joshua's Complaint (11:28–30)
          Yahweh's Fresh Provision of Meat (11:31–32)
          Plague upon the People: With Meat in their Mouths
             (11:33–34)
          Second Stage of the Journey: Kibroth Hattaavah to Hazeroth
             (11:35)
      (5) Third Rebellion: Challenge to Moses' Authority (12:1–16)
          Miriam and Aaron's Challenge of Moses (12:1–3)
          God Speaks to Moses, Aaron, and Miriam (12:4–8)
          The Judgment against Miriam (12:9–13)
          God's Reply to Moses, Miriam, and Aaron (12:14–15)
          Third Stage of the Journey (12:16)
EXCURSUS: THE LITERARY STRUCTURE OF NUMBERS 13–14
      (6) Fourth Rebellion: Rejection of the Promised Land
          (13:1–14:45)

Geographical Setting: Arabah of Moab along the Jordan
across from Jericho (22:1)
Cycle I: First Messengers Sent to Balaam (22:2–14)
  Balak Sees—Moses Fears the Numerous Israelites (22:2–4)
  First Messengers Sent (22:5a)
  The Message: Curse the Mighty Israel (22:5b–6)
  Elders of Moab and Elders of Midian Journey to Pethor to
    Meet Balaam (22:7)
  Balaam's Response (22:8)
  God's Encounter with Balaam (22:9–12)
  Balaam's Response of Refusal (22:13)
  Messengers Return Home to Moab (22:14)
Cycle II: Second Set of Messengers Sent to Balaam
  (22:15–21)
  Messengers Again Sent to Balaam (22:15–17)
  Balaam's Response to Balak's New Messengers (22:18–19)
  God's Second Encounter with Balaam (22:20)
  Balaam Departs with Messengers (22:21)
Cycle III: God's Messenger Sent to Balaam (22:22–38)
  Introduction: God's Anger with Balaam (22:22a)
  The Angel of Yahweh Appears (22:22b)
  The Donkey Responds (22:23)
  The Angel of Yahweh Appears Again (22:24)
  Donkey Responds Again (22:25)
  The Angel of Yahweh Appears the Third Time (22:26)
  Donkey Responds the Third Time (22:27)
  God's Third Encounter with Balaam (22:28–35)
  Balak Goes out to Meet Balaam (22:36–38)
Preparation for the First Oracular Event (22:39–40)
Balaam's First Oracle (22:41–23:10)
  Balak Leads Balaam to Bamoth Baal (22:41)
  Balaam Instructs Balak to Prepare Sacrifices (23:1)
  Balak Obeys Balaam (23:2)
  Balaam to Balak: Stand Beside Your Burnt Offering (23:3)
  God Manifested Himself to Balaam (23:4–5)
  Balaam Returns to Balak (23:6)
  Balaam Obeys Yahweh: Speaks the First Oracle (23:7–10)
Balak's Response to Balaam and the Rejoinder (23:11–12)
Balaam's Second Oracle (23:13–26)
  Balak Sacrifices Animals on Seven Altars (23:14b)
  Balaam to Balak: Stand Beside Your Burnt Offering (23:15)
  God Manifested Himself to Balaam (23:16)

## II. THE REBELLIOUS GENERATION IN THE WILDERNESS (10:11–25:18)

Part two of the first volume of the Book of Numbers commences with the departure from Mount Sinai, the setting of revelation to the faithful community, and concludes with the nation at Abel-Shittim in Transjordan, a place of idolatry and immorality. This section contains the heart of the wilderness experience of Israel (from which the Hebrew title of the book, *běmidbār*, "in the wilderness," derives) and presents not merely a geographical movement from Sinai but a theological movement away from God during a period of continual rebellion. Unity turns to disunity, righteousness to rebellion, order to disorder, holiness to harlotry, and hope to despair. The people of God reject his lordship, his land, and his leader.

The rebellion of Israel is presented in three movements: (1) from Sinai to Zin, containing four rebellions and climaxing with the rejection of the land, (2) in the Zin Wilderness, highlighting the rebellion of Korah and Reubenites against the Aaronic priesthood, and (3) from Zin to the Moabite plain, during which Moses rebels, Balaam brings blessing upon Israel, and the people again falter in their idolatry. This extended section, juxtaposed between the two cycles of faithfulness and harmony on one side (1:1–10:10) and the two cycles that look forward to the Promised Land (27:1–36:13), contains two climactic failures, the rejection of the land and the rebellion of Moses. These accounts serve to warn the people that if they continue to reject Yahweh's leadership and that of his prophets as they prepare to enter the Promised Land, their end will be destruction like that of the wilderness generation. On the other hand, if they will serve him faithfully and pursue righteousness and holiness, God will bring great blessing upon his people in and through the land. The Balaam oracles provide an amazing demonstration of God's sovereignty in that even if all the people rebel, including their great prophet Moses, God will work to bring blessing to his chosen ones and manifest his dominion over the nations.

### 1. Rebellion Cycle A: From Sinai to Zin—Decline and Fall of the First Generation (10:11–15:41)

The first rebellion cycle is structured as follows:

1. Historical Setting—The Movement from the Sinai Wilderness to the Wilderness of Paran (10:11–13,29–32).

2. Twelve Tribes—Departure from Sinai (10:14–36),[1] Spies Sent into the Land (13:1–16).

3. Cycle development—Four Rebellions: Grumbling, Quail, Leadership, Land (11:1–12:16; 13:17–14:45).

4. Laws Relating to the Community of Faith: Offerings from the Land, Sin, and Garment Tassels (15:1–41).

This cycle does not contain a separate section dedicated to the priests and Levites and their roles in the community; however, the subsequent cycle has as its major focus the priests and Levites.

The compounding of insurrection accounts would have a resounding effect on future readers and listeners as they heard the text move from the beginning of the victorious march to the successive complaints about gen-

---

[1] This cycle contains a second twelve-tribe listing in 13:1–16, which delineates each of the leaders who were sent from the Wilderness of Paran to explore the land and report back their findings.

eral hardships, food supply, leader, and land. Such rebellion leads to judgment, hardship, and even death. Yet the cycle concludes with a promise and a portentous warning: God will bring them into the land eventually and bless them abundantly, but though unintentional sins may be atoned, outright rebellion and rejection of God's commands will result in severe judgment.

## *(1) Historical Reference: From Mount Sinai to the Paren Desert (10:11–13)*

**¹¹On the twentieth day of the second month of the second year, the cloud lifted from above the tabernacle of the Testimony. ¹²Then the Israelites set out from the Desert of Sinai and traveled from place to place until the cloud came to rest in the Desert of Paran. ¹³They set out, this first time, at the LORD's command through Moses.**

**10:11–13** The introductory historical reference in the cycle outlines the time frame, the parameters of the geographical movement, and the initial response of the people in journeying in obedience to the Lord's command. A triple inclusio (using *wayĕhî, wayyisᶜû,* and *ᶜānān*) brackets the full context of 10:11–36. The introductory *wayĕhî* ("and it came about") extends to 10:35 (first word), with transition into the following section in 11:1. The contexts of these occurrences provide a considerable contrast in spirit and purpose. In the first the people depart Sinai in following the Lord's leadership in the cloud, which was before them and over them. In the second the people are complaining about the hardships of the desert. The bracketing of the journey commencement with *wayyisᶜû* ("and they set out") in 10:12,28 exhibits a people faithfully responding in tribal unity to the Lord's command through Moses. The cloud *(ᶜānān)* provided direction for the people in their journey and protection from the harshness of the sun. After the dialogue between Moses and Hobab, the use of the term in 10:33 reiterates this theme. Then the three terms converge in 10:34–35, *ᶜanan* YHWH *ᶜălêhem ... bĕnāsᶜām / / wayĕhî binsoaᶜ* ("and the cloud of YHWH was over them ... when they set out // and it came about when they set out"), thereby adjoining the themes of God's presence, God's leadership, and the journey of the faithful children of Israel.

The departure from the Sinai Desert takes place on the twentieth day of the second month of the second year after the departure from Egypt, or about a month after the celebration of the Passover described in 9:1–14 and less than two months after the initial setting up of the tabernacle (Exod 40:17). They had camped there for almost a year, seen Moses ascend and descend the mountain, built and dedicated the tabernacle, taken a military census before beginning their victory march toward the Promised Land, and celebrated God's great deliverance in the Passover.

### CALENDAR OF EVENTS FROM THE EXODUS TO THE PLAINS OF MOAB

| Year | Month | Day | Event | Biblical Reference |
|------|-------|-----|-------|--------------------|
| 1 | 1 | 14 | Exodus: Departure from Egypt | Exod 12:1–50 |
| 1 | 3 | 14 | Arrival in Sinai Desert | Exod 19:1 |
| 2 | 1 | 1 | Tabernacle Erected | Exod 40:17 |
| 2 | 1 | 1–12 | Israelite Tribe Dedication Offerings | Num 7:1–89 |
| 2 | 1 | 14–22 | Passover & Unleavened Bread Celebration | Num 9:1–14 |
| 2 | 2 | 1 | First Tribal Military Census | Num 1:1–46 |
| 2 | 2 | 14 | Passover Alternative for Unclean and Distant | Num 9:6–13 |
| **2** | **2** | **20** | **Departure from Sinai Desert** | **Num 10:11** |
| 2 | 2 | 23 | Kibroth Hattaavah (Quail) | Num 10:33; 11:34 |
| 2 | | | Spies Sent from Kadesh in Paran Desert | Num 13:3,26 |
| 40 | 1 | | Miriam Dies in Kadesh in Zin Desert | Num 20:1 |
| 40 | 5 | 1 | Aaron Dies | Num 20:22–29; 33:37–39 |
| 40 | 11 | 1 | Moses Speaks to the People | Deut 1:3 |

The geographical parameters of this initial movement are the Sinai and Paran Deserts (*midbār*, "wilderness, desert"). According to the cycle progression and the travel itinerary (33:16–18), the Israelites camped at Taberah (11:3), Kibroth Hattaavah (11:34–35), and Hazeroth (12:16) on their way to the Paran Desert. As with defining precisely the Sinai Desert and the mountain of Horeb or Sinai, the perimeter of the Paran Desert is difficult to outline. No cartographic mapping remains from this period identifying these regions. From the data described in biblical usage,[2] Paran was west of Midian, east of Egypt, extending southward (or southwestward) toward Mount Sinai, northward toward Kadesh (Barnea), and eastward to the Arabah. Kadesh is associated with both the Paran (13:26) and Zin (20:1) Deserts. Paran seems to encompass a broader geographical area, which would include in its northeast quadrant, the Zin Desert, which is more narrowly defined by the Nahal Zin and its water drainage basin. Hence, the text shifts from the general Paran Desert region (10:17; 13:26) to a context in which greater specificity is needed, as in the listing of the itinerary of the spies (13:21) and the rebellion of Moses (20:1–13; 27:14).

Milgrom notes that in the manner in which the Lord leads the people during the wilderness experience, "the Lord renews the wonders of the Exodus: manna (Num 11:7–9; Exod 16:14–36), quail (Num 11:31; Exod 16:11–13), water from the rock (20:2–13; Exod 17:1–7). And the victories in the Negeb

---

[2] Cf. Gen 14:6; 21:21; Num 10:12; 12:16; 13:3,26; Deut 1:1; 33:2; 1 Kgs 11:18; Hab 3:3. Additionally, the LXX reads Paran instead of Maʿon in 1 Sam 25:1. If Mount Sinai is to be located in the south-central Sinai peninsula (Jebel Musa), then the Paran Desert would include the northeast quadrant of the peninsula. If Mount Sinai is identified with Jebel Sin Bisher, Paran would be more northward and associated with the present-day location of the Wilderness of Paran.

and Transjordan anticipate those in Canaan."[3] Milgrom also notes that 10:11–12:16 functions as a literary unit bracketed by an inclusio regarding the geographic context of the Desert of Paran (10:12 and 12:16). The full context of the cycle within the overarching framing of the Book of Numbers is defined by an inclusio built on the concept of obedience to the Lord's commands, in 10:13; 13:3; 14:41 (negative–disobedience); and 15:40. The net literary structure of the cycle is as follows:

A. Triumphal March from Sinai Begins in Tribal Array (10:11–36)
   "Set out at the Lord's command through Moses"
B. Three Rebellions: The People Complain against God (11:1–12:16)
   General Complaint   Taberah        Burning Fire
   Food Supply   Kibroth Hattaavah   Graves of Craving
   Leadership                         Miriam's Disease
C. Fourth Rebellion Climax: Rejection of the Promised Land
   (13:1–14:45)
   Sending out the Twelve Spies "at the Lord's Command"
   Report of the Spies
   Rebellion and Judgment of the People
D. Sovereign Promise: Offerings from the Land for Yahweh (15:1–41)
   Offerings of Consecration and Communion
   Offerings for Sin
   Garment Tassels: Identity of the People of the Covenant
   "I am the Lord your God!"

*(2) The Departure from Sinai (10:14–36)*

[14]**The divisions of the camp of Judah went first, under their standard. Nahshon son of Amminadab was in command. [15]Nethanel son of Zuar was over the division of the tribe of Issachar, [16]and Eliab son of Helon was over the division of the tribe of Zebulun. [17]Then the tabernacle was taken down, and the Gershonites and Merarites, who carried it, set out.**

[18]**The divisions of the camp of Reuben went next, under their standard. Elizur son of Shedeur was in command. [19]Shelumiel son of Zurishaddai was over the division of the tribe of Simeon, [20]and Eliasaph son of Deuel was over the division of the tribe of Gad. [21]Then the Kohathites set out, carrying the holy things. The tabernacle was to be set up before they arrived.**

[22]**The divisions of the camp of Ephraim went next, under their standard. Elishama son of Ammihud was in command. [23]Gamaliel son of Pedahzur was over the division of the tribe of Manasseh, [24]and Abidan son of Gideoni was over the division of the tribe of Benjamin.**

---

[3] J. Milgrom, *Numbers*, JPS Torah Commentary (Philadelphia: Jewish Publication Society, 1990), 75. Cf. T. Ashley, *The Book of Numbers*, NICOT (Grand Rapids: Eerdmans, 1993), 190–228.

²⁵Finally, as the rear guard for all the units, the divisions of the camp of Dan set out, under their standard. Ahiezer son of Ammishaddai was in command. ²⁶Pagiel son of Ocran was over the division of the tribe of Asher, ²⁷and Ahira son of Enan was over the division of the tribe of Naphtali. ²⁸This was the order of march for the Israelite divisions as they set out.

THE ISRAELITE TRIBES DEPART IN ORDERLY ARRAY (10:14–28). **10:14–28** The first rebellion cycle commences with the orderly departure of the tribes of Israel from the Sinai Desert. The names of the tribal leaders are the same as those delineated as assistants for the census taking in 1:5–15, but in the order of the tribal march outlined in 2:1–3:38. The entire marching order was as follows:

ISRAELITE MARCHING ORDER

| Tribe | Leader | Priestly/Levitical Division |
|---|---|---|
| | | MOSES, AARON, AND PRIESTS |
| Judah | Nahshon ben Amminadab | |
| Issachar | Nethanel ben Zuar | |
| Zebulun | Eliab ben Helon | |
| | | Gershonites and Merarites (carry tabernacle parts) |
| Reuben | Elizur ben Shedeur | |
| Simeon | Shelumiel ben Zurishaddai | |
| Gad | Eliasaph ben Deuel | |
| | | Kohathites (carry holy articles of tabernacle) |
| Ephraim | Elishama ben Ammihud | |
| Manasseh | Gamaliel ben Pedahzur | |
| Benjamin | Abidan ben Gideoni | |
| Dan | Ahiezer ben Ammishaddai | |
| Asher | Pagiel ben Ocran | |
| Naphtali | Ahira ben Enan | |

Seven groups in all followed the cloud/pillar as they journeyed from Mount Sinai into the surrounding wilderness. The order and symmetry of the beginning of the journey from the mountain of God, the place where the nation has been constituted, to the Promised Land, where the fulfillment of that nationhood was to be confirmed, echo the essential themes of the first two cycles of the Book of Numbers: unity and harmony, purity and faithfulness. The people of God move out in harmonious accord, faithful to the Lord's leading through the cloud pillar and the ark of the covenant, the symbols of his presence with them in a miracle of nature and in the focal point of the relationship between God and his people. The ark of the covenant was the place of ultimate mediation between God and humanity, symbolized in the ritual activity of the Day of Atonement (Lev 16:1–34) and in the verbal expression of the covenant in the two tablets placed within the chest covered by the mercy seat. Revelation through the natural world and through his word have been essential elements in the relationship between God and man since the creation, when God conversed with Adam in the garden. Despite Israel's rebellion, God continued to reveal himself in nature and through history in his prophetic revelation to bring about the ultimate promise of redemption in Christ Jesus.

**[29]Now Moses said to Hobab son of Reuel the Midianite, Moses' father-in-law, "We are setting out for the place about which the LORD said, 'I will give it to you.' Come with us and we will treat you well, for the LORD has promised good things to Israel."**

**[30]He answered, "No, I will not go; I am going back to my own land and my own people."**

**[31]But Moses said, "Please do not leave us. You know where we should camp in the desert, and you can be our eyes. [32]If you come with us, we will share with you whatever good things the LORD gives us."**

HOBAB: DEPARTURE OR GUIDANCE IN THE WILDERNESS? (10:29–32). **10:29–32** Both the content and the placement of this passage in the narrative raise several questions for the reader and interpreter. The first concerns the identity of Hobab ben Reuel in light of other passages in Exodus and Judges. The second concerns the literary function(s) of the pericope in the Book of Numbers. The third concerns why Hobab finally agreed to journey with Israel to the land of Canaan. The fourth pertains to the relationship between Israel and the Midianites in Numbers and the Pentateuch.

Hobab is identified by the typically full Hebraic threefold description, "son of Reuel" *(ben Rĕʿuʾēl)*, "the Midianite" *(hammidyānî)*, "father-in-law of Moses" *(ḥōtēn Mōšeh)*. The construct relationship of these three elements, however, raises several question when passages from Exodus and Judges are considered. What is the relationship between Jethro, Reuel, and Hobab? Milgrom has noted three potential solutions: (1) Hobab and Jethro are the same person and Reuel is their father, taking father and daughter in Exod 2:16,18 to mean grandfather and granddaughter; (2) the term *ḥōtēn* means a relation of the bride, hence father-in-law as well as brother-in-law; and (3) Reuel is a clan name, making Hobab the young desert scout of the Midianite clan of Reuel, Moses' son-in-law.[4]

The title "son of Reuel" can mean that he was the direct "offspring" of Reuel or that he belonged to the "clan" of Reuel. The latter definition of clanship is preferred here.[5] The relationship of Reuel to Moses as *ḥōtēn*, usually translated as "father-in-law" is echoed in Judg 1:16 and 4:11, in

[4] Milgrom, *Numbers*, 78.
[5] With Milgrom, *Numbers*, 78.

which these relatives of Moses by marriage are also identified with the Kenites.[6] By comparison with Exod 2:18–3:1, where Reuel is also called Jethro, who is also called the *ḥōtēn Mōšeh*, here he is obviously the "father-in-law" of Moses. Mitchell has demonstrated that the term *ḥōtēn* refers to a "relation by marriage."[7]

The dual identification of Reuel and Hobab as both Midianite and Kenite evidences that the Midianites were not a single clan. As Milgrom notes, they were a "confederation of peoples, one of which is the Kenites."[8] Some earlier scholars took the use of the two names Jethro and Reuel as an indication that Exod 2:18 and 3:11 were from different Pentateuchal sources.[9] But the use of dual names in the Bible and ancient Near Eastern texts has been demonstrated by C. H. Gordon and others to be a common practice in poetic and prose contexts.[10] Wenham's summary provides the simplest solution: "that Moses invited his brother-in-law Hobab to accompany Israel on their journey through Canaan. His father-in-law Reuel or Jethro had earlier given Moses valuable advice about organizing the people."

Moses appealed to Hobab's experience in the desert regions of Sinai and Paran to provide valuable assistance to the Israelites in the harsh conditions

---

[6] The Hebrew construct chain in Num 10:29 is ambiguous, in that *ḥōtēn Mōšeh* may describe either Reuel, the immediate antecedent, or Hobab, the secondary antecedent, or both. See T. C. Mitchell, "The Meaning of the Noun *ḥtn* in the Old Testament," *VT* 19 (1969): 93–112. The NIV (also NAB, NEB, NLT) text hence takes מֹשֶׁה חֹתֵן here as related to Reuel, translating it as "father-in-law of Moses," whereas in Judg 4:11 the same phrase is translated as "brother-in-law of Moses" where the relationship with Hobab is noted. However, the phrase in Judg 4:11 is translated "father-in-law" in NASB, RSV, NKJV.

[7] Ibid.

[8] Also W. J. Dumbrell, "Midian: A Land or a League?" *VT* 25 (1975): 323–37. Milgrom (*Numbers,* 78) notes similarly that Enoch was both a Kenite ("son of Cain," Gen 4:17) and a Midianite (Gen 25:4). Since the term קֵינִי can be translated "smiths," some have taken the Kenites to be a clan of mine workers and copper ore processors, working the accessible copper ore deposits of the eastern Sinai region and the Paran wilderness of the southern Negev. Hence the excavation at Timnaᶜ has evidenced Midianite mining activity in the region at the end of the LB and beginning of the Iron I period.

[9] Cf. G. B. Gray, *A Critical and Exegetical Commentary on Numbers,* ICC (Edinburgh: T & T Clark, 1903), 93; B. Levine, *Numbers 1–20, A New Translation with Introduction and Commentary* AB (New York: Doubleday, 1993), 311; P. Budd, *Numbers,* WBC (Waco: Word), 113. Levine suggests that "we encounter for the first time in the book of Numbers selections from the JE historiographic archive. These sources, generally considered to be earlier than the priestly texts of Numbers, preserve distinctive traditions about the wilderness period, characterized as a time in which relations between the Israelites and their God were generally harsh" (311).

[10] C. H. Gordon, *Before the Bible* (London: Collins, 1962), 236–38. For a thorough treatment of the complexities of this text, see R. K. Harrison, *Numbers,* 177; W. F. Albright, "Jethro, Hobab and Reuel in Early Hebrew Tradition," *CBQ* 25 (1963): 1–11 (Albright suggested that Reuel was the ancestral clan name and not the personal name in Exodus and Numbers); Ashley, *Numbers,* 195–97.

they would face during the coming journey. This setting provides a model of shared human leadership under the ultimate direction of God through the cloud and the positioning of the ark of the covenant. Moses functioned as the director of the people ("by the Lord's command through Moses," v. 13), Hobab provided the desert tracking services ("you know where we may camp in the desert, and you can be our eyes," v. 31), and the Lord led the way ("the ark of the covenant went before them," v. 33).

The positioning of the Hobab dialogue raises several questions about the narrative flow of Numbers. It provides additional background to the historical setting of the cycle, but the content relating to the Midianites also provides another function. A dimension of polarity in the overarching structure of the three rebellion cycles can be observed. On the one hand, the Midianite Hobab can become a participant in and a recipient of the good things Yahweh has promised to his people Israel. The fruit of this promise is evidenced in the later Judges narratives. But on the other hand, another Midianite, the woman Cozbi, would be instrumental in bringing evil through plague and death to Israelites. She was among those (Moabites as well) who enticed many Israelite men into idolatrous worship of the Baal of Peor in the Shittim region near the Jordan River (Num 25:1–18). In the final cycle of Numbers, retribution against the Midianites is carried out because they had been instrumental in leading Israel into idolatry at the instigation of Balaam of Pethor.

Another literary function of the position and content of the present narrative is the close juxtapositioning of the statements regarding God's beneficence ("the Lord has promised good things [*hatôb*, 'the good'] for Israel" v. 29) and his promise of victory ("Rise up, O Lord! May your enemies be scattered," v. 35) opposite the people's rebelliousness in the initial phraseology of chap. 11 ("Now the people complained about their hardships [*ra'*, "evil"]).[11]

The open-ended question raised by the narrative, Will Hobab acquiesce to Moses' request and help lead Israel through the wilderness? provides another literary element to the narrative flow of Numbers in light of the coming events. Will Hobab and this generation of Israelites faithfully follow the Lord through the wilderness to the place that the Lord had said, "It (the Promised Land) I am giving to you"? Or will they grumble, complain, and rebel against God and experience his judgment? Yahweh is willing to lead them and bless them, but will they experience the fullness of his blessing by being his special and unique people and obeying faithfully his commands? The answer would surface in the following chapter.

---

[11] See commentary below on 11:1–3.

<sup></sup>³³So they set out from the mountain of the LORD and traveled for three days. The ark of the covenant of the LORD went before them during those three days to find them a place to rest. ³⁴The cloud of the LORD was over them by day when they set out from the camp.
³⁵Whenever the ark set out, Moses said,
"Rise up, O LORD!
May your enemies be scattered;
may your foes flee before you."
³⁶Whenever it came to rest, he said,
"Return, O LORD,
to the countless thousands of Israel."

FIRST STAGE OF THE JOURNEY (10:33–36). **10:33–36** Just over thirteen months had transpired since God demonstrated his love through the fulfillment of the promise to deliver them from bondage and oppression in Egypt in the Exodus. As they set out on this initial stage of the victory march to the Promised Land, they would travel for three days under the leadership of the Lord through the cloud and the ark of the covenant. Moses functioned as their human commander. The ark moves from the center of the camp (2:17) to the front of the march. As Ashley notes, "The new stage of the journey would have not only the continuity of the old cloud, but also the development of the ark's leadership, symbolizing Yahweh on his throne, to assure people of the divine leadership in the days ahead."[12] The cloud also would serve as shade to protect them through the harshness of the late spring in the Sinai region, where May temperatures rise to 90–100 degrees.

The phraseology "three days' journey" *(derek šělošet yamîm)* is similar to the "eleven days journey" in Deut 1:2 that describes the distance from Mount Horeb (Sinai) to Kadesh Barnea. This kind of phraseology was commonly used in the ancient Near East to indicate distance traveled by armies or caravans, in which the average distance was about fifteen miles per day. Various groups may have traveled more or less than that distance in a given number of days, hence an "eleven days' journey" (=about 165 miles) may take as little as nine or ten days or perhaps as much as eighteen to twenty days, depending on the progress of the group. Hence, the Israelites probably traveled forty to forty-five miles on this initial leg.

The sense of joyous excitement and the hope of victory in the march echoed through the air as the great prophet shouted what R. Allen calls the "Battle Cry of Moses."[13] Fifteen verses later (11:14–15) Moses' victory shout would turn to lament before God because of the rebelliousness of the meat-hungry crowd. Verses 34–36 in the Hebrew text are enclosed in special signs called "inverted *nuns*," which has been taken by many scholars as an

---
[12] Ashley, *Numbers,* 198.
[13] R. B. Allen, "Numbers," EBC (Grand Rapids: Zondervan, 1986), 2:784.

indication that the contents were believed by the Massoretes to be out of their original context and possibly to be transposed.[14] However, the dual acclamations fittingly conclude not only this section of the Numbers narrative but the entire Sinai narrative that began in Exodus 19. There they had witnessed God's miraculous power and experienced the revelatory relationship in the establishment of the nation in the Mosaic covenant. The words proclaimed at the outset of each stage of the journey announced that Yahweh as Lord of the armies of Israel and the heavens would shatter and scatter the enemies of God. In the second colon of the poem in the NIV, the phrase "may your foes flee before you" translates the Hebrew *wĕyānūsû mĕsanʾêkā mippānêkā*, "may they flee—the ones who hate you—from before you," a phraseology that reflects the holy war motif in passages such as Ps 68:1.[15]

The final refrain—"Return, O Lord, to the myriads of thousands of Israel!"—bespeaks the magnitude of the forces of Israel as they prepare to launch into the victory march leading to holy war against Canaan. The parallelism of the dual declarations strikingly proclaims that Yahweh God of Israel is not only Lord of the armies of the heavens but also Lord of the innumerable armies of the children of Israel.[16] Together they are an invincible force as long as they act in unity, harmony, purity, and faith.

Just when things look the brightest and most promising, with the Lord leading the people by the cloud of his presence in a glorious march from the mountain where they have encountered him toward a Promised Land of abundance and freedom, the story takes a dramatic turn. The children of Israel have departed Sinai just forty days after taking the census for the military conscription. Less than a month had transpired after having celebrated God's great deliverance in the Exodus from Egypt during the feasts of Passover and Unleavened Bread and less than a week after the observance of the second month Passover (9:11) for those who had been unclean during the first month celebration. Then suddenly the story veers from victorious march to grievous grumbling and rebellious resistance to God's plan for blessing and fulfillment of promise.

### (3) First Rebellion: General Murmuring (11:1–3)

**[1]Now the people complained about their hardships in the hearing of the LORD, and when he heard them his anger was aroused. Then fire from the LORD**

---

[14] See E. Tov, *Textual Criticism of the Old Testament* (Grand Rapids: Fortress/John Knox, 1992); B. J. Roberts, *The Old Testament Texts and Versions* (Cardiff: University of Wales Press, 1951), 34; *IBHS* 1.5.3c, 18.

[15] Cf. also Josh 7:4; 10:11; etc.

[16] Note "Excursus 1: The Large Numbers in Numbers" in the commentary on 1:44–46. Taking the Hb. *ʿeleph* as armed units, the translation might be rendered "the myriads (countless) battalions of Israel."

burned among them and consumed some of the outskirts of the camp. [2]When the people cried out to Moses, he prayed to the LORD and the fire died down. [3]So that place was called Taberah, because fire from the LORD had burned among them.

**11:1–3** The initial rebellious incident cited in the text sets the stage and pattern for the successive acts of sedition. As noted previously, this method of introducing a section with a formative case is typical of the Book of Numbers and other Pentateuchal texts.[17] As Milgrom notes, "This short section of three verses contains all of the essential elements of all the subsequent narratives describing Israel's complaints: complaint (11:4–5; 12:1–2; 14:1–4; 17:6–7; 20:3–5; 21:5), divine punishment (11:33; 12:9–10: 14:20–37; 16:32; 17:11; 21:7), and immortalizing the incident by giving a name to the site (11:34; 20:13; 21:3; Exod 15:23; 17:7)."[18] This pattern is parallel to the complaint patterns of Exodus and Judges.[19] In most cases Moses also acts as an intercessor before the Lord on behalf of the people.

Direct apposition of 11:1–3 is made with 10:29–36 through linguistic and chiastic features. The first word in the Hebrew text of 11:1, *wayĕhî* ("and so it happened") is also the first word in 10:35. In the earlier text the focus is on the ark of God leading the people out from Sinai with the promise of "good things to Israel" (10:29–32). In the present text the people are complaining continually about the "hardship" (lit. "evil," *ra*) of the desert. Hence the following chiastic (contrastive) outline is presented:

A  Yahweh has promised good things *(tōb)* for Israel (10:32)
   B  *wayĕhî* So it happened that the ark set out (10:35)
      C  Rise up, O Lord (10:35b)
      C'  Return, O Lord (10:36)
   B'  *wayĕhî* So it happened that the people complained (11:1)
A'  Evil *(ra)* in the hearing of Yahweh (11:1)

The murmuring and complaining by the people of the hardships of the wilderness had been a continuous character trait since the initial stage of their departure from Egypt. They complained when the Egyptians approached just before the sea was parted before their eyes (Exod 14:10–18). They grumbled at Marah because of the bitterness of the waters (Exod 15:22–26). Additional parallels have been noted by Milgrom in that the grumbling at Marah occurred after a three-day march from Egypt, followed

---

[17] See above comments on 1:1. Cp. also the pattern of the Othniel pericope in Judg 3:7–11.
[18] Milgrom, *Numbers,* 82.
[19] See Exod 16:2–16; 17:1–7; Judg 3:7–11; etc. The expanded pattern of this form in Numbers is as follows: (1) complaint or rebellion of the people, (2) judgment from Yahweh, (3) people cry out to God (or Moses) in the midst of danger, (4) Moses intercedes on behalf of the people, (5) God mercifully responds by removing or lessening the judgment, (6) the location is given a memorial name representing the nature of the event.

by the quail incident (Exod 16:1–36). The Taberah grumbling occurred after a three-day march from Sinai, then followed by the quail provision and judgment (11:4–34).[20] The people complained soon after they had seen God's miraculous work in the crossing of the Red Sea and again soon after leaving the place where they had encountered him and entered into a special covenant relationship with him. In the Book of Numbers this action constitutes a shift in the structural and theological movement of the book from one of unity, faithfulness, holiness, and celebration to one of discord, rebellion, and dissatisfaction with who they were as the people of the covenant. The text translates literally "and so the people became like those murmuring evil in the ears of Yahweh." God had promised goodness and blessing; the people responded with rebellious complaints.[21]

The Lord was merciful in sending his purging fire only to the perimeter of the Israelite camp. Many could have been consumed had the judgment been meted out in the midst of the encampment. The outskirts of the camp were where uncleanness and ceremonial impurity were relegated.[22] A judgment of fire from the Lord often comes by means of lightning, though the mode of igniting the fire is not specified. This form of judgment parallels that meted out against Nadab and Abihu (Lev 10:1–3), though that fire came out from the midst of the tabernacle.

Faced with the potential disastrous circumstances of an all-consuming fiery judgment, the people quickly shifted from complaining before God to pleading with Moses to intercede with God on their behalf. The verb *wayyitpallēl*, translated "and he prayed" in the NIV, denotes intercessory prayer that was a continuous action on the part of God's chosen leader. The Lord in his mercy was responsive to the fervent prayer of this righteous man, whom Milgrom calls the "archetype of prophetic intercessor,"[23] and the fiery judgment abated (lit. "sank down," *tišqaʿ*). Further destruction and death were

---

[20] Milgrom, *Numbers*, 82; and "Excursus 24: The Structure of Chapter 11–12," 376–80. Note the following structure observed by Milgrom:

| Complaint 1: Taberah (11:1–3) | Complaint 2: Hazeroth (12:1–15) |
|---|---|
| a People complain (11:1a) | a' Miriam and Aaron Complain (12:1–2a) |
| b God hears, fumes, punishes (11:1b) | b' God hears, fumes, punishes (12:2b,4–5,9–10) |
| c People appeal to Moses (11:2a) | c' Aaron appeals to Moses (12:11–12) |
| d Moses intercedes (11:2ba) | d' Moses intercedes (12:13) |
| e Appeal answered (11:2bb) | e' Appeal answered (12:14) |
| f March delayed | f' March delayed (12:15) |

[21] Hb. כְּמִתְאֹנְנִים is a *hithpoel* participle from the root ʾnn (only here and Lam 3:39) with the *k* preformative. Allen rightly describes this preformative as asseverative (see R. Williams, *Hebrew Syntax* [Toronto: University Press, 1968], sec. 261). Hence the translation, "Yet the people became truly murmurous" is derived.

[22] Exod 19:16; Lev 14:8; 16:26,28; Num 5:1–4.

[23] Milgrom, *Numbers*, 83.

diverted from the people, who were saved by the mercy and grace of God.

The place was memorialized as Taberah ("burning" or "it [the fire] burns") because the fire of Yahweh had burned the outskirts of the camp in judgment against his people. The site is mentioned again only in Deut 9:22, in the context of Moses' recounting the history of Israel's unfaithfulness in a challenge to the people to fear the Lord and to obey, serve, and love him (Deut 10:12–13). Taberah is omitted in the journey itinerary of Numbers 33:16–17, perhaps being subsumed under the heading of Kibroth Hattaavah in the subsequent context.

### (4) Second Rebellion: Complaint about Food (11:4–35)

Complaints about food and water supply were among the most common reasons for the dissatisfaction that festered among the people and led to outright rebellion against God and his appointed leader Moses. The present passage closely parallels both Exod 16:1–36 and 18:15–26, the former in the provision of manna after the entire community voiced its discontent concerning their lack of food in the Sin Desert just a month after their Exodus from Egypt,[24] and the latter in the appointment of leaders to aid in dealing with legal matters among the people. In Exodus 16 food came as a blessing from God after the murmuring of the people; however, in Numbers 11 the provision of the quail after the inordinate craving of the people was a form of punishment.[25] In Num 11:10–30 the seventy elders are endowed with the Spirit of God and prophesy as a result, whereas in Exodus 18 the focus is on the need for settling legal disputations.

The structure of the chapter, with the intertwining of the two themes of food supply and leadership, has presented a challenge to interpreters. The material has been analyzed variously in recent studies. Ashley has outlined the material of Num 11:4–12:15 in three cycles of three basic thematic elements in the structure of the story. Using the designations A = Food Theme, B = Leadership, T = Transition, he outlines the section as follows:

| | | |
|---|---|---|
| A 11:4–13 | A' 11:18–20 | A" 11:31–34 |
| T 11:14–15 | T' 11:21–23 | T" 11:35 |

---

[24] Source critics have generally assigned the present text to JE and Exod 16 to P, though Gray theorized that the reference to manna in Num 11 may have been "due to an editor who composed it freely on the basis of tradition or transferred it from the account in JE of the first giving of the manna" (*Numbers*, 101). Budd suggested that the Yahwist took "a story of the provision of the quail and elaborated it" (*Numbers*, 125). More recently B. Levine suggested that the use of הָעָם in the Book of Numbers was an indicator of the JE source (*Numbers 1–20*, 319). The deconstructive approach of source critics such as Gray, Budd, and Levine ignores the consistent internal structures within the given chapters of Exodus and Numbers. The canonical text reflects unity of structure and theology rather than disparate sources or embellished traditions.

[25] Ashley, *Numbers*, 207.

B 11:16–17      B' 11:24–30        B" 12:1–15

Milgrom presented a basic chiastic structure to 11:4–34 in his "Excursus 24: The Structure of Chapters 11–12." God's answer to the complaints of the people and Moses was discerned as the focal point of the chiasm.[26]

A People's Complaint: Meat (11:4–10a,b)
  B Moses' Complaint: Assistance (11:10b–15)
    X God's Answer to Both Complaints (11:16–24a)
  B' God Authorizes Elders: Diminishes Moses (11:24b–30)
A' God Supplies Meat: Punishes Complainers (11:31–34)

An alternative structural analysis of the text, however, evidences a slightly different focus for the pericope: a crisis of belief in the dialogue between Moses and Yahweh over the nature of the people and the ability of the Lord to supply the needs of his people. The following chiastic outline gives rise to this central element. Highlighted are several of the Hebrew terms derived from the root *ʾāsap* ("to gather"), which are keys to understanding the structure and interpreting the content of the passage. Note the following outline of usage: (1) a "gathered group" of people (11:1) instigate the murmuring; (2) Yahweh instructed Moses to "gather" seventy elders (11:16) who were spiritual leaders; (3) at the crux of the chiasm, Moses uses the term in a rhetorical question regarding the inadequacy of "gathering" all the fish in the sea to satisfy the cravings of the people; (4) Moses faithfully "gathered" the seventy elders (11:24); and (5) the term is used twice to describe the gluttonous group who "gathered" no less than thirty-eight bushels of quail per person. A second key term is *taʾăwāh* ("craving, desire"), used in v. 4[27] to describe the intense desires of the people, and in vvv. 34 and 35 for the naming of the site. One might call this form of derived nomenclature a talionic toponym, in which the name matches the form of judgment and the original sinful desires of the people.

A second factor contributing to this interpretation is the larger balancing of the elements that compose the larger chiastic structure of the combined three cycles of rebellion. The complaint and disbelief of Moses in this chapter finds its chiastic parallel in Numbers 20. In the latter passage Moses' frustration, evidenced throughout his travels with the Israelites, turns to outright rebellion in which he violates the holiness of God. Furthermore, the Miriam and Aaron rebellion in Numbers 12 is paralleled by the death of both brother and sister of Moses in Num 20:1 and 22–29.

---

[26] What is presented is a simplified version of Milgrom's outline (*Numbers*, 377–78).

[27] The term is used twice in v. 4, verbal + cognate accusative nominal forms, and twice at the end of the pericope.

Chiastic Structure of the Second Rebellion:
A Crisis of Belief for Israel and Moses

A  Complaint of the People (*hā'sapsūp*): Craving (*hit'awwū ta'ăwâ*)
Meat (vv. 4–6)
  B  Yahweh's Former Provision: Manna Quality (vv. 7–9)
    C  Moses' Complaint about People: Why Trouble (*hărē'ōtā*) Your
    Servant? (vv. 10–15)
      D Yahweh Responds: Assemble (*'espâ*) Seventy Elders (vv. 16–17)
        E  Preparation for Provision of Meat: Purification and Confession
        (vv. 18–20)
          F    Moses Expresses Disbelief to Yahweh (vv. 21–22)
          F'  Yahweh Responds to Moses' Disbelief (v. 23)
        E'  Preparation for Blessing: Elders Assembled (*wayye'ĕsōp*)
        (v. 24)
      D'  Yahweh Sends Spirit upon the Seventy Elders (vv. 25–27)
    C'  Moses Responds to Joshua's Complaint (vv. 28–30)
  B'  Yahweh's Fresh Provision of Meat *(wayya'aspū . . . 'āsap)*
  (vv. 31–32)
A'  Plague upon the People (*qibrōt hata'ăwâ,* "Graves of Craving")
(vv. 33–34)

**⁴The rabble with them began to crave other food, and again the Israelites
started wailing and said, "If only we had meat to eat! ⁵We remember the fish we
ate in Egypt at no cost—also the cucumbers, melons, leeks, onions and garlic.
⁶But now we have lost our appetite; we never see anything but this manna!"**

THE RABBLE'S COMPLAINT (11:4–6). **11:4–6** The second rebellion
was instigated by an assembly *(hā'sapsūp)* of those who had departed from
Egypt along with the Israelites, and the discontent spread rapidly through
the camp of the children of Israel.[28] The initial term used to describe this
mutinous group is a hapax legomenon built on the verb *'āsap,* "to gather."
This faction seems to be distinguished in the text from the Israelites. The
group's offense is described as an intense craving (lit. "they were craving a
craving") for meat and other produce that they had eaten in Egypt. In the
midst of their austerity in the desert setting, they had become nostalgic over
their former food supply while forgetting the bondage and oppression from
which the Lord had so dramatically delivered them. The failure to remember
God's grace and faithfulness was the second aspect of their rebellion.

Goshen in the eastern Nile delta was practically the breadbasket of Egypt,
lush with vegetation[29] and abounding with natural and man-made canals

---

[28] Exod 12:38; Deut 29:1; Josh 8:35.
[29] Deut:11:10.

whose waters teemed with fish and were replete with nutrients for abundant crop production. The foods listed were among the most commonly grown in the region, namely cucumbers *(qiššūʾîm)*, melons *(ʾăbaṭṭiḥîm)*, leeks *(ḥāṣîr)*, onions *(běṣālîm)*, and garlic *(šûmîm)*.[30] All require ample amounts of water via irrigation for abundant crop production. But now the arid desert setting was taking its toll on the people, for their bodies were becoming dehydrated. The Hebrew phrase *napšēnû yěbēšâ,* translated in the NIV as "we have lost our appetite," is better translated "our bodies are dried up" or "our lives are vanquished." The claim that they saw nothing but manna was perhaps an exaggeration, considering the goods that were brought from Egypt. But the description of manna that follows in the text demonstrates that their claims were spurious.

**[7]The manna was like coriander seed and looked like resin. [8]The people went around gathering it, and then ground it in a handmill or crushed it in a mortar. They cooked it in a pot or made it into cakes. And it tasted like something made with olive oil. [9]When the dew settled on the camp at night, the manna also came down.**

YAHWEH'S PROVISION OF MANNA (11:7–9). **11:7–9** Over against the people's lustful yearning for a variety of foods, the reader is reminded of God's faithful provision of the life-sustaining manna, which he had commenced providing just a month after their departure from the land of bondage. Concerning this inclusion, Milgrom has noted, "This botanical and culinary description of the manna was deliberately inserted here to refute each point in the people's complaint."[31] The manna, which had been God's gracious gift to his people, had now become detestable to them.

Precise identification of the substance called manna with known agricultural products of ancient or modern times is somewhat tentative. The association with coriander seed is likely, since the seed is used for flavoring similar to sesame or poppy seeds.[32] Physical description seems to be intended in the comparison to bdellium, a loan word in English from the Semitic root *budulchu* (Akk.) via the Greek *bedellion,* generally associated

---

[30] For a summary of data on these vegetables in ancient Israel and Egypt, see O. Borowski, *Agriculture in Iron Age Israel* (Winona Lake: Eisenbrauns, 1987), 137–38.

[31] Milgrom, *Numbers,* 84.

[32] W. E. Shewell-Copper, "Coriander," *ZPEB* 1:960; Borowski, *Agriculture in Iron Age Israel,* 98; *Fauna and Flora of the Bible* (New York: United Bible Societies, 1980), 110–11. Also cf. J. M. Renfrew, *Palaeoethnobotany: The Prehistoric Food Plants of the Near East* (New York: Columbia University Press, 1973), 171, who notes that though coriander has not yet been found in excavations of Syro-Palestine, samples have been unearthed in the tomb of Tutankhamun in the Valley of the Kings and in the Neo-Assyrian fortress of Nimrud.

with a pale yellow or white aromatic resin.[33] Generally manna has been associated with a by-product of the tamarisk tree found in northern Arabia. B. Childs notes: "There forms from the sap of the tamarisk tree a species of yellowish-white flake or ball, which results from the activity of a type of plant lice *(Trabutina mannipara and Najococcus serpentinus)*. The insect punctures the fruit of the tree and excretes a substance from this juice. During the warmth of the day it (the substance melts), but it congeals when cold. It has a sweet taste. These pellets or cakes are gathered by the natives in the early morning and, when cooked, provide a sort of bread. The food decays quickly and attracts ants. The annual crop in the Sinai Peninsula is exceedingly small and some years fails completely."[34] The present passage also assumes prior knowledge of the substance based upon their initial and continuing experience, first described in Exod 16:4–35. Whether this known modern food source is or is not equivalent to the manna of the Israelite desert sojourn experience, the provision for the host of Israel was a miraculous gift of God, an outpouring of his gracious, loyal love for his people.

The hardened resinous manna could be ground on millstones or in a mortar, typically made from basalt or very hard limestone, and then boiled and formed into cakes. The taste is compared to the rich creamy olive oil that comes from the upper layer of the first pressing of the olives.[35] In Exod 16:31 the taste of manna cakes is compared to honey.[36] As in Exodus 16 the manna appeared in the early morning, blown in from the heavens (sky) during the night so that enough could be gathered for the daily consumption after the morning dew had evaporated.

**[10]Moses heard the people of every family wailing, each at the entrance to his tent. The LORD became exceedingly angry, and Moses was troubled. [11]He asked the LORD, "Why have you brought this trouble on your servant? What have I done to displease you that you put the burden of all these people on me? [12]Did I conceive all these people? Did I give them birth? Why do you tell me to carry them in my arms, as a nurse carries an infant, to the land you promised on oath to their forefathers? [13]Where can I get meat for all these people? They keep wailing to me, 'Give us meat to eat!' [14]I cannot carry all these people by myself; the burden is too heavy for me. [15]If this is how you are going to treat me, put me**

---

[33] See Milgrom, *Numbers*, 84,308; D. Bowes, "Bdellium," *ZPEB* 1:494; *Fauna and Flora of the Bible*, 96.

[34] B. S. Childs, *The Book of Exodus*, OTL (Philadelphia: Westminster, 1974), 282. See also F. S. Bodenheimer, "The Manna of Sinai," *BA* 10 (1947): 2–6.

[35] The former term in the Hb. phrase לְשַׁד הַשָּׁמֶן refers to cream (cf. Akk. *lishdu*, CAD, "L," 9:215), hence "the cream of the olive oil." The term occurs only here and in Ps 32:4, "My juices were sapped as in the drought days of summer."

[36] The LXX apparently conflates Num 11:8 and Exod 16:31, translating the Hb. as ἐγκρὶς ἐξ ἐλαίου, "a cake made with oil."

to death right now—if I have found favor in your eyes—and do not let me face my own ruin."

MOSES' COMPLAINT ABOUT THE PEOPLE (11:10–15). **11:10–15** Upon hearing the cries of dissatisfaction from the people, God was considerably angered,[37] and Moses was distressed (lit. "and in the eyes of Moses evil/contemptible"). The widespread nature of the discontent is highlighted by the phrase "every family wailing," as the initial grumbling of the rabble spread like wildfire through the camp. Moses is incensed at the people for making his role as a leader an unbearable one and toward Yahweh for assigning him this overwhelming burden of leadership. His reaction is pointed primarily toward God, challenging the divine decision to place him in the parental role of providing for this nation. It was not he who gave birth to the nation, and hence it was not he who bore the responsibility for their welfare.

R. Allen calls this passage "Moses' Lament" and outlines the poetic character of the verses.[38] But the words of Moses reflect more than standard lament; they contain the emotive effusion of discontent, despair, and even the seeds of rebellion. In most psalms of lament, expressions of faith and hope come forth out of the midst of desperation. Here Moses has lost sight of God's greatness and grace, of his ability to provide for the needs of his people. The Hebrew phraseology of Num 11:11 is the same as that of Exod 5:22, except there Moses evidences a selfless concern for his oppressed brethren. Now the focus is on his own misery.[39] The usage of pronouns and pronominal suffixes in these verses heightens the effect of Moses' disavowing of his perceived role of a nurse caring for an unweaned child:

"Why have **You** brought this evil *(hăreʿōtā)* upon **Your** servant? (v. 11)
What have **I** done to displease **You**,
That **You** put the burden of all **this** people on **Your** servant?
Did **I** conceive *(hārîtî)*[40] all **these people**? (v. 12)
Did **I** give them birth??
Why do **You** tell **me** to carry them in **my** arms as a nurse carries an infant,
   to the land **You** promised on oath to **their** forefathers?
Where can **I** get meat for all **these people**? (v. 13)
**They** keep wailing to **me**, Give **us** meat.
**I** cannot carry all **these people** by **myself**, the burden is too heavy for **me**! (v. 14)
If this is how **You** are going to treat **me**, (v. 15)

---

[37] Note the burning anger of God יְהוָה אַף־חַר וַיִּחַר parallels 11:1, and later 11:33.

[38] Allen, "Numbers," 791–92.

[39] Milgrom, *Numbers,* 85. Cf. Exod 5:22 הַזֶּה לָעָם הֲרֵעֹתָה לָמָה to the present context in Num 11:11 לְעַבְדֶּךָ הֲרֵעֹתָ לָמָה.

[40] The term הָרִיתִי is from the root הרה rather than רעע but seems to be a play on words with the vocalization of הֲרֵעֹתָ in v. 11. Was Moses calling the conception of this people by God a baneful deed?

Put **me** to death right now
If **I** have found favor in **Your** eyes,
then do not let **me** face *(ʾerʾeh)*[41] **my** own ruin *(bĕrāʿātî).*

The movement starts with Moses emphatically blaming God (you, your) for bringing evil upon his servant, moves to him disavowing any relationship to his fellow Israelites (these, them), and ends with him desiring that Yahweh take his life (I, me, myself) so that he would not have to face further tribulation. Note also how the twofold use of forms of the Hebrew *raʿ* ("evil, calamity, ruin") in the subsection vv. 11 and 15 form an internal inclusio.

Moses' despair concerning his life's lot parallels those of other notables in Israel's history. Job cursed the very day of his birth in the midst of his season of suffering, and Jeremiah likewise bemoaned his conception and birth in the midst of the shame he experienced in being beaten and imprisoned by Pashhur in Jerusalem.[42] At this point in his leadership ministry, Moses faced a crisis of faith and dependency, preferring death as a favor from God rather than continue to have the responsibility of directing such a rebellious rabble. The Lord responds with grace and yet also with judgment. Moses would get some relief, but in the long run this was just the beginning of troublesome years to come.

[16]**The LORD said to Moses: "Bring me seventy of Israel's elders who are known to you as leaders and officials among the people. Have them come to the Tent of Meeting, that they may stand there with you. [17]I will come down and speak with you there, and I will take of the Spirit that is on you and put the Spirit on them. They will help you carry the burden of the people so that you will not have to carry it alone.**

YAHWEH RESPONDS: ASSEMBLE SEVENTY ELDERS (11:16– 17). **11:16–17** The Lord instructed Moses to appoint seventy elders from among the leaders who were also officers among the Israelites. The Hebrew term *šōtēr* ("official" or "scribal assistant") is attested in the Akkadian *šatāru*, "to write," and Aramaic *šĕtārāh*, "document," suggesting a kind of official with scribal function within a given group. The term is also used of the Israelite foremen whose responsibility it was, under the pharaoh's taskmasters, to meet the daily quotas of mudbrick production in Egypt (Exod 5:14–19). These men probably would have had a recording function in their service for maintaining records of production.[43] Harrison has suggested that the *šōtĕrîm* were responsible for the compilation of the Book of Numbers

---

[41] Similar to the earlier play on words, Moses is asking not to see, ראה, his own demise, רעע.
[42] Job 3:1–13; 10:1–7; Jer 20:1–18.
[43] Cf. also their function in Deut 16:18 as judges. See also R. D. Patterson, "שׁטר," *TWOT* 2:918–19.

from smaller sections of scroll material.[44] Seventy of these men, a number suggestive of a full complement of persons, would be endowed with the Spirit of God for assisting Moses in bearing the burdens of the people as spiritual leaders. The spiritual dimension differentiates this group from those appointed for administrative and judicial tasks in Exod 18:25–26.

Moses' role was to gather (*'espâ*) the seventy elders and present them before the Lord at the entrance to the Tent of Meeting, the standard place for revelatory activity from the Lord and where priests and Levites were anointed and commissioned for service.[45] The Lord would then descend in the cloud and speak to Moses, the key individual in the revelatory activity of Yahweh. In the process he would impart to them some of his spirit, which heretofore had been endowed only upon Moses. The descending of the Lord to speak with his servant face-to-face is described in Exod 33:9–11, when the cloud pillar would settle on the Tent of Meeting that Moses originally pitched outside the Israelite camp.[46]

[18]"Tell the people: 'Consecrate yourselves in preparation for tomorrow, when you will eat meat. The LORD heard you when you wailed, "If only we had meat to eat! We were better off in Egypt!" Now the LORD will give you meat, and you will eat it. [19]You will not eat it for just one day, or two days, or five, ten or twenty days, [20]but for a whole month—until it comes out of your nostrils and you loathe it—because you have rejected the LORD, who is among you, and have wailed before him, saying, "Why did we ever leave Egypt?"'"

PREPARATION FOR PROVISION OF MEAT: PURIFICATION AND CON-FESSION (11:18–20). **11:18–20** After instructions for Moses' appointment of the elders, directions for the larger populace ensued. Consecration was required prior to receiving the blessing from the Lord, but this blessing would have dreadful repercussions. Milgrom notes that the Hebrew term *hit-kaddĕshû* ("sanctify yourselves") is a "technical term used by the non-priestly texts for the process of purification through bathing in order to receive the presence of the Lord the following day in the sanctuary or in a

[44] Harrison, *Numbers,* 15–21.
[45] Lev 8:2–3; Num 8:9; 16:18; 20:6; 27:3; etc.
[46] Note also the "descending of the LORD" in Gen 11:5; 18:21; Exod 3:8; 19:20; Num 11:25; 2 Sam 22:10; Ezek 44:2; Zech 14:4, by which the Lord enters into the realm of humanity to observe and to act, sometimes to empower certain individuals. Several of the judges of Israel experience the empowerment of the Spirit of God, such as Othniel (Judg 3:10), Gideon (Judg 6:34), Jephthah (Judg 11:29), and Samson (Judg 14:19; 15:14). Cf. also 1 Sam 10:6; 2 Kgs 2:9,15; Isa 63:11; Joel 2:28. The Spirit of God descended in the form of a dove at Jesus' baptism (Matt 3:16–17; Mark 3:10–11; Luke 3:22; John 1:32–33), and then as a mighty wind on those gathered in the upper room at Pentecost (Acts 2:1–4).

theophany."[47] Ritual purity was necessary before offering sacrifices, or as preparation for celebrating festivals like Passover, the wondrous memorial to God's deliverance of the people from bondage in Egypt.[48] Now many wanted to return there. In this context ritual bathing and clothes washing were the obligatory prerequisites for theophany. The same manner of preparation was carried out by the people when they readied themselves for God's descending upon Mount Sinai and the Ten Commandments were issued (Exod 19:10–11).

The contrast between the true source of blessing is heightened further when the people ascribe "goodness" to their situation in Egypt. When the people were preparing to leave Sinai, Moses told Hobab that God had promised good things to Israel. God was Israel's true source of goodness, but now they claimed things were better for them in Egypt (lit., "For goodness is for us in Egypt"). To attribute goodness to the land of bondage, oppression, and despair was blasphemous, evidence of their brazen rebellion against God; they had rejected his goodness. Now he would turn that which was formerly a means of great blessing, the abundant provision of quail for their meat supply, into a means of cursing and plague. The supply from God would be far more than abundant, lasting for a whole month. The pattern in the dialogue comes to a dramatic climax in the intensifying sixfold enumeration of the supply period for the quail—not one, two, five, ten, or even twenty days, but for an entire month (over twenty-nine days) they would experience the oxymoronic fullness of God's wrathful blessing. The savory meat they so lusted after would become loathsome to them.[49] The nature of the punishment would echo their rejection of God.

**[21]But Moses said, "Here I am among six hundred thousand men on foot, and you say, 'I will give them meat to eat for a whole month!' [22]Would they have enough if flocks and herds were slaughtered for them? Would they have enough if all the fish in the sea were caught for them?"**

MOSES EXPRESSES DISBELIEF TO YAHWEH (11:21–22). **11:21–22** The dialogue between Moses and Yahweh continues, with the servant prophet despairing over both the magnitude of the crowd of people that must

---

[47] Milgrom, *Numbers*, "Excursus 27, Sanctification: Preparation for Theophany," 384–85. Milgrom (p. 88) also notes that underlying this instruction is the intimation that the coming sacrifice will be Israel (vv. 33–34).

[48] Exod 12:Num 9:6–13.

[49] Ashley noted a play on words between אַפְּכֶם, "your nostrils [noses]," and the term מְאַסְתֶּם, "you have rejected, forsaken" (*Numbers*, 212). Milgrom suggests that the language describing effusiveness of the meat coming out of the nose is a reference to the stench that will permeate the atmosphere of the camp as a result of the rotting flesh of so many quail in the camp (*Numbers*, 88).

be fed with this promised supply of quail and the inability to satisfy the continuous craving and grumbling, even if God himself is the supplier. First Moses reminds the Lord concerning the matter of the six hundred thousand footsoldiers, plus the women, children, Levites, and others, a potential total of two to two and a half million people.[50] An overabundance of meat for a month for twenty thousand would have been an unbelievably miraculous phenomenon in the midst of the Sinai desert, where occasional quail runs may number ten thousand or more in a season. For over two million such a surfeit of poultry would have been an even greater incomprehensible and astronomical quantity. But the fact was that the people were simply looking for an opportunity to complain about their lot in life. Moses noted that even their full cattle, sheep, and goat supplies that they had brought forth out of Egypt, as well as the totality of the fish in the sea, would not have been sufficient to quench the lustful and ravenous appetites of this company.

**[23]The LORD answered Moses, "Is the LORD's arm too short? You will now see whether or not what I say will come true for you."**

YAHWEH RESPONDS TO MOSES' DISBELIEF (11:23). **11:23** In his dolor and disbelief Moses had challenged God's ability to meet the needs of the people in the wilderness. He had questioned God's essential beneficent nature. But the Lord responds quickly and succinctly to the disputation with a rhetorical question, "Is the hand of the Lord shortened?" Has somehow the right hand and arm of Yahweh, which delivered the Israelites from the bondage of Egypt and brought them through the sea on dry ground, been reduced in power and capacity? Absolutely not! So now the reluctant Moses and the recalcitrant people were about to experience once more the magnitude of God's power of blessing and the veracity of his promise to supply the needs of his people. In spite of the numerous life illustrations the Israelites and the assembly had experienced, they had not yet come to the realization of the promise the apostle Paul later echoed in Phil 4:19, "My God will supply all your needs according to his glorious riches in Christ Jesus."

**[24]So Moses went out and told the people what the LORD had said. He brought together seventy of their elders and had them stand around the Tent.**

---

[50] As for the comments on the size of the Israelite company and the census of the military in chaps. 1 and 26, see commentary on Num 1:46 and the "Introduction." Taking אֶלֶף literally as "1,000," the total given here as 600,000 would be a round figure, rounded downward similar to that delineated in Exod 12:37. If אֶלֶף is taken alternately (also literally) as "military troop or division," then the number would be rounded upward from the specific 598 military division comprised of 5,550 soldiers, with a total Israelite population of 20,000. Cf. C. Humphreys, "The Number of People in the Exodus from Egypt: Decoding Mathematically the Very Large Numbers in Numbers I and XXVI," *VT* xlvii/2 (1998): 196–213.

PREPARATION FOR BLESSING: ELDERS ASSEMBLED (11:24).
**11:24** Though Moses had serious doubts about the outcome of the events ahead, he responded in obedience and followed through with the first stage of the instructions the Lord had given him (11:16). He instructed the people in that which the Lord had instructed him. The term used is *wayyĕdabbēr*, which when used with Yahweh as speaker means "revelatory instruction" and with Moses as speaker indicates his faithful obedience in relating those instructions to the people.[51] He presumably went out from the entrance to the tabernacle to gather a group of seasoned assistants. In contrast to the ravenous assembly *(hā'sapsūp)*, that insatiable assembly who incited rebellion throughout the camp, a group of devout elders was assembled *(wayye'ĕsōp)* who would aid Moses in the spiritual oversight of the people.[52]

[25]Then the LORD came down in the cloud and spoke with him, and he took of the Spirit that was on him and put the Spirit on the seventy elders. When the Spirit rested on them, they prophesied, but they did not do so again. [26]However, two men, whose names were Eldad and Medad, had remained in the camp. They were listed among the elders, but did not go out to the Tent. Yet the Spirit also rested on them, and they prophesied in the camp. [27]A young man ran and told Moses, "Eldad and Medad are prophesying in the camp."

YAHWEH SENDS SPIRIT UPON THE SEVENTY ELDERS (11:25–27).
**11:25–27** The promise of the sharing of the Spirit of God with the seventy elders, as delineated in v. 17, is now fulfilled. With Moses in his traditional position at the entrance to the tent, the place of revelatory activity, and with the elders of the people stationed around the Tent of Meeting in close proximity, the symbolic presence of the Lord in the form of the cloud descends and speaks with Moses. As the Lord conversed with his special servant, he apportioned some of his Spirit with which he had endowed Moses among the surrounding elders. The language of the Hebrew text evidences that this distribution of the Spirit was carried out by God and as such did not diminish that portion of the Spirit that had rested upon Moses previously.[53] The elders' authority was derived through Moses, and as such they functioned as an extension of the ultimate authority endowed upon Moses by the Lord. It was God's Spirit who was disseminated among the seventy elders, not that of Moses, and thus not lessened. This impartation was a unique gift of God upon the leaders and scribes that would enable them to assist Moses in giv-

---

[51] See Num 17:6 (17:21 Hb.).

[52] Note the play on words using the two forms of the root אסף in 11:4 הָאסַפסֻף and in the present context וַיֶּאֱסֹף.

[53] The Hb. phraseology in v. 25 indicates that some of the Spirit that was "upon" Moses was placed by God "upon" the seventy, שׁ אִישׁ שִׁבְעִים עַל וַיִּתֵּן עָלָיו אֲשֶׁר מִן־הָרוּחַ וַיָּאצֶל הָרוּחַ עֲלֵיהֶם כְּנוֹחַ וַיְהִי הַזְּקֵנִים.

ing spiritual oversight and supervision to this large rebellious congregation.

The immediate impact of the impartation of the Spirit of God that came to rest upon the seventy elders was an outpouring of prophetic activity by its recipients. The meaning of the term "prophesy" *(wayyitnabĕʾû)* in this verse has been interpreted variously. Many scholars take it as an example of the early form of ecstatic prophetic activity,[54] parallel to 1 Sam 10:6–13 and 19:18–24, when Saul (and his men) was endowed with the Spirit of God and began to prophesy in such a manner that was identifiable as prophetic activity. Some "abnormal" behavior resulted when the Spirit of God came upon Saul, whereby he stripped off his clothes, prophesied in some fashion, and then fell asleep in that condition and remained so all that night (19:23–24). The immediate behavior of the seventy elders upon receiving the Spirit, whereby they could be identified as prophets, soon subsided. The text itself does not give an indication of ecstatic activity or any other clear picture of the behavior that accompanied their engaging in prophetic utterance.[55] After that one occasion in which spiritual endowment resulted in a prophetic manifestation, the text says they did not continue to exhibit that activity.[56] That is not to say that their newly appointed role of spiritual leadership was discontinued, but only that this identifiable evidence of their spiritual anointing was not repeated.

The process of the bestowing of the Spirit and the response of the seventy reflects a pattern of God's working that is carried out in ultimate fashion in the outpouring of the Holy Spirit upon those who were gathered in Jerusalem on the Day of Pentecost.[57] When the manifestation of the Spirit in what appeared to be tongues of fire came to rest upon the believers, they began to speak ecstatically in a number of foreign languages that were understood by the mixed multitude of Diaspora Jews who were gathered for this pilgrimage festival.

---

[54] Milgrom, *Numbers,* 89; Levine, *Numbers,* 313,325; Gray, *Numbers,* 113. Contra, see Harrison, *Numbers,* 189.

[55] The *hithpael* form used here, וַיִּתְנַבְּאוּ, is also employed in 1 Kgs 22:8 of Micaiah giving advice to Jehoshaphat; of Uriah (of Kirjath Jearim) in Jer 26:20; of Jeremiah himself in Jer 29:27. Yet it is also used in conjunction with non-Israelite prophets, such as those of Baal and Asherah on Mount Carmel (1 Kgs 18:29), and the false prophets of Jeremiah's day who prophesied by Baal (Jer 23:13).

[56] The Hb. וְלֹא יָסָפוּ, translated in the NIV as "but they did not do so again," is a common usage of the verb יָסַף. It is often used in combination with other verbs to denote a continuation or repetition of the given action of the primary verb. Cf. Gen 8:12, וְלֹא־יָסְפָה שׁוּב־אֵלָיו עוֹד, "and it (the dove) did not return to him again." See also GKC §120d, on the usage of the term to denote the nonrecurrence of an action; *IBHS* §36.3.1b, 656.

[57] If the number of believers gathered in Jerusalem in Acts 1:15 can be carried over into the Pentecost context of Acts 2:1–12, then the number receiving the Holy Spirit on that occasion would have been about 120.

The efficacy of this impartation of the Spirit was realized when two of the men who had been registered among the seventy elders, yet who had not joined the others when they gathered around the Tent of Meeting, were also empowered and prophesied in the same manner. Why they remained in the camp is not revealed in the text, but the inclusion of this account evidences the power of God in accomplishing his purposes among his people. Eldad and Medad became witnesses to the larger community of the manifestation of the Spirit among the elders. An unknown young man (perhaps Joshua, who voices the complaint of v. 28) gave witness of this phenomenon back to Moses, who was still gathered at the Tent with the other sixty-eight. Since a young person was able to observe and report the prophetic activity of Eldad and Medad, undoubtedly many others in the neighborhood of their tents were witnesses to the event. Eldad and Medad apparently had been registered (*baktūbîm*, "among those written") among the chosen elders who were appointed to this position of spiritual leadership.[58] The outward manifestation of the Spirit validated their appointment, evidenced their anointment, and evoked an announcement.

The Hebrew terminology used to describe the movement in this passage has led a number of scholars to posit that the Tent of Meeting was a separate facility outside the camp from the tabernacle, which stood in the center of the camp. In v. 26 Eldad[59] and Medad were said to have not "gone out" to the Tent but remained "in the camp" *(bammaḥăneh)*, where they prophesied. At the conclusion of the episode, Moses and the elders returned to the camp. Based upon source-critical interpretation, Gray suggested that the combined evidence of vv. 24,27, and 30, paralleling Exod 33:7–11, "implies that the tent was outside the camp."[60] Yet in Exodus 33 the placement of the Tent of Meeting outside the camp preceded the construction of the tabernacle (Exod 40:1–38) and the organization of the Israelite camps around the combined tabernacle and Tent of Meeting (Num 2:1–3:38). In v. 24 Moses "went out" *(wayyēṣē)* from his encounter with the Lord and told the people of the coming intervention, which seems to view the encounter as taking place at a point of revelation within the camp. In summary, the Hebrew verb *yāṣāʾ* describes the movement "out of" one context into another, and not necessarily toward the inside or outside of the camp.

**[28]Joshua son of Nun, who had been Moses' aide since youth, spoke up and said, "Moses, my lord, stop them!"**

---

[58] The registration of the seventy elders seems to have involved an official written record, perhaps carried out by someone from the larger group of shoterim among the Israelites.

[59] The name Medad occurs as "Modad" in the Samaritan Pentateuch and the LXX.

[60] Gray, *Numbers,* 114–16; and commentary on Num 12:5. See also Levine, *Numbers 1–20,* 329; Cf. Milgrom, *Numbers,* 94; also "Excursus 28, The Tent of Meeting: Two Traditions," 386–87. Similar use in Num 12:5 of the Hb. אצי is cited in support of this argument.

²⁹But Moses replied, "Are you jealous for my sake? I wish that all the LORD's people were prophets and that the LORD would put his Spirit on them!" ³⁰Then Moses and the elders of Israel returned to the camp.

MOSES RESPONDS TO JOSHUA'S COMPLAINT (11:28–30). **11:28–30** Joshua ben Nun was introduced as a leading warrior in the first battle against the Amalekites (Exod 17:8–14). When Moses met with the Lord at the Tent of Meeting, which was at first outside the camp of Israel (Exod 33:7–11), the young Joshua remained at the Tent even after Moses had departed. Only a few months later Joshua acted as an assistant to Moses when the Spirit came upon the seventy elders. He became defensive when the report came concerning Eldad and Medad's prophetic activity, for he presumably felt he was acting on behalf of Moses, the Lord, and the elders gathered at the Tent, defending the exclusivity of this divine act.[61] Calling for his master Moses to force Eldad and Medad to cease and desist their prophesying, Joshua perhaps sees these two men who were not directly under Moses' supervision as a threat to Moses' leadership.

Moses' resonant response to Joshua contrasts considerably with that of his earlier expressions of complaint and despair. Instead of condoning his servant's zeal in defending his position of authority, Moses commends the Lord's movement among the two elders and expresses the desire that all the people would be so endowed with his Spirit. In doing so they would evidence the aspirations of a closer relationship to God. An undercurrent in Moses' response may be his own desire for further relief from the heavy responsibility of leadership. Centuries later the prophet Joel would echo the words of Moses as he proclaimed to the people of Judah concerning the coming Day of the Lord:

I will pour out My Spirit on all people,
  Your sons and your daughters will prophesy,
  Your old men will dream dreams,
  Your young men will see visions.
Even on my servants, both men and women,
  I will pour out My Spirit in those days. (2:28–29)

Peter recalled these words in his sermon in Jerusalem on the Day of Pentecost when the Spirit was poured out on the believers gathered (Acts 2:16–21). Later the apostle Paul would seem to reiterate Moses' sentiment when he shared with the struggling church at Corinth that Christians would "eagerly desire the greater gifts," especially the gift of prophecy (1 Cor 12:27–31; 14:1–5).[62] Had

---

[61] The Hb. הַמְקַנֵּא suggests that Moses interprets Joshua's reaction as one of jealousy in which the accusing party strongly desires to possess something another person possesses.

[62] Cf. Paul's desire that all speak in tongues and even more that they prophesy, that the church would be edified (1 Cor 14:5).

the people of Yahweh been responsive to the Spirit of God rather than to their sinful appetites, the wilderness journey would have taken on a totally different atmosphere.

**[31]Now a wind went out from the LORD and drove quail in from the sea. It brought them down all around the camp to about three feet above the ground, as far as a day's walk in any direction. [32]All that day and night and all the next day the people went out and gathered quail. No one gathered less than ten homers. Then they spread them out all around the camp.**
**[35]From Kibroth Hattaavah the people traveled to Hazeroth and stayed there.**

YAHWEH'S FRESH PROVISION OF MEAT (11:31–32).    **11:31–32**    As a divinely ordained gale had blown across the sea, bringing deliverance to the Israelites and destruction to the pursuing Egyptian army, so now a wondrous wind brought a quintessential quantity of quail to blow across the camp, bringing sustenance to the faithful but destruction to the craving. A strong east wind parted the sea, and now an east wind and a south wind from the heavens descended upon the camp with mounds of meat. The psalmist described in greater detail the account:

> He let loose the east wind from the heavens,
> and led forth the south wind by his power.
> He rained meat down on them like dust,
> lying birds like sand on the seashore.
> He made them come down inside their camp,
> all around their tents.
> They ate till they had more than enough,
> for he had given them what they craved.
>
> But before they turned from the food they craved,
> even while it was still in their mouths,
> God's anger rose against them,
> he put to death the sturdiest among them,
> cutting down the young men of Israel. (Ps 78:26–31)

The passage builds upon the parallel usage of the Hebrew *rûaḥ* as spirit or wind. The Spirit of God had blessed the seventy elders with prophetic gifts, and now the wind of God would bless the people with food provisions. The magnitude of the two forms of blessing was copious. God had previously supplied his people with quail in the early days of their journey from Egypt to Mount Sinai (Exod 16:13). Now in the early days after their departure from the mountain of God, he supplied them with an even greater outpouring of his power than they imagined or wanted. Writers throughout history have described the movement of quail across the Sinai generally northward in the spring, as we have in the present context, and southward in the fall. Arabs earlier in this century are known to have had between one and two million quail in the autumn migration of these small birds, known by the genus *coturnix coturnix* or *coturnix vulgaris*.[63] The extraordinary quantity of quail were swept in from the sea, probably from the Gulf of Aqaba (Elath) if the wind were from the east, and then downward toward the encampment of Israel.

The magnitude of the quail is measured in three ways: the breadth of distribution, the depth of the piles, and the amount of individual collection. The wind left behind (*wayyiṭōš*, "leave, let lie") the quail that fell upon the camp and its environs for a day's journey in each direction. The phrase "a day's journey" *(kĕderek yôm)* defines a distance of about twelve to fifteen miles, hence the flurry of quail spread over an area of more than four hundred square miles.[64] The reference to a height of "about three feet (two cubits) above the ground" *(kĕʾammātayim ʿal-pĕnê hāʾāreṣ)* may refer to the height of the birds' flight—two cubits above the face of the ground"—or the depth of the piles of quail—two cubits upon the face of the ground.[65] The latter is to be preferred on the basis of context, which seems to have the intent of portraying the volume of small fowl, and the former demands that the verb be repointed as *wayyiṭōś* from the rare Hebrew verb *ṭûś*, meaning "flutter," as in the flight pattern of the birds. Each person gathered at least ten homers of the birds over a two-day period, a volume estimated at between thirty-eight and sixty-five bushels. The homer, which was composed of ten ephahs, was the largest dry volume measure in the Hebrew vocabulary.[66] Some of the birds were eaten right away, while most of them were spread out around the camp, presumably for drying the meat after cleaning and salting them.[67] The Greek

---

[63] For a discussion of quail, see O. Borowski, *Every Living Thing: Daily Use of Animals in Ancient Israel* (Walnut Creek: AltaMira, 1998), 151–55. Fowling using low-slung nets is known from several Egyptian tomb murals, including those of Kagemni at Saqqarah dating to the sixth dynasty and two New Kingdom reliefs from Deir el-Bahri. Israelite fowling using nets is mentioned in Hos 7:12. The fourteenth century Arab writer Al-Qazwini described the fowling activity of the people El-ʿArish in the north coastal Sinai. Cf. J. Gray, "The Desert Sojourn of the Hebrews and the Sinai-Horeb Tradition," *VT* 4 (1954): 148–54. Cf. also Aristotle, *The History of Animals* in *The Complete Works of Aristotle: The Revised Oxford Translation,* ed. J. Barnes, Bollingen Series LXXI.2 (Princeton: University Press, 1984), I:934.

[64] Milgrom notes that Ibn Ezra suggested that the terminology of "around the camp" means that the quail fell outside the camp and thus were a curse to Israel, whereas the manna from God fell within the camp where the Lord's presence resided.

[65] Those interpreting the reference to the height of flight include Ashley, *Numbers,* 218; Budd, *Numbers,* 129; Harrison, *Numbers,* 190–91. Among those taking the reference as depth include Levine, *Numbers,* 314; Wenham, *Numbers,* 109; Milgrom, *Numbers,* 92.

[66] Estimates for the volume of the חֹמֶר range from 3.8–6.5 bushels. Cf. M. A. Powell, "Weights and Measures," *ABD* 6:903; and O. R. Sellers, "Weights and Measures," *IDB* 4:834–35. Milgrom notes *Targ. Jon.* with 5.16 bushels or 220 liters. Cf. Wenham–500 gallons=2,200 liters, 109; Harrison–60 bushels, 191; and Gray–100 bushels, 119; Josephus–175 liters/homer, *Ant.* 3.6.6§142.

[67] For further background on the phrase שָׁטוֹחַ סְבִיבוֹת הַמַּחֲנֶה, "spread them out around the camp" (for drying), cf. the use of שָׁטַח, "to spread out for drying" in Ezek 26:5 and possibly Jer 8:12.

historian Herodotus described the Egyptian practice of salting and laying the fish and fowl out on the sands in the hot sun for drying the meat.[68]

<sup></sup>**<sup>33</sup>But while the meat was still between their teeth and before it could be consumed, the anger of the LORD burned against the people, and he struck them with a severe plague. <sup>34</sup>Therefore the place was named Kibroth Hattaavah, because there they buried the people who had craved other food.**

PLAGUE UPON THE PEOPLE: WITH MEAT IN THEIR MOUTHS (11:33–34). **11:33–34** While the people were processing and eating the quail, the Lord's anger burned against many of the rabble *(hāʾsapsūp,* v. 4) who had gathered *(wayyaʾaspû,* v. 31) too much, and many were struck by a severe plague and died. While the meat was still between their teeth and the supply most plenteous, they were struck down with a disease, probably food poisoning, since the derived toponym of the site (Kibroth Hattaavah) was based on the term used to describe their sinfulness *(taʾăwâ,* "craving"). Talionic justice, judgment fitting the offense, was the portion of those who had protested against the Lord. Like so many places in Israel's history, place names reflected their experience with their God. As Bethel ("house of God") derived from Jacob's encounter with God in the central hill country, and Taberah ("burning") reminded the Israelites of Yahweh's fiery holocaust, so now the graves of the ravenous would become a didactic memorial to the results of rebellion against Yahweh their God.

SECOND STAGE OF THE JOURNEY: KIBROTH HATTAAVAH TO HAZEROTH (11:35). **11:35** The rebellion cycles in the Book of Numbers recall the process of the Israelite journey from their close encounter with God at Mount Sinai to the plains of the Jordan Valley across the river from Jericho and the Promised Land. The next stop in the story of rebellion would be Hazeroth, where the brother and sister of Moses would challenge his divine authority. The precise location of either site is conjecture, and both are dependent upon the location of Mount Sinai. If Mount Sinai is located at Jebel Musa in south central Sinai peninsula, then the location of Hazeroth might be associated with the Wadi Hudeirat region, forty miles northeast of Jebel Musa. If Mount Sinai is to be located at Jebel Sin Bisher or the environs, then Kibroth Hattaavah and Hazeroth would be situated along the route eastward across the central Sinai region toward Elath and Mount Seir.

The reverberating succession of rebellion narratives in this first cycle of insurrections against God continues with a challenge to the leadership authority and the special character and calling of the prophet Moses. Milgrom even suggests that "the uniqueness of Moses is the sole theme of this

---

[68] Herodotus, 2.77.

chapter."[69] The first rebellion was a general complaint against God in the setting of the wilderness, and the second was a protest over the quality of the food supply God had so faithfully provided in that austere desert location. Now the protest becomes more narrowly focused. Now it is a struggle within the family of Moses concerning his position within the community and his unique relationship with God. If the event recounted in this chapter follows in chronological order that of the previous chapter, the physical setting is at Hazeroth, on the way from Mount Sinai to the Wilderness of Paran, in the northeast quadrant of the Sinai peninsula.

The narrative begins in a manner reflecting the typical human attempt to camouflage one's true intent by stating an issue that might gain a more sympathetic hearing. Complaints about ethnicity were presented to hide the true challenge to the authority of God's chosen leader, a rebellion that was ultimately a challenge to the sovereignty of God over the affairs of humanity. The initial stated basis of the complaint was an ethnic question concerning Moses' wife and perhaps the issue of the purity of the Israelite community. This pretense of a principle of purity might gain a more sympathetic hearing from God, Moses, and the people, especially in light of the previous context of rebellion, in which a mixed multitude (11:4) of Israelite and non-Israelites instigated the insurrection that resulted in numerous deaths from a severe plague brought by the Lord. Their perception that ethnic purity might have been the key issue in this previous instance might have led them to believe that they had spiritual insight equivalent to that of their younger brother. Another connection between this and the previous chapter is the example provided by Eldad and Medad receiving prophetic insight directly from God and independent of Moses (11:26–27). But the real reason for their disputation was a deeper one with potentially more grave consequences.

### (5) Third Rebellion: Challenge to Moses' Authority (12:1–16)

[1]Miriam and Aaron began to talk against Moses because of his Cushite wife, for he had married a Cushite. [2]"Has the LORD spoken only through Moses?" they asked. "Hasn't he also spoken through us?" And the LORD heard this.

[3](Now Moses was a very humble man, more humble than anyone else on the face of the earth.)

---

[69] Milgrom, *Numbers*, 93. He notes furthermore that this theme "is reflected in the challenge to his authority (v. 2); his humility (v. 3); God's affirmation of his uniqueness (vv. 6–8); the punishment of Miriam (vv. 9–10); and Moses' successful intercession on her behalf (vv. 11–15). The previous chapter (11:14–17,24–31) has contrasted Moses with the ecstatics. This chapter contrasts him with the prophets, in particular Miriam and Aaron who, based on their own prophetic gifts, contest Moses' leadership.

MIRIAM AND AARON'S CHALLENGE OF MOSES (12:1–3).   **12:1** The section begins with the feminine singular form of the verb *watĕdabber*, implicating Miriam as the leader in this endeavor. As noted numerous times in the earlier chapters, the masculine singular form *wayĕdabber* is used regularly to refer to the process of divine instruction from Yahweh, or of Moses' response in subsequent instruction of the people.[70] Hence the very use of verb form draws the attention of the reader/hearer to that which is distinctive or out of the ordinary in the flow of the narrative. The literary structure of this passage is highlighted by the variant use of the preposition *b-* with the verb *dibber*, which can be translated "speak with" or contrastingly, "speak against" depending upon the context. She was backed by her brother Aaron, who previously had supported the seditious acts of the people in the erection and worship of the golden calf.[71] Wenham notes that this protest "was not just a case of petty family jealousy, for Aaron, Moses' brother, was also the high priest, and therefore a supreme religious leader and most holy man in Israel; while Miriam, his sister, was a prophetess and thus head of the spirit-filled women (Exod 15:20f.). Here, then, is an alliance of priest and prophet, the two archetypes of Israelite religion, challenging Moses' prophetic position as sole revelatory mediator between God and Israel."[72]

Miriam's questioning the Cushite origin of Moses' wife was but a smokescreen for her central concern, but the ethnic issue was a timely one for the Israelites. The rabble of mixed origins had instigated a rebellion that led to considerable loss of life for the community. Miriam may have been suggesting that a little ethnic cleansing might be beneficial to the survival of the Israelites. The identity of this Cushite woman has been debated by scholars. First, on the basis of Gen 2:13; 10:6; Ps 68:31; and Isa 18:1, Cush, the first son of Ham, is identified with Nubia (or perhaps Ethiopia), which bordered ancient Egypt on the south. If this connection is assumed, Moses' Cushite wife would have been a woman other than Zipporah, his Midianite wife from the clan of Jethro and Reuel. Some have suggested that Zipporah had died, and the Cushite wife was of a recent marriage.[73] On the other hand, the synonymous parallel cola in Hab 3:7 would evidence an association of Cushan with the Midianites, giving credence to the identity of the Cushite woman with Zipporah. A third suggested possibility is that the term Cushite refers to distinguishable physiological features that would have made her distinctive, in which case the deeply tanned Midianites from northwest Arabia could be implied by the text. Whichever was intended in the case raised by Miriam, the questioning of Moses' exclusive right as Israel's leader was

---

[70] Note "Introduction: Structure and Outline" and commentary on 1:1.
[71] Exod 32:1–5,21–24.
[72] Wenham, *Numbers*, 110.
[73] Allen, "Numbers," 797–98.

at the heart of the issue, though based on a questioning of his wife's ethnicity. Milgrom suggests that the *kî* be taken as introducing direct speech, hence the words from Miriam are a quote, perhaps emphatically, "He married a Cushite woman!" Milgrom further states, "Regardless of whether Moses' wife was Ethiopian or Midianite, the objection to her, it is to be implied, was ethnic (Lev 24:10).

Ethnic purity was an important issue in ancient Israel, as is evidenced in the commands to drive out and/or annihilate the Canaanites from the Promised Land[74] and later in the instructions of Ezra to the formerly captive Israelites to separate themselves from their pagan foreign wives because they potentially could lead their husbands into idolatry.[75] Throughout the Pentateuch, however, there are explicit instructions that there was to be one code of law for the native Israelite and the sojourning foreigners in the land. In Num 9:14 aliens living among the Israelites could even celebrate the Passover if they did so according to the statutes related to its commemoration, including that of circumcision as an indicator of that individual's coming under the covenant relationship with the God of Israel.[76] Zipporah had of course circumcised her son on the way from Midian to Egypt, bringing him under the covenant umbrella. It also would seem strange for Miriam to bring up a case against Zipporah after so much time had transpired, yet humans with a contentious mind will look far and wide in time and space to find something on which to base their grievances. Again, Miriam's complaint against Moses on the basis of ethnicity is undermined further, supporting the view that this was not the real reason for her objections to Moses.

**12:2** The primary reason for Miriam and Aaron's complaint was now clearly stated in the resonant parallel rhetorical questions, "Has the Lord spoken only through Moses? Hasn't he also spoken through us?" The Hebrew text is emphatic regarding this matter of exclusivity that is being raised by Moses' siblings:

| *hăraq* | *'ak-bĕmōšeh* | *dibber* | YHWH |
|---------|---------------|----------|------|
| Has only | indeed—by Moses | spoken | Yahweh |
| Has not | also—by us | spoken | (He) |
| *hălō'* | *gam-bānû* | *dibbēr* | — |

Should only Moses hold the position of leadership in the prophetic community of Israel as well as the community at large? Should he hold such a unique status while yet having a foreign wife? That Miriam and Aaron possessed prophetic gifts was not the issue. Both are described in prophetic terms in the Old Testament.[77] In the ancient Near East a number of professions like that of pro-

---

[74] Num 33:51–56.
[75] Ezra 10:2–12; cf. also Num 26:1–6; 1 Kgs 11:1–13.
[76] Exod 12:48–49; also cf. Lev 24:22; Num 15:14–16,29.
[77] Miriam, Exod 15:20–21; Aaron, Exod 4:16; both Mic 6:4.

phetic counsel and priestly oversight were handed down within families, much as in craft and trade skills.

The gravity of Miriam and Aaron's objections is amplified in the terse ominous conclusion to the verse. With two Hebrew words the reader or hearer is called upon to take seriously the challenge being raised against Israel's divinely appointed leader. The Lord always hears, and in this case one is assured that he will respond in judgment in his own time. The parenthetic note of v. 3 adds to the dramatic effect being created in this passage, as the divine silence reverberates. The expected reaction of anger from the Lord is withheld until v. 9.

**12:3** A parenthetic statement by the narrator concerning the character and quality of Moses as a man and as a leader of Israel is interjected into the flow of the narrative, heightening the dramatic effect of the passage. The position of the first term *věhāʾîš* ("now the man") in the Hebrew text emphasizes Moses' humanity, but as an ordinary human being he had demonstrated extraordinary character in the area of humility. The term *ʿānāw* used is not the normal Hebrew word for humility, meekness, or weakness but one that conveys an individual's devout dependence upon the Lord.[78] It may also describe a state one must experience before one is honored by God or man.[79] In his first encounter with the Lord at Horeb in the burning bush, Moses realized his human limitations—"Who am I that I should go to Pharaoh and bring the Israelites out of Egypt?" (Exod 3:11). But with the assurance of the divine presence—"I will be with you" (Exod 3:12)—he went forth by faith, even though initially reluctant, and was used by God in ways that far surpassed human comprehension. His humility in this manner far exceeded that of any other person on the earth. Ashley notes further that "Moses himself would probably have let this challenge go unanswered. It was Yahweh who heard it and who took it upon himself to answer it."[80]

**[4]At once the LORD said to Moses, Aaron and Miriam, "Come out to the Tent of Meeting, all three of you." So the three of them came out. [5]Then the LORD came down in a pillar of cloud; he stood at the entrance to the Tent and summoned Aaron and Miriam. When both of them stepped forward, [6]he said, "Listen to my words:**

**"When a prophet of the LORD is among you,**

---

[78] Zeph 2:3 (2x); Ps 22:26.

[79] Prov 15:33; 18:12; 22:4. Allen ("Numbers," 798–99), following C. Rogers ("Moses: Meek or Miserable?" *JETS* 29/3 [1986]: 257–63), suggests an alternate translation of "miserable" instead of "meek' or "humble" in Num 12:3. This so-described miserable state came as the result of continued opposition from the people, now from his brother and sister, and is echoed in his propensity at times toward self-pity, in which he voices to God his frustrations in dealing with the overwhelming burdens of his leadership position.

[80] Ashley, *Numbers,* 224.

I reveal myself to him in visions,
I speak to him in dreams.
⁷But this is not true of my servant Moses;
he is faithful in all my house.
⁸With him I speak face to face,
clearly and not in riddles;
he sees the form of the LORD.
Why then were you not afraid
to speak against my servant Moses?"

GOD SPEAKS TO MOSES, AARON, AND MIRIAM (12:4–8). **12:4–5**
The Lord interjected himself into the dispute suddenly and awesomely.
Allen describes the Lord's entrance into the situation as "an abrupt response
of the Lord that was pregnant with terror."[81] All three siblings are summoned to come out to the Tent of Meeting, probably to the entrance of that
central locale of divine revelation.

Some scholars have suggested that the terminology in v. 4 (ṣĕ'û from
yāṣa', "come out") gives credence to an alternative tradition that there was
a Tent of Meeting outside the encampment of Israel, as well as the one in the
center of the tribal assembly (Num 2:1–3:38).[82] In the use of the Hebrew
term yāṣa' in the Old Testament, however, the outward direction of movement is often a matter of whose perspective is being envisioned in the text.
In the tribal military conscription census of Num 1:20–45, those counted
were the ones who were able to *kol yōṣē' ṣābā'*, which could be translated
"everyone going out to war" or "everyone entering the army," the latter preserving better the meaning of *ṣābā'* as "host" or "army." Hence, one can
envision Yahweh speaking to Moses, Miriam, and Aaron from the context of
the Tent of Meeting, summoning them to come out from that first circle of
encampment in which the priests and Levites dwelled and to come in toward
the entrance of the Tent of Meeting, a meeting place for divine instruction.[83]

The hearing took place in the context of the visible evidence of the presence of the Lord, for the cloud pillar descended and stood erect at the
entrance to the Tent of Meeting. From the cloud pillar the Lord called forth
the dissident sister and brother for a special revelatory session. The Lord
normally spoke only with Moses (v. 8), but this time he directed his words
toward the prophetic challengers to Moses' authority. The two of them
stepped forward.

**12:6–7** In poetic proclamation the Lord affirms Moses' position as the

---

[81] Allen, "Numbers," 800. Cf. Prov 3:25; Job 22:10; Isa 30:13; 47:11; Jer 4:20.
[82] Levine, *Numbers 1–20*, 329; cf. Milgrom, *Numbers,* 94; also "Excursus 28. The Tent of
Meeting: Two Traditions," 386–87. Similar use in Num 11:24–27 of צֵא is cited in support of this
argument.
[83] Lev 1:1; 16:7; Num 1:1; 8:9; 11:16; 16:18–21.

uniquely commissioned confidant of Yahweh. The poetic form and style augment the effect of the words. The chiastic structure of the passage has been noted by several scholars, here presented with my own translation:

A   Introduction: Hear my words (6)
   B   If your prophet is of Yahweh,[84]
     C   In a vision to him I make myself known
       D   In a dream I speak to him.
         E   Not so my servant Moses (7)
         E′   In all my household he is trustworthy
       D′   Face to face I speak with him (8)
     C′   And in[85] a presence[86] that is not in riddles
   B′   And the form of Yahweh he beholds
A′   Rhetorical Conclusion: How then were you not afraid,
      To speak against my servant Moses?

At the focal point (E-E′) of the literary structure one can seen the emphasis in the passage is on the uniqueness of Moses as a prophet of Yahweh, a man who stands above the others among the Israelites, such as the recently endowed seventy elders, as well as above Miriam and Aaron. His calling was to a unique role as the mediator of the covenant.[87] He elucidated the relationship between God and his people. He was the spokesman of instruction and revelation from God to the nation and the one who related to God in a uniquely clear way. Other prophets among the Israelites might receive revelation through visions (Isaiah or Ezekiel)[88] or dreams and their interpretation (Joseph or Daniel),[89] or they might express themselves through ecstatic utterance (Saul)[90] or hymnic recitation (Miriam);[91] but Moses transcended all of those types of prophets in the manner subsequently delineated.

Moses is distinguished as a unique prophet of God first in his character

---

[84] Note the variant translations of אִם־יִהְיֶה נְבִיאֲכֶם יְהוָה, which literally might be rendered, "If your prophet is Yahweh," as Allen, "If there is one of your prophets–I am Yahweh," Harrison, "When there is a prophet among you, I the Lord (reveal Myself)," Ashley, "If there is a prophet of Yahweh among you." Milgrom takes the Hb. text as a broken construct chain, resulting in the following rendering: "If either of you (Aaron or Miriam) is (or claims to be) YHVH's prophet" (*Numbers,* 308, n. 23). The Hb. expression נְבִיאֲכֶם denotes the relationship between Moses and the people, here particularized in the address as Miriam and Aaron.

[85] The addition of the preposition "in" (בְּ) follows the reading of several manuscripts, including the LXX, Syriac, Targums, and SamPent.

[86] The Hb. text presents a play on words with מַרְאָה in v. 6b and מַרְאֶה in v. 8 as a means of showing a distinction between the two types of visionary prophets.

[87] Cf. the statement in Deut 34:10–12 concerning the unsurpassed uniqueness of Moses.

[88] Cf. Isaiah's vision of the glory of the Lord in 6:1–13 or Ezekiel's in 1:1–28.

[89] See Gen 37:5–10; 41: 32; Dan 2:18–45; 4:6–27; 7:1–28; etc.

[90] 1 Sam 10:11–12.

[91] Exod 15:20–21.

role as a trustworthy servant of God and second in the straightforward manner in which God revealed himself to him. Calling Moses "my servant" puts him in a limited category of persons in biblical history.[92] When the Lord conferred the promise of multitudinous descendants to Isaac as he had made to his father Abraham, the Lord refers to the founding patriarch as "my servant."[93] Caleb is called "my servant" by God in 14:24 because of his faithful spirit and wholehearted devotion to God's instruction to enter and inherit the Promised Land. In the Servant Songs of Isaiah 42–53, Yahweh's servant was one whom God would strengthen by his Spirit to bring justice, righteousness, and salvation to the nations.[94] To be called a faithful or trustworthy servant by God is the highest honor that can be bestowed upon a child of God, indeed upon any human being.[95]

**12:8** The three lines at the beginning of the verse provide a picture of the unique relationship between Yahweh and Moses within which the faithful prophetic servant encountered some visible manifestation of the presence of God. The terminology related to the "form" *tĕmūnat)* of Yahweh used here is echoed also in Exod 20:4 (=Deut 5:8) of the iconographic form the Israelites were forbidden to make of their God. Similarly in Deut 4:12,15–16,23,25 it describes that form of God that the people had not seen, as had Moses, and therefore should not fashion as a visible representation of their God. Yet David, in a state of righteous yearning, prayed that he might see this likeness of his God (Ps 17:15). Moses had indeed been graced with a special relationship with the Lord, to see that which Isaiah saw only in the smoky trail of his glory in his visionary temple call experience (Isa 6:1–2). Moses had seen plainly and openly, more than any other human had ever envisioned, that which God had allowed of himself to be observed. In Exod 33:11 the Lord is said to have spoken to Moses "face to face, as a man speaks to his friend." This does not mean that Moses literally saw God's face, for if he had done so he would have surely died (33:20). Earlier in v. 9 the communication between God and Moses is seen in the process of the cloud descending upon the tent and God talking with Moses. Later in that context Moses is said to have seen the back side of God's glory as he passed over Moses, who was positioned in the cleft of the rock (vv. 17–23). Only Jesus, the Incarnate Son of God, had seen the Father in his fullness of glory. He became that which even Moses would have longed to see. Those who seek him and learn from him partake of the Bread of Life (John 6:44–51).

The encounter closes with the same language (*dabbēr b-*, "speak against") of the original complaint in 12:1. Since God spoke 'to' and 'with'

[92] Cf. Deut 34:5; Josh 1:1,2,7,13,15; 11:12,15; 12:6; 13:8; 14:7; 18:7; 22:2,4,5; 24:29.
[93] Gen 26:24.
[94] Note the "Servant Songs" of Isa 42:1–4; 49:1–7; 52:13–53:12.
[95] Note the teaching of the "Parable of the Talents" in Matt 25:21,23.

Moses, how could Miriam and Aaron dare to speak "against" him. To speak against God's servant in this case was tantamount to speaking against God himself, and he surely would respond.

⁹**The anger of the LORD burned against them, and he left them.**

¹⁰**When the cloud lifted from above the Tent, there stood Miriam—leprous, like snow. Aaron turned toward her and saw that she had leprosy;** ¹¹**and he said to Moses, "Please, my lord, do not hold against us the sin we have so foolishly committed.** ¹²**Do not let her be like a stillborn infant coming from its mother's womb with its flesh half eaten away."**

¹³**So Moses cried out to the LORD, "O God, please heal her!"**

THE JUDGMENT AGAINST MIRIAM (12:9–13). **12:9–10** The immediate response of the Lord to Miriam was one of anger, followed by withdrawal. The terminology of the heated response of God to the situation parallels that in 11:1 and 33. The Lord had revealed himself to Miriam and Aaron in a special way at the entrance to the Tent of Meeting. His presence in the encounter was not only one of revelation, but also one of protection while the countercharges were outlined in the indictment. The charges against the plaintiff Moses had been dismissed with resounding affirmation of his character by the ultimate Judge of all of humanity. Now the judgment against the false accuser would be meted out. When the cloud of God's presence withdrew from over and from within the Tent of Meeting, Miriam and Aaron stood in alarmed disbelief at what they observed.

As the billowing cloud lifted, Moses and Aaron witnessed the horror that had spread over the body of their beloved sister, the dreaded skin disease that would require her withdrawal from the proximity of the tabernacle and from the environs of the community itself. The Hebrew ṣōraʿat was used to designate a class of serious cutaneous diseases that cause a white flaking of the skin. Harrison probably is right in suggesting that "ṣōraʿat is a generic term for a group of pathological conditions and serves the same sort of function as the term *cancer,* which covers a wide range of degenerative tissue states."[96] Several modern diseases have been suggested that would be similarly described, including psoriasis, leucoderma, shingles, or leprosy, the modern Hansen's disease (Hansen's bacillus). The latter would have been the more chronic of the potential identifying afflictions, though the skin deformity in leprosy is seldom "white as snow" in its manifestation. Leprosy in the ancient Near East and in the Bible was often seen as punishment for offenses against God (or the gods).[97]

That Miriam rather than Aaron was plagued by the disease reinforces the

---

[96] Harrison, *Numbers,* 197. See also his article "Leper, Leprosy," in *ISBE* (rev) 3:103–6.

[97] J. Milgrom, *Cult and Conscience: The Asham and the Priestly Doctrine of Repentance,* SJLA 18 (Leiden: Brill, 1976), 80–82.

gender specific implication of the initial verb in v. 1 that Miriam was the chief instigator of the dispute. That this is not the biased statement of a male-dominant society, reflected in what some might call a "man-God wrath against women,"[98] is proven by Aaron's appalled response upon observing his stricken sister and Moses' impassioned plea to God for her healing. Whatever the actual skin disease was that Miriam contracted, she would become an outcast from society, forced to live outside the holy camp of Israel. The laws regarding various skin diseases required the afflicted to live on the outskirts of the camp or town so as to not defile the purity of the community. Indeed the interior of the community was where Yahweh dwelled in their midst, and its sanctity of purity and holiness was to be maintained. Knowing this, Aaron's reaction may have been a combination of his dismay at Miriam's physical disfigurement, his realization that she would have to be separated from Moses and himself, and his fear that he might subsequently be struck with this heinous disease and suffer the same disgrace from the community.

**12:11-12** With deep emotion Aaron immediately apologized to Moses, addressing him as lord and submissively confessing his sin of rebellion. He who had opposed Yahweh's servant so presumptuously, promptly placed himself in the servant position under that very same individual. Perhaps attempting to lighten the potential judgment against himself, he characterized his transgression as foolishness. The Hebrew *yā'al* is a rare term used in Isa 19:13 and Jer 5:4 and 50:36 to refer to a person who acts in a delusional manner as a result of ignorance, of one lacking knowledge of God and his ways. As such his offense could be expiated through a propitiatory act of intercession. Intentional rebelliousness was punishable by banishment or death by stoning.[99] Out of concern for his stricken sister, he begged Moses not to hold Miriam culpable for their sin, by which she might be afflicted even further with chronic leprosy. He asked that God not afflict Miriam such that she might have the appearance of a stillborn child, whose scaly flesh would sometimes peel off with the amniotic fluids when handled after birth. The Hebrew phrase at the beginning of v. 12 literally reads, "Please do not let her be like the dead," which heightens Aaron's appeal; he realized that if she continued in this state, she might die.

**12:13** Like Aaron's distressed appeal, Moses turns to the Lord with a great emotive entreaty, "O God, please heal her!" Faced with the dilemma of letting Miriam suffer the consequences of her rebellion against him or pray for her restoration, Moses graciously becomes the intercessor on behalf of his accuser. The close familial ties are evidenced in his

[98] Allen, "Numbers," 802.
[99] Num 15:30-31.

response.[100] The urgency of his plea is reflected in this terse request through his use of the short form *El* in referring to God and the imperative verb form in pleading for her physical restoration.[101] The prayer is stated in monosyllables and in an introverted structure in the Hebrew text: *ʾēl nāʾ rĕpāʾ nāʾ lāh,* with the pivotal focus being on the term for healing *(rĕpāʾ).*[102]

**[14]The LORD replied to Moses, "If her father had spit in her face, would she not have been in disgrace for seven days? Confine her outside the camp for seven days; after that she can be brought back." [15]So Miriam was confined outside the camp for seven days, and the people did not move on till she was brought back.**

GOD'S REPLY TO MOSES, MIRIAM, AND AARON (12:14–15). **12:14– 15** Grace and mercy are evidenced in the Lord's response to Moses, for Miriam survives the ordeal. With chronic leprosy she would have been banished from the community for life. She would have to endure, however, the consequences of her rebellion: public humiliation and isolation from the camp of the community for seven days. The Lord raises an apparent analogous case law from which to draw her due discipline. This punishment would be equal to that which she would have experienced if her father had spat on her face in contempt.[103] The seven days of separation were the standard period for the purification process for a leper. Although we are not informed about whether other elements of the cleansing ceremony outlined in Lev 14:1–32 were followed, such as animal sacrifice, ritual sprinkling, bathing, and shaving of the head, one might assume this standard practice was followed.

While Miriam was going through her required period of separation and ritual purification, the Israelite camp remained at Hazeroth. This delay was perhaps out of some respect or admiration for Miriam and her noble place within the community leadership. But also Israel would not disembark on the next stage of the journey to the Promised Land until the Lord would lead them by the cloud. Hence the seriousness of the rebellion of one of Israel's leaders is magnified, and the consequences of such an act would affect the

---

[100] Note also that Moses' sin in violating the holiness of God by striking the rock at Meribah (Num 20:2–13) comes immediately after the death of his beloved sister.

[101] Allen, "Numbers," 803.

[102] Milgrom, *Numbers,* 98.

[103] Since this statement has no direct parallel in Pentateuchal law or in any legal literature yet uncovered from the ANE, inference can be drawn from Lev 15:8 and Deut 25:9 (cf. Isa 50:6) regarding the uncleanness brought on by sputum in a context of public humiliation. This implication was apparently an understood community practice not recorded in the halakhah of the Torah. Note also that within the Qumran sectarian community, spitting in the assembly was punishable by a period of thirty days of penance, during which the transgressor was separated from the purity of the congregation and his food ration was reduced (1QS VII:13).

entire community. They must all wait upon the Lord until he leads them. In the period of Israel's entrance into Canaan under Joshua, the sin of one man's (Achan) family resulted in their being defeated in the strategic battle at Ai (Josh 7:1–5). Only after the restoration of one of their key leaders would the people of Israel be allowed to move toward their final destination, the promised Holy Land.

**16After that, the people left Hazeroth and encamped in the Desert of Paran.**

THIRD STAGE OF THE JOURNEY (12:16). **12:16** After the fulfillment of Miriam's seven days of separation and purification, the Israelite community departs from Hazeroth and moves on to the Wilderness of Paran in the modern southern Negev, or northeast Sinai region.[104] The Paran Wilderness was the goal of the first phase of the journey (10:11), and from that area the spies were to be sent to explore the Promised Land (13:3).

## (6) Fourth Rebellion: Rejection of the Promised Land (13:1–14:45)

Following three successive seditious actions by the people of Israel, each resulting in dramatic judgment from God, the first rebellion cycle reaches its climax in the people's rejection of the land God had promised since he called them into being through a promissory oath to Abraham. Ashley has noted that in each case the punishment was "related directly to the words of the people involved."[105] The previous sections provide the general historical context of rebelliousness without noting the specific time frame of each. They function as precursors to the *fait de compli* that ensues: the rejection of the Promised Land and the rejection of God's leadership through Moses.

Excursus: The Literary Structure of Numbers 13–14

These two chapters constitute a literary unit that is based upon the following factors: (1) utilization of chiastic structures, (2) repetition and wordplay on several key terms and phrases, and (3) narrative dialogue involving Yahweh, Moses, and the people. Milgrom has outlined one such structural analysis of the passage that is based on broad thematic and discourse developments within the text (with details omitted):

---

[104] From a synthesis of biblical passages, the Wilderness of Paran seems to have denoted a large arid region in the NE Sinai, extending northward to Kadesh Barnea and the Nahal Zin drainage basin (Num 13:3,26; 20:1; Deut 1:1), eastward to the Arabah and the regions of Mount Seir (Edom) and also the Midianites (Gen 14:6; 1 Kgs 11:18).

[105] Ashley, *Numbers,* 230. He notes that the gluttonous demand for meat resulted in an over-abundance to the people's detriment (11:4–34); Miriam's complaint against Moses' dark-skinned wife ended in Miriam's being turned "white as snow" with leprosy (12:1–12).

A   The Scouts' Expedition (13:1–24)
 B   The Scouts' Report (13:25–33)
  C   The People's Response (14:1–10a)
 B'   God's Response (14:10b–38)
A'   The People's Expedition (14:39–45)[106]

The key question in the literary analysis of a complex unit such as this is that of the center of the chiasmus. What is the focal turning point and hence the central theme of the pericope? Is it the people's response, God's intervention, or the contrast between the responses of the faithful minority (Joshua, Caleb, Moses, and Aaron) and the unfaithful majority? The answers to these and other questions are the goals of the literary analysis.

The literary outline below highlights the key terms and themes that are the vehicles through which the theological developments within the passage are emphasized. Each theme or subtheme has a positive and a negative development and result.

**The Land as Gift.**   First is the theme of God's blessing in the gift (*'ănî nōtēn*, "I am giving," 13:2) of the Promised Land, the Land of Canaan. Even though the first generation would reject the Promised Land, the promise would not be nullified. He would promise the land to the children of that rebellious generation (14:31), and then bless their land abundantly, as Num 15:1–21 evidences. A subtheme related to the giving of the land is that of its quality. Under the instructions from Moses and the Lord, the scouts were sent to evaluate the quality of the land and assess the cities and their inhabitants. The essential question regarding the land was whether it was good (*hăṭôbâ*) or bad (*'im-rāʿa*).[107] When the scouts returned, they described the land as good, describing it as flowing with milk and honey, a key phrase used throughout the Old Testament to characterize the quality and productivity of the Promised Land. The tenor of the report, however, suddenly shifted from one of prospective prosperity to one of foreboding fear as the majority of the scouts announced the seeming insurmountability of the people and their heavily fortified cities (13:28–29). This fear turned to rebellion when they described the land in terms of death, hence evil or bad, and described a potential return to Egypt as "good" (13:31–14:4).

**Sending the Scouts.**   Second is the theme of the sending of scouts to explore the Land of Canaan, the Promised Land. Moses sends them (*šālaḥ*) to explore (*tûr*) the land, and they ascend (*ʿālâ*) into the hill country under the direction of the Lord (13:2–25). These terms are repeated several times in the narrative, which portrays the scouts as faithfully following the commands of God through Moses. But when they attempt to ascend into the hill country on their own, they are soundly defeated (14:40–45).

**Leadership.**   Third is the theme of leadership in the persons of Moses and Aaron, Joshua and Caleb, as well as and in contrast to the scouts, who were all

---

[106] Milgrom, *Numbers*, "Excursus 29: The Structure of Chapters 13–14," 387–88.

[107] Note this passage echoes the goodness of God's creation as first proclaimed in Gen 1:10,12,18,21,31.

leaders from their respective tribes. Moses received instruction from the Lord concerning the reconnoitering of the land, which he then relates to the twelve scouts (13:1,17; 14:5). Note that Hoshea (Joshua) is highlighted in the delineation of the names of the tribal scouts, for his name recurs at rhetorically important points in the account, such as in his support of Moses and Caleb and in his assertion of the need to go up into the land and inherit what the Lord has given Israel (13:8; 14:6–9,30). The other ten scouts who were sent to explore the land go up obediently, but then at the pivotal point in the narrative, they rebelliously counter Caleb's report and lead the people to fear entry into the land and the peoples living therein (14:31–33). In the end they are judged severely for their sedition (14:36–37). Only the faithful visionary scouts, Joshua and Caleb, who believed in God's ability to bring the nation in and bless them abundantly, would survive to experience the promise. Only two of the countless thousands who were counted in the military conscription census of 1:1–46 would live to see the handiwork of the Lord (14:38; Josh 1:2; 14:6–15; 19:49–50).

Moses exemplified his leadership ability through his role as intercessor in this account. When faced with the potential annihilation of the people he had led out of bondage in Egypt, Moses appealed to God on the basis of God's glory, including his reputation among the nations. He appealed to God's forgiving nature, and the imminent disaster was averted for the moment. He also fulfilled his prophetic leadership role as one who forewarns the people of impending judgment when he advised them not to try to enter the land after their entry had been denied. A true prophetic leader must evidence a close relationship to God and a thorough knowledge of his word, whereby he or she understands God's full nature. Then out of that understanding that person may speak for him a message of forgiveness and love and/or judgment and justice in a given situation.

**Nature of God.** Following the first three rebellion cycles, each of which begins with a statement of the rebellious activity of the persons involved, this cycle commences with divine instruction and obedient responsiveness of the people. The scouts go forth to search out the Promised Land, which God had promised to the descendants of Abraham. The nature of God as divine beneficiary to his people is in view (the land is called "exceedingly good" by Joshua and Caleb), and the fulfillment of that promise of a homeland was anticipated. When the majority of the scouts return with a negative report, however, and lead Israel to rebel and reject the land, another side of God's nature is evidenced. In rejecting the Promised Land, the people reject the God of the promise, and hence they are subject to his judgment. When the people ascribe death and destruction to God by suggesting that he had led them purposefully into the wilderness to die, they disparage his essential life-giving character. When Joshua and Caleb warn the people that they should not rebel against the Lord or be fearful of the inhabitants of the land, he characterizes the Lord as One who would *lead* them into the land, give the land to them, and protect them by manifesting his presence with them during the process of gaining their inheritance. But when the people turn against their leaders and try to stone them, the Lord intervenes in a dramatic way.

The glory of the Lord appears in the form of a fiery cloud over the Tent of Meeting, which is visible to the entire assembly, bringing the message that God's justice in judgment is to be meted out against a rebellious people. Communication of this desire comes through Moses, who is challenged to exercise his role as revelatory intercessor. In intervening on behalf of the people, he appeals to God's attributes of love and forgiveness, as well as his long-suffering nature. Moses notes that God's glory as displayed through the miraculous signs in Egypt, the deliverance of the nation from bondage, the crossing of the sea, and provisions for the people in the desert is at stake in this endeavor. The balance between God's love and God's justice and judgment must be maintained in theological tension. God's love and long-suffering would be preserved in his allowing the rebellious generation to survive in the wilderness for forty years, wherein he would still provide for them faithfully. But this was also their judgment, in that all those of the former generation would eventually die in that desolate world and not inherit the Promised Land or experience the fullness of God's blessing.

**Rebelliousness of the People.**   This passage marks the fourth stage of rebellion among the people in this third cycle of the Book of Numbers, coming in rapid succession and producing a hammering staccato effect upon the hearer or reader.[108] If one takes into account the parallel passage in Deut 1:19–46, the idea of sending scouts originated with the people as they were situated on the southern edge of the Amorite hill country. The idea seemed good to Moses, and the Lord then laid out the instructions for reconnoitering the region, by utilizing leaders from each of the tribes of Israel.

Some early tension is created in the account with the very question of whether the land was good or bad, since the land has been previously characterized as good and flowing with milk and honey.[109] The scouts returned with an initial report about the goodness of the land, but they instigated rebelliousness and fear by describing the people of the land as more powerful than Israel. Caleb and Joshua knew that the power of Israel lay not in their military might and the numbers of their armies but in the power of their God. But fear of the world and its seemingly insurmountable power caused Israel to lose sight of the vision and promises of God. The scouts described the people of the land as descendants of the Nephilim. The majority of ten scouts led the congregation to reject the gift of the land and mutiny against its leaders (Moses, Aaron, Joshua, and Caleb) and against God himself. In their grievous grumbling they despised God and his beneficent deliverance by ascribing goodness to the land from which they had been delivered and by outwardly stating their preference for death over life. One of the hallmarks of a life of sin and rebellion is a person calling "evil" what God has deemed as good and calling "good" that which is inherently evil, which amounts to a confusion of ultimate reality. (In following outline, words in bold print evidence the thematic emphases outlined.)

---

[108] The first was a general evil complaint (11:1–3), the second about food (11:4–35), and the third was about Moses' position of leadership (12:1–16).

[109] Exod 3:8,17; 13:5; 33:3; Lev 20:24.

STRUCTURAL OUTLINE OF NUMBERS 13–14

**Intro: Yahweh Instructs Moses: Send the Scouts to Explore the Land**
(13:1–2)
Moses Instructs and **Sends** Scouts (13:3–20)
A  Intro: Moses Instructs and **Sends** at the Word of Yahweh
[ʿal-pî **YHWH**](13:3)
**Paran Wilderness**
B  Tribal Scout Leaders Enlisted: "These Are the Names" Inclusio (13:4–16)
**Hoshea => Joshua**
C  Moses **Instructs/Sends** Scouts: "**Go Up** Thru Hill Country"
(13:17)
a  **See** What **Land** Is Like
b  What **People** Are Like: Strong/Weak, Few/Many
c  What **Land** Is Like: **Good** or **Bad**
b′  What **Cities** Are Like: Unwalled or Fortified
a′  What **[Land]** Soil is Like: Fertile or Poor
Sample: Trees or Not—Bring Back Some Fruit
D  Scouts **Explore** the Land: Zin [S] to Rehob [N] (13:21–25)
a  **Went Up and Explored the Land**: Geographical (13:21)
b  **People** of the Land: Anakites of Hebron (13:22)
b′  **Land**'s Fruit: Grapes, Pomegranates, Figs (13:23–24)
a′  **Return after Forty Days from Exploring the Land**
**(13:25)**
C′  Moses, Aaron, and Congregation Receive the Report (13:26–29)
Report at Kadesh in **Paran Wilderness** (Geographical) (13:26)
a  **Land**: Fruit Shown—**Milk and Honey Description** (13:27)
b  **But on the Other Hand** (ʾepes) (13:28)
**People** Powerful
**Cities** Large and Fortified—Anakites There
**People**  Amalekites—Negev (13:29)
Hittites, Jebusites, Amorites—Hill Country
Canaanites—Coastal and Jordan Valley
B′  **CALEB: We Are Able** to Go and Take Possession (13:30)
**OTHERS: We Are Not Able—They Are Mightier** (13:31–33)
**BAD REPORT** of the Land—Devours the Living
Nephilim of the Anakim—We Are Like Grasshoppers
C″  **Congregational Response to the Report (14:1–4)**
**People Mourn**—Raise Voices and Weep
Grumble against Moses and Aaron
Why Is Lord Bringing Us to Land to Die?
Better **(Good)** to Go Back to Egypt
Choose a **Leader** and Go Back to Egypt
B″  **Leadership Response to the People (14:5–10a)**
Moses and Aaron Fall on Their Faces
**Joshua and Caleb—Tear Clothes**
**Land Is Very, Very Good**

Yahweh Will Lead Us into That Land –
**Land of Milk and Honey**
He Will Give It to Us
Do Not Rebel versus Yahweh
**People of the Land**: Do Not Be Afraid of Them
We will Swallow Them Up
Their Protection Is Gone
Yahweh Is with US
Do Not Be Afraid of Them

**A″ God Intervenes: Glory of Lord Appears (14:10b–12)**
**Promise of Destruction**
People Talk of Stoning Leaders
**GLORY OF LORD** Appears at Tent of Meeting
Yahweh: (ʿad-ʾānâ) How Long Will They Treat
Me with **Contempt**? (14:11)

**B‴ Moses Intercedes with Yahweh for the People (14:13–19)**
Plea Basis: God's Reputation [=Glory] (14:13–16)
a **Egyptians Will Hear**
b **You** Brought Them out by Your Power
a They (Egypt) Will Tell Inhabitants of the Land
The (Inhabitants of the Land) Have Heard
b′ **You** Are with Them
**You** Meet with Them Face-to-Face ("Eye-to-Eye")
**You** Are a Cloud over Them—Pillar before Them
a″ **Nations Who Heard** Will Say—**Lord Is Not Able**
b″ May Lord's Strength Be Displayed (14:17–19)
Lord Is Slow to Anger—Loving—Forgiving
Not Leave Guilty Unpunished—Third/Fourth
Generation
**Moses: Forgive Them** by Your Love
You Pardoned Them before, Now Do So Again

**A‴ Yahweh Responds: Promises Forgiveness and Judgment
(14:20–35)**
**Yahweh Forgives Them** as Moses Asked (14:20–25)
**Swears by Himself and His Glory**
None Who Saw **MY GLORY** in Egypt and Desert
They Tested/Condemned Me Ten Times (Disobeyed)
None Will See the Land I Promised to Their Forefathers
All Those Who Had Contempt for ME
None Will See It

**B‴ Leaders: Caleb My Servant Will Live (14:24)**
I Will Bring Him into the Land He Went Into ++ Descendants
Amalekites and Canaanites Are There—Turn Back to Way of
Red Sea (14:25)

**A‴ Yahweh Continues: Community Will Die (14:26–35)**
a **How Long** (ʿad-mātay) **Will the People Grumble**

          against Me?
          b  I will Do What You Said
            c  People of Israel: Your Bodies Will Fall in the Desert
              None Will Enter the Land I Promised
            c'  Except Caleb and Joshua
              (a)  Of Your Children You Said Would Be Plundered
                (b)  I Will Bring Them into the Land
              (a')  Your Children—Shepherds Forty Years
                (One Year/Day)
            b'  I Am Against You
            I Yahweh Have Spoken
          a'  A? Not Long—They Will Meet Their End in the Desert
        B'''''  Leaders: Joshua and Caleb versus Others Sent
          (14:36–38)
        Those Sent Who Gave **BAD REPORT—Death**
        **Joshua and Caleb (Good Report)—Survived**
**Conclusion: Moses Reports Judgment—Israel Mourns (14:39–45)**
        **People Mourn**
          a  **Attempt to Go Up** into Hill Country—We Sinned
            To Place Yahweh Promised
            Moses: Why Disobey Yahweh? (*ʿābar ʾet-pî* **YHWH**)
          b  **Do Not Go Up**—Yahweh Is NOT with You
            Amalekites and Canaanites Will Defeat You
          b'  **You Have Turned away from Yahweh**—He Will NOT Be
            with You
            You Will Fall by the Sword
          a'  **Attempt to Go Up** into Hill Country—Defeat
            Moses and Ark of Covenant Remain in Camp
            Amalekites and Canaanites of Hill Country Defeat Israel
            Beaten to Hormah

[1]**The LORD said to Moses,** [2]**"Send some men to explore the land of Canaan, which I am giving to the Israelites. From each ancestral tribe send one of its leaders."**
[3]**So at the LORD's command Moses sent them out from the Desert of Paran. All of them were leaders of the Israelites.**

INSTRUCTIONS FROM YAHWEH TO EXPLORE THE PROMISED LAND (13:1–3).  **13:1–3**  The literary form of the instructions to search out the Promised Land are given in the same manner as previous directives, utilizing the introductory formula of divine speech.[110] The revelatory nature of God's interaction with Moses and other Israelite leaders has been observed as a major theological theme throughout the Book of Numbers, as well as being

---

[110] See discussion above on וַיְדַבֵּר יְהוָה אֶל־מֹשֶׁה לֵּאמֹר in "Introduction: Title" section.

the key literary structural element.[111] God revealed himself through Moses in the dynamic of that faithful relationship, and when the nation acted in harmonious response to God's instructions, life would go well for them. They would live in freedom in the Promised Land and experience the abundance of this land "flowing with milk and honey." When they grumbled or rebelled against his commands, however, dire consequences came to pass. The phrase "at the Lord's command" (ʿal-pî YHWH, "by the mouth [=word] of Yahweh") recalls the journey hymn in Num 9:17–23. It is repeated in semantic parallels in 14:28 (nĕʾūm YHWH) and 14:41 (ʾet-pî YHWH) in contexts of judgment and warning.

In light of Moses' rehearsal of the sequence of events in the sending of the spies in Deut 1:19–46, in which we learn that the initiative to spy out the land came from the people, not from God, one should likely put the instruction from the Lord to "send some men to explore" subsequent to the initial request of the people.[112] Moses thought well of the idea and chose the men for the reconnaissance mission under God's direction. In retrospect he realized that the Lord was also angry with him because of this incident (Deut 1:37–38). A second reason for this prohibition is provided in Num 20:2–13, where Moses strikes the rock in contempt and impiety toward God (and the people) in the place where God promised to supply water and again demonstrate his providential care for Israel.

In the earlier generations this land was a promised inheritance; now it was about to become a reality as possession, for the text emphasizes using the present participle: "The land of Canaan which I (myself) am giving to the children of Israel."[113] But though the promise of land is never rescinded, possession of and prosperity in the land will be highly dependent on Israel's faithfulness.[114] The geographical setting of the instructions was the Wilderness of Paran, that large desert expanse in northeast Sinai, which as noted above probably included the region around the Nahal Zin and its wilderness area, as well as Kadesh Barnea to the west.[115] The more precise locale of

---

[111] See the "Introduction" sections on the "Structural Outline" and "Structural Theology," which develop these themes.

[112] In the SamPent version of Num 13, Deut 1:20–23a is inserted at the beginning of the chapter in a seeming attempt to resolve the inherent difficulty. A number of critical scholars delineate two sources or traditions, the first a Caleb-Hebron tradition that suggests the spies only searched out the Hebron region and the second that only Caleb spoke against the majority report (reflected in Deut 1:24–36 and Josh 14:6–12). But Josh 14:6 refers to both Joshua and Caleb ("concerning me and concerning you"—Caleb speaking to Joshua), and Deuteronomy is selective in rehearsing the events of the journey from Egypt to the Plains of Moab across from the Promised Land.

[113] The same phraseology is in Deut 1:20, where Moses reviews the sending out of the spies.

[114] See discussion of "The Land" in the "Introduction: Theology of the Book of Numbers."

[115] See discussion on the Wilderness of Paran in commentary on Num 10:12. The LXX version adds the gloss εἰς τὴν ἔρημον Φαραν, αὕτη ἐστὶν Καδης, hence supporting this association.

Kadesh is provided at the conclusion of the mission as the place where the spies make their report to Moses and the nation.

⁴**These are their names:**
**from the tribe of Reuben, Shammua son of Zaccur; ⁵from the tribe of Simeon, Shaphat son of Hori; ⁶from the tribe of Judah, Caleb son of Jephunneh; ⁷from the tribe of Issachar, Igal son of Joseph; ⁸from the tribe of Ephraim, Hoshea son of Nun; ⁹from the tribe of Benjamin, Palti son of Raphu; ¹⁰from the tribe of Zebulun, Gaddiel son of Sodi; ¹¹from the tribe of Manasseh (a tribe of Joseph), Gaddi son of Susi; ¹²from the tribe of Dan, Ammiel son of Gemalli; ¹³from the tribe of Asher, Sethur son of Michael; ¹⁴from the tribe of Naphtali, Nahbi son of Vophsi; ¹⁵from the tribe of Gad, Geuel son of Maki.**

¹⁶**These are the names of the men Moses sent to explore the land. (Moses gave Hoshea son of Nun the name Joshua.)**

TRIBAL SCOUTS ENLISTED (13:4–16). **13:4–16**   In his usual faithful manner in responding to God's commands, Moses commits to sending representative leaders from each of the twelve tribes to search out the territory God had promised to their ancestors Abraham, Isaac, and Jacob. The standard phraseology for introducing a group of ancestral leaders or a genealogical record, "these are the names," is utilized in vv. 4 and 16, thus marking the passage off as an inclusio, bracketing the beginning and end of the section. The names of those enlisted vary from those enlisted to aid in the census taking in chaps. 1–2, where the clan chieftains are called "head of their fathers' household" *(rōʾš lĕbêt-ʾăbōtāyw).*[116] Because of the nature of the task laid before them, these men probably were from among those listed in the military conscription of chap. 1 and hence able to go to war in the coming conquest of the land.

Additional emphasis is evidenced in the overall structure of the Book of Numbers since this listing of the twelve tribes is the second such occurrence within the first rebellion cycle. The first (10:14–29) is in the delineation of the tribal departure from Mount Sinai, and the phrase "at the LORD's command" *(ʿal-pî YHWH)* occurs there also (10:13). As representatives of their respective ancestral tribes, they were to provide direction for the nation. In this case their assigned responsibilities were military in nature.

### Scout Leaders from the Israelite Tribes

| Tribe | Name | Father |
|---|---|---|
| Reuben | Shammua[117] | ben Zaccur |
| Simeon | Shaphat[118] | ben Hori |

---

[116] Hb. רֹאשׁ לְבֵית־אֲבֹתָיו, "head of the house of his fathers."
[117] Shammua means "one who is heard," perhaps "report of God" (Allen, "Numbers," 807).
[118] Shaphat means "he judged."

| Judah | Caleb[119] | ben Jephunneh |
| Issachar | Igal[120] | ben Joseph |
| Ephraim | Hoshea (=Joshua)[121] | ben Nun |
| Benjamin | Palti[122] | ben Raphu |
| Zebulun | Gaddiel[123] | ben Sodi |
| Manasseh | Gaddi[124] | ben Susi |
| Dan | Ammiel[125] | ben Gemalli |
| Asher | Sethur[126] | ben Michael |
| Naphtali | Nahbi[127] | ben Vophsi |
| Gad | Geuel[128] | ben Maki |

At the conclusion of the list of the scouts' names, emphasis is given to the person of Joshua, whose former name was Hoshea. The inclusion here serves several purposes in the narrative: (1) to highlight his role as a leader, (2) to portend his role as a spokesman for God, and (3) to provide a structural marker for the chiastic rhetorical structure of the passage in which contrast is made between the faithful leaders—Moses, Aaron, Joshua, and Caleb—and the faithless ten scouts who held sway over the Israelite congregation.

**[17]When Moses sent them to explore Canaan, he said, "Go up through the Negev and on into the hill country. [18]See what the land is like and whether the people who live there are strong or weak, few or many. [19]What kind of land do they live in? Is it good or bad? What kind of towns do they live in? Are they unwalled or fortified? [20]How is the soil? Is it fertile or poor? Are there trees on it or not? Do your best to bring back some of the fruit of the land." (It was the season for the first ripe grapes.)**

MOSES INSTRUCTS THE TRIBAL SCOUTS (13:17–20). **13:17–20** Moses faithfully reiterated to the tribal scouts the instructions given him by the Lord.[129] They were directed to explore the land of Canaan from

---

[119] Caleb is generally derived from כֶּלֶב, meaning "dog." The term often is used in a derogatory sense in describing lowly persons, but in ANE literature (Amarna Tablet 61.2; 71.6, of Egypt, where certain dogs were deified) they were symbols of servanthood. Cf. 2 Kgs 8:13. Note Num 14:24, where Caleb is referred to by God as "My servant."

[120] Igal, or better Yiga'al, means "he redeems."

[121] Hoshea means "salvation, deliverance." His name is altered with the theophoric expansion to Joshua or Jehoshua יְהוֹשֻׁעַ, meaning "Yahweh delivers."

[122] Palti means "my safety."

[123] Gaddiel means "my fortune is God."

[124] Gaddi is a short form of the previous name Gaddiel, meaning "my fortune."

[125] Ammiel or ('Ammi'el) derives from two words 'Ammi (עַמִּי), "my people," and (אֵל) "God"—hence the derived meaning "God of my people."

[126] Sethur means "secret" or "hidden," perhaps a longer theophoric form existed as Sethurel, "hidden in God."

[127] Nahbi, if derived from חָבָא, would mean "my hiding place." The name also could be derived from a Semitic root נחב.

[128] Geuel may mean "majesty of God" (Allen, "Numbers," 807) or "loftiness of God."

[129] Cf. the use of the terms שָׁלַח and תּוּר in 13:2–3,17.

which their ancestral tribal leaders had journeyed some four hundred years earlier during a time of famine. They were to head northward through the hill country regions later to be known as Judah, Samaria, and Galilee ("go up") starting in the Negev ("southlands"). They would reach as far north as Rehob of Lebo-Hamath in southern Lebanon. Biblical texts indicate that the Negev region stretched southward from Hebron (Qiryat Arba) into the Zin Wilderness region,[130] whereas in modern times the term denotes the region from Arad and Beersheba southward to Elat on the Gulf of Aqaba.

The scouts' primary objective was to reconnoiter the land to provide the answers to a series of questions Moses posed concerning the quality and productivity of the land and the military strength of its inhabitants. Though the specific time (day/month) frame is not provided, seasonal data was noted in the instructions and in the produce brought back by the scouts. This was the time of the first harvest of the vineyards (v. 20), hence late summer or early fall (late July to early September), several months after the departure from Mount Sinai in early spring.[131] The questions move from general to specific in a pattern of pairs that focus on the land and its peoples. As noted above, the very questions portend the possibility of a negative response. The land as a gift from God would surely be good, as suggested by the phrase "flowing with milk and honey." At the center of the chiasm, noted in the "Structural Outline of Numbers 13–14" in the above excursus, was the question, "Is it good or bad (evil)?" Their response at the conclusion was one of both/and rather than either/or. The land is good, but the people are bad news.

[21]So they went up and explored the land from the Desert of Zin as far as Rehob, toward Lebo Hamath. [22]They went up through the Negev and came to Hebron, where Ahiman, Sheshai and Talmai, the descendants of Anak, lived. (Hebron had been built seven years before Zoan in Egypt.) [23]When they reached the Valley of Eshcol, they cut off a branch bearing a single cluster of grapes. Two of them carried it on a pole between them, along with some pomegranates and figs. [24]That place was called the Valley of Eshcol because of the cluster of grapes the Israelites cut off there. [25]At the end of forty days they returned from exploring the land.

SCOUTS EXPLORE THE LAND (13:21–25). **13:21–25** The account begins with a summary statement and concludes likewise: The scouts went up to explore the land from the Wilderness of Zin and returned from exploring after forty days. The language is consistent with the instructions God

---

[130] Gen 12:9; 13:3,14; 20:1; 24:62; Num 21:1; 33:40; etc.

[131] In the Temple Scroll from Qumran the sectarians described the celebration of the firstfruits festival on the third of Ab, seven weeks after Shevuoth, which would likewise suggest a date in the last week of July or the first two weeks of August (11QTemple 19:11–20:10; G. Vermes, *Dead Sea Scrolls in English*, 4th ed. [New York: Pelican, 1995], 156–57).

gave to Moses and Moses gave to the scouts, indicating initial faithfulness to their assigned task.

Their mission took them from the Zin Wilderness, in the northeastern corner of the larger Paran Wilderness, to the vicinity of Rehob of Lebo-hamath. They would return to make their report to Moses and the Israelites at Kadesh in the northwestern region of the Paran Wilderness. The exact location of this Rehob is unknown, though the region of Lebo Hamath suggests a site in southern Lebanon, such as Beth Rehob near Tel Dan on the southern flank of Mount Hermon.[132] This would distinguish the site from other sites named Rehob,[133] such as Rehob in the Jordan Valley, located four miles south of Beth-Shean. Lebo Hamath (or perhaps "Lebo of Hamath") has generally been identified with modern Lebweh on the Orontes River, on the southern border of the ancient kingdom of Hamath, and about fourteen miles north-northeast of Baalbek. Lebo is recounted as a city on the northern border of the Promised Land (Num 34:7–8) and later of the Israelite kingdom of David and Solomon (1 Kgs 8:65).

Particulars of the scouts' journey begin with the Negev region, which they travel through on the way to Hebron. The ancestry of the Hebronites is highlighted by the mention of three clans of the Anakim or Anakites, namely Ahiman, Sheshai, and Talmai. These names are Semitic in origin, reflecting the fact that the inhabitants of the land spoke a Semitic dialect, though they might have necessarily been of Semitic ancestral stock. The name Anak was associated with a people famed and feared for their great size and military prowess and may also be associated with the ethnic phrase *Iy-ʿanaq* found among the Egyptian Execration Texts of the early second millennium B.C. In v. 33 in the Septuagint the term was translated as "giants," and they were associated with the Rephaim in Deut 2:11.[134] Remnants of these giants survived into the time of the Judges and the beginning of the Israelite monarchy. In Josh 12:21–22 the Anakim were noted as having lived in the Hebron region, as well as to the west in the Shephelah in such cities as Gath, and in the coastal plain in Gaza and Ashdod. Some have suggested that the famous Goliath, who was defeated by David, was one of the surviving descendants of these exceptionally tall individuals.[135] Four others were killed by David's men in a battle recounted in 2 Sam 21:15–22. Though the three names of the Anakites are not mentioned again in the biblical text, they were no doubt heads of prominent Anakite clans to have been included at this point. Caleb and his army drove the three clans out of Hebron, according to the account in Josh 15:14. Later in the scouts' report

---

[132] Cf. J. Simons, *GTTOT*, 7; G. W. Van Beek, *IDB* 1:396.

[133] "Rehob means "wide place," "pass," or "plaza."

[134] Cf. also Deut 9:2.

[135] Milgrom, *Numbers*, 103.

to Moses the Anakites were associated with the Nephilim, the descendants of offspring that resulted from the illicit union between the "sons of God" and the "daughters of men" in Gen 6:4.

A geographical and historical parenthesis is set forth concerning the historical context of the building of Hebron in relationship to the construction of Zoan in Egypt. Hebron was said to have been fortified seven years before Zoan, which was in the eastern Nile delta, about one hundred miles northeast of Cairo. The Hebrew Zoan is the equivalent of the Egyptian Dja‘net (or d‘nt), which was vocalized by the Greeks as Tanis.[136] Hebron, formerly known as Qiryath ‘Arba, is located about twenty miles south of Jerusalem in the central hill country, and it must have been a prominent city at this time due to its comparison with the Egyptian stronghold of Zoan.

The scouts explored the area west or north of Hebron, known as the Nahal Eshkol, from which they brought back the exemplary produce of the region, a voluminous cluster of grapes, along with a complement of pomegranates and figs. The name of the valley, Eshkol, means "cluster (of grapes)" and was also the name of the brother of Mamre the Amorite, an associate of Abraham and the one for whom the town on the northwestern outskirts of Hebron was named (Gen 14:13). Hence the valley may have been named originally according to the family name of Eshkol, and then developed as a prime region for viticulture.[137] On the other hand, the Valley of Eshkol may have been so named by the scouts who explored the region somewhere north of Hebron according to the magnificent clusters of grapes that were growing there. The duration of the scouts' exploration of the land was recounted as forty days, the approximate time it would have taken for such a journey on foot, assuming the men kept a good pace throughout the expedition. The number forty often is used in the Bible for an indefinite period in excess of a month. Having trekked from the Zin Wilderness, through Hebron and the central hill country, all the way to Lebo Hamath and back again, would mean that they would have covered a minimum of three hundred and fifty miles and perhaps as much as five hundred miles in their lateral movement in reconnoitering the hill country and valleys.

**[26]They came back to Moses and Aaron and the whole Israelite community at Kadesh in the Desert of Paran. There they reported to them and to the whole assembly and showed them the fruit of the land. [27]They gave Moses this account:**

---

[136] The former association of Tanis/Zoan with Avaris, the capital of the Hyksos, is no longer accepted. Cf. J. K. Hoffmeier, *Israel in Egypt: The Evidence for the Authenticity of the Exodus Tradition* (New York: Oxford University Press, 1996), 117–19; K. A. Kitchen, *New International Dictionary of Biblical Archaeology* (Grand Rapids: Zondervan, 1983), 384; and Harrison, *Numbers*, 204–6.

[137] See Milgrom, *Numbers*, 103.

"We went into the land to which you sent us, and it does flow with milk and honey! Here is its fruit. [28]But the people who live there are powerful, and the cities are fortified and very large. We even saw descendants of Anak there. [29]The Amalekites live in the Negev; the Hittites, Jebusites and Amorites live in the hill country; and the Canaanites live near the sea and along the Jordan."

[30]Then Caleb silenced the people before Moses and said, "We should go up and take possession of the land, for we can certainly do it."

[31]But the men who had gone up with him said, "We can't attack those people; they are stronger than we are." [32]And they spread among the Israelites a bad report about the land they had explored. They said, "The land we explored devours those living in it. All the people we saw there are of great size. [33]We saw the Nephilim there (the descendants of Anak come from the Nephilim). We seemed like grasshoppers in our own eyes, and we looked the same to them."

REPORT OF THE SCOUTS (13:26–33). *Group Report* (13:26–29). **13:26–29** In typical Hebrew literary pattern, the report begins with a summary statement utilizing three verbal concepts. They came back[138] to the camp that was now at Kadesh in the Paran Wilderness; they reported ("brought back to them a word") their findings; and they showed them the grape cluster, figs, and pomegranates they had brought from the land. So the first part of their report focused on matters related to the land and its productivity, followed by matters related to the people and their military capabilities. Their accounting of the quality of the land was a faithful representation of that which they had seen and partaken from the regions into which they had been sent. It was indeed an exceptionally fertile land, worthy of being described as "flowing with milk and honey." But as quickly as they gloried over the produce of the land, they began to grumble about the power of the people of the land. The solemn report turned sour; the wondrous picture turned piteous; the glorifying words became gloomy.

The contrastive report concerning the people of the land marks a major turning point in the narrative and is introduced by the emphatic and restrictive Hebrew adverbial phrase *'epes kî*, which could be translated as "however, on the other hand," or "but."[139] The divergent context is further emphasized by the placement of the noun for strength, *'az*, at the beginning of the nominal clause: "strong are the people who inhabit the land." Furthermore, their cities were described as extremely well fortified, seemingly impregnable to these unbelieving observers. This portion of the report concludes with a listing of the various Semitic and non-Semitic tribes living

---

[138] The וַיֵּלְכוּ וַיָּבֹאוּ is an emphatic double verb pattern, with וַיֵּלְכוּ denoting the general movement and וַיָּבֹאוּ giving direction; hence, the meaning "they went forth and entered [into the camp] unto Moses, Aaron, and the entire congregation of the Israelites."

[139] Contra B. K. Waltke and M. O'Connor, who suggest that אֶפֶס or כִּי אֶפֶס restrict the preceding material but that the "emphatic use is missing" (*IBHS*, 39.3.5e; p. 672).

throughout the country. The Amalekites and the Canaanites, who later would defeat the Israelites in their attempt to enter the land against God's will, lived in the Negev ("southlands") and coastal plains respectively. The power of the Canaanites, who controlled many cities in the valleys and plains at the conclusion of the conquest under Joshua and during the period of the Judges,[140] would later be acclaimed in referring to their possession of "iron chariots." The Semitic Amorites and Jebusites lived in the hill country, along with some of the non-Semitic Hittites who had migrated into the region from eastern Anatolia.[141] The term Amorite can refer in general to a number of the inhabitants of the Levant, including those in areas known today as Syria, Lebanon, Jordan, Israel, and Palestine. It may also refer more specifically to ethnic descendants of Canaan as delineated in Gen 10:16.[142] The Jebusites lived in Jerusalem, as they had throughout the Middle Bronze Age (2000–1550), and would remain in control of the city through most of the early history of Israel until the time of the Davidic conquests.[143]

*Caleb's Rejoinder (13:30).* **13:30** The faithful servant Caleb promptly spoke out against the negative report in the face of the people's grumbling. Speaking firmly with a visionary declaration to the Israelite audience, Caleb issued a trifold emphatic challenge: "Let us indeed go up," (as the scouts had done initially), "and we will possess it" (as God had promised), "for we are certainly capable of it" (by God's power).[144] As noted above, Caleb here serves as the spokesman in the narrative for the faithful leadership represented by Moses, Aaron, and Joshua. His faithfulness in this circumstance will earn him and his descendants a special allocation of land when the Israelites would finally enter it, as well as the assurance that he would survive, unlike all of the others but Joshua, to see the fulfillment of God's promise.

*The Majority's Surrejoinder* (13:31–33). **13:31–33** As readily as Caleb had challenged the people to mount a campaign to conquer the land, the other ten scouts debunked the idea that they could be successful against the formidable foes of Canaan. They used the same terms as Caleb but negated them. Caleb had emphatically said, "Let us indeed go up ... for we are certainly capable of it." But the majority responded with fear and trepidation, "We are not able to go up against the people, for they are stronger than we are!" Their words stood in direct opposition to not only the words of the faithful servant Caleb but against Moses, Aaron, Joshua, and ulti-

---

[140] See Josh 16:10; 17:12; Judg 1:27–33.

[141] The Samaritan Pentateuch and the LXX add the Hivites to the list of peoples living in the hill country.

[142] The later annals of Sennacherib list the kings of Phoenicia, Edom, Moab, Ammon, and Philistia among the Amorites he conquered in his campaign of 701 B.C. *ANET*, 3rd ed., 287.

[143] Josh 15:8,63; 18:16; Judg 1:8,21.

[144] Alt. translation: "We will surely overcome it."

mately against God. They renounced God's promise to accompany them with his awesome presence, to grant them decisive victory in what seemed, humanly speaking, to be overwhelming odds, and henceforth to confer upon them their rightful inheritance as the people of God—a homeland of abundant prosperity. But the full possession of the Promised Land in freedom and fortune was, and would always be, dependent upon the people's faithfulness.

Their message of apprehension and distrust was disseminated throughout the Israelite camps that surrounded the tabernacle, the central sanctuary and symbol of Yahweh's faithful presence. Focusing fearfully upon the outward feasibility in the face of the world's power rather than upon their inward faith in God's omnipotence, they lost perspective of the boundless possibilities that awaited them. Suddenly all of the peoples of the land were acclaimed to be like that limited group of descendants of the Anakim who were abnormally large. They began to see themselves as lowly insects, as grasshoppers to be stepped upon on the ground or pinched from the stalks of the fields of the land, to be easily beaten by those inhabitants like the giant Nephilim. Like the later Israelites who trembled before the colossal Goliath and the Philistines, until a devoted youth named David stepped forth to answer the challenge, the Israelites saw themselves being consumed rather than being conquerors through their God.

[1]That night all the people of the community raised their voices and wept aloud. [2]All the Israelites grumbled against Moses and Aaron, and the whole assembly said to them, "If only we had died in Egypt! Or in this desert! [3]Why is the LORD bringing us to this land only to let us fall by the sword? Our wives and children will be taken as plunder. Wouldn't it be better for us to go back to Egypt?" [4]And they said to each other, "We should choose a leader and go back to Egypt."

CONGREGATIONAL RESPONSE TO THE REPORT (14:1–4). **14:1–4** The Israelite community reacted to the majority report with fear and frenzy, discounting totally the credibility of Caleb's minority report and his visionary challenge to go forth and conquer the land with God's power and presence. The collective congregation of the tribes of Israel and the accompanying non-Israelite rabble (11:1) now moaned vociferously against the divinely ordained leadership of Moses and Aaron, precipitating an all-night session of weeping and wailing because of their perceived plight. Looking only through the eyes of their human frailty, they felt they had nowhere to turn. They had departed Egypt under dramatic circumstances, but now they somehow thought slavery would be better than facing Canaan, which seemed like a mighty invincible fortress, or simply dying in the wilderness.

The outcries of the people were dramatic, and the language of the first verse heightens the effect. Two standard Hebrew expressions for the lifting

of one's voice are conflated, *wattiśśāʾ kol-hāʿēdâ wayyittěnû ʾet-qôlām,* followed by a clause describing their intense mourning. Normally one of two
synonymous expressions would be used, either that of "they raised their
voice" *(watisāʾ ʾet-qôl)* or "they uttered their voice" *(wayyitěnû ʾet-qôl).*
Both are used in contexts of lament in the Old Testament.[145] The former
phrase is used of Hagar lifting her voice as she wept over the potential death
of Ishmael, after they had been driven into the desert by Sarah (Gen 21:26);
and it is used of Esau's bitter outcry after he found out that his brother Jacob
had received the family blessing from Isaac (Gen 27:34–38). The latter
phrase is employed in Joseph's weeping before his brothers when he
revealed his identity to them in Egypt (Gen 45:2), as well as Jeremiah's
lament over the wicked reign of Jehoiakim (Jer 20:22). In the present context the two phrases are merged into one expression of intense lament as the
people bemoaned their situation, brought upon themselves by their unbelief
in God's promise and power.

The intensity of the lament was heightened further by their stated preference for a return to Egypt, where they might have preferred to die in a state
of subjection and oppression.[146] The very people who had seen first hand
the marvelous and miraculous demonstration of God's omnipotence against
one of the most powerful nations of the second millennium B.C. now longed
to return to a world of bondage rather than believe a word of blessing. The
sinful human tendency, even among Christians, to lapse back into the addic-
tive ways of sin and despair after having seen the outward demonstration of
God's working on their behalf was evidenced in this setting. Often in a state
of rebellion against God, one loses the benefit of spiritual mooring, whereby
wisdom and discernment become elusive and proper decision making is
made extremely difficult. Worry and fear dominate one's thought patterns.
The Israelites had thus renounced and rejected God's beneficence, by now
suggesting that a return to Egypt would be a *good thing* rather than marching into a land that even the cynical scouts deemed as *good.* Further evidence of their stupefaction can be seen in the statement in v. 3, where they
suggested that God might have led them into the desert to die. They made
the God of life and hope to be one of death and despair. Wenham notes: "By
this time they actually propose returning to Egypt, thereby rejecting the
whole plan of redemption. From Exodus 1 to the mission of the spies is but
one plot: how Israel was brought out of Egypt to the borders of Canaan.
Now within sight of their goal they suggest giving it all up."[147]

In order to return to Egypt, they would need to choose new leadership to

---

[145] Both expressions, נשׂא את־קוֹל and נתן את־קוֹל, are used in the context of laments with
בכה.

[146] Note Milgrom, *Numbers,* 107.

[147] Wenham, *Numbers,* 120.

replace Moses, Aaron, Joshua, and Caleb. They now could only remember the good food they ate in Egypt, like the cucumbers, leeks, melons, and onions. They seemed to forget the tyrannous oppression they had so long experienced at the hand of its pharaonic leadership. As noted in the previous structural outline, the recurring theme of leadership and the correlative fellowship of the people are keys to understanding the development of the narrative. They had rejected Caleb's word, and now they must reject their divinely appointed leader, Moses, in order to accomplish this reversal of goals. Their godly leaders, however, would not simply stand by in silence while the program of promise collapsed; they had to respond with every fiber of their physical and spiritual beings to try to thwart this potential disaster.

**⁵Then Moses and Aaron fell facedown in front of the whole Israelite assembly gathered there. ⁶Joshua son of Nun and Caleb son of Jephunneh, who were among those who had explored the land, tore their clothes ⁷and said to the entire Israelite assembly, "The land we passed through and explored is exceedingly good. ⁸If the LORD is pleased with us, he will lead us into that land, a land flowing with milk and honey, and will give it to us. ⁹Only do not rebel against the LORD. And do not be afraid of the people of the land, because we will swallow them up. Their protection is gone, but the LORD is with us. Do not be afraid of them."**

**¹⁰But the whole assembly talked about stoning them.**

LEADERSHIP RESPONSE TO THE PEOPLE (14:5–10a). **14:5–10a** The righteous leadership of the nation responded in exemplary fashion. The prophetic and priestly leaders, Moses and Aaron, fell facedown upon the ground in humble submission before God and in merciful propitiation before the people. Then in concerted response to their leaders' self-humiliation,[148] the two faithful scouts Joshua and Caleb ripped open their cloaks in an act of great remorse and contrition, and then exhorted the people to focus upon the beneficence of God in provision of the Promised Land and to abandon this evil notion of rebellion and jettison their fears of the people of the land. The rending of one's garments was practiced widely in cultures of the ancient Near East as an outward expression of mourning for the dead, of expressing deep lament over disaster or plague, or of prefacing a prophetic message of judgment to an individual or a nation. According to Wenham, this act may presage the mourning for the death of the unfaithful scouts and the generation that would die in the wilderness.[149]

At this point in the narrative Joshua chimes in and corroborates the positive witness of Caleb regarding the exceeding goodness of the land they had

---

[148] Cf. Milgrom, *Numbers,* 108.
[149] Wenham, *Numbers,* 121.

scouted and the powerlessness of the peoples of the land before the faithful people of God. The reminder that Joshua and Caleb were among the scouts serves the narrative purpose of connecting them with the earlier events—the scouting theme as these two men had witnessed the same land that the other ten had—and of emphasizing their role in the present context. For the first time in the narrative all four of the faithful leaders are mentioned together, and the antithesis between the righteous few (remnant) and the innumerable nation of rebels is heightened. In a rare expression of ultimate value, the land is emphatically deemed "exceedingly good," or literally *ṭôbâ hāʾāreṣ měʾōd měʾōd*, "good is the land exceedingly exceedingly."[150] The basis of the scouts' optimistic declaration is clarified by the prophetic proclamation of faith that Yahweh was the One who would lead them into this exceptionally good land and grant it to them as an inheritance, thus also reiterating the theme of the gift of the land. But the statement has a qualifier; the granting of the gift can come only as a result of his pleasure *(ḥāpēṣ)*. God takes pleasure in an individual or a community who evidences an intimate knowledge of him, who exercises loving-kindness, justice, and righteousness in holding fast the covenant and ultimately doing his will (Isa 56:4; Jer 9:24; Ps 40:7). He was not, is not, and will not be pleased with those who do evil and who bring sacrifices and gifts with unclean hearts (Isa 1:11; 65:12; Mal 2:17). Hence the warning, "Do not rebel against the LORD."

The statement regarding the impotence of the Amorites and Canaanites before a faithful Israel was accompanied by a dual challenge to stand fearless before their foes and a statement of confidence in the Lord's presence, by which victory would be gained. A series of contrastive statements with emphatic elements highlight the literary structure of vv. 9–10. The Hebrew accentuation might be translated into English (in bold-face type) in the following chiastic pattern:

**Only against Yahweh**
  **You must not rebel**
    **You must not fear** the people of the land
    For our food are they
    Their shade has disappeared from over them
    Indeed Yahweh is with us!
  **You must not fear** them
    Then the whole congregation said to stone them with stones **(rebellion)**
**But the Glory of Yahweh** appeared in the Tent of Meeting to all the Israelites.

Instead of the land devouring the people, as the unfaithful scouts had threat-

---

[150] The doubling of מְאֹד as in the present nominal clause טוֹבָה הָאָרֶץ מְאֹד מְאֹד is found in about eight other contexts in the OT (Gen 7:19; 30:43; Exod 1:7; 1 Kgs 7:47; 2 Kgs 10:4; Ezek 9:9; 16:13; 37:10) as expressions of maximal or exceptional quantity or quality.

ened, Israel and God would consume those giants and occupy their land, for
the time of the Amorites was at hand. But instead of reaching out for this
opportunity for victory, they reacted ominously. Fear of the world was the
foundation of their rebellion. Confidence in a faithful covenant God was their
only hopeful recourse.

The Israelites chose insurrection over submission as they passed the word
to gather stones to kill their faithful leaders in whom they had lost faith.
Their fomenting fear erupted in a riotous act of attempted murder, for they
intended to stone Joshua and Caleb and Moses and Aaron. Death by stoning
was prescribed in Leviticus for those offering idolatrous sacrifices (20:2),
practicing bestiality (20:16), engaging in divination (20:27), speaking blas-
phemy against the Lord (24:14,23) or one's father and mother (Deut 21:21),
and in Numbers for the violation of the Sabbath (14:35). Later in the Book
of Numbers the point is made that murder defiles the land in such a way that
no atonement was possible (35:33–34). The people were about to defile their
land, their leaders, and ultimately their Lord; thus only God himself could
intervene to rectify the situation. He did so in such a dramatic way that it
defied the rebellious to do anything but stand in true fearful awe.

**Then the glory of the LORD appeared at the Tent of Meeting to all the Israel-
ites. [11]The LORD said to Moses, "How long will these people treat me with contempt? How long will they refuse to believe in me, in spite of all the miraculous
signs I have performed among them? [12]I will strike them down with a plague and
destroy them, but I will make you into a nation greater and stronger than they."**

GOD INTERVENES: GLORY OF LORD APPEARS (14:10b–12).  **14:10b–
12**  At pivotal points in the Bible, when humanity's sinful rebellion reached
an uncontrollable crisis, God would intervene through wondrous means to
demonstrate his power and glory, and then manifest his justice and grace by
endeavoring to draw his crowning creation back to himself. From Noah and
Abraham, to Moses and Elijah, and finally and incomparably in Jesus, the
story of his redemptive power has resonated through his word to challenge
those whom he desires to call his own to faith and fulfillment. But redemption often was prefaced by judgment, so from the cloud of the Lord's presence came the revelation that God intended to ravage the Israelite nation
with plague and destruction and rebuild a new and greater kingdom through
Moses. This potential of starting over through Moses had been raised by
Yahweh when the people constructed the golden calf soon after the Exodus
(Exod 32:10).

Structurally, this section concludes the first chiastic cycle, which focused
on the scouting of the Promised Land and concluded with the responses of
the people to their leaders, but it also commences the second cycle in which
the focus is on the judgment against the unfaithful scouting leaders. In the

larger pericope of 13:1–14:45, this is the pivotal point of the narrative, for here God intervenes and interacts with his appointed leaders. The message of destruction was introduced by the repeated rhetorical question, "How long?" (*ʿad-ʾānâ*, twice),[151] which evidenced God's long-suffering nature and attitude toward his recalcitrant people. How long will they revile me? How long will they not trust in me? The question would continue to be asked throughout Israel's history. How many times would God's people reject him in spite of the wonders that were performed before their very eyes and on their behalf? Why would Solomon, who was granted exceptional wisdom and who built the Temple, later pursue the gods and idols of the surrounding nations, even to the point of building temples to worship the false deities on the hills opposite the temple to the One True God? Why was there not a great revival of Yahweh worship after the dramatic demonstration of God's power on Mount Carmel in the days of Elijah's ministry? Eventually God's perseverance and long-suffering nature must be balanced by his justice in the form of judgment. And but for the intercessory activity of Moses as the leader of the nation, the people might have perished.

The "miraculous signs" *(hāʾōtôt)* by which their faith should have been founded and confirmed were the plagues upon Egypt, the crossing of the Red Sea, and the provision of food and water in the arid desert. Though expressions of faith are not as explicitly common in the Old Testament as they are in the New Testament, such as Heb 11:1–12:2, they were intrinsically implicit throughout the words of Moses, the prophets, and the poets. Faith in God and his word was a fundamental presupposition underlying all of the actions, attitudes, and aesthetic reflections of faithful biblical persons. To believe God was to accept his precepts, his teachings, and his general revelation in nature, and then to act accordingly in obedient faith. This was what it meant for Israel to be the people of God on an individual or community basis, so that in the midst of social, political, and economic endeavors in an unbelieving world they might fully be a blessing to the nations. To live in blessing and to be a blessing was what God had intended for this people when he called forth into being this new nation through his faithful servant Abraham. Would he now start the process over?

**13Moses said to the LORD, "Then the Egyptians will hear about it! By your power you brought these people up from among them. 14And they will tell the inhabitants of this land about it. They have already heard that you, O LORD, are with these people and that you, O LORD, have been seen face to face, that your cloud stays over them, and that you go before them in a pillar of cloud by day and**

---

[151] The usage of עַד־אָנָה here is paralleled in the literary structure by the equivalent phrase עַד־מָתַי in v. 27, bracketing by inclusio the section in which the dialogue between Yahweh and Moses regarding the people's fate takes place.

a pillar of fire by night. [15]If you put these people to death all at one time, the nations who have heard this report about you will say, [16]'The LORD was not able to bring these people into the land he promised them on oath; so he slaughtered them in the desert.'

[17]"Now may the Lord's strength be displayed, just as you have declared: [18]'The LORD is slow to anger, abounding in love and forgiving sin and rebellion. Yet he does not leave the guilty unpunished; he punishes the children for the sin of the fathers to the third and fourth generation.' [19]In accordance with your great love, forgive the sin of these people, just as you have pardoned them from the time they left Egypt until now."

MOSES INTERCEDES WITH YAHWEH FOR THE PEOPLE (14:13–19). **14:13–16**  The narrative takes another sharp turn as Moses again carries out his role as intercessor for the people before Yahweh, and the prayer by which he did so evidences the depth of his knowledge of God and his ways. This role had been exercised previously in 11:2, when fiery judgment came down from the skies, and in 12:13, when Miriam was struck with a leprous disease. In the quail incident (11:4–34) his leadership was reflected in a different way in a dialogue with the Lord concerning the heavy load of responsibility that had been laid upon his shoulders. The key issue of Moses' initial appeal was that of God's reputation among the nations, a question of how God's dealing with his people might be misconstrued by the Egyptians and the surrounding nations. This would continue to be an age-old question of how a benevolent God can bring harsh judgment upon his people and still maintain his reputation with honor. The prophet Habakkuk would ask a similar question centuries later about how God could use an evil nation to chasten and humiliate Israel, who had been so unfaithful. The question remains a vital one today as to how a beneficent God could allow atrocious treachery and heinous violence to continue sometimes unabated in our world, upon which the atheistic and agnostic forces in our world question the very existence of such a God. But God's attributes cannot be juxtaposed against each other; they must remain in balance. His love and faithfulness cannot be pitted against his justice and righteousness, such that sin and rebellion might ultimately go unanswered and unpunished.

Rhetorically, the threefold use of the second person pronoun in emphatic position echoes Moses' depth of passion in his appeal to God concerning his present and future reputation among the peoples of Egypt and Canaan, saying: *You* are in their midst, *You* appear to them and over them, and *You* go before them day and night. These expressions brilliantly portray the intimacy of the relationship between God and his people, through his abiding presence, his providential protection, and his power. With such mighty deeds renowned among the nations, Moses beseeched the Lord to allow his vengeance to acquiesce to his forgiveness based upon the possibility that defamation might come to his Name.[152] To allow the Israelites to suffer great loss or be annihilated in one fell swoop of vengeance might convey to the nations that Israel's God was unable to bring them into the Promised Land,[153] casting a detrimental reflection on his character rather than on the real problem, an insolent nation. The terminology of ability here *(yākôl)* reminds the reader of similar usage in the contrasting reports of Caleb *(yākôl nûkal,* "we are surely able") versus the ten other scouts *(loʾ nûkal,* "we are not able"). The Egyptians would echo the words of the unfaithful spies who were deserving of judgment rather than continue to stand in awe of Yahweh because of his continued miracle working on behalf of his people. God might be seen as unfaithful to his people.

**14:17–19** With this foundation laid, Moses takes his entreaty to a second level now based upon God's attributes of long-suffering, faithfulness, loyal love, and forgiveness, while still maintaining the balance with his justice and righteousness. Moses understood that God's strength could be magnified through the balanced application of his attributes to their current situation. On one hand he recalled the words of the Decalogue, which spoke of God's judgment of idolatry lasting to the third and fourth generations of the rebellious, while his loyal love would endure to a thousand generations of the faithful (Exod 20:5–60).[154] Additionally, he remembered that Yahweh was a gracious God, who through His compassion, abundant love, and long-suffering could forgive the sinful and rebellious (Exod 34:6–7). So often the God of the Old Testament has been presented errantly and misguidedly as a God of wrath and destruction, while asserting that the God of the New Testament in Jesus was one of mercy and love. The present appeal of Moses demonstrates that the God of the Old Testament also embodied mrecy and love. It furthermore evidences that Moses' understanding of God and his nature had advanced to a level of keen discernment that can only come as a result of an intimate relationship with him.[155]

---

[152] That God's reputation among the nations was at stake with respect to his people is later reflected in several OT contexts. (1) The King of Arad heard of Israel's advance (Num 21:1). (2) Balak sent for the assistance of a Mesopotamian divination expert named Balaam because he saw in Israel what God had done (Num 22:2–6). (3) Rahab sought concessions for her family in Jericho because of the awe of God in his miraculous works in Egypt and Transjordan (Josh 2:8–14). And likewise (4) the Gibeonites entered into a subservient treaty relationship with Israel on the basis of similar reports.

[153] If one takes the LXX reading of τὸ ὄνομά σου (= שְׁמֶךָ, "your name") instead of שִׁמְעֲךָ ("your report" or "your reputation"), then the flow of the narrative in vv. 15b–16 would read: "Thus the nations who have heard of your Name will say, 'On account of Yahweh's inability to bring this people to the land which he swore to them, he slew them in the wilderness.'"

[154] Cf. other such examples and forms of this liturgical confession in Isa 65:6–7; Jer 32:18; Jonah 4:2; Pss 103:8; 109:14; Neh 9:17–19,27–32.

[155] Cf. Allen, "Numbers," 819.

Moses then requested that God forgive this rebellious generation in the manner that he had pardoned them in the past. From the murmurings about water supply at Rephidim (Exod 17:1–7) and the incident of the making of a golden calf (Exod 32:1–35), to the more recent complaints about food supply and shared leadership (Num 11:4–34), Moses had witnessed God's grace in not bringing immediate judgment upon this rebellious generation. The term for "forgive" had not been used in responses of God to previous Israelite instances of discontent and rebellion, but Moses had intervened several times and seen the Lord relent from bringing destruction to the entire nation by punishing only the instigators of the insurrections. The present text (vv. 18–19) shares a number of similarities with Exod 34:6–7, indicating that Moses drew directly from the revelation in the previous incident with the golden calf. God had said he would forgive iniquity, transgression, and sin, though not leaving the guilty unpunished. The Exodus passage contains as well the challenge to obedience for the people to be faithful to the Lord so that they might see his wondrous works in driving out the inhabitants of Canaan (Exod 34:10–14).

**[20]The LORD replied, "I have forgiven them, as you asked. [21]Nevertheless, as surely as I live and as surely as the glory of the LORD fills the whole earth, [22]not one of the men who saw my glory and the miraculous signs I performed in Egypt and in the desert but who disobeyed me and tested me ten times— [23]not one of them will ever see the land I promised on oath to their forefathers. No one who has treated me with contempt will ever see it.**

YAHWEH RESPONDS TO MOSES' PRAYER (14:20–23).    **14:20–23** The Lord responded graciously and in concert with the theological tenets proffered by Moses' plea for forgiveness for the intractable Israelites. But forgiveness based upon God's grace and covenant love does not imply that divine retribution has been or will be dismissed fully. By God's grace the annihilation of the rebellious nation was alleviated, but by his justice they must be recompensed for their sins. The phraseology for forgiveness here, *sālaḥtî kidbārekā*, "I have forgiven [them] according to your word,"[156] utilizes the normal verb for forgiving or pardoning sin or the sinner; but in context it does not carry the meaning of total absolution from sin. God forgives, but he does not forget the long history of the waywardness of his people and simply exculpate them. God spoke of the Israelites testing him "these ten times," an expression that denotes consistent action over a long period of time. Though the Babylonian Talmud delineated ten specific occasions of

---

[156] Note that the Samaritan Pentateuch and several other MSS read the plural כדבריך, "according to your words."

Israelite sedition,[157] the number probably was used figuratively and in contrast to the ten plagues that God brought against the Egyptians. Indeed those were the ten signs by which their deliverance and redemption was accomplished. None of that generation who experienced firsthand the incomparable miracles of God would survive the wilderness experience to see firsthand the provision of God in the Promised Land. So the answer comes to the question asked rhetorically by Yahweh in 14:11, "How long will this people treat me with contempt?" This people, those who over and over treated me with contempt, will no longer do so! That generation would experience firsthand the justice-through-judgment side of Yahweh's character through a form of talionic justice. They rejected the land, so they will not see the land.

**²⁴But because my servant Caleb has a different spirit and follows me wholeheartedly, I will bring him into the land he went to, and his descendants will inherit it. ²⁵Since the Amalekites and Canaanites are living in the valleys, turn back tomorrow and set out toward the desert along the route to the Red Sea."**

CALEB MY SERVANT WILL LIVE (14:24–25). **14:24–25** Only Caleb and Joshua did not join in the rebellion in rejecting the land, but instead they had pleaded with the people to go forth into the land and claim their inheritance. Only these two will see the fulfillment of the promise from among the thousands who were counted in the military conscription census of Num 1:1–46 and among the twelve tribal representatives who explored the land. In this reiteration of the leadership theme, the faithful Caleb is acclaimed by God as his servant. Up until this time, only Moses had been afforded this prestigious honor by having the Lord bestow upon him the epithet "My servant."[158] A true servant of God is one who believes in God and trusts his word implicitly, who speaks of God and for God words of deliverance and hope to the peoples and who carries out the will of God even in the face of a world that denies and defies him. The text literally reads, "But my servant Caleb, because he has a different spirit within him, and he remained loyal to me, so I will bring him into the land wherein he entered, and his seed will inherit it."

Caleb would be granted a tract of land within the tribal allocation for the Judahites, in the region of Hebron, the town mentioned explicitly in the text as the abode of the giant Anakites and the area near where the enormous

---

[157] These are (1) at the Red Sea (Exod 14:11–12); (2) at Marah (15:23); (3) in the Sin Wilderness (16:2); (4–5) twice at Kadesh (16:20,27); (6) at Rephidim / Massah / Meribah (17:2–7); (7) at Sinai (32:1–35); (8) at Taberah (Num 11:1); (9) at Kibroth Hattaavah (11:4–34); and (10) here at Kadesh in the Zin Wilderness (13:1–14:45) ('Arakin 15b). The rabbis described them as two at the Red Sea, two for water, two for food, two for flesh, one for the idolatry of the golden calf, and one for the spies. Cf. also Ashley, *Numbers,* 260–61; Gray, *Numbers,* 158.

[158] Num 12:7; and later in Deut 34:5; Josh 1:1–2.

cluster of grapes was procured. This promise came to fulfillment in the allocation of territory for the tribe of Judah (Josh 15:13–19) and in the later conquest narrative (Judg 1:9–15). Joshua would be included specifically in this
statement of blessing and assurance in vv. 30 and 38. Caleb had spoken up
first (3:30), and hence Caleb would receive the blessing first.

This section of Yahweh's speech to Moses concludes with an instruction
to turn back, literally to "turn the face around and depart," and head back
down in the wilderness by the way of the Red Sea. In that the same phraseology, "Way of the Sea of Reeds," is used in this directive, Milgrom has suggested that this geographical reference "illustrates the measure for measure
principle" [talionic justice]. … If Israel desires to return to Egypt (v. 4), then
it should turn back—but only to die in the wilderness (vv. 28–29)."[159] The
usage may carry this force on a literary level, since in Exod 13:18 this is the
"way" or route they followed when they departed from Egypt.[160] But it is
also a geographical statement in that the Way of the Red Sea Wilderness was
the name of a road through the wilderness, connecting the northwestern corner of the Red/Reed Sea (Migdol/Pi-hahiroth area above the Gulf of Suez)
with the town of Ezion Geber on the northeastern corner of the Red/Reed
Sea, as well as the road from Kadesh Barnea in the Zin Wilderness to Ezion
Geber on the Gulf of Aqaba.

**26The LORD said to Moses and Aaron: 27"How long will this wicked commu-
nity grumble against me? I have heard the complaints of these grumbling Israelites. 28So tell them, 'As surely as I live, declares the LORD, I will do to you the
very things I heard you say: 29In this desert your bodies will fall—every one of
you twenty years old or more who was counted in the census and who has grumbled against me. 30Not one of you will enter the land I swore with uplifted hand to
make your home, except Caleb son of Jephunneh and Joshua son of Nun. 31As for
your children that you said would be taken as plunder, I will bring them in to**

---

[159] Milgrom, *Numbers,* 113.

[160] Note the variant order of the phrase in Exod 13:18, דֶּרֶךְ הַמִּדְבָּר יַם־סוּף, "the Way of
the Wilderness of the Red (Reed) Sea, and that of Num 14:25, הַמִּדְבָּר דֶּרֶךְ יַם־סוּף. Note also
that the translation of the location of the sea crossing in Exod 13, namely יַם־סוּף as either "Reed
Sea" or "Red Sea," is acceptable. This phrase has a wide ranging semantic domain, since it is used
to refer to the sea into which Solomon's ships sailed from Ezion Geber on the northern shoreline
of the modern-day Gulf of Aqaba (Elat). Hence the terminology seems to have the broad range of
geographical application to either the northern finger of the Red Sea, including the Gulfs of Suez
and Aqaba, and the extension of the lowlands and marshy regions north of the tip of the Gulf of
Suez. Note also that the region of the Bitter Lakes, Lake Timsah, and vicinity may have been a
meter deeper in the second millennium B.C., giving an occasional tidal connection between the
Gulf of Suez and the Bitter Lakes (~18 km). This channel of lowlands was cut in the digging of the
Suez Canal. Cf. J. Hoffmeier, *Israel in Egypt: The Evidence for the Authenticity of the Exodus Tra-
dition* (New York: Oxford, 1996), 176–222; and H. H. Lamb, *Climate: Present, Past, and Future*
(London: Methuen, 1977), 2:347.

enjoy the land you have rejected. ³²But you—your bodies will fall in this desert. ³³Your children will be shepherds here for forty years, suffering for your unfaithfulness, until the last of your bodies lies in the desert. ³⁴For forty years—one year for each of the forty days you explored the land—you will suffer for your sins and know what it is like to have me against you.' ³⁵I, the LORD, have spoken, and I will surely do these things to this whole wicked community, which has banded together against me. They will meet their end in this desert; here they will die."

YAHWEH SPEECH: THE UNFAITHFUL COMMUNITY WILL DIE IN THE WILDERNESS (14:26–35). **14:26–35** The third section of the Yahweh speech begins with the standard revelatory formula used throughout the Book of Numbers, *wayĕdabbēr YHWH*, indicating divine instruction for the leadership of the faithful community.[161] This is the first time the phrase has been employed in the narrative since 13:1. Now the divine adjudication concerning the case of the rebellious Israelites is spelled out to Moses the prophet and Aaron the priest with alarming clarity. As noted in the earlier outline of the literary structure, these verses are set forth in a chiastic structure in which the central theme is the survival and deliverance of the faithful scouts Joshua and Caleb (14:30) in contrast to the male militia whose bodies will all fall in the wilderness from whence they were sent.

A reiteration of the rhetorical questions asked in 14:11 introduces the second cycle of response, in which the answers provided expand upon the previous statement. This literary style of expanding layers or cycles of material, in which additional details are provided concerning a given issue, is a common literary style in the Pentateuch.[162] Source critics claim that this section from the supposed P source (Priestly author) breaks the flow of the narrative between vv. 25 and 36. The continuous flow of the narrative in the parallel passage in Deut 1:40–41 is posited as support of this hypothesis. P. Budd, for example, called vv. 26–38 "a major elaboration of the tradition by the priestly author."[163] The reiteration of the material and themes within this section, however, need not be seen as extraneous but as a vital part of the rhetorical structure of the account, since it emphasizes with reverberating clarity the message of obedience and faith for this and future generations. The Hebrew phrase *'ad mātay* ("How Long??") would be used by Elijah (1 Kgs 18:21) in the ninth century B.C., Hosea (8:5) and Isaiah (6:11) in the eighth century, and Habakkuk of the sixth century, with each asking the "how long?" question concerning the duration of the patient and long-suffering nature of God before judgment comes.

---

[161] See the longer discussion of this subject in the "Introduction" and the commentary on 1:1.

[162] Cf., e.g., the layers of material in the discussion of the ritual on the Day of Atonement as outlined in Lev 16:1–34. In that context there are at least three layers: Introduction (vv. 1–5), Initial Sacrificial Offerings (vv. 6–10), Expansion (vv. 11–28), and Conclusion (vv. 29–34).

[163] Budd, *Numbers*, 153. Cf. also Levine, *Numbers 1–20*, 369.

The Lord then swore by himself and his very nature as the One True Living God that every one of those men twenty years of age and older would perish in the wilderness. The phraseology of avowal, "As surely as I live!" which often introduced a divine oracle, speaks of God as the Living One, from whom life flows and to whom all life belongs. On the other hand, all of those enlisted according to the military conscription census of 1:1–46, indeed every one of those recruited to conquer the land but who were now guilty of rejecting the generous geographical gift, would die. Israel rejected their ultimate source of livelihood in rejecting the gift of the land, choosing the way of death instead. The wages and consequences of sin and rebellion are death and destruction, whereas the gift of God is eternal life in Christ Jesus our Lord (Rom 6:23).[164]

The theme of faithful leadership is again reiterated, and this literary ploy of repetition would reverberate vibrantly in the ears and hearts of the hearers for generations to come.[165] Only Caleb ben Jephunneh and Joshua ben Nun from among the Israelite troops would survive the judgment of a slow death in the desert. God promises a reward to the two faithful scouts who gave a good report concerning the quality of the Promised Land and challenged the people to enter it with vision and faith. Caleb will be granted a tract of land in the vicinity of Hebron,[166] and Joshua will receive an inheritance in the hill country of Ephraim at Timnath-Serah, north of Mount Gaash.[167] The others will die in the desert. The term used here for their dissipated bodies is *pigrêkem*, which often is used to describe human corpses that would be scattered on the ground after a great battle.[168]

In the present situation most would die not as a result of a battle against the nations but as the result of their contending with God. The actual number included in this judgment, however, might be smaller. Milgrom noted that in the delineation of those who would die in the desert, the text specifies those age twenty and older who were eligible for military service. Therefore the Levites were not counted in the census or represented among the tribal leaders who scouted out the land.[169] This selective meting out of the punishment may be followed if within the larger pericope of 14:20–38 the movement is

---

[164] Cf. Heb 3:16–19.

[165] This is the fifth time Caleb is mentioned in the narrative (previously 13:6,30; 14:6,24; here in 14:30; and again in 14:38 for the sixth time) and the fourth for Joshua (13:8,16; 14:6; here in 14:30; and again in 14:38 for the fifth occurrence).

[166] See commentary on 14:24.

[167] Josh 24:29–30.

[168] Cf. Jer 31:40 and 33:5, which speak of the bodies of Israelites who were said to have died at the hands of the Lord rather than God's agent Nebuchadnezzar. In Ezek 6:5 the prophet speaks of the corpses of the idolatrous Israelites who were laid before the worthless idols they had worshiped.

[169] Milgrom, *Numbers*, 113.

from the general statement to the more particular, a common literary technique in the Pentateuch. Such a progression would develop in three stages as follows: (1) none of those who saw God's miracles in Egypt and the desert and treated him with contempt would see the land (14:21–24), (2) none of the men who were conscripted in the military census would enter the land (14:29–30), and then (3) the men sent into the land for exploration but who returned with a bad report died of a plague (14:36–37). Yet in v. 35 the judgment is enlarged again in a manner similar to that of part (1) above—"I will surely do these things to this whole wicked community." And though there is no suggestion in the account that the Levites supported the minority report of Caleb and Joshua, in several subsequent texts the extent of the punishment of Israel in the wilderness was specified in terms of that entire generation of fighting men.[170] In the second rebellion cycle of Numbers 16–19, some of the Levites from the Korah clan were punished severely because of their rebellion. The 250 who led the mutinous effort died in fiery judgment, and thousands of others died in a plague in the aftermath of a rebellion against Moses and Aaron (Num 16:1–50).

As with Caleb and Joshua, the Israelite children would not perish in the wilderness; they would be punished less severely. They would suffer deprivation and various temptations in the austerity of the desert. Punishment for the sins of the fathers could last for generations, as noted before in the Moses and Yahweh speeches.[171] Those whom they thought would be taken into slavery in the wars against the Canaanites and Amalekites would instead continue in the traditional role of pastoral nomads, shepherding their flocks of sheep and goats in the austerity and barrenness of the Paran Wilderness. The children of the unfaithful Israelites would bear this lengthy punishment for the gross infidelity of their fathers. The term used to describe this infidelity is zĕnûtêkem, which is normally used in the context of sexual immorality and (metaphorically) for idolatry.[172] The text reads literally, "They [your children] shall bear your fornications [harlotries]," a form of guilt Milgrom called the "consequential asham." Bearing the guilt of their fathers' spiritual adultery meant that the forty years in the wilderness was the necessary reparation or punitive consequence of their rebellion.[173]

Another talionic element in the judgment is reflected in the statement of the length of time that the Israelite community would have to endure the harshness of the desert because of their rejection of Yahweh and the land. A year of punishment would be meted out for each day of the injurious journey of the scouts,

---

[170] Num 26:63–65; Deut 2:14–16; Josh 5:1–6.

[171] Cf. the words of Moses (Num 14:18) and Yahweh (Exod 34:7).

[172] Cf. Exod 34:16–17 with Lev 19:29; Jer 3:2,9; 13:27; Hos 4:11; 6:10.

[173] Milgrom, *Cult and Conscience: The Asham in the Priestly Doctrine of Repentance*, Studies in Judaism in Late Antiquity (Leiden: Brill, 1976), 3–7.

an assessment utilized later in the history of God's dealing with Israel in prophetic judgment oracles.[174] The number forty also carried with it the connotation of the general length of a generation,[175] though the specific length of the judgment was thirty-eight years according to Deut 2:14.[176]

The next statement by Yahweh reveals one of the harshest realities of this judgment pericope. If God is for us, who could stand against us? But if God is against us, there is no hope. Israel was about to learn what it meant to have God against them, a situation where even the feeblest of foes would triumph over the armies of Israel.

**[36]So the men Moses had sent to explore the land, who returned and made the whole community grumble against him by spreading a bad report about it— [37]these men responsible for spreading the bad report about the land were struck down and died of a plague before the LORD. [38]Of the men who went to explore the land, only Joshua son of Nun and Caleb son of Jephunneh survived.**

JUDGMENT AGAINST THE LEADERS: THE TEN VERSUS JOSHUA AND CALEB (14:36–38). **14:36–38** Once again in the cycles of this lengthy pericope a comparison is made between the unfaithful ten scouts and the faithful Joshua and Caleb, only this time the contrast included the final judgment against the obstinate majority. The treasonous acts were rehearsed once more in a succinct repetitive and chiastic fashion before the punishment was administered. The reiterated phrase, which brackets the focal point of the chiasmus, focuses on the act of spreading a bad report about the land. The center of the statement was the death of the spies. Note the following literary structure, which represents the Hebrew word order in the translation:

A   The Men Sent by Moses to Explore the Land
  B   Who Returned and Made the Congregation Grumble
    C   And Spread Defamation concerning the Land
      D   They Died (by a Plague before YHWH)
    C'   The Men Who Spread Defamation of the Land—for Evil
  B'   Joshua and Caleb Lived
A'   Of the Men Who Went to Explore the Land

---

[174] Cf. the forty days Ezekiel lay on his side for the forty days of Judah's sinfulness. A parallel can also be seen in the prophecy of the seventy weeks in Dan 9:20–27, in which a week represents a year.

[175] Deut 2:14; Josh 5:6; Judg 3:11; thirty (eighty yrs. = two generations); 5:31; 8:28; etc.

[176] Though a more precise time frame is not delineated, the Israelites departed Sinai "on the twentieth day of the second month of the second year" after the Exodus (Num 10:11). They arrived back at Kadesh in the Zin Wilderness in the first month (of the fortieth year?), after which Miriam died, Moses sinned, and then Aaron died. Then the events of chaps. 21–35 and the Book of Deuteronomy took place, and then the preparation for Passover took place on the tenth of the first month (year not specified) after they had crossed the Jordan and entered the land.

Those ten died almost immediately from a plague. The wicked community that had banded together in an attempt to overthrow their divinely appointed leaders by stoning them to death (14:10a) experienced an untimely death in the desert. Those whom they sought to slay, the steadfast Joshua and Caleb, would survive.

**³⁹When Moses reported this to all the Israelites, they mourned bitterly. ⁴⁰Early the next morning they went up toward the high hill country. "We have sinned," they said. "We will go up to the place the LORD promised."**

**⁴¹But Moses said, "Why are you disobeying the LORD's command? This will not succeed! ⁴²Do not go up, because the LORD is not with you. You will be defeated by your enemies, ⁴³for the Amalekites and Canaanites will face you there. Because you have turned away from the LORD, he will not be with you and you will fall by the sword."**

**⁴⁴Nevertheless, in their presumption they went up toward the high hill country, though neither Moses nor the ark of the LORD's covenant moved from the camp. ⁴⁵Then the Amalekites and Canaanites who lived in that hill country came down and attacked them and beat them down all the way to Hormah.**

CONCLUSION: MOSES REPORTS JUDGMENT—ISRAEL MOURNS (14:39–45). **14:39–45** The account ends with a reversal of the fortunes for Israel due to their rejection of God and the resultant divine punishment. In the introduction Yahweh instructed Moses *(wayĕdabbēr mōšeh)*[177] to send scouts into the land to explore that which he had promised their forefathers. Moses sent the scouts according to the command of the Lord (*ʿal-pî YHWH*, "according to the word/mouth of Yahweh"), and the phraseology used means this leader of the people was following in faithful obedience. Now the same Moses instructs *(wayĕdabbēr mōšeh)* the people concerning the judgment of the Lord against the ten unfaithful scouts. After their response of remorse to this revelation, they attempt to enter the land against the command of the Lord (*ʿōbĕrîm ʾet-pî YHWH*, "transgressing the word of Yahweh"). To attempt to advance into the land of blessing without the Lord's blessing is to set a course for failure.

The conclusion is replete with antithetical statements in relationship to the initial instructions given by God and Moses. In Yahweh's instruction to Moses, he stated that he was giving them the land; but now when they attempt to enter "the place the Lord promised," they are warned against doing so. Moses instructed the Israelites to "go up" into the land (13:17); now they are commanded, "Do not go up!" In earlier episodes of rebellion,

---

[177] Note the use of the standard formula for instruction here, usually used with Yahweh as the subject (see 13:1 above, the commentary on Num 1:1, and "Introduction: The Structure and Outline of the Book of Numbers"). Moses became God's spokesman for the revelation of judgment that had already begun with the death of the ten scouts.

Israelite remorse often led to Moses interceding with Yahweh to withdraw his punishment of the nation or at least to lighten its effect.[178] But in this case the prophet proclaimed further warning if the people should respond rebelliously again and attempt to conquer the land. In the end the Amalekites and Canaanites, whom they would have easily conquered with Yahweh the Divine Warrior on their side, would soundly defeat them.

This passage follows a simple chiastic style: A B / B' A":

A  Attempt to Go up into Hill Country—We Sinned
   To Place Yahweh Promised
   Moses: Why Disobey Yahweh? (*'bar 'et-pî YHWH*)
   B  Do Not Go up—Yahweh Is NOT with You
      Amalekites and Canaanites Will Defeat You
   B'  You have Turned away from Yahweh—He Will NOT Be with You
      You Will Fall by the Sword
A'  Attempt to Go up into Hill Country—Defeat
   Moses and Ark of Covenant Remain in Camp
   Amalekites and Canaanites of Hill Country Defeat Israel in the Land

As Ashley notes, "The children of Israel rose up early in the morning, that is, the day in which they had been commanded to turn and depart into the wilderness by the way of the Reed Sea (v. 25). They have disobeyed God once again and mistaken the seriousness of his judgment for something amenable to change if only they will do what was originally commanded."[179] Sometimes the consequences of sin and rebellion are irreversible, and one must endure the experience of God's judgment before a new course of action brings blessing. Sometimes those consequences endure for a lifetime, but even in those settings we must continue in faith so that our lives reflect redemption rather than further reproach.

### (7) Offerings from the Land of Promise: Covenant Hope (15:1–41)

The material in chap. 15 addresses three key subjects in relationship to the previous material within the first rebellion cycle; hence it holds a strategic contextual position in the cyclical thematic outline of the Book of Numbers. The covenant relationship between Yahweh God and his people Israel is in full view. Many scholars have noted the puzzling abrupt transition from the rebellious spy incident of chaps. 13–14 and the Korah rebellion of chap. 16, yet few have considered the broad structural outline in this assessment. Gray simply stated: "What reasons induced the editor to refer

---

[178] Num 11:2; 12:13–15.
[179] Ashley, *Numbers*, 271.

this particular group of laws, like those of c. 19, to the period of wandering cannot be determined."[180] The same positional question derives from the placement of priestly instructions in chaps. 5–6; 19; 28–29. As noted previously in the "Introduction: Structural Outline and Contents," each of the offerings sections functions within the sequential outline to focus the reader and hearer on the proper relationship between God and humanity in the context of the preceding material of the given cycle.

Because of the priestly nature of the material, most source critical scholars have dated the compilation of this chapter to the postexilic period, partially on the basis of a comparison with the parallel content of Ezek 46:3–15. There in the context of the New Jerusalem and the New Temple, the burnt offerings for the Sabbath, feast days, and other occasions are delineated with their accompanying grain and oil sacrifices. Gray presumed that the Numbers 15 scale of grain and oil accompaniments to the various animal sacrifices were more recent than those of Ezekiel 46, because Ezekiel's legislation addressed public offerings and those of Numbers 15 applied to private as well as public offerings. Yet later in the same discussion Gray acknowledges the antiquity of the general content of Numbers 15, stating, "Considerably more ancient than the exact regulation of the amounts to be offered was the practice of associating meal, wine, and oil with animal offerings."[181] P. Grelot dated the extension of the legislation to the resident alien to the latter half of the fifth century B.C.[182] M. Noth suggested that this section may be one of the latest pieces of legislation in the Pentateuch.[183] More recently Levine dated the Priestly source as having its initial impetus in the late sixth century B.C.E. and continuing well into the postexilic era.[184] As will be argued separately below, however, each piece of legislation included in Numbers 15 fits well within the milieu of the original wilderness setting. Though the final edited form of the text as we have it may date to later in the preexilic period, the content has parallels in the art and literature of the ancient Near East of the second millennium B.C. in

---

[180] Gray, *Numbers*, 169. Cf. Budd, *Numbers*, 166–67; Levine, *Numbers 1–20*, 385–86. Yet Wenham rightly considers the placement of Numbers 15 in the overall arrangement of the book. He notes that "these laws have been placed here as a deliberate comment on the preceding narrative." (127) Cf. also Allen, "Numbers," 824.

[181] Gray, *Numbers*, 170–71.

[182] P. Grelot, "La Dernière Étape de la Rédaction Sacerdotale," *VT* 6 (1956): 174–89.

[183] M. Noth, *Numbers: A Commentary,* OTL (Philadelphia: Westminster, 1968), 114.

[184] Levine, *Numbers 1–20*, 103–8. He furthermore dates Numbers 30 to the fifth or fourth century B.C.E.

locations like Ugarit and the Hittite capital of Hattusas.[185]

The first section (vv. 1–21) delineates the various offerings to be presented to the Lord when the covenant people enter the Promised Land rejected in the previous chapter. By way of divine directive, the rejection of the land by the majority of the spies and the people will be surmounted. God will bring them into the land of promise (15:2–3,18–19) in spite of their rebellious rejection of that gracious gift, and he will bless them so abundantly that they will in turn bring multitudinous sacrifices and offerings with which to honor and worship him. The accompaniment of animal sacrifices with grain and oil offerings, plus the wine libations, were quite appropriate considering the previous setting of the land exploration. The scouts examined the quality of the agricultural produce of the land and even brought back a spectacular sample from the vineyard. The vineyard was often a symbol of God's richest blessing upon the land.[186] The offerings from the grain fields were to be of the firstfruits, the earliest and choicest of the crops the Lord bestowed. The issue behind the singular requirements for the bringing of these offerings by either a native Israelite or a resident alien (vv. 13–16) may be presented at this point in the context of the mixed multitude or rabble who instigated the uprising over food supply (11:4).

The second section (vv. 22–36) contains rules pertaining to purification rituals in the context of unintentional sins and the ultimate punishment for intentional or defiant sins. This material is presented in response to the defiance of the people, especially the ten unfaithful scouts. They provide the means for symbolically addressing the issue of failing to follow God's instruction. Unintentional sins require restitution or reparation offerings, but flagrant, overt rebellion against God carries dire consequences, even death. Hence, in vv. 32–36 an example of intentional sin and its consequences is recounted. Since the Sabbath was a sign of the covenant relationship between God and man, the inclusion here is emphatic in light of the breach of the covenant in the immediate context. In the larger context this section would remind the people of the consequences of rebellion against the covenant commandments, namely judgment and loss of the land. For generations to come they would hear the story of the loss of a whole generation of their forefathers because of rebellion and sin. The abuse of the Sabbath would be decried throughout the history of Israel, especially by the latter prophets

---

[185] For evidence that grain and libation offerings were offered in conjunction with other types of sacrifices, see the Ug. "Keret Epic," in *ANET*, 144, lines 156–75; or V. Matthews and D. Benjamin, *Old Testament Parallels*, 78, I.ii.5–24. For Mesopotamian parallel see "The Gilgamesh Epic," *ANET*, 94–95, Tablet XI, lines 145–62; *Old Testament Parallels*, 27–28, col. iv.145–98. For similar Hittite ritual texts see "Ritual for the Erection of a New Palace," *ANET*, 358, iii.14–27.

[186] Deut 6:11; Isa 27:2. Cf. also negative impact when used metaphorically of Israel in Isa 5:1–4; Jer 2:21.

such as Amos, Hosea, Isaiah, and Jeremiah. At the end of the history of the Southern Kingdom of Judah, Jeremiah would prophesy the destruction of Jerusalem because of the breaking of the Sabbath.[187]

The chapter concludes (vv. 37–41) with instructions regarding the tasseled garments that were to be worn as a reminder of the covenant stipulations, whereby they might live in an obedient, faithful relationship to the God of the covenant. They set forth a means (garment fringes) for having a constant physical reminder of the special relationship between God and his people so they might not defy him as the generation represented by the ten timid spies had done. In Deuteronomy that outward sign of the covenant between God and man was the wearing of phylacteries bound to the forehead and forearm, which were symbols of their subservience in the covenant relationship to God. The epilogue to the chapter presents the great covenant proclamation of Yahweh as the Sovereign Lord, who delivered his people from slavery and oppression. The people must acknowledge him as their rightful King by being obedient to his commands.

Like many sections of the Torah,[188] this chapter contains a key word that provides a unifying element to the entire chapter, namely the verb ʿāsāh, meaning "to make" or "to perform."[189] After the introduction in vv. 1–2, the Israelites were instructed to make various fire offerings to the Lord, and the verb is used eleven times in vv. 3–16 in delineating the sacrificial elements or in describing the process by which they were offered. It does not occur in the section dealing with the presentation of the firstfruits of the dough (vv. 17–21), though in the following expansion of laws related to inadvertent and defiant sins (vv. 22–36) the term is employed six times. In the final section (vv. 37–41) the Israelites were instructed concerning the "making" of the garment tassels as a covenant reminder.

**¹The LORD said to Moses, ²"Speak to the Israelites and say to them: 'After you enter the land I am giving you as a home ³and you present to the LORD offerings made by fire, from the herd or the flock, as an aroma pleasing to the LORD— whether burnt offerings or sacrifices, for special vows or freewill offerings or festival offerings— ⁴then the one who brings his offering shall present to the LORD a grain offering of a tenth of an ephah of fine flour mixed with a quarter of a hin of oil. ⁵With each lamb for the burnt offering or the sacrifice, prepare a quarter of a hin of wine as a drink offering.**

**⁶"'With a ram prepare a grain offering of two-tenths of an ephah of fine flour mixed with a third of a hin of oil, ⁷and a third of a hin of wine as a drink offering.**

[187] Jer 17:21–27. Cf. also Isa 58:13–14.
[188] Cf. the use of עלה and שלח in chaps. 13–14 and לקח in chaps. 16–17.
[189] Forms of the verb עָשָׂה occur twenty-one times in chap. 15, in vv. 3(2x),5,6,8,11,12 (2x),13,14(3x),22,24(2x),29,30,34,37,39,40.

Offer it as an aroma pleasing to the LORD.

<sup>8</sup>"'When you prepare a young bull as a burnt offering or sacrifice, for a special vow or a fellowship offering to the LORD, <sup>9</sup>bring with the bull a grain offering of three-tenths of an ephah of fine flour mixed with half a hin of oil. <sup>10</sup>Also bring half a hin of wine as a drink offering. It will be an offering made by fire, an aroma pleasing to the LORD. <sup>11</sup>Each bull or ram, each lamb or young goat, is to be prepared in this manner. <sup>12</sup>Do this for each one, for as many as you prepare.

<sup>13</sup>"'Everyone who is native-born must do these things in this way when he brings an offering made by fire as an aroma pleasing to the LORD. <sup>14</sup>For the generations to come, whenever an alien or anyone else living among you presents an offering made by fire as an aroma pleasing to the LORD, he must do exactly as you do. <sup>15</sup>The community is to have the same rules for you and for the alien living among you; this is a lasting ordinance for the generations to come. You and the alien shall be the same before the LORD: <sup>16</sup>The same laws and regulations will apply both to you and to the alien living among you.'"

OFFERINGS FROM THE LAND (15:1–16). **15:1–2** The chapter divides into three sections of divine instruction, similar to Lev 6:1–30, with each commencing with the familiar revelatory phraseology found throughout the Book of Numbers.[190] The first verse begins with the full Hebrew version of the didactic introduction, "Then Yahweh instructed Moses, saying: 'Instruct the children of Israel, and thus you shall say to them.'" Typically this extended formal introduction is found in specific priestly legislation,[191] though it also occurs in the introductions to the two challenges to enter the Promised Land and drive out its inhabitants.[192] In this one chapter it was utilized three times, thus adding further emphasis to the content in light of the contextual situation.

The content of the instruction stands in deliberate contrast to the previous context of rebellion in which the land was rejected. Note the following comparative emphases in this amplified translation: "When you shall enter the land of your habitations [which you have so recently rejected] which I myself am giving to you [as I have promised time and time again], then you shall perform a fire offering to the Lord [from the abundant produce of flock and field with which I myself shall bless you—and in spite of your recent rebellion]." The Hebrew phrase *ʾăšer ʾănî nōtēn lākem* ("which I am giving to you [Israelites]") exactly duplicates the message in 13:2 in the instruc-

---

[190] Cf. the three sections of Lev 6:1–11,12–16,17–23, each of which commence with וַיְדַבֵּר יְהוָה אֶל־מֹשֶׁה לֵּאמֹר, and the present passage in which the division of Num 15 into 1–16,17–36,37–41 results. The concluding section begins in v. 37 with the alternate form אֶל־מֹשֶׁה לֵּאמֹר וַיֹּאמֶר יְהוָה. For further discussion of this phraseology and its use in the Book of Numbers, see "Introduction: Structure and Outline of the Book of Numbers" and commentary on Num 1:1.

[191] Num 5:11–12; 6:1–2; 8:1–2; 9:9–10; 16:23–24; 18:25–26; 29:1–2; 35:9–10.

[192] Num 33:50–51 and 34:1–2.

tions to send scouts to explore the land. In commenting on this remarkable introduction, Allen notes: "The grace and mercy of the Lord are magnified as he points to the ultimate realization of his ancient promise to Abraham (Gen 12:7) and his continuing promise to the nation that they would indeed enter the land."[193] The land belonged to the Lord, and he would grant it to Israel as an inheritance according to his unconditional promise to Abram. But he would not allow a recalcitrant and rebellious generation of his people to experience the fullness of his blessing; that would be left to the next generation.

**15:3–12** When the next generation of leadership (those under the military conscription age of twenty years old plus Joshua and Caleb) would enter the land, work it, and reap its blessings from God, then they would sacrifice offerings from the land in celebration of their relationship to God. The offerings noted are those made by fire, namely the whole burnt offering *(ʿōlâ)* or sacrifice *(zebaḥ),*[194] for fulfilling a vow *(lĕpallēʾ neder),* the freewill offering *(nĕdābâ),*[195] or the festival offerings *(mōʿădêkem).* Notably excluded are the purification or sin offering *(ḥaṭāʾat)* and the reparation or guilt offering *(ʾāšām).* According to Lev 22:17–25, animals for such offerings were generally of unblemished quality and taken from the cattle, sheep, or goats.[196] The whole burnt offering *(ʿōlâ)* was presented to the Lord in an act of consecration or general atonement by which one entered into or maintained a quality relationship with God. In the ritual process an individual laid his hand upon the head of the sacrificial animal, achieving identification with the animal, which then would be offered in its totality upon the altar as a symbol of the offerer's rendering his life to God in relationship and service. The peace, vow, and freewill offerings were of the communion type, in which certain portions of the animals were offered to God[197] and the remainder provided for the priests and the offerer,[198] who consumed them in the communal setting of the tabernacle or Temple. Hence the totality of the Israelite community, composed of God, the priests, and the people, would engage in a corporate meal that celebrated the unity of the community of faith. Such would be needed desperately in the context of Israel's woeful

---

[193] Allen, "Numbers," 825.

[194] Probably the sacrifice of well-being, or peace offering, usually listed as the זֶבַח־שְׁלָמִים as in the parallel verse of Lev 22:21, which lists also the vow fulfillment and freewill offerings in a triad of gifts for burnt offerings.

[195] The נְדָבָה is missing from the Syr. and Vg manuscripts.

[196] Lev 22:23 allows for a physically deformed ox or sheep in the case of the freewill offering, but not in the fulfillment of a vow.

[197] E.g., the fat and the blood were always presented to the Lord at or upon the altar (Lev 7:22–27). In the case of the fellowship/peace offering, the breast was presented as a wave or elevation offering before the Lord and then given to the Aaronic priests along with the right thigh portion.

[198] Lev 6:29; 7:6,14–18; 28–38 Cf. Lev 2:3,10; 6:18 for grain offerings provided for the priests.

rejection of their inheritance, both now at Kadesh and in the future days of rebellion.

Each of the sacrificed animals was to have an accompanying offering of a portion of fine flour mixed with oil, plus a proportional wine libation *(nesek)* that would be poured out as unto the Lord during the ritual process. Procedures are minimal in this passage, and the people presumably would have followed those methods or steps delineated in Lev 1:1–3:17; 6:8–23; 7:11–38. Instead the focus is upon the produce of the land that the Lord would grant as an inheritance to the second generation. The picture of a burning sacrifice is presented in anthropomorphic terms, whereby the combined elements would render a sweet-smelling sacrifice into the symbolic nostrils of God. Certain portions of the animal, such as the entrails, might produce a pungent odor, but the accompanying cakes and wine would mollify such smells and produce a pleasant fragrance. Three times, the number of completeness, the phraseology "an aroma pleasing to the LORD" is used in the delineation of the various offerings, and then twice more in the discussion of the equal application of the law to both native born Israelites and resident aliens in the land. That such sacrifices were to be presented by the offerer out of a faithful, humble, and subservient heart is evidenced by the later prophetic condemnation of the detestable multitude of sacrifices that were brought before the Lord by a morally and ethically corrupt people.[199]

The proportions of grain and oil offerings as well as the wine libations are listed as follows, with comparative amounts delineated in Ezekiel 46:

| Animal | **Num 15:1–16**<br>Grain + Oil | Wine | **Ezek 46:4–15**<br>Grain + Oil (only) |
|---|---|---|---|
| Lamb | 1/10 ephah + 1/4 hin | 1/4 hin | 1/6 ephah + 1/3 hin[200] |
| Ram | 2/10 ephah + 1/3 hin | 1/3 hin | 1 ephah + 1 hin |
| Young Bull | 3/10 ephah + 1/2 hin | 1/2 hin | 1 ephah + 1 hin |

Comparative weights and measures (approx.)
| Ephah (~ 1 bushel) | 1/10 eph = 2 qts | 2/10 eph = 4 qts liters | 3/10 eph = 6 qts |
|---|---|---|---|
| Hin (~ 1 gallon) | | 1/4 hin = 1 qt | 1/3 hin = 1.3 qts_ hin = 2 qts |

The antiquity of this practice of proportional grain and wine offerings is evidenced in 1 Sam 1:24, where Hannah brought a three-year-old bull along with an ephah of flour and a skin of wine for a dedication offering to the Lord on behalf of her son Samuel.[201] Hence, the legislation presented here need not be

---

[199] Cf. Isa 1:10–17; Jer 7:1–26; Amos 5:7–15; 21–27.

[200] According to Ezek 46:4–15, with its purview being the New Temple in the New Jerusalem, only the lambs that would be offered as the daily burnt offering were to have specific requirements of grain and oil Other lamb burnt offerings were to be accompanied by optional amounts, of the equivalent of what one could gather with the hands.

[201] Cf. also 1 Sam 10:3.

dated to the postexilic age, as is assumed by many literary source critics.[202] The section concludes with a summary statement regarding the number of animals offered and the number of accompanying grain and wine sacrifices. Each separate animal is to be presented to the Lord with its own grain and oil cakes and its own wine libations.[203]

**15:13–16** Throughout the Torah emphasis is given to the principle of equal application of halakhic statutes to the native Israelite (*ʾezrāḥ*) and the resident alien (*gēr*).[204] Earlier in Numbers the celebration of Passover was extended to resident aliens who sought identity with Israel and their God through following the festival statutes, such as ritual purification (Num 9:6–13) and circumcision (Josh 5:2–11). According to Lev 19:34 the alien was to be treated as a native Israelite, to be loved as oneself, remembering that the Israelites were once strangers in Canaan and Egypt. The use of the term *ʾezrāḥ* here points to the time when Israel would be settled in the land, an experience reserved for the second generation Israelites and their progeny. Each person in the company of Israel, present and future, was to have equal access to God within the prescribed manner of sacrificial worship.

The proper extension of justice and righteousness to the resident alien was an important element of Israel's existence as a unique people of God and of their calling to be a source of blessing and light to the world (Gen 12:3; Isa 42:6; 49:6). A variety of non-Israelites had come out from the bondage of Egypt with the descendants of the sons of Jacob, and though some of them (among the "rabble," Num 11:4) had helped instigate the rebellious murmuring concerning their food supply, the opportunity for repentance under the umbrella of the covenant relationship would always be there. After all, there were no "native-Israelites"—that is, those born in the land—when God delivered his people from bondage and oppression. So the door was always to be open to proselytes who would desire to identify with Israel, their faith, and their God.

[17]The LORD said to Moses, [18]"Speak to the Israelites and say to them: 'When you enter the land to which I am taking you [19]and you eat the food of the land,

---

[202] The presumption that the present legislation postdates Ezek 46 is based on the assumption that later legal materials would evidence more complexity and standardization. This assumption, e.g., stands behind Gray's threefold reasoning for the later dating of Num 15 (*Numbers*, 170; cf. Budd, *Numbers*, 266; Levine, *Numbers 1–20*, Sturdy, *Numbers*, 108). The opposite at times may in fact be the case, and the exilic or early postexilic material in Ezek 46 more likely suggests a simplification from earlier practices of ancient Israel.

[203] V. 12 contains a simple A B::B A chiastic word construction: "According to the number which you perform, thus you shall perform for each according to their numbers." The verb עשׂה, used twice here, carries the meaning "You shall perform [the sacrifice]."

[204] For an expanded treatise on the meaning of גר see Milgrom, "Excursus 34: The 'Ger,'" 398–402. Milgrom translates the term as "resident stranger."

present a portion as an offering to the LORD. <sup>20</sup>Present a cake from the first of your ground meal and present it as an offering from the threshing floor. <sup>21</sup>Throughout the generations to come you are to give this offering to the LORD from the first of your ground meal.

OFFERINGS OF THE FIRSTFRUITS (15:17–21). **15:17–21** The second section of divine instruction begins as the first, with the expanded version of the revelatory formula.[205] As noted earlier, this chapter is replete with emphasis, such that even a short five-verse section dealing with a special grain offering is pregnant with meaning. Emphases in both content and style within the pericope and in the larger context include: (1) reiteration of the divine promise to bring the children of Israel into the Promised Land (13:2; 15:2), (2) that Yahweh will bless them with abundant grain fields from which they may bring their offerings, (3) that the law of the firstfruits as a gift to God—and hence for the priests—extended even to the very first kneaded dough of the season, and (4) the resounding staccato effect of the repetition of the terms *tĕrûmâ* ("contribution, [elevation] offering") four times and *tārîmû* ("you shall lift up, you shall set aside") three times. Even the most seemingly mundane daily practice of kneading dough for making bread was to be a time of worship and celebration of God's benevolence and faithfulness. The first or choicest dough *(rēšît ʿărisōtēkem)* made from the first coarsely ground flour of the season was set aside for honoring God. Bread was the essential food staple of life, and hence a sacred sacrifice was rendered back unto God as the giver of life and the provider of grain from which the bread was made. Similarly, wine as well as grapes from the vineyard, olive oil as well as olives from the orchard, and fruit juices from the fall fruit harvest were offered to God. According to Num 18:11–16, all firstfruits and products brought in devotion to the Lord were supplied to the priests.

In the previous two chapters, issues concerning the quality of the land and its produce were central to understanding the nature of God's promises to Israel and their rebellious response to him. Now he takes the promise one step further by vowing to take action to bring them into the land. His grace and mercy became a causative reality in the life of the nation that had recently rejected this blessing. Further, God gives Israel the food, or produce, of the land. The land "flowing with milk and honey" (13:27; 14:8), meaning that which was abundantly productive, would be the resource by which God would bless the faithful inhabitants. A holistic continuum in the relationship between God and humanity is in view here: God supplied the land and blessed it with abundant productivity; man responded in faith by honoring God with the first and choicest of its produce and by keeping the covenant stipulations; God continued to bless the land and the nation. Dis-

---

[205] See above comment on 15:1.

obedience, however, such as exemplified in the recent rejection of God and his gift of the land, would break the continuum.

This practice of honoring God with the first of the dough from the kneading bowl was meant to be an object lesson throughout the history of Israel. Gratefully honoring God with this offering becomes one of the means of reminding every generation of the goodness and faithfulness of God.

²² "'Now if you unintentionally fail to keep any of these commands the LORD gave Moses— ²³any of the LORD's commands to you through him, from the day the LORD gave them and continuing through the generations to come— ²⁴and if this is done unintentionally without the community being aware of it, then the whole community is to offer a young bull for a burnt offering as an aroma pleasing to the LORD, along with its prescribed grain offering and drink offering, and a male goat for a sin offering. ²⁵The priest is to make atonement for the whole Israelite community, and they will be forgiven, for it was not intentional and they have brought to the LORD for their wrong an offering made by fire and a sin offering. ²⁶The whole Israelite community and the aliens living among them will be forgiven, because all the people were involved in the unintentional wrong.

²⁷"'But if just one person sins unintentionally, he must bring a year-old female goat for a sin offering. ²⁸The priest is to make atonement before the LORD for the one who erred by sinning unintentionally, and when atonement has been made for him, he will be forgiven. ²⁹One and the same law applies to everyone who sins unintentionally, whether he is a native-born Israelite or an alien.

³⁰"'But anyone who sins defiantly, whether native-born or alien, blasphemes the LORD, and that person must be cut off from his people. ³¹Because he has despised the LORD's word and broken his commands, that person must surely be cut off; his guilt remains on him.'"

³²While the Israelites were in the desert, a man was found gathering wood on the Sabbath day. ³³Those who found him gathering wood brought him to Moses and Aaron and the whole assembly, ³⁴and they kept him in custody, because it was not clear what should be done to him. ³⁵Then the LORD said to Moses, "The man must die. The whole assembly must stone him outside the camp." ³⁶So the assembly took him outside the camp and stoned him to death, as the LORD commanded Moses.

OFFERINGS FOR INADVERTENT VERSUS INTENTIONAL SINS (15:22–36). This passage breaks down into five sections: (1) introduction (vv. 22–23), (2) offerings for inadvertent sins of the community (vv. 24–26), (3) offerings for inadvertent sins of the individual (vv. 27–29), (4) penalty for defiant sin (vv. 30–31), and (5) application of the penalty for defiant sin— the breaking of Sabbath law (vv. 32–36). In a succinct manner this section restates the sacrifices required for atonement for inadvertent sins delineated in Lev 4:1–5:19. Unmitigated violation of God's commandments, however, could not be atoned for through sacrifice. Anyone who performed such an act of defiance against God would bear the penalty for his sin by being cut off from the community of faith. Maintaining the unity and holiness of the community is a key theme of the Book of Numbers.[206]

For several reasons this section is somewhat of a continuation of the previous context. First, a form of the verb ʿāśâ recurs in the introduction and an additional five times in this pericope. Second, there is a connection between the antecedent to the definite pronoun in the phrase, "these commandments," and the contextual background of the conditional particle wĕkî ("Now if ..."), which introduces the case law. If "these" does not refer to the immediately preceding context, then it must refer to some other unknown corpus of halakhic legislation,[207] and the referent has been lost in antiquity. A third indication of the continuity is the reference in v. 24 to the "prescribed grain offering and drink offering," which were to accompany the sacrifice of a young bull for a burnt offering. The amounts were specified in 15:9–10 as three-tenths ephah of fine flour mixed with one-half hin of oil, plus one-half hin of wine as a libation (drink) offering. The legislation is distinguished from the previous context by the addition of the sin offering given for inadvertent failure by the community or an individual to keep the covenant stipulations. Third, certain phrases speak of the continuous application of the law throughout their generations to both native Israelites and resident aliens.

**15:22–23** The introduction to this section can be translated literally, "If you sin inadvertently in that you do not perform all these commandments which Yahweh spoke to Moses."[208] One must ask What was the context of unintentional or inadvertent sin? What did it mean that an accidental mistake was made in ritual observance? Leviticus 4:1–5:19 gives several examples of these unintentional abrogations of covenant stipulations. Several settings are envisioned, including: (1) sin of an anointed priest due to lack of knowledge of proper cultic procedures or a lack of knowledge of some facet of covenant law, (2) intentional act by the community or an individual in which they are made aware of the breach of law subsequent to the act by another individual or by the priests who had been given the responsibility of teaching the law to the community (Lev 10:11), (3) accidental act by which an individual or group is rendered impure by cultic standards, through touching unclean animals, human or animal corpses, (4) accidental death or manslaughter (Num 35:11), or (5) through the violation of the priestly protocol or sanctity of the Tent of Meeting. These were expiable through proper sac-

---

[206] See "Introduction: Structural Theology of the Book of Numbers."

[207] Cf. Milgrom, *Numbers,* 122; "Excursus 35: The Two Sections on the Purification Offering," 402–5.

[208] Or more simply translated, "So if you stray and do not do." The Hb. verb form תִשְׁגּוּ from שָׁגָה (v. 22)—and equivalent verbs שׁוּג and שָׁגַג—and the noun form שְׁגָגָה (vv. 24–29) all carry the same idea of unintentionality or inadvertence. In 35:11 the same Hb. term בִּשְׁגָגָה that is found in 15:26 is used to describe an accidental death or manslaughter.

rificial ritual of atonement, conveying the general principle that neither ignorance of the law nor inadvertent breaking of the law is entirely excusable. Such acts were contrasted with the intentional rebellious acts for which no atonement was feasible.

The purification ritual was to be applied not only to the recently delineated commands concerning the burnt offerings, communion offerings, and first dough offerings covered under this heading of sinful acts, but to any commandment God had issued through Moses since the beginning of his prophetic ministry. Such would be the case for the remainder of the history of Israel, hence the time frame phraseology, "continuing throughout your generations." Not only were the priests given the responsibility of teaching the statutes and commandments of God to the present and future generations of the community of faith, but so also were the fathers of the various households. This is particularly emphasized in Deut 6:1–9, a foundational passage for the educational responsibilities of the family.[209]

**15:24–26** The community setting of an inadvertent infraction is described as one in which the wrongful act was done by a group of people outside the notice of the larger congregation or literally "away from the eyes of the congregation" (*'im mēʿênê hāʿēdâ*).[210] Such an infraction also might have occurred by the unwitting activity of the entire assembly. The priest was to perform the ritual sacrifice of the young bull[211] with its accompanying grain and wine libation offerings, and thus atonement (*kipper*) was accomplished. One is left to assume that the amounts of grain, oil, and wine were the same as those delineated in 15:8–11, though these additions are not included in the ritual descriptions of Leviticus 4.

The normal order for the various types of offerings is the purification or sin offering first, followed by the burnt offering of consecration, and then consequently the communion offering when desired. Here the normal order for the burnt and sin offerings is reversed, though this sequence is not unknown.[212] The present order may be to emphasize the additional grain, oil, and wine supplements, which would be presented to the Lord out of the bountiful produce of the Promised Land. That was the very land that the nation had just rejected but which God had promised again as a gift and had purposed to bring them into as a testimony to his grace and mercy.

---

[209] Cf. Prov 1:8 and the context of instructions in wisdom by the fathers in Prov 1:1–7:27.

[210] The phraseology is very similar to that of Lev 4:13, וְנֶעְלַם דָּבָר מֵעֵינֵי הַקָּהָל, "that the matter is hidden from the eyes of the assembly."

[211] The sacrificial animal for the community in the case of inadvertent sin is the same as in Lev 4:13–21. In that passage the detailed process of performing a sacrifice of atonement is spelled out more explicitly.

[212] The normal order is reflected in Lev 5:7–10; 14:22; 15:15,30; 16:5; Num 6:11; etc; whereas, the reverse is found also in Lev 12:6.

The Hebrew verb *kipper* was the standard term for the atonement achieved through the offering of a sacrifice for sin or for some other form of ritual impurity. Its usage ranged from that which was accomplished on the Day of Atonement to purification ritual after being healed from some skin disease.[213] Though the idea of propitiation, or the appeasement of God's wrath or punishment, may be in view in several texts in which *kipper* is used, the predominant usage of the term is for expiatory purposes, signifying the removal of sin or impurity.[214] Thus with the proper atonement ritual, and presumably with the proper attitudinal response of the community, forgiveness was achieved. As in the earlier legislation of vv. 13–16, the efficaciousness of the ritual act was extended to the resident alien as well as the native Israelite, for the community of faith is viewed holistically and harmoniously rather than ethnically divided.

**15:27–29** In typical Hebraic style, the legislation moves from the general to the particular, from the community infraction to the individual who has committed some inadvertent breach of the statutes and laws of the covenant. The sacrificial requirement in this case for the average individual in the community of faith, whether native Israelite or resident alien, was one female goat. This is similar to the stipulation outlined in greater ritual detail in Lev 4:27–31. Two variations in the present context are notable. In the present context the age of the goat is specified as a "year-old" animal or, more precisely, a goat in its first year (*ʿēz bat-šĕnātāh,* "goat [that is] a daughter of her [first] year"), a detail not specified in Leviticus. One would assume that the requirement that the goat be unblemished, or "without defect," was in effect since this was a sin offering. Also no burnt offerings are mentioned as in the previous case of the community infraction. In the sacrificial process the priest acted on behalf of the sinful person who would thus have come in a state of uncleanness to the Holy Place.

**15:30–31** The thrust of the entire passage reaches its climax in the broader context of Israel's rebellion in rejecting the Promised Land and hence rejecting God. The nation's defiance was an example of a sin of "a high hand" in that they had symbolically raised their fists in defiance of God, and for this there was no means of sacrifice that could deliver them from judgment. In the previous contexts of inadvertent infractions of the law by the community as a whole or by the individual, forgiveness was attainable through prescribed ritual sacrifices. But in the case of outright and deliberate rebellion, nothing could compensate for the people's sin, nothing could remove the impurity except the manifestation of the grace and mercy of God.

---

[213] Cf. the Yom Kippur purification rituals of Lev 16:15–22 with those of Lev 14:3–20 regarding the offering of a sin sacrifice for atonement cleansing from infectious skin diseases.

[214] R. L. Harris, "כָּפַר (*kāpar*)," *TWOT* 1:452–53.

The introduction to this section varies slightly from the parallel in 15:27, but builds on the conditionality stated there, *ʾim nepeš ʾaḥat teḥĕṭāʾ*, "if one person should sin." In this case the protasis is stated simply as follows: *wĕhanepeš ʾăšer-taʿăśeh bĕyād rāmâ*, "but the person who acts with a high hand." The raised right hand with the outstretched arm was a common symbol of strength and power in ancient Near Eastern literature and iconography.[215] Two further qualifiers follow in the text, thereby clinching the indictment against the person or persons who would sin in such a manner. First is the phrase *ʾet-YHWH hûʾ mĕgaddēp* ("Yahweh he blasphemes") in which the name of God is placed in the initial emphatic position. Second is a pair of phrases exhibiting poetic style in perhaps a formal accusation form, with each having the object of the offense in the emphatic position: *kî dĕbar-YHWH bāzâ*, "for the word of Yahweh he has despised,"[216] and *wĕʾet-miṣwātô hēpar*, "and his commandment(s)[217] he has violated." Concerning the depth of resolution toward sin expressed by such a person, Ashley notes, "This kind of rebellion therefore differs from the intentional sin described in Lev 5:20–26[Eng. 6:1–7] for which a reparation offering may be made, 'when the offender feels guilty' (5:23,26[Eng. 6:4,7])." The sinner with a high hand feels no guilt; therefore the offense is not sacrificially expiable."[218] The one who sins defiantly may not feel the guilt of his violation, but he is nonetheless guilty before God and man.

Such a defiant person must suffer the ultimate of judgment, the *karet*. Such a form of judgment, by which God would eradicate an offender's line of descendants[219] or deny a person's life in the hereafter, was reserved for the most heinous or sacrilegious offenses.[220] Milgrom delineates five categories of infractions in which the *karet* was meted out: (1) violation of sacred time, as in the neglect of certain holy days, (2) violation of sacred substance, such as in the consumption of blood, (3) neglect of purification ritual, such as circumcision, (4) illicit worship, such as idolatry or sorcery, and (5) illicit sexual activity, such as incest or bestiality.[221] In some cases

---

[215] See "Poems of Baal and Anath," *ANET*, 130–35, IIIAB/B., lines 38–40; also IIAB.vii.38–41. Common in the iconography of Baal is the standing form with the raised right hand wielding a sword, lightning bolt, or a club.

[216] Alternate translations are "disdain, revile, or treat with contempt."

[217] Several MSS, including the Samaritan Pentateuch, the LXX, the Vg, and the Targums have the plural form.

[218] Ashley, *Numbers*, 288.

[219] Such as the extension of the punishment to the third or fourth generation; see above Num 14:18. Cf. also Lev 23:30; Deut 7:24; 29:19; Ruth 4:10; Ps 109:13.

[220] For an expanded treatment of this means of punishment, see Milgrom, "Excursus 36: The Penalty of 'Karet,'" 405–08; also D. J. Wold, "The Biblical Penalty of Kareth," Ph.D. diss. University of California at Berkeley, 1978.

[221] Milgrom, *Numbers*, 406.

the community would carry out the death penalty via stoning.[222]

**15:32–36** The passage concludes with an exemplary adjudication of the case law delineated in vv. 30–31, which relates to a deliberate violation of Sabbath statutes. This case is pregnant with meaning for the community in the wilderness and for the communities of faith for generations to come. First, all forms of work and creative activity were prohibited on the Sabbath. Not even one's servants or animals could do work on this holy day, and the penalty for transgression of Sabbath was death (Exod 35:2; Deut 5:13–15). The holiness of the Sabbath was established by God on the basis of creation, and this one day of the weekly cycle was to have been set aside as a day for celebration of God and his creative activity by ceasing from one's own creative activity (work), even as God did (Gen 2:2–3; Exod 20:8–11). Gathering wood for building a fire was just such a form of work and a deliberate violation of the covenant. Second, the Sabbath was also a day to remember the covenant relationship between Yahweh and Israel and was the ultimate example of God's faithfulness in delivering the people from Egypt (Deut 5:15).

In the earlier chapters of the Book of Numbers, emphasis was placed upon several themes, including covenant faithfulness, holiness, and purity among the members of the community. The unclean and the adulterous were to be restricted from the sanctity of the community gathered by tribes around the tabernacle as the holy epicenter. God in the tabernacle, which reflected his presence and providence, was the focal point of the community life in work and worship. Now the nation stood at the crossroads of faith and futility. They had not done as Yahweh had commanded in their rejection of the Promised Land (13:1,31–32; 14:9–11). Korah and his followers would violate the holiness of the sanctuary with their presumptuous attempt to usurp the priesthood (chaps. 16–17). Disharmony ran rampant when the rabble started the camp murmuring (11:4), when Aaron and Miriam challenged Moses' authority (12:1–2), and then the majority of the scouts incited the people to rebel against Joshua and Caleb, Moses and Aaron, and reject the land (13:30–14:10). The penalty for the leaders of the rebellion was death by plague (14:37), and for the generation of followers it was destitute life in the wilderness.

Therefore the inclusion at this point of an exemplar of adjudication in the case of a key covenant violation was most appropriate. This juxtapositioning of material in chaps. 11–14 with that of chap. 15 would serve to remind the younger generation that survived the forty-year desert experience and the many future generations that God would bless abundantly the faithful and obedient people of God, but the rebellious would experience only hardship

---

[222] Cf. Lev 24:10–17,23; Deut 21:18–2. This penalty was also unjustly carried out against Stephen; see Acts 6:8–15; 7:58.

and death. This same implicit challenge would be issued explicitly by
Joshua after the land had been divided among the various tribes, when he
proclaimed boldly: "Fear the Lord and serve him with all faithfulness. ...
But if serving the Lord seems undesirable to you, then choose this day
whom you will serve" (Josh 24:15).

[37]The LORD said to Moses, [38]"Speak to the Israelites and say to them:
'Throughout the generations to come you are to make tassels on the corners of
your garments, with a blue cord on each tassel. [39]You will have these tassels to
look at and so you will remember all the commands of the LORD, that you may
obey them and not prostitute yourselves by going after the lusts of your own
hearts and eyes. [40]Then you will remember to obey all my commands and will be
consecrated to your God. [41]I am the LORD your God, who brought you out of
Egypt to be your God. I am the LORD your God.'"

COVENANT EPILOGUE: GARMENT TASSELS AND GROWING FAITH
(15:37–41). **15:37–41** Humans often need physical reminders of matters
of spiritual importance. Essentially all religions possess outward forms of
dress, adornment, or iconography that serve the purposes of self-identity,
stimulation of faith, and solemn witness to outsiders. Sometimes these man-
ifestations identify group members in other geographical settings who otherwise would not be easily distinguished from those outside the group. For
Orthodox Judaism such identifiers and reminders of the faith include the
side curls and dress codes of the Hassidic communities, the phylacteries
worn on the head and the *tefillin* on the wrist or forearm during special
prayer times, and the *mezuzot* symbols of the Decalogue placed on doorposts. In the ancient Near East as well, special garments were made for
priests and royalty that identified them within their communities and to the
outside world.[223] The appendage of a section dealing with just such an outward reminder of the covenant relationship between Yahweh and his people
was thus a fitting conclusion.

The passage commences with the familiar phraseology of divine instruction in its expanded form, which was noted earlier as a structural and theological key to understanding the entire canonical book as well as the present
chapter.[224] The second connecting element to the immediately preceding

---

[223] For an expanded treatment of these garment fringes, see Milgrom, *Numbers*, "Excursus 36:
The Tassels 'Tsitsit,'" 410–14. Cf. also S. Bertman, "Tasseled Garments in the Ancient East Mediterranean," *BA* 24 (1961): 119–28; and F. J. Stephens, "The Ancient Significance of Sitsith," *JBL*
50 (1931): 59–70.

[224] This concluding section begins in v. 37 with the alternate form וַיֹּאמֶר יְהוָה אֶל־מֹשֶׁה
לֵאמֹר instead of the more often used phrase וַיְדַבֵּר יְהוָה אֶל־מֹשֶׁה לֵּאמֹר. For further discussion
of this phraseology and its use in the Book of Numbers, see "Introduction: Structure and Outline
of the Book of Numbers" and commentary on Num 1:1.

context is the use of the verb ʿāśâ, which was used eighteen times in the previous thirty-six verses and three times more in the present pericope. The first occurrence appears in the plural imperative form, "Make for yourselves tassels" (v. 38), followed by two second-person plural perfect forms (vv. 39–40). In the chiastic structure of vv. 38–39 (see n. below) the first perfect form carries equal didactic and compulsory force as the imperative "you shall make them [the tassels]," and the second usage transitions into the function of the tassels, "and you may obey [do] all my commandments."

Chiastic Structure of Num 15:37–41

A Divine Instruction (vv. 37–38a)
  B Holiness Object Lesson: Violet Thread in Each Tassel (v. 38b)
    C Threefold Purpose of the Tassels (v. 39a)
      See Tassels—Remember Commandments—Do Them
      D Threefold Antithesis >> Not go: (v. 39b)
        After Your Heart—After Your Eyes—Prostituting after Them
    C' Purpose Reiterated (v. 40a)
      Remember and Do All My Commandments
  B' Holiness of the Community (v. 40b)
A' Divine Proclamation: I am Yahweh Your God (v. 41)
  I am Yahweh Your God
    I brought you forth from the land of Egypt—To be for you God
  I am Yahweh Your God

At the center of this structure is one of the central themes of the Book of Numbers, the struggle of the people of God to be obedient to the instructions from God in the midst of a world that would constantly lure them into idolatry and rebellion. The reference to the heart and the eyes is a Hebrew way of describing the full realm of human cognitive and emotive being. The first generation of Israel that had seen and experienced the most dramatic display of God's nature and power had failed to follow through on this most basic of precepts. The same challenge lay ahead for the next generation, who would again see God's handiwork in the conquest of the land as they had seen his power demonstrated in the Exodus when they were but children. Would they be obedient to God and see the fullness of his blessing? Or would they suffer hardship like their forefathers due to their own disobedience? God would remain faithful and long-suffering with his people.

Would they be faithful?[225]

The purpose of the tassels was to remind the people to be obedient to Yahweh's covenant commandments, including its laws, statutes, precepts, and principles. The violet color, often associated with royalty (Esth 1:6; 8:15),[226] here denotes holiness as well in the context of the extensive use of violet in the construction of the tabernacle, including the protective veil at the entrance to the Holy of Holies.[227]

By noticing them continuously and remembering who they were as a people of God, they would recall why they were there: to be lights in a world of darkness. Only then could they preserve the holiness of God in and amongst themselves, thereby fulfilling the requirement of "being consecrated"[228] to the Lord, their only true source of salvation, hope, and fulfillment. In Lev 12:44–45 the nation was instructed to be holy even as their God was holy, abstaining from all forms of iniquity, idolatry, and impurity.

Milgrom concludes:

> To recapitulate: The *tsitsit* are the epitome of the democratic thrust within Judaism, which equalizes not by leveling but by elevating. All of Israel is enjoined to become a nation of priests. In antiquity, the *tsitsit* (and the hem)

---

[225] Note the following chiastic pattern of the Hb. text in vv. 38–39

וַיֹּאמֶר יְהוָה אֶל־מֹשֶׁה לֵּאמֹר׃                                    37
דַּבֵּר אֶל־בְּנֵי יִשְׂרָאֵל וְאָמַרְתָּ אֲלֵהֶם                          38

דַּבֵּר אֶל־בְּנֵי יִשְׂרָאֵל וְאָמַרְתָּ אֲלֵהֶם                          38
וְנָתְנוּ עַל־צִיצִת הַכָּנָף פְּתִיל תְּכֵלֶת׃

וְהָיָה לָכֶם לְצִיצִת                                                39
וּרְאִיתֶם אֹתוֹ וּזְכַרְתֶּם אֶת־כָּל־מִצְוֹת יְהוָה
וַעֲשִׂיתֶם אֹתָם

וְלֹא־תָתֻרוּ אַחֲרֵי לְבַבְכֶם
וְאַחֲרֵי עֵינֵיכֶם אֲשֶׁר־אַתֶּם זֹנִים אַחֲרֵיהֶם׃

לְמַעַן תִּזְכְּרוּ וַעֲשִׂיתֶם אֶת־כָּל־מִצְוֹתָי                          40
וִהְיִיתֶם קְדֹשִׁים לֵאלֹהֵיכֶם׃

אֲנִי יְהוָה אֱלֹהֵיכֶם אֲשֶׁר הוֹצֵאתִי אֶתְכֶם מֵאֶרֶץ מִצְרַיִם          41
לִהְיוֹת לָכֶם לֵאלֹהִים אֲנִי יְהוָה אֱלֹהֵיכֶם׃  פ

[226] As per Milgrom, *Numbers*, 127.

[227] Cf. Exod 25:4; 26:1,4,31; 27:16; 35:6,35; 36:8,11,35,37: 38:18; etc. Also the breastplate and various garments worn by the high priest were adorned with violet thread (Exod 28:6,8,15,28,37; 39:1–3,5,8; etc.). Note the wording of Exod 39:1: "From the blue, purple and scarlet yarn they made woven garments for ministering in the sanctuary. They also made sacred garments for Aaron as the LORD commanded Moses."

[228] Note the participle form of קדשׁ in וִהְיִיתֶם קְדֹשִׁים לֵאלֹהֵיכֶם, "so you shall be consecrated ones to your God."

were the insignia of authority, high breeding, and nobility. By adding the violet woolen cord to the *tsitsit*, the Torah qualified nobility with priesthood: Israel is not to rule man but to serve God. Furthermore, *tsitsit* are not restricted to Israel's leaders, be they kings, rabbis, or scholars. It is the uniform of all Israel.[229]

The section and cycle conclude with the acclamation of Yahweh's Lordship over the nation of Israel, whom he had delivered from bondage to Egypt. The Exodus was the miracle by which the Lord laid claim upon Israel's allegiance and thankfulness. Now at the end of this cycle of material, which recounted the people's repeated rebellion against God and the abrogation of that covenant allegiance, the nation is reminded of that unique position they held by God's grace. The verse commences and concludes with the profound and emphatic statement of God's existence and his relationship to Israel, *'ănî YHWH 'ĕlōhêkem*, "I am Yahweh your God," the very words that conclude the two Sinai cycles in Num 10:10. These words also echo the promise of deliverance of Exod 6:2–8, which they experienced with such marvelous signs and wonders. That promise had included the pledge to bring the people into the land of Canaan, so as to fulfill the promise made to Abraham, Isaac, and Jacob. Yet the marvel of God's grace was that though this first generation had rejected the promised gift, the promise had not been nullified. God would again demonstrate his Lordship by bringing to culmination Israel's inheritance of the land.

## 2. Rebellion Cycle B: Korah and Company Challenge Moses (16:1–19:22)

### Excursus: Source Critics and Numbers 16–19

Recent source critics typically have assigned most of the material of chaps. 16–19 to the Priestly school, revising and expanding an original core of Yahwistic-Elohistic tradition. G. B. Gray discerned multiple strands of priestly and non-priestly tradition, based on the overarching priestly emphasis and the variant lists of rebels found within and without the Book of Numbers. Reasoning that since only Korah is referred to in Num 27:3, and in Deut 11:6 only Dathan and Abiram appear, these texts represent variant sources. Such a dissection of the texts results in the following components:

JE  16:1b,2a,12–15,25,26b,27b–32a,33–34
    Reubenites>>Dathan and Abiram instigated the rebellion versus Moses
Pg  16:1a,2b,3–7a,18–24,26a,27a,35,41–17:13
    Layman Korah
Ps  16:1a,7b–11,16–17,32b,36–40
    Levites protesting Aaron's high priesthood[230]

---

[229] Milgrom, *Numbers,* 414; id., "Of Hems and Tassels," *BAR* 9/3 (1983): 61–65.

Positing a more complex segmentation of the account, Budd suggests a creative literary history of the Korah rebellion: (1) Pre-Yahwistic tradition of Dathan and Abiram refusal to enter Canaan from the South (v. 12), (2) Yahwist tells the story from Transjordan as unwillingness to wait on Moses, tantamount to an overt challenge to his leadership, which results in the ground swallowing them up (vv. 1b,21,12–15,25,27b–31,33a), (3) some elaboration of the disaster (vv. 32a,33b,34), (4) early priestly story about 250 laymen who were refused opportunity to offer incense is integrated into the tradition (vv. 2b,4–7,18,35), (5) the author of Numbers introduces Korah as a rebel of Levite lineage to distinguish Aaronic priests from the Levites (vv. 1a,3,8–11,16–17,19–24,26–27a,32b, 33b).[231]

More recently Levine has espoused a simpler approach than Gray's dual priestly conflict traditions. He outlines the source-critical makeup as follows:

JE—Num 16:1–2 (rewritten by P), 12–15,25–34

P —Num 16:3–11,16–24,35, and chap. 17[232]

Ashley discerned two concurrent stories of rebellion, one of Korah and the Levites and the other of Dathan, Abriam, and On, which were interwoven by the narrator in the movement from scene to scene.[233] The resultant complex of narrative has unity as a whole with the common theme of the primacy of the Aaronic priesthood from both the Levitical and lay standpoints. The two standpoints and physical settings necessitate some repetition and result in some superficial "inconsistencies," which are interpreted by critical scholars as representing separate literary sources. For example, Gray states: "Certain features in the story, such as the redundance in vv. 32–34 and the presence of distinctive marks of both J and E, make it probable that it is in itself a composite."[234] Levine sees the statement in 16:35 (from what he and others call the P source) that fire from the Lord consumed the 250 men as "indirect contradiction to the account of JE (16:25–34)." Several of the so-called inconsistencies are simply the result of the Hebraism of representing the whole and the parts, whereby partial lists of individuals or practices represent the whole as set forth elsewhere in the narrative. For example, Korah's fate in particular is not noted until Num 26:11, in which he is said to have died in the fire from the Lord that killed 250 of his cohorts.[235]

---

[230] (Key: JE = combined Yahwist/Elohist source; Pg = original Priestly source; Ps = Priestly source.) Cf. Gray, *Numbers,* 186–88 and de Vaulx, *Les Nombres,* 190–91.

[231] Budd, *Numbers,* 184.

[232] Levine, *Numbers 1–20,* 405–6.

[233] Ashley, *Numbers,* 296.

[234] Gray, *Numbers,* 190.

[235] In other biblical accounts reference is made to one or more of the insurgents, though all were killed as a result of God's judgment. Cf. Korah in Num 16:8,31 and 27:3 (cf. Jude 11), yet Deut 11:6 refers only to Dathan and Abiram. The variations should be viewed as variations in narrative intent rather than disparate sources.

CYCLE OUTLINE

The second rebellion cycle focuses on issues of the priesthood and the roles of the priests as leaders and teachers of Israel. If they are faithful in their service to the Lord and the people, the nation will flourish and prosper in the fullness of God's blessing. Hope for the future in the wilderness as well as the land of promise will be bright, thus fulfilling the purpose for which Yahweh called them forth from Egypt and adopted them as his unique creation. But should the children of Israel continue to manifest a rebellious attitude toward God and his appointed leaders, the disastrous consequences of rebellion experienced thus far only portend a future of struggle and deprivation for this fledgling nation.

This cycle commences with a rebellion led by Korah, of the Kohathite Levitical clan, with the support of dissident leaders from Reuben and other tribes. The text provides no specific time reference as to how long after the report of the spies and the failed attempt to attack the land from the south that this rebellion occurred. Yet the Korah rebellion serves structurally as the historical setting of the cycle outline, providing also the basis for the cycle development. The focus of the cycle is the challenge to the leadership of Moses and Aaron in the Israelite community and the confirmation of the divine appointment of the Aaronic priesthood. This insurrection ultimately contests God and his sovereignty in choosing Aaron and his progeny as cultic leaders, and hence God acts miraculously to validate his choice before the tribal leaders and ultimately the nation. After the judgment is meted out against the leaders of the rebellion, the primacy of the Aaronic priesthood by divine election is vindicated in the very setting of the tabernacle. Chapter 17 ends on a somber note with a question concerning the survival of the people in the aftermath of their continued rebelliousness.

The section on matters relating to the priests and Levites (chap. 18) contains several elements deriving from the previous context: (1) the role of the priests as guardians of the holiness of the sanctuary, (2) provisions for the priests and the Levites from the tithes and offerings from the larger Israelite community, and (3) the responsibility of the priests and Levites in tithing from their provisions in the manner of the community as a whole. The cycle concludes with laws relating to impurity derived from proximity with the dead, juxtaposed with the context of the Levites and Israelites who died in the Korah rebellion (chap. 19). God's holiness cannot tolerate the impurity of death and sin, and graciously he provides a means of

cleansing and purification from that which would separate a person from
fully experiencing God's blessing within the context of the faithful community.

## (1) Rebellion of Korah and the Reubenites (16:1–50)

¹Korah son of Izhar, the son of Kohath, the son of Levi, and certain Reubenites—Dathan and Abiram, sons of Eliab, and On son of Peleth—became insolent
²and rose up against Moses. With them were 250 Israelite men, well-known community leaders who had been appointed members of the council. ³They came as a
group to oppose Moses and Aaron and said to them, "You have gone too far! The
whole community is holy, every one of them, and the LORD is with them. Why
then do you set yourselves above the LORD's assembly?"

KORAH INSTIGATES REBELLION VERSUS MOSES AND AARON (16:1–
3). **16:1–3** The cycle is introduced in an unusual way for the Book of
Numbers, for it commences with a preterit form of the verb *laqaḥ* ("to
take") and without an object of the verb to follow.[236] A survey of the
Hebrew text of the cycle evidences the key role this term plays in understanding the movement and theological import of the section. Korah desired
to take control of the Israelite camp with the aid of his associates Dathan,
Abiram, and On, usurping the roles of both Moses and Aaron. In vv. 6,17,
and 18 the 250+ rebellious leaders take up censers at the entrance to the Tent
of Meeting as instructed by Moses. After the disastrous judgment is meted
out by the Lord, Eleazar took the 250+ censers left by the dead insurgents
and had them hammered into an additional overlay for the altar of the tabernacle (16:39,46,47). Then Aaron took the true priestly censer and used it to
bring atonement and purification on behalf of the Israelite camp so that the
plague brought on by the insurrection could be averted. Further demonstration of the primacy of the Aaronic priesthood is accomplished when Moses,
in obedience to the Lord, took staffs from the twelve tribes and placed them
in the tabernacle. In 18:6 the Lord said to Aaron, "I myself have selected
[taken] your fellow Levites from among the Israelites as a gift to you." This
verse, which echoes the theme of divine choice, stands then in opposition to
the "take control" attitude of Korah in the rebellion. Korah was not only
challenging Moses and Aaron but God himself. Additional atonement is
accomplished when the priest takes the red cow and sacrifices and burns it
for the purification offering for uncleanness caused by contact with the dead
(19:2b,4,6,17,18).

---

[236] Note the following introductory phrases: (1) in 1:1; 26:1; and 31:1 וַיְדַבֵּר יְהוָה אֶל־מֹשֶׁה
("then Yahweh spoke to Moses")—in 26:1 following the reading of the Samaritan Pentateuch vs.
the MT וַיֹּאמֶר. In 7:1 and 10:11 וַיְהִי ("then it came about") and in 20:1 וַיָּבֹאוּ בְנֵי־יִשְׂרָאֵל ("then
the Israelites entered").

As a prominent leader Korah's lineage is traced back fully through three major figures in the Levitical line. As a Kohathite, Korah was among the favored clan of the Levites whose responsibility it was to transport the sacred furnishings of the tabernacle after they had been packed by the Aaronic priests (Num 4:1–20).[237] As indicated by the use of the term *lqḥ,* Korah attempted to usurp authority from Moses and Aaron, aided by three prominent leaders from the tribe of Reuben, namely Dathan, Abiram, and On. Apart from this singular text, On is not mentioned in the Book of Numbers or elsewhere in the Hebrew Bible. These three men cultivated a following of 250 Israelites from the various tribes of Israel.[238] Harrison suggests that Korah's motives "may have been the product of jealousy because his cousins Moses and Aaron had been appointed to the highest positions in the covenant community."[239] Reubenites such as the three mentioned may have joined the rebellion in seeking preferential status for the firstborn of the tribe of Jacob. But according to Gen 49:3–4, Reuben had forfeited the birthright due to his impetuous and power-wresting act of sleeping with his father's concubine Bilhah, who gave birth to Dan after being provided by Rachel in her unfruitful state. Kohathite and Reubenites alike were attempting a power play against God's appointed leaders (Exod 3:1–4:17; 28:1–4), attempting to usurp authority they perhaps felt theirs by right of lineage. Hence, the rebellion was not only against Moses and Aaron, but against God and his divine right to choose and anoint whom he so desires.

The common assertion of this mutinous assembly of leaders against Moses and against Aaron was, "You have gone too far!" *(rab-lākem)* or literally, "You have [too] much!" Milgrom describes this proclamation of the holiness of the entire congregation as "a clever application of the command to 'be holy'" that is found at the conclusion of the previous cycle.[240] The Israelites had been instructed to wear garment tassels as a reminder of their covenant relationship to the Lord, so they might keep his commandments and live holy lives before God and the world. In addition Yahweh had said at Sinai that the children of Israel were to be "a kingdom of priests and a holy nation" (Exod 19:6). But those words were based on the faithful obedience to the covenant stipulations and not an unconditional promise. The rejection of the Promised Land in the previous cycle was evidence enough of the people's forsaking of the special covenant relationship it was to have enjoyed. The group furthermore asserted that Moses and Aaron were self-appointed

---

[237] Cf Exod 6:16–25, where the early lineage of the Levites is found, including the name of Korah in vv. 21–24.

[238] As indicated by the reference to Zelophehad of Manasseh having not joined in this rebellion (Num 27:3).

[239] Harrison, *Numbers,* 232.

[240] Milgrom, *Numbers,* 131.

rather than divinely ordained, an accusation far more true of those registering the complaint. But whereas sanctification in 15:40 was related to the
people's obedience to all God's commands over against their seeking to fulfill their own lusts and desires, their rebelliousness had blinded them to their
own lack of holiness. As a result this congregation of rebels who rose up in
unison would die together, for the earth would soon consume them.[241]

**⁴When Moses heard this, he fell facedown. ⁵Then he said to Korah and all his
followers: "In the morning the LORD will show who belongs to him and who is
holy, and he will have that person come near him. The man he chooses he will
cause to come near him. ⁶You, Korah, and all your followers are to do this: Take
censers ⁷and tomorrow put fire and incense in them before the LORD. The man
the LORD chooses will be the one who is holy. You Levites have gone too far!"**

MOSES' INITIAL RESPONSE: YAHWEH WILL DEMONSTRATE (16:4–
7).   **16:4–7**   As was so often the case, Moses' response before this band of
rebels was that of a true servant prophet. He fell upon his face before the
people as he prayed for wisdom from above, surrendering his will to that of
his God.[242] His response to Korah came after an unspecified period of time,
but when he arose his words were poignant. Moses would leave it up to God
to vindicate the relative holiness of the various parties through an experi-
mental test involving a priestly ritual, a function to which the insurgents
aspired. Only one whom God himself deemed qualified to serve in the
priestly role would be granted access to serve in the capacity of an incense
bearer. Any attempt by one who is not holy to perform such cultic ritual
resulted in grave consequences. According to Lev 10:1–2, even the priests
(Nadab and Abihu, sons of Aaron) who offered incense improperly were
subject to judgment by death.

Moses' words are introduced (v. 5) with the preterite form *wayĕdabbēr,*
"then Moses spoke to ...", so often used in the introduction of divine
instruction,[243] after which Moses speaks *(wayyōʾmer)* twice to Korah (vv. 8,
16) and then again *wayĕdabbēr* to the congregation in relating the instruction given him by God. Twice before Moses' speech to the congregation
Yahweh speaks *(wayĕdabbēr)* to Moses [and Aaron], giving instructions to
be relayed to the Israelites concerning the coming judgment. Moses concludes with a retort using the same words Korah used against Moses and
Aaron, "You have [too] much *[rab-lākem]*, you sons of Levi!"

**⁸Moses also said to Korah, "Now listen, you Levites! ⁹Isn't it enough for you
that the God of Israel has separated you from the rest of the Israelite community**

---

[241] Cf. Wenham, *Numbers,* 135.

[242] Cf. Num 11:2; 14:5; 20:6.

[243] See above commentary on 1:1, etc., on the use of וַיְדַבֵּר.

and brought you near himself to do the work at the LORD's tabernacle and to stand before the community and minister to them? <sup>10</sup>He has brought you and all your fellow Levites near himself, but now you are trying to get the priesthood too. <sup>11</sup>It is against the LORD that you and all your followers have banded together. Who is Aaron that you should grumble against him?"

<sup>12</sup>Then Moses summoned Dathan and Abiram, the sons of Eliab. But they said, "We will not come! <sup>13</sup>Isn't it enough that you have brought us up out of a land flowing with milk and honey to kill us in the desert? And now you also want to lord it over us? <sup>14</sup>Moreover, you haven't brought us into a land flowing with milk and honey or given us an inheritance of fields and vineyards. Will you gouge out the eyes of these men? No, we will not come!"

<sup>15</sup>Then Moses became very angry and said to the LORD, "Do not accept their offering. I have not taken so much as a donkey from them, nor have I wronged any of them."

MOSES' CONFRONTATION WITH REBELLIOUS LEADERS (16:8–15). **16:8–15** Moses' second address to Korah confronts the Levites among the rebellious lot. He strikes at the heart of the matter, pointing to the Levites' desire for position, power, and prestige instead of being satisfied with the special role God had granted them previously. The Levites had been set apart *(hibdîl)*[244] from the other tribes to perform the service of the tabernacle and to be a special possession of the Lord (Num 8:14). Moses asks Korah rhetorically if this special appointment was so insignificant a function that he felt he should aspire to a higher position, which highlights the fact that Korah was acting out of selfish ambition rather than holy intentions. Ultimately, Korah's company of Levites, Reubenites, and others had joined forces not against Moses and Aaron but against God himself, who had delineated the various appointments to position and responsibility for the Aaronic priests and the Levite assistants. God had "brought them near"—given them the privileged access to the tabernacle in their special services—but they desired to seize control of the priesthood.

Their response enraged Moses. The generation that had experienced the dramatic and miraculous wonder of God's deliverance from the enslavement and harsh cruelty of Egypt now reflects with blind nostalgia on their past situation, deeming it one of blessing and abundance. Their minds now confused the place of despair and death with the quality land God had promised and they had rejected. Disobedience in refusing to enter and inherit the Promised Land had resulted in death and defeat, and now they sought to

---

[244] בדל is used in the creation contexts of separating light (and its luminaries) from darkness and dividing the waters of the heavens from those of the earth (Gen 1:4,6,7,14,18). The term is also used to describe the function of the veil in the tabernacle as a divider between the Holy of Holies and the other courts and in the process of distinguishing between holy and unholy articles (Exod 26:33), including ascertaining clean from unclean animals (Lev 10:10; 11:47; 20:24–26).

blame Moses for their current situation instead of accepting the responsibility themselves—so common a human sinful trait. The ploy in their retort, "Will you gouge out the eyes of these men?" was an attempt to equate Moses' leadership with deliberate deception, for this Hebrew idiom is tantamount to our modern sayings "to pull the wool over their eyes" or "to hoodwink" one's opponents.[245] Dathan and Abiram were saying they would not be fooled by Moses' leadership, perhaps even a veiled reference to the days of Moses' status as a prince in Egypt, during which he killed an Egyptian. They would continue their support of the rebellion from a distance, perhaps remembering the judgment meted out against Nadab and Abihu.

[16]Moses said to Korah, "You and all your followers are to appear before the LORD tomorrow—you and they and Aaron. [17]Each man is to take his censer and put incense in it—250 censers in all—and present it before the LORD. You and Aaron are to present your censers also." [18]So each man took his censer, put fire and incense in it, and stood with Moses and Aaron at the entrance to the Tent of Meeting. [19]When Korah had gathered all his followers in opposition to them at the entrance to the Tent of Meeting, the glory of the LORD appeared to the entire assembly.

MOSES' FURTHER INSTRUCTIONS TO KORAH (16:16–19). **16:16–19** The challenge of vv. 6–7 to perform the priestly function of incense burning is reiterated to Korah. He and his 250 rebellious supporters are ordered to appear at the entrance to the tabernacle, each carrying a bronze censer, and to stand there with Moses and Aaron. Milgrom notes that in v. 18 the men put fire and incense into the censer, but the fire was not taken from the altar. Therefore they "were guilty of offering *ʾēš zārâ,* 'unauthorized fire,' not from the altar—the sin of Nadab and Abihu (Lev 10:2). It is hardly accidental that when Moses asks Aaron to offer incense on a fire pan he specifies that the fire be taken from the altar (17:11[Hb. 16:46])."[246]

As the scene unfolds with the rebellious gathered in a stance of opposition to Moses and Aaron and the entire congregation of Israel within sight, the glory of the Lord appeared to the entire congregation. As the wonder and splendor of God's presence was revealed in that moment, the full assembly became aware of his eminence and soon the imminence of the judgment that

---

[245] Wenham (*Numbers,* 136, n. 1) has noted the chiastic structure in the words of Dathan and Abiram that emphasize the issue of their expectations of blessing:

A  We will not come up (12)
  B  Brought out
    C  From a land of milk and honey (13)
    C′  To a land of milk and honey
  B′  (Not) Brought into
A′  We will not come up (14)

[246] Milgrom, *Numbers,* 134.

awaited them. Such a display of God's glory had earlier resulted in the death of those who counseled the people to reject the gift of the Promised Land and the promise of death to the generation that heeded their unfaithful words (Num 14:10–37).

**20The LORD said to Moses and Aaron, 21"Separate yourselves from this assembly so I can put an end to them at once."**

**22But Moses and Aaron fell facedown and cried out, "O God, God of the spirits of all mankind, will you be angry with the entire assembly when only one man sins?"**

YAHWEH'S JUDGMENT AND MOSES' APPEAL (16:20–22). **16:20–22** Moses and Aaron were to distance (*hēʿālû missābîb*, "go up from around") themselves from Korah, his allies, and the larger assembly so that the Lord could dispense immediate judgment upon the unholy challengers and their many followers.[247] But again Moses and Aaron, the true prophetic and priestly leaders of the Israelites, instead of seeking offense against their opposition, humbled themselves as servants by interceding with God on behalf of the people. They pleaded with God not to destroy the entire assembly because of the rebellious leadership of one man, namely Korah. Numerous times the community seemed easily swayed by the outward cries of a small minority, but now the humble supplications of two men would save the majority from annihilation. Similar counsel was echoed much later by Caiaphas, who advised the Jewish leaders that it would be better for one man to die, namely Jesus of Nazareth, than the whole nation to perish (John 11:50; 18:14).

Moses appealed to Yahweh by addressing him as "O God, God of the spirits of all mankind" (*ʾēl ʾĕlōhê hārûḥōt lĕkol-bāśār* — "O God, God of the spirits [breath] of all flesh"). The appositional title is found only here and in Num 27:16 in the Hebrew Bible, though in the latter the name Yahweh appears instead of ʾEl, the generic Semitic term for God.[248] This form of address in Moses' prayer emphasizes that God is the creator, giver, sustainer, and sovereign Lord over all flesh, especially the humanity whose lives were suspended over the fulcrum of life and death due to their sinful actions (cf. Isa 42:5; Zech 12:1). Moses' subsequent plea therefore was an

---

[247] Milgrom notes the contrasting movement of the warning to the people to "go up from around" (הֵעָלוּ מִסָּבִיב, vv. 24,27) the tents of the rebels because those evil men would soon "go down" (וַיֵּרְדוּ, v. 33) to destruction (*Numbers*, 135).

[248] Ashley, *Numbers*, 313. On the use of El in the OT and ANE, see M. Pope, *El in the Ugaritic Texts*, SVT 2 (Leiden: Brill, 1955); W. F. Albright, *Yahweh and the Gods of Canaan* (reprint, Winona Lake: Eisenbrauns, 1981); F. M. Cross, "אֵל ʾēl," *TDOT*, 242–62. Other similar epithets for God using אֵל include אֵל אֱלֹהֵי יִשְׂרָאֵל, "God, God of Israel" (Gen 33:20); הָאֵל אֱלֹהֵי אָבִיךָ, "God, God of your father" (Gen 46:3).

appeal to God's mercy, longsuffering, pardoning grace, and forgiveness (cf. Num 14:17–20).

²³Then the LORD said to Moses, ²⁴"Say to the assembly, 'Move away from the tents of Korah, Dathan and Abiram.'"
²⁵Moses got up and went to Dathan and Abiram, and the elders of Israel followed him. ²⁶He warned the assembly, "Move back from the tents of these wicked men! Do not touch anything belonging to them, or you will be swept away because of all their sins." ²⁷So they moved away from the tents of Korah, Dathan and Abiram. Dathan and Abiram had come out and were standing with their wives, children and little ones at the entrances to their tents.
²⁸Then Moses said, "This is how you will know that the LORD has sent me to do all these things and that it was not my idea: ²⁹If these men die a natural death and experience only what usually happens to men, then the LORD has not sent me. ³⁰But if the LORD brings about something totally new, and the earth opens its mouth and swallows them, with everything that belongs to them, and they go down alive into the grave, then you will know that these men have treated the LORD with contempt."

YAHWEH'S RESPONSE AND MOSES' WARNING: JUDGMENT IS IMMINENT (16:23–30). **16:23–30** This time Moses and Aaron were instructed to tell the people[249] to distance themselves from the tent compounds of the leaders of the rebellion. As a Kohathite, Korah would have been living in close proximity on the southern side of the tabernacle with the Reubenites, such as Dathan and Abiram, who were in the adjacent camp (Num 2:16). They refused Moses' earlier summons and remained in the vicinity of their tents. So Moses and the Israelite elders went out to the tents of these rebellious leaders to warn the Israelites to flee from that area surrounding the "tents (ʾohălê) of these evil men" and away from the dwelling place (miškan, tabernacle) of Korah, Dathan, and Abiram.[250] The people in the vicinity were directed, "Do not touch anything belonging to them, or you will be swept away because of all their sins!" Contact with unclean articles, those belongings rendered impure by the sinfulness of the fathers Dathan and Abiram, would incur uncleanness and render the people culpable of the same punishment about to come upon the leaders' households. Continued support for the mutinous rebels would result in their being "swept away with all their sins"

---

[249] The term translated "congregation" (עֵדָה) has been used throughout the text to refer to various groups, such as the 250, the larger full assembly of the children of Israel, and now those living in the vicinity of the leaders of the rebellion, lit. "all Israel who were around them" (וְכָל־יִשְׂרָאֵל אֲשֶׁר סְבִיבֹתֵיהֶם), as noted by v. 34.
[250] Budd proposed that Korah, Dathan, and Abiram had set up their own tent / tabernacle (מִשְׁכָּן) to rival the tabernacle of Yahweh (also often referred to as a מִשְׁכָּן), an interpretation that would heighten the tension over control of the priestly duties (Numbers, 180,183).

*(tissāpû bĕkol-ḥaṭṭōʾtām).*[251] Then the test was explained further by Moses as one in which God himself would judge between the calling and authority of Moses and Aaron and that of the challengers.

The people responded immediately and moved up and away (cf. 24) from the area surrounding the tents of Korah, Dathan, and Abiram. The two men who earlier had refused Moses' summons came to the entrances to their tents along with their families to confront Moses. Similar to vv. 5–7 and 16–17, Moses proposed a test to demonstrate the legitimacy of his divine calling over against the opposition. His pointed words were qualified by the phrase "that [it is] not from my heart" *(kî-lōʾ millibbî),* meaning that he had not acted on his own accord or out of personal desire for power or prestige but because God had directed him and given him words to speak.[252] The negative side, from Moses' standpoint, of the test is presented first. That Moses acted on his own would be evidenced by the men surviving to die by natural causes (lit. "like of death of all humanity") or by some other "visitation" such as was common to men.[253] But if Yahweh were to do something new and totally different (lit. "create a creation," *bĕrîʾâ yibrāʾ)*[254] than what might normally occur, such as the earth swallowing up the rebels, then the evidence would be overpowering in favor of Moses. The obverse of this is presented clearly, that the death of the opposition would demonstrate absolutely that they had rejected Yahweh, God of Israel, inasmuch as they had rebelled against the leadership of his servants, Moses and Aaron.

[31]As soon as he finished saying all this, the ground under them split apart [32]and the earth opened its mouth and swallowed them, with their households and all Korah's men and all their possessions. [33]They went down alive into the grave, with everything they owned; the earth closed over them, and they perished and were gone from the community. [34]At their cries, all the Israelites around them fled, shouting, "The earth is going to swallow us too!"

[35]And fire came out from the LORD and consumed the 250 men who were offering the incense.

YAHWEH'S JUDGMENT (16:31–35). **16:31–35** As Moses concluded his address to Korah, Dathan, and Abiram, the prophetic words resonated

---

[251] This phraseology is parallel to that used in Gen 19:15,17 in the potentiality of Lot's family being "swept away with the iniquity of the city" (Sodom and Gomorrah) when God destroyed them. Cf. also 1 Sam 12:25; 26:10. The directive "Do not touch" is also given in Exod 19:12–13 concerning touching the holy mountain where Moses had ascended.

[252] One can trace this theme through Exodus and Numbers, beginning at the call of Moses in Exod 3:–20; Num 12:6–8. Similar words are echoed by Balaam in the third rebellion cycle, who claims that his prophetic words were of divine origin. Cf. Num 22:13,18–20; 23:8,16; 24:13.

[253] The varieties of death envisioned in these two phrases would include death as a result of old age, perhaps human tragedy such as fatal accident, war, disease, famine, or other natural calamity

[254] That this particular phraseology is unique; cf. also Exod 34:10; Isa 45:8; 48:6; Jer 31:22.

with cataclysmic consequences. As Harrison notes, "The tension must have been overwhelming when the earth shook and split open beneath the rebels. Verse 32 emphasizes the scope of the calamity from the standpoint of an eyewitness, describing the demise of Korah and his confederates. Their descent alive into the grave *(šĕʾōl)*, and immediate entombment, was a fate the Israelites had never witnessed before."[255] Sheol at this point in Israel's history seems to have been the grave, or perhaps a shadowy, unknown realm where one was gathered to his fathers at death. Normally one would place the dead in a cave or man-made tomb where the body slowly deteriorated, and then later the bones of the more recently deceased were added or gathered to those of one's ancestors in the ancestral burial site. But in this incident the bodies of the rebels and perhaps their families as well as their possessions plummeted into the gaping abyss that soon closed over them with collapsed dirt and rock of the desert terrain.[256] Though Korah's name is not mentioned here in the judgment, the second census informs us that his fate was the same as that of Dathan and Abiram (26:10).

The awe-struck Israelites fled in horror, frightened for their very lives as they frantically reflected on Moses' words about being near or touching that which belonged to the rebels. Fire burst forth from the Lord and consumed the 250 national leaders who had sought priestly status in burning incense before the Lord. This death was similar to that which befell Nadab and Abihu, who though being Aaronic priests offered incense using an unclean or impure fire source, a prime example of talionic justice (Lev 10:1–2).

[36]The LORD said to Moses, [37]"Tell Eleazar son of Aaron, the priest, to take the censers out of the smoldering remains and scatter the coals some distance away, for the censers are holy— [38]the censers of the men who sinned at the cost of their lives. Hammer the censers into sheets to overlay the altar, for they were presented before the LORD and have become holy. Let them be a sign to the Israelites."

[39]So Eleazar the priest collected the bronze censers brought by those who had been burned up, and he had them hammered out to overlay the altar, [40]as the LORD directed him through Moses. This was to remind the Israelites that no one except a descendant of Aaron should come to burn incense before the LORD, or he would become like Korah and his followers.

YAHWEH'S INSTRUCTION TO THE PRIESTS (16:36–40[17:1–5]).
**16:36–40** In the English Bible this passage is the natural conclusion of the

---

[255] Harrison, *Numbers*, 238.

[256] Evangelical scholars debate the fate of the family members in this dramatic destruction. Ashley suggests most in the families are included in the "them with their households" of v. 32, though he mentions that some of the sons survived so as to be counted in the second census in 26:11 (*Numbers*, 319–20). Harrison focuses solely on the Num 26:11 passage in making the determination as to who died along with Korah, Dathan, and Abiram, as well as the 250 leaders who died in the consuming blaze that followed.

Korah rebellion, and hence chap. 16 continues, whereas in the Hebrew Bible 17:1 (= 16:36 English) begins a new chapter that includes the making of the hammered bronze covering for the altar from the material of the 250 censers and the final test to confirm the Aaronic priesthood. In both cases there is continuity in the narrative ample to warrant either division. Both the Hebrew and the English chapters commence with the familiar introductory phrase of divine speech, *wayĕdabbēr YHWH ʾel-mōšeh lēʾmōr,* one of the key phrases for the organization and the theology of the entire biblical book.[257] Divinely ordained instruction is given to the priestly leadership through the prophetic servant Moses, whose position and authority have just been vindicated. Now the time has come for the full confirmation of the Aaronic priesthood.

Eleazar, eldest surviving son of the high priest Aaron,[258] was given the responsibility of collecting the bronze censers that were left in the aftermath of the inferno that swept through the entrance to the tabernacle and consumed the 250 rebels who had joined with Korah, Dathan, and Abiram. At this point Eleazar began assuming some of priestly duties in place of his father, under divine direction through Moses. Eleazar's service would also prevent the high priest Aaron from becoming unclean due to contact with the dead.[259] Because the bronze censers had been utilized in a cultic ritual act, and perhaps purged of impurity by the divine judgment, the material could be utilized in forming a special bronze covering for the sacrificial altar that stood in the court of the tabernacle. Each of the 250 censers was hammered into thin sheets of bronze and then molded by hammer to the shape of the altar.

The outer casing would serve as a reminder of the sanctity of the tabernacle, the supremacy of the Aaronic priesthood, and the seriousness of encroaching upon the holy sanctuary. Any attempt at profaning the holiness of the sanctuary, whether by unrighteous acts (Nadab and Abihu) or by unqualified personnel would be judged severely. How this covering fit in relation to the original bronze covering (Exod 27:2; 38:2) remains unexplained.[260] But the object lesson is self-evident, as are others in the Book of Numbers: tassels on garments were a reminder to be obedient to the commandments of God (Num 15:37–41), Aaron's rod was a sign not to grumble against the Lord and his anointed (Num 17:10), and the bronze serpent was

---

[257] See again commentary on 1:1 and "Introduction: Structural Outline."

[258] Num 3:1–4; Lev 10:1–2.

[259] See Budd, *Numbers,* 195; Ashley, *Numbers,* 324.

[260] Many scholars follow this interpretation that the altar was covered a second time, including: Milgrom, *Numbers,* 140; P. Heinisch, *Das Buch Numeri, Ubersetz und Erklärt, Die Heilige Schrift des Alten Testament* (Bonn: Hanstein, 1936), 68; Wenham, *Numbers,* 138; Noordzij, *Numbers,* 154; and Ashley, *Numbers,* 325–26. Others focus on the text as a conflation of priestly accounts without attempting to resolve the obvious question as to which altar is meant (see Gray, *Numbers,* 208; Budd, *Numbers,* 194).

a sign for deliverance from snakebite (21:4–9).

The coals from the collected censers were scattered outside the camp so as to not render others impure by contact with the remnants of the dead. In chap. 19 purification from ritual uncleanness brought about by contact or proximity to the dead is addressed. Many Israelites in the aftermath of this judgment would need ceremonial cleansing to be able to come before the Lord.

**⁴¹The next day the whole Israelite community grumbled against Moses and Aaron. "You have killed the LORD's people," they said.**

**⁴²But when the assembly gathered in opposition to Moses and Aaron and turned toward the Tent of Meeting, suddenly the cloud covered it and the glory of the LORD appeared. ⁴³Then Moses and Aaron went to the front of the Tent of Meeting,**

PEOPLE'S RESPONSE: GRUMBLING (16:41–43[17:6–8]).         **16:41–43** Amazing as it seems, the Israelites failed to comprehend fully the gravity of rebellion for even twenty-four hours. The very next day after the dramatic demise of Korah and his friends, the whole congregation was back grumbling against Moses and Aaron that they were responsible for the deaths of these they called "the LORD's people" (*'am YHWH*). Their complaint was similar to that of Korah and company. They maintained their own holiness and put the responsibility and blame for the deaths of more than 250 leaders upon Moses rather than acknowledge that Yahweh himself had brought judgment upon those mutinously sinful men.

This second complaint of the people brought a second theophany as they gathered at the entrance to the tabernacle. The glory of the Lord descended upon the sanctuary for the second successive day. Milgrom suggests that the pillar of fire within the cloud, which continually covered the sanctuary when it was stationary, intensified so as to be seen in its brilliance during the daytime, since the fire was normally visible during the night.[261] The cloud that had directed them thus far through the desert, giving hope for the future, now became an ominous sign of what was about to occur.

**⁴⁴and the LORD said to Moses, ⁴⁵"Get away from this assembly so I can put an end to them at once." And they fell facedown.**

**⁴⁶Then Moses said to Aaron, "Take your censer and put incense in it, along with fire from the altar, and hurry to the assembly to make atonement for them. Wrath has come out from the LORD; the plague has started." ⁴⁷So Aaron did as Moses said, and ran into the midst of the assembly. The plague had already started among the people, but Aaron offered the incense and made atonement for them. ⁴⁸He stood between the living and the dead, and the plague stopped. ⁴⁹But 14,700 people died from the plague, in addition to those who had died because of**

---

[261] Milgrom, *Numbers*, 139.

**Korah.** **⁵⁰Then Aaron returned to Moses at the entrance to the Tent of Meeting, for the plague had stopped.**

YAHWEH DISPENSES JUDGMENT (16:44–50[17:9–15]). **16:44–50** As Moses and Aaron went to the entrance to the tabernacle, the Lord instructed Moses to get away (lit. "rise up from the midst") from the vicinity of the defiant crowd so that he could annihilate them. Yet as before (16:20–21), Moses instead fell upon his face in subservience and prayer before the Lord, always a true servant of the people. By this action he also was putting himself at risk of judgment, but God is continually mindful and willing to respond to the submissive hearts of his faithful servants. While in this posture Moses directed Aaron to take *(qaḥ)*[262] the censer and place fiery coals from the altar in it and add incense so as to make atonement *(kappēr)* for the sinful murmuring of the people, thus attempting to avert the imminent destruction of all of those assembled. Here the term *kpr* clearly means "propitiation" or "appeasement of the wrath of God." In the cultic contexts of the ancient Near East, incense often was offered to pacify or appease the wrath of gods and goddesses and soothe their spirits. Incense enhanced the sweet smelling aroma of burning sacrifices that ascended into the heavens, symbolically entering into the nostrils of God (or the gods).[263]

Judgment in the form of a plague had started when Aaron returned with the censer full of burning coals and incense. Though the kind of plague is unspecified, Aaron's role in averting the resultant onslaught of death is clear. He physically stood between the living and the dead, though as high priest he would normally avoid all possible contact with the dead (Lev 21:11).[264] But for the sake of the survival of the living, he humbled himself and was willing to sacrifice his ritual purity and his own life for the sake of the people. He was a true intercessor. This image of a priestly intercessor had its ultimate expression in the work of Christ, who as a Priest of a higher order—Melchizedek—sacrificed his own life and took upon himself the sin of humanity through his death on the cross, for the sake of gaining life eternal for a rebellious human race.

Prior to Aaron's intercession the plague had taken its toll on the seditious Israelites. The account totals 14,700 in addition to the more than 250 leaders who died in the judgment against Korah and his associates.[265] At the conclusion of the plague, Aaron returned to join Moses at the entrance to the tabernacle. The literary form highlights the physical movement in the account and the role of Aaron as intermediary, with the inclusio of the Tent of Meeting bracketing both ends (vv. 42,50). Note the symmetry and literary devel-

---

[262] See commentary on the term לְקַח on 16:1 and the introduction to this cycle of material.

[263] Note the often-used phraseology of Lev 1:9,13,17; 2:2,9,11; 3:5,16; etc.

[264] The term עָצַר occurs in the rare *niphal* form twice here: וַתֵּעָצַר and הַנֶּעֱצָרָה. Cf. also Num 25:8 and Ps 106:30, where the plague at Baal Peor/Shittim was halted; 2 Sam 24:25 and 1 Chr 21:22, where the plague resulting from David's census was checked.

opments in the following chiastic inclusio:

A  Gathering at the Tent of Meeting (v. 42a)
  B  Glory of the Lord Appears (vv. 42b–43)
    C  Move Away Instructions (v. 45)
      D  Censer Preparation Instructions (v. 46a)
        E  Aaron to Hurry into the Assembly (v. 46b)
          F  Make Atonement for the Plague (v. 46c)
        E'  Aaron Ran into the Assembly (v. 47)
      D'  Incense Offered for Atonement (v. 47b)
    C'  Stood between Living and Dead (v. 48a)
  B'  Plague Stopped with 14,700 Dead (vv. 48b–49)
A'  Aaron Returned to the Tent of Meeting (v. 50)

One more demonstration of the position and role of the Aaronic priesthood would answer the questions of the people once and for all.

### (2) Aaron's Budding Staff: Primacy of the Aaronic Priesthood Reconfirmed (17:1–13)

Following the rebellion against Moses and Aaron, led by Korah and three men of the tribe of Reuben and supported by 250 Israelite community leaders, the need emerged for demonstrating the divine sanction of the priestly leadership of Aaron and the Levites. Judgment had been meted out against the seditious instigators and their supporters, and confirmation of God's selection was in order. Furthermore, the manifestation was intended to subdue the grumbling, complaining, and unruly nature that had become a habitual characteristic of the people of God. Numbers 17 contains the third and climactic account of the vindication of the Aaronic precedence.

The Hebrew text order varies from the English and Septuagintal translations. The MT 17:1–15 is equivalent to the English 16:36–50, following the tradition of the LXX, and therefore the English 17:1–13 contains the MT 17:16–28. The purpose in the MT sequence is to link without a major break Korah's rebellion and the Lord's response in setting forth this conclusive demonstration. Based on the sequence of the key revelatory forms *wayĕdabbēr*, "The LORD/Moses spoke" (vv. 1,6) and *wayyōmer*, "The LORD/children of Israel said" (vv. 10,12), the pericope divides as follows: (1) commands and purpose of the test, (2) compliance of leaders and results of the test, (3) charge and compliance of Moses, (4) consternation and fear of the people.

---

[265] On the large number of people who died as a result of the plague, see the excursus "The Large Numbers in Numbers" in the commentary on 1:44–46. Note also the methodology of C. Humphreys and others in suggesting that fourteen clans were affected by the plague, resulting in the death of seven hundred individuals in addition to the initial 253+ who died with Korah. See "The Number of People in the Exodus from Egypt: Decoding Mathematically the Very Large Numbers in Numbers I and XXVI," *VT* XLVIII/2 (1998): 196–213.

¹The LORD said to Moses, ²"Speak to the Israelites and get twelve staffs from them, one from the leader of each of their ancestral tribes. Write the name of each man on his staff. ³On the staff of Levi write Aaron's name, for there must be one staff for the head of each ancestral tribe. ⁴Place them in the Tent of Meeting in front of the Testimony, where I meet with you. ⁵The staff belonging to the man I choose will sprout, and I will rid myself of this constant grumbling against you by the Israelites."

REQUIREMENTS: INSTRUCTIONS AND COMMANDS (17:1–5[17:16–20]). **17:1–5** Moses' administrative leadership and Aaron and the Levites' priestly priority had been challenged on several fronts, from the case of the report of the spies (13:2) to the Korah rebellion (16:1–2). The Lord saw the need to establish finally and ultimately the preference and preeminence of Aaron as high priest and the Levites as the curators of the Israelite cult. The divine directive to Moses is delineated in the threefold imperatival instructions, which together provide emphasis to the process: Speak >>> Get ... Write ... Place.

Each of the twelve tribal leaders' staffs (*maṭṭeh maṭṭeh,* "tribal staff") was symbolic of the larger tribe and the authority of its possessor, and the name of the current tribal leader was to be carved on the wooden rod. The double entendre in use of the term "rod, staff" is intentional and key to the account. This instruction would enable the heads of the clans to distinguish the one whom God had set apart, demonstrating the Lord's sovereign selection and allaying the objections of the others. Aaron's name, for example, was carved on the rod representing the tribe of Levi, rather than that of Moses, the younger brother. The others were quite possibly those listed in 1:5–15, where the tribe of Levi is not recorded. With the given total of twelve, the two tribes of Joseph, Ephraim and Manasseh must have had one representative leader's staff.[266]

The twelve staffs[267] were to be brought "in front of the Testimony," inside the Tent of Meeting (tabernacle). That these rods were to be placed inside the Holy of Holies, in front of the ark, which represented the very presence of the Living God, bespeaks the solemnity and seriousness of the occasion. Only Moses or Aaron could enter without the consequence of immediate death. Moses would carry out the ritual test, to ensure no tampering by his brother. The object lesson of the divine trial would be evidenced in the manifestation of the sprouting to life of a dead wooden staff. Only

---

[266] Probably Ephraim, according to the priority pronounced by Jacob in Gen 48:12–20.

[267] The language script of the inscription remains an enigma because no Proto-Hebrew epigraphic materials are known from this early period. Possibilities include the Proto-Canaanite script of King Ahiram and other Canaanite-Phoenician inscriptions of the Late Bronze Age or Iron IA, as well as less likely Egyptian hieroglyphs. The earliest Israelite texts of the Iron II period reflect an adapted form of the Syro-Phoenician script of the twelfth–tenth centuries B.C.

God can impart life to that which is dead, and this test would show to the combined tribes of Israel that Yahweh had conferred a special blessing upon the tribe whom he would choose. The resultant intent was the alleviation of the grumbling spirit and open criticism that had so characterized the Israelites. Kaiser notes:

> The true nature of this murmuring is seen in that it is an open act of rebellion against the Lord (Num 14:9) and a stubborn refusal to believe God's word and God's miraculous works (Num 14:11,22,23). Thus the right attitude in real difficulty is unconditional acceptance and obedience.[268]

**[6]So Moses spoke to the Israelites, and their leaders gave him twelve staffs, one for the leader of each of their ancestral tribes, and Aaron's staff was among them. [7]Moses placed the staffs before the LORD in the Tent of the Testimony.**

READY COMPLIANCE OF THE PEOPLE AND MOSES (17:6–7[17:21–22]). **17:6–7** Moses faithfully complies with the Lord's instructions and the twelve staffs are placed "before the Lord" (="in front of the Testimony" of v. 4) in the "Tent of the Testimony." This phraseology is an abbreviated variant form referring to the ark of the covenant, which housed the two tablets of the law. The law upon the tablets also is referred to as the "testimony" (Exod 31:18; 34:29). This setting was the seat of revelation (Exod 25:22), and thus the outcome of the test was to be interpreted as divine revelation.

**[8]The next day Moses entered the Tent of the Testimony and saw that Aaron's staff, which represented the house of Levi, had not only sprouted but had budded, blossomed and produced almonds. [9]Then Moses brought out all the staffs from the LORD's presence to all the Israelites. They looked at them, and each man took his own staff.**

RESULTS OF THE TEST (17:8–9[17:23–24]). **17:8–9** The evidence of divine disclosure and designation surpassed even Moses' expectations. The following morning Moses entered the inner Tent of the Testimony and observed the miraculous handiwork of the Lord in demonstrating his sovereignty over nature and humanity in resounding fashion. In literary response to the threefold instructions of vv. 2–4, a fourfold manifestation of God's power over nature is displayed, as Aaron's almond wood staff matured through the production cycle: sprouted –> budded –> blossomed –> produced almonds.

The almond tree, chosen by Aaron to fashion his tribe's staff, may have been a symbol of the Levite clan. The almond is one of the earliest trees to bud and blossom in the spring, and the fruit ripens in early to midsummer. But for a formerly dead limb to sprout, bud, blossom, and produce ripe

---

[268] Kaiser, *TWOT,* "לוּן," 475.

almonds overnight was a remarkable wonder, a natural process with supernatural timing. The almond branch in Israelite art and literature was a symbol of life that derived from their Maker. For Jeremiah it was a symbol of God's guarding his word so as to bring it to pass and accomplish his purpose (Jer 1:11–12). The bud and flower were shaped so elegantly that the three golden bowls on each side of the tabernacle lampstand were patterned after them (Exod 25:31–40).

Moses subsequently returned with the twelve staffs from the Tent of God's presence so that the Israelites might observe the results. The term translated "looked" (yir°ū from rā°â, "to see") often means "look with discernment, understanding."[269] Those scrutinizing the rod Moses displayed and then distributed, each one to its tribal representative, could readily see the manifestation of the divine selection. The priority of the Aaronic priesthood had been vindicated, and the other tribal leaders must have acknowledged the outcome, some with shame who earlier had rebelled and some with humble submission to God.

**[10]The LORD said to Moses, "Put back Aaron's staff in front of the Testimony, to be kept as a sign to the rebellious. This will put an end to their grumbling against me, so that they will not die." [11]Moses did just as the LORD commanded him.**

RENEWED INSTRUCTIONS (17:10–11[17:25–26]). **17:10–11** The subsequent set of divine instructions to Moses would establish a symbolic memorial to God's sovereign decision. Aaron's produce-yielding almond staff was to be placed in front of the ark of the Testimony as a sign to the present and future generations of this significant encounter with the Almighty. The rod, like the manna in Exod 16:33–35, resulted from a rebellious situation and would serve as a testimony to God's provision for his people in the Aaronic priesthood. The priests and the Levites represented the people before God in the cult and facilitated their worship of him, and this intermediary role demanded holiness and faithfulness. The succeeding chapter outlines the tithe and offering provisions for this distinct class of religious leaders.

Aaron's budded staff would serve also as a sign to the rebellious, literally "the sons of rebellion,"[270] so they would no longer murmur and complain against God and thereafter reap the disastrous consequences that had been experienced in previous circumstances. Moses' compliance as a faithful prophet and servant is no minor response in the structural scheme of the Book of Numbers.

---

[269] Cp. Elijah's revelation in 1 Kgs 19:3 or God's words concerning his people in Isa 6:10.

[270] The particular phraseology is unique to this verse, though similar phrases combine מְרִי, "rebellion," with other terms, such as Isaiah's "people of rebellion" (30:9) and Ezekiel's "house of rebellion" (2:5,6,8; 3:9,26,27; 12:2,3,9,25; 17:12; 24:3). Such phraseology is a degrading rhetorical metonym for the common referent "children of Israel."

This is the last time the phrase is used of Moses before the great lawgiver himself joins the Israelites in their rebelliousness (20:2–13). Eight times previously Moses had carried out the Lord's commands in faithful adherence to the stipulations. Later at Kadesh in the Wilderness of Zin, the loyal servant would succumb to the temptation to react in an unholy manner toward his God.

**<sup></sup>¹²The Israelites said to Moses, "We will die! We are lost, we are all lost! ¹³Anyone who even comes near the tabernacle of the LORD will die. Are we all going to die?"**

RHETORICAL RESPONSE OF THE ISRAELITES (17:12–13[17:27–28]). **17:12–13** Realization of the gravity of the issue of rebellion and the questioning of God's anointed reverberated in the hearts and minds of the people. Their obstinacy was turned to despondent cries for mercy, exhibiting a tone that implies anything but hope or confidence in God's forbearing compassion. They believed they were about to perish at the hand of a holy God. The Hebrew verbs reflect the people's certainty of their ensuing demise, a hopeless situation with a futile future. The Hebrew text reads *hēn gāwaʿnû ʾābadnû kūlānû ʾābādnû* (lit., "Behold we expire, we perish! All of us perish!"). The mortal danger of merely approaching[271] the tabernacle would likely discourage further dissension or insurrection. The unanswered final question of the people concerning their fate will be resolved in the following two chapters, which contain the instructions from the Lord concerning a proper approach to a holy and just God.

Reference is made in the New Testament (Heb 9:4) to the placement of Aaron's budded staff in front of the ark of the covenant. The writer of Hebrews outlines the ultimate preeminent priesthood, that of Jesus Christ, the High Priest of the "greater and more perfect tabernacle" and the Mediator of the new covenant. Whereas the Lord formerly restricted entry into the Holy of Holies to the Aaronic high priesthood, so only Jesus could enter the Most Holy Place of the heavenly tabernacle and bring reconciliation between mankind and God, setting forth himself as the quintessential sacrificial offering. Furthermore, the stipulation of Jesus concerning those who would desire entry into the presence of God is explicitly recorded in the Gospel of John (14:6): "I am the Way and the Truth and the Life. No one comes to the Father except through me."

### (1) The Priests and the Levites: Additional Responsibilities and Provisions (18:1–32)

The second rebellion cycle concludes with two chapters that complement the distress and harsh realities recounted in chaps. 16–17. Following the

---

[271] כֹּל הַקָּרֵב הַקָּרֵב אֶל־מִשְׁכַּן יְהוָה יָמוּת. The dittography here probably is original, echoing the repetition of אָבַדְנוּ in v. 27.

Korah rebellion and the judgment upon its leaders and followers and the three-fold public vindication of the Aaronic priesthood, additional responsibilities of and provisions for the priests and Levites are outlined in the present chapter. The final chapter in the cycle (chap. 19) contains the essential purification ritual for expurgating the uncleanness associated with the dead, as was necessary when the 14,950+ perished in the Korah rebellion. These chapters complete the cyclical structure of the second rebellion cycle. Chapter 18 reconfirms the Aaronic priestly leadership as demonstrated in chap. 17 and the service roles of the Levites as presented in chaps. 3 and 4. At the same time this material sets forth principles that provide the foundation for answering the open rhetorical question at the conclusion of chap. 17 regarding the potential death of the rebellious congregation. One additional purpose is within the larger framework of the Book of Numbers. The extensive description of offerings brought by the Israelites, and which would be used in support of the priesthood, stands parallel to chap. 15 in that there is implicit assurance that Yahweh will bring his people into the Promised Land and abundantly supply their needs—in spite of their continued rebelliousness.

The present chapter readdresses and expands the role of the Levites as guardians of the tabernacle. They were to preserve the sanctity of the holy place and to prevent encroachment from Israelites outside the Levitical line, as well as from rebellious and unclean Israelites even from within, such as Korah and his associates. If impure or unauthorized persons were allowed by the Levites to enter the sanctuary, they would suffer blame and retribution for neglect of duty. Thus it answers the question about the protection and survival of the people in the face of potential judgment before God. Violation of the holy precinct by unauthorized persons was punishable by death. Even the Levites, as delineated in chaps. 2; 4; 8, and demonstrated in chaps. 16–17, were not permitted to enter the Tent of Meeting proper. Only the Aaronic priesthood and Moses were eligible for that sacred privilege.

The phraseology "they shall bear the iniquity of the sanctuary" emphasized this point. In a very real sense, the gift of the priesthood was a gift of grace to the nation of Israel, whereby they might live in holiness and righteousness in their relationship to God and not suffer death as a result of violating his holiness. As Milgrom has noted, the Levites functioned as a "lightning rod to attract God's wrath upon themselves whenever an Israelite has encroached upon the sancta."[272] Hence, they functioned as both physical and spiritual intermediaries between God and the people.

M. Douglas has outlined the Book of Numbers in a cyclical structure, which is based on alternating sections of story and law, to be read in "rungs" of faith-defilement, holy times, and purification. The law sections, such as

---

[272] Milgrom, *Numbers*, 371.

chaps. 15; 18–19, develop in parallel fashion the theme of the constitution of the nation as a holy and undefiled people and define its prophetic destiny as the people of God in the midst of a defiled world. As a general overview, the parallel structure is outlined as follows:[273]

| Numbers 15 | Structural Theme | Numbers 18–19 |
|---|---|---|
| 15:1–21 | A. Holy things for priests and Levites | 18:1–32 |
| 15:22–29 | B. Purification from unintended sin | 19:1–19 |
| 15:30–36 | C. Intention: deliberate sinners cut off | 19:20 |
| 15:37–41 | D. A statute forever—perpetual | 19:21–22 |

This pattern analysis, however, does not address the intricate poetic and rhetorical devices employed throughout these and the surrounding chapters, which are addressed in the following commentary.

### Excursus: The Literary Structure of Numbers 18 and Its Meaning

The chapter builds upon previous material related to the Aaronic priests and the Levites related in chaps. 3; 4; and 8, with an additional piece of legislation in the final section related to the Levite tithe of the tithe to the priesthood (vv. 25–32). At the conclusion of this chapter is a "Literary and Structural Outline of Numbers 18," which highlights the rhetorical emphases of each section within the overall structure of the chapter. Metrical calculations are included that further suggest that the passage has a poetic substructure that facilitated memorization and recitation of this passage.

In Part I the structural emphasis is on the delineation of duties and responsibilities between the priests and the Levites, through which they bear the consequences of any iniquity, violation, or trespass against the sanctity of the Tent of Meeting. Protective service of the Levites extended only to the Tent, where they accompanied the priests but not to the holy objects within the Tent, which were under the full watchcare of the priests. Encroachment by any unauthorized person, whether by a non-Levite upon the sanctuary or by a Levite upon the holy objects, was punishable by death. Priests were also culpable of violating the sanctity of the Holy Place if they allowed an unauthorized person within its defined sacred space. Even the priests were prohibited from going beyond the veil and entering the Holy of Holies; only the high priest was permitted to enter that sanctum on the Day of Atonement.

In Part II the various means of tribute support for the priesthood are outlined. Since neither the Levites nor the Aaronic priests would have territorial allocations within the Promised Land, having been set aside for the sacred service of the tabernacle, some means was necessary for providing for the well-being and sustenance of those in their households. The material is presented in cyclical fashion, moving from the general to the specific in typical Pentateuch style of presenting stipulations. First the statement is made about the general tribute

---

[273] M. Douglas, *In the Wilderness: The Doctrine of Defilement in the Book of Numbers*, JSOT-Sup 158 (Sheffield: Academic Press, 1993), 144–52.

(v. 8), then to the various offering types by which the material would be received (vv. 9–10), and then to the specific plant, animal, and human elements that would be dedicated or contributed to the priests and Levites. Throughout this section emphasis is made on the fact that the tribute given to Yahweh was a gift from Yahweh and for the priests and Levites with the constant repetition of the respective phraseology. In a mere twelve verses the following tabulation of these indicative phrases emerges. That the gifts were presented to Yahweh is expressed seven times, usually *l-YHWH*. Yahweh's giving of the tribute, using a form of *nātan* is stated four times. The second person pronominal suffix abounds in such phrases as "for you" (*ĕkā or lāk*, 15x), "with you" (*'itkā*, 3x), "for your sons" or "daughters" (*lĕbānêkā, libnōtêkā*, 6x), "for your household" (*bêtkā*, 2x), and "for your offspring" (*lĕzar'ăkā*, 1x), for a total of twenty-seven times. The complete expression of this principle is found in the concluding verse of the section, "All of the holy presentation offerings, which the Israelites have presented to Yahweh, I have given for you, and for your sons, and for your daughters with you as an everlasting covenant."

In the third section an inclusio is formed by statements concerning the Levite lack of a territorial inheritance in the Promised Land. Within the bracketed context the poetic narrative moves from the pronouncement that Yahweh was their share of the inheritance in the midst of the Israelites (vv. 20,24b), and hence that which was his share via the annual tithe was to be their inheritance (vv. 21,24a), to the focal point in the chiastic structure, that this gracious provision was in compensation for their guardianship service of the Tent of Meeting (vv. 22–23).

Part IV presents the new legislation regarding the Levite tithe of the tithe to the priesthood, via a concluding summary of tribute portions mentioned in the previous sections. At the center of the modified chiastic form is the highlighting of the fact that this special share was the best of the best of the tribute collected from the Israelite threshing floors and wine vats. The concluding verse of the chapter completes the chapter-long inclusio regarding the matter of bearing[274] "the responsibility for offenses" (lit., "iniquity," *'āwōn*) against the sanctuary or not bearing the guilt (lit. "sin," *hēṭ'*) of abusing the offerings brought by the Israelites.

**[1]The LORD said to Aaron, "You, your sons and your father's family are to bear the responsibility for offenses against the sanctuary, and you and your sons alone are to bear the responsibility for offenses against the priesthood. [2]Bring your fellow Levites from your ancestral tribe to join you and assist you when you and your sons minister before the Tent of the Testimony. [3]They are to be responsible to you and are to perform all the duties of the Tent, but they must not go near the furnishings of the sanctuary or the altar, or both they and you will die. [4]They are to join you and be responsible for the care of the Tent of Meeting—all the work at the Tent—and no one else may come near where you are.**

**[5]"You are to be responsible for the care of the sanctuary and the altar, so that wrath will not fall on the Israelites again. [6]I myself have selected your fellow Lev-**

---

[274] Note the use of the verb form תִּשְׂאוּ in v. 1 and וְלֹא־תִשְׂאוּ in v. 32.

ites from among the Israelites as a gift to you, dedicated to the LORD to do the work at the Tent of Meeting. ⁷But only you and your sons may serve as priests in connection with everything at the altar and inside the curtain. I am giving you the service of the priesthood as a gift. Anyone else who comes near the sanctuary must be put to death."

PRIESTS AND LEVITES: GUARDIANS OF THE SANCTUARY (18:1–7).
**18:1–7** The section commences with the introductory formula for divine instruction, *wayyōmer YHWH*, "and Yahweh spoke,"[275] but this time the directions are addressed to Aaron alone.[276] Following the vindication of the Aaronic priesthood, the role of the Aaronic priests and the Levites as guardians of the Holy Place takes on additional significance. The holiness and purity of the sanctuary may be at risk should a people become rebellious and attempt to usurp the power of the divinely ordained priesthood or endeavor to present impure or unclean sacrifices in the realm of the holy.

This passage reiterates and builds upon certain aspects of the priestly regulations outlined previously in Numbers 3–4 (see also Lev 8–10). The basic responsibility is to bear the consequences of violations against the sanctuary or, in other words, be culpable or accountable for any potential sacrilege against the Holy Place. Levine defined the phrase *ʿăwōn-hammiqdāš* ("offenses against the sanctuary") and its proper adjudication as "infractions against the purity of the sanctuary. ... Impurity was viewed as an external force which entered the person or attached itself to him. The primary purpose of expiation was, therefore, to rid oneself of this foreign force."[277]

The reference to "your ancestral tribe" (lit. "your father's household") may narrow the application to the Kohathites, following Milgrom and the commentary of R. Rashi and Ibn Ezra,[278] though this restriction is not self-evident. The phrase may refer to the collective clans of Kohath, Gershon, and Merari in the Levitical line, since the text moves progressively from the priesthood to the Levites. The detailed responsibilities of the three Levite clans were delineated in Num 3:5–4:33, and since the Numbers 3 passage begins with a reminder (vv. 2–4) of the consequences of profaning the sanctuary, there obtains here in v. 7 an implicit warning concerning any such

---

[275] On the use of the divine revelatory formula וַיְדַבֵּר יְהוָה אֶל־מֹשֶׁה לֵּאמֹר and the present alternative וַיֹּאמֶר יְהוָה אֶל־אַהֲרֹן in the Book of Numbers, see above discussion in "Introduction: Structure and Outline" and commentary on Num 1:1.

[276] Only here and in Lev 10:8 does Aaron function as the sole recipient of the divine instruction, and only in Lev 10:8 and Num 18:8 is the term וַיְדַבֵּר used. The following pattern emerges וַיֹּאמֶר in 18:1, then וַיְדַבֵּר in 18:8 with instruction to Aaron, and 18:25 with instruction to Moses.

[277] Levine, *In the Presence of the Lord: A Study of Cult and Some Cultic Terms in Ancient Israel*, Studies in Judaism in Late Antiquity (Leiden: Brill, 1974), 5:76–77.

[278] Milgrom, *Numbers*, 146, n. 2, 315; id., *Studies in Levitical Terminology*, also Ashley, *Numbers*, 339. Ashley suggests that the use of שֵׁבֶט אָבִיךְ implies a tribal subunit.

abuses in the future. Since everyone but the priests is prohibited from entering the Holy Place beyond the veil, the priests must monitor themselves with respect to their service within the sancta. In v. 5 there is the added comment that "wrath will not fall on the Israelites again," or more literally "there will not be any longer wrath upon the Israelites," which would recall the recent deaths of those who had violated the sanctuary restrictions among the Korah-led rebels and the sons of Aaron, Nadab, and Abihu.[279]

The terminology of the presentation of the Levites in service of the priesthood, namely that they be "brought near" *(haqrēb)* to accompany the Aaronic priesthood, is the same as that in which a person presents a sacrificial animal or other offering in the sanctuary. The Levites were a tribe of servants offered as a sacrifice from the Lord to the priests for carrying out the service of the Tent of Meeting. Even the Levitical Kohathites, however, who transported the holy vessels of the tabernacle during its mobile days in the wilderness (Num 3:31; 4:4–16), could not touch the vessels or the altar until they had been properly covered. Violation of this ordinance was punishable by death, as was the consequence for anyone who was not divinely ordained to serve in the priesthood.

The Hebrew construction in v. 7 is difficult for a precise rendering of the translation, especially in the use of the verb and noun forms from *ntn* ("to give, appoint"):

| | |
|---|---|
| *wĕʾattâ ûbānêkā ʾittĕkā* | So you and yours sons with you |
| *tišmĕrû ʾet-kĕhūnnatkem //* | shall guard your (pl) priesthood |
| *lĕkol-dĕbar hammizbēaḥ* | in every matter of the altar |
| *ûlĕmibêt lapārōket — waʿăbadtem* | and beyond the veil—you shall serve. |
| *ʿăbōdat mattānâ* | The service of the gift |
| *ʾetēnʾ et-kĕhūnnatkem* | I have given your priesthood |
| *wĕhazzār haqqārēb yûmāt* | But the stranger who approaches shall die. |

The difficulties for the interpreters of the text have been the meaning of the phrase "service of the gift" and "I have given."[280] Milgrom suggests that *mattānâ* implies subordination and that the priests are never set forth in such a subordinate position, hence the problematic phraseology. Neither are the priests ever assigned a service defined by the term *ʿăbōda*. It is also notable that in Num 4:5–20 the priests had extensive work responsibilities in preparing the various holy implements for transportation by the Kohathites, but these tasks are never described as *ʿăbōdâ*.

---

[279] Nadab and Abihu in Lev 10:1–5; Korah rebellion in Num 16:46–17:11.

[280] For a summary of the problems of some interpreters, see Ashley, *Numbers,* 343–44; Budd, *Numbers,* 200–202.

The priesthood was given as a gift to the Aaronic priests, and the Levites were given as a gift to the Aaronic priesthood. But the priests were not given to anyone or any group. Though perhaps improperly calling the phrase a gloss, Milgrom rightly concludes that the usage here is "to anticipate the priests' *mattānâ* of 'gifts' (rather than 'dedication') and it would mean that the priests are rewarded with gifts (vv. 9–20) for incurring mortal dangers in their *ʿăbōdâ* of guarding the inner sancta, just as the Levites are rewarded with the tithes for their hazardous *ʿăbōdâ* in transporting the sanctuary."[281] That the giving of this *ʿăbōdâ* in v. 7 has as its focus the offerings that follow in vv. 8–19 is supported by the function of the twice-used verbal form *nātatî* in v. 8. A similar phraseology to Num 18:1,7 occurs in Exod 28:38, where Aaron is said to bear the iniquity of the holy things, which the Israelites consecrate in all the gifts of their holy things. The high priest was to wear a small golden plaque, engraved with the phrase "holiness to YHWH," that was tied to his forehead by a blue chord so that he could bear the iniquity of the holy things.

In the wonder of the sacrificial system of ancient Israel, it was nothing short of amazing how in the presentation of sin and guilt offerings on behalf of the individual or the community, of that which was offered through an identification (laying the hand on the head) and substitutionary process on behalf of the offerer(s), could then bear the iniquitous consequences of the misdeed from the realm of the unholy and impure to the realm of holiness and purity. Sacrifices for sin and guilt were rendered as holy before the Lord. Hence only clean (proper type) and unblemished (proper quality) sacrificial elements were to be presented to the Lord in any kind of sacrificial setting, whether it be in communion, consecration, or atonement. Implied in the Levitical texts, but explicitly proclaimed throughout the prophets, proper representation of the gift for the offerer could only be efficacious if the offerer came with a clean heart and mind. Otherwise, the blood of bulls and rams and goats and lambs was an abomination to God.[282]

**⁸Then the LORD said to Aaron, "I myself have put you in charge of the offerings presented to me; all the holy offerings the Israelites give me I give to you and your sons as your portion and regular share. ⁹You are to have the part of the most holy offerings that is kept from the fire. From all the gifts they bring me as most holy offerings, whether grain or sin or guilt offerings, that part belongs to you and your sons. ¹⁰Eat it as something most holy; every male shall eat it. You must regard it as holy.**

**¹¹"This also is yours: whatever is set aside from the gifts of all the wave offerings of the Israelites. I give this to you and your sons and daughters as your regu-**

---

[281] Milgrom, *Numbers,* 315, n. 18.
[282] Isa 1:10–31; Amos 5:21–27; Jer 7:1–11.

lar share. Everyone in your household who is ceremonially clean may eat it.

<sup>12</sup>"I give you all the finest olive oil and all the finest new wine and grain they give the LORD as the firstfruits of their harvest. <sup>13</sup>All the land's firstfruits that they bring to the LORD will be yours. Everyone in your household who is ceremonially clean may eat it.

<sup>14</sup>"Everything in Israel that is devoted to the LORD is yours. <sup>15</sup>The first offspring of every womb, both man and animal, that is offered to the LORD is yours. But you must redeem every firstborn son and every firstborn male of unclean animals. <sup>16</sup>When they are a month old, you must redeem them at the redemption price set at five shekels of silver, according to the sanctuary shekel, which weighs twenty gerahs.

<sup>17</sup>"But you must not redeem the firstborn of an ox, a sheep or a goat; they are holy. Sprinkle their blood on the altar and burn their fat as an offering made by fire, an aroma pleasing to the LORD. <sup>18</sup>Their meat is to be yours, just as the breast of the wave offering and the right thigh are yours. <sup>19</sup>Whatever is set aside from the holy offerings the Israelites present to the LORD I give to you and your sons and daughters as your regular share. It is an everlasting covenant of salt before the LORD for both you and your offspring."

PROVISIONS OF TRIBUTE FOR THE PRIESTS (18:8–19). Since the priests bore the grave responsibility for maintaining the holiness of the sacred precinct and its various implements, special provisions were made for them via the tribute offerings brought by the Israelites. As noted in the discussion of 3:9–13,38, the Levites provided guardianship and maintenance service for the sanctuary, to ward off potential offenders who might profane the sanctuary by encroachment or other unholy acts. Such offense was evident in the case of the rebellion led by Korah, Dathan, and Abiram. The pericope moves from the general statement concerning the offerings constituting compensation for the priests, to the specific types of offerings rendered, to the consumption by those among the priesthood.

**18:8** The passage commences with a formal introduction, utilizing the formula for divine revelatory instruction, *wayĕdabbēr YHWH ʾel–* ("then Yahweh instructed ..."), here used in one of the rare occurrences where Moses is not included as one of the recipients of the instruction.[283] Then in a general statement the responsibility and perquisite compensation for the priesthood is described. In a simple chiastic structure utilizing two common usages of the verb *nātan* ("to give"), emphasis is placed on the personal decision of the Lord to bless the Aaronic lineage with the keeping of his tribute, those contributions made to him by the Israelites. The first use of *nātan* carries the meaning of appointment or putting someone in charge of a specific responsibility. God had placed under the charge of the Aaronic priesthood all the holy things of the Israelites *(kol-qādĕšê bĕnê-yiśrāʾēl)*, that is,

---

[283] See comment on 18:1 above.

all of their sacred offerings. In the second use of *nātan* emphasis is placed on the giving of the tribute for compensatory provision for the priests, supplying their sustenance.[284]

The phrase used to describe the general responsibility of the priests in regard to these gifts is *mišmeret tĕrûmōtāw*, generally translated "service of my presentation offerings." The question arises as to the nature of this service. Is it one of guardianship, preservation, oversight, or simply keeping? A variety of the derived meanings of the verbal form *šāmar* may apply at the various points in the process. In a general overview an individual or community group presented the tribute to the priests in the sanctuary, during which it came under their supervision. They performed or supplied oversight to certain required ritual acts with various portions of the given offering: assuring and guarding the sanctity of the offerer, offering, and sacred precinct, and then they were allowed to keep designated portions of many of the offerings as compensation[285] for their services. Hence a broad range in usage may be in view.

**18:9–10** The priestly tribute is divided into two levels of sanctity, the "most holy offerings" (*qōdeš haqqŏdāšîm*, "holy of the holy things," vv. 9[2x],10) and the generally holy offerings, the *tĕrûmat mattānām* ("tribute of their gifts," vv. 11–18). The particular holiest of the offerings, which were to be consumed by the priests, were all their dedicated offerings presented at the sanctuary for their cereal offerings, plus their sin (purification) and guilt (reparation) offerings. The cereal grain offering, as described in 2:1–13 and 6:14–23, was an unleavened mixture of fine flour, oil, and incense. A memorial portion was burned on the altar as a sweet aroma to the Lord, and the remainder was eaten by the Aaronic priests.

The particular animals offered as sin or purification offerings, as described in 4:1–35 and 6:24–30, were specified according to one's ranking within Israelite society. They ranged from a bull sin offering for the high priest, as that which was sacrificed by the high priest for himself and his family on the Day of Atonement (16:3–14), to the two turtledoves or pigeons brought by a poor person (5:7–10), or even a tenth of an ephah[286] of fine flour for a destitute individual (5:11–13). The guilt or reparation offering, brought as a result of the violation of someone's property or the inadvertent

---

[284] The rabbis listed twenty-four compensatory elements for the priests and Levites. See P. Levertoff, *Midrash Sifre on Numbers* (London: Society for Promoting Christian Knowledge, 1926), 163–64. See also H. Basser, ed., *Pseudo-Rabad Commentary to Sifre Numbers,* USF Studies in the History of Judaism 189 (Atlanta: Scholars Press, 1998), 126–49. Cf. Milgrom, *Numbers,* 148–49.

[285] מֶחְשָׁה refers to a sacred measure or portion allotted to the priests, used only here in this manner in BH.

[286] One-tenth of an ephah would amount to about two quarts.

breaking of a covenant stipulation, usually consisted of a ram or its equivalent in silver shekels, plus a penalty of one-fifth of the value of the animal (5:14–19; 7:1–10). For the various animals the slaughtering and sacrificial process included the ritual slaughtering of the animal, the disposition of the drained blood upon the altar or its sides, the burning of assigned portions such as the fat and entrails upon the large bronze altar, and the setting aside and then consumption of priestly portions. In keeping with 6:29 and 7:6, only the males among the priests and their families were permitted to consume these most holy of offerings.

**18:11–18** The second level of tribute consisted of the variety of firstfruits and firstborn of Israelite production. The first fruit from the trees[287] and offspring from the womb were treated as special gifts from God that were to be returned to him. This section delineates the particular offerings from plants (vv. 12–14) and from animals and humans (vv. 15–18). Verse 19 offers a summary of the functions of the holy tribute as a gift to the priesthood and as a covenant of salt, which speaks of the pledge of permanence and preservation of this meritorious arrangement for the well-being of Israelite society. Because the other tribes supported the one tribe that provided oversight to the central Holy Place, the sanctity of the sanctuary and hence the holiness of God were preserved and elevated, and the ongoing blessed livelihood of the Israelite society could be a lighthouse to the nations of the holiness and goodness of their God.

The contributions are translated in the NIV as that which was "set aside from the gifts all of the wave offerings of the Israelites," literally rendered as "the tribute of their gifts, and of all the elevation offerings of the Israelites." First the tribute, or *tĕrûmat*, refers to the nonsacrificial gifts dedicated to the Lord outside the sanctuary, such as many of the firstfruit and tithe contributions. The elevation offerings, or *tĕnûpōt*, were those sacrificial elements that were rendered to the Lord in a special presentation ceremony in which the offerer or priest lifted the representative elements as unto the Lord as part of a larger ritual process. Often the breast or right thigh of the animal was lifted as an elevation offering. This offering was associated with the peace offering (Lev 7:30,34; 23:20), the consecration of the priests (Exod 29:26; Lev 8:29), the dedication of the Levites (Num 8:11–13,21), and the purification ritual for the Nazirite (Num 6:20). In Lev 10:15 the thigh of the heave offering and the breast of the elevation offering were ordained as gifts for the Aaronic priesthood. Grain and oil offerings were also presented in this fashion, as in the consecration of the priests (Exod 29:23–24; Lev 8:27),

---

[287] According to Lev 19:23–25 the fruit from recently planted trees was not to be consumed until the fifth year (after three years of restriction from eating its fruit and the fourth year in which all of the fruit from the tree was holy and dedicated to the Lord), hence the first of the fruit as implied in the present passage.

cleansing ritual for lepers (Lev 14:12,21,24), and the sheaf of grain and two loaves for the Feast of Weeks (Lev 23:15,17). The classification of these elements as a secondary level of *qodāšîm* enabled them to be eaten by the female members of the priestly family as well as the male members, to whom the "holiest" of the offerings were restricted.

The three plant products specified under the *qodāšîm* classification of offerings were literally the cream of the crop, namely the very finest of the olive oil, wine, and grain production. These first produced *(rē'šît)* or processed offerings were distinguished from the normal first fruit *(bikkûrîm)* offerings of the first ripe olives, grapes, and grain.[288] The first yields of the production of oil from the olive crushing vats, newly pressed wine *(tîrôš)*, and freshly ground flour from the choicest wheat were to be returned to the Lord, the owner and giver of all produce of the earth. The quality of the produce was deemed as the best or choicest *(ḥēleb,* "fat" or "cream") of the crops, hence the origin of the expression "the cream of the crop." Just as the fat of any animal sacrificed or otherwise slaughtered for consumption was not to be consumed, so the fat of the produce from field, orchard, or vineyard was not to be eaten but devoted to the Lord. Only the ritually pure or "ceremonially clean" in the household of Aaron were allowed to partake of the holy offerings.

The paramount type of offering for the Lord and the sanctuary was called the *ḥērem* or "devoted" offering. Unlike many of the animal and human firstborn offerings delineated in vv. 15–18, anything that was presented as *ḥērem* could not be redeemed for payment or substitution. All *ḥērem* material reverted to the priests, whether a field, beast, or human (Lev 27:21, 28).[289] The totality of the *ḥērem* of the fields or flocks was granted to the priests, and humans or unclean animals that were not sacrificed or consumed could be used in the service of the sanctuary.

The discussion of these goods and their status as gifts to the Lord and to the priesthood assumes the Israelite occupation of Promised Land in which these are produced—contra the rejection of the land in Numbers 14 and the challenge to the Aaronic priesthood in Numbers 16–17. The cycle of blessing in Israelite agricultural society, through which the fellowship between God and humanity in the community of faith found its continual expression, was as follows:

---

[288] For an expanded discussion of the רֵאשִׁית and the בִּכּוּרִים, see Milgrom, *Numbers,* "Excursus 43: First Fruits," 427–28. The first processed foodstuffs included also fruit syrup, leavening, and kneaded dough (Num 15:20–21). From the sheep came the first sheared wool. Cf. also Exod 23:16–19; Lev 2:14; 23:17–18; Deut 18:4; 26:1–11.

[289] Cf. those things that were devoted to destruction in Lev 27:29; Deut 7:28; 13:18.

### Israelite Cycle of Blessing

Blessing from God in Growth of Crops and Harvest
In the Promised Land

| | |
|---|---|
| Firstfruits and first ripe consumed by the priests after portions sacrificed to God | Obedience of Israel to the Covenant in sowing and reaping rules |
| Firstfruits and first produce presented to the Lord special portions sacrificed on altar | Reaping of the firstfruits |
| | Production of oil, wine, flour, etc. |
| Portions separated and dedicated to God | |

If the cycle of blessing was broken by the unfaithfulness of the people or the impure acts of the priests, then the errant parties were subject to the penalty of profaning God's holiness, namely death. Later in the history of the Israelite kingdoms prophets such as Hosea illustrated the nation's unfaithfulness by using the imagery of abused firstfruits of the fig season that went to Baal Peor instead of Yahweh: "I found Israel like grapes in the wilderness; I saw your fathers as the firstfruits on the fig tree in its first season. But they went to Baal-peor, and consecrated themselves to that shame; so they became an abomination like the thing they loved" (Hos 9:10). The cycle of blessing had been broken by the Israelites in rejecting the land, yet in v. 13 it is still called "their land." The Lord still held to his promise, which he brought to pass in the next generation of Israel.

The second part of the tribute list for the priests related to animals and humans brought to the sanctuary for offering or dedication. The firstborn were the first male issue from the womb of the mother *(kol-peter reḥem lĕkol-bāśār)*,[290] whether human or animal. Animals defined by Levitical law as clean, such as cattle, sheep, and goats, were to be offered as sacrifices. Since humans could not be sacrificed physically, nor could unclean animals be sacrificed, a redemption price was established by which a substitutionary value was rendered to the priesthood. In the simple chiasmus of v. 15b, the language of human firstborn redemption is emphatic *(pādōh tipdeh)*, whereas the language used to describe the redemption of the animals is simply "you must redeem" *(tipdeh)*. Milgrom states that human firstborn redemption was mandatory, whereas animal firstborn redemption was optional, thus reading the imperfect as permissive rather than imperative.[291] According to Exod 34:19 the unclean donkey could be redeemed with a lamb, otherwise its neck was to be broken. Other unclean animals are not discussed, probably because they were of little use to the priesthood or the average Israelite. Animals sacrificed or redeemed were always those that had

---

[290] This phraseology is found elsewhere only in Exod 13:2,12–15; 34:19; Num 3:12; 8:16; and Ezek 20:26. The male firstlings are specified in Exod 34:19–20.

[291] Milgrom, *Numbers*, 152; also "Excursus 45: The First-Born," 431–32.

the potential for human usage or consumption. The process of human and animal redemption had a didactic purpose of reminding the Israelites of their redemption from Egypt, an object lesson of history that could be rehearsed in every generation so that the people might not forget the Lord's benevolence and the heavy price that was paid for their deliverance unto freedom and blessing.

Based on the principle of Exod 11:1–10 and 13:2,11–16, namely that Israel was redeemed and delivered from Egypt through the death of the firstborn men and animals (Exod 12:29), the firstborn of all of Israel, whether man or beast, were to be consecrated to Yahweh.[292] In the census taken in preparation for the journey from Mount Sinai to the Promised Land, the firstborn of Israel's tribes who were at least one month old were counted and then redeemed via a man-for-man substitution by the Levites. The excess number of 273 firstborn males of the Israelite community beyond the number of the Levites were redeemed via the set redemption price of five shekels each (Num 3:40–50).[293] The same phraseology of 3:37 is used in this passage in establishing the redemption price for future firstborn in Israel at the same price and age.[294]

After setting forth the firstborn human redemption price, the instructions move to the produce of the herds and flocks of which Israel would be blessed in the Promised Land. Cattle, sheep, and goats were sacrificeable, and hence not redeemable. Appropriate to all animal sacrifices, the blood was to be tossed or sprinkled upon the altar or its sides,[295] the physical focal point of divine-human mediation, since the blood was representative of the life of the animal.[296] In that the life of the flesh was in the blood, it was always to be rendered back to God, the source, sustainer, and owner of all life. The fat and other set portions were to be burned with fire on the altar, producing that sweet-smelling aroma with which Yahweh was pleased, if of

---

[292] For an extensive discussion of the firstborn legislation in Exodus, Leviticus, and Numbers, see G. Brin, *Studies in Biblical Law: From the Hebrew Bible to the Dead Sea Scrolls,* JSOTSup 176 (Sheffield: Academic Press, 1994), 165–281.

[293] Five sanctuary shekels were equivalent to about two ounces of silver, which was about equal to five or six months' pay in ancient Israel, according to Harrison, *Numbers,* 250. Cf. Wenham, *Leviticus,* 338; *Numbers,* 144.

[294] Another form of redemption was rendered when humans or animals were vowed to the Lord's service. In Lev 27:2–8 avowal redemption prices were set by the age and gender:

| AGE | MALE | FEMALE |
|---|---|---|
| 60+ years | 15 shekels | 10 shekels |
| 20–60 yrs | 50 shekels | 30 shekels |
| 5–20 yrs | 20 shekels | 10 shekels |
| 1 mo – 5 yrs | 5 shekels | 3 shekels |

[295] Lev 1:5,15; 3:2,8,13; 4:5–7; etc.

[296] Lev 17:6,11–14.

course the offerer brought the sacrifice in a state of ritual, moral, and ethical purity. This subsection concludes with a simple chiastic reiteration of the Levitical law concerning priestly ownership of the breast and thigh from the sacrificial animal offerings.

> So its flesh — belongs — to you
> Like the elevated breast
> Like the right thigh
> To you — it belongs.

**18:19** In summary fashion, utilizing an inclusio framing that brackets the overall chiastic structure of vv. 8b–19,[297] the emphasis is placed again on the fact that the tribute from Israel was a gift from God for the priestly families, both male and female. This perpetual statute concerning the tribute donation for priestly support is deemed a "covenant of salt" *(bĕrît melaḥ)*. Though the origin of this phraseology is unknown, the concepts of preservation and permanence are conveyed by the function of salt in ancient Near Eastern society. Salt as a preservative ensured the quality of the meat or other consumable or nonconsumable goods, as well as enhancing the taste when used in cooking. Salt, which accompanied many Israelite sacrifices, was used physically in the seasoning of the elements, but it also contributed to the quality of the covenant relationship between humanity and God (Lev 2:13).[298] In Ezra 4:14 the Sanballatide leaders in Samaria pledged their loyalty to the Persian government by using the expression "we have salted the salt of the palace."[299] With these concepts in mind, the covenant of salt between Yahweh and the Aaronic priesthood emphasized the quality and permanence of the relationship. That relationship was evidenced outwardly through the perpetual statute of the Israelite supplying of tribute to Yahweh, which then provided the means of sustenance for the priests and their families.

**²⁰The LORD said to Aaron, "You will have no inheritance in their land, nor will you have any share among them; I am your share and your inheritance among the Israelites.**

**²¹"I give to the Levites all the tithes in Israel as their inheritance in return for**

---

[297] See "Literary Structure and Outline of Numbers 18" below.

[298] Note the connection between the expressions in Lev 2:13, "Every offering of your grain you shall season with salt; you shall not allow the salt of the covenant of your God to be lacking from your grain offering" (NRSV). Cf. also Ezek 43:24.

[299] The Aramaic expression מְלַחְנָא הֵיכְלָא דִּי־מְלַח, "that the salt of the palace we have salted," was used in the context of demonstrating their loyalty to the king and suggesting that the Jews of Jerusalem might rebel and not submit their required tribute. As a result the royal household would thus suffer damage (v. 13) both financially and politically. Implied of course is that the Samaritans had demonstrated their loyalty by paying the required tribute.

the work they do while serving at the Tent of Meeting. [22]From now on the Israelites must not go near the Tent of Meeting, or they will bear the consequences of their sin and will die. [23]It is the Levites who are to do the work at the Tent of Meeting and bear the responsibility for offenses against it. This is a lasting ordinance for the generations to come. They will receive no inheritance among the Israelites. [24]Instead, I give to the Levites as their inheritance the tithes that the Israelites present as an offering to the LORD. That is why I said concerning them: 'They will have no inheritance among the Israelites.'"

PROVISIONS FOR THE LEVITES (18:20–24). Note that the text has been divided here between vv. 19 and 20, whereas many translations, following the division in the Masoretic Text, separate between vv. 20 and 21.[300] As was argued in the "Introduction: Structure and Outline of the Book of Numbers," the phraseology of divine revelatory instruction, namely *wayĕdabbēr YHWH* and *wayyōmer YHWH* constitute major organizational markers in the Book of Numbers and in most cases introduce new instructions or legislation. In the present chapter these expressions are used four times in alternating sequence, perhaps for lexical variety, but in each case they introduce new material. The matter at hand, the issue of the tithe inheritance over against the noninheritance of land, applies to the entire tribe of the Levites, of which the Aaronic priesthood was a distinctive part. The term "inheritance" *(naḥălâ)* is one of the key words of this section. Verse 20 could function as a concluding colophon for the material in vv. 8–19 and thereby provide a transitional verse into the following material. Perhaps that is the reason for the Masoretic division, but the use of the introductory phraseology seems to argue for the section division as followed presently.

As noted in the "Literary and Structural Outline" below and the following chiastic outline, the focal point of the passage is the weighty responsibility the Levites carried in bearing the consequences of sin and trespass against the sanctuary. Bracketing the section on the Levite service are the pair of dual declarations that the Israelite tithes are their compensatory inheritance (vv. 21,24a) and that this inheritance is a substitute for the territorial inheritance promised to the other tribes of Israel. This balanced outline provides additional support for the verse division examined above.

H  No Inheritance of Land (v. 20b)
 I  Tithe Inheritance for the Levites (v. 21)
  D'''  Levite Service (vv. 22–23)
 I'  Tithe Inheritance for the Levites (v. 24a)
H'  No Inheritance of Land (v. 24b)

---

[300] Those separating between vv. 20 and 21 include the NKJV, NASB, RSV, and NRSV. Cf. commentaries of Budd, *Numbers,* 200; Ashley, *Numbers,* 353; Wenham, *Numbers,* 144; de Vaulx, 211–12; Gray, *Numbers,* 233; and the Pentateuch and Haftorahs, 647. Those dividing the text at the end of v. 19 include the NIV and KJV. Cf. commentaries of Harrison, *Numbers,* 251; Milgrom, *Numbers,* 154; Noth, *Numbers,* 137.

This section builds off the introductory material set forth in vv. 2–6 of Part I, which addressed the matters of Levite service under the supervision of the Aaronic priesthood. In Part II the priestly provisions were delineated, and now in Part III the Levites are recompensed.

**18:20**  Following the introductory phrase *wayy³ōmer YHWH*, which marks the beginning of a new section, the subject matter of this pericope is set forth with a general statement concerning the Levite and priestly inheritance. Their inheritance was not one of territorial ownership like that which would be apportioned to the other tribes of Israel.[301] Their estate was a holy one, and the Lord of the covenant was their inheritance. This is not to say that the priests and Levites somehow owned Yahweh, but instead what physically accrued to Yahweh from the territorial inheritance of the Israelites would belong to them. The tangible evidence of this relationship was the tribute brought by the Israelites. These gifts became their birthright in the land instead of territorial grant. This restriction on the priests and Levites concerning land ownership does not confute the allocation later of forty-eight cities and their surrounding areas for the Levites support.[302] They would be granted these for constructing their dwellings and pasturing their herds and flocks, as well as for providing geographical locations for the collection and distribution of the tithes, tribute, and devoted commodities offered by other twelve tribes of the Israelites. These allocations would quite literally be "in the midst of the Israelites," but they would be owned by the sanctuary and not the individual priests or Levites.[303]

**18:21**  The Levites are addressed specifically in the continued instruction directed to Aaron by the Lord, with reference to their receiving the tithes brought by the Israelites. The language is emphatic, "Behold I have given," in Yahweh's designating all the tithes of Israel for Levite inheritance. They would not own property of land in the manner of the other Israelite tribes, but they would be granted a tenth of the produce from those tribal properties in exchange[304] for their protection and transportation services

---

[301] For further discussion of the concepts of "inheritance" (נַחֲלָה) and "share" (חֵלֶק), see M. Tsevat, " חלק," *TDOT* 4:447–51; D. J. Wiseman, "חלק," *TWOT* 1:292–93; L. J. Coppes, "נחל," *TWOT* 2:569–70; D. M. Howard, "Excursus: Israel's Inheritance of the Land in Joshua," in *Joshua*, NAC (Nashville: Broadman & Holman, 1998), 300–307. Milgrom (*Numbers*, 317, n. 53) notes that the two terms are used in synonymous parallelism in poetic texts and in equivalent expressions in prose, e.g., Gen 31:14; Deut 10:9; 12:12; 14:27; 18:1; 32:9; 2 Sam 20:1; Job 20:9; 27:13.

[302] Num 35:1–8; the cities and the Levitical clan assignments are delineated in Josh 21:1–42.

[303] Cf. a similar arrangement for the New Temple state in Ezek 44:1–45:5.

[304] The distinctive term in the phrase עֲבֹדָתָם חֵלֶף, "exchange for their services," is used in this manner only here and in v. 31 below. חָלַף derives from the *hiphil* function of the verb, meaning "to change, exchange" as in the prohibition in Lev 27:10 against exchanging one sacrificial animal for another. See S. Tengström, "חָלַף," *TDOT* 4:432–35.

rendered on behalf of the sanctuary and its priesthood.[305] The tithe or "tenth" *(ma'ăšēr)* was the required percentage of the productivity of Israelite labors that was to be rendered to the Lord at the sanctuary. In Lev 27:30–32 the tithes are described as "the grain from the soil or fruit from the trees" and "of the entire herd and flock—every tenth animal which passes under the shepherd's rod,"[306] all of which was holy to the Lord. Hence forth the Levites would have an ample supply of animal and plant products for their livelihood while performing their services for the sanctuary under the auspices of the Aaronic priesthood.

The statutes on tithing and the relationship between the Levites and the other Israelites were expanded in Deut 12:17–19 and 14:22–29. When the Temple would be completed as the place which the Lord would choose for his name to abide, portions of the tithes of grain, oil, wine, and the firstlings of the flocks and herds would be consumed jointly by the Levites and the offerers in the vicinity of the sanctuary. Provision was made for those who might have to journey some length to bring their tithes to the city of God's choosing, later of course Jerusalem, whereby they could sell their titheable goods and bring the equivalent monetary value to the city, and then purchase that which they desired for the community tithing celebration. Again this presents a wondrous picture of the Israelites in communion with God and one another, in the context of the holy place that represented his presence on earth, rejoicing before the Lord who had so richly blessed them. This was the portrait of the community of faith in coordinated harmony and celebration set forth in Num 1:1–10:10 but which had been fractured by the series of rebellious acts. Due to continual complaints about God's provisions and challenges to his appointed leaders, Israel was floundering in discord and despair. But Yahweh was faithful to his promise to their forefathers. He would bring them into the land and bless them abundantly, so that this picture of joy and harmony might be restored in celebration of the relationship between God and humanity.[307]

The concept of the giving of a tithe is known from ancient Near Eastern sources from the Levant and Mesopotamia. Not only were agricultural

[305] For detailed discussion of the services rendered by the Levites, see text and commentary on Num 1:47–53; 3:5–39; 4:1–33.

[306] The expression "that which passes under the shepherd's rod" describes the careful counting process the shepherd would engage in regularly to insure against loss of cattle, sheep, goats, camels, or donkeys.

[307] Note that some scholars see a contradiction between Numbers and Deuteronomy concerning the tithing legislation, with Numbers describing the mandatory tithe for the Levites and priests and Deuteronomy describing consumption by the persons offering the tithes at the sanctuary. This variance is perhaps the reason for the later rabbinical designation of a "first tithe" for the Levites, who lived throughout the land in their designated cities, and the "second tithe," which was to be consumed in Jerusalem.

goods tithed, but also various commodities such as metals and goods produced by craftsmen. The usage of the Ugaritic $m^c\check{s}rt^{308}$ evidences a royal temple societal structure in which contributions to the given sanctuary could be utilized by the royalty. A kind of royal priesthood is evidenced in the account of Melchizedek in Gen 14:18–24. In Babylon of the sixth century B.C., cattle contributed as tithes were branded for the temple treasuries, and other goods were earmarked on storage jars and other receptacles.[309] In the Iron II Israelite kingdom period goods collected for the royal provision were inscribed with the term *lmlk* ("for the king"). Whether some of these might have been dedicated for the temple stores is unknown, but there is little doubt that some means of identifying the tithed goods was employed during the First Temple period.

**18:22–23** At the focal point of this section is the reiteration of the critical and dangerous role the Levites served on behalf of the Israelite community. During the wilderness journey the three clans of the Levites and the Aaronic priests would camp in the immediate vicinity of the four sides of the sanctuary, between it and the three other tribes that were encamped on the perimeter. They acted first as a positional barrier between the holy geocentral position of the Tent of Meeting and the community at large, ensuring its sanctity by guarding against encroachment by unauthorized persons, including any unclean persons of their own Levite clans. As stated previously in vv. 2–5, they would bear the consequences of sin and iniquity against the sanctuary, so that no longer—as had happened as a result of the recent Korah rebellion—would anyone die because of such a violation of the holy precinct of the Tent of Meeting. This responsibility was to be a perpetual one, such that they were to be solely dedicated to the Lord and not encumbered by the territorial responsibilities of their Israelite brothers. This was their inheritance, as Yahweh's inheritance, in the present and in days to come, when Yahweh would bring Israel into the land of their inheritance.

**18:24** The chiastic structure of this section is completed by the reiteration of the two statements of vv. 20 and 21 concerning the tithe being the Levite inheritance (v. 24a) instead of territorial allotment (v. 24b). The contributions of the Israelites to Yahweh were in turn his gifts to them for their dedicated service.

**[25]The LORD said to Moses, [26]"Speak to the Levites and say to them: 'When you receive from the Israelites the tithe I give you as your inheritance, you must present a tenth of that tithe as the LORD's offering. [27]Your offering will be reckoned to you as grain from the threshing floor or juice from the winepress. [28]In**

---

[308] Perhaps vocalized as *ma^c\check{s}\bar{a}rtu* similar to the Hb. *ma^{\check{a}}\check{s}er;* see C. Gordon, *UT,* 462.

[309] For an extensive discussion of the tithe in Israel and the ANE, see Milgrom, *Numbers,* "Excursus 46: The Tithe (18:21–32)," 432–36.

this way you also will present an offering to the LORD from all the tithes you receive from the Israelites. From these tithes you must give the LORD's portion to Aaron the priest. [29]You must present as the LORD's portion the best and holiest part of everything given to you.'

[30]"Say to the Levites: 'When you present the best part, it will be reckoned to you as the product of the threshing floor or the winepress. [31]You and your households may eat the rest of it anywhere, for it is your wages for your work at the Tent of Meeting. [32]By presenting the best part of it you will not be guilty in this matter; then you will not defile the holy offerings of the Israelites, and you will not die.'"

TITHES AND OFFERINGS OF THE LEVITES (18:25–32).   One new piece of legislation emerges from this section. The Levites would be responsible to tithe to the Lord and thus to the priesthood out of the tithes received from the Israelites as their regular tribute. Furthermore, the Levites are to contribute in this tithe of the tithe the very best of the best that was bestowed upon them as gifts to God from the Israelites and from God to the Levites. As noted in the commentary on Num 15:1–21 and v. 23 above, this material would serve as a reminder to the people of God's faithfulness. Together chaps. 15 and 18 resound in a kind of staccato effect in a crescendo of proclamation to all future generations that Yahweh will bring to consummation his promise of a land flowing with milk and honey, even if one generation should falter in its faithfulness. He was and always would be their God and they his people.

**18:25**   As with the three previous sections of chap. 18, the final portion commences with the extended introductory formula for divine instruction, *wayĕdabbēr YHWH el–*, but the recipient is Moses instead of Aaron.[310] Milgrom suggests this was "in order to avoid the conflict of interest that would result if Aaron were told to collect the tenth of the Levitical tithe assigned to him."[311] In turn Moses instructed the Levites about the process of collection of the tithes from the Israelites and their duty of tithing the best and holiest to Aaron. These issues are at the focal point of the structure of this section.

**18:26**   Repetition of previous phraseology from this chapter abounds in this verse, with a few notable distinctions. The original tithe, which had been designated as the Levite inheritance in exchange for their service on behalf of the sanctuary, is treated like income similar to that which the average Israelite earned through his farming activities (vv. 21,24a). Therefore that which God had enabled the Levites to appropriate through the compulsory tribute was subject to the tithe statute. That representative portion was contributed again to the Lord first, and secondarily to the Aaronic priests. The text is careful to make the distinction that the Levite tithe is rendered first to Yahweh and then to Aaron.

---

[310] Note the commentary and notes on Num 15:1–2.s
[311] Milgrom, *Numbers,* 156. Cf. Ashley, *Numbers,* 358.

**18:27,30–31** These two verses bracket in a brief inclusio the focal point of the section, which is that the choicest of the choicest was to be the source of the Levite tithe that would support the Aaronic priests. Hence, they were accounted to the Levites as if they had produced them on their own. The Levites were a select tribe, set apart by the Lord for special services, and hence were the initial recipients of that which was the best of the Israelite productivity. The sons of Aaron, the priests, were the select clan from among the select tribe and hence would be due the tribute of only the very finest of that with which God had so blessed his people.

Two key agricultural products, which were the result of processing the raw materials, were to be set aside by the Levites for this tithe, the best grain from the threshing floor and the finest juice from the wine vat after the initial pressing of the grapes. These two items are perhaps used as exemplars for the contributions of the Levites due to their special attributes evidenced throughout the Hebrew Scriptures as well as in the literature and iconography of the ancient Near East. From the painted wall murals of Egypt to the hewn murals of the Hittites in central and eastern Anatolia and the Assyrians of Mesopotamia, the activities and products of grain processing and wine production were esteemed as sacred aspects of human endeavor in utilizing these gifts from the gods. Rites associated with bread and wine held significant places in ancient cultic activities, as they did in ancient Israel. Cultic activities were associated with threshing floors and wine presses, as well as olive presses (see v. 12). In the Book of Numbers particular attention is given to the bread, oil, and wine accompaniments to a number of animal sacrifices.[312]

**18:28–29** At the center of this chiastic construction is the giving of the Levite tithe of their collected tithes to Aaron, the high priest and representative of the entire priesthood. The tribute from the Levites was from the very best, literally "its fat" *(ḥēleb),* the same word used to describe the best of the oil, grain, and wine processing in v. 12. Thus only the *creme de la creme* was fitting for the Levite contribution to the priesthood. All of the tribute described in this chapter was deemed "holy" (vv. 8, 9,17), and thus the best was also the holiest.

**18:32** The conclusion is a reminder of the seriousness of the service laid before the priests and Levites. They were responsible for oversight of the holy sanctuary and the holy gifts, to ensure that no unauthorized or unclean person encroach upon the sancta or profane the holy gifts made to the Lord. Anyone violating the holiness of the sacred precinct or its paraphernalia would surely die. Additionally, the Levite rendering of the holiest of the holy tithed goods to

---

[312] See 15:1–21; 18:8–12; 28:1–29:40. Nazirites, however, were restricted from touching or using any products of the vineyard as part of their vow (6:2–4) until after the completion of their period of avowal. At that point sacrifices of bread and wine were offered by the Nazirite in addition to the animals of the purification (sin) and peace offerings (6:14–17,21).

Yahweh was to ensure that at the end of the tithing sequence only those goods of the ultimate quality would be rendered unto the Holy Lord and his holy servants. In following this stipulation, the holy gifts of the Israelite tribes to the sanctuary would not be profaned. A loss of quality control could lead to the loss of life by one of Yahweh's faithful servants.

In the New Testament the principle of support for ministers of the gospel of Jesus Christ obtains from this and other Old Testament examples. As any workman was worthy of his wages or provisions (Matt 10:9–10), so ought those who preach the gospel have their needs supplied (1 Cor 9:2–18). The calling to the gospel ministry is likewise a high and holy calling, worthy of the very best that an individual can render unto the Lord in following him faithfully, by giving one's life as a continual living sacrifice to God (Rom 12:1–2).

### Literary and Structural Outline of Numbers 18

### Part I: Service of Priests and Levites

A **Introduction 1: Yahweh to Aaron**
   Then YHWH said to Aaron
   B **Priesthood:** You - and you r sons - and your father's household - with you
      You shall **bear** - the iniquity - of the holy place
         You - and your sons - with you
      You shall bear - the iniquity - of your priesthood
      C **Levites:** Your brothers - the tribe of Levi -
                     the tribal-clan of your father
         Bring them near - with you - that they may accompany – you
         And they may serve you
         You - and your sons - with you
         Before (*liphney,* "in service of") the Tent of Meeting
         D **Levite Service: They shall guard your service –**
                           and the service of all the Tent
         But to all the holy things -
         And to the altar - they shall not come near –
         So they shall not die - Neither they - nor you
      C' **Levites:** So let them accompany - you (or join with you)
         That they may guard the service of the Tent of Meeting
         For all - the service of the Tent
            But an unauthorized one - shall not come near - to you
         D' **Levite Service:** So you shall guard - the service -
                              of the holy place
         - and the service - of the altar
         So there will not be - anymore wrath - upon the Israelites
      C'' **Levites:** But I - Behold - I have **taken\*** - your brothers the Levites
         From among - the Israelites -
         for you - from the gift - of things given - to YHWH
         To serve the service - of the Tent of Meeting
   B' **Priesthood**: But you - and your sons - with you
   You shall guard - your priesthood

and every matter of the altar - and inside the curtain (veil) -
                                    also you will perform
The service - of the gift - I am giving - your priesthood
But the unauthorized person - who comes near - he will die.
*key word chap. 16

### Part II: Tribute for the Priests

**A′ Introduction 2: Yahweh to Aaron**

Then Yahweh Instructed - Aaron (spoke to Aaron)

**E  Tribute for Priests**

Indeed I - behold - I have given you (put in charge of) -
   the keeping (guarding) - of my **tribute**
   for all the holy things - of the Israelites -
To you - (I am) **giving** (providing) - as a compensatory portion
To your sons - as an everlasting statute

    **F  Holiest Offerings:** This - will be - for you -
      From the **holiest - of the holy things** - from the fire
      All of their offering - and all of their cereal offering -
      and all of their sin offering - and all their reparation offering
      which they have rendered (returned) to me
      Holiest of the holy things - to you - are they - and to your sons

**G  Offerings Consumed**

In/With the **holy of the holiest** things -
   you shall eat it
   Every male - shall eat it
holy it is to you

**E′  Tribute Given**

And **This** is for you - **every tribute** of their gift
(For belong) every elevation offering of the Israelites
   To you - I am **giving** them -
   To your sons - and your daughters - with you - an everlasting statute
Every **clean** (ritually pure) person - in your household - shall eat - it.

**F′  Offerings Specified**

**a  Plants**

All the cream - of the olive oil -//-
And all the cream (best) - of the new wine - and grain
    Their firstfruits - which they **give** - to YHWH
      To you - I have **given** them
    The firstfruits - of everything which [is] - in their land
    Which they bring - to YHWH
    For you - it shall be

**G  Offerings Consumed**

    Every **clean** person - in your household - shall eat it
Every devoted thing -in Israel -//- belongs - to you

**b  Animals and Humans**

    **(A)  General Statement**

      Every opening - of the womb - of all flesh
      Which they bring near - to Yahweh
      Whether from human - or beast - it belongs to you

**(B) Exceptions for Redemption**
**Except** - that you shall indeed - redeem (2x)
    - the firstborn of the human
    - the firstborn of the unclean beast
You shall redeem
    **(C) Redemption Price**
    Its redemption-price - from one month old - you shall redeem
    By your value - of silver -//- five shekels
    By the shekel of the sanctuary -
    Twenty gerahs each
**(B′) Redemption Exceptions Specified**
**Except** - Firstborn - bull
    Or firstborn lamb
    Or firstborn goat
You shall not - redeem -//- Holy are they
    Their blood - you shall toss - upon the altar
    And their fat - you shall burn
    A fire of savory smoke - to YHWH
  **(A′) Conclusion:** Then its flesh - belongs to you
    Like the elevated breast -
    And like the right thigh
  To you- it belongs
**E″ Tribute Summary: All the tribute** - of the holy things
which contributed - the Israelites - to YHWH
I have given - to you
and to your sons - and to your daughters - with you for everlasting statute
A covenant - of salt -//- everlasting - it is
Before - YHWH
To you - and to your seed (offspring) - with you

### Part III: Levite Tithe Inheritance
**A‴ Instruction: Then Yahweh said to Aaron**
  **H No Inheritance of Land for the Levites**
  In **their** land - you shall not inherit
    A share (property) - there will not be - for you -in their midst
  I am - your share - and your inheritance
    In the midst of - the Israelites.
  **I Tithe Inheritance for the Levites**
    Now for the sons - of Levi
    Behold - I have **given** - every **tithe** - in Israel - for an **inheritance**
    In return (exchange) for - their service
    Which they - are serving (rendering) - service - of the Tent of Meeting
  **D Levite Service**
    They shall not come near - any longer -//- the Israelites
    To the Tent of Meeting
    So as to bear - the sin (mistake/error/) - to die (death)
        So he shall serve -> the Levite
        the service of the Tent of Meeting
        and they shall bear - their iniquity (guilt)

An everlasting - statute - to your generations
In the midst of the Israelites -
They shall not **inherit** - an **inheritance**.
**I' Tithe Inheritance for the Levites**
For - the **tithe** - of the Israelites
Which they contributed - to YHWH - as tribute
I have given - to the Levites - as an **inheritance**
**H' No Inheritance of Land**
On account of this (therefore) - I said - to them
In the midst of - the Israelites
Not - they shall **inherit** - an **inheritance**.

**Part IV: Tithe of the Tithe**

**A''' Instruction: Then instructed - YHWH - Moses - saying:**
    **I'' Tithe Inheritance**
Now to the Levites - you shall instruct
And you shall say - to them:
When - you **take** - from the Israelites - the tithe
    Which I have **given** - to you - from them - as your inheritance
You shall **contribute** - from it - the **tribute** - of YHWH

**A tithe - from the tithe.**

    **E Tribute from Grain and Wine**
Thus it will be accounted - for you - as your **tribute**
    As the grain - from the threshing floor
    And as the fullness - of the wine vat
    **J Contribution and Collection of the Levite Tithe**
    When you **contribute** - even you -//- the tribute of YHWH
    From all your tithes -
    which-you have **taken** -//- from - the Israelites
    Then you will **give** - from it
    The **contribution** -of Yahweh -//- for Aaron - the priest
    From all - your **gifts** - you shall **contribute**
    (From) Every tribute - of YHWH
    From all its best (fattest) - its holiest part - from it
**E Tribute from Grain and Wine**
Thus, you shall say - to them
    When you **contribute** - its best - from it
    Then it shall be accounted - for the Levites
    As the produce (yield) - of the threshing-floor
    And as the produce (yield) - of the wine-vat
**G Offerings Consumed**
Thus you shall **eat** - **it** - in every place
You - and your household
For a wage - it is - for you
Exchange - for your service -
of the Tent of Meeting

A'''' **Conclusion: But you shall not bear - upon you - the sin**
  when you contribute - its best - from it
  and the holy things - of the Israelites
  Not - you shall profane (pollute) -//- & Not - you shall die.

## (4) Red Heifer Ashes and the Waters of Purification (19:1–22)

The conclusion to the second rebellion cycle, which focused on the rebellion of the Levites under Korah and the Reubenites, outlines special purification rites related to death. The ceremonial process of water purification rites outlined for the priests was extended to the common people in the subject of contact with the dead. Priests were rendered unclean by contact with the dead (Lev 21:1–3; 22:4–7), and Nazirites were restricted from contact with the dead (Num 6:6), lest they be rendered unclean and their period of sanctification be terminated. The common people became unclean if they touched anything ceremonially unclean, including a human corpse, and they were to live outside the camp during such periods of uncleanness (Lev 5:2–3; Num 5:2). Death carried a higher level of impurity, as is evidenced by the numerous ritual washings and bathings delineated both in the preparation phase and in the application procedures. Since death was such a common exposure for all persons, a special pragmatically feasible ritual was established for addressing this problem. Numbers 19 details the ritual purification process that would be continuously available to the people without having to sacrifice an animal every time there was a death in the family, so it facilitates the maintenance of a holy community of faith. Maintenance of purity and sanctity as a reflection of individual and community holiness in separation from the world's forces is important for all who desire a healthy relationship with a holy God. At this point in the history of revelation, the means of maintaining this relationship included a special ritual process.

The positioning of this chapter after the challenge to the priesthood serves several purposes.

First, in chap. 18 the duties and responsibilities of priests and Levites were presented to ward off potential encroachment and sacrilege offenses against the Tent of Meeting. The present context outlines the select ritual for a specific source of uncleanness: that which results from the contact with a dead person or with property in the proximity of a recently deceased individual. In the overall structure of the Book of Numbers, the historical context of this ritual is that of the death of 14,700 in the plague that followed the Korah rebellion (16:36–40). Contact with or having proximity to the bodies of the nearly fifteen thousand dead would require a massive application of purification codes.

Another connection between chap. 19 and chaps. 16–17 is the use of the key word *lāqaḥ*, "take," in vv. 3,4,6,17,18. Korah had tried to take control of the priesthood with a group of rebels (16:1), but when they took their censers of burning incense to the entrance to the Tent of Meeting, they were consumed by the earth (16:16–34). Then Aaron took his censer and stood between those being struck by the plague and the rest of the Israelites, preventing further death and destruction. In the confirmation of the priesthood, each of the representatives from the twelve tribes took their staffs and placed them in the Tent of Meeting, and the next day Aaron's staff had evidenced God's work on behalf of the Aaronic clan. In Yahweh's speech in 18:6 the divine directive is seen in the statement that he had taken the Levites from among the Israelites to serve the sanctuary and the priesthood. Then the Levites would take the tithe from the Israelites, which in turn God granted to them in compensation for their service. In the present chapter the Israelites are instructed to take[313] a red heifer to Aaron (v. 2), who then gives it to Eleazar who slaughters it outside the camp and then takes some of the blood to be sprinkled at the entrance to the tabernacle. Then as the heifer is burning the priest takes the cedar, hyssop, and scarlet wool and tosses them on the sacrifice. Later in the ritual cleansing ceremony the priest *takes* some of the ashes and mixes them with water, and then a clean person *takes* some hyssop, dips it into the mixture, and sprinkles all the necessary household items and persons rendered unclean by exposure to death. Though some of these uses may seem mundane, collectively they present a contrast of usage between the initial usage in Korah's rebellious attempt to usurp the power of the priesthood and those occurrences that follow, each indicating the faithful response of the priests and people to the instructions from the Lord. Aaron and Eleazar have retaken control of the priesthood with divine imprimatur and impetus. As Ashley notes, "This chapter forms a fitting conclusion to the section on the causes and consequences of rebellion in chaps. 11–19. Death is the final consequence, but heirs of the promise may have fellowship with God by following the divinely given procedure here included."[314]

Second, in the cyclical structure of the Book of Numbers, this chapter provides the important section on "laws governing the community of faith." Later in Jewish history this passage would serve as the basis for a variety of applications of purification ritual beyond that of cleansing for the dead. A parallel passage is found in Deut 21:1–10, which details the community ritual for the expiation of sin and impurity caused by an unsolved murder or death. Third, this passage provided additional warning to future generations

---

[313] Usually translated "bring" in the expression וְיִקְחוּ אֵלֶיךָ, "that they should bring [take] to you" a red cow.

[314] Ashley, *Numbers,* 362.

concerning the grave consequences of rebellion against the Lord, as their forefathers experienced in the wilderness.

LITERARY STRUCTURE. Scholars have traditionally divided the chapter into its two distinct movements, with the first focused on the ritual methods associated with the sacrifice of the red cow and the disposition of its ashes (chaps. 1–10) and the second on the application of the ashes in the ritual purification procedures (chaps. 1–22). Yet as Milgrom has rightly observed, literary analysis evidences a bifid or "binary" structure, with the break in the text between vv. 13 and 14, with each section beginning with the phrase "this is the law" (*zō᾽t ḥūqqat hattôrâ*, "this is the statute of law" in v. 2a, and *zō᾽t hattôrâ*, "this is the law" in v. 14a). Note the following outline from Milgrom's "Excursus 46: The Structure of Chapter 19":[315]

| Panel A (19:2a–13) | Panel B (19:14–22) |
|---|---|
| "This is the ritual law" (19:2a) | "This is the ritual" (19:14a/a) |
| Preparation of the ashes | Touching corpse or its derivatives |
| Renders impure (19:2b–10) | Renders impure (19:14–16) |
| Purification procedure (19:11–12) | Purification procedure (19:17–19) |
| Penalty for nonpurification (19:13) | Penalty for nonpurification (19:20) |
| | "Law for all time" (19:21a) |
| | [Addition (21b–22)][316] |

Further parallel is seen in the concluding statements concerning the penalty for failure to adhere to the ritual requirements:

| | |
|---|---|
| "… does not cleanse himself | "… fails to cleanse himself |
| defiles the Lord's tabernacle | that person will be cut off from the |
| | congregation |
| that person will be cut off from Israel | for he has defiled the Lord's sanctuary |
| Since the water of purification | The water of purification |
| was not dashed on him | was not dashed on him |
| he remains unclean" (v. 13) | he is unclean" (v. 20) |

Several chiastic patterns are evident in both the micro and macro structures of this chapter, which both enhance the literary flavor of the material and contribute to the particular emphases made therein. Repetition of terms and phrases complete the stylistic features of this text. The following emphases emerge from the literary analysis. (1) Torah statute // perpetual statute: both sections of this chapter commence and are completed with equivalent phrases, highlighting that which was legally binding for both this generation in the wilderness and for the many generations to come. (2) Ritual ablutions: four types of

---

[315] Milgrom, *Numbers,* 437–38.

[316] See below "Literary Structure of Numbers 19" for a detailed outline of the bifid structure of this chapter. The layout of the bifid structure of Num 19 is based on Milgrom's outline (*Numbers,* 437–48), with revisions and expansion.

cleansing and purification are outlined: sprinkling of blood, washing clothes, bathing of the body, sprinkling of unclean persons and objects. (3) Impurity of death: touching and even general proximity to the dead can render persons and objects unclean and therefore in need of ritual purification. If persons continue in their state of uncleanness, the sanctuary is in danger of defilement. Impurity is extremely pervasive. (4) Paradox of impurity: the handling of each element in the preparation of the ashes renders each person unclean until evening, yet ashes plus fresh water when sprinkled properly upon an unclean person renders them clean.

M. Douglas has outlined the Book of Numbers in a cyclical structure, which is based on alternating sections of story and law, to be read in "rungs" of faith defilement, holy times, and purification. The law sections, such as chaps. 15; 18–19, develop in parallel fashion the theme of the constitution of the nation as a holy and undefiled people and define its prophetic destiny as the people of God in the midst of a defiled world. As a general overview, the parallel structure is outlined as follows:[317]

| Numbers 15 | Structural Theme | Numbers 18–19 |
|---|---|---|
| 15:1–21 | A. Holy things for priests and Levites | 18:1–32 |
| 15:22 29 | B. Purification from unintended sin | 19:1–19 |
| 15:30–36 | C. Intention: deliberate sinners cut off | 19:20 |
| 15:37–41 | D. A statute forever perpetual | 19:21–22 |

This pattern of thematic analysis is fruitful, but it does not address the intricate poetic and rhetorical devices employed throughout these and the surrounding chapters, which are addressed in the following commentary.

**[1]The LORD said to Moses and Aaron: [2]"This is a requirement of the law that the LORD has commanded:**

INTRODUCTION: DIVINE INSTRUCTION AND FIRST STATUTE (19:1–2a). **19:1–2a** The chapter begins with an extended version of the introductory formula for divine instruction, *wayĕdabbēr YHWH ʾel-mōšeh wĕʾel-ʾahărōn lēʾmōr*, "and Yahweh spoke to Moses and Aaron, saying …"[318] "The inclusion of Aaron with Moses is most fitting in that the entire cycle has been devoted to matters of the priesthood and the tribe of Levi and in that chap. 19 focuses on matters related to purification. Further emphasis on the divine origin of this legislation is found in the second verse, with the statement that "this statute of Torah" *(zōʾt ḥūqqat hattôrâ)* was commanded

---

[317] M. Douglas, *In the Wilderness: The Doctrine of Defilement in the Book of Numbers,* JSOT-Sup 158 (Sheffield: JSOT Press, 1993), 144–52.

[318] On the use of the divine revelatory formula וַיְדַבֵּר יְהוָה אֶל־מֹשֶׁה לֵאמֹר in the Book of Numbers, see above discussion in "Introduction: Structure and Outline" and commentary on Num 1:1.

*(ṣiwwâ)* by Yahweh. The sequence of *wayĕdabbēr* and *ṣiwwâ* is found else-where in the Book of Numbers to introduce some special legislation.[319] The particular phrase *zōʾt ḥuqqat hattôrâ* occurs only here and in 31:21, which addresses impurity from corpse contamination resulting from warfare. Exposure to death in warfare rendered one unclean for seven days. The abbreviated form, *zōʾt hattôrâ*, introduces the latter section of this chapter, which deals with the application of the ordinances presented in the former.

**Tell the Israelites to bring you a red heifer without defect or blemish and that has never been under a yoke. ³Give it to Eleazar the priest; it is to be taken out-side the camp and slaughtered in his presence. ⁴Then Eleazar the priest is to take some of its blood on his finger and sprinkle it seven times toward the front of the Tent of Meeting. ⁵While he watches, the heifer is to be burned—its hide, flesh, blood and offal. ⁶The priest is to take some cedar wood, hyssop and scarlet wool and throw them onto the burning heifer. ⁷After that, the priest must wash his clothes and bathe himself with water. He may then come into the camp, but he will be ceremonially unclean till evening. ⁸The man who burns it must also wash his clothes and bathe with water, and he too will be unclean till evening.**

**⁹"A man who is clean shall gather up the ashes of the heifer and put them in a ceremonially clean place outside the camp. They shall be kept by the Israelite community for use in the water of cleansing; it is for purification from sin. ¹⁰The man who gathers up the ashes of the heifer must also wash his clothes, and he too will be unclean till evening. This will be a lasting ordinance both for the Israelites and for the aliens living among them.**

PREPARATION OF THE ASHES OF THE RED HEIFER (19:2b–10). **19:2a–3** The process began with the selection of a quality red cow that was unblemished and that had never been harnessed with a yoke. The red cow *(pārâ ʾădūmmâ)* was a roan or reddish brown color,[320] the perfect quality of which was defined as "unblemished" and "never been under a yoke." Almost all sacrificial animals were required to be unblemished, hav-ing no observable physical deformities or surface defects that might indicate disease or genetic imperfection. The rabbinical interpretation extended the red and perfect *(tĕmîmâ)* characteristics to mean the cow in its entirety was of red color and not spotted, mottled, or blended with other colors.[321] In the Israelite system all sacrificial animals had to be of such quality that they were potentially edible. In that the cow had never been yoked for farming or

---

[319] Num 5:1; 28:1–2; 34:1–2; 35:1–2,9–10. Only here is the verb not in the imperative form, though in the context the following verb יְדַבֵּר carries the imperatival mood.

[320] For further explanation of this color, see A. Brenner, *Colour Terms in the Old Testament,* JSOTSup 21 (Sheffield: JSOT Press, 1982), 62–65.

[321] It was said that "two hairs of another colour on its body were sufficient to disqualify it" (J. H. Hertz, ed., *The Pentateuch and Haftorahs,* 2d ed. [London: Soncino Press, 1978], 652).

other physical tasks, it was probably young and strong.[322] Ashley has suggested on the basis of 1 Sam 6:7 that the cow might have been previously calved,[323] so the translation would not be entirely proper.[324] Elsewhere the bull was sacrificed as a sin offering for the high priest and his family (Lev 4:3–12; 16:6,11) or on behalf of the community as a whole (Lev 4:13–21), and so the female is specified here such that there be no confusion of purification agents or rituals. Additionally the cow would offer the maximum potential yield of purification ashes so the ritual need not be repeated as often.[325] The redness of the cow reflected the color of blood, as did the other sacrificial elements burned with the cow. Finally, the female of a given species is usually indicated as the animal of choice for a sin offering by an average individual (Lev 4:27–5:6).

When the qualified cow had been selected, it was then presented to Eleazar, the priest and son of Aaron. Why would Eleazar be chosen instead of Aaron? Several reasons have been suggested. First, Aaron was the high priest, and all caution was taken to ensure that the high priest not become unclean so as to render him unqualified to perform regular ritual activities prescribed for him. The high priest was not to defile himself by going near a corpse, even that of his mother or father (Lev 21:11). Second, this ordinance was directed not only to the present but also to future generations. Aaron was now aging and would soon die in the latter stage of the forty-year wilderness experience (Num 20:22–29). Also this preparation took place outside the camp, the normal realm of uncleanness where persons having skin diseases and other infirmities were remanded. The high priest was prohibited from going outside the sanctuary, lest he potentially return with some unknown or inadvertent impurity (Lev 21:12).[326] As the next in charge of the priestly corps, Eleazar escorted the cow outside the proximity of the tabernacle and then outside the camp of the twelve tribes of Israel to a designated area for the enactment of the ritual preparation. The cow was ritually slaughtered by another individual in the presence of Eleazar (*lĕpānāyw*),[327] thereby indicating priestly supervision of the slaughtering and other ritual preparation of the ashes.

---

[322] *Parah* 2.3: "It was invalid even if someone rode on, leaned on, crossed the river with its help, had a cloak draped across it, or even had its lead rope doubled across its back, it was considered invalid. ... if aught be done for the sake of the heifer it is valid, but if for the sake of a person, it is invalid.

[323] This matter was debated by the Tannaitic rabbis. See *Parah* 2.1.

[324] Ashley, *Numbers*, 364.

[325] So remarks Milgrom, *Numbers*, "Excursus 48: The Paradox of the Red Cow," 440. Cf. Ashley, *Numbers*, 364.

[326] Some rabbis suggested Aaron was prohibited from carrying out this ritual because of his connection with the golden calf incident (*Pentateuch and Haftorahs*, 652).

[327] The Hb. לִפְנֵי (here as לְפָנָיו, "before him") often carries the idea of service when an individual is the object of the preposition.

**19:4–6** As the blood dripped from the neck of the cow, Eleazar dipped his fingers into the blood and sprinkled it seven times in the direction of the entrance to the Tent of Meeting, which was often the location of revelatory activity (Num 12:5; 16:18). So from the eastern outskirts the priest would splash the blood toward the west with the flick of his fingers, and hence also toward the altar where blood was normally poured out or sprinkled. The repetition of the act seven times, the number of completeness, parallels this activity with other sin or purification offerings, such as the sprinkling of the blood inside the Holy Place on the Day of Atonement (Lev 16:14–19; cf. Lev 4:6,17).

The cow was burned in its entirety, including the "offal" or that which was contained within the stomach and intestines, but not including any excrement that might have exuded from the animal and thus have contributed contaminants to the offering or the procedures.[328] This process and elements were very similar to that carried out on the bull of the sin offering of the priest or the community (Lev 4:11,21) or in the cleansing of the leper in which the identical items are used in the sprinkling process but are not burned (Lev 14:3–9). Eleazar is commanded to take red cedar wood, crimson wool, and hyssop and cast them on the burning red cow. Only here in all of the offerings is the blood of the sacrificial victim burned on the altar. The burning of the blood with the remainder of the animal enhanced the purifying efficacy of the ashes, which were gathered from the ground after the total incineration of the carcass.[329] The red, bloodlike color of the additional burned elements, the crimson red[330] woolen material and the reddish cedar wood, also contributed to the visible imagery and hence to the detergent capacity of the ashes.[331] The plant species translated "hyssop" was probably not the Greek *hussōpos* (from which the English was derived), which was not native to this region. The plant known in the Hebrew as *ʾēzôb* is believed to have been either marjoram, sage, or thyme, the leaves of which are very absorbent.[332]

---

[328] Cf. Budd, *Numbers*, 208. Contra Gray, *Numbers*, 250.

[329] *Zebachim* 14.1 describes the physical layout of the place of burning as a pit during the second Temple era, and the red cow was led across the Kidron Valley by members of the priesthood on a causeway or bridge constructed by the priests (cf. *Parah* 3.6). The rabbis also funded the construction of the bridge across to the Mount of Olives, and the animal was burned in a nearby pit.

[330] שָׁנִי probably is an Egyptian loan word.

[331] Crimson red dye was derived from the crimson worm *(Kermes bilicus)* and was also used in the production of priestly garments and curtains for the Tent of Meeting (Exod 36:8,35,37; 39:1–2).

[332] *Fauna and Flora of the Bible*, 2d ed. (London: United Bible Societies, 1980), 129–30. The species *origanum maru or origanum majorana* grows in Syria and Palestine to a height of about one m. from the ground or rock crevices. Its leaves and branches are hairy, and its flowers are white. Its aromatic leaves when dried are used as a condiment. When collected in bunches, it can be used for sprinkling, for its hairy leaves would hold the liquid for application, whether sprinkling or painting.

**19:7–8** One of the repetitious features of the sacrifice of the red cow was the number of washings and bathings that took place during the ritual preparation process and later in the application of the ash and water mixture. This is paralleled by the number of ritual ablutions that took place on the Day of Atonement (Lev 16:4,24,26,28). All persons involved in the preparation of the ashes, who had by prescription entered the process in a ritually pure state *(ṭāhôr)*, had to bathe their bodies and wash their clothes because of contamination or impurity contracted during the performance of their assigned tasks. The priest (Eleazar) who carried out the slaughtering and sprinkling (v. 7), the assistant[333] who burned the cow (v. 8), and the one who gathered and stored the ashes (v. 10) would be rendered unclean by their touching of this purification (sin) offering—the red cow ashes. But this was a lesser state of uncleanness than one who would touch a dead body. After taking the prescribed ritual bath, they would remain unclean just until evening.[334] After washing and bathing they were permitted to reenter the camp, though they would remain in a state of uncleanness until sundown. After sundown, their period of impurity satisfied, they could fully reenter the realm of the community purity and holiness.

**19:9–10a** The ashes were carefully collected by a ritually clean person into a clean vessel and stored in a clean location outside the camp for safekeeping until they were needed. The term translated "kept" *(mišmeret)* may have a more emphatic meaning here, that of "safeguarding service" similar to the usage in Num 3:28–38 and 4:27–32. Those responsible would ensure the purifying ashes were carefully stored in a ritually pure container, placed in a clean locale, and guarded against any contamination that would render them useless for further application.

The ashes were safeguarded for use in the water of cleansing for purification from sin or other form of impurity. The "water of cleansing" *(mê niddâ,* "waters of removal") would be made efficacious for ritual cleansing by the addition of the ashes of the red cow and other burned products that were also cleansing agents. In a very real sense the purification property of blood and other reagents was reconstituted when the fresh ("living") waters were added, making the mixture ready for sprinkling as a purification offering.

**19:10b** In future generations this purification offering and ritual would be one of the more commonly applied purification offerings because of the continual potentiality of becoming unclean due to the death of someone in

---

[333] Whether this person (or the one who gathered the ashes) was a priest, Levite, or layperson is unspecified in the text. He simply had to be ritually clean to handle the purification (הַחַטָּאת) elements.

[334] Though not explicitly stated, I agree with Milgrom (*Numbers,* 162) that bodily cleansing for the person who collected the ashes was understood, as well as explicitly stated for the other two individuals.

the family, of a neighbor, or of a sojourner in the land. This statement is concluded by the phrase "perpetual statute" *(ḥūqqat ʿôlām)*, as is the second section of the book (v. 21). Hence the heretofore prescribed process of preparing the ashes was a perpetual statute for the future generations of Israel. As with other expressions of community faith, the ritual guidelines applied to both the native Israelite and to resident aliens. Previously in the Book of Numbers, other such legislation was equally applied in the areas of Passover celebration (9:14), offerings made by fire (15:14–15), offerings for inadvertent sins (15:26,29), and sins of a high hand (15:30). Again the openness of Israelite ritual law to resident aliens who desired to identify with the community of faith stands in contrast to some other religious practices in the Ancient Near East. For example, Hittite temple ritual prohibited foreigners from bringing anything to the gods or even approaching the gods.[335]

Finally, there are important parallels between the rituals associated with the dead outlined in Num 19:1–10 and Deut 21:1–10. In Deuteronomy the focus is on the absolution of community guilt in the case of an unsolved murder. The elders of the city nearest where the slain person was discovered would wash their hands over a heifer which was taken into a valley with flowing water and killed by breaking its neck. Note the following parallels:

| **Deut 21:1–10** | **Num 19:1–10** |
|---|---|
| Association with death | Association with death |
| 1. Heifer / cow | 1. **Red** heifer / cow |
| | 2. Without defect or blemish |
| 2. Not worked nor worn the yoke | 3. Never worn the yoke by Eleazar |
| 3. Taken to flowing stream in valley | 4. Taken outside the camp |
| 4. Heifer killed - elders break neck | 5. Heifer sacrificed by Eleazar |
| 5. Levitical priests oversee / bless / settle | 6. Eleazar sprinkles blood seven times toward front of Tent of Meeting (tabernacle) |
| | 7. Heifer burned totally, including blood |
| 6. Elders ritual wash hands over dead cow | 8. Ritual bathing of priest and clothes, unclean |
| 7. Pray God atone for innocent blood | 9. Ashes of heifer stored later mixed with water for ritual purification of death |

**[11]"Whoever touches the dead body of anyone will be unclean for seven days. [12]He must purify himself with the water on the third day and on the seventh day; then he will be clean. But if he does not purify himself on the third and seventh days, he will not be clean. [13]Whoever touches the dead body of anyone and fails to purify himself defiles the LORD's tabernacle. That person must be cut off from**

---

[335] "Instructions for Temple Officials," ii.9–11, *ANET,* 2d ed., 208.

Israel. **Because the water of cleansing has not been sprinkled on him, he is unclean; his uncleanness remains on him.**

GENERAL RULE FOR APPLYING RED HEIFER ASHES (19:11–13). **19:11–13** In the customary Pentateuchal pattern, the halakhic legislation begins with a general statement of the guidelines for applying the purification offering of the red cow, and then details of the application procedures are delineated. The questions of Who? What? Why? How? and What if / if not? are set forth in rudimentary fashion.

| | |
|---|---|
| Who? | Anyone who comes into contact with a dead person's body |
| Why? | Renders unclean, ritually impure for seven days |
| How? | Purification with water of cleansing on third and seventh days |
| What if/not? | Failure to comply renders one impure; defiles sanctuary |
| | Anyone who remains impure must be cut off from the community |

The literary structure of this section unfolds as follows:

A  Touching the dead renders one unclean seven days (19:11)
  B  Purification on third and seventh days makes one clean (19:12)
  B'  Failure to purify on third and seventh days >> unclean
  A'  One who touches the dead [=unclean] (19:13)
    B"  Failure to purify
      C  Defiles the sanctuary
      C'  Must be cut off from Israel
    B"'  Failure to purify: Waters of cleansing not applied
  A"  Uncleanness remains

Several key issues can be discerned from this structure. First, uncleanness that comes from contact with the dead carries with it a high level of impurity. As Ashley notes, "This double application of the waters may have indicated the seriousness of the pollution of contact with a corpse."[336] The time period of the impurity states the common maximum length for persons who have become unclean. Yet with some forms of impurity, such as contact with the red cow during the preparation process, one is rendered impure only until sundown. Second, emphasis on matters related to uncleanness abounds. In these three verses the Hebrew term for "unclean" ($t\bar{a}m\bar{e}^{\,}$) occurs four times versus only two times for the term for "clean" ($t\bar{a}h\hat{o}r$). Third, the seriousness of this impurity is heightened by the focus of each of the chiastic structures in this section. The variant in the center of v. 12 is the issue of compliance or noncompliance with the purification rites. In the second cycle of v. 13 only the matter of noncompliance is addressed, and the focal point is that of the consequence for failure to undergo the ritual cleansing.

---

[336] Ashley, *Numbers,* 371.

[14]"This is the law that applies when a person dies in a tent: Anyone who enters the tent and anyone who is in it will be unclean for seven days, [15]and every open container without a lid fastened on it will be unclean.

[16]"Anyone out in the open who touches someone who has been killed with a sword or someone who has died a natural death, or anyone who touches a human bone or a grave, will be unclean for seven days.

[17]"For the unclean person, put some ashes from the burned purification offering into a jar and pour fresh water over them. [18]Then a man who is ceremonially clean is to take some hyssop, dip it in the water and sprinkle the tent and all the furnishings and the people who were there. He must also sprinkle anyone who has touched a human bone or a grave or someone who has been killed or someone who has died a natural death. [19]The man who is clean is to sprinkle the unclean person on the third and seventh days, and on the seventh day he is to purify him. The person being cleansed must wash his clothes and bathe with water, and that evening he will be clean. [20]But if a person who is unclean does not purify himself, he must be cut off from the community, because he has defiled the sanctuary of the LORD. The water of cleansing has not been sprinkled on him, and he is unclean. [21]This is a lasting ordinance for them.

"The man who sprinkles the water of cleansing must also wash his clothes, and anyone who touches the water of cleansing will be unclean till evening. [22]Anything that an unclean person touches becomes unclean, and anyone who touches it becomes unclean till evening."

SECOND STATUTE: APPLYING THE WATERS OF PURIFICATION FOR DEATH IMPURITY (19:14–22).  **19:14a**  The second section of the chapter begins with the abbreviated form of the phrase that introduced the legislation in the chapter that defined the preparation of the ashes and the general guidelines governing its usage. "This is the Torah" (*zōʾt hattôrâ*, "This is the instruction") commences the specific areas of application of the purification offering of the ashes of the red cow. This section divides into four parts: (1) answers the questions as to who, what, and how uncleanness is contracted (vv. 14–16), (2) addresses the issue of procedure in rectifying the uncleanness state (vv. 17–19), (3) affirms the consequences of noncompliance (v. 20), and (4) asserts the matter of cleansing for the person who carries out the ritual cleansing process.

**19:14b–16**  The two realms of life in which this form of uncleanness may be contracted are examined, the interior, the tent or dwelling place and the exterior, the open field. Within the dwelling place, the tent being the most applicable in the wilderness setting, everyone and everything openly exposed to the death within the tent was rendered unclean for seven days. Those attending the person who died, anyone within the dwelling place, and anyone who enters while the dead body is lying within is rendered impure and must undergo the ritual cleansing process. Vessels containing food or other commodities that had been left uncovered[337] when the person died or even opened after the death occurred contracted the impurity of death. This stipulation is parallel to that of Lev 11:32–34, which prescribes the destruction of a vessel and its contents, which have become unclean as a result of contact with a dead unclean animal.

In the open field (lit. "upon the face of the field") or perhaps simply "outside," one may contract the uncleanness of death through one of the following means: (1) physical contact with someone who has been slain by a sword, (2) touching someone who has died in the open field while working or walking along a road or path, (3) handling bones (or even a single bone) from human remains of someone whose death and decay may have gone unnoticed for a considerable length of time, or (4) contact with a grave, whether it be a cemetery or cave. Contact may have been intentional, such as when a soldier or other person attended an injured person after a battle or when carrying a dead body to the proper burial site, or one may have stumbled accidently upon a body or bones while traveling through an overgrown field or through a forest. Each of the cases rendered the person or vessel unclean for seven days.

**19:17–19** The purification procedures involved a three-stage process, the making of the purification mixture, the sprinkling of the unclean person, and the cleansing of the one performing the purification ritual. The person performing the ceremonial cleansing or decontamination process must simply be one who is ritually clean; it does not necessarily involve the application or oversight by a priest, who was a necessary attendant to the process of preparation of the ashes. The mixture of ashes from the red cow, hyssop, cedar, and crimson wool were placed in a bowl, and fresh (lit. "living," *ḥayyîm*) water was then added to the ashes making a muddy looking emulsion. The agent would then take some leaves of marjoram,[338] dip it into the

---

[337] These types of vessels would have included pottery vessels such as storage jars for dry or wet goods (wheat, barley, almonds, water, olive oil, or wine), which might have stoppers or flat or concave lids, and smaller jugs or juglets for various liquids (foods or ointments). Some storage jars had pointed bases that enabled them to be stacked by inserting the base of the upper jar inside the rim of the lower, thereby sealing the lower container. Other vessels had earthenware covers that could be attached using cords laced through handles of the vessel and small holes in the lids. Milgrom remarks, "A tightly closed vessel will not admit the 'vapors' of impurity given off by a corpse; its contents remain pure" (*Numbers,* 161). According to the Temple Scroll from Cave 11 near Kh. Qumran, vessels that were not tightly closed with affixed lids were rendered unclean permanently and had to be destroyed (11QTemple 49:8–9). Perhaps because of the porous nature of earthenware, allowing it to absorb that which was unclean, that vessel had become unclean and could not be made pure again.

[338] As before in v. 6, the reference to "hyssop" is probably to the more absorbent leaves of marjoram, sage, or thyme. Later rabbis specified that three stalks of plant were used in the sprinkling process.

mixture, and then sprinkle it upon the tent exterior and interior, upon the open vessels that had been rendered unclean, upon the persons who were within the tent when the person died as well as those who entered afterward, and/or upon the person who has come in contact with a dead body in a field. Emphasis is given to the manner of sprinkling by means of the waters over the items to be cleansed by the movement of the arm and hand, highlighted by the fourfold use of the preposition ʿal ("upon"), which is then followed by the fourfold list of the exterior contaminating contacts.[339] Two Hebrew terms are used for describing the distribution of the waters of purification over the unclean person or objects, and they are used in vv. 13,18,19,20 in chiastic structure, which emphasizes the sprinkling application. Note the order below in that the term zōraq is used for the sprinkling process in the exclusionary cases because of noncompliance, and hizzâ is used in the case of active sprinkling for purification:

v. 13   zōraq, "sprinkling," exclusion because the waters were not "poured/ sprinkled" on the unclean
   v. 18 hizzâ purification by "sprinkling" the waters upon persons and objects
   v. 19 hizzâ purification by "sprinkling" the waters on third and seventh days
v. 20   zōraq, "sprinkling," exclusion of defiled persons for not having waters "poured/sprinkled" on them[340]

This structure adds further emphasis to the need for carrying out the ritual sprinkling procedures. Presumably, those unclean vessels that were purified in the process would then be washed to complete their purification.

The order of the exterior elements of v. 18, which repeat those from v. 16, create another simple chiastic construction as follows A B C D::D B A C:

| A pierced | B dead | C bone | D grave |
| C bone | A pierced | B dead | D grave |

The application of the waters of purification were to be performed on the third and seventh days of the period of uncleanness. Again the seven-day period of impurity parallels that prescribed for Nazirites who had become unclean by contact with the dead (Num 6:9) and for those having various skin diseases such as psoriasis or leprosy (Lev 13:5; 14:9; 15:13). Each of those, however, prescribed a sacrificial act on the eighth day following the week-long separation. Also unlike the purification rituals for the leper and one having a bodily discharge, this passage does not delineate a requirement that the person be sep-

---

[339] Note the arrangement of these two sets of four elements in the literary outline below in this chapter.

[340] Cf. Ashley, who believes that the two verbs described different ritual processes (*Numbers*, 372). But in the LXX the semantically equivalent Gk. terms περιρραντίζω and περιρραίνω are used for זרק and הזה respectively. Likewise, if someone comes into contact with an unclean individual, that person becomes impure. Cf. vv. 21–22 comment below.

arated from the community for the duration of their uncleanness.[341] They would not be allowed to mingle regularly with the ritually pure public. In fact the family would generally mourn for at least the seven-day period, but it apparently was not required that they be excluded from the camp.

At the conclusion of the ritual sprinkling of the ashes and water mixture, the previously clean person who had applied the purifying potion was to undergo the same ritual bathing process as the priest and his assistants who prepared and gathered the ashes (vv. 7,8,10). That person would wash his garments, then bathe himself with pure water, yet remain in a state of uncleanness until sundown. Then he could reclothe himself with the purified garments, and he could be deemed as clean and able to participate in the holiness of the community.

**19:20** In parallel with v. 13, the gravity of noncompliance with the purification ritual requirements is emphasized by repetition. This pattern of setting forth casuistic law is common in Leviticus and Numbers. In v. 13 the excommunication and extermination penalty was exacted as being away from the nation Israel (*miyyiśrāʾēl*), whereas in v. 20 the exclusion from the midst of the congregational assembly (*mittôk haqqāhāl*)[342] is in focus. The parallelism in the literary structure and in the content of each of the verses would suggest these are equivalent statements. Death brings with it a heightened degree of impurity, but God provided a simple means of reconciliation through the sprinkling of water mixed with ashes. Failure to submit to his statutes in faith, simply by following the prescribed process outlined in this chapter, resulted in the continued defilement of the individual. The contamination also reached inward toward the tabernacle, which was at the heart and center of the community life and well-being.

**19:21–22** A summary statement recapitulates the basic principles of uncleanness caused by contact with the purifying agents. It is introduced by the reiteration of the phrase found in the concluding statement of the first section of the chapter (v. 10b), that these stipulations remain a perpetual statute throughout the generations of Israel. The person who performed the ritual sprinkling and the one on whom the ritual was performed would wash their garments and then bathe themselves, but both would remain unclean until evening. In fact, anyone who would come into contact with the waters of purification would be rendered unclean and thus be required to undergo the ritual cleansing procedure. Any such persons rendered unclean, and who

---

[341] Cf. Lev 13:4–6; Num 5:1–4.

[342] The noun קָהָל is used here (and in 14:5; 15:15; 16:33; 17:12; 20:6) over against the normal עֵדָה used extensively throughout the Book of Numbers (81x). It was into the "midst of the congregation" (same phrase as here in 19:20) that Aaron ran with his censer and incense to make atonement for Israel and stand between those stricken by the plague and those who survived the judgment of God meted out against Korah and his followers among the congregation of Israel.

had endured the ritual cleansing process, would remain unclean until sundown. Furthermore, anything those persons touched prior to sundown would also become unclean, and so they would need to remain in a state of virtual isolation until sundown so as to not contaminate other persons or objects.

In conclusion, the writer of the Book of Hebrews compared the cleansing a person received by application of the ashes of the red heifer to that of the cleansing efficacy of the blood of Jesus Christ, noting that the work of Christ ultimately superseded that of the Old Testament purification rituals. The ashes of the red heifer could only cleanse the outward man, "for the purifying of the flesh" (NKJV), but the blood of Christ accomplished the cleansing of the conscience, the inward man. Jesus accomplished this purification act, once and for all, so that we might be delivered from that which leads to death, and instead live to serve him, the living God (Heb 9:13–14).

### LITERARY BIFID STRUCTURE OF NUMBERS 19

| | |
|---|---|
| **Introduction: Divine Instruction (v. 1)**<br>**A "This is the statute of Torah" (v. 2a)**<br>Which Yahweh commanded saying,<br>"Speak to the Israelites." | **A' "This is the Torah" (v. 14a)** |
| **B Preparation of the Ashes: Uncleanness**<br>**(vv. 2b–10a)**<br>**Presentation and Slaughtering (vv. 2b–3)**<br>1. **TAKE** — They shall — to you a perfect red cow (v. 2b) w/o blemish — which a yoke has not been put on it<br>2. You shall give it to Eleazar the priest<br>3. He will bring it outside the camp<br>4. He shall slaughter it before him | **B' Unclean Entities (vv. 14b–16)**<br>1. A man—who dies—in a tent (v. 14)<br>Any one — who enters — the tent<br>Any one — [who is] in the tent<br>He shall be **unclean** for seven days<br>2. Any open vessel upon which no lid (v. 15)<br>**Unclean** — it is<br>3. Anyone — who touches — in open field (v. 16)<br>One pierced by a sword<br>Or dead person  or human bones<br>Or a grave<br>**Unclean** seven days |
| **Blood and Burning (vv. 4–6)**<br>1. Eleazar the priest **shall take** some blood w/ his fingers (v. 4)<br>2. He shall sprinkle toward opening of Tent of Meeting some of the blood seven times<br>3. He shall burn the cow before his eyes (v. 5) with its hide, its flesh, its blood concerning its refuse he shall burn<br>4. The priest shall **TAKE** — cedar, hyssop, scarlet wool (v. 6) and cast into the midst of the burning cow | |

## LITERARY BIFID STRUCTURE OF NUMBERS 19

| | |
|---|---|
| **Bathing and Washing (vv. 7–8)**<br>1. **Then he shall wash** — his clothes >> the priest (v. 7)<br>**and bathe** — his flesh — with water<br>2. Afterward he may enter the camp<br>So **unclean** — is the priest — until evening<br>3. Also the one who burns it (v. 8)<br>**He shall wash** — his clothes — with water<br>**Bathe** — his flesh (body) — with water<br>So he is **unclean** — until evening | |
| **Safe-Keeping of the Ashes (v. 9)**<br>1. **Gather** — a clean (pure) man — the ash of the cow<br>2. **Set Aside** — outside of the camp — in a place clean (pure)<br>3. So it **Shall Be** — for the assembly of the children of Israel<br>for it is service of the waters of purification for sin<br><br>Bathing and Washing (abbreviated) (v. 10a)<br>1. So he will wash — one who gathers the ashes — his clothes<br>and he is unclean until evening | **C′ Specific Purification Procedures (vv. 17–19)**<br>1. They shall **take** — for the unclean one (v. 17)<br>Some ash of burned purification offering<br>Put on it living/fresh water—in a vessel<br>2. Then clean person shall **take** hyssop (v. 18)<br>Dip in water -//- and He shall sprinkle<br>Upon the tent<br>and upon all vessels<br>and upon the persons there<br>and upon one touching<br>on bone(s)<br>on one pierced<br>on a dead person<br>on a grave |
| **C Perpetual Statute (v. 10b)**<br>1. So it shall be — for the children of Israel and for the sojourner sojourning among you<br>**For a perpetual statute** | |
| **D General Rule: Purification Procedures (vv. 11–12)**<br>1. One who **Touches** — when dead — any human body (v. 11)<br>He shall be **unclean** — seven days<br>2. He — will purify himself — on third day and seventh day — he will be **clean** (v. 12)<br>2′. **IF NOT** — he purifies himself — on third day and seventh day<br>**NOT** — he will be **clean** | 3. **A Clean** person shall sprinkle (v. 19)<br>Upon the **unclean** person on third and seventh days and **Purify** him on the seventh day<br>He shall **wash** his clothes<br>**bathe** with water<br>He will be **clean** in the evening |

## LITERARY BIFID STRUCTURE OF NUMBERS 19

| | |
|---|---|
| **E 1′ Anyone who Touches** a corpse, a body that died (**v. 13**) and **DOES NOT purify himself** The sanctuary of YHWH — he **defiles** and that man **SHALL BE CUT OFF** — from Israel Because **waters of purification** were not poured on him **Unclean** — he is Still his **uncleanness** is in him | **E′ BUT** a man who is **Unclean** (v. 20) and **DOES NOT purify himself** He shall be **CUT OFF** from assembly For the sanctuary of YHWH — he **defiles** For **waters of purification** were not poured on him He is **unclean** |
| | **D′ Perpetual Statute (vv. 21–22)** So it shall be for them **perpetual statute** (v. 21) One who sprinkles the **waters of purification** he shall wash his clothes and one who touches the **waters of purification** shall be unclean until evening and anyone who touches unclean is unclean (v. 22) and the person who touches [it] is unclean until evening |

## 3. Rebellion C: From Zin to Moab—The Rebellion and Replacement of Moses (20:1–25:19)

The third rebellion cycle encompasses a wide variety of material with the most enigmatic structure of all seven cycles in the Book of Numbers. The historical setting involves a series of movements from the Wilderness of Zin to the borders of Edom and into the Plains of Moab, during which there are triumphs and tragedies as well as victories and defeats. Instead of referencing the nation by the usual listing of the twelve tribes, the Israelites are viewed en masse using a new phraseology, "the children of Israel, the whole congregation" (20:1,22). Matters related to the priests and Levites are subsumed under the priestly and prophetic activity of the prophet-diviner Balaam, that is, until the end of the cycle when Eleazar's son Phinehas rises to the occasion as a defender of the faith. A structured set of laws governing the community of faith is lacking, though implicitly a series of halakhic issues emerge out of the incident involving the bronze servant and the Balaam oracles. Rather, this cycle includes a series of blessings upon the community of faith through the oracles of Balaam.

Building upon Wenham's observation of a general pattern in the three travelogues of Exodus–Numbers, which recount the travels in stages from Egypt and the Red Sea to Mount Sinai (Exod 12:29–19:25), from Mount

Sinai to Kadesh (Num 10:11–12:16), and from Kadesh to the Plains of
Moab opposite Jericho (Num 20:1–21:35), the following structural outline
results.[343] The recurring pattern in these two chapters is as follows: (1) historical event, (2) people's murmuring, (3) God provides, and (4) persons
punished. Parts (3) and (4) are reversed in chap. 21. The common elements
include: victory over Israel's enemies; journey march in stages; complaints
and grumbling of the people concerning food and water; songs of victory;
manifestation of the Glory of God; miraculous provisions; judgment from
God; leadership through Moses, Aaron, and Miriam; and the need for faith.

Milgrom has delineated the two parallel units of material in Num 20:1–
29 and 21:1–35 to demonstrate the literary contrast being made between the
"Failure of the Leaders" in the former and the "Failure and Deliverance of
the People" in the latter. The pivotal point in these two chapters is when the
people cry out to the Lord for deliverance and he grants great victory. Milgrom outlines the material as follows:

| Failure of the Leaders (chap. 20) | Failure and Deliverance of the People (chap. 21) |
|---|---|
| A Miriam's Death (v. 1) | A' Victory over the Canaanites (vv. 1–3) |
| B People murmur for water (vv. 2–6) and leaders rebel vs. God (vv. 9–11a) | B People murmur for water and they rebel vs. God (vv. 4–5) |
| C God provides water (vv. 11b,7–8) | C' People punished (v. 6) |
| D Leaders punished (vv.12–29) | D' God shows mercy to Israel (vv. 7–35) |
| 1. No entry (vv. 12–13) | 1. He heals (vv. 7–9) |
| 2. No passage (vv. 14–21) | 2. He provides water (vv. 16–18) |
| 3. Aaron's death (vv. 23–29) | 3. Three victories vs. Amorites (vv. 21–35) |

Each of these sections is bracketed by an inclusio; in the first it is death, and in
the second it is victory. Concerning the arrangement of the material, Milgrom
concludes that it "is not haphazard but follows a structural scheme that is both
aesthetic and logical. It reveals symmetry and purpose and, viewed as a whole
and from a distance, satisfactorily resolves all the apparent problems that characterize the text when it is viewed from up close as a series of discrete
parts."[344]

A comparison of the three journey passages evidences very different
development of themes and didactic purposes. In the Exodus narrative victories over the Egyptians and the Amalekites and the manifestation of the
glory and power of God bring deliverance, hope, and blessing to Israel.
Despite their complaints, God is gracious in faithfully providing for the
needs of the people along their desert journey. Moses, Aaron, and Miriam

---

[343] Wenham, *Numbers*, 148.
[344] Milgrom, "Excursus 55: The Redaction of Chapters 20–21," 466–67.

provide dedicated leadership to the nation and challenge them to faithfulness in God. Yahweh the Warrior fought for Israel against the Amalekites, one of those peoples who would become one of the archenemies of God and his people. There is no judgment of the people until later in Exodus in the aftermath of the idolatry involving the gold calf. In the second journey narrative, the tenor is decisively different.

## Excursus: The Journey Motif in Exodus and Numbers

| Journey I<br>Egypt to Mount Sinai<br>Exod 12:29–19:25 | Journey II<br>Mount Sinai to Kadesh<br>Num 10:11–14:45 | Journey III<br>Kadesh to Moab Plains<br>Num 20:1–21:35 |
|---|---|---|
| V Vs. Egypt (12:29–42) | M Mount Sinai to Paran Desert (10:11–34) | M Arrival at Kadesh (20:1a) |
| M Succoth – Red Sea (13:17–14:9) | S Moses' Song of Victory | L Miriam Dies (20:1b) |
| C Egyptian Army Advance (14:10–12) | C General Complaint (11:1a) | C No Water (20:2–5) |
| | | L Moses and Aaron Intercede (20:6a) |
| L/F Moses Appeals for Israel to Believe (14:13) | J Fiery Judgment (11:1b) | G Glory of Lord – Instructions Given to Speak to Rock (20:6b–8) |
| V Vs. Egypt (14:14–31) | L Moses Intercedes– Fire Recedes (11:2) | L Moses [and Aaron] Strikes Rock (20:9–11) |
| G Glory of Lord Manifested in Pillar Cloud and Angel of God (14:19–25) | C Complaint about Food (11:4–9) | J Judgment vs. Moses and Aaron (20:12–13) |
| F Israel Saw and Believed (14:31) | L Moses Intercedes w/ Complaint (11:10–23) | M Journey through Edom Denied; Travel to Mount Hor (20:14) |
| S Moses and Miriam (15:1–21) | G Lord Descends in Cloud – Spirit upon Elders (11:24–30) | L Death and Burial of Aaron (20:22–29) |
| M Red Sea to Shur Desert (15:22) | P Provision of Quail (11:31–33) | V Vs. Arad (21:1–3) |
| C Bitter Waters – Marah (15:22–24) | J Plague Strikes – Kibroth Hataavah (11:33–34) | M Mount Hor around Edom (21:4) |
| P Waters Made Sweet (15:25) | M Kibroth Hataavah to Hazeroth | C No Food or Water (21:5) |
| F Faith Challenge (15:26) | C Miriam and Aaron Vs. Moses (12:1–2) | J Fiery Serpents (21:6) |
| M Elim and Sin Desert (15:27–16:1) | L Moses Most Humble (12:3) | F People Appeal and Repent to Moses (21:7) |
| C Food Supply (16:2–3) | G Lord Descends in Cloud (12:4–5) | L Moses Makes Bronze Serpent (21:8–9) |
| G Glory of Lord in Cloud (16:10) | S Song about Moses (12:6–8) | M Oboth to Land of Moab and Amorites (21:10–13) |
| P Manna and Quail (16:11–36) | J Miriam Struck w/Leprous Disease (12:9) | S Songs of Victory in Transjordan (21:14–18a) |
| M Sin Desert to Rephidim (17:1) | L Aaron to Moses, Moses to God (12:10–13) | M Mattanah - to Pisgah; Request Passage through Amorite Land (21:18b–20) |
| C No Water (17:2–3) | | |
| L Moses Intercedes (17:4) | | |

| | | |
|---|---|---|
| **P** Water at Meribah / Massah (17:5–7) | **P** Healing but Isolation for Miriam (12:14–15) | **V** Vs. Amorite Sihon of Heshbon (21:21–26) |
| **V** Vs. Amalekites (17:8–16) | **M** Hazeroth to Paran Desert (12:16) | **S** Song of Victory vs. Amorites (21:27–30) |
| **L** Moses and Jethro (18:1–27) | **L** Moses Sends Spies (13:1–16) | **M** Journey to Bashan (21:31a) |
| **M** Rephidim to Mount Sinai (19:1–2) | **F** Assess the Quality of the Land (13:17–25) | **V** Vs. Og of Bashan (21:31b–35) |
| **G** Glory of Lord at Mount Sinai (19:3–25) | **F** Report: Good and Bad Challenge of Faith (13:26–33) | **M** Plains of Moab (22:1) |
| | **C** Fear of the Ten Spies and Israel (14:1–4) | **V** God vs. **Balaam: Cursing turned to Blessing** (22:2–24:25) |
| | **L/F** Moses and Aaron, Joshua and Caleb Intercede; Faith Challenge (14:5–9) | |
| | **G** Glory of Lord Appears (14:10) | |
| | **L** Moses Intercedes (14:11–19) | |
| | **G** Glory of Lord Promised (14:20–22) | |
| | **J** Judgment vs. Unfaithful (14:23–38) | |
| | ***V*** Defeated by Amalekites (14:39–45) | |

| | | |
|---|---|---|
| V=Victories over Israel's Enemies | G=Glory of God Manifested | S=Songs and Celebration |
| C=Complaints and Grumbling | P=Miraculous Provision of Food / Water | F=Faith Demonstrated or Needed |
| J=Judgment from God | L=Leadership of Moses, Aaron, and Miriam | M=Journey March |

The account of the departure from Mount Sinai begins on a positive note, with Moses telling Hobab that God has promised good things for Israel, and Moses sings a song of the victory march with Yahweh leading the nation forth and vanquishing their enemies. But the account quickly turns sour as the people complain in an ever-increasing manner and rapidity. Each case then is followed by the meting out of judgment upon the rebellious lot. The first time the Lord descends upon the people, the results are beneficial, for the seventy elders are endowed with the Spirit and prophesy. Miriam and Aaron then contend with Moses over the leadership status held by the prophet, and judgment upon Miriam ensues. The second time the glory of God descends it is for judgment, bringing a message of death and destruction (14:10b–12). Moses rises to the occasion as the intercessor for Israel, and most of the people are saved from immediate death. God's glory, his reputation, among the nations is at stake, and the full manifestation of his glory would one day come. At the conclusion of this journey narrative, the Israelites are defeated by the Amalekites, a people they had defeated in the first journey account.

The third journey narrative contains an admixture of gloom and hope. Miriam dies, Moses and Aaron rebel, and then Aaron dies. The Israelites are denied passage though the region east of the Arabah by Edom, yet they are victorious against the Canaanites at Arad, and then later against Sihon of the Amorites at Heshbon and against Og of Bashan. Songs are composed to declare God's fighting on behalf of his people Israel. Yet Moses' rebellion in striking the rock, violating the holiness of God, had reverberating repercussions through the extended narrative. He was denied entry into the Promised Land, punished like the rebellious first generation that rejected the land. God uses a pagan divination expert named Balaam, against the will of this prophet for hire, to pronounce gloriously the wonder of the God of Israel and his beneficence.

The two key individuals of this cycle fall into the seditious pattern of the nation: Moses and Balaam. Moses' defiance in striking the rock, thereby violating the holiness of God, represents the final collapse of the seditious nation; the greatest of the prophets has joined in the rejection of God's sovereignty over the lives of his people. The pagan prophet Balaam on the other hand moves from a rebellious sorcerer to an obedient servant, even if against his own will and the will of his employer, Balak of Moab. In the beginning Moses' sister Miriam dies, and then following Moses' profaning act and Edom's denial of passage of Israel, Aaron dies. Only a few still remained from the aging adult generation of Israel that experienced God's dramatic saving activity in the Exodus. After a brief victory at Arad, the community repeats its pattern of rebellion, only to be saved by looking upon a bronze serpent mounted on a pole. But the journey motif quickly resumes, and they travel through the Plains of Moab, in which God gives victories over Sihon and Og of the Amorites in Heshbon and Bashan respectively. After these victories the scene changes dramatically.

Balaam, the pagan sorcerer of Mesopotamian origin, whom one might expect to rebel against the God of Israel (and he does), now becomes an unexpected spokesman for God. Moses is silent in the narrative. Yet even if the most faithful, devoted leader of the people of God should fall into sin, God will use whatever resource is necessary to communicate with and for his people. Jesus said in response to the Pharisees who requested that his disciples be rebuked, "I tell you if they keep quiet, the stones will cry out."[345] That a donkey should be the most spiritually observant character in

---

[345] Luke 19:39–40.

this section stands in sharp contradistinction to the nations and the individual leaders, a slap in the face toward any humanly originated means of conceiving of God and his ways. God will ultimately accomplish his will by whatever means and agency necessary. What echoes from the mouth of this most unusual servant of God are some of the most extraordinary words of praise for God and his purpose for his people. Reversal of fortunes reverberates through several episodes of the story: a persistent pagan prophet learns from a donkey, a Moabite king's desires are thwarted by God, and Balaam's intent to curse and bring condemnation upon Israel is turned by God into an opportunity to bring blessing beyond compare for the near and distant future. God reveals his character and his intent to bless abundantly all of humanity, both Hebrews and Gentiles.

The third rebellion cycle concludes with another collapse of Israel's character, despite the wondrous revelation through the prophet Balaam. The account of the idolatrous activity at Shittim and its consequences, while standing at the doorstep of the land of promise, served several didactic functions: to show that God will continue to bring judgment on a sinful and rebellious generation, to warn that and future generations of the consequences of rejecting God's law, and to seal the status of the Aaronic priesthood as God's choice for spiritual leadership. Temptations toward idolatry would plague Israel throughout their future in the land. Lest one think that the Balaam of chaps. 22–24 turned toward this God who had used him so wondrously, we find out later that the illustrious prophet was the instigator of the means by which Israel fell. The story of the first generation ended in tragic judgment, and the new generation would continue to be faced with the issue of faithfulness to God, that which would determine the course of their future as either blessed or bedeviled, reverent or rebellious.

### (1) From Kadesh of Zin to Mount Hor: The End of an Era (20:1–29)

The material in this chapter describes events in the northeast Sinai region during the advance from Kadesh in the Zin Wilderness to Mount Hor on the border of Edom. The time frame cited is simply the first month, which has traditionally been interpreted as the conclusion of the forty-year punishment of Israel in the wilderness. This section recounts the rebellion of Moses in response to the repeated grumbling of the people of Israel and the Edomite denial of passage for the Israelites. These two episodes come between the deaths of Miriam and Aaron. In the overall structure of the three rebellion cycles, this section is the counterpart to the rebellion of Miriam and Aaron against Moses in chap. 12. Only now the focus is on Moses, who rebels with some encouragement from Aaron. By the end of the chapter two of the three have died, and Moses has received a sentence not unlike that of the generation that rejected the land. Even the greatest of the prophets must endure the judgment of God when he rebels.

**¹In the first month the whole Israelite community arrived at the Desert of Zin, and they stayed at Kadesh. There Miriam died and was buried.**

HISTORICAL SETTING: KADESH OF ZIN AND THE DEATH OF MIRIAM DIED (20:1). **20:1** The historical and geographical setting provide a fitting conclusion to the story of judgment against the first generation that experienced the wonders of God's deliverance. Though the year is not specified, the mention of the first month brings the setting into conformity with the month of the deliverance from Egypt,[346] the month in which they should have been celebrating the Passover and the Festival of the Unleavened Bread in the Promised Land. Instead they found themselves back at Kadesh after some forty years of wilderness nomadic shepherding, and again they grumbled about their water supply as that first generation had done soon after they had crossed the Red Sea (Exod 15:23–26; 17:1–7).[347] At Kadesh the twelve scouts returned after a forty-day reconnaissance of the Promised Land (Num 13:26), but then the people were judged because of their rebellion against God and their rejection of the land. A group of ten who rebelled by giving a report about the land that was based on fear rather than faith affected an entire nation for an entire generation. They became an example for the future history writers and tellers of Israel, as well for Christianity, of the disastrous effects of unfaithful leadership on a community of faith.[348]

Now the generation of those who were twenty years of age or more had nearly all passed away. Israel found themselves at Kadesh ("holy place") in the Zin Wilderness. In 13:26 the reference is made to Kadesh being in the Paran Wilderness, but as was argued earlier these references are compatible. The Zin Wilderness, which encompassed the area of the drainage basin of the Nahal Zin, was likely the designation for a northeastern subregion of the larger Paran Wilderness, which covered much of the northeastern Sinai peninsula. The reference to the Israelites as "the whole Israelite community" (*běnê-yiśrāēl kol-hāʿēdâ*, "the children of Israel, the whole congregation") recalls the references in 13:26; 14:1,2,5,10 where the same phraseology is used for the collective assembly that heard the report and rejected the land. Now the collective assembly would once again contend with their divinely appointed leader.

Miriam's death and burial is reported with simple reverence. She was a leader among the Israelites, a prophetess and songstress (Exod 15:20–21),

---

[346] Gray, *Numbers*, 259–60; Budd, *Numbers*, 217. Since the Israelites move soon afterward from Kadesh to Mount Hor and then northward through the Transjordan highlands, most interpreters assume these events took place at the conclusion of the forty years in the wilderness.

[347] According to the detailed itinerary in Numbers 33 of the victory march from Egypt to the Plains of Moab, Aaron died on Mount Hor on the first day of the fifth month of the fortieth year after the Exodus (33:38–39).

[348] Note the use of the account of Numbers 13–14 in Heb 3:7–19. Cf. also Deut 1:26–46.

sister of the divinely chosen high priest and prophetic leader of the nation, who demonstrated her compassionate character soon after Moses was born (Exod 2:4–9). Miriam was gone, the only woman whose death has been remembered from that generation.[349] The love Moses had for Miriam was demonstrated when she was struck with a leprous skin disease after she challenged Moses' authority (Num 12:1–13). Appalled by what he saw affecting his beloved sister, he dramatically cried out for the Lord to heal her. Then in honor of Miriam, the nation delayed its march for the required period of seven days for her purification before it continued on its divinely led journey from Hazeroth to the Paran Wilderness. What effect Miriam's death had on Moses' rebellion in the verses that follow one can only speculate. I would suggest that these events are juxtapositioned purposefully in the text, and were thus at least a contributing factor to the prophet's demise. The death of Moses' dear sister Miriam may have caused the prophet to enter a period of depression or even despair, which might have led him to respond so negatively in the following account.

**[2]Now there was no water for the community, and the people gathered in opposition to Moses and Aaron. [3]They quarreled with Moses and said, "If only we had died when our brothers fell dead before the LORD! [4]Why did you bring the LORD's community into this desert, that we and our livestock should die here? [5]Why did you bring us up out of Egypt to this terrible place? It has no grain or figs, grapevines or pomegranates. And there is no water to drink!"**

**[6]Moses and Aaron went from the assembly to the entrance to the Tent of Meeting and fell facedown, and the glory of the LORD appeared to them. [7]The LORD said to Moses, [8]"Take the staff, and you and your brother Aaron gather the assembly together. Speak to that rock before their eyes and it will pour out its water. You will bring water out of the rock for the community so they and their livestock can drink."**

**[9]So Moses took the staff from the LORD's presence, just as he commanded him. [10]He and Aaron gathered the assembly together in front of the rock and Moses said to them, "Listen, you rebels, must we bring you water out of this rock?" [11]Then Moses raised his arm and struck the rock twice with his staff. Water gushed out, and the community and their livestock drank.**

**[12]But the LORD said to Moses and Aaron, "Because you did not trust in me enough to honor me as holy in the sight of the Israelites, you will not bring this community into the land I give them."**

**[13]These were the waters of Meribah, where the Israelites quarreled with the LORD and where he showed himself holy among them.**

MOSES' REBELLION AT MERIBAH KADESH (20:2–13). **20:2–5** The general setting of Moses' rebellion was a familiar one, involving the recur-

---

[349] According to *Targum Jonathan*, Miriam died on the tenth day of the first month of the fortieth year.

ring theme of a lack of water supply on the western side of the arid Zin Wilderness.[350] The sequence of events in vv. 2–5 closely parallels those of Exod 17:2–3, though the wording of the need is slightly different.[351] In both cases the people contended *(wayyāreb)* with Moses, but in this case the complaint is more extensive. Not only did they ask the rhetorical question concerning whether they were brought out of Egypt to die in the wilderness, as they had asked before, but they also expressed the wish that they had died as their rebellious brethren had before and claimed that where the Lord had led them was "this evil place" *(hammāqôm hārāʿ hazzeh)*. The use of the term "evil" here recalls the evil grumbling of the people in 11:1, the bad report brought by the ten scouts in 13:19,32, and the Lord's declaration that the generation that rejected the Promised Land was "this whole wicked community which has banded together against me" (14:35). To ascribe evil to the place where God had guided them was dangerous ground for the people to tread.

Two statements regarding the lack of water supply provide an inclusio (vv. 2,5) for the people's complaint, which was directed against Moses and Aaron. A full complement of three issues were raised by the people, providing a comprehensive view of their rebellious and confused nature. Contradiction exuded from their words when they claimed that they would have preferred death over life. They blamed Moses and Aaron for their predicament. After all, how could their God have led them into this forbidden desert to die an untimely death? They were God's chosen people, the congregation of the Lord *(qĕhal YHWH)*, and so it must have been Moses' fault that they faced this crisis of survival in a place with no grain, fruit, or water. The fruit listed were those very fruits that the scouts had brought back from the land forty years before (13:23). They still suffered from the same syndrome of unbelief. How easily they had forgotten the numerous times when God had miraculously provided them food, water, and shelter in the desert!

**20:6** Moses and Aaron retreated to that sacred locale where God so often revealed himself, and they fell prostrate upon their faces in their usual position of entreaty and intercession.[352] As they lay face down at the front of the Tent of Meeting, the glory of the Lord appeared to them in the form of the fire-encased cloud,[353] demonstrating quite visibly the divine presence and imprimatur upon

---

[350] See commentary on 13:26.

[351] Cf. אֵין מַיִם לִשְׁתֹּת הָעָם, "There was no water for the people to drink" in Exod 17:1 with Num 20:2, which reads וְלֹא־הָיָה מַיִם לָעֵדָה, "There was no water for the congregation."

[352] The entrance to the tabernacle so often had been the place of divine manifestation and instruction, as well as the place for presentation of sacrifices (cf. Exod 29:4,11,32,42; 33:9–10; Lev 1:3; 3:2;4:4,7,18;8:3–4; Num 6:10,13,18; 10:3; 12:5; 16:18–19,27). The prone position during intercession was exercised when the Israelites suggested appointing a new leader to replace Moses when they had rejected the land (14:5) and when Korah and his followers tried to usurp the priesthood from Aaron (16:4).

[353] Milgrom, *Numbers*, 165.

his servants. When one demonstrates the attitudes of humility and servanthood, God's presence and blessing are realized most fully.

**20:7–8** Directions as to what rite to perform for the rocks to yield the needed water are introduced by the standard formula for introducing divine revelatory instruction, *wayĕdabbēr YHWH ʾel-mōšê lēʾmōr* ("so YHWH instructed Moses, saying …").[354] Though the contention with the people involved both Moses and Aaron, and later both Moses and Aaron acted unrighteously and suffered punishment, only Moses is addressed directly in the introduction. The instructions were threefold: take the rod, assemble the congregation, and speak to the rock. Though whose rod was intended to be used was not specified, v. 9 indicates that the rod or staff was taken "from the Lord's presence" (*millipnê YHWH*, "from before Yahweh"), suggesting that the rod was that of Aaron which budded, blossomed, and produced almonds in the divine confirmation of Aaron's priestly authority.[355] It was to be kept before the ark of the testimony as a sign to any future grumbling rebels so that their murmurings might be summarily dismissed (Num 17:10). This interpretation probably would not have been challenged had not the rod Moses wielded in v. 11 been designated as "his rod." Therefore Milgrom has suggested that "it was more likely the rod of Moses which had been employed in the performance of God's miracles in the wilderness," especially in the case of Moses' striking of the rock to produce water in Exod 17:5–6.[356] The stated purpose of the rod in 17:10, which coincides with the present context of the rod's usage, seems to argue for the identification with Aaron's rod. As Harrison notes, "If this was the case, it would presumably be meant to indicate that there was no dichotomy between the leadership functions of the two men.

Together the prophet Moses and the priest Aaron were to gather the congregation of Israel in front of the rock, and then they were to speak to the rock that which the Lord had instructed them. Thus they would be agents of the miraculous provision of water, so that people and animals would be amply supplied. The human agency of the miracle is emphasized by the use of the second person singular pronoun in the two forms "you will bring forth" (*hôṣēʾtā*) and "you shall cause them to drink" (*hišqîtā*).[357]

---

[354] For further information on the use of the divine revelatory formula for instruction, see "Introduction: Structure and Outline of the Book of Numbers" and commentary on Num 1:1.

[355] Those identifying the rod as Aaron's include Harrison, *Numbers,* 264; Gray, *Numbers,* 262; Budd, *Numbers,* 218; Wenham, *Numbers,* 149; Noordtzij, *Numbers,* 176.

[356] See also Exod 14:16. Milgrom, *Numbers,* 165. Cf. Noth, *Numbers,* 145; Levine, *Numbers 1–20,* 489; de Vaulx, *Les Nombres,* 222–23.

[357] In the instructions "thus you shall speak" the second person plural was used, followed by two verbs in the second person singular, the latter two uses thus functioning as a collective form for the two men. Cf. Harrison, *Numbers,* 264–67.

**20:9** In his usual faithful manner, Moses began by dutifully following the Lord's command by taking the rod (staff) from the presence of the Lord in the tabernacle. The phraseology "just as he commanded him" has been employed numerous times through the Book of Numbers to this point to emphasize the faithful obedience of Yahweh's servant to his instructions.[358] The scene was set for another demonstration of God's mercy, benevolence, and longsuffering, but the account would soon take a sudden tragic shift.

**20:10–11** The faithful following of the Lord's instructions would continue in the second step with their joint gathering of the Israelite constituency in front of the rocky crag. The death of his dear sister Miriam was no doubt a contributing factor to his demise,[359] but what Moses said, what he did, and how he did it were such that he was without excuse before God. Yet as Moses began to speak, the tenor of his speech changed dramatically, and he committed several rebellious infractions of his own. Instead of addressing the rock, he launched into a diatribe against the complaining community, calling them "rebels" (*hammōrîm*, "ones who behave obstinately"). Retellings of the event use the same term to describe Moses' and Aaron's actions in this episode (20:24; 27:14). That which they declaimed of their adversaries they had become. Budd notes that the word for rebellion here *(mārâ)* is always used in the Pentateuch of defiance against God.[360] Moses earlier had shared his frustration with God concerning the implacable Israelites when they grumbled about the monotonous food supply (11:1–15). That time he complained to the Lord about the responsibility of overseeing thousands of continuously rebellious and complaining people. He felt God was afflicting him with this overwhelming burden, even to the point of asking the Lord to take his life rather than allow him to experience the shame and humiliation of failure. This time the fullness of his frustration was manifest before God and the whole assembled congregation. Moses did not simply call the people rebels, a mere statement of truth (though perhaps out of anger), but he took the Lord's instructions and used them as a means to justify his self-interest and self-pity. The Lord had said that Moses and Aaron would be the agents for the delivery of the water from the rock, but then the prophet's self-centered attitude erupted as he usurped the words of God for his own glorification, saying, "Shall we bring forth from this rock for you water?" Such presumption would have the general effect, notes Budd, that "they have prevented the full power and might of Yahweh from becoming evident to the

---

[358] Examples from Exodus and Numbers include Exod 39:1,7,21,32; 40:16,32; Num 1:19,54; 2:33,34; 3:16; 4:37,41,45,49,49; 5:4; 8:20,22; 9:5,23;10:13; 15:35; 17:11; 20:27; 26:4; 27:11,22,23; 29:30; 31:7,31; 33:2; 36:5.

[359] See comment above on 20:1.

[360] Budd, *Numbers*, 218.

people, and have thus robbed him of the fear and reverence due to him."[361]

Moses struck the rock not once but twice as he vented his anger and frustration over this ever-rebellious lot. As in previous circumstances of this kind, the rock was a symbol of God's mercy and benevolence, so striking the rock was in a sense a striking out against God. Moses had damaged severely the intimate personal relationship he had with God. His actions were detrimental to the maintaining of a reverence for God and his mercy in Israel. The trusted servant had fallen into the same trap as the many rebellious people he had complained about to God. Harrison calls Moses' actions "an unpardonable act of insubordination."[362]

Milgrom has examined Moses' actions against the backdrop of Egyptian and Mesopotamian magicians and diviners as well as in the context of the nature of God revealed in the Pentateuch. Moses' actions were tantamount to that of an idolatrous pagan magician, and thus Milgrom notes, "Here, in a direct address to his people, Moses ascribes miraculous powers to himself and Aaron. Indeed by broadcasting one word, *nôṣîʾ,* "we shall bring forth"— Moses and Aaron might be interpreted as having put themselves forth as God. ... Israel had to be released from more than chains; it still had to be purged of its pagan background.[363] In summary, Milgrom states, "Against the backdrop of the Pentateuchal sensitivity to man's usurping of God's powers, Moses' act is manifestly shocking."[364] The collapse of character was so critical that he would suffer severely for his actions and his attitudes. He would not experience the fullness of God's promise, the ultimate goal of his divinely ordained mission. He had been used dramatically and wondrously by God to bring his people Israel out of Egypt, but he would not bring them into the Promised Land.

God's mercy and grace were evidenced when the waters gushed forth from the rocky crag, in spite of Moses' actions. He fulfilled his promise to provide ample water for the people, and Moses was used as an agent in the miracle. Geographers and biblical interpreters have written for years of the extensive aquifers that exist beneath the surface rock strata of the Sinai peninsula. The several oases such as at Serabit al-Khadem, Ain Hawarah, Ain Khadra, and Ain el-Qudeirat (Kadesh Barnea) are examples of such abundant water supplies.[365] So at the moment of Moses' sin in striking the rock,

---

[361] Ibid.

[362] Harrison, *Numbers,* 267.

[363] Milgrom, *Numbers,* "Excursus 50: Magic, Monotheism, and the Sin of Moses," 452. Note also the context of God's blessing at Meribah within the psalmist's calling of Israel to repentance because of their idolatrous activities (Ps 81:6–10).

[364] Ibid., 454.

[365] Note the discussions in N. Glueck, *Rivers in the Desert* (New York: W. W. Norton, 1968), 22, and C. S. Jarvis, *Yesterday and Today in Sinai* (Edinburgh: Blackwood, 1931), 174–75.

God caused the water to erupt from underground water source, more than amply supplying the needs of the Israelite population. The Lord continued to demonstrate, as he continues to do today, his essential benevolent nature, fulfilling his promise to supply the needs of his people. Even the failure of his leaders would not thwart his will to bless his people. The rebellious, however, would fail to fully experience the abundance of his blessing.

**20:12** The announcement of judgment against Moses and Aaron commences with the secondary formula for divine instruction, with the *waw* of the preterit form functioning as an adversative, *wayyōʾmer YHWH ʾel-mōšeh wĕʾel-ʾahărōn* ("However, the Lord said to Moses and Aaron, …").[366] First the rationale for the punishment is stated, followed by the sentence itself. Moses and Aaron had failed to fully trust in the Lord's instructions in the situation at hand, whereby they would have demonstrated their faith before the people and addressed the rock. Instead they addressed the people harshly and intentionally struck the rock. This failure to follow instructions, coupled with a rebellious and invective attitude against God's people, was a violation of the holiness of God. In Exod 17:2–6 Moses was instructed by God to strike the rock in order to produce water, and he did so faithfully in the presence of the elders of Israel. He acted faithfully and God was glorified. This time the situation was similar, but the instructions and results were quite dissimilar. That Moses "did not trust in me enough to honor me as holy" means that he had let the Lord down by his rash unfaithfulness and obstinate attitude toward the Lord and his people. The prophet who previously had been called "more humble than any other man on the face of the earth" (Num 12:3) had acted haughtily; the servant of Yahweh who was the exemplar of faithfulness (12:7) had fallen; and the one who was said to have spoken with the Lord "face to face" (12:8) had brought defamation to his Lord.

Earlier the people had contended with Moses, Aaron, and God. The result of their rebellion was condemnation to live the rest of their lives in the desert and not see the Promised Land. But here near the end of the story of the nation's rebellions, the contentious words and actions of Israel's great prophet and priest lead to their experience of the same condemnation. The wording is pregnant with poignant and paradoxical implications. Moses and Aaron would not fulfill their original obligations or dreams of experiencing God's fullest blessing in the land.[367] "This congregation" whom they now seemed to loathe so deeply would enter the land that God was going to give them. These words reverberated with the glorious memories of the earlier

---

[366] On the use of the divine revelatory formula וַיְדַבֵּר יְהוָה אֶל־מֹשֶׁה לֵּאמֹר and the present alternative וַיֹּאמֶר יְהוָה אֶל־אַהֲרֹן in the Book of Numbers, see above discussion in "Introduction: Structure and Outline" and commentary on Num 1:1.

[367] Cf. also Moses' punishment as described in Num 27:12–14; Deut 1:37; 3:23–28; 4:21.

promises of the gift of land that the Lord had spoken to Abraham and Isaac, Jacob and Joseph, and more recently Moses and Aaron. Moses would only be allowed to see the land from a distance, from the peak of Mount Pisgah in Transjordan. Aaron would not see it at all.

**20:13** The spring produced by God at Kadesh became known as the Waters of Meribah, later described as the Waters of Meribah Kadesh in Num 27:14.[368] As in Exod 17:7 the site was named Meribah *(mĕrîbâ)* because the people contended *(rîb)* with the Lord. But there also Yahweh manifested his holiness, literally "show[ed] himself holy" *(wayyiqqādēš),* among the congregation. He demonstrated that he indeed was God over the situation by abundantly supplying the needed water and by rightly bringing judgment against Moses and Aaron because of their sin.

[14]Moses sent messengers from Kadesh to the king of Edom, saying:

"This is what your brother Israel says: You know about all the hardships that have come upon us. [15]Our forefathers went down into Egypt, and we lived there many years. The Egyptians mistreated us and our fathers, [16]but when we cried out to the LORD, he heard our cry and sent an angel and brought us out of Egypt.

"Now we are here at Kadesh, a town on the edge of your territory. [17]Please let us pass through your country. We will not go through any field or vineyard, or drink water from any well. We will travel along the king's highway and not turn to the right or to the left until we have passed through your territory."

[18]But Edom answered:

"You may not pass through here; if you try, we will march out and attack you with the sword."

[19]The Israelites replied:

"We will go along the main road, and if we or our livestock drink any of your water, we will pay for it. We only want to pass through on foot—nothing else."

[20]Again they answered:

"You may not pass through."

Then Edom came out against them with a large and powerful army. [21]Since Edom refused to let them go through their territory, Israel turned away from them.

EDOM DENIES PASSAGE TO THE ISRAELITES (20:14–21). As the end of the forty-year period of judgment drew near, an alternate route

---

[368] Cf. also Deut 32:51; Ezek 27:19; 48:28.

around Southern Canaan was sought since they had been defeated by the Amalekites and Canaanites near Hormah in the biblical Negev (14:35). From Kadesh Barnea they decided to move eastward through the Nahal Zin basin in the Zin Wilderness, onward across the Arabah toward the realm of the Edomites. The Edomite territory extended from the Wadi Zered (mod. Wadi el-Hasa) on the north to the Gulf of Aqaba (Elath) on the south and to the Arabian Desert on the east. It was characterized by reddish-purple mountains in the south along the Arabah Valley, to intermittent sections of arable land in the northern half, extending from near Petra and the Wadi Musa to Bozrah and the Wadi Zered. Deep valleys such as the Wadi Rum provided east-west passage across the region. The Israelites might have been seeking passage from the south along the Kings' Highway from its beginning on the Gulf of Aqaba, and then northward through the Transjordan table lands of Edom and Moab. More likely their intentions were to enter the region from the Arabah near Tamar into the Edomite highlands through one of the wadis, such as the Wadi Feifa toward Zalmonah or Punon, and then past Bozrah, the Edomite capital city during the Iron Age.[369] The exact route remains unknown. The request for safe passage was denied, despite an impassioned plea.

That Edom should possess a king during this period in history has caused concern for interpreters since the publication of N. Glueck's definitive works on the settlement of Transjordan during the Bronze and Iron Ages.[370] As a result of his surface surveys in the area while living as a spy among the bedouin of what is now southern Jordan between 1934 and 1940, he observed that there was a gap in the material remains during the MB to Iron IA periods, hence he and others concluded that the accounts about Edomite sovereignty mentioned in Numbers and Deuteronomy were retrojected into the Israelite wilderness period by later Israelite sources of the Iron II.[371] More recent surveys and excavations in Transjordan, however, have yielded evidence of seminomadic and sedentary populations

---

[369] For an analysis of the travel itineraries through Edom found in Num 20:14,22–23; 21:1–3,4,10–13 as compared with Num 33:36–45, see Aharoni, *The Land of the Bible*, 200–209. Cf. also T. Brisco, *Holman Bible Atlas* (Nashville: Broadman & Holman, 1998), 71–73.

[370] N. Glueck, *Explorations in Eastern Palestine*, II & III, AASOR, XV, XVIII–XIX (New Haven: ASOR, 1935, 1938–39). Other earlier publications included "The Boundaries of Edom," *HUCA* 11 (1936): 141–57; "The Civilization of the Edomites," *BA* 10 (1947): 74–83; *Rivers in the Desert* (New York: Norton, 1968); *The Other Side of the Jordan* (New Haven: ASOR, 1940).

[371] These materials are typically assigned by source critical scholars to the supposed JE source. Noth even noted that "this, then, is the first appearance, at least the first that can be certainly proved, of the 'Elohist' in the book of Numbers" (*Numbers*, 149). Cf. also Gray, *Numbers*, 264–67; Budd, *Numbers*, 222–24; Levine, *Numbers 1–20*, 491.

during the very periods Glueck suggested were unoccupied.[372]

Still the question remains as to whether the Edomites could have been organized into what modern socio-political analysts would deem a 'nation' with a centralized monarchy, complete with bureaucratic structure. Ashley has observed that the use of the Hebrew term for king *(melek)* may range from a reference to the great internationally acclaimed kings of Egypt, Assyria, Babylon, or Persia of the ninth to fifth centuries B.C. to simply the rulers of lesser towns such as Sodom and Gomorrah (Gen 14:2) or Jericho, Ai, Jerusalem, Yarmuth, Lachish, Debir, and others of the period of the Israelite conquest (Josh 1:1–5; 12:7–24). Edom seems to have been organized under chieftains at this time,[373] the head of which might have been designated broadly as a king. Along this line Ashley notes that "a diplomatic letter addressed to 'the king of Edom' could not fail in stroking the ego of a petty ruler in that territory."[374] It is also true that the word may have a general meaning of "ruler" here.

Although the text does not mention that a written document was involved in the communication process, the terminology, content, and structure of the sending of the messengers to the king of Edom follows classical Hebrew epistolary form and protocol.[375] If the correspondence entailed only oral communication, the same protocol was utilized. Such correspondence usually was delivered by royal messengers and generally contained the following elements: introductory greeting, rehearsing of past relationship, current circumstances for the correspondence, the formal request, stipulations for the new relationship, and conclusion with the imprimatur of the sender.[376] The adaptation of the form herein is outlined in the ensuing structure:

| | |
|---|---|
| A. Introduction | [Assumed: To the King of Edom] |
| B. Past Relationship | Thus says your brother Israel (v. 14b) |
| C. Historical Setting / | You know the hardships that have come upon us, |
|    Present Circumstances |   how our forefathers went down to Egypt |
| |   we lived there many years |
| |     the Egyptians mistreated us and our fathers |

---

[372] Cf. J. R. Bartlett, *Edom and the Edomites* (Sheffield: JSOT Press, 1989), 55–82; "The Land of Seir and the Brotherhood of Edom," *JTS* 20 (1969): 1–20; "The Rise and Fall of the Edomite Kingdom," *PEQ* 104 (1972): 26–37; J. A. Dearman, *Studies in the Mesha Inscription and Moab* (Atlanta: Scholars Press, 1989); P. Bienkowski, ed., *Early Edom and Moab,* Sheffield Archaeological Monographs 7 (Sheffield: JRS Collis, 1992); B. Macdonald, *Ammon, Moab, and Edom* (Amman, Jordan: Al–Kurba, 1994); D. V. Edelman, ed., *You Shall Not Abhor an Edomite for He Is Your Brother* (Atlanta: Scholars Press, 1995).

[373] Note the use of אַלּוּפֵי אֱדוֹם, "chieftains of Edom," in Exod 15:15. See Gen 36:15ff.

[374] Ashley, *Numbers,* 389.

[375] The Samaritan Pentateuch expands upon v. 14 with details from Deut 2:2–6.

[376] Note also that an abbreviated form of this correspondence form is found in 21:21–22. More lengthy correspondence is found in Aramaic in Ezra 4:9–16,17–22; 5:6–17.

But we cried out to the Lord:
  He heard our cry
  He sent an angel
  He brought us out of Egypt (vv. 14b–16a)

Now we are here at Kadesh, a town on the edge of
  your territory (v. 16b)

D. Formal Request            Please let us pass through your country (v. 17a)

E. Stipulations Offered      We will not go through any field or vineyard
                             We will not drink water from a well
                               by the King's Highway we will travel
                             We will not turn to right or to the left until we have
                               passed through your territory (v. 17b)
F. Conclusion                [missing / Peace and Salutations]

Several features are notable in this composition, which has all the earmarks of
diplomatic correspondence but with distinctive Hebraic style. Analyzing the
Hebrew syntactical structures, there are three sets of three elements in the
communiqué, giving emphasis to those portions. The recounting of the wondrous deliverance from Egypt is set forth in two triads, each presenting a terse
but complete rehearsing of the past events in a pattern of physical movement:
went down/were mistreated; sent an angel/brought us out; let us pass through.
In the second of these two triads, the unique relationship between Yahweh and
Israel is emphasized, in that Yahweh was a God who was not aloof but
intensely interested in the well-being of his people. The movement of the text
through the use of personal pronouns in chiastic form is artfully presented,
providing further focus on the role of Yahweh, God of Israel. Note the resulting arrangement:

  A **Your** brother
    B **We / Us** went down to Egypt … **We** cried
      C **He /** Yahweh heard … he sent … he brought us out of Egypt
    B' **We** are at Kadesh
  A' **Your** territory (*gĕbûlekā*)
    B" **Let us** pass through
  A" **Your** land (*ʾarṣekā*)
    B" **We** will not pass through / not drink / not turn right or left
      Until **we** have passed through
  A'" **Your** country (*gĕbûlekā*)

Terms used in v. 17 to refer to the territory of Edom through which they
desired to pass are also presented in a simple chiastic layout.

**20:14**  The statement of the prior relationship sets forth the basis upon which the request was made, brotherhood. The kinship went back to the days of Jacob and Esau, and as it was in the days of the two sons of Isaac, so it was throughout the history of the two nations. Sometimes they were friends and allies, but more often they were bitterest enemies.[377] This relational basis of entreaty was more than simply kinship; it was also an egalitarian statement. Normally one would address the recipient of such a letter as "servant," placing oneself in the subordinate position before the addressee. Moses makes a tacit assumption about the Edomite knowledge of Israel's past history of hardship,[378] from the circumstance of famine that led the sons of Jacob to migrate to Egypt with their families, to the experience of slavery and bondage at the hands of the Egyptian taskmasters, and finally along the journey from Egypt to the wilderness.

The use of the singular verb or pronoun to refer collectively to an ethnic group like Israel or Edom is common in Hebrew style. Thus Noth's suggestion that the changing of the singular to plural could be an example of "carelessness in the manner of expression," which was perhaps the result of unrefined conflation of the J (Yahwist) and E (Elohist) sources,[379] is unfounded. Gray argues, "The personification of a whole class or people so that it is spoken of or represented as speaking in the singular is frequent in Hebrew. In these cases the pronouns referring to the class or person are naturally in the singular, as in the present passage (v. 19)."[380] Thus the personification of the collective Edom (=Esau) as the singular brother of Israel (=nation, or person Jacob) is quite natural, and not a sign of the editing of sources.

**20:15–16**  This brief sketch of Israel's suffering and deliverance became stylized through the history of recounting the story of God's great redemption of his people from Egypt. The kernel of the story would be recounted for the scores of generations up to the present time through the celebration of Passover, the pilgrimage festivals of Pentecost (Shavuoth) and tabernacles (Sukkoth), and the ancient ritual of the bringing of the firstfruits and in numerous hymns.[381]

---

[377] Jacob/Israel and Esau/Edom as friends: Gen 33:1–17; Deut 23:7. Jacob/Israel and Esau/Edom as enemies: Gen 27:1–46; Num 24:18; Deut 2:4; 2 Sam 8:14; 1 Chr 18:11–13; 1 Kgs 14:7; 22:47; Obad 1–21; Jer 49:7–22; Ezek 25:12–14; Amos 1:11–12.

[378] Moses used the same term for hardship (הַתְּלָאָה) in describing to his father-in-law Jethro the difficulties Israel encountered along the way from Egypt to Sinai. The term bespeaks the wearying and bitter struggle one faces in a destitute and desperate situation. Cf. Neh 9:32; Lam 3:5; Mal 1:13.

[379] Noth, *Numbers,* 149.

[380] Gray, *Numbers,* 265; cf. also Ashley, *Numbers,* 390; Milgrom, *Numbers,* 167.

[381] Examples of this and other adapted forms are found in Deut 26:5–8; Josh 24:4–8; Pss 106:1–15; 136:1–26; etc. An expanded form is recounted by Stephen in Acts 7:9–36.

What emphasis was being placed in the mentioning of the agency of the angel of God in the deliverance of Israel is not explicitly evident. What theological concepts and responses might have been aroused among the Edomites through this correspondence? Might they have feared the power of angels or divine messengers, such that they might think twice of denying passage to a people blessed with angelic accompaniment? In the Exodus the angel acted on behalf of Israel and against Egypt in several ways. The angel went before Israel on the initial march and then went behind the people by the sea as the Egyptian army approached from the rear, first guiding and then protecting them (Exod 14:19). The angel led them through the wilderness and would lead them into the Promised Land (Exod 23:20–23). On a personal level one other contributing factor may be at work in the narrative. Moses had just rebelled and been judged for his failure to maintain the holiness of God before the people, so perhaps he was suffering some personal reticence about his leadership ability. Asserting the angelic accompaniment made the request a stronger one in his mind. The Israelites were poised to advance through their region, still marching with their angelic direction and authority. Finally, the introduction of the angel as a character at this point in the narrative would pave the way for the introduction of another angel, the angel of Lord in the Balaam account in Num 22:22–35.

The citing of the point of origin for the letter at "Kadesh, a town on the edge of your territory," made the king of Edom aware of the immediacy of the need for passage. That Kadesh (interpreted as Kadesh Barnea on the western edge of the Zin wilderness) was on the border of the Edomite territory has been taken by some scholars in the past to suggest that this narrative is a later insertion, perhaps during the late eighth century B.C. or later, since the Edomites were not known to have exercised dominion over the lands west of the Arabah until well into the Iron II period.[382] In response, Wenham has suggested that Kadesh of Num 20:16 (called Meribah Kadesh) lay further to the east than Kadesh Barnea, which was near the Arabah. Certainly this possibility is plausible, considering Kadesh, meaning "holy place," was a common toponym in the ancient Near East. This would also address the problem of Israel's general movement in returning in 20:1 to the exact same place where they were forty years earlier. Ashley takes a different approach to the issue, positing that the geographical statement need not carry the precision some interpreters claim for it. Instead, he notes, "When Kadesh is called *a city on the outskirts of your border* it means no more than that the Israelites are near to

---

[382] Levine, *Numbers 1–20*, 492; Noth, *Numbers*, 151; Bartlett, *Edom and the Edomites*, 90–93; Gray, *Numbers*, 266.

Edom as opposed to far away from it."[383] If indeed Edom was at a stage of transitioning from a seminomadic to sedentary culture, the defining of borders (or "outskirts," Ashley) would have been rather fluid. Similar to the Midianite presence in the Sinai peninsula, Edomite clan incursions across the Arabah may have occurred during the end of the Bronze and into the early Iron ages.

**20:17** The actual request carried three negative stipulations whereby the Israelites would be respective of Edomite dominion should passage be permitted. They would not pass through their fields or vineyards. If the timing of this request followed closely the previous account, it would have been springtime, and the grain fields would be at or near harvest time. Vine dressing for the summer and fall crops would have just begun. Water rights were of great concern in the ancient Near East, as they are even in present-day negotiations between the Israelis, Palestinians, and Jordanians. The Israelites would presumably bring their own water supply from Kadesh during their brief passage of perhaps two days through the Edomite highlands. Hence the appeal was predicated on Israel's not being a burden to Edom or disturbing their agricultural activities. They would journey straight through Edom in order to reach the Kings' Highway, not turning aside for any reason. The Kings' Highway was the famous passage that connected the Damascus trade center with Arabia, Sinai, and Egypt via a route through the Transjordan tablelands (Golan, Bashan, Gilead, Ammon, Moab, and Edom) and the southern mountains, paralleling the Arabah on the eastern side. Egyptian kings such as Thutmosis III passed along this road in their conquests of Transjordan and the eastern Levant.[384] From southern Arabia the caravaneers brought the highly prized commodities of incense, spices, perfumes, and precious jewels, as well as copper from the Sinai and Paran Wilderness sources.

**20:18** A derisive disapproval from the Edomite leadership came without any protocol or diplomatic subtlety. In spite of the Edomite rejection, the Israelites would explore again possible diplomacy even after the first rejection by the Edomite leader, but further approaches would receive increasingly hostile responses. Edom's initial refusal was accompanied by a threat of war. Edom at this point seems to have possessed no fear of Israel, their angelic overseer, or their God, despite the appeals contained within the ini-

---

[383] Ashley, *Numbers*, 391. Ashley cites additionally Num 34:3–5 and Josh 15:1–12 as corroborating evidence that the statements imply general proximity, since the border of Judah was said to be touching the border of Edom.

[384] Note remarks by C. R. Krahmalkov, "Exodus Itinerary Confirmed by Egyptian Evidence," *BAR* 20/4 (1994): 54–62,79. Note also contra Krahmalkov, D. Redford, "A Bronze Age Itinerary in Transjordan (Nos. 89–101 of Thutmoses III's List of Asiatic Toponyms," *Journal of the Society of Egyptian Archaeology* (1982): 55–74.

tial message. The threat of war with Edom would lead to a second attempt at diplomacy rather than to a deployment of troops, since the Edomite region was not a part of the territory promised by God. Israel as yet had no dispute with Edom; besides, they were distant relatives of one another. Perhaps, as the rabbis much later suggested, Edom was exacting revenge for the earlier conflict between Esau and Jacob. The Esau-Jacob animosity served as the type scene for later Edomite-Israelite acrimony. The accusation of Amos 1:11 against Edom carries the same basic message, that God would judge Edom because "he pursued his brother with the sword." Some source critics have suggested that Num 20:18,20 is dependent on Amos 1:11, which is viewed as supportive of an eighth century B.C. date for the present narrative.[385] Rather, the Amos text seems more likely to be an abbreviated form of the account of Num 20:14–21, a terse form of an ancient rivalry used in the oracles against the nations surrounding Israel and Judah.

**20:19–21** The attempt at diplomatic correspondence carried alternative stipulations, the only part of which is preserved in the text of v. 19. Israel again vowed to ascend into the mountainous territory of Edom by the most direct route, that of the "main road" (*bamsillâ*, "by the highway, prepared road"), that which was used by trade caravans and military troops.[386] They swore they would recompense the Edomites for any water they might consume on the way, but the Edomites again flatly refused passage. The suggestion of payment for safe passage was in keeping with ancient Near Eastern protocol, as often tolls or tribute were exacted from trade caravans while traversing the regions of Mesopotamia and the Levant. Hence this was not an unusual request, though the response to the second appeal was out of the ordinary. The Edomites reacted with a show of military force, emphasized by the use of the phrase "strong hand," a symbol of power and judgment in the ancient Near East. Not wanting to engage in a battle over undesired territory, the Israelites decided to retract their offer and seek another route in which to circumnavigate the region of Mount Seir and Edom. Harrison aptly notes that in this account there is no directive from the Lord in regard to the diplomatic correspondence, though nothing is made of this issue in the text as it is in Josh 9:14–15 when Joshua failed to consult the Lord regarding entering into a treaty with the Gibeonites. But in that the rejection of Israel by Edom is couched between the two pericopes that highlight the rebelliousness of Moses and Aaron and the resultant punishment, this chapter would provide an awesome historical lesson to later Israel. Sin and rebellion will lead to rejection, denial, and defeat.

---

[385] Levine, *Numbers 1–20*, 491–93.

[386] Milgrom compares the מְסִלָּה to the *harran zukinim*, "infantry road," of Assyrian records. But the Samaritan Pentateuch reads מְסַלָּה (also LXX), "rocky road," perhaps a less traveled route through the mountains.

<sup>22</sup>The whole Israelite community set out from Kadesh and came to Mount Hor. <sup>23</sup>At Mount Hor, near the border of Edom, the LORD said to Moses and Aaron, <sup>24</sup>"Aaron will be gathered to his people. He will not enter the land I give the Israelites, because both of you rebelled against my command at the waters of Meribah. <sup>25</sup>Get Aaron and his son Eleazar and take them up Mount Hor. <sup>26</sup>Remove Aaron's garments and put them on his son Eleazar, for Aaron will be gathered to his people; he will die there."

<sup>27</sup>Moses did as the LORD commanded: They went up Mount Hor in the sight of the whole community. <sup>28</sup>Moses removed Aaron's garments and put them on his son Eleazar. And Aaron died there on top of the mountain. Then Moses and Eleazar came down from the mountain, <sup>29</sup>and when the whole community learned that Aaron had died, the entire house of Israel mourned for him thirty days.

THE DEATH AND BURIAL OF AARON (20:22–29). Following the introductory journey citation, this section focuses on the death of Aaron in initial fulfilment of God's judgment issued in 20:12. Moses' turn would come some months later. Moses' death, recorded in Deut 34:1–12, has several parallels. Both died in the mountains and were buried there. Moses accompanied Aaron on his last journey, but when Moses' time came, he made that trek alone. Out of respect for the persons and the positions, the death of Israel's first great high priest was marked by a period of thirty days of national mourning, as was the death of Moses (Deut 34:8). These deaths mark the transition of leadership from Aaron to Eleazar and Moses to Joshua (Deut 34:9). But the two death accounts serve different purposes in their given contexts. In the account of Aaron's death, the Lord provided instructions for preparation for the end with the passing of the priestly mantle to Eleazar, and he reminded them both of the reason for their not continuing on to fulfill the promise of the entry and conquest of the land of Canaan. The transition into the high priesthood of Eleazar, elder surviving son of Aaron, had already begun, for Eleazar supervised the disassembly and care of the tabernacle and its furnishings (Num 3:32; 4:16) and prepared the ashes of the red cow for purification rituals (Num 19:3–7). In the account of Moses' death on Mount Nebo, the reminder of the judgment is more implicit, with emphasis given to God's providing him a momentary glimpse of the wondrous Promised Land.

Now the process of handing over the symbols of authority of the priesthood make the transition complete. Furthermore, in the concluding episodes of this rebellion cycle another kind of priest will emerge at the behest of Yahweh, God of Israel. Balaam will become priest and prophet used by God to bless his people, though quite against his own will and the will of his employer Balak of Moab. But before the encounters of Balaam, there would be both blessing in victory and judgment through a plague of serpents.

**20:22** The pericope commences with a geographical note concerning the journey from Kadesh to Mount Hor, whereby they circumnavigated the Edomite territory. Again the Israelites move en masse ("the whole Israelite community")[387] to a mountainside whose location has eluded biblical geographers for centuries.[388] The location of Mount Hor is dependent upon the defining of the route followed by the Israelites on their journey from Kadesh, around Edom, and eventually into the Plains of Moab. As with Kadesh (20:16), Mount Hor was on the border with Edom, according to Num 33:37, so the Israelite movement was skirting the territorial boundaries of the militant Edomites. Suggested mountains have included the traditional Islamic identity of Jebel Nebi Harun ("Mount of the Prophet Aaron") near Petra,[389] Jebel Medra about six miles east-northeast of Kedesh, ʿImaret el-Khurisheh, about eight miles north of Kadesh, or Jebel Madurah about fifteen miles northeast of Kadesh Barnea. Jebel Nebi Harun fits neither the physical setting described in this pericope nor the territorial setting since it is located in the heart of ancient Edom. The Jebel Madurah suggestion has received the widest scholarly support because it is generally on the way from Kadesh Barnea to the Arabah along the route of the Atharim, and the surrounding terrain fits the general picture where the Israelites could observe the initial events from afar.[390] In any case, absolute certainty concerning the precise location of this Mount Hor will remain an enigma, as will the identities of mountains like Sinai, Pisgah, and the Mount of the Temptation of Jesus.

A second factor in locating Mount Hor is interpreting the unusual toponymic phraseology utilized here, *hōr hāhār* (Hor the mountain), which if taken as a toponym would be the only case in which the name of the mountain preceded the word for mountain.[391] Ashley offered a possible alternative that Hor was an archaic form of *hār*, based on the Old Canaanite shift from *ā* to *ô*, which may also provide the basis for the LXX reading of *to oros to oros* ("the mountain the mountain" or perhaps "the summit of the mountain").[392]

**20:23–24** The instructions from the Lord as to the preparation for the death of Aaron are introduced by the short form of the alternative divine revelatory formula used throughout the Book of Numbers.[393] The material

---

[387] See the commentary and note above on the use of this phraseology in Num 20:1f.

[388] According to Deut 10:6 Aaron died after the journey from Bene Jaakan to Moserah, which Harrison suggested was an etiological toponym based on the events there (*Numbers,* 272).

[389] This identification is at least as old as the first century A.D. See Josephus, *Antiquities* 4.4.7.

[390] This identification is favored by Harrison, *Numbers,* 272.

[391] Here and in reference to the mountain of the same name on the northern boundary of the Promised Land in Num 34:8. The normal order is הַר XXX as in הַר הַכַּרְמֶל (Mount Carmel, 1 Kgs 18:20) or הַר עֵיבָל (Mount Ebal, Josh 8:30).

[392] Ashley, *Numbers,* 394–95.

[393] For further discussion on the use of the present introductory clause וַיֹּאמֶר יְהוָה אֶל־מֹשֶׁה and its primary counterpart וַיְדַבֵּר יְהוָה אֶל־מֹשֶׁה לֵּאמֹר וְאֶל־אַהֲרֹן לֵאמֹר, see the commentary on Num 1:1 above and "Introduction: Structure and Outline of the Book of Numbers."

is addressed to both Moses and Aaron, since both leaders of Israel would carry out the instructions accompanied by Eleazar, son of Aaron. Aaron was about to be "gathered to his people" in the manner of the biblical patriarchs. The death and burials of Abraham (Gen 25:8), Ishmael (Gen 25:17), Isaac (Gen 35:29), Jacob (Gen 49:29,33), and then later Moses (Num 27:13; Deut 32:50) were described in this phraseology, which is unique to the Pentateuch. General gathering (or lack thereof) of one or more individuals upon death is seen in Jer 8:2; 25:33. Several concepts have been applied to this terminology in its interpretation. In general, the phrase conveys the idea of being reunited with one's ancestors who had entered the realm of Sheol previously, which is an intimation of immortality.[394] One is not to be left unburied or "ungathered" since that was viewed as an ignominious end of life, so the prophet Jeremiah used this imagery to convey condemnation upon the leaders of Judah (Jer 8:2). One hypothesis is that this process described the secondary burial, when one's bones were moved from the burial chamber to the ossuary chamber where earlier family members' bones had been gathered.[395] But both Aaron and Moses were buried on separate mountains in a land that had not belonged to nor been promised to their forefathers because they had rebelled against the word of God. Hence Wenham takes the phrase to mean that Moses and Aaron were united with their ancestral families in Sheol, the place of the dead, which "describes a central Old Testament conviction about life after death."[396] And though the two great leaders of Israel would die and be buried outside the Promised Land because of their unholy rebellion at the Waters of Meribah, they would be honored in their deaths with all the status and dignity afforded the great patriarchs of Israel. Structurally, the use of the phrase in vv. 23 and 26 provides an inclusio bracketing the instructions.

**20:25–26** Moses led ("Take," *qaḥ*)[397] Aaron and Eleazar up on the mountain and there presided over the public ceremonial transference of the high priesthood. Milgrom has suggested that this was done on the mountain rather than at the tabernacle so that Aaron would remain high priest until the final moments before his death.[398] Aaron would not return to the community in his state of having had the high priestly investiture removed both physically and spiritually. This was a momentous and emotional occasion for the

---

[394] *Pentateuch and Haftorahs,* 658.

[395] Levine, *Numbers 1–20,* 494.

[396] Wenham, *Numbers,* 153.

[397] Note the usage of לקח in relation to the collective usage in Num 16:1,6,17,18; 17:4,11,12,17,24 (Hb. versification), where the concept of "taking control" of the situation at hand is implicit.

[398] Milgrom, *Numbers,* 170.

nation and for Eleazar as they observed from a distance the departure of
their first great high priest, the preeminent mediator of the sacral life of the
nation in its relationship to Yahweh their God. For Eleazar it was no doubt a
moment filled with emotional upheaval, a literal and metaphorical mountaintop experience in being inaugurated as the new high priest; but on the
other hand it was a familial nadir, since his honorable father was about to
die. The old era was passing; the generation was nearly gone that had witnessed the numerous miracles of God in Egypt, in the Exodus, at the Red
Sea, at Mount Sinai, and all along the journey through the wilderness. A new
generation of leadership was taking the reins over the nation and under God,
and prospects of the new life in the Promised Land were looming ever
nearer. According to Num 35:25–32, in the generations to come a person
who had sought asylum in one of the cities of refuge because he had committed manslaughter or unintentionally killed another person would be
released from confinement within the city after the death of the high priest,
providing a new lease on life for that individual.

**20:27–28** As he so often had done before, Moses followed Yahweh's
instructions faithfully,[399] though no doubt this process was a heart-rending
event as he removed the ceremonial priestly garments from his beloved
brother. He removed the tunic, the ephod, and the bejeweled breastplate that
Aaron wore to symbolize his role as intermediator on behalf of the twelve
tribes of Israel.[400] They ascended Mount Hor with the congregation observing the steps of the three men on this final journey before the passing of their
high priest.

Aaron died on the mountain, gathered to his people on the first day of
the fifth month of the fortieth year after the Exodus, as the period of judgment for the first generation drew to a close. The date of his death and his
age (123 years) as recounted in the journey itinerary in Num 33:38 coin-
cide with the data given in Exod 7:7, which states that Moses was eighty
years of age and Aaron eighty-three when they first spoke to the pharaoh
in Egypt. The first high priest of Israel was an enigmatic figure in the Old
Testament. On one hand he functioned as a spokesman for Moses before
the pharaoh (Exod 4:14; 5:2–3; 7:6,10); at the command of the Lord
through Moses he held out his hand over the Nile River and a swarm of
frogs emerged (Exod 8:5–9); he stretched out his rod and the dust turned

---

[399] Note the function of the phrase וַיַּעַשׂ מֹשֶׁה כַּאֲשֶׁר צִוָּה יְהוָה and its key function throughout the Book of Numbers as a statement of obedience in service in 1:19,54; 2:33,34; 3:39,42,51;
4:49; 8:3–4,20,22; 9:5,8; 15:23,36; 17:11; 19:2; 20:9,27; 26:4; 27:11,22,23; 30:1,2;
31:7,21,31,41,47; 36:10,13. An alternate expression of obedience, עַל־פִּי יְהוָה, occurs in
3:16,39,51; 4:37,41,45,49; 9:18,20,23; 10:13; 13:13; 22:38 [23:5,12,16 variations in Balaam ora-
cles]; 33:2; 33:38; 36:5.

[400] As so vividly described in Exod 28:1–43.

to lice throughout the land (Exod 8:16–17). Later during the judgment against the rebellious gang led by the Levite Korah, Aaron literally stood wielding his censer between the living and the dead, acting as their exemplary mediator (Num 16:48; Heb 17:13). On the other hand he succumbed to the whims of the people in the production of the golden calf, which led to idolatrous worship and eventual judgment (Exod 32:1–35), and he followed Moses' example in the rebellion at the Waters of Meribah (Num 20:10). In the Book of Hebrews, Aaron serves as a prototype of the high priesthood of Jesus Christ, though his priesthood was deemed inferior to that of the Melchizedek typology that was applied to Jesus (Heb 7:1–9:28). As Harrison remarks, "Human types are necessarily imperfect, however, and so the Christian can rejoice in the sinless perfection of Jesus, who obtained our redemption on Calvary, not by the blood of bulls and goats but by his own blood (Heb 9:11–15)."[401] Aaron supervised an earthly priesthood and cult that was but a mere shadow of things to come, in which the sacrifice of animals and plants symbolized the rendering of the life of the offerer when the life of the element was presented to God. Christ's sacrifice was the ultimate and perfect example of life rendering by a perfect high priest, offering a perfect sacrifice of himself, not in the Temple in Jerusalem but once for all time in the perfect heavenly sanctuary, the ultimate Holy Place in the very presence of God. Thus he obtained for humanity salvation, deliverance, forgiveness, and freedom from the guilt of sin, the foundations of our joy and eternal hope.

**20:29** When only Moses and Eleazar descended from the mountain, the assembled congregation of Israel knew that their beloved high priest was dead. They had not actually observed his death and burial, but they fully realized it when they saw Eleazar wearing the complete array of priestly garments and vestments. The period of mourning for the two greatest leaders of Israel was thirty days, whereas others were typically mourned for seven days.[402] Concerning the impact of the death of Israel's first high priest on the nation, Milgrom cites the rabbinical tradition from Targum Jonathan: "When Aaron's soul rested, the clouds of Glory moved away, on the first of the month of Av. And the entire congregation saw Moses descend from the mountain with rent garments. And he was weeping and saying, 'Woe is me for you, my brother Aaron, the pillar of Israel's prayer.' And they too wept for Aaron thirty days, the men and women of Israel."

---

[401] Harrison, *Numbers,* 273.

[402] Based on the prescribed period of uncleanness following the death of a member of the family (Num 19:14–19) and on examples from the death of Jacob (Gen 50:10) and Saul and his sons (1 Sam 31:13).

## (2) Victory over the Canaanites of Arad Hormah (21:1–3)

¹When the Canaanite king of Arad, who lived in the Negev, heard that Israel was coming along the road to Atharim, he attacked the Israelites and captured some of them. ²Then Israel made this vow to the LORD: "If you will deliver these people into our hands, we will totally destroy their cities." ³The LORD listened to Israel's plea and gave the Canaanites over to them. They completely destroyed them and their towns; so the place was named Hormah.

The divergence of material in this the third of the rebellion cycles is no more evident than in the present chapter. As is observable in the outline of thematic development in chaps. 20–21, there are both high and low points in these two chapters. But whereas the events of chap. 20 are rather somber, with the deaths of Miriam and Aaron bracketing the rebellion of Moses and Aaron and the rejection by the Edomites of Israelite passage, chap. 21 starts and ends on a more positive note. The rebellion of Israel concerning water supply on the way around Edom, which itself ends with a message of deliverance via the bronze serpent, is placed between the victories over Arad/Hormah (vv. 1–3) and those over Amorite kings of Sihon (vv. 21–31) and Og (vv. 32–35). God's leading the Israelites along a circuitous route around Edom is a reminder of his faithfulness in providing and protecting his people on their way to the Promised Land. In contrast to the rejection of Israelite passage around Edom and the turning away of Israel in their dejected state, when a similar response came from Sihon of Heshbon, Israel rose to the occasion and was victorious over the Amorite kings in the Transjordan highlands from the Arnon River to Gilead and Bashan. Though this region was not part of the original Promised Land (see Num 34:10–12), it would come under the control and settlement of the tribes of Reuben, Gad, and half of Manasseh (32:1–42).

Milgrom has delineated the two parallel units of material in Num 20:1–29 and 21:1–35 in order to demonstrate the literary contrast being made between the "Failure of the Leaders" in the former and the "Failure and Deliverance of the People" in the latter. The pivotal point in these two chapters is when the people cry out to the Lord for deliverance, and he hears them and brings healing (v. 9) and victory over their enemies (vv. 24–25, 32–35).

After the death of Aaron and the thirty days of mourning, the Israelites set out from Mount Hor to circumnavigate Edom along a route known as the Way of the Atharim. While the Israelites were on the journey, the King of Arad received word of Israel's advance and responded with his militia in the manner that the Edomites had responded to the second request for passage from Moses (20:20–21). The unnamed king of Arad was successful in capturing some of the Israelites, and this time they responded by asking for help from the Lord who granted them a convincing victory over their enemies. In the very locale where in a state of rebellion they had once suffered a resounding defeat at the hands of the Canaanites and Amalekites, at Hormah of the Negev (Num 14:45), now triumph was theirs because the Lord was with them rather than against them.

**21:1–3** The references to Arad, Hormah, and the Way of the Atharim have provided biblical historians, geographers, and archaeologists considerable difficulties. If the reference to Arad means the city of Arad, as identified with Tel Arad in the eastern Negev, then the problem is quite perplexing. Tel Arad was a substantial urban center during the Early Bronze Age, destroyed ca. 2650 B.C., but then remained unoccupied until the early Israelite monarchy.[403] Since no remains exist that might be identified with this Arad in the latter part of the Late Bronze Age (or early Iron I), many modern commentators have taken the reference to a King of Arad as a later gloss in the text based on Josh 12:14.[404] Alternative suggestions have been made to solve this dilemma. First, the reference to the King of Arad may be a regional designation, like the aforementioned "King of Edom" in Num 20:14, who may have ruled from the city of Hormah (v. 3) or even in the vicinity of Yeroham.[405] Hormah has been identified by some with Tel Malhata (Tel el-Milh),[406] a city of the Middle Bronze and Iron Ages about eight miles southwest of Tel Arad.[407] Others simply place the city of Arad at the site of Tel Malhata at this point in history, in keeping with the occasional transference of a city name to another location, and then locate Hormah at Tel Masos (Kh. el-Meshash), three miles to the west of Tel Malhata.[408] The occupational history of Tel Masos is similar to that of Tel Malhata.[409] One must note that Hormah, meaning "destruction," is a name given to the site after the defeat of the Canaanites in this part of the Negev. Multiple cities (ʿārêhem, "their cities") are said to have been completely or utterly

---

[403] R. Amiran, O. Ilan, M. Aharoni, "Arad," *NEAEHL*, 1:75–87. Cf. Y. Aharoni, "Arad: Its Inscriptions and Temple," *BA* 31 (1968): 31–32; R. Amiran, O. Ilan, A. Herzog, "Arad," *OEANE*, 1:169–76.

[404] Gray, *Numbers*, 283; Budd, *Numbers*, 229–30; Noth, *Numbers*, 154–55; J. Sturdy, *Numbers*, CBSC (New York: Cambridge University Press, 1976), 146; de Vaulx, *Les Nombres*, 234.

[405] An Arad *yrchm* (pronounced Yerucham perhaps) is known from the tenth century B.C. annals of Shishak and provides an example of two cities having the same toponymic preface. Arad *yrchm* is often identified with Jerahmeel of 1 Sam 27:10; 30:27 but perhaps could be a site near the modern Israeli town of Yerocham, eighteen miles SSE of Beersheba, twenty-four miles SSW of Tel Arad, and seventeen miles SSW of Tels Masos and Malhata. E.g., a second Arad is known from the annals of Shishak, called Arad *yrchm*, or perhaps Yerucham.

[406] M. Kochavi, "Tel Malhata," *NEAEHL*, 3:934–37.

[407] This would be compatible with the Early Date of the Exodus and Conquest according to the revised chronology of J. Bimson, *Redating the Exodus and Conquest* (Winona Lake: Eisenbrauns, 1980), 203–5.

[408] Y. Aharoni, *The Land of the Bible* (Philadelphia: Westminster, 1979), 201.

[409] A. Kempinski, "Tel Masos," *NEAEHL*, 3:986–89. V. Fritz, "Tel Masos," *OEANE*, 3:437–39.

destroyed by the Israelite armies, and the use of the toponym Hormah in 21:3 may designate a single key city of this campaign or the region of the defeated towns.[410]

The "Way of the Atharim" *(derek hāʾătārîm)* was described by Y. Aharoni as "leading from Kadesh-barnea to Arad," along which the fortresses of Bir Hafir, Oboda, and Aroer were built during the Israelite monarchy.[411] The meaning and location of *hāʾătārîm* apparently were lost early in history, and the later Syriac and Targums took this as the "Way of the Spies" from *tārîm* ("those who scouted, explored"). This gave rise to the tradition that the Israelites under Moses tried to enter the land through the same route as the previous generation. But this identification is untenable on linguistic, historical, and literary grounds. An expansion of the term *tārîm* to *(hā)ʾătārîm* would have been highly improbable.[412] Second, the naming of a trade route after a portion of the pathway taken by the scouts seems unlikely. If such a toponymic designation had occurred at such a dark moment in the wilderness journey of Israel, it most likely would have been recounted in history in the manner of such sites as Meribah, Kibroth Hataavah, Taberah, and here Horah. Third, the evidence is lacking for the tradition that Moses and the Israelites were attempting to enter the land from the Negev along the pathway in which they were thwarted nearly forty years before, or even that Moses was trying to enter the land from the South against the expressed will and judgment of the Lord (20:12), both on literal and literary readings of the text. There is no hint in the text of Moses even attempting to circumvent Yahweh's directive against him leading the Israelites into the Promised Land, though no doubt he would have desired to do so. Otherwise, after the Lord gave them a resounding victory at Hormah, it would have seemed quite natural to proceed northward into the upper reaches of the Negev (even to Arad itself) and into the central hill country. Instead, in the literary movement through the chapter, the victory over the Canaanites of Arad provided the new generation a foretaste of great things to come when they would enter the Promised Land under the power of God and the leadership of Joshua. The key statement in this passage is that the Israelites, when faced with the adversity of an ambush by the Canaanites, consulted the Lord and vowed to put their enemies under the destructive condemnation of holy war.[413]

Budd has offered a better suggestion that the Way of the Atharim may be

---

[410] By the time of Joshua's southern campaign, Arad and Hormah are known to be separate towns with individual kings (Josh 10:40; 12:14). These would probably be included among those defeated in the Negev, described in general in Josh 10:40.

[411] Aharoni, *Land of the Bible,* 58

[412] Note also BDB, 85–86.

[413] Cf. D. Olson, *Numbers,* INT (Louisville: John Knox, 19961), 34.

a reference to the road leading to Tamar, or Ein Tamar, located about ten miles south of the Dead Sea.[414] Such a desert road from Kadesh would have followed a line east northeast across the southern Negev to the basin of the Nahal Avedat and the Nahal Zin, south of the Machtesh Gadol. Modern Israeli mapping has labeled a mountain along this route as Hor Hahar (Mount Hor, Num 20:22; 21:4) about eighteen miles southwest of Ein Tamar. Along this route the Canaanites of the Arad (and Arad Yerocham) region may have perceived that the Israelites were encroaching upon their territory and hence came down to attack them, perhaps also ascertaining that since they had defeated them a generation before (14:35), they would again seek to demonstrate their territorial control and sovereignty. According to Num 21:4 the Israelites journeyed from Mount Hor, via the Way of the Red Sea *(derek yam-sûp)*, which Aharoni ascertained was the trade route extending from Elath on the eastern finger of the Red Sea in the Gulf of Aqaba northward through the Arabah to the Dead Sea. Hence the desert route would have them approaching the northern end of the Arabah from the west southwest, and then crossing the Arabah between Tamar and Zalmonah.[415]

## (3) Rebellion and Judgment (21:4–9)

[4]They traveled from Mount Hor along the route to the Red Sea, to go around Edom. But the people grew impatient on the way; [5]they spoke against God and against Moses, and said, "Why have you brought us up out of Egypt to die in the desert? There is no bread! There is no water! And we detest this miserable food!"

[6]Then the LORD sent venomous snakes among them; they bit the people and many Israelites died. [7]The people came to Moses and said, "We sinned when we spoke against the LORD and against you. Pray that the LORD will take the snakes away from us." So Moses prayed for the people.

[8]The LORD said to Moses, "Make a snake and put it up on a pole; anyone who is bitten can look at it and live." [9]So Moses made a bronze snake and put it up on a pole. Then when anyone was bitten by a snake and looked at the bronze snake, he lived.

**21:4–5** Once more, as the Israelites journeyed along the Way of the Red Sea, going out of their way to circumnavigate the northwest corner of the territory of the Edomites, the people grew impatient and ungrateful for that which the Lord had provided them. As at Kibroth Hataavah (11:4–10), they openly expressed their soul-felt dissatisfaction to God and Moses about the monotonous diet of manna they had been eating and the lack of water during this lengthy journey through the deserts. This verse is one of the few times in the Book of Numbers that the verb form *wayĕdabbēr* is used with the

---

[414] Budd, *Numbers,* 230.
[415] See Brisco, *Holman Bible Atlas,* 72, map 32.

people as the subject instead of God or Moses, which perhaps sharpens the seriousness of their rebellion.[416] They described their food supply as "miserable" (*haqqĕlōqēl*, "worthless, contemptible"), thereby deploring and degrading that which God had so graciously given to them for some forty years. When a person's heart is intent on rebellion and beset by discontent, even the best of gifts from the Lord can lose their savor; nothing will fully satisfy until the heart is made right. The structure of this pericope parallels the simplicity of the first rebellious incident in 11:1–3 and outlines as follows: (1) historical setting (v. 4a); (2) sin of the people (vv. 4b–5); (3) judgment from the Lord (v. 6); (4) response of the people (v. 7a); (5) intercession of Moses (v. 7b); (6) response of the Lord in deliverance (vv. 8–9). Unlike other rebellion accounts, no toponymic designation is made for identifying the site of the incident. This rebellion account structure closely parallels the accounts of the Israelite judgeships throughout Judges 3–16, and it is perhaps surprising that source critics have not ascribed this account to the supposed Deuteronomic historians and editors.

**21:6** In response to the people's uprising, the Lord sent forth "fiery serpents" (*hannĕḥāšîm haśśĕrāpîm*, "burning snakes"), whose poisonous venom soon resulted in death to the many who were bitten. Distinct from the previous protestation concerning the food and water supply, no impassioned response came from Moses, and the fierce anger of the Lord was embodied in the serpents. The adjective "burning" may refer to the burning sensation and pain brought about by the lethal injection of venom through the serpents' fangs. In comparing this phrase, however, with the usage of the term *śārāp* in v. 8, the reference may be to a specific species of snake whose bite caused such a burning sensation.[417] Because the roots for the terms "serpent" (*nāḥāš*), "enchantment" (*naḥaš*), and "copper/bronze" (*nāḥûš* or *nĕḥōšet*) are so closely related, this account has been taken by a number of source critical scholars as etiological, a didactic story built upon an event and/or word association that may or may not have a basis in reality.[418] Many of these scholars have interpreted this account in Numbers 21 as a retrojection from the late eighth century B.C. during the reign of Hezekiah, when the king began destroying the idolatrous worship centers through the realm of Judah. At that time the Judahites worshiped a bronze serpent called Nehushtan (2 Kgs 18:4). However, these two stories have quite the opposite impact

---

[416] The phrase "speak against" (-בְּ דִּבֶּר) recalls the challenge to Moses' leadership by Miriam and Aaron in 12:1 (וַתְּדַבֵּר מִרְיָם וְאַהֲרֹן בְּמֹשֶׁה) that resulted in her contracting a leprous skin disease.

[417] Ashley, *Numbers*, 404–5. D. J. Wiseman translated הַשְּׂרָפִים as "venomous" (*TB* 23 [1972]: 108–10). The former view of this term referring to a species seems more likely in the broader context.

[418] Budd, *Numbers*, 233; Gray, *Numbers*, 274–75; Noth, *Numbers*, 156–57.

on the people. Rather than being like the bronze iconographic serpent Nehushtan of the eighth century that had a disastrous effect on the people of Judah, the *nĕḥaš nĕḥōšet* (bronze serpent) Moses produced and mounted on a pole had a miraculous healing effect on those who looked upon it. More likely than retrojection from the monarchial period to the wilderness, the Nehushtan of Hezekiah's day was simply one of many forms of iconography the Israelites produced during periods of rampant idolatry that had their basis in the formative period of Israel's history. In a similar manner Jeroboam I of northern Israel revived a form of worship utilizing the imagery of a calf like the one produced by the Israelites and Aaron when Moses first ascended Mount Sinai (Exodus 32).

Several species of snakes have been posited as the possible identity of these fiery serpents. T. E. Lawrence described his encounters with horned vipers, puff-adders, cobras, and black snakes in eastern Jordan.[419] The "carpet viper" (*Echis carinatus* or *Echis coleratus*) is a highly poisonous viper known from Africa and the Middle East and thus is a likely candidate.[420] Other suggestions for identity of the serpent include the puff-adder and sand viper, neither of which is as lethal as the carpet viper. R. J. Wolff advanced the idea that the serpentine creatures were nematodes known as Guinea worms that the Israelites contracted by drinking contaminated water in the desert, but his suggestion has not received scholarly support.[421] On the identity as the carpet viper, Harrison concludes: "Since the incident was a natural event actuated by supernatural considerations, the most poisonous desert reptile would be eminently suitable for inflicting divine punishment upon the rebellious Israelites."[422]

**21:7** Also unlike previous rebellion accounts, the Israelites respond with repentant hearts, confessing their sinfulness in speaking seditiously against God and Moses. Though driven in part by the desperate circumstances of facing death by snake bite, they seem to have realized genuinely the seriousness of their indiscretion.[423] Having experienced several times through their history in the wilderness that the effectual fervent prayer of a righteous man like Moses avails much, they appeal to their divinely appointed leader to intercede with God on their behalf.[424] Unlike the way he reacted with unrighteous anger at Keribah Kadesh (20:10–11), Moses

---

[419] T. E. Lawrence (of Arabia), *Revolt in the Desert* (New York: G. H. Doran, 1927), 93.

[420] See discussion in Harrison, *Numbers,* 276.

[421] R. J. Wolff, *ISBE,* 4:1209–10.

[422] Harrison, *Numbers,* 276.

[423] Cf. Aaron and Miriam's impassioned pleas for Moses to intercede when she was struck with the leprous disease (Num 12:11).

[424] At Meribah in the Sin Wilderness (Exod 17:3–6); at Taberah (Num 11:2); and at Hazeroth with Miriam (12:12–14).

responded to their penitent pleas with an equally humble heart and prayed *(wayyitpallēl)* on behalf of the people.[425]

**21:8–9** The Lord graciously responded to the pleas of Moses and the people by giving instructions for preparing a homeopathic antidote for the snakes' venom. Yahweh's response commences with the secondary formula for divine instruction, *wayyōʾmer YHWH ʾel-mōšeh,*[426] and the message was that Moses should produce a *sārāp* ("winged serpent" or "fiery serpent")[427] and mount it on a signal pole (*nēs,* "sign, banner, placard") for people to see. Anyone who had been bitten by the snakes could then look at the serpent-bearing sign and would live rather than die. The verb translated "look" *(rāʾâ)* often carries with it the idea to see with belief or understanding, and it is to be so interpreted in this context. The function was a form of homeopathic and apotropaic ritual whereby a votive form of the source of the disease (homeopathic element) is used in a ritual to ward off evil (apotropaism), or in this case death from snake bite.[428]

The use of the copper or bronze serpent form in the worship context of the Sinai region has been attested through the excavated remains of a temple at Timna, located on the west side of the Arabah about fifteen miles north of Elat and Aqaba on the gulf. The Beno Rothenberg expedition carried out surveys and excavations in the area intermittently from 1959–1969.[429] This Bronze and Iron Age copper mining site was exploited by the Egyptians, who left behind evidence of their activities in the mining shafts, smelting facilities, wall carvings, and a small cultic center dedicated to Hathor, the patron deity of Egyptian artisans. Among the remains in the temple unearthed in 1969 from the period of Midianite occupation was a five-inch long copper snake with a gilded head, no doubt representative of some deity in the local cult and of a typology of cultic activity well attested in Egyptian

---

[425] The *hithpael* form here (וַיִּתְפַּלֵּל) is the normal form used with the verb פלל ("to plea"), though it still carries the continual or iterative sense.

[426] See previous examples and commentary on 3:40; 7:11; 11:16,23; 12:4,6,14; 14:11,20; 15:35,37; 17:10; 18:1,20; 20:12. For detailed analysis of the usage of the two formulae from divine instruction, see "Introduction: The Structure and Outline of the Book of Numbers."

[427] The LXX adds χαλκοῦν, "copper, bronze," here for further explanation. Samaritan Pentateuch has the form שָׂרוּף.

[428] A biblical parallel to this ritual is found in the case of the plague that killed so many Philistines after they had captured the ark. Votive gold offerings in the form of the disease (perhaps boils like those formed on the body from bubonic plague) and the determined instrument of the disease (mice) were offered to the Lord by placing them in the ark of the covenant, after which the ark was returned to the Israelites at Beth Shemesh (1 Sam 5:6–6:18).

[429] B. Rothenberg, *Timna: Valley of the Biblical Copper Mines* (London: Thames & Hudson, 1972), esp. 125–207, fig. 41 and Color Plates XIX–XX; *The Egyptian Mining Temple of Timna* (London: Thames & Hudson, 1988). See also Rothenberg and J. Glass, "The Midianite Pottery," in *Midian, Moab, and Edom,* ed. by J. F. A. Sawyer and D. J. A. Clines, JSOTSup 24 (Sheffield: JSOT, 1983), 65–124.

literature and iconography.[430] An eight-inch-long coiled copper snake form was excavated at Tel Mevorakh in the northern Sharon Plain and has been dated to the Late Bronze Age.[431] K. R. Joines notes that the Egyptians wore miniature models of serpents in order to prevent snake bite.[432]

The use of the mounted copper serpent by Moses and the people under the direction of the Lord carries a higher level of meaning and implication. Wenham noted several contrasting elements when comparing Num 21:7–9 with the verbal and visual records of the ancient Near East. First, the utilization of the mounted copper serpent was to take place after one had been bitten by a snake, not to ward off an attack. A person was in mortal danger if he neglected to look with faith upon the mounted serpent, literally standing between life and death at the point of decision to follow what might on the surface seem like a simple magic ritual. The repetition of the phraseology of life and death in vv. 8 and 9 emphasizes the crucial role the symbol held in the faith life of the people. Second, there existed a paradox of function here as was true in the case of most of animal sacrifices for sin and guilt in the Israelite system.[433] Blood, which by contact could render one unclean, could on the other hand bring ritual purification. This paradox is no more vividly pictured than in the ritual of the red cow (Num 19:1–22), whereby purification is affected for a person made unclean by death through the sprinkling of that which has rendered everyone else impure.[434] So looking with hope for salvation and healing upon a form of that which has rendered one in a position of living or dying was a wondrously paradoxical act of faith in a God who controlled all power over life or death.

In the New Testament, Jesus used the imagery of the copper serpent to demonstrate that he must be lifted up on the cross in order to accomplish the salvation of humanity. Just as the people in the wilderness looked with faith upon an uplifted serpent so that they might live, so through the paradox of faith in the efficacy of the death and resurrection of Jesus, those who believe in him should not perish but have eternal life (John 3:14–16; 12:32–33).[435]

---

[430] For an analysis of the role of serpent iconography in the history of the cults of Israel and Egypt, see K. R. Joines, "The Bronze Serpent in the Israelite Cult," *JBL* 87 (1968): 245–56; *Serpent Symbolism in the Old Testament* (Haddonfield, N.J.: Haddonfield House, 1974), 85–96; D. J. Wiseman, "Flying Serpents," *TynBul* 23 (1972): 108–10.

[431] E. Stern, "A Late Bronze Age Temple at Tell Mevorakh," *BA* 40 (1977): 89–91.

[432] Joines, "The Bronze Serpent in the Israelite Cult."

[433] Wenham, *Numbers*, 157–58.

[434] Note Milgrom's assessment of this ritual paradox in "The Paradox of the Red Cow (Num 19)," *VT* 31 (1981): 62–72; also found in his JPS tome, *Numbers*, "Excursus 48," 438–43.

[435] Cf. Harrison, *Numbers*, 278–79.

*(4) Journey through Moab (21:10–20)*

[10]The Israelites moved on and camped at Oboth. [11]Then they set out from Oboth and camped in Iye Abarim, in the desert that faces Moab toward the sunrise. [12]From there they moved on and camped in the Zered Valley. [13]They set out from there and camped alongside the Arnon, which is in the desert extending into Amorite territory. The Arnon is the border of Moab, between Moab and the Amorites. [14]That is why the Book of the Wars of the LORD says:

"... Waheb in Suphah and the ravines,
   the Arnon [15]and the slopes of the ravines
that lead to the site of Ar
   and lie along the border of Moab."

[16]From there they continued on to Beer, the well where the LORD said to Moses, "Gather the people together and I will give them water."
[17]Then Israel sang this song:

"Spring up, O well!
   Sing about it,
[18]about the well that the princes dug,
   that the nobles of the people sank—
   the nobles with scepters and staffs."

Then they went from the desert to Mattanah, [19]from Mattanah to Nahaliel, from Nahaliel to Bamoth, [20]and from Bamoth to the valley in Moab where the top of Pisgah overlooks the wasteland.

This section contains two alternating genre of material from the journey motif, the march itinerary and songs from the journey, as recorded in the Book of the Wars of Yahweh, a document long lost in antiquity except for occasional excerpts included in canonical Scripture. The geographical movement is predicated on the material in 20:14–23, in which the Israelites are said to have traveled around Edom because their king refused Moses' request for passage through their territory. Concerning these verses Wenham writes, "Extracts from the travel log interspersed with fragments of old poems convey the sense of elation as the goal of their wanderings comes into sight."[436]

**21:10–13** The journey motif resumes with the Israelites disembarking from the region of Mount Hor and the Way of the Atharim and setting up camp at Oboth, and then traveling on to Iye Abarim[437] on the edge of the Moabite territory. According to the wilderness march itinerary of Num 33:41–44, intermediate encampments were established at Zalmonah and

---

[436]Wenham, *Numbers*, 159.
[437]Also called simply *Iyyim* ("ruins"). Num 33:44–48 uses collectively the terminology of Iye Abarim, Iyim, and the mountains of Abarim.

Punon before they reached Oboth.[438]

The intent of the narrative in 21:10–11 is to progress quickly through the region, circumnavigating Edom, arriving at the eastern side of Moab on the edge of the desert, and then proceeding on to the Amorite regions of Sihon of Heshbon and Og of Bashan. From there they moved northward along the perimeter of Moab to a camp in the Zered Valley and then the Arnon Valley. The upper reaches of the Arnon River were situated on the edge of the Jordanian desert and marked the frontier boundary between the Moabites to the south and the Amorites to the north. The fourfold verbal sequencing of terms meaning "moved on, set out" (*wayyisĕʿû* [2x] and *nāsāʿû* [2x], "they set out, disembarked") and "camped" (*wayyaḥănû* [4x]) recalls the words of the original song of the Israelite march as recorded in Num 9:17–23 that "at the Lord's command the Israelites set out, and at his command then encamped." Having sought the Lord faithfully in the case of the bronze serpent, they were prepared to follow him faithfully on their journey through Transjordan and to experience again the joy of victory.

Most source critical scholars have long suggested that the itinerary stages of Numbers 20–21 are a conflation of sources, including JE and P and that chap. 33 is primarily of priestly origin. Verses 10–11 are described as P material, yet vv. 12–13 are identified as JE material, even though, as Ashley has pointed out, the vocabulary is essentially the same. The differences are largely geographical in terms of the number of campsite names preserved in a given region. Numbers 33 includes more of the sites between Kadesh and the border of the Amorite country (five vs. two), but Numbers 21 contains more names of cities within the Amorite region (seven vs. three).[439] The differences are to be regarded as variations based on geographical and literary context and purpose rather than hypothetical sources, and in fact neither of the texts is exhaustive. The geographical movement and sites mentioned in Numbers 21 reflect a concern in the narrative of Israel moving from Mount Hor to the region, all to show how God fought for Israel in the Transjordan. Numbers 33 on the other hand is a travelogue of Moses recounting the victory march from Egypt to the Plains of Moab, the front door of the Promised Land. Hence it only summarily addresses the region of the Amorites in its literary groupings of itinerary stages.[440]

---

[438] The location of Zalmonah is problematic, though Aharoni suggests the name of the site was preserved in a Roman fortress in the Arabah called Calamona (*Land of the Bible*, 202); "Tsalmonah," in J. Simons, *GTTOT*, 259, §439. Punon is generally identified with Feinan, an ancient copper mining site of the Bronze-Roman (Phaenon) periods, in the wadi of like name.

[439] Ashley, *Numbers*, 408–9.

[440] Note the work of Wenham in grouping the sites of Numbers 33 into six columns of seven sites each (*Numbers*, 217–18). See the discussion and chart in commentary on chap. 33, noting that the journey itinerary there was not meant to be an exhaustive list but a select collection of representative sites along the journey to final victory in the Promised Land.

**21:14–15**   The first song excerpt derives from the *Book of the Wars of Yahweh,* an ancient text heretofore unknown, though the second song excerpt in vv. 17–18 may have been drawn from it as well. The reason for this tribute from a book apparently dedicated to the great victories ascribed to Yahweh the God of Israel seems to be the geographical citations concerning the great gorge of the Arnon River and the border towns of the region of Moab, through which the Israelites were about to enter on their way to greater victories against the Amorites. The initial portion in vv. 14b–15a has no verb, only place names and geographical features. Thus the excerpt enhances the journey motif since it was God who was leading the Israelites through and around the terrain of the land of the Moabites. In the literary structure this song and the one quoted in vv. 17–18 are anticipatory of the great victory song of vv. 27–30 when Israel defeated the Amorite king Sihon of Heshbon. Together these three songs provide an overarching inclusio near the end of the rebellion cycles with the song Moses sang when Israel first departed Sinai (10:35–36). Indeed hymnic composition in conjunction with victory marches was a common tradition throughout the history of Israel. It seems to have begun with Moses and Miriam after the crossing of the Sea (Exod 15:1–21), continued with the marching and camping song when the Israelites were preparing to depart Mount Sinai (Num 9:16–23),[441] and is evident in the numerous psalms composed by David in response to the great victories the Lord wrought on his behalf.

The identity of Waheb in Suphah[442] in the vicinity of the Arnon River is unknown, though the description of the ravines is quite similar to much of the Arnon Gorge as it stretches from the desert to about midway down the eastern shore of the Dead Sea. The plural form of ravines (*hannĕḥālîm,* "the wadis, brooks, rivers") probably refers to the entire drainage basin of the eastern Arnon system with its numerous tributaries. The upper reaches of the Wadi al-Wala, a northern tributary of the Arnon, could also be included in the picture.[443] The deep gorge and precipitous ravines formed a very distinctive and formidable boundary for the northern part of Moab, though later the Moabites would expand into the tablelands, hills, and valleys in the area of Heshbon. Additionally some of the ravines led to the dwelling or seat of

---

[441] See commentary above on Num 9:15–23 for a hymnic and metrical analysis of this song.

[442] Perhaps meaning "Waheb in a Storm-wind / whirlwind." D. Christensen's reconstruction of the text from its consonantal base at this point is inviting, though it adds little to the meaning and function of the present reading. In repointing and reconstructing portions of the text, the phrase "Waheb in Suphah" became "Yahweh came in a whirlwind." The war motif would be more explicit than the implicit meaning in the Masoretic Text arrangement. See "Num 21:14–15 and the Book of the Wars of Yahweh," *CBQ* 36 (1974): 359–60.

[443] For further analysis of the northern border of Moab during the Iron Age, see "Moab's Northern Border: Khirbat al-Mudayna on the Wadi ath-Thamad," by P. M. Michele Daviau, *BA* 60/4 (1997): 222–28.

Ar, which was located near the Moabite border. This site probably is to be equated with Ar of Moab, a city (Num 21:28), district, or region (Deut 2:9; Isa 15:1).[444] The complete original song may have included more geographical data, and hence a fuller context.

**21:16–18a** On the edge of the desert the Israelites came to a site named Beer ("well") that would be remembered throughout their history because of the Lord's gracious supply of water once more in an arid region. Though some commentators have equated this site with the Moabite Beer Elim of Isa 15:8, this term for well is used so generically that any such identification would at best be tenuous.[445] The song that follows this note on the journey celebrates the wondrous gift of water provided by the Lord, this time without a preface of the people's rebellion.[446] With such a long history of complaining about the lack of water, the celebration of God's granting of water by instruction to Moses marks another turning point in the narrative of God's dealing with Israel. The recent occasion of Moses gathering the people to see God supply their need ended in judgment and despair for the prophet (20:2–13). Death was meted out to the last group who grumbled (21:5–6). Now Israel was given further incentive to continue toward the goal of the Promised Land.

The song reflects the quality leadership of the princes *(śārîm)* and nobles of the people *(nědîbê hāʿām)* who engaged in the digging of the well. The former term probably refers to the tribal chieftains or clan leaders, and the latter provides a poetic parallel to the princes, suggesting they willingly gave of themselves to engineer this worthy endeavor.[447] Milgrom notes the work of A. Musil, who described the digging of wells or water pits by bedouins in the riverbed of the Wadi el-Thamad (W. eth-Themed), pits known in the Arabic as *bir* or *biyar*.[448] J. Sturdy cites a Bedouin refrain that echoes similar sentiment about well digging:

> Flow water, spread abundantly; Wood, camel, do not scorn it!
> With sticks we have dug it.[449]

**21:18b–20** In seven verbless clauses the epic narrative (or perhaps poem) continues the journey motif from this well of Beer and the desert

---

[444] See also Deut 2:9,18,29. In Is 15:1 Ar is paralleled with Kir of Moab, a title for the capital of the Moabites. The destruction of Ar and/or Kir (קִיר) represents the destruction of the entire country.

[445] For examples see Gray, *Numbers,* 288; Noordzij, *Numbers,* 190; Harrison, *Numbers,* 281.

[446] Note the classical choral meter of 3–3–3–2 in the word count. The metric structure continues through the end of this pericope in v. 20, as 2–2–2, 2–3–2–3. Cf. John 4:10–15 in which Jesus described a well of living water that would quench humanity's eternal thirst.

[447] The term נְדִיב derives from the root נָדַב meaning "to be willing, generous, noble," as does the term for the free-will offering (נְדָבָה) is likewise derived.

[448] Milgrom, *Numbers,* 178; from A. Musil, *Arabia Petraea* (Vienna: A. Hölder, 1908), 259.

[449] Sturdy, *Numbers,* 151.

regions to the sites of Mattanah ("gift"), Nahaliel ("river of God"), Bamoth ("high place, cultic center"), the valley that is in the Moabite countryside, and the peak of the Pisgah mountains, which overlooks the wasteland (Jeshimon). Translators and commentators alike have faced the problem of whether these are place names or descriptive terms that should be translated. Translating several of the toponyms (e.g., Mattanah may be translated "gift" in v. 18b as part of the conclusion to the song, hence the phrase would further describe the gift of the well from God in the midst of the wilderness) yields the following versification of vv. 17b–20:

> "Spring up, O well; Sing about it!
> The well dug by princes;
> > its excavation by the nobles of the people, with scepter and with staves;
> from the wilderness a gift (Mattanah),
> > from a gift the river of God,
> > and from the river of God a high place;
> > from the high place the valley which is in the field of Moab,
> > the top of the Pisgah [range], which is overlooking the face of the
> > wasteland."[450]

Poised on the mountaintop of Nebo, the prominent peak of the Pisgah mountains, Moses would late be granted a glimpse of the Promised Land. For now the Israelite congregation celebrated with great joy the gift from God. The sites probably were remembered by these toponyms in the generations that followed, but by the postexilic period they were lost in antiquity.

Mattanah has not been identified, though Khirbet el-Medeiyineh (Madaynah) has been suggested.[451] Yet Y. Aharoni identified Kh. el-Medeiyineh with Iye Abarim (Iyyim).[452] The mound is located about eleven miles northeast of Diban (or southeast of Madaba) and contains pottery from the end of the Late Bronze Age and Early Iron I. Likewise, Nahaliel has not been located, though this could be a reference to the Wadi Zerqa-ma`in that flows from the central highlands to the Dead Sea, about ten miles south of its northern end. Bamoth ("high places, cultic centers") has not been identified, though it could have been preserved in the longer form Bamoth Baal (Num 22:41) or Beth Bamoth of the later Mesha inscription.[453] Bamoth was a toponym, often combined with names or titles of deities in the naming of important worship centers among Canaanites and Amorites. According to this poetic narrative, this Bamoth seems to have been located somewhere

---

[450] My translation taking vv. 19–20 as a continuation of the song, since no verbs of journey, namely וַיִּסְעוּ and וַיַּחֲנוּ, are included here.

[451] Cf. Simons, *GTTOT,* 62; Harrison, *Numbers,* 282.

[452] Aharoni, *Land of the Bible,* 436.

[453] Line 27, *ANET,* 320. Beth-baal-meon of line 30 could be another possibility since it is mentioned with Madaba and Beth Diblathen, which are also in this general vicinity.

near Mount Nebo in the Pisgah range. The Pisgah peak provides an excellent vantage point over the wilderness areas on the northwestern, northern, and northeastern sides of the Dead Sea. On a clear winter day from the traditional Mount Nebo, one can see where the Jordan River flows into the Dead Sea, the northern end of the Judean wilderness and the Jericho oasis, as well as the regions to the north on both sides of the Jordan.

Several commentators have suggested that the valley mentioned in v. 20 should be identified with the Wadi ʿAyûn Mûsā, about two miles northeast of the corner of the Dead Sea.[454] Finally, the term translated "wasteland" *(hayěšîmōn)* is also taken as a place name and identified by Y. Aharoni with Beth Jeshimoth, part of the realm of Sihon of the Amorites that was conquered by Israel (Josh 12:3).[455] The Way of Beth Jeshimoth descended from Heshbon westward toward the Jordan River, through the region opposite Jericho and near which the Israelites later encamped.

### (5) Victory over the Amorites of Transjordan (21:21–35)

A second attempt at diplomacy for gaining safe passage through the territories of Transjordan was undertaken by the Israelites in engaging the Amorites ruled by Sihon of Heshbon. The previous such endeavor at negotiation with their "brothers" the Edomites had ended in rejection and intimidation, forcing the Israelites to circumnavigate the region of Mount Seir for fear of war (20:14–21). This time the story begins much the same, and the initial response of the Amorites was like that of the Edomites to the south, but the repartee of Israel and the final outcome are quite the opposite. Victory, conquest, and celebration became the allotment for Israel, especially when Yahweh their God gave them confidence and fought for them. This account became one of the most remembered victories in the history of Israel.[456] The account of this campaign in Deut 2:24–37 details the direction Moses was given by the Lord before sending the messengers to Sihon, so the engagement that followed was not done without the Lord's blessing.

**[21]Israel sent messengers to say to Sihon king of the Amorites:**

**[22]"Let us pass through your country. We will not turn aside into any field or vineyard, or drink water from any well. We will travel along the king's highway until we have passed through your territory."**

**[23]But Sihon would not let Israel pass through his territory. He mustered his entire army and marched out into the desert against Israel. When he reached**

---

[454] Gray, *Numbers*, 291; Ashley, *Numbers*, 415.

[455] Aharoni, *Land of the Bible*.

[456] Cf. also the recounting of this event in Num 32:33; Deut 2:24–37 (expanded form); 3:6; 29:7–8; 31:4; Josh 2:10; 9:10; 12:21; 1 Kgs 4:19; Pss 135:10–12; 136:17–19.

Jahaz, he fought with Israel. ²⁴Israel, however, put him to the sword and took over his land from the Arnon to the Jabbok, but only as far as the Ammonites, because their border was fortified. ²⁵Israel captured all the cities of the Amorites and occupied them, including Heshbon and all its surrounding settlements. ²⁶Heshbon was the city of Sihon king of the Amorites, who had fought against the former king of Moab and had taken from him all his land as far as the Arnon.

²⁷That is why the poets say:

"Come to Heshbon and let it be rebuilt;
let Sihon's city be restored.

²⁸"Fire went out from Heshbon,
a blaze from the city of Sihon.
It consumed Ar of Moab,
the citizens of Arnon's heights.
²⁹Woe to you, O Moab!
You are destroyed, O people of Chemosh!
He has given up his sons as fugitives
and his daughters as captives
to Sihon king of the Amorites.

³⁰"But we have overthrown them;
Heshbon is destroyed all the way to Dibon.
We have demolished them as far as Nophah,
which extends to Medeba."

³¹So Israel settled in the land of the Amorites.

VICTORY OVER SIHON OF HESHBON (21:21–31). **21:21–22**  Only a terse summary of the correspondence[457] is preserved in this passage. Israel sent forth messengers *(wayyišlaḥ yiśrāʾēl malʾākîm),*[458] or diplomatic envoys, to negotiate passage northward along the Kings' Highway in the Transjordan highlands and then westward down the hillsides to the shores of the Jordan River.[459] The stipulations were essentially the same, with Israel promising neither to invade the farmlands of the Amorites for their own food supply nor access the wells along the way for their water. An additional request from this message was included in Deut 2:28, which was the opportunity to purchase food supplies while passing through the land.

**21:23–26**  Sihon's response was the same as the king of Edom, refusal of passage and the dispatching of troops to ward off Israel's advance (20:20–21). The account in Deuteronomy notes that the Lord had hardened the heart of Sihon in the manner of the pharaoh in Egypt so that the power of God

---

[457] Num 20:14–17 preserves a more complete example of the form of typical diplomatic correspondence.

[458] The phraseology מַלְאָכִים יִשְׂרָאֵל וַיִּשְׁלַח nearly duplicates that of 20:14, except that in the previous account Moses was the initial agent in dispatching the emissaries.

[459] See comment on the "Kings' Highway" above on 20:17.

might be demonstrated in the defeat of the Amorite king (2:30). The Amorite army launched an all-out military campaign against Israel, who was encamped near the edge of the wilderness of Kedemoth, and the armies met at a site named Jahaz. Though the identity of its locale is somewhat uncertain, the biblical and extrabiblical evidence locates it somewhere between Dibon and Madaba.[460] It later became one of the Levitical cities in the tribal territory of Reuben.[461] The armies of Sihon and the Amorites suffered a resounding defeat, with the Israelites carrying out the methodology of holy war as they "put him to the sword"—utter destruction—and "took over his land"—possession.[462] The Amorite "kingdom" of Sihon is said to have spread from the Arnon River to the Jabbok River, a length of about forty-five to fifty miles, but it apparently was flanked by the fortified towns of the Ammonites on the eastern and northern sides. The early existence of the Ammonite kingdom seems evidenced by the discovery and excavation of a Middle to Late Bronze Age temple near the Amman airport[463] as well as other sites in the region, such as Tel el- Umeiri,[464] Hesban,[465] Jalul, and Tell el-Jawa.

Heshbon was said to have been the key city of Sihon at the time of the Israelite conflicts,[466] though remnants are meager from the Middle or Late Bronze ages at Tel Heshban, located about eleven miles southwest of Amman. Only a few LB potsherds and no architectural remains were uncovered at the site during the excavations carried out under the auspices of

---

[460] The Mesha stele (lines 18–20) mentions a Jahaz (here יַהְצָה, "toward Jahaz") close to Dibon, which belonged to the Moabites during their expansion northward in the late tenth to early ninth century B.C. Cf. Josh 13:18 (Reubenite city); Judg 11:20; and the oracles against Moab in Isa 15:4 and Jer 48:34. Aharoni located it at Kh. el-Medeiyineh (also Iye Abarim), eleven miles NE of Dibon and the same distance SE of Madaba. Other suggestions for the location include Kh. et-Teim, Umm el-Walid, Tel Jalul (currently under excavation), and Kh. Umm el-Idham. See Snaith, *Leviticus and Numbers,* 173; Budd, *Numbers,* 246. Cf. also Simons, *GTTOT,* 262.

[461] 1 Chr 6:78; listed as Jazer in Josh 21:39.

[462] The phrases וַיַּכֵּהוּ יִשְׂרָאֵל לְפִי־חָרֶב, "So Israel struck him with the face/mouth of the sword," and וַיִּירַשׁ אֶת־אַרְצוֹ, "and he took possession of his land," are phrases of holy war used in Deut 7:2 and Num 33:53 respectively as well as numerous other passages. On the former cf. Num 31:8; Deut 13:16; 20:13; 28:22; Josh 10:28,30,32,35,37,39; 11:10,11,12,14; 19:47; Judg 1:8; etc. On the latter cf. Num 13:30; 21:32,35; 33:53; Deut 1:8,21,39; 2:21,22,24,31; 3:18,20: 4:1,5,14,22,26,47; 6:1,18; 7:1;8:1; 9:1,4,5,6,23; 10:11; 11:8,10, etc.

[463] L. Herr, "The Amman Airport Structure and the Geopolitics of Ancient Transjordan," *BA* 46 (1983): 223–29. Herr also edited *The Amman Airport Excavations,* 1976; ASOR Annual, 48 (Winona Lake: ASOR/Eisenbrauns, 1983).

[464] See L. Geraty, "'Umeiri, Tell el-," *OEANE,* 5:273–74; Geraty, et al., *The Madaba Plains Project: The 1984 Season at Tell el-`Umeiri and Vicinity and Subsequent Studies* (Berrien Springs: Andrew University, 1989), as well as subsequent volumes.

[465] Geraty, "Hesban," *OEANE,* 3:20–22; "Heshbon," *ABD,* 3:181–84; R. Boraas, S. Horn, L. Geraty, et al.; "Heshbon," 1968–76, vols. 1–10, Andrews University Monographs, 1969–78.

[466] Heshbon was listed among the cities of the Levites in Josh 21:39.

Andrews University in 1968–76. The archaeological record at Tel Hesban parallels that of Arad, Ai, Hebron, and other sites of the Israelite campaigns, which leads some critical scholars to deny the historicity of these events, suggesting that they have been retrojected into Israel's formative period by the JE authors from later victories by kings such as Omri.[467] The name Heshbon, however, may have been used by the Amorites for another locale. S. Horn suggested that the Heshbon of Sihon could have been located at Jalul,[468] and other nearby sites that have occupational strata from the LB period would be possible candidates. R. W. Younker has demonstrated the complexity of the social and political structures of early Moab, as well as the adjacent Ammonite and Amorite populations, and hence cautions against ascribing aspects of formal statehood to these early tribal oriented groups.[469] Perhaps continued surveys and excavations in the Madaba Plains Project will clarify this situation in the near future.

An earlier conflict between the Amorites of Sihon and the former king of the Moabites, by which Sihon gained control of this region, is alluded to in v. 26. The geopolitical history of the region between the Wadi Zered and the Jabbok River was a tumultuous one, with ever shifting boundary disputes and continual battles for territorial supremacy from the Late Bronze Age through the Iron Ages. The Egyptians, Moabites, Ammonites, Amorites, the Israelites of the tribes of Reuben and Gad, the later Israelites under Omri and Ahab, and the Arameans all waged war in this region. They were soon followed by the super powers of the Assyrians, Babylonians, and Persians. The earlier battle remembered in this text probably was one of those at the formative stage of these two peoples, who were still developing entities when Israel marched through the area.

**21:27–31** The provenance of this song of victory has puzzled scholars of this century, and three distinct approaches have been delineated. As mentioned above, some source critical scholars have tended to set this song in the context of Omri's conquest of Moab in the first half of the ninth century B.C.,[470] while others have taken it as an even earlier song mocking Moab. Budd's recent comment is typical of this view, suggesting that "the Yahwist has taken up an old taunt song against Moab which was probably, though not

---

[467] Budd, *Numbers,* 244–45. See also J. M. Miller, "Ancient Moab: Still Largely Unknown," *BA* 60/4 (1997): 194–204.

[468] Horn, "Heshbon," *EAEHL,* 510–14; J. A. Dearman, "Roads and Settlements in Moab," *BA* 60/4 (1997): 205–213.

[469] R. W. Younker, "Moabite Social Structure," *BA* 60/4 (1997): 237–48. Cf. also, G. Mattingly, "The Culture-Historical Approach and Moabite Origins," in *Early Edom and Moab: The Beginnings of the Iron Age in Southern Jordan,* ed. by P. Bienkowski, Sheffield Archaeological Monographs 7 (Sheffield: J. R. Collis, 1992), 55–64.

[470] Sturdy, *Numbers,* 153–54.

certainly, of Israelite origin. The version available mentioned Heshbon as
the city of Sihon. He took this Sihon to be an Amorite king and assumed that
he had previously dispossessed the earlier Moabites. Since in his view this
was Israelite territory, he constructs the story of the defeat of Sihon by the
Israelites."[471] Budd simply calls the song a "literary construct" and suggests
that the Book of Judges supports this proposition, since it seems to indicate
that only small enclaves of settlers lived in the region (Judg 3:12–20; 8:4–
17; 10:17–12:6). Thus for Budd the song need not be grounded in historical
reality. Nothing in the present context, however, demands the kind of kingdom that was in existence in the ninth to eighth centuries B.C. that would
necessitate placing the historical narrative into a later period. This kind of
etiological interpretation disregards both the content of the song and its
chronological and literary context. There is no known destruction of Heshbon by Omri, though he controlled Moab during the second quarter of the
ninth century B.C. Instead the Mesha Stele was etched and erected in celebration of Moab's successful rebellion against Israel shortly after the death
of Ahab (2 Kgs 3:4–27). Under Joram and Jehoshaphat many cities of Moab
were destroyed, but their armies finally withdrew after Mesha sacrificed his
son on the walls of Kir Hareseth. The song itself calls for the rebuilding of
Heshbon, to be established as the city of Sihon's kingdom (v. 26). The woe
oracle denounced the Moabites and their god Chemosh, who was supposed
to be a protector of the people but who instead allowed Sihon to take the
Moabite children captive. Israel, under the leadership of Yahweh their God,
had defeated all the forces of the Amorites during this latter stage of the wilderness experience, and hence the song was composed and sung in the subsequent history of the nation.

The traditional Jewish interpretation is that the song is of Amorite origin
and that it was adopted and adapted by the Israelites to show their supremacy over the Amorites, who had earlier conquered Moab. The song had been
sung by the Amorite bards, but their glorious victory had been shamed by
the Israelite conquest of the Amorite territory. The song must be viewed in
the literary context of the inclusio formed by the usage of the clauses "Israel
dwelt in all the cities of the Amorites" in v. 25 and "Thus Israel dwelt in the
land of the Amorites" in v. 31.[472] Israel, by the hand of their God (Deut
2:31–33), had triumphed over the Moabite region the Amorites had conquered. The Amorite song of victory was used against them to bring shame
and to discredit the once-powerful king. The account of the battle and the
words of this song, which recalled the Amorite victory over Moab, would

---

[471] Budd, *Numbers,* 244–45;

[472] Note the parallels in the clauses from vv. 25 and 31:
(31) וַיֵּשֶׁב יִשְׂרָאֵל בְּכָל־עָרֵי הָאֱמֹרִי (25) and וַיֵּשֶׁב יִשְׂרָאֵל בְּאֶרֶץ הָאֱמֹרִי.

later give Jephthah his rationale for refusing to return peacefully the region of Gilead to the Ammonite king (Judg 11:13–33). Israel possessed the land not by confiscating it from the Ammonites or Moabites but by utterly conquering the Amorites who had previously dispossessed the former inhabitants. They had not entered the Ammonite or Moabite realms of that time period, only that of the stubborn and belligerent Sihon the Amorite.[473] The mention of the territory and towns of Moab also prepares the reader for the Balaam oracles, set in the context of King Balak's ever-growing fear of the Israelites. Portions of this song also would be recounted in the prophets' oracles against Moab in the eighth to sixth centuries B.C., including Isa 15:1–14 and Jer 48:1–47.

The song itself has all the earmarks of a classical epic lyric, with the summons to the Amorite audience to "come" *(bōʾû)* and rebuild Heshbon as the new capital of its lead conqueror Sihon. The fiery destruction that was Heshbon's extended all the way to Ar of Moab, mentioned also in 21:15 above. The translation of the final colon of this verse has been problematic, in that one would expect a parallel to "it consumed" *(ʾākĕlâ)* instead of "lords," which has no precedent or parallel. Several modern translations have followed the LXX translators, who apparently read the Hebrew *baʿălê* ("lords, masters") as *bālʿâ* ("it consumed").[474] In the woe oracle against Moab, the lyricist denigrated the Moabites and their patron deity, Chemosh, saying boastfully that they had perished and that captives were taken from the young men and women for the use and abuse of the Amorites. The name Chemosh is recited twelve times in the Mesha stele, including in the appellation Ashtar-Chemosh, as the god who enabled Mesha to break the yoke of Israel's domination and recapture and rebuild a number of his cities, including Jahaz (L19 and Num 21:23) and Dibon (L21, also Dibon Gad in Num 33:45–46), Beth-diblathen ("Almon Diblathaim," NIV) (L30 and Num

---

[473] Milgrom outlined a variation on this viewpoint, suggesting that "the boundaries of Sihon and Og described in Deuteronomy and Joshua reflect the administrative redistricting of Transjordan under Solomon: Og's kingdom and Transjordan Manasseh correspond to Solomon's seventh and twelfth districts (1 Kgs 4:14,19)" (*Numbers,* "Excursus 54: The Song of Heshbon," 463). But excavations in Jordan over the past five decades have evidenced that the situation in the Late Bronze Age in the Transjordan was one in which territorial boundaries of the various groups such as the Moabites and Ammonites were less firmly fixed. Statements regarding boundaries in Numbers probably refer only to the historical setting of that given time, before the classical territorial boundaries were established. For Israel's descendants it was crucial to establish that Israel had not violated God's command to abstain from attacking and dispossessing the descendants of their common ancestors the Moabites (Gen 19:36–38).

[474] Gk. καὶ κατέπιεν, "as it devoured." The reading requires scribal metathesis and the changing of the ʾ to ה, neither of which would be an unusual inadvertent scribal error. Translations that have followed this reading include the NEB and GNB, with commentary support from Budd, *Numbers,* 242 ; Wenham, *Numbers,* 162; and Ashley, *Numbers,* 416,425. This may simply be an example of poetic ellipsis of a verb in the second colon.

33:46–47), and Madaba (L30 and Num 21:30).[475] Interestingly Heshbon is not preserved in the Mesha inscription, though it remained a vital city of this period in Moab's history. Woefully the worship of Chemosh of Moab was brought into the environs of Jerusalem in the tenth century B.C., where the once-wise Solomon built a temple to Chemosh on the hill opposite that upon which the Temple of Yahweh was built earlier in his reign. The seeds of idolatry were planted in the city where the one true God was to have been worshiped exclusively.

**[32]After Moses had sent spies to Jazer, the Israelites captured its surrounding settlements and drove out the Amorites who were there. [33]Then they turned and went up along the road toward Bashan, and Og king of Bashan and his whole army marched out to meet them in battle at Edrei.**

**[34]The LORD said to Moses, "Do not be afraid of him, for I have handed him over to you, with his whole army and his land. Do to him what you did to Sihon king of the Amorites, who reigned in Heshbon."**

**[35]So they struck him down, together with his sons and his whole army, leaving them no survivors. And they took possession of his land.**

VICTORY OVER OG OF BASHAN (21:32–35). **21:32–35** Two subsequent victories over the Amorites are recounted as the Israelites continued northward through the region against Jazer and vicinity and finally against Og the king of Bashan. Moses is reintroduced into the text as the one who sent forth the spies to scout out the situation in Jazer, which was followed by another victory over the Amorites who were living there. The final clause of v. 32, "the Amorites who were there," may suggest that Jazer was not an Amorite town originally, but it may have come under Amorite dominion in the expansion efforts of Sihon or Og into the Ammonite region. Jazer was both the name of a region (Num 32:1) and its principal city (32:3). Noth suggested the land of Jazer was located in the valley of the Wadi Kefrein,[476] which flows down toward the Jordan. The city was located by Simons with Khirbet Gazzir (Jazer), about ten miles west northwest of Amman.[477]

The account here of the victory over Og of the Bashan region reads quite similar to the beginning verses of the extended version in Deut 3:1–11, though Deuteronomy recounts the story in the first person voice of Moses. The battle does not seem to have been provoked initially by Israel, though their northward advance was perceived as a threat to Og's sovereignty over the region. Hence the armies were dispatched straightaway, and the battle ensued at Edrei, generally associated with modern Derʾā on the Syrian-

---

[475] Cf. translation of W. F. Albright, "The Moabite Stone," *ANET*, 320–21.

[476] Noth, *Numbers*, 236–37.

[477] Simons, *GTTOT*, 119, §300.

Jordanian border and thirty miles east of the Sea of Galilee.[478] The capital of the kingdom of Og of Bashan was located at Ashtaroth, situated on a northern tributary of the Yarmuk River (Deut 1:4). Later Edrei would be included in the tribal territorial allocation of the Machirites of the eastern half of the tribe of Manasseh (Josh 13:31). Though no other battles are recounted in Numbers, perhaps suggesting that the Israelites moved northward through Gilead uncontested, this need not be concluded. In Deut 3:4–6 it is noted that sixty cities from the kingdom of Og of Bashan were subjected to the stipulations of holy war.

**21:34** The counsel from the Lord is introduced by the secondary introductory formula for divine instruction used in the Book of Numbers *(wayyo>mer YHWH >el-mōšeh).*[479] The message from the Lord, that they should not fear the oncoming enemies, was the same one given to the people by Moses, Aaron, Caleb, and Joshua when they were faced with the prospects of entering the Promised Land, a task that seemed to them frightening and formidable (Num 14:9). To hesitate in fear would be to rebel against God, but to advance against a foe just like the one they had just defeated would afford evidence of their faith in a God who fights for them.

**21:35** Only a brief summary of the complete conquest is provided here, for the more extensive version is recounted in Deut 3:3–11. The important feature to this account was that Moses and the Israelites faithfully obeyed the instructions from the Lord, and victory was theirs. Og's dynasty over Bashan had come to an abrupt end, and no descendant of the king would be there to take his rightful place on the throne. The concluding aspect of holy war, that of taking possession of the land, parallels the phraseology of v. 24. The concluding words of the chapter prepare the reader for the coming instructions in Num 33:50–53 and the concomitant warning not to retract in fear like the first generation. The series of victories in chaps. 20–21 would provide the Israelites with the foundation for a faith in Yahweh their God that would give them courage and hope as they would go forth across the Jordan River to the Promised Land.

*(6) The Book of Balaam (22:1–24:25)*

### Introduction to the Balaam Oracles

The stories of Balaam, his donkey, and his oracles of blessing upon Israel have both fascinated and intrigued readers young and old throughout history.

---

[478] Cf. Simons, *GTTOT,* 124, §302; Mattingly, "Edrei," *ABD,* 2:301. This site, which is located sixty miles S of Damascus on an eastern tributary of the Yarmuk River, contains remnants of a Late Bronze occupation, which would befit this historical context.

[479] On the use of the divine revelatory formula וַיְדַבֵּר יְהוָה אֶל־מֹשֶׁה לֵּאמֹר and the present alternative וַיֹּאמֶר יְהוָה אֶל־מֹשֶׁה in the Book of Numbers, see above discussion in "Introduction: Structure and Outline" and commentary on Num 1:1.

Wenham remarked: "The charming naivete of these stories disguises a brilliance of literary composition and a profundity of theological reflection. The narrative is at once both very funny and deadly serious."[480] For most scholars these accounts have seemed out of place, an anachronistic and puzzling legend of ninth or eighth century B.C. origin and retrojected into the conquest tradition for the purpose of showing God's care for his people and justifying their exploits against the Moabites. Yet, as has been argued in the "Introduction" and expanded below, this material stands with amazing relevance to the structural and theological outline of the Book of Numbers. Balaam becomes for a brief moment the revelatory instrument of God, replacing Moses, who mysteriously is nowhere present. Israel is talked about and seen from a distance. The positioning of the Balaam oracles at the conclusion of the third cycle of Israel's rebellion presents a remarkable picture of God working on behalf of his people in spite of their almost complete failure to follow him faithfully. God will continue to reveal himself to and pronounce blessing upon his people, even if the instrument of blessing is a pagan divination expert of international reputation.

As noted earlier the third rebellion cycle is the most enigmatic; here the rebellion cycles take a striking turn and come to a perplexing conclusion with implications for the rest of the book and for the future history of Israel. The historical setting is the Plains of Moab across the Jordan from Jericho following the deaths of Miriam and Aaron, the rebellion of Moses, and then the victories over the Amorites in Transjordan. Now only Joshua, Caleb, and Moses remain from the leadership that saw God's incomparable, mighty acts displayed in Egypt and the Exodus. Yet now Moses' has fallen into the seditious pattern of the nation by his defiance of God in striking the rock, thereby violating the holiness of Yahweh. Moses now represents the final collapse of the seditious nation except for a remnant of the two faithful spies. The picture of God's sovereign and faithful intent to bless his people is striking in contrast to their almost total rebellion against him. His grace abounds against all attempts to thwart it.

Balaam, a pagan sorcerer of Mesopotamian origin, whom one might expect to rebel against the God of Israel—and he does—now becomes the unexpected spokesman for God. Moses is silent here, absent from the narrative. Yet even if the most faithful devoted leader of the people of God should fall into sin, God will use whatever resource is necessary to communicate with and for his people. The greatest of the prophets has joined in the rejection of God's sovereignty over the lives of the people, and the plot turns as God uses Balaam instead of Moses (and Aaron) to bestow blessing and glory upon his people as a prophet and to worship God with sacrifices and offer-

---

[480] Wenham, *Numbers,* 164.

ings as a priest. Jesus said that if the children of the faith were silenced, the stones would cry out (Luke 19:40; cf. Luke 3:8; Matt 3:9). The narrative arrangement creates discontinuity in the character plot yet continuity in the thematic developments. Balaam is a rebellious instrument of God, a paradoxical and oxymoronic character himself in the story.

That a donkey should be the most spiritually observant character in this section stands in sharp contradistinction to the characterization of the nations and the individual leaders, a literary slap-in-the-face toward any humanly conceived means of defining God and his ways. God will ultimately accomplish his will by whatever means and agency necessary. What echoes from the mouth of this most unusual servant of God are some of the most striking words of praise for God and his purpose for his people. Reversal of fortunes reverberates through several episodes of the story: a persistent pagan prophet learns from a donkey; a Moabite king's desires are thwarted by God; and Balaam's intent to curse and bring condemnation upon Israel is turned by God into an opportunity to bring blessing beyond compare for the near and distant future. God reveals—the central theme of the Book of Numbers—his character and his intent to bring abundant hope and beneficence to all of humanity, indeed to the Jews and to the Gentiles.

The third rebellion cycle concludes with another collapse of Israel's character, in spite of the wondrous revelation through the prophet Balaam. Idolatry at the doorstep of the land of promise serves to warn future generations of the consequences of rejecting God's law: judgment, plague, disease, and finally death. Temptations toward idolatry would plague Israel throughout their future in the land. Lest one think that the Balaam of chaps. 22–24 turned in faith toward this God who used him in such an amazing manner, we find that the illustrious prophet was the instigator of the means by which Israel would fall. The first generation ends in tragic judgment, and the new generation is faced with the matter of faithfulness to God, which will determine the course of their future.

In the final rebellion cycle, Aaron has died and Moses has disregarded God's holiness. Ritual activity is performed only by a reluctant and antagonistic sorcerer. Yet as Balaam states in the second oracle:

> There is no sorcery against Jacob,
>    no divination against Israel.
> It will now be said of Jacob
>    and of Israel, "See what God has done!" (23:23)

Three times Balaam has seven altars built with seven sets of bull and ram sacrifices, followed by pronouncement of blessing upon Israel. A fourth oracle of ultimate blessing, the promise of a glorious messianic ruler, ensues without a concomitant ritual act as the Spirit of God comes upon him. The Balaam oracles stand as a testimony of God's faithfulness to Israel and his commitment to work on behalf of his people, even though they rebel against him. He will eventually bring them back to himself.

### Balaam in the Setting of the Ancient Near East

From a variety of ancient Near Eastern texts from Mari, Babylon, and Anatolia have come cuneiform texts that illustrate the roles prophets and divination experts played in society during the Bronze and Iron Ages. From counselors to chiefs and kings to consultants for individuals and their families, these professional purveyors of portentous proficiency plied their skills in addressing matters that ranged from those of international importance to individual idiosyncrasy.

### Balaam: Prophet, Diviner, or Sorcerer?

In the Old Testament certain forms of divination were permissible while other forms, especially that of sorcery, were summarily condemned. Sorcery was not only prohibited but was punishable by death (Exod 22:18; Lev 19:26; 20:27; Deut 18:10). Sorcery *(kešāpîm)* was a means of using black magic, incantations, necromancy, or manipulation of deity to affect change in the course of events set forth by God (or the gods). In the ancient Near East such a practice was predicated on the belief that the will of the gods and goddesses of one's pantheon could be manipulated by human activity whereby they would change their minds and accomplish the desired response. The God of Israel was no deity whose course of action was at the whim of human desire. Attempts to use God in this way were disastrous for the Israelites, as when they brought the ark of the covenant down into their battle against the Philistines (1 Sam 4:1–22). Yet certain forms of sorcery, such as casting an evil spell on someone that resulted in death, were also capital crimes. Divination on the other hand was a means of discerning the will of the gods via reading omens in nature, earthly and heavenly, and providing this information to inquiring individuals. Acceptable forms in the Old Testament of discerning the will of God include interpreting patterns of oil or water (Gen 44:5,15) or casting lots (1 Sam 14:41–43). The most widely acceptable form was the consulting of the Urim and Thumim by the high priest who carried them on his ephod over his heart (Exod 28:30–35; 1 Sam 2:28; 14:3; 23:6,9; 28:6; 30:7). In each of these cases the "diviner" priest was attempting to discern the will of God in the given situation.

Balaam falls into the category of a diviner who emerges as a prophet. His initial oracles are derived after performing ritual sacrifice and other divining activities on the heights of the mountains, exercising the skills in which he was trained. Later his oracles come directly from the Lord without ritual preface. His expressed abilities include *naḥaš*, "to seek an omen" (23:23;

24:1) and *qesem*, "divination by casting lots" or "clairvoyance" (22:7; 23:23). The method of *naḥaš* was that practiced by Joseph during his leadership role in Egypt (Gen 44:5,15); and *qesem* is known from the practice of visionary diviners among the false prophets of Israel (Ezek 12:9; Zech 10:2). Balaam gave no pretense of being a sorcerer who might actually change the will of the God (or even the gods); for he proclaimed, "I could not do anything great or small to go beyond the command of the LORD my God" (22:18), and again, "I must speak only what God puts in my mouth" (22:38). Balak's expectations were quite the contrary. He had hired Balaam expressly to change the course of Israel's pathway of God's blessing which they had heretofore experienced. What Balak wanted was a sorcerer's skill, but what he acquired was a diviner's Divine direction. In the end Balak became the recipient of that which he had intended for Israel, in fulfillment of the promise the Lord made to Abram, "I will bless those who bless you, but whoever curses you I will curse" (Gen 12:3). In this context Milgrom concludes, "Thus Israel's blessing moves from the present to the future, from a description of Israel's potential to its eventual fulfillment, reaching its crescendo in the full retribution it will exact from Balak (through his nation) for defying God by attempting to destroy Israel."[481]

But lest one think that Balaam became a faithful believer in Yahweh, God of Israel, one only has to look to the succeeding chapters of Numbers and additional texts from the Hebrew Bible and the Christian New Testament. Though his acclamation of "Yahweh my God" in 22:18 might on the surface evidence such faith, the continuing saga of Balaam as the pagan diviner reveals otherwise.

### Balaam and the Texts from Deir ʿAlla

While excavating the tel of Deir ʿAlla, which lay on the alluvial plain of the ghor terrace where the Jabbok River flows into the Jordan River Valley, the Dutch excavation team under the direction of H. J. Franken uncovered a remarkable inscription recounting the activities of a Balaam son of Beor. The texts were written in red and black ink on a plastered wall or stele, possibly in a temple or other cultic context. On the basis of paleography and linguistics, as well as the stratigraphic context, the texts have been dated from the mid-eighth to the seventh century B.C.[482] and hence several centuries

---

[481] Milgrom, "Excursus 59, Balaam: Diviner or Sorcerer?" 473.

[482] Cf. an eighth century date proffered by J. Naveh, "The Date of the Deir ʿAlla Inscriptions in Aramaic Script," *IEJ* 17 (1967): 256–58; a seventh century date by F. M. Cross, "Notes on the Ammonite Inscription from Tell Sīrān," *BASOR* 212 (1973): 12–15; and in contrast to the original dating by the excavator to the Persian sixth century, H. J. Franken, "Texts from the Persian Period from Tell Deir ʿAllā," *VT* 17 (1967): 480–81.

after the events narrated in the Book of Numbers. The script is that of Aramaic and the language Ammonite at the point where the Ammonite Aramaic script was diverging from mainline Aramaic.[483]

The fragmented plaster sections have been pieced together into twelve combinations, only two of which are substantial enough to conjecture a translation. Though Combinations I and II have a number of lacunae, several conclusions can be drawn from the contents. One Balaam son of Beor, who is described as a "seer of the gods" *(hzh ʾlhn)*, had a frightening night vision that he shared with his colleagues in the midst of his fasting and grief. He foretells a period of drought and darkness, of mourning and death, and in which the natural order is upended. Small birds like the swift and the sparrow attack larger ones like the eagle and the pigeon; the deaf hear at a distance, and fools have insightful visions. Balaam then perhaps exercises his prophetic-divination expertise to confront or curse the gods and goddesses who have brought on this calamity, and he implores the goddesses Ashtar (consort of Chemosh in Moab) and Sheger (known from Ugarit and Phoenician sources) to bring light, rain, and fertility to the land. Milgrom suggested that "perhaps the temple on whose walls this inscription was written was founded to honor the gods (Sheger and Ashtar) who heeded Balaam's plea/sacrifice."[484]

The translation of Combinations I and II reads as follows with notes from Hackett (H) and Milgrom (M). Two types of gaps in the text are denoted; brackets ([ ]) mark reconstructions based on comparative texts, and three dots (...) denote lacunae lacking sufficient data for reconstruction.

## Combination I

1.  The account of [Balaam son of Beo]r, a man who was a seer of the gods. The gods came to him in the night, and he envisioned (saw, H) a vision

2.  like an oracle of El. Then they said to [Balaa]m, son of Beor: "Thus he will do [...] afterward (in the future? M).

3.  And Balaam arose on the next day [...] from [...] and he wept

4.  deeply. And his people came to him [and said to] him[] "Balaam son of Beor, why are you fasting and weeping?" And he

5.  said to them, "Sit down. I will tell to you what the *šadda[yin* are about to do.] Come and see the wonders of the gods. The go[d]s gathered together

6.  and the *šaddayin* stood in the assembly and said to *Š[eger* ...], 'Sew up; bolt up the heavens with your dark cloud; appoint darkness and not

---

[483] See the paleographic discussions in J. Hackett, "The Balaam Text from Deir ʿAllā," HSM 31 (Chico, Cal: Scholars Press, 1984), 1–19. Note also Milgrom, *Numbers,* Excursus 60, "Balaam and the Deir ʿAllā, Inscription," 473–74.

[484] Milgrom, *Numbers,* 476.

7. eternal light, and set the dark [ cloud's se]al on your bolt, and do not remove it forever! For the swift shall

8. reprove the griffin-vulture (eagle, M), and the voice of the vulture shall sing out. [...], the son of the *naḥaṣ* bird shall claw up young herons, and the swallow shall tear

9. at the pigeon, and the sparrow [...] the staff; and at the place where the ewes are brought, the rabbits shall eat laurel branches (?wolf? H).

10. [...] drink wine and hyenas listen to instruction. The whelps of the f[ox ...

11. ...] to the wise he takes you. The poor woman prepares myrrh and the priestess

12. [...] for the prince a tattered loincloth. The esteemed person indeed esteems (others),
    and the one esteeming is es[teemed

13. ...] Deaf ones shall hear from a distance [

14. ... the eyes of ] a fool shall see visions. Sheger and Ashtar for [ .

15. ...] the leopard. The piglet chases the son of

16. [the ...]

## Combination II

1. [...]
2. ? to the *Šadd*[*ayin* ...]
3. ? he has eaten [...]
4. Young woman full of love [drink ...][485]
5. ? Why do the seed (offspring - M) and the firepit contain foliage(?) [...]
6. El will be satisfied. Let him cross over to the house of eternity, the hou[se ...]
7. the house where the traveler does not go and the bridegroom does not go there, the house [...]
8. and the worm from the tomb, from those who have arisen among human beings (H)[486] and from the graves of [...]
9. [...] Will he not take counsel with you; or will he not take advice from one dwelling [ .. ]
10. [...] You will cover him with a garment. If you are contentious with him, he will faint. If you [...]
11. I will put [...] under your head. You will lie down on your eternal resting

---

[485] P. K. McCarter, with Caquot and Lemaire, translates the line phrase as "young woman, drink your fill of love!" ("The Balaam Texts from Deir ʿAlla," *BASOR* 239 [1980]: 49–60; A. Caquot and A. Lemaire, "Les textes araméens de Deir ʿAlla," *Syria* 54 [1977]: 202).

[486] Wide disagreement on this clause; note Milgrom, "From the testicles of men, from the thighs of ..." (*Numbers,* 475).

place to perish, to [...]
12. [...] in their heart. The offspring sings in his heart [...]
13. [with a he]art of gladness, kings will see visions [...] Death will take the newborn child
14. [...] ? [...] ? ? the heart of the offspring grows weary because he comes to [...]
15. to his end [...] ? ? [...] ? [...] inquire of the king ? ?
16. ? [...] a distant vision [...] ? your inquiry, Why [...]
17. to make known the account which he spoke orally to his people judgment and punishment[487]
18. and I shall not drink (to the king?) [...]

## Critical Scholarship

For most literary and source critical scholars, the story of Balaam was one of the more ancient portions of the Pentateuchal narrative material derived from the early conflation of Yahwistic and Elohistic sources. Noth, for example, discerned a source variation in the Balaam oracles, suggesting that the "two self-contained sections 22.41–23.26 and 23.28–24.19 present obvious doublets; the former, with two 'Balaam discourses,' forms the main part of the E-version, while the latter, again with two 'Balaam discourses,' forms the main part of the J-version." He found difficulty in discerning sources in chap. 22, ascribing the story of Balaam's donkey in 22:21–35 to the J-narrative and the remainder of the material in chaps. 22–24 to either the total conflation of J and E or later editorial insertions and additions.[488] Gray assigned 22:2–22 to the Elohistic source, based primarily on what he described as the prevalent use of Elohim in reference to God in that section.[489] Yet even critical scholars such as Noth and A. W. Jenks have pointed out that the divine names are used inconsistently in the Balaam accounts and should not be used to differentiate sources, as was noted earlier by W. F. Albright.[490] Yet, as will be demonstrated below in the literary analysis of these chapters, the shifting between divine names is by no means inconsistent or arbitrary, but instead it functions as one of the elements in the devel-

---

[487] Last phrase *l lšn mšpt wmlqh* possibly "tongue (=mouth) of judgment and punishment."

[488] Noth, *Numbers,* 171–72. Cf. Gray, who presented a detailed analysis of all three chapters based on these alleged sources, noting themes and characteristics, character development in each of the sources (*Numbers,* 309–22). See also A. Dillmann, *Numeri, Deuteronomium, und Josua,* 135–67; Snaith, *Leviticus and Numbers,* 10; de Vaulx, *Les Nombres,* 262–63; Budd, *Numbers,* 256–61; Levine, *Numbers 1–20,* 62–63.

[489] Gray, *Numbers,* 312.

[490] Noth, *Numbers,* 172; A. W. Jenks, *The Elohist and North Israelite Traditions* (Missoula: Scholars Press, 1977), 55–57; and W. F. Albright, "The Oracles of Balaam," *JBL* 63 (1944): 207–53.

opment of the literary structure.

A second critical issue related to the Balaam accounts is the suggestion that this material, though from an ancient Pentateuchal source, is a late insertion into the flow of the narrative of the Book of Numbers, retrojected from the eighth or seventh century B.C. into the Late Bronze or Iron I historical context of the Israelite conquest tradition. Milgrom stated: "Clearly the rabbis believed that the Balaam story was composed independently and only later inserted into the Pentateuchal corpus. Indeed, these chapters are totally distinct from the larger context: Neither the personalities nor the events in them appear in the adjoining chapters."[491] After the literary analysis section detailing the internal cohesion of the narrative and poetic portions, an outline of the recurrent themes in the Balaam oracles and the remainder of the Book of Numbers will be presented. I will also demonstrate how the Balaam material has been intricately interwoven into the adjoining chapters utilizing several basic Hebrew verbs.

### LITERARY ANALYSIS OF NUMBERS 22–25

The following literary analysis will show the internal cohesiveness of the narrative, which includes the Baal Peor incident of chap. 25, and provide the foundation for demonstrating the continuity with the remainder of the Book of Numbers. This analysis will serve as the basis for addressing the parallels and developments in the areas of structure (both micro and macro levels), theme, narrative plot, characterization, and theology through the commentary on the Book of Balaam.

### OUTLINE OF THE BALAAM ORACLES

GEOGRAPHICAL SETTING: Arabah of Moab along the Jordan across from
    Jericho (22:1)

| | |
|---|---|
| CYCLE I: FIRST MESSENGERS SENT TO BALAAM | (22:2–14) |
| Balak Fears Israel; Sends First Messengers to Balaam | (22:2-7) |
| Balaam's Response to the Messengers | (22:8) |
| God's First Encounter with Balaam: Don't Go | (22:9–12) |
| Balaam Refuses to Go to Moab | (22:13) |
| Balak's Messengers Return Home to Moab | (22:14) |

| | |
|---|---|
| CYCLE II: SECOND SET OF MESSENGERS SENT TO BALAAM | (22:15–21) |
| Balak Sends More Messengers to Balaam | (22:15–17) |
| Balaam's Response to the New Messengers | (22:18–19) |
| Balaam's Second Encounter with God: Go and Speak | (22:20) |

---

[491] Milgrom, *Numbers*, 185.

## Excursus: Recurrent Themes and Literary Structures in the Balaam Oracles and the Book of Numbers

Many source critical scholars, while acknowledging the relative antiquity of the poetics of the Balaam oracles, have suggested that the materials is discontinuous from the remainder of the Book of Numbers. Based upon their discernment of variant "historical" sources in the narrative as compared to the preceding and succeeding materials, they have posited that Numbers 22–24 represent the conflation of the proposed Yahwistic (J) and Elohistic (E) sources with epic poetry, whereas most of the material in the Book of Numbers is said to have derived from the priestly source (P). Baruch Levine claimed, "The generic diversity of Numbers, when considered together with its varied sources, compounds the problem of establishing its coherence and makes Numbers the most loosely organized of all the Torah books."[492] In the previous section I have attempted to demonstrate the internal coherence of this material on the basis of literary analysis. This section will outline the numerous theological themes, including the precise Hebrew wording, which are recurrent in the Balaam oracles when compared to other so-called P materials in the Book of Numbers, whereby showing the theological coherence in this pivotal book of the Torah.

### The Deliverance from Egypt

The theme of Yahweh's miraculous deliverance of the Israelites from bondage in Egypt rings throughout the Hebrew Scriptures, including numerous allusions in the Book of Numbers. References are made in three contexts to this theme in the Balaam accounts, twice in the context of the initial correspondence between Balaam and Balak (22:5,11), and in oracles two and three of Balaam (23:22; 24:8). These four verses are complemented by five explicit references to the Exodus in the Book of Numbers in the chapters preceding the Balaam material (1:1; 9:1; 14:23,13–22; 15:41; 20:14–16), and then in two succeeding passages (32:11; 33:1–8). For Balak this reference serves as the historical setting of his request of the services of the divination prophet Balaam. In the second oracle the statement that "God brought them out of Egypt" (23:22) is the chiastic center of the passage, serving as the basis for the proclamation that God was with Israel, and therefore no cursing or condemnation could be brought against such a powerful nation. In the third oracle, like the previous, God's deliverance provides the

---

[492] Levine, *Numbers 1–20*, 72.

exemplar of his power in providing for his people. Israel under God's blessing was as powerful as the wild ox or the lion, able to conquer and devour any foe.

### The Nations' Fear of Israel

Out of a dreadful fear Balak sent an entourage of elders from Moab and Midian to the renowned Mesopotamian prophet seeking divine assistance against the ominous hoard of the Israelites (22:2–3). That fear is reflected in the words of Balaam in the second oracle, when he described the sons of Jacob as rising "like a lioness" that "devours ... prey and drinks the blood of ... victims" (23:23–24). A similar anxiety among the enemies of Israel is proclaimed by Moses when the Israelites first embarked on their journey from Sinai, "Rise up, O LORD! / May your enemies be scattered; / may your foes flee before you" (10:35). However, the same fear could befall the people of God. When the Israelites became fearful of the inhabitants of Canaan after the scouts' report, the nations no longer were fearful of Israel, and the people suffered defeat at the hands of the Amalekites and Canaanites at Hormah (14:45) Likewise Edom, following the sins of Moses and Aaron at Kadesh, expressed no fear in rejecting the Israelite request to traverse their territory on the journey into Transjordan highlands (20:14–21). Later when the Israelite spies were sent into Jericho just prior to the crossing of the Jordan by the nation, Rahab recounted to them the terror that had gripped the town of Jericho since God had delivered the Israelites from Egypt and given over Sihon and Og to them in recent battles (Josh 2:9–13).

### The Vast Numbers of Israel

One of the expressed fears of the Moabite king that served as a basis for his request for help from Balaam was over the vast population of Israel and the potential harm for his own people. The Israelites had defeated the formidable foes in Sihon of the Amorites and Og of Bashan, and Balak saw a similar fate for his armies and territorial dominion (22:2–4). Furthermore, in the first oracle of Balaam the prophet-diviner announces rhetorically, "Who can count the dust of Jacob, or number a fourth of Israel?" These words echo the theme of God's blessing delineated in Numbers 1–2, in which the census is described of the Israelite armies that came forth from Egypt. Later this theme is reiterated in the Book of Numbers in 26:1–62 and 31:4.

### Blessing and Cursing of Israel

The several pronounced blessings of Israel via the prophet Balaam as the spokesman for Yahweh are simply the latest in the long line of accounts threaded through the Pentateuch. J. Sailhammer has noted that "their placement at this point in the book is part of the writer's plan to develop a central theological thesis. The first planks of this thesis were laid down in Genesis 1, where the writer shows that the center in God's purpose for creating humankind was his desire to bless them. ... Even after they fell away from God's protective care in the Garden of Eden, God let it be known that his plan for their blessing would not be thwarted by this act of disobedience."[493] Even when the leadership of the nation

---

[493] Sailhammer, *The Pentateuch as Narrative*, 405.

fails, as in the case of Moses' sin of violating the holiness of God (Num 20:11–
12), God will use whatever means necessary, even a pagan divination expert, to
accomplish his desire of blessing the nation.[494] The reversal of the plans of
human agents such as Balak to bring cursing and destruction to the people of God
is a theme that echoes throughout the pages of Scripture. Whether the enemy be
personified in an Egyptian pharaoh, Nebuchadnezzar of Babylon, Haman the
Agagite, or even the rebellious people of Israel in rejecting the gift of the Promised Land, God will act to accomplish his ultimate will for Israel and indeed for
all of humanity. The ultimate example in the Bible is evidenced in the crucifixion
of Jesus, in that what the Romans and Jews accomplished in putting to death the
one they thought to be a seditious individual named Jesus brought about the ultimate good for all of humanity.

Within the Book of Numbers the blessing and cursing theme in the ministry
of Balaam is the focus of 22:12; 23:7–11,13–26; and 24:1–19. The theme of
blessing is evidenced likewise in the terminology of Num 6:24,27, the priestly
blessing, and in the general sense in the varied themes of the vast population of
the Israelites that God delivered from Egypt, the gift of the Levitical priesthood,
the supply of the needs of the people in the wilderness, the gift of the Promised
Land, victory over their enemies, among others.

### Expressions of God's Anger

When God confronted Balaam while he was on his journey to Moab, God was
very angry with the prophet (lit., "the anger of God burned" — *wayyiḥar-ʾap
ʾĕlōhîm*).[495] Similarly Balaam turned his anger toward his donkey and beat him
in the pathway when the animal lay down under him (22:22,27). Later Balak
expressed his anger with Balaam for pronouncing blessing over Israel rather than
cursing (24:10). Only in 22:22 does the expression *ʾap ʾĕlōhîm* occur; in all
seven other cases in the Book of Numbers *ʾap YHWH* is employed in reference
to God's anger. The alternative use of *ʾĕlōhîm* in 22:22 rather than *YHWH* is due
to the literary structure as noted above.

### God's Sovereignty over the Nations

Throughout the Balaam oracles references are made to God's acts on behalf
of Israel and against the nations that surrounded them. Yahweh brought forth the
Israelites from the bondage of Egypt, and he would subdue any foreign power
that sought to conquer or oppress his chosen people (22:5,11; 23:22). The final
prophecy over Israel speaks of the One who would rise out of Israel to conquer
Moab (24:17), the immediate enemy in the historical context of the account, as
well as Edom (24:18–19). The concluding oracles denounce a variety of enemies
of Israel, including the Amalekites, Kenites, and Assyria (24:20–24). This theological tenet also relates to the above blessing and cursing theme, as God had
promised since the time of the call of Abraham to bless those who would bless

---

[494] Cf. Saul and the witch of Endor (1 Sam 28:1–25).

[495] Cf. the phraseology describing God's anger with Balaam (וַיִּחַר־אַף אֱלֹהִים) in 22:22 is
paralleled by that of Balaam's anger with his donkey (וַיִּחַר־אַף בִּלְעָם) in 22:27. Similarly the
expression וַיִּחַר־אַף יְהוָה and its equivalents are found in 11:1,10; 12:9; 25:3; 32:10,13,14.

Israel and curse those who cursed them. This theme would be reiterated through the history of the nation, even in the context of God's use of peoples like the Amalekites (Num 14:45), Assyrians, and Babylonians to exact discipline upon his people.[496] Israel would not be immune to this principle; they too would reap the curse of God if they rebelled against him (14:20–23,26–38; 34:55–56).

Elsewhere in the Book of Numbers God's dealing with the nations is seen in relationship to Egypt (noted above), the land of Canaan and its inhabitants (13:17–30; 21:1–3), and the Amorites (21:21–32) in the preceding chapters. In the concluding cycles of the Book of Numbers this theme is reiterated in the matter of the Midianites (31:1–11), the Egyptians (33:1–8), and in the challenge to drive out the Canaanites from the Promised Land (33:50–56).

### Sacrifices and Offerings

Not only does Balaam functions as prophet in the narrative, but he also performs priestly duties in the sacrificing of animals prior to the pronouncement of the first three oracles (23:1–6; 14–17; 27–29). The burnt offerings of bulls and rams are mentioned specifically in each of the passages, which were typically offered as acts of consecration by priests on behalf of themselves, the king, or the nation as a whole (Lev 1:2–17; 4:3–31). Elsewhere in the Book of Numbers, references to burnt offerings are made in the context of the offerings in the land (15:3–12) and in the list of the various festival offerings (28:1–29:40).

### God Reveals Himself

Expressions of God's revelatory encounters with Balaam utilize the same phraseology as that employed through the remainder of the Book of Numbers. In 22:8 Balaam responds to the emissaries from Balak in saying that he would only return with the message that God had spoken to him (*ka²ăšer yĕdabbēr YHWH ²ēlāy,* "just as Yahweh speaks to me"). Similar phraseology using the verb *dibbēr* ("he spoke, instructed") is used more than forty times in the book, providing one of the major organizing elements of the text.[497] Introductory phraseology to God's speaking with Balaam, whether directly, through his messenger, the angel of Yahweh, or through the donkey, and which uses the alternate Hebrew verb *²āmar* ("he said"), occurs in 22:9,12,20,28,30,32,35. The use of *²āmar* in this context continues the use of the same verb in the immediately preceding context following the rebellion of Moses and Aaron. In 20:7 Yahweh instructed Moses *(wayĕdabbēr YHWH ²el-mōšeh),* but after the irreverent striking of the rock, he spoke *(wayyō²mer YHWH)* with the prophet in 20:12,23; 21:8,16,34. The use of *²āmar* continues in 25:4 but then is reversed in 25:10, using the more familiar *wayĕdabbēr YHWH ²el-mōšeh* following the faithful response of Phinehas in adhering to Moses' instruction to kill the unfaithful idolaters of Baal Peor. Thus the verb usage enhances the whole reversal theme of the accounts of Balaam within the larger context of the Book of Numbers. Note the layout of the use of

---

[496] Cf. 2 Kgs 17:5–41; 24:17–25:21; Jer 7:1–8:3; Hab 1:5–8; etc.

[497] Cf. commentary on 1:1 and examples in 1:48; 2:1; 3:5,11,14,44; 4:1,21; 5:1,5,11; 6:1,22; 8:1,5,23; 9:1,9; 10:1; 13:1; 14:26; 15:1,17; 16:20,23; 17:1,16; 18:8,25; 19:1; 20:7; 25:10,16; 26:1,52; 28:1; 31:1; 33:50; 34:1,16; 35:1,9.

the Hebrew verbs *dbr* and *'mr* in "Appendix A: The Use of *dbr* and *'mr* in Num 19:1–26:1."

Now that the great prophet and leader had been restored, Yahweh revealed himself as he had done in the former times. But he would still suffer the consequences of his failure at the waters of Meribah Kadesh.

**¹Then the Israelites traveled to the plains of Moab and camped along the Jordan across from Jericho.**

GEOGRAPHICAL SETTING: ARABAH OF MOAB ALONG THE JORDAN ACROSS FROM JERICHO (22:1). **22:1** The conclusion to the journey motif in the Book of Numbers also serves as a historical introduction to the Balaam oracles. The geographical setting of "the plains of Moab along the Jordan across from Jericho" would be that of the remainder of the Book of Numbers, as well as that of Deuteronomy. The phraseology is repeated as the ending to the canonical book (36:13).

The Book of Balaam is introduced with the historical and geographical setting that connects the narrative with the previous and succeeding material. Following Israel's traversing the land of the Moabites, which had been conquered earlier by Sihon of the Amorites, the Lord had delivered the great kings Sihon of Heshbon and Og of Bashan into the hands of Moses and the Israelites (Num 21:10–35). With the hill country from the Arnon to the Yarmuk Rivers then secured and the Moabites now freed from Sihon's dominion, the Israelites positioned themselves in the plains of Moab, having come through the mountains of Abarim (Num 33:48). The phrase "plains of Moab" (*'arbôt mô'āb*) describes the southern Jordan Valley on the east side of the river opposite Jericho and just north of the Dead Sea. Geologically the potentially arable lands of the Jordan Valley between the Dead Sea and the Galilee has two levels due to the parallel fault lines running generally in a north-south direction. The lower terrace closest to the river is called in the Arabic the *zhor,* and the upper terrace is known as the *ghor.* Together these plateaus immediately opposite Jericho (lit., "the Jordan of Jericho") are about eight to ten miles wide, narrowing to the north to about four to five miles. Two towns in the area are noted elsewhere in Numbers, namely Shittim (25:1, or Abel Shittim in 33:49) and Beth Jeshimoth (33:49). While encamped on the northwestern corner of the Moabite territory, the leader of the nation senses a need to act expeditiously to address this potentially threatening mass of people. The phraseology recurs with some minor variations in 26:3; 33:48,50 and as the conclusion to the book in 36:13.

**²Now Balak son of Zippor saw all that Israel had done to the Amorites, ³and Moab was terrified because there were so many people. Indeed, Moab was filled with dread because of the Israelites.**
**⁴The Moabites said to the elders of Midian, "This horde is going to lick up**

everything around us, as an ox licks up the grass of the field."

So Balak son of Zippor, who was king of Moab at that time, [5]sent messengers to summon Balaam son of Beor, who was at Pethor, near the River, in his native land. Balak said:

"A people has come out of Egypt; they cover the face of the land and have settled next to me. [6]Now come and put a curse on these people, because they are too powerful for me. Perhaps then I will be able to defeat them and drive them out of the country. For I know that those you bless are blessed, and those you curse are cursed."

[7]The elders of Moab and Midian left, taking with them the fee for divination. When they came to Balaam, they told him what Balak had said.

[8]"Spend the night here," Balaam said to them, "and I will bring you back the answer the LORD gives me." So the Moabite princes stayed with him.

[9]God came to Balaam and asked, "Who are these men with you?"

[10]Balaam said to God, "Balak son of Zippor, king of Moab, sent me this message: [11]'A people that has come out of Egypt covers the face of the land. Now come and put a curse on them for me. Perhaps then I will be able to fight them and drive them away.'"

[12]But God said to Balaam, "Do not go with them. You must not put a curse on those people, because they are blessed."

[13]The next morning Balaam got up and said to Balak's princes, "Go back to your own country, for the LORD has refused to let me go with you."

[14]So the Moabite princes returned to Balak and said, "Balaam refused to come with us."

CYCLE I: FIRST MESSENGERS SENT TO BALAAM (22:2–14). The process of procuring the services of the renowned Balaam of Pethor is recounted in three cycles, with the first two focused on the dispatching of Moabite and Midianite emissaries to the prophet-diviner who receives direction from the Lord regarding his due response, and the final devoted to the encounter with the emissary from Yahweh (the angel of the Lord). As shown in the literary/rhetorical outline of this material, the focal point of each chiastically structured pericope is the revelatory encounter between the Lord and Balaam. In the final ironic and satiric encounter Balaam is shown to be less perceptive than his donkey as the angel of the Lord appears to them on their journey to Moab, yet it is he who the Lord will use to pronounce resplendent blessing upon his chosen people Israel.

*Balak Sees—Moab Fears the Numerous Israelites (22:2–4).* **22:2–4** In the beginning Balak is introduced simply as the son of Zippor who had observed the movement and success of Israel against the Amorites who had formerly controlled the Moabites during the reign of Sihon of Heshbon (21:26). He is only identified as the king of Moab at the end of this secondary inclusio, which structurally outlines as:

So he observed    Balak son of Zippor    all that Israel had done to the Amorites
  Moab dreaded greatly    from before the people because they were numerous
  Moab was alarmed    from before the children of Israel
    Moab allies with Midian (proverbial description)
Now Balak son of Zippor was king of Moab at that time.

The description of Balak as king does not necessarily mean that Moab was organized as a national entity as this time, since the Hebrew term *melek* can refer to a tribal chieftain, the head of a city within a larger region of cities with common ethnic origin, or a national king.[498]

One of the keys in this passage is found in the use of the Hebrew verb *rāʾâ*, which means "to see with understanding" and "to have a clear comprehension of the matters at hand." Balak has not only watched literally the movement of the vast population of the Israelites, but he has been made aware of the dramatic victories and potential threat of this people who were now encamped within the reaches of his fledgling domain. Balak's seeing of Israel is amplified by the two ominous verbs that follow, for Moab was filled with terror and dread as they were faced with the prospect of a fate similar to that of the kingdoms of Sihon and Og. Thus he saw as his only resort to reach beyond the confines of his kingdom and thus the realm of his god Chemosh and his consort Ashtar for obtaining divine intervention into his impossible situation. His gods had been ineffective against Sihon of the Amorites and would have thus been even less effective against the Israelites and their God Yahweh.

The vast numbers of the Israelites and their potential to cause considerable damage to the peoples and economies of Moab and Midian is enhanced by the reciting of a proverbial figure concerning the effect of an ox upon the land. As the powerful ox consumes the grasses of the land, so Israel was occupying the fertile plateau of the Moabite plains along the east side of the Jordan opposite Jericho. The Moabites were concerned enough to share their need with the leaders of Midian, with whom we soon learn the Moabites were allied in sending for help from Balaam of Pethor. The effect of the alliance on Israel will recur in the Baal Peor incident of Numbers 25 in which both Moabite and Midianite women served to draw Israelite men into immorality and idolatry. That incident would then provide rationale for the retribution taken against the Midianites in Numbers 31, in which Phinehas functions as the priestly leader and Balaam is killed in the military engagement.

*First Messengers Sent (22:5a).* **22:5a** The language used of the sending of messengers is that of formal diplomatic correspondence, often includ-

---

[498] E.g., "king of [city]" in Gen 14:18; 20:2; Josh 10:3; 11:1; 12:1,9–24. For "king of [a people], which can be tribal, see Gen 36:31ff., and for "king of [region] see Josh 10:3; 11:10.

ing written communication. Hence, Balaam is a prophet-diviner of eminent proportion to have received this group of official emissaries from an alliance of peoples such as Moab and Midian.[499] Through the history of interpretation, several attempts have been made to further denigrate the character of Balaam by suggesting an ignominious meaning to his name. Allen suggested the name was a corruption by the prophetic writers of the Old Testament, meaning "devourer of the people."[500] But whether or not the name was originally of a pejorative nature, the evidence from the Deir ʿAlla inscription views him in a positive light as a seer of the gods.

Balaam is said to have resided in "Pethor, near the River" (22:5), a site that has been identified with the city Pitru, situated almost thirteen miles south of Carchemish on the Sajur River tributary of the Euphrates.[501] The NIV phraseology "his native land" translates *ʾereṣ běnê-ʿammô* ("land of the sons of his people"), which some have identified alternately as "the land of the sons of Amau."[502] Though some scholars have posited the possibility that *ʿammô* may refer to the nearby region of Ammon, Deut 23:4 is quite explicit in placing Balaam's homeland in Aram Naharaim, the region of the upper Euphrates and its twin tributaries, the Khabur and the Balikh. The identification of Pethor with Pitru would make the journey between Moab and Pethor a distance of approximately 420 miles, probably taking twenty-two to twenty-five days each direction. Four such legs, with even brief time in between treks of the various entourages, would then mean that the correspondence process would have taken nearly four months minimum. Meanwhile the Israelites are inhabiting the valley plains within sight of several mountain peaks overlooking from the southeast.

*The Message: Curse the Mighty Israel (22:5b–6).*   **22:5b–6** Balak's correspondence with Balaam commences with a statement regarding Israel's deliverance from Egypt, a prominent theme of Numbers and the rest of the Old Testament, though his words do not acknowledge that it was the God of Israel who delivered them from bondage. That might indicate an affirmation of the existence and power of the Israelite deity. Israel is compared to a locust plague that is devouring the resources of the land (lit, "conceals the eye of the land") on the northwestern perimeter of Moab.[503] Similar phrase-

---

[499] Balaam texts of Deir ʿAlla, Combination I, lines 1,4.

[500] Allen, "Numbers," 887.

[501] Note Pedru of the annals of Thutmose III ca. 1467 B.C.; later Pitru in the annals of Shalmaneser III (859–24); *ANET*, 278.

[502] This alternative derives from a possible reading of Egyptian and Mari (Akk.) texts. See W. F. Albright, "Some Important Recent Discoveries: Alphabetic Origins and the Idrimi Statue," *BASOR* 118 (1950): 11–20, esp. 15–16, n. 13. Idrimi, the fifteenth–fourteenth century B.C. king of Alalakh, is said to have ruled over the regions of Mukishkhe (later Meshech?), Ni, and Amau.

[503] Milgrom, *Numbers,* 186.

ology is used in Exod 10:5,15 to describe the imminent locust plague upon Egypt that Moses predicted should the pharaoh refrain from setting the Israelites free from bondage. Though in his entreaty Balak does not ascribe Israel's deliverance to their God, the assistance he seeks from Balaam has everything to do with the divine. He wants Balaam to invoke a divine curse upon Israel that would weaken both them and their God enough to allow him to gain victory and drive them from his territory.

Ancient Near Eastern texts recount the power of priests and prophets to discern, intervene, and even manipulate the will of the gods through means of augury, special sacrificial rituals, and oral pronouncement of blessing or cursing.[504] Knowledge of the ways, works, and the occasional whims of the divine and the skill at cajoling or manipulating these various deities into bringing benefit to the human realm (or detrimental effects toward one's enemies) was a highly prized craft. The power to curse one's enemies via ritual and oral pronouncement would be an invaluable gift whereby the upper hand could be gained on the divine level and military victory achieved in the human sphere. A parallel to the use here of the Hebrew *ʾārar* ("to pronounce a curse") is found in an Akkadian text, which reads:

> May the great gods of heaven and the nether world **curse** him *(li-ru-ru),* his descendants, his land, his soldiers, his people, and his army with a baneful curse; may Enlil with his unalterable utterance **curse** him with these curses so that they speedily affect him.[505]

Balaam had apparently achieved international fame for his ability to carry out such activity, and thus Balak could commend him in recognition of the effectiveness of his prophetic practice, saying, "I know that those you bless are blessed and those you curse are cursed." This element of acknowledgment and praise for the one being entreated would often come earlier in the letter, but the direness of the situation warranted the presentation of the ominous circumstances. If Balaam could successfully invoke a curse upon Israel, his territory would be delivered from potential defeat and destruction, and the Moabites would have the freedom they enjoyed before being overwhelmed by Sihon of the Amorites.

*Elders of Moab and Elders of Midian Journey to Pethor to Meet Balaam (22:7).* **22:7** The Moabite and Midianite elders journey to Pethor with the communiqué in hand in order to procure the services of Balaam. These men were somehow versed in divination or associated with this discipline, for the Hebrew phrase reads "and divinations were in their hands." The NIV

---

[504] See M. Weinfeld, "Ancient Near Eastern Patterns in Prophetic Literature," in *The Place Is Too Small for Us: The Israelite Prophets in Recent Scholarship* (Winona Lake: Eisenbrauns, 1995), 32–49.

[505] CAD, I, "A" Part II, 235; R. Harper, "Code of Hammurabi," xliv, 83,89.

translation, "taking with them the fee for divination," may seem inappropriate since 22:37 and 24:11 indicate that Balaam was to be rewarded following his successful cursing of Israel. Milgrom suggested that these men possessed some skill or perhaps even divination instrumentation that might somehow help in the negotiations with Balaam.[506] Ashley notes on the other hand that the Hebrew qĕsāmîm can mean either the divination practice or elements or the fees charged for the exercising of the trade.[507] Gray suggested this was a form of remuneration that was to be offered as a down payment or, as he called it, "an earnest of what he might receive."[508] The practice of divination was condemned summarily in Deut 18:10 along with a host of other practices, such as acts of sorcery, interpreting omens, engaging in witchcraft, casting spells, or conjuring up the dead.[509] Fees for such activities, however, are generally called gifts (minḥâ), and the former suggestion of Milgrom is to be preferred. After the journey of several weeks, the elders met with Balaam and formally presented their message and case to him.

*Balaam's Response (22:8).* **22:8** The initial meeting with Balaam is recounted in summary fashion with focal point. The actual details of such a meeting would have entailed the standard hospitality process of formal greetings, the sharing of preliminary gifts, the sharing of a meal, and probably an extended discussion of the events precipitating this visit, and then the formal presentation of the letter. However enticing the personal and professional opportunity might have seemed to Balaam, he evidences caution in responding to the elders of Moab and Midian. He must consult with the divine prior to answering their request, especially since the job would entail an encounter with the God of Israel.

As noted above in the parallels between the Book of Balaam and the rest of Numbers, the terminology denoting the revelatory encounter closely resembles that used of Yahweh's revelatory encounters with Moses and the great prophet's faithful response to his God. The typical phraseology in Numbers for the Lord revealing himself to Moses is wayĕdabbēr YHWH ʾel-mōšeh lēʾmōr ("Then Yahweh spoke to [instructed] Moses, saying").[510] In this verse Balaam utilizes the same verb-subject sequence in saying yĕdabbēr YHWH ʾēlāy ("Yahweh speaks to [instructs] me"). Now Balaam

---

[506] Milgrom, *Numbers*, 187.

[507] Ashley, *Numbers*, 447, following a large number of scholars, including A. Dillmann, *Das Bücheri Numeri, Deuteronomium und Joshua* (Leipzig: Hirzel, 1886), 143; Gray, *Numbers*, 329; Noordzij, *Numbers*, 203; Noth, *Numbers*, 176; Sturdy, *Numbers*, 163; de Vaulx, *Les Numbres*, 266; Budd, *Numbers*, 249; Harrison, *Numbers*, 295.

[508] Gray, *Numbers*, 329.

[509] Cf. also Deut 18:14; 1 Sam 15:23; 2 Kgs 17:17; Isa 2:6; Ezek 21:29; Mic 3:6–7.

[510] See 1:1; 2:1; 3:5,11,14; etc. See comment on 1:1.

as the substitute Moses encounters the One True God who reveals himself to mankind.[511] The encounter is set in a simple chiastic form, with the revelatory clause at the focal point of the verse.

Balaam said, Sleep here tonight and I will return to you
The word according to that which Yahweh speaks (instructs) to me.
So the princes of Moab dwelled with Balaam.

Balaam was about to encounter deity in a way that would transcend any other manner he had experienced. References to Yahweh and divine speech have led some interpreters to believe that Balaam was a believer in Yahweh, the God of Israel, particularly in the phraseology of 22:18, "I could not do anything great or small to go beyond the command of the LORD my God." Allen takes Balaam's words here and elsewhere as braggadocio.[512] But the writer uses them to preface the idea that Balaam is about to become a somewhat unwitting instrument of God for revelation and blessing for Israel. It is also possible that the actual message sent from Balak via the elders of Moab and Midian may have been more extensive than the portion recorded in vv. 5b–6, including a reference to the God of Israel. Being a prophet who had encountered a variety of deities during his extensive career, Balaam may have been saying that he would seek an initial word from the deity whom the enemies of Balak worshiped. Though he names the name of Yahweh God of Israel, he is not a devotee of Yahweh but only his agent in the revelatory process. Thus Balaam became an instrument of the One True God who desires to reveal himself to humanity and to teach these non-Israelites something of his incomparable character.[513] Later this prophetic-diviner would show his true colors by instigating the idolatrous immorality at Baal Peor, and for the rest of biblical history his name would be synonymous with moral and ethical degradation.[514]

*God's Encounter with Balaam (22:9–12).* **22:9–12** God comes to Balaam—and not Balaam to God—at the beginning of this revelatory relationship, and in the process of God revealing himself to Balaam, the name of God is always Elohim instead of Yahweh. Balaam again is a substitute for Moses, but not his replacement. The question posed to Balaam was rhetorical, since God obviously knew who these men were and why they were there. This method of commencing an encounter between God and man

---

[511] Note the Hb. כַּאֲשֶׁר יְדַבֵּר יְהוָה ("just as Yahweh instructs me') in this verse as compared to the phraseology of כַּאֲשֶׁר צִוָּה יְהוָה ("just as Yahweh commanded ...") in 1:19,54; 2:34; 5:4; 8:22; 26:4; etc.

[512] Allen, "Numbers," 887.

[513] Cf. the response of Abimelech and his men to Isaac in Gen 26:28.

[514] Cf. Num 31:8,16; Deut 23:3–6; Josh 13:22; 24:9–10; Neh 13:1–3; Mic 6:5; 2 Pet 2:15–16; Jude 11; Rev 2:14. See also the discussion of the role of Balaam in Allen, "Numbers," 888.

recalls similar expressions in Gen 3:9 between God and Adam and Gen 4:9 between God and Cain. Balaam's response to God echoes the words of the message sent by Balak of Moab, with only slight variation, such as in the use of two synonyms for cursing, namely *ʾārâ* ("to pronounce a curse") in v. 6 and in v. 11 *qābâ*. Repetition of this type is quite common in Hebrew narrative.[515]

God's word to Balaam was to refuse the invitation of Balak's emissaries. Milgrom notes that three times in the Hebrew Bible God appears to non-Israelites "in order to warn them not to carry out their intentions."[516] The Israelites as descendants of the patriarchs Abraham, Isaac, and Jacob had been promised unending blessing by God through their history, and in the initial blessing by God in Gen 12:3, Abram was promised that any attempt to curse his future descendants would be reverted back to the one cursing. God himself would carry out retribution against any person, nation, or other entity who would endeavor to execrate or exterminate his people. He had rescued Joseph from prison and delivered this fledgling nation from the hand of the Egyptian pharaoh, the head of one of the most powerful nations on earth in that day. Time after time he would act faithfully to his promise in preserving, delivering, providing for, and blessing his people. What God has blessed, no human can curse.

*Balaam's Response of Refusal (22:13).* **22:13** Like Balaam of the Deir ʿAlla texts, the prophet arose that morning after his encounter with God and returned with the essence of the word he had received from on high in that night dream. As in Balaam's initial response to Balak's emissaries, the prophet is said to have spoken the name of Yahweh, the God of Israel. He did not repeat the matters related to cursing or blessing but simply stated that Yahweh had refused to grant him permission to journey with them back to Moab.

*Messengers Return Home to Moab (22:14).* **22:14** In the coordinating element with vv. 22:5a,7 in the structure of this passage that forms an inclusio, the Moabite messengers whom Balak had sent to Balaam are seen returning dejectedly to their leader. They repeated the very words that Balaam had ascribed to Yahweh in his refusal to acquiesce to their request. Balaam responded obediently to the revelation granted him by God, but Balak knew only that the prophet had refused his invitation, not that it was Israel's God who had revealed himself to Balaam.

**15Then Balak sent other princes, more numerous and more distinguished than the first. 16They came to Balaam and said:**

---

[515] E.g., Gen 22:1–18; Exod 9:8–9; Lev 16:6,11; Num 7:1–89 (repetition nearly identical for each of the twelve tribes); Josh 13:1; etc.

[516] Milgrom, "Numbers," 187. Cf. Gen 31:24 with Laban and Gen 20:3 with Abimelech.

"This is what Balak son of Zippor says: Do not let anything keep you from coming to me, [17]because I will reward you handsomely and do whatever you say. Come and put a curse on these people for me."

[18]But Balaam answered them, "Even if Balak gave me his palace filled with silver and gold, I could not do anything great or small to go beyond the command of the LORD my God. [19]Now stay here tonight as the others did, and I will find out what else the LORD will tell me."

[20]That night God came to Balaam and said, "Since these men have come to summon you, go with them, but do only what I tell you."

[21]Balaam got up in the morning, saddled his donkey and went with the princes of Moab.

CYCLE II: SECOND SET OF MESSENGERS SENT TO BALAAM (22:15–21). *Messengers Again Sent to Balaam (22:15–17).* **22:15–17** Dissatisfied with the initial response from Balaam, Balak sends a second diplomatic corps of higher ranking officials from his administration. In the cyclical structure of the initial encounters with Balaam, this verse compares to v. 5 in which the messengers are deemed *malʾākîm*, the generic term for diplomatic couriers who would convey correspondence between kings or high ranking officials. These men are described as "high princes who were greater than these," that is, in comparison to the former envoy. The phraseology *śārîm rabbîm wĕnikbādîm mēʾēlleh* could be translated "more noble and honorable princes than these," meaning that they were honored *(nikbādîm)* chieftains or leaders from the clans of Moab who were sent to offer Balaam exceedingly great honor (*kî-kabbēd ʾăkabbedkā mĕʾōd*, "For I will indeed bestow honor upon you greatly," v. 17), which would be conferred by Balak upon Balaam when the prophet had accomplished the desire of the king. The monetary implications of this honor is reflected in Balaam's response in v. 18. An abbreviated form of the original message requesting Balaam's expertise in pronouncing a curse upon Israel is reiterated here. The message commences with the phraseology often referred to as the messenger formula, "Thus says Balak," often used by the latter prophets in introducing an oracle from Yahweh.[517]

*Balaam's Response to Balak's New Messengers (22:18–19).* **22:18–19** In the succeeding narrative the diplomatic engagement of these honored officials with Balaam is now telescoped by comparison with the initial encounter, moving directly to Balaam's response. Balaam's initial answer addressed the issue of the honored reward offered by these nobles on behalf of Balak; the Moabite king's palace could not contain enough gold and sil-

---

[517] C. Westermann, *Basic Forms of Prophetic Speech* (Philadelphia: Westminster, 1967), 90–96; cf. among the scores of examples Jer 2:1,5; 6:6,9,16,21; Ezek 16:3,36,59; 25:8,12,15; 26:7,15,19; Amos 1:3,6,9,11,13; 2:1,4,6; etc.

ver to convince the prophet to prevail upon the command of Yahweh. He
could do absolutely nothing that would transgress or violate the revelation
he would receive from Yahweh. The phraseology used here to describe Balaam's inability to transgress the word or command of Yahweh, *la'ăbōr 'et-
pî YHWH* (lit., "to cross over the mouth of Yahweh") compares exactly with
that used in Num 14:41 of the Israelites who had disobeyed the Lord's command not to try to enter the land after they had rejected his gracious gift at
the advice of the majority of the spies.[518] In Num 24:13 the same terminology is used in a similar context of Balaam's inability to transgress the word
of Yahweh. Similar phraseology, using the verb *mārâ* ("rebel"), is used of
Moses and Aaron's violation of the holiness of God in the striking of the
rock at the Waters of Meribah.[519] Thus Balaam's bold proclamation in
22:18–19:

> I would not be able to violate the word of the LORD (Yahweh) my God
> In doing little or much. So now you shall indeed stay here tonight,
> And I will know what more Yahweh may instruct (speak to) me."

Several authors have suggested that the narrator's use of Elohim in contrast to placing the name Yahweh in Balaam's words is meant to convey the
narrator's intent to denigrate Balaam's character. Noordzij saw the narrator's
use of *'ĕlōhîm* when referring to a pagan god or the multiplicity of gods
who were at Balaam's disposal as a polytheist, and thus Balaam's use of the
name of Israel's God was one of fraudulent boasting.[520] As Ashley rightly
points out, however, the use of the intensive plural in forms such as *'ĕlōhîm*
all occur in the construct state with suffixes or with reference to a person, a
group of people, or a place. Ashley summarizes, "Had the narrator intended
to convey that Balaam was fraudulently claiming visions from Yahweh,
while actually being inspired by a pagan 'evil spirit,' he could have been
much plainer about it."[521] Instead Balaam's words echo the reality that he
had indeed had an encounter with the God of Israel, through which the true
Elohim had confronted and revealed himself to the pagan diviner. Yahweh
God of Israel will use whatever means he desires to reveal himself to
humanity, even if it is an individual who seems the absolute antithesis of
what kind of an instrument he would normally utilize. In the narrative he has
become the substitute for the great prophet Moses, who had recently fallen.
In a similar manner God had revealed himself to the Egyptian pharaoh in the
days of Joseph (Gen 41:1–40) and later to Nebuchadnezzar (Dan 2:17–
19,45).

---

[518] Cf. also 1 Sam 12:14–15; 15:24; 1 Kgs 13:21.
[519] Cf. אֲשֶׁר־מְרִיתֶם אֶת־פִּי in Num 20:24 with לַעֲבֹר אֶת־פִּי יְהוָה in the present passage.
[520] Noordzij, *Numbers*, 203–4.
[521] Ashley, *Numbers*, 448.

*God's Second Encounter with Balaam (22:20).*  **22:20**  As was likely
the case in the initial episode, the second encounter of God *('ĕlōhîm)* with
Balaam occurred at night, a time often recounted in the Hebrew Bible for
revelations, dreams, visions. Such was the setting for Abimelech of Gerar
(Gen 20:3–7), Laban (Gen 31:24), Nebuchadnezzar (Dan 2:1–30; 4:1–8),
Daniel (Dan 2:19), and Zechariah (Zech 1:8), and the same is told of Balaam
in the Deir 'Alla inscriptions.[522] The narrator again does not tell us what
means if any Balaam might have used to attempt to engage Yahweh in this
encounter. In the reverse of typical Hebrew Bible narration where stories,
didactic, and halakhic materials are often told in expanding circles, the story
here is abbreviated.

Unlike the result of the first encounter with God, this time Balaam is permitted to make the journey to the land of Moab, but his role will remain the
same. He would be authorized only to speak the word God revealed to him.
The NIV text loses the literary flavor of the repetition from vv. 8,18–19.
Note the wording parallels below:

22:8      I will bring back to you the **word** according to what Yahweh **speaks** to me
22:18     I am not able to transgress the word (mouth) of Yahweh my God, to **do**
22:19     I will know what more Yahweh **speaks** to me
22:20     Only the **word** which I **speak** to you, that you will **do**

Balaam is and will be on the journey constrained by Yahweh to reveal and
accomplish only that which the God of the blessed nation Israel will allow. At
this point in the narrative the reader might ask the question, If God has relented
on his prohibition of Balaam making the journey to Moab at the behest of
Balak, might he now change his mind and permit Balaam to curse this nation
he had punished in times past? As Ashley notes, "This kind of ambiguity
maintains reader interest and prolongs the drive to the climax of the story (as
does the story of the donkey that follows in vv. 22–35)."[523]

*Balaam Departs with Messengers (22:21).*  **22:21**  In response to the
newly revealed message from God, Balaam prepares for the journey of four
hundred miles from Pethor to Moab in the southern Levant, a trek of perhaps
three weeks' duration. This verse completes the second cycle of correspondence between Balak and Balaam involving diplomatic messengers, and it
introduces the reader to the next key character in the story, that of his female
donkey *('ātôn).* As Ashley has observed, only in Judg 5:10 and 2 Kgs 4:22
are female donkeys described as riding animals, usually the male donkey
*(ḥămôr)* was utilized.[524] This element may also serve to heighten the irony
and satire of the story to follow—that a female pack animal is more attuned

---

[522] Combination 1, line 1; see "Balaam and the Texts from Deir 'Alla" (above).
[523] Ashley, *Numbers,* 451.
[524] Ibid.

to the ways and means of Yahweh than one of the noblest of the world's prophetic divination experts.

²²But God was very angry when he went, and the angel of the LORD stood in the road to oppose him. Balaam was riding on his donkey, and his two servants were with him. ²³When the donkey saw the angel of the LORD standing in the road with a drawn sword in his hand, she turned off the road into a field. Balaam beat her to get her back on the road.

²⁴Then the angel of the LORD stood in a narrow path between two vineyards, with walls on both sides. ²⁵When the donkey saw the angel of the LORD, she pressed close to the wall, crushing Balaam's foot against it. So he beat her again.

²⁶Then the angel of the LORD moved on ahead and stood in a narrow place where there was no room to turn, either to the right or to the left. ²⁷When the donkey saw the angel of the LORD, she lay down under Balaam, and he was angry and beat her with his staff. ²⁸Then the LORD opened the donkey's mouth, and she said to Balaam, "What have I done to you to make you beat me these three times?"

²⁹Balaam answered the donkey, "You have made a fool of me! If I had a sword in my hand, I would kill you right now."

³⁰The donkey said to Balaam, "Am I not your own donkey, which you have always ridden, to this day? Have I been in the habit of doing this to you?"

"No," he said.

³¹Then the LORD opened Balaam's eyes, and he saw the angel of the LORD standing in the road with his sword drawn. So he bowed low and fell facedown.

³²The angel of the LORD asked him, "Why have you beaten your donkey these three times? I have come here to oppose you because your path is a reckless one before me. ³³The donkey saw me and turned away from me these three times. If she had not turned away, I would certainly have killed you by now, but I would have spared her."

³⁴Balaam said to the angel of the LORD, "I have sinned. I did not realize you were standing in the road to oppose me. Now if you are displeased, I will go back."

³⁵The angel of the LORD said to Balaam, "Go with the men, but speak only what I tell you." So Balaam went with the princes of Balak.

³⁶When Balak heard that Balaam was coming, he went out to meet him at the Moabite town on the Arnon border, at the edge of his territory. ³⁷Balak said to Balaam, "Did I not send you an urgent summons? Why didn't you come to me? Am I really not able to reward you?"

³⁸"Well, I have come to you now," Balaam replied. "But can I say just anything? I must speak only what God puts in my mouth."

CYCLE III: GOD'S MESSENGER SENT TO BALAAM (22:22–38). *Introduction: God's Anger with Balaam (22:22a).*    **22:22a**    Balaam's third encounter with the God of Israel commences with a statement of God's becoming angry with the prophet's going to Moab. Scholars for ages have attempted to understand the motive for God's anger with Balaam, since

Balaam presumably was making the journey at the behest of God. Ashley and Milgrom offered a solution in taking the Hebrew particle *kî* as temporal, hence "while he was going" God became angry with him.[525] Still the problem remains as to the cause of the anger. The phraseology (*wayyiḥar-ʾap* *ʾĕlōhîm*[526]) recalls the expression of God's anger with persons in a rebellious state, as with the people at Taberah (11:1), with Miriam and Aaron (12:9), and later with the people at Abel Shittim in the Baal Peor incident (25:3). The rabbinical tradition in the Targumic literature interpreted this sequence as evidence of Balaam's personal rebelliousness in embracing the idea that he might eventually be successful in pronouncing a curse on Israel. Thus taking Ashley and the rabbis in tandem, the verse would refer to God becoming angry with Balaam while he was on the journey because he still thought he might curse the people of Yahweh. That Balaam was lacking spiritual insight at this point in the journey narrative is evident from the context that follows.

That God would become angry and engage one of his servants on a journey directed by him follows the enigmatic pattern echoed in the Pentateuch in the lives of Moses on his way back to Egypt (Exod 4:24–26) and Jacob at Peniel (Gen 32:22–32). These incidents seem to serve the purpose of reminding these men that a holy God is in control of the situation and the lives of his people and that they as his servants should be faithful to the tasks assigned to them to carry out God's plans. Lest Balaam think he might ply his prophetic trade of his own accord and reap a considerable reward from the king of Moab, God confronted him in his rebellious state of mind—that state of mind that prevented him from seeing God's emissary in the road three separate times. A female donkey, presumably the epitome of stupidity and stubbornness in that day, was more spiritually perceptive than this renowned prophet. That an angel with a sword would appear to Balaam and his donkey recalls the similar motif of the cherubim with the flaming sword in the Garden of Eden after the fall of man (Gen 3:24), of the emissary who confronted Joshua on the way to Jericho (Josh 5:13–15), and the angel sent to destroy Jerusalem and confront King David (1 Chr 21:14–30). These theophanies served to remind humanity of the absolute holiness of God and the subservient role of men before a sovereign deity.

---

[525] Milgrom likewise notes the use of כִּי־הֹולֵךְ here as a "verbal reference to v. 21b, illustrating the technique used by the redactor to lock the ass episode into place here. For other similar examples of this editorial technique, see Josh 3:17; 4:1–10; Judg 6:6,7–10; 1 Sam 17:57; 18:6; 23:14,15–18" (*Numbers,* 320, n. 59). Milgrom cites the investigative and interpretive work of A. Rofé, *The Book of Balaam* (סֵפֶר בִּלְעָם) [Hebrew](Jerusalem: Sinai, 1979), 56.

[526] Note the BHS suggestion to read Yahweh with the Samaritan Pentateuch and several Masoretic and Septuagint manuscripts. This would bring the phraseology into conformity with the expressions of Yahweh's anger in 11:1; 12:9; and 25:3.

*The Angel of Yahweh Appears (22:22b).*   **22:22b**   The emissary of Yahweh, the *malʾak YHWH*,[527] positioned himself in front of Balaam and his female donkey as an angelic adversary, *śāṭān*, wielding a sword in his hand. This is not an explicit or even veiled reference to the Satan of the heavenly court depicted in the Book of Job (Job 1:6–2:10)[528] who questioned the faithfulness of men to God. Nor is this figure what Gray referred to as "a temporary appearance of Yahweh in human form."[529] Harrison rightly called him the "surrogate for the Lord Himself," who is distinguished from God (v. 31).[530] Yet clearly this messenger speaks the words of God as echoed in the familiar refrain in v. 35, "That which I speak to you, it shall you speak."[531] Balaam was accompanied by two of his servants (*ûšĕnê nĕʿārāyw*, "and two young men"), the standard number of men who attended a leading individual on a long journey.[532] Several critical scholars have suggested that the shift from the attendant "princes of Moab" in v. 21 to "his two servants" in v. 22 represents a change in source materials, from the Elohist to the Yahwist.[533] The diplomatic envoys from Balak have not disappeared; as accessory characters in the story they simply are not in focus at this juncture of the narrative. The key characters are Balaam, Balak, the donkey, Yahweh God, and his emissary the angel of Yahweh.

*The Donkey Responds (22:23).*   **22:23**   Upon each of three occasions the donkey evidences clear perception of the appearance of the messenger from the Lord, and she turns aside presumably in fear of its life. Each time the pathway of diversion grows narrower, from an open road, to a rock-pile walled pathway through the vineyards, to a narrow passage in which there was no possibility of circumventing the divine emissary. There off the side of the road in open country the incognizant and self-absorbed prophet responds negatively to the astute animal by beating the animal with perhaps a rod, stick, or staff. A righteous man would care for the needs of his animal (Prov 12:10), yet Balaam would later threaten to kill the donkey with a sword (v. 29). An astute prophet who studied animal behavior should have realized that something extraordinary was happening. But his pride was severely injured in the presence of his young attendants, and he responded like an infidel.

---

[527] This phrase occurs ten times in vv. 22–35.

[528] A similar scenario is envisioned in the Apocryphal Genesis text from the Qumran caves in the account of Abraham and Isaac in the Moriah mountain region. In that text the request of Abraham to sacrifice Isaac resulted from a Satanic challenge to the faithfulness of the patriarch.

[529] Gray, *Numbers*, 333. Cf. also Noordzij, *Numbers*, 208; Noth, *Numbers*, 179; Snaith, *Numbers*, 176.

[530] Harrison, *Numbers*, 298.

[531] Cf. v. 20, See also 22:8,19.

[532] As with Abraham and Isaac on the three-day journey to the land of Moriah (Gen 22:2–5).

[533] E.g., see Budd, *Numbers*, 256–65; de Vaulx, *Les Nombres*, 256–65.

*The Angel of Yahweh Appears Again (22:24).*   **22:24**   The second cycle
in the encounter between the emissary of Yahweh and the pagan diviner took
place in the context of a vineyard, and hence a more arable region typical of
the area near Pethor or in proximity to the Transjordan region of the southern Levant such as in the Golan/Bashan region or the highlands of Gilead.
These areas were known in ancient times, as they are today, for their vineyards and high quality wine production. Walls made of piled stones were
created in the process of clearing the land for planting and also marked the
boundaries between neighboring vineyards.

*Donkey Responds Again (22:25).*   **22:25**   In this narrow passageway
the donkey again rightly perceived the intent of the Lord's emissary block-
ing the further advance of the prophet. Having little room to avoid the
sword-wielding angel, the donkey pressed against the rock wall to the point
where Balaam's foot was squeezed severely between the side of the donkey
and the stones. The prophet's raised ire resulted in a second whipping of the
observant beast for what the injured Balaam perceived to be a case of progressive disobedience.

*The Angel of Yahweh Appears the Third Time (22:26).*   **22:26**   As so
often is the case in Hebrew narrative, stories are recounted in three cycles
with the third receiving considerable expansion over the preceding contexts.[534] In this case at the conclusion of the third encounter between God
and Balaam stands the third encounter between the angel of Yahweh and
Balaam with his donkey. The intensity of the narrative is heightened as this
revelatory experience receives considerable expansion, revealing that only
as a result of divine intervention is the prophet finally enabled to see Yahweh's emissary. God's intervention takes on extraordinary proportions
through the opening of the heretofore unintelligible mouth of a lowly female
donkey who is enabled to communicate with a human, and through the
unveiling of the eyes of an incognizant prophet whose training and expertise
in the ways of deity had not equipped him to see the divine representative
standing directly in front of him.

*Donkey Responds the Third Time (22:27).*   **22:27**   Unable to find even
the slightest gap between the appearance of the angel of Yahweh and the
sides of this narrow alleyway, the donkey collapses onto its knees and then
to its belly and lay down with the prophet still mounted in his riding position. Now instead of Yahweh being angry with Balaam (v. 22), Balaam
became extremely angry with the seemingly self-consumed animal.[535] But
it was Balaam who was focused on his own wants, desires, and problems

---

[534] Cf. Gen 1:1–3:24. Note also Harrison, *Numbers,* 299; G. Wenham, *Numbers,* 170–71. Harrison notes a variety of threefold repetitions in this account.

[535] Note the verbal parallel between v. 26, בִלְעָם אַף־וַיִּחַר, and v. 22, אֱלֹהִים אַף־וַיִּחַר.

and as a result was even more unseeing in the weightier issue of God's presence. He beat the animal a third time and now more severely, "with his staff."

*God's Third Encounter with Balaam (22:28–35).*  **22:28–35**  The story of the revelatory process between God and Balaam then took a dramatic turn filled with ironic and comedic dimensions. Not only was the female donkey more observant spiritually, but her normally unintelligible braying mouth was opened in such a manner that as she spoke Balaam understood her. Harrison remarked, "Balaam's insensitivity to the Lord's presence made it necessary for God to open the mouth of the donkey before Balaam's own eyes could be opened."[536] As a result of this final encounter with God along the journey, Balaam would realize fully his role of speaking only that which Yahweh had revealed to him.

This marvelous account of God using whatever means he so desires to reveal himself has enamored readers from the laity to the scholars, and the response to the occurrence has ranged widely. The interpretations generally fall into one of three categories as outlined below.

1. That the donkey's mouth was mobilized so as to speak in an audible human voice. Milgrom suggests that God "gave the ass the power of speech" in the manner that he empowered Ezekiel to speak after a period of silence (Ezek 3:27; 33:22) and Balaam himself later in the account.[537]

2. That the donkey's normal process of braying was heightened such that it was perceived and interpreted by Balaam in a human verbal manner. In Harrison's opinion, "As the donkey brayed, she conveyed a message of anger and resentment that the seer understood in his mind in a verbal form and to which he quite properly responded verbally. ... Through her opened mouth the braying animal retaliated against her undeserved treatment by uttering sounds that were unintelligible to the other onlookers but that Balaam was able to comprehend through processes of mental apperception that are not well understood." Harrison compared the phenomenon to the sound many perceived as thunder when the voice came from heaven confirming the coming glorification of the Father through the death of Christ (John 12:27–33), to that of early Christian charismatic speech, which was intelligible only through an interpreter (Acts 2:3–13; 1 Cor 12:10), and to the voice of Jesus as he spoke to Saul of Tarsus on the road to Damascus (Acts 9:4).

3. That the story was a legendary account created for didactic purposes and as such has no basis in a factual event. In this case the phenomenon need not be explained.

Either of the first two options acknowledges the reliability of the event,

---

[536] Harrison, *Numbers,* 300.
[537] Milgrom, *Numbers,* 191.

since Balaam heard the voice of the donkey in a way that was interpretable in a verbal manner. Wenham suggested that "it is immaterial to the story whether the donkey really spoke, or whether Balaam just imagined it talking." On the other hand he clearly states that "if men were able to utter God's words, why should not the same be true of animals?"[538]

Wenham emphasizes the threefold nature of the encounters: "The ass was caught three times between the angel's sword and Balaam's stick. Soon Balaam will find himself trapped three times between Balak's demands and God's prohibitions."[539] Balaam's conversation with God via the donkey occurs in three stages, and in the third round the angel of the Lord commences his dialogue with the prophet by asking a question similar to that which the donkey posed in her first speech, "Why have you beaten your donkey these three times?" The elements of reversal in the story are further enhanced by the statement that apart from the spiritual insight of this animal Balaam would have been the one killed rather than his donkey. The brief chiasmus in vv. 31–33 also enhances the narrative effect.

Then Yahweh uncovered Balaam's eyes and said "Why?"
(a)   Behold I have come out as your adversary,
  (b)   The donkey saw me and turned away from
(a')  So now I should kill you, and yet let her live."

Having had an authentic encounter with the truly Divine, Balaam responded in the manner that anyone who so meets with God is constrained to respond. He bowed his head and fell prostrate (*wayyištaḥû lĕʾapāyw*, "and he fell prostrate upon his face" or "he worshiped") before the emissary of Yahweh as a servant would before his master.[540] Once he had comprehended the full significance of this extraordinary situation, he confessed the error of his ways. Based on the nature of the usage of the Hebrew verb *ḥāṭāʾ* and the statements of Balaam following this confession, one derives that Balaam was simply stating that he had made a mistake in not perceiving that Yahweh's emissary was positioned in front of him in the various pathways he had traversed. As in this case the confession need not carry with it connotations of moral or ethical turpitude from the expressed statement of the prophet, though we would make such an assessment of his character based upon his later actions in advising the Moabites in the idolatrous incident at Abel Shittim (Num 25).

The words of the final instructions to Balaam by Yahweh's emissary are

---

[538] Wenham, *Numbers*, 171.
[539] Ibid.
[540] Ashley notes the word pair וַיִּקֹּד וַיִּשְׁתָּחוּ is used in Gen 24:26,48; 43:28; Exod 4:31; 12:27; 34:8; 1 Sam 24:9; 28:14; 1 Kgs 1:16,31 in reference to the actions of a person of a lower societal echelon before one of greater status (as derived from *HALAT* 283–84; *Numbers*, 458).

couched in a simple chiastic structure, which once again emphasize the role of the prophet as an instrument for divine revelation.[541]

> (a) "Go with the men;
> **(b) but only the word I speak to you, you shall speak."**
> (a') So Balaam went with the princes of Balak

Now having encountered the Lord in the daytime after two previous nighttime revelations and fully cognizant of his divinely ordained role in the coming days, Balaam dutifully continues his journey to meet with Balak. He has learned, as D. Olson has put it, "that the life of a prophet is like riding a donkey. Balaam's own personal ability to steer the course of history and see what lies ahead is minimal, less than the animal on which he rides. Lest Balaam have any thought he can make an end run around God, the angel teaches Balaam that he must lay down his own initiative in cursing or blessing Israel and allow God to use him as God sees fit."[542]

*Balak Goes out to Meet Balaam (22:36–38).*  **22:36–38**  Balak, having finally received word that the reluctant Balaam was nearing his kingdom, journeys out to meet and welcome the famous prophet at the town of Ir (or Ar)[543] of Moab on the edge of his realm.

The Arnon River gorge functioned as the classical northern limit of the ancient Moabite territory (21:26), though in the Iron II period, the Moabites expanded northward to Heshbon and beyond. Allen notes a comedic element in the story of Balak going out to meet the prophet. The sense of urgency is evident in Balak's rush to meet Balaam so that he can begin the job of cursing Israel, but he berates the prophet by his critical questioning concerning the delay. Balak's personal involvement in the greeting ceremony was a means of paying high honor to the visiting prophetic dignitary. He could have simply sent his servants to the territorial border to formally greet the party and then have them escorted into the king's presence in the capital city's royal residence. Instead Balak accompanied Balaam along the stages of the journey to the point where Balaam would begin performing his prophetic divination service.

Balak's greeting commenced with stern questions concerning Balaam's

---

[541] See above vv. 8,18,20.

[542] Olson, *Numbers,* 145.

[543] The NIV reads "the Moabite town," which translates עִיר מוֹאָב, similar to NKJV and others as "the city of Moab" (NEB). Cf. Gen 24:10. The Hb. phrase could refer to a town known as ʿIr-Moab or simply ʿIr and could perhaps be the equivalent in the Moabite dialect of ʿAr-Moab of Num 21:15,28, in the proverbial sayings concerning Sihon and Moab (Milgrom, *Numbers,* 193). Harrison rightly notes that none of the ancient versions follows this alternate reading. A suggested identification for ʿIr (ʿAr) is El-Medeiyim, which overlooks the Wadi es-Sfei, a NE tributary just to the east of Aroer. Other historical geographers place ʿAr well south of the Arnon and thus would not fit the current criteria for this city to be on the border of Moab. Cf. Num 21:28.

initial reluctance to come as a result of the diplomatic messengers sent in the first round of negotiations. The Moabite king's next question gave indication of his own interpretation of the prophet's turn down of his first offer. He believed that the issue of reward was at the heart of the matter, but in fact Balaam's real concern was that he speak on that which had been revealed to him by the God he was being asked to confer with regarding the Israelites.

> Now am I in fact able to speak anything?
> The word which God places in my mouth
> That I will speak.

For the fourth time in the Book of Balaam, the prophet confesses that he could only speak that which Yahweh revealed (lit, "the word which God puts in my mouth, it I will speak"; *haddābār ʾăšer yāśîm ʾĕlōhîm bĕpî ʾōtô ʾădabbēr*).[544] He apparently has now come to the full realization that he will simply be God's instrument of revelation; he will be a spokesman for this God of Israel and not one who could even attempt to manipulate him. He does not, however, inform Balak at this point of his earlier revelation, that God had said he could not curse Israel because they were to be the recipients of his blessing. Ordinarily he might think that with the right sacrifices, incantations, and cultic manipulations the desired result could be accomplished. But Yahweh God of Israel was a different kind of deity from any he had ever or would ever encounter in his ministry.

**39Then Balaam went with Balak to Kiriath Huzoth. 40Balak sacrificed cattle and sheep, and gave some to Balaam and the princes who were with him.**

PREPARATION FOR THE FIRST ORACULAR EVENT (22:39–40). **22:39–40** Balaam and Balak journeyed to Kiriath Huzoth, where they prepared for the next divine encounter by which the Moabite king still expected the prophet to fulfill his commissioned duty of cursing Israel. Balaam still had not informed Balak of the content of the message he had first received from Yahweh, that he must not pronounce a curse upon Israel because they were a blessed people (22:12).

The name and location of "Kiriath Huzoth" (lit., "city outside [plazas]") presents an enigma in light of recent excavations from Tel Dan in northern Israel. In the excavations around the perimeter of the plaza of the Iron II gate area, the director A. Biran notes the discovery of several buildings that may have served the city in an official capacity, for oversight of daily commercial activity.[545] Were these the offices of city officials who were overseers of the

---

[544] Cf. 22:8,18,19, plus once by God in 22:20, and the angel of Yahweh in 22:35.

[545] A. Biran, "New Discoveries at Tel Dan," presentation at the Annual Meeting of the American Schools of Oriental Research and the Society of Biblical Literature, Boston, November 1999.

bartering and selling of agricultural goods and crafted wares in the gate courtyard? Were they smaller shops adjacent to the wider plaza? So was this a city of shops, bazaars, or just the proper name of a Moabite town whose toponymic derivation was that of its original function? Harrison suggested that the town probably was in close proximity to the Kir of Moab, the probable capital of Moab.[546]

In Kiriath Huzoth the king slaughtered cattle and sheep for the celebration, which would have been the normal hospitable practice for visiting dignitaries. The sacrifices probably were the peace offerings, which were of the communal type eaten by the worshiper, the priests, and any guests.[547] Admittedly Ashley is correct in stating that "there is no proof ... that the Moabite cult was anything like the Israelite cult in sacrificial matters";[548] the slaughtering of animals for a ceremonial banquet was common to Semitic peoples. Peace offerings are known among the Northwest Semitic peoples of Ugarit and Aram, and because of the commonality of cultures these offerings were likely practiced among most of them. Similar hospitality practices are known in the New Testament in the study of the return of the wayward son in Luke 15:11–32.

Another approach to the interpretation of the sacrifices has been taken by several scholars, that the sacrifices described in v. 40 were actually preparatory sacrifices for the divination process that would follow the next morning. Allen and Harrison have suggested that Balak delivered to Balaam and his attendants certain portions of the slaughtered animals, such as the liver or other entrails, which they could examine according to the principles of their profession.[549] The context, however, does not necessarily warrant the importing of divination ritual into this setting. Those who were present with Balaam are called princes *(śārîm)*, perhaps leaders from one of the sending peoples, the Moabites or Midianites, or even royal attendants and not necessarily priestly agents of Balaam or Balak. Part of the question lay in the function of *wayĕhî* at the beginning of v. 41. If it functions disjunctively, since *wayĕhî* often commences a new development in the story, then the connection between the sacrifices (or slaughtering) that evening and the rituals of the following day is lessened. If the function is one of succession, then perhaps a connection may be made between the two periods of action in the story.[550] Preference here is for the sacrifices of Balak

---

[546] Harrison, *Numbers,* 304. Kir of Moab has been equated with the biblical Kir Hareseth and identified by Aharoni with el-Kerak in the west-central Moabite plateau *(Land of the Bible,* 56).

[547] Cf. Exod 18:12; 1 Sam 9:22–27; Neh 8:9–12. See also Milgrom, *Numbers,* 193; Gray, *Numbers,* 339.

[548] Ashley, *Numbers,* 462.

[549] Allen, "Numbers," 895; Harrison, *Numbers,* 304. Note also perhaps Olson, *Numbers,* 145. Hepatoscopy, e.g., is known among the baru prophets as a means of determining omens, along with the reading of the patterns of the internal lining of other organs such as the intestines or stomach.

being a ceremonial meal of hospitality and the activities of the following day (NIV, "The next morning" (lit. *wayĕhî babbōqer*, "and it happened in the morning") were the commencement of the sacrificial activity to determine the will of God. In the former case only Balak is said to be slaughtering the animals, and Balaam would surely have overseen the ritual slaughtering of the bulls and rams if they were intended for prophetic use.

[41]The next morning Balak took Balaam up to Bamoth Baal, and from there he saw part of the people.

[1]Balaam said, "Build me seven altars here, and prepare seven bulls and seven rams for me." [2]Balak did as Balaam said, and the two of them offered a bull and a ram on each altar.

[3]Then Balaam said to Balak, "Stay here beside your offering while I go aside. Perhaps the LORD will come to meet with me. Whatever he reveals to me I will tell you." Then he went off to a barren height.

[4]God met with him, and Balaam said, "I have prepared seven altars, and on each altar I have offered a bull and a ram."

[5]The LORD put a message in Balaam's mouth and said, "Go back to Balak and give him this message."

[6]So he went back to him and found him standing beside his offering, with all the princes of Moab. [7]Then Balaam uttered his oracle:

"Balak brought me from Aram,
    the king of Moab from the eastern mountains.
'Come,' he said, 'curse Jacob for me;
    come, denounce Israel.'
[8]How can I curse
    those whom God has not cursed?
How can I denounce
    those whom the LORD has not denounced?
[9]From the rocky peaks I see them,
    from the heights I view them.
I see a people who live apart
    and do not consider themselves one of the nations.
[10]Who can count the dust of Jacob
    or number the fourth part of Israel?
Let me die the death of the righteous,
    and may my end be like theirs!"

BALAAM'S FIRST ORACLE (22:41–23:10). The oracular events in which Balaam responds to his encounter with Yahweh by speaking forth the message which has been revealed to him are recounted in three cycles with an epilogue of additional oracles completing this most dramatic revelatory event. The cyclical pattern of the three phenomenal occurrences follows a basic structure as outlined below:

---

[550]*IBHS*, 33.2 (547–54).

1. Balak takes Balaam to an observation point to view Israel
   (22:41; 23:13–14a; 23:27–28)
2. Balaam instructs Balak to offer sacrifices (23:1; missing; 23:29)
3. Balak obeys Balaam by sacrificing the prescribed animals
   (23:2; 23:14b; 23:30)
4. Balaam tells Balak to stand by his offering altars (23:3;
   23:25; missing)
5. Balaam goes alone and Yahweh reveals himself (23:4–5; 23:16;
   24:1–2)[551]
6. Balaam returns to Balak, who is standing by his offering
   (23:6; 23:17; missing)
7. Balaam obeys Yahweh and speaks the oracle (23:7–10; 23:18–24;
   24:3–9)

The focal point of the structure of these three cycles is the revelatory encounter
between Yahweh and Balaam. In 23:5 and 16 Balaam's central role as a spokesman for Yahweh reiterates that which has been spoken of previously in
22:8,18–20,35,38. Balaam would be able to speak only that which Yahweh had
spoken to him. In the third oracular cycle the complementary elements 4 and 6
are absent though the oracle itself is as long as that of the second event. Since
the text tells us that Balaam no longer resorted to divination practices in the
third period of preparation (24:1), the practice of "standing by the offering"
may have been part of the special ritual activity Balaam dispensed with on this
third occasion. In the process and at the conclusion of these events, Balak king
of Moab would discover that subservience to Yahweh the God of Israel was the
key to success. Balak was obedient to Balaam in hope of gaining the desired
response, but Balaam was in turn constrained to be obedient only to Yahweh,
who reigns over all kings and kingdoms.

*Balak Leads Balaam to Bamoth Baal (22:41).*    **22:41** From an elevated location known as Bamoth Baal (*bāmôt bāʿal,*"the cultic centers of
Baal")[552] from which he could observe the outer fringe (*qĕṣēh hāʿām*) of
the populous Israelites, Balaam would commence his service of the king of
Moab. Positioning himself at vantage point from which he could see the
object of cursing ritual was necessary for the pronouncement to be efficacious. Some have associated Bamoth Baal with Bamoth of Num 21:19–20
from which the Israelites sent messengers to Sihon requesting permission to
pass through his territory and with Bamoth Baal of Josh 13:17 in the territo-

---

[551] In the structure of the third oracle, Balaam does not journey off alone to encounter God.

[552] The KJV reads "high places of Baal," which is followed by the NASB in translating the term
בָּמוֹת בָּעַל. The LXX reads the singular ἐπὶ τὴν στήλην τοῦ βααλ ("upon the stone [stele] of
Baal"), and hence not a proper name. Noth concurred: "That *bāmôt baʿal* is to be understood as a
proper name of a place is, in spite of Josh 13.17, quite unlikely" (*Numbers,* 182).

rial list of the tribe of Reuben. Whether or not this phrase is descriptive of the site of the proper name, the function is clear. The ubiquitous northwest Semitic deity Baal had been worshiped at the site for some time, and hence at a site dedicated to the veneration of a pagan deity, the pagan divination prophet Balaam and his royal beckoner Balak were about to learn of the ways and words of the One True Deity.

*Balaam Instructs Balak to Prepare Sacrifices (23:1).* **23:1** Balaam provided instructions for Balak to construct seven altars to carry out the sacrifices that were preparatory for the encounter with the divine. The special significance of the number seven as a symbol of fullness or completeness is attested throughout the Scriptures, as well as in ancient Near Eastern and Greco-Roman literature. From the seven days of creation in Genesis 1–2 to numerous references to various groups of seven in Revelation,[553] the number is prominent throughout the Bible.[554] The building of multiple altars in a single setting is unattested elsewhere in the Old Testament, though a close parallel is known from Mesopotamian literature. R. Largement cites the reference to a Babylonian text in which a worshiper is instructed to "erect seven altars before Ea, Shamash, and Marduk, to set up seven censers of cypress, and then pour out [as a libation offering] the blood of seven sheep."[555] When these rituals had been performed, the worshiper then appeared before the deity and announced to him or her that the offerings had been properly presented. The deity or deities then were obliged to respond to the individual in whatever manner desired.

In the Israelite sacrificial system, offering of bulls and rams represented the upper echelon of society. A bull was offered as a sin offering by a priest

---

[553] E.g., the seven churches addressed in Revelation 1–3, seven seals, the Lamb with seven horns and seven eyes which were the seven spirits of God, the seven angels with seven trumpets, seven plagues, and the seven bowls of God's wrath.

[554] See also from the Hebrew Bible, the importance of the seventh month (Tishri) for the festival calendar (Day of Trumpets—Rosh Hashanah, Day of Atonement—Yom HaKippurim, and the week-long Feast of Booths—Sukkoth in Num 29:1–39), the counting of the omer for seven weeks (sevens) connecting Passover with Shavuoth—Pentecost (Lev 23:15–18), the Sabbath day, the sprinkling of the blood of the sacrificial animal seven times for a sin offering (Lev 4:6; 16:14,19), the seven days of isolation or seven days of purification for various kinds of uncleanness (Lev 13:5,21,26,32,50; Num 6:9; 19:12,14,16,19; etc.), and numerous other examples. The first oracle of Balaam also is composed of seven lines of short parallel clauses.

[555] R. Largement, "Les oracles de Bileam et la mantique suméro-akkadienne," in *Memorial du cinquantenaire 1914–1964* (Paris: Travaux de l'Institut de Paris, 1964), 46. Cf. also Virgil's *Aeneid* 6,38–39, in which seven head of cattle and seven sheep were offered, and Job 42:7–9. M. S. Moore has cited several parallels between the Book of Job and the Book of Balaam, including "(1) emphasis on proper facilitation of *dābār*, (2) wrath of Yahweh, (3) presence of *śāṭān*, (4) employment of the seven bulls and seven sheep, (5) both describe the ritual as a ʿōlâ, and (6) tandem activity (Balaam and Balak // Job and Eliphaz/Bildad/Zophar" (*The Balaam Traditions: Their Character and Development,* SBLDS 113 (Atlanta: Scholars Press, 1990), 105, n. 27.

(including the high priest) who had committed an unintentional sin or on behalf of the whole Israelite community (Lev 4:3,14), and guilt offerings included the sacrifice of an unblemished ram (Lev 5:14–6:6). The offering of seven bulls and/or seven rams is paralleled in Gen 21:27–28; 1 Chr 15:26; Job 42:7–9; and Ezek 45:23. As in the present context, the sacrifices of Job 42 and Ezekiel 45 are deemed burnt offerings, those that were offered for consecration or sanctification of the presenting party.

*Balak Obeys Balaam (23:2).* **23:2** Balak's faithful obedience to the instruction of Balaam, who is functioning now as a divine intermediary, recalls the same phraseology used of Moses and the Israelites responding to Yahweh's commands in Numbers 1–17.[556] Balak had no idea that he was forwarding the cause of those whom he sought to destroy, abetting the pronouncement of blessing upon his enemies. Through the Balaam material, the prophet has said and would continue to say that he could speak only in accordance with what God had revealed to him. Now Balak too becomes an inadvertent agent of the God of Israel. The purpose of such offerings in the ancient Near East was twofold: to gain the favor of the deity by the performing of purification ritual and to obtain from the bodies of the sacrificial victims the portions necessary to determine the will of the gods. In that Balak and Balaam offered up a bull and a ram on each altar, the divination artiste would have had considerable animal entrails to examine in preparing to encounter the incomparable God of Israel. The Hebrew text does not provide the details of such divination activity, since biblical writers in general were reticent to offer such information on ritual incantation.[557]

*Balaam to Balak: Stand Beside Your Burnt Offering (23:3).* **23:3** The ritual of standing by one's offering is attested in the Mesopotamian *āpilu* practice of having a proxy such as the king's representative "stand by" the slaughtered animal. In this case the king himself, since the king often functioned as high priest in Semitic cultures, offered the sacrifices on behalf of his people, whom he thought were threatened by the mighty Israel. As Balaam prepared to go off alone to a nearby locale in expectation of meeting with God, he spoke the words now all too familiar to the company of hearers: "The word which he reveals to me I will tell you." Earlier he had encountered God twice during the night while alone in his house and then later during the day through Yahweh's emissary. The use of the Hebrew particle *ʾûlay* ("perhaps, perchance") denotes a degree of

---

[556] The Hb. phraseology וַיַּעַשׂ בָּלָק כַּאֲשֶׁר דִּבֶּר בִּלְעָם parallels that of Num 5:4 in which the Israelites did as Yahweh spoke in matters of purification כַּאֲשֶׁר צִוָּה יְהוָה. Cf. בְּנֵי יִשְׂרָאֵל כַּאֲשֶׁר דִּבֶּר יְהוָה אֶל־מֹשֶׁה כֵּן עָשׂוּ in Num 1:19 and אֶת־מֹשֶׁה כֵּן עָשׂוּ וַיַּעֲשׂוּ בְּנֵי יִשְׂרָאֵל כְּכֹל אֲשֶׁר צִוָּה יְהוָה of 1:54; in addition to 2:34; 3:51; 4:49; 5:4; 8:4,20,22; 9:5,23; 10:13; 15:36; 17:11.

[557] B. Levine, *In the Presence of the Lord: A Study of Cult and Some Cultic Terms in Ancient Israel,* SJLA 5 (Leiden: Brill, 1974), 23.

contingency in the words of Balaam, for he desired a meeting with Yahweh in the manner of his former encounters. But he had come to realize through the confrontation with his donkey and the angel of Yahweh that this God can reveal himself in some unexpected ways. The use of the *niphal* form of *qārā²* ("he met") also implies a degree of chance. Milgrom notes, "It is used deliberately here and in vv. 3,15,16 and in the context of a divine manifestation elsewhere only in Exod 3:18; 5:3, in an address to a foreigner whose encounter with God cannot be counted on."[558] The text leaves the option of responding to Balaam in the hands of God.

Where Balaam went after leaving the presence of Balak and the sacrifice-laden altars is somewhat of an enigma. The NIV reads "barren height" in taking the Hebrew term *šepî* as singular of the plural term *šĕpāyîm* used in Isa 41:18; 49:9; Jer 3:2,21; 4:11 to describe desolate areas without vegetation, often arid hills in or near deserts.[559] Some translators take the term to mean "alone" rather than a geographical locale.[560] But in fact the usage of the term may not refer to an elevated location at all, only a barren place. The poetic parallelism of Isa 41:18 would indicate that it could actually be an arid lowland.

I will make rivers flow unto [upon] the *šĕpāyîm*,
    And springs within the valley;
I will turn the desert into pools of water,
    And the parched ground into springs.

If Balaam left Balak and moved toward the Israelite encampment in the valley, he could have moved to an even lower elevation.

*God Manifests Himself to Balaam (23:4–5).* **23:4–5** Balaam's somewhat tentative expectations were realized when God met him at this barren place. According to the ritual sequencing of his tradition, he announces to God that he has performed his ritual duty.[561] The phraseology of Yahweh's

---

[558] Milgrom, *Numbers,* 320, n. 12.

[559] As found in the NIV, NKJV, NRSV, or the NASB version, "bare hill." Note also another possible occurrence in the singular in the *ketiv/qere* reading of Job 33:21. That such a location was an elevated mound or hill is not demanded by the singular or plural usage of the term in those few occurrences in the Hebrew Bible; contra Milgrom, who argues against the "barren height" because he thinks that if this were intended a form of the verb עלה would be used to describe Balaam's movement toward such an elevated location (*Numbers,* 195). But this is not the same term or phrase (בָּעָה גִּבְהָה) that is most used to refer to the hills where idolatrous activity was so prolific, mentioned in Deut 12:2; 2 Kgs 14:23; 2 Kgs 16:4; 17:10; 2 Chr 28:4; Jer 2:20; 13:27; 17:2; Hos 4:13. The term may simply describe a barren setting for Balaam's meeting with God. Noordzij offers another alternative that demands some textual emendation. Interpreting the MT as representing the result of haplography, he emends the text to read וַיֵּלֶךְ לכשפו, thus meaning "Then he went to his sorceries." Though the alternative is creative and perhaps appealing from the standpoint of Balaam's profession, there is no textual attestation to support this reading.

[560] Milgrom with support from the Tgs and R. Rashi.

[561] See comment on 23:1 above.

revelation and instruction to Balaam, whereby he "put a message in Balaam's mouth" *(wayyāśem YHWH dābār bĕpî bilʿām)* that he was return to Balak and speak *(tĕdabbēr)*, echoes the earlier statements by Balaam that he could not transgress the word of Yahweh (22:18) but speak only the word God put in his mouth (22:38). The cycle of material reflecting the preparation of the prophet to fulfill God's intention in proclaiming blessing upon his people was now complete. Note the following structural outline of the revelatory clauses up to this point.

*lōʾ ʾûkal laʿăbōr ʾet-pî YHWH ʾĕlōhāy* (22:18)
> I am not able to transgress the mouth of Yahweh my God

*wĕʾak ʾet-haddābār ʾăšer-ʾădabbēr ʾēleykā ʾōtô taʿăśeh* (22:20)
> But only the word that I speak to you, it shall you do

*wĕʾepes ʾet-haddābār ʾăšer-ʾădabbēr ʾēleykā ʾōtô tĕdabbēr* (22:35)
> Nothing but the word which I speak to you, it shall you speak

*wayyāśem YHWH dābār bĕpî bilʿām* (23:5)
> Then Yahweh put a word in the mouth of Balaam

The idiom of having Yahweh put a word in the mouth of an individual, denoting the receiving of a direct revelation from Yahweh, is used of several of the Hebrew prophets. In Deut 18:18 it is used of prophets in general, and then specifically of Yahweh to Jeremiah (Jer 1:9) in his call experience. In Ezekiel an alternate form of this idiomatic expression is portrayed in the prophet's eating a scroll, after which he spoke God's message to the house of Israel (Ezek 3:1–11). The ultimate expression of this phrase is found in Num 12:8, where Yahweh describes his communication with the great prophet Moses as *peh ʾel-peh*, "mouth to mouth." In the Balaam material the phraseology of Balaam speaking the mouth of Yahweh is repeated in vv. 12,16.

*Balaam Returns to Balak (23:6).*  **23:6**  Upon his return Balaam finds Balak and his Moabite princes faithfully standing by their altars and their accompanying sacrifices, eagerly awaiting those longed-for words that Balaam has been able to pronounce a curse upon their enemy Israel, enabling them to mount a victorious attack against their dreaded foe. As Allen notes, however, "They received a word from heaven all right, but it was far from what they expected."[562]

*Balaam Obeys Yahweh: Speaks the First Oracle (23:7–10).*  Each of the oracles conforms to the following basic pattern: (1) introductory formula, "Balaam took up his oracle," (2) statement of purpose, (3) message of the oracle—blessings upon Israel in the first three oracles, transition in the fourth from blessing Israel to cursing Moab and Edom, followed by three oracles of cursing against the Amalekites, Kenites, and Assyrians. Each of the seven oracles is called a Hebrew *māšāl*, to perhaps distinguish these

---

[562] Allen, "Numbers," 896.

pagan-sourced pronouncements from the normal prophetic oracle. The term *māšāl* commonly denotes a proverb or short parable from the wisdom sources, such as the Book of Proverbs, but it is never used to designate the dicta from the biblical prophets of Yahweh.[563] Gray has elucidated various usages of the term beyond that of the proverb, citing the use of the term to introduce lament in Job 27:1ff.; 29:1ff.; or to denote bywords or objects of taunting in Isa 14:4; Mic 2:4; Deut 28:37. In the present context the term denotes a prophetic figurative discourse in poetic form, which Noordzij describes as having "a deep meaning or with more or less cryptic allusions, which is easily memorized by its form, and creates curiosity and stimulates reflection because of its content."[564]

The antiquity of the language of theses oracles has been argued since the landmark literary work of Albright in a 1944 in an article entitled "The Oracles of Balaam." Albright cited terms, literary structures, and grammatical nuances that would support the dating of the oracular material to the twelfth century B.C. and the final composition of the narrative framework by the end of the tenth century B.C., after a considerable period of oral transmission.[565] Harrison, on the other hand, suggested that the Hebrew *šōṭĕrîm* had probably collated the oral and written traditions and updated many of the expressions by the time of Samuel in the late twelfth to early eleventh centuries B.C. In a forthright statement Wenham summarizes the issues related to the antiquity of the material, "The archaic Hebrew spelling of these poems and their metre prove the early date of their composition."[566] Freedman dates the present text of the Balaam oracles to the eleventh century B.C.[567]

The initial oracle is composed of seven lines of short parallel clauses, each having somewhat condensed content and poignant stylistic word order. The broad literary outline of the oracle is as follows:

### Literary Structure of the First Oracle of Balaam

A  Setting: Balak Summons Balaam to Curse Israel          (23:7b)
  B  Balaam Cannot Curse what **God (El)** has not cursed.  (23:8)
  B′ Israel Incomparable among the Nations                 (23:9–10a)
A′ Balaam Longs to be like Israel                          (23:10b)

The ensuing translation reflects the microstructure of the individual lines.

---

[563] Often in the former and latter prophets the phrase יְהוָֹה נְאֻם is employed, but also in Num 14:28 and six times in the Balaam oracles (24:32,4,152,16).

[564] Noordzij, *Numbers*, 216. Cf. also BDB, מָשָׁל, 605.

[565] Albright, "The Oracles of Balaam," *JBL* 63 (1944): 207–33. Cf. also D. Vetter, *Seherspruch und Segensschilderung*, CTM 4 (Stuttgart: Calwer, 1974).

[566] Wenham, *Numbers*, 173.

[567] D. N. Freedman, "Divine Names and Titles in Early Hebrew Poetry," in *Pottery, Poetry, and Prophecy* (Winona Lake: Eisenbrauns 1980), 90.

| | | | |
|---|---|---|---|
| 1. From Aram | he brought me | Balaq | (23:7b) |
| The king of Moab | from the mountains of Qedem (the East) | | |
| 2. "Come | curse for me | Jacob | (23:7c) |
| and Come | Denounce | Israel | |
| 3. How can I curse | [what is] not accursed | of God | (23:8) |
| and How can denounce | [what] has not denounced | Yahweh | |
| 4. For from rocky peaks | I see him | | (23:9a) |
| and From the heights | I watch him | | |
| 5. Behold a people | distinctive | are dwelling | (23:9b) |
| and Among the nations | not | is he reckoned | |
| 6. Who has counted | the dust of Jacob | | (23:10a) |
| Or numbered | [even] a fourth of Israel? | | |
| 7. May it die | my life (soul) | the death of the upright | (23:10b) |
| and May it be | my end | like his! | |

Structurally, the first couplet contains a brief chiasmus in complementary parallelism with the second line expanding on the first as to the geographical origin of Balaam. At the emphatic center is the beckoning king who instigated this whole episode. The second reflects synonymous parallelism, highlighting the word pair Jacob/Israel, which is repeated in line six and then twice in the second oracle and once in each of the final two oracles. In the third line the rhetorical questions couched in explanatory synonymous parallelism highlight the prophet's inability to countermand the intent of God to bless Israel. These questions are a reprise of the original response received by Balaam from Yahweh when the messengers were sent to procure his services (22:12). In lines 4–6 the prophet declares in resounding fashion the distinctiveness of Israel among the nations as a result of his distant observation and his unique experience in receiving revelation from a most distinctive God. In the explanatory parallelism of the final stich the prophet proclaimed that he wished he could be as blessed as Israel.

**23:7b** Aram denotes the general region of the upper Euphrates from which Balaam has journeyed.[568] The term is qualified in Scripture in the toponyms Aram Naharaim ("Aram of the Two Rivers"), from which Rebekah was brought as a bride for Isaac (Gen 24:10),[569] and Paddan Aram ("Field of Aram"), the region where Rebekah's brother Laban resided (Gen 25:20).[570] Balak has summoned Balaam from his homeland, perhaps some four hundred miles away, to pronounce a curse upon Israel and to denounce (zā'am, "indignant speech") them so that he might be victorious over them.

**23:8** Balaam retorted rhetorically that the cursing of Israel was an utterly impossible proposition in light of the divine blessing Yahweh had

---

[568] More specifically Aram Naharaim in Deut 23:4.

[569] Also the region from which the oppressor Cushan Rishathaim came (Judg 3:8). See also Deut 23:5.

[570] Cf. also Gen 28:2,5–7; 31:18; 33:18; 35:9,26.

bestowed upon his people. As Balak had noted in his original request to Balaam, this prophet-diviner was internationally renowned as one who was effective in exacting both blessing and cursing on individuals and groups. He would do so by sacrificial activity accompanied by imprecations and execrations through which the gods and goddesses might be conjured into accomplishing that which his employers desired. But now he had encountered an incomparable God who had promised to bless an unparalleled people.

**23:9** As Balaam viewed the populous Israelites from his vantage point, he observed that they were a "people who live apart" *(ʿām lĕbādād yiškōn)*, which means that they lived apart from the other nations in safety and security as recipients of Yahweh's blessing.[571] Israel's election by God to be his own demonstrated to the nations that they were a distinctive and peculiar people who belonged to a jealous God who was like none others from among the nations. According to the foundational covenant conditions recorded in Exod 19:5–6, Israel was Yahweh's treasured possession, who as a result of this election were to obey fully the stipulations of the covenant and be a holy nation and a kingdom of priests.[572] Although they had endured the trials and tribulations as a consequence of their rebellions in the wilderness, God was intent on bringing the nation into the Promised Land and blessing them abundantly.

**23:10a** Evidence of God's election of Israel and the fulfillment of his promise to Abram to make a great nation through him and bless him was the dramatic growth of the population while enduring the hardship and oppression in Egypt (Gen 12:2–3; 13:16; Exod 1:7,10; 12:37). This theological point is reiterated in the initial military census of Num 1:1–46 and 2:1–32, and again in the second census of Num 26:1–51. In the Book of Balaam this issue was initially raised by Balak in his message to Balaam (22:3–5). Now it has been confirmed by the prophet himself.

The parallel clauses of counting the dust of Jacob and numbering the fourth part of Israel result from a minor emendation of the second colon of the Masoretic Text, which literally reads "and the number of the fourth of Israel." The Samaritan Pentateuch (and the LXX) contain evidence of a variation from the Masoretic *mispār*, which is divided into two words with *spr* being read as a verb form rather than a noun *(mî sāpār*, "who can number"). Albright suggested that the text be further emended to read *turbaʿat yisrāʾēl*, "the sands/dust-cloud of Israel," since the particle *ʾet* does not elsewhere occur in ancient Hebrew poetry.[573] Keil suggested that the Masoretic

---

[571] Cf. the use of this clause in Deut 33:28, Ps 4:9; Jer 49:31; and Mic 7:14.

[572] Note also Deut 7:6; 10:14–15; 14:2; 26:18; Ps 135:4; Mal 3:17. This theology carries over into the NT in Rom 9:2–11:36; Eph 1:14; Titus 2:14; and 1 Pet 2:9.

[573] Albright, "The Oracles of Balaam," *JBL* 63 (1944): 213, n. 28.

reference to the "fourth" part of Israel was an allusion to the fourfold division of the nation as described in Numbers 2.[574] Balaam's ability to see the outskirts of Israel (22:41) would refer to one of the groups of three tribes and perhaps one of the corps of the Levites or the priests themselves. The point being made was that Israel was so numerous that one could not even count a small fraction (one-fourth) of their population since they raised a dust cloud during their trek through the Moabite plains.[575]

**23:10b** In the final stich of Balaam's first oracle, consisting of a couplet in complementary parallelism, the prophet reflects upon his life in light of what he has observed and the revelation he has received. Noordzij has stated the matter most astutely: "Balaam sees the divine blessing that rests on Israel as surpassing anything he has seen thus far; he would consider it his good fortune to die as the children of Israel can die, not only because his own death would then not be premature and violent (cf. Job 4:7), but also because he would then have the assurance that his offspring would belong to a blessed nation and would continue to live in safety and peace, a blessing that was even rarer then than it is in our own time."[576] He dearly wanted what Israel possessed, but would he be willing to submit to the covenant stipulations and obey God fully? For a moment as he realized that he did not have Israel's number in order to condemn them, he may have thought of making a full commitment to this new deity. But we know that at the end of the story he was not willing to submit to God's plan for blessing, for he counseled the Moabite leaders to subvert Israel through idolatry and immorality (25:1–18). For this he would die the death of violence in retribution (31:8,16) rather than the death of the upright[577] as expressed in the present passage.

> [11]Balak said to Balaam, "What have you done to me? I brought you to curse my enemies, but you have done nothing but bless them!"
> [12]He answered, "Must I not speak what the LORD puts in my mouth?"

BALAK'S RESPONSE TO BALAAM AND THE REJOINDER (23:11–12). **23:11–12** Balak's furious response came as expected, since he as the king of Moab had spent so much time and money personally working toward the desired end of condemning Israel to destruction. He took Balaam's actions and words as a personal and professional affront, yet his

---

[574] C. F. Keil, *The Book of Numbers* (Edinburgh: T & T Clark, 1869), 180.

[575] Milgrom, *Numbers,* 197.

[576] Noordzij, *Numbers,* 218.

[577] Noordzij may be right in seeing a play on the words "Israel" (*isrāʾēl* , "he struggles with God") and the reference here to Israel as the "righteous / upright" (*yĕšarîm*). He wanted to be upright, but in the end he struggled with God.

words express the reality of the situation. God will accomplish the reversal of fortunes for any who would try to destroy his people. Balaam then reminded Balak of that which he had communicated from the beginning; what Yahweh instructs he must do. The phraseology of v. 12, lit., "What he puts in my mouth I must be careful to speak," forms an inclusio with v. 5, completing the first cycle of oracular material and connecting this section to 22:18. The narration and poetic portions of the text have been meshed cohesively.

¹³Then Balak said to him, "Come with me to another place where you can see them; you will see only a part but not all of them. And from there, curse them for me." ¹⁴So he took him to the field of Zophim on the top of Pisgah, and there he built seven altars and offered a bull and a ram on each altar.

¹⁵Balaam said to Balak, "Stay here beside your offering while I meet with him over there."

¹⁶The LORD met with Balaam and put a message in his mouth and said, "Go back to Balak and give him this message."

¹⁷So he went to him and found him standing beside his offering, with the princes of Moab. Balak asked him, "What did the LORD say?"

¹⁸Then he uttered his oracle:
"Arise, Balak, and listen;
    hear me, son of Zippor.
¹⁹God is not a man, that he should lie,
    nor a son of man, that he should change his mind.
Does he speak and then not act?
Does he promise and not fulfill?
²⁰I have received a command to bless;
    he has blessed, and I cannot change it.

²¹"No misfortune is seen in Jacob,
    no misery observed in Israel.
The LORD their God is with them;
    the shout of the King is among them.
²²God brought them out of Egypt;
    they have the strength of a wild ox.
²³There is no sorcery against Jacob,
    no divination against Israel.
It will now be said of Jacob
    and of Israel, 'See what God has done!'
²⁴The people rise like a lioness;
    they rouse themselves like a lion
that does not rest till he devours his prey
    and drinks the blood of his victims."

²⁵Then Balak said to Balaam, "Neither curse them at all nor bless them at all!"

²⁶Balaam answered, "Did I not tell you I must do whatever the LORD says?"

BALAAM'S SECOND ORACLE (23:13–26). Following the failed first attempt at cursing Israel through means of divination at Bamoth Baal, the undeterred Balak perceived that perhaps the location was improper for carrying out the precise rituals that would bring him success against Israel. Another locale might bring them into closer proximity to the gods or goddesses who often were understood to have some topographical preferences or even geographical limitations. He thought perhaps a vantage point from which Balaam could observe a smaller portion of Israel might enable the prophet to gain the upper hand in this challenge to the divine. The Moabite king does not yet fully understand that the blessing of Yahweh upon Israel has no limitations by physical geography or prophetic manipulation. The structure of the introduction to the second oracle is patterned after that of the first, with the exception that Balaam does not need to instruct Balak to offer the necessary sacrifices. He understood his role in the ritual procedures.[578]

*Balak Leads Balaam to Sedeh Zophim on Pisgah (23:13–14a).* **23:13–14a** The name Sedeh Zophim ("field of Zophim") derives from the topographical term *śādeh* ("field, pasture") and the plural participle of the verb *ṣāpâ* ("keep watch over"), hence a "field of watchmen." The site is not otherwise known from the Hebrew Bible. Several scholars interpret this locale as a known place for observing heavenly omens or making astrological observations.[579] Pisgah was one of the prominent peaks in the Abarim range which extended from the northwest perimeter of the Moabite plateau to the region just northeast of the Dead Sea (33:47–48). In Num 21:20 Pisgah is described as overlooking Jeshimon ("wasteland"). Later in the Abarim mountains on Mount Nebo atop Pisgah, Moses would lay his hands upon Joshua and commission him to lead the Israelites into the Promised Land (27:12–23), and he would have the opportunity to see the land from the distant peak (Deut 3:21–28). There he would die and be buried (Deut 34:1–12). The verse follows a simple chiastic structure as outlined below:

a  Come with me to another place
  b  Where you may see them from there,
    c  But only its outer edge you will see,
    c'  But all of it you will not see.
  b'  Curse him for me from there."
a'  He took him to Sedeh-zophim, to the top of the Pisgah

*Balak Sacrifices Animals on Seven Altars (23:14b).* **23:14b** In the cycles of introductory material this line compares to 23:2 and later 23:30.

---

[578] See the above outline in the introduction to the first oracle of Balaam.

[579] E.g., Noordzij, *Numbers,* 219; Dillmann, *Die Bücher Numeri,* 152; Milgrom, *Numbers,* 198. Milgrom notes that the Phoenicians referred to an astrologer by a similar phrase, *ṣope šamem,* "watcher of the skies." See also W. H. Propp, who suggests the term *śādeh* can refer to various highland hills for pasturage; "On the Hebrew *śāde(h),* 'Highland,'" *VT* 37 (1987): 230–36.

Balak dutifully offers sacrifices in the prescribed manner he perceives as necessary to gain the desired response from the object deity. Again Balak had no idea that he was forwarding the cause of those whom he sought to destroy, abetting the pronouncement of blessing upon his enemies. Again Balak becomes an inadvertent agent of the God of Israel.

*Balaam to Balak: Stand Beside Your Burnt Offering (23:15).*
**23:15** Balak performed his required duty of representing his people by standing by the sacrificial altars. Only now there is no contingency in the words of Balaam about whether Yahweh will appear. The prophet anticipates a fifth encounter with God and by now probably was anticipating a similar response from God. See the commentary on 23:3 above.

*God Manifested Himself to Balaam (23:16).* **23:16** The narrative nearly duplicates the words of 23:4–5 as God again revealed himself to this pagan diviner. His ritual is abbreviated since he no longer feels the need to announce that he has performed the proper ritual sacrifices of his trade. Again as in the manner of Moses and the later Hebrew prophets, Yahweh put a word in the mouth of Balaam, denoting the receiving of a direct revelation from Yahweh (22:38; 23:5,12). In the later oracles the revelation would come via the Spirit of God moving upon and within the prophet (24:2). See the commentary above on 23:4–5.

*Balaam Returns to Balak (23:17).* **23:17** The wording of this verse follows closely that of 23:6. Balaam went back to where Balak had been waiting expectantly by the smoldering sacrificial altars, awaiting those longed-for words that Balaam has been able to pronounce a curse upon their enemy Israel. As he saw the prophet coming, he asked, "What did Yahweh speak?" Balak's question now echoed the revelatory elements Balaam had spoken from the very first encounter with the Moabite and Midian messengers while at home in Pethor, "I will bring you back the answer the LORD gives me" (22:8). Balak realized that the whole situation depended exclusively on the will of Yahweh, whose name he had become accustomed to hearing. But he still did not realize that blessing was the only possible outcome of Balaam's second encounter.

*Balaam Obeys Yahweh: Speaks the Second Oracle (23:18–24).* **23:18–24** The second oracle of Balaam enlarges upon the central theme of the first, that of the divine blessing upon Israel that has rendered them indomitable. The introduction to the oracle in v. 18a is the same as that of the first oracle. (See the commentary above on 23:7.) Again the oracle type denoted by *māšāl* is a prophetic figurative discourse in poetic form.

In the literary structure of the second oracle as outlined below one can observe the general chiastic structure that focuses on the dynamic relationship between Yahweh and his people Israel. That relationship has had its most miraculous and irrefutable demonstration in the deliverance of the nation from bondage in Egypt. Therefore blessing has been Israel's destiny because no force on the earth or in the heavens could countermand that which God has established by his power and through his faithfulness. The oracle is composed of eleven lines of parallel cola, highlighted by the use of several word pairs common to Hebrew poetry, such as listen/give ear, do/fulfill, observe/see, misfortune/trouble, augury/divination, and lion/lioness. The poetry contains synonymous, explanatory, and antithetical parallelism, as well as chiasmus on the micro- and macro-structural levels.

### Literary Structure of the Second Oracle of Balaam

**Introduction: Balaam Addresses Balak**　　　　　　　　　　　　　　**(23:18)**

| Arise | Balak | Listen! | |
|---|---|---|---|
| | Give ear to me | Son of Zippor! | |

**E  God is Immutable**　　　　　　　　　　　　　　　　　　　　　　**(23:19)**

| No man | [is] God | that He could lie! | |
| Nor son of man | | that He should be repentant! | |
| Has He said | and not done? | | |
| Or spoken | and not fulfilled? | | |

　**F  God's Blessing Is Irrevocable**　　　　　　　　　　　　　　**(23:20–21a)**

| Behold | To Bless | I have received [command] | |
| | He has blessed | and I cannot countermand it | |
| | There is no observing | misfortune in Jacob | |
| | and there is no seeing | trouble in Israel | |

　　**G  God's Presence with Israel Means Victory**　　　　　　**(23:21b–22)**

| | Yahweh his God | | is with him |
| | The acclaim of a King | | is in him. |
| | God (El) | brings them out | from Egypt |
| | Like the towering horns | of a wild ox | is [He] for him! |

　**F′ God's Blessing Nullifies Divination**　　　　　　　　　　　**(23:23)**

| | For there is no augury | against | Jacob |
| | and no divination | against | Israel. |
| | Now it is said | on behalf of Jacob | |
| | and on behalf of Israel | What God (El) has done! | |

**E′ Israel is Like a Lion**　　　　　　　　　　　　　　　　　　　**(23:24)**

| Behold a people | | like a lioness | rises |
| | | Like a lion | he raises himself up |
| He does not rest | | until he has devoured | [his] prey |
| and the blood of the slain ones | | he has drunk." | |

**23:18**　Balaam hearkened Balak to attention as he commenced his oracle. The imperative verb *qûm,* translated "Arise!" has the effect of calling the king to attention, since he was already standing beside his offerings. The ensuing word pair listen/give ear complete a triple imperative statement, producing the maximum effect in Hebrew literary style. The prophet was endeavoring to prepare the Moabite king to receive the coming phenomenal pronouncement. The poetic parallelism of Balak son of Zippor derives from the introduction to the Book of Balaam in 22:2.

**23:19** God is different and separate from mankind, transcendent beyond the realm of humanity with all of its tendencies toward falsehood, deceit, misfortune, and calamity. Therefore he has no need to repent of any moral or ethical turpitude or misdeed. God is immutable, and his word bespeaks his incomparable integrity. On the other hand, Balaam and Balak were the antithesis of God, men of banal character. Concerning this pagan prophet Allen remarks, "He is himself the prime example of the distinction between God and man."[580] Balaam's words were ineffective before God, for as the prophet often explained, "I can speak only what Yahweh speaks to me!" On the other hand, God's word is entirely efficacious; what he says he will do, what he speaks he will accomplish." His word is never uttered into the void and never fails to produce what he intends (Isa 55:11).

The word for God used here for the first of three times in this oracle is *ʾēl*, which derives from the basic word for deity in Semitic languages. Most often in the Hebrew Bible the term occurs in the plural form Elohim, denoting the power or majesty of the One True God (though occasionally of the multiple gods of the nations), or *ʾēlîm*, the plural form often used in reference to the plethora of gods and goddesses of the nations. The short form *ʾēl* often occurs in epithets that highlight some aspect of the relationship between God and his people, such as *ʾēl-šadday* ("God Almighty," Gen 17:1), *ʾēl-ʾĕmet* ("God of Truth," Ps 31:6).[581] The present form *ʾēl* occurs by itself most often in the poetic materials of the wisdom, hymnic, and prophetic literature such as the Books of Job, Psalms, and Isaiah.

**23:20–21a** The recurrent theme of the Book of Balaam, that God has and will continue to bless Israel,[582] now reverberates through the mouth of the prophet. God's blessing is so powerful and irrevocable that even the most renowned divination expert of the day could not counter its effectiveness. Only God could rescind his blessing upon Israel, and he would not because such an act would violate his character.

The first part of v. 21 corresponds to the beginning of v. 23 in the literary structure, with each of the four cola beginning with the negative particle *lōʾ* ("not"), outlined as follows.

| Not | does one observe | misfortune | in Jacob | (21a) |
|-----|------------------|------------|----------|-------|
| Not | does one see | trouble | in Israel | |
| For Not[is there] | | augury | in Jacob | (23a) |
| Nor | [is there] | divination | in Israel | |

---

[580] Allen, "Numbers," 901.

[581] For a more extensive treatment of the term *ʾēl* and its various forms, see J. B. Scott, "אלה," *TWOT* 2:41–45; F. M. Cross, "אל," *TDOT* 1:242–60; H. Ringgren "אלהים" *TDOT* 1:267–84.

[582] Num 22:12; 23:8–10 (neg. implication); 24:5,9,11.

The term ʾāwen, translated "misfortune" in the NIV and many other versions,[583] often carries with it the implication of moral or ethical perverseness (Isa 1:13; Jer 4:14; Hos 6:8). In the prophets it is associated with the rites and iconographic forms used in worship of other gods (Isa 41:29; Hos 12:11). As found in the present context, the term ʾāwen is often paired with ʿāmāl ("trouble, sorrow, misery").[584] Milgrom has suggested rightly that the connotations of moral evil and iniquity are not in view here[585] because these have been evidenced often in Israel's wilderness experience.[586] Yet in spite of Israel's rebelliousness, God has reiterated his purpose of blessing Israel by saving them from total destruction and vowing to bring them into the Promised Land (14:31,38; 15:1–5; 16:47–50; 20:12). In the structural context this word pair is juxtapositioned with augury and divination, which Balaam practiced. Allen then is probably accurate in observing that these words "are not used to refer to moral issues but to mantic concerns. That is, God does not look on his people with "an evil eye" or a hostile glance. ... When Israel is presented in the context of a hostile environment, then it is the blessing of Israel that is maintained,"[587] The next section establishes the foundation for Israel's blessing, that Yahweh God was in their midst as the great and mighty and liberating King!

**23:21b–22** What set Israel apart was not their population, their power, or their perseverance in the wilderness over the past forty years; what set Israel apart was their God. The statement that Yahweh God is with his people means that no form of opposition can overcome them. He was their invincible King and Warrior, who demonstrated his royal nature by delivering his people from bondage to one of the most powerful nations in the ancient Near East. Ashley notes that the present participle form of yāṣāʾ, typical of the hymnic context, meant that "the action of God's bringing Israel out from Egypt was not something that was completed historically until the conquest."[588] In the broader scope of Israel's history, as would be demonstrated through the periods of the judges, kings, and prophets, God was and still is in the process of bringing his people out of bondage.[589] This is the central theme of Israel's salvation history, as repeated numerous times through the Hebrew Bible.[590]

---

[583] NRSV, NASB; contra NKJV.

[584] E.g., Isa 59:4; Pss 10:7; 55:11; 90:10; Job 4:8; 5:6; 15:35; Isa 10:1; Hab 1:3.

[585] Milgrom, *Numbers,* 199.

[586] E.g., Num 11:1; 13:28–14:43; 16:1–17:13; 20:1–12. Also after the Balaam oracles, the Baal Peor incident of Num 25:1–18.

[587] Allen, "Numbers," 902.

[588] Ashley, *Numbers,* 479.

[589] Cf. Pss 115:9–14; 118:1–29; Judg 3:10,30; Isa 61:1; Amos 9:11–15; Luke 4:16–21; etc.

[590] E.g., Ps 105:23–45; Jer 2:6; 23:1–8; Hos 11:1.

The power of Yahweh is compared to the wild ox, in particular the powerful and protruding "horns" of the animal. The Hebrew term here is *tôʿăpōt*, a rare and obscure word used only here and in Num 24:8 (third oracle), Job 22:25, and Ps 95:4. Perhaps the idea of eminence, glory, or strength is in view here since it enhances the nature of Yahweh as the delivering King.[591]

**23:23** Israel did not need augurs, diviners, sorcerers, or magicians to have success against their various enemies. The term "augury" *(naḥaš)* refers to the practice of reading omens in the skies through clouds and movements of birds. "Divination" practices for the purpose of determining the will of the gods was often accomplished through the casting of lots via dice or darts, the consulting of teraphim, or in reading the patterns of entrails via hepatoscopy (liver dissection) or colonoscopy (intestinal examination). The first line of the verse corresponds to the second line of v. 21 in the chiastic structure of the oracle (see comment above).

The disclaimer regarding Israel's possession or adherence to divination practices is remarkably juxtaposed with the positive acclamation of what God has done on behalf of Israel. The first line contains a simple stich of synonymous parallelism, using the terms "sorcery" and "divination." The second line consists of two cola in simple chiasmus that build the crescendo of thought, erupting in the compelling confession, "What God has achieved!" God had done marvelous miracles for Jacob and for Israel because he is for his people.

**23:24** In the concluding verse to the oracle, the imagery turns to that of the lion on the hunt for prey, but instead of Israel being the hunted they are the hunter. God brings a reversal of fortunes for the enemies of his people through his power and presence. This verse portends the more explicit statements in the third and fourth oracles (24:8–9,17). Balaam advises Balak not to contend with Israel lest the Moabites be consumed by the ravenous lion of Judah and Israel, who was and would continue to be his nation's neighbor (Num 24:17; Isa 15:9; Jer 48:1–47; Mic 5:7).[592] Yahweh God of Israel is also compared to a lion who would devour the enemies of Israel (Jer 49:19; Hos 5:14; Nah 2:12–13). In the chiastic structure this verse parallels v. 19, which in its effect emphasizes that Israel will be victorious against Moab only because God provides their lionlike power.

Imagery of forcefulness and brute strength are conveyed through the use of terms for "lion" in the Old Testament. The lion represents both raging power when it is on the hunt for prey, but it can also denote a firm but quiet force when pictured in a posture of repose. Iconographic forms of lions are

---

[591] See also Deut 33:17; Ps 22:21.
[592] Cf. also Gen 49:9; Deut 33:20,22.

prolific throughout the ancient Near East, from Ethiopia and Egypt to Hazor and Ugarit and from Assyria and Babylon. The distinction between the pair of Hebrew words for lion in this text and again in 24:6 *(lābî' // 'ări)* is probably minimal due to their use in synonymous parallelism.[593]

*Balak's Second Response to Balaam and the Rejoinder* (23:25–26). **23:25–26** Balak's response to Balaam's second proclamation exceeds that which followed the pronouncement of the first oracle (23:11). After this occasion the Moabite king decides he would prefer silence over either blessing or cursing. Balaam's rejoinder to Balak, in the words he was now growing weary of hearing but would hear again after the third oracle, reverberated through the mind and heart of Balak (22:38; 23:3,12; 24:13). These words again remind the reader that this pagan divination prophet was an instrument of God's revelatory process, that he was constrained to proclaim everything and only that which Yahweh intended for him.

[27]Then Balak said to Balaam, "Come, let me take you to another place. Perhaps it will please God to let you curse them for me from there." [28]And Balak took Balaam to the top of Peor, overlooking the wasteland.

[29]Balaam said, "Build me seven altars here, and prepare seven bulls and seven rams for me." [30]Balak did as Balaam had said, and offered a bull and a ram on each altar.

[1]Now when Balaam saw that it pleased the LORD to bless Israel, he did not resort to sorcery as at other times, but turned his face toward the desert. [2]When Balaam looked out and saw Israel encamped tribe by tribe, the Spirit of God came upon him [3]and he uttered his oracle:
"The oracle of Balaam son of Beor,
    the oracle of one whose eye sees clearly,
[4]the oracle of one who hears the words of God,
    who sees a vision from the Almighty,
    who falls prostrate, and whose eyes are opened:

[5]"How beautiful are your tents, O Jacob,
    your dwelling places, O Israel!

[6]"Like valleys they spread out,
    like gardens beside a river,
like aloes planted by the LORD,
    like cedars beside the waters.
[7]Water will flow from their buckets;
    their seed will have abundant water.

---

[593] For a comprehensive study of the seven terms for 'lion' in the OT, see G. J. Botterweck, "אֲרִי," *TDOT*, 374–88. אֲרִי is one of the most common words for lion and occurs thirty-five times in the OT, whereas לָבִיא is found only eleven times. Botterweck suggests that the latter term may refer to the Asian lion as opposed to the African lion, but this is somewhat conjectural.

"Their king will be greater than Agag;
their kingdom will be exalted.

[8]"God brought them out of Egypt;
they have the strength of a wild ox.
They devour hostile nations
and break their bones in pieces;
with their arrows they pierce them.
[9]Like a lion they crouch and lie down,
like a lioness—who dares to rouse them?

"May those who bless you be blessed
and those who curse you be cursed!"

[10]Then Balak's anger burned against Balaam. He struck his hands together and said to him, "I summoned you to curse my enemies, but you have blessed them these three times. [11]Now leave at once and go home! I said I would reward you handsomely, but the LORD has kept you from being rewarded."

[12]Balaam answered Balak, "Did I not tell the messengers you sent me, [13]'Even if Balak gave me his palace filled with silver and gold, I could not do anything of my own accord, good or bad, to go beyond the command of the LORD—and I must say only what the LORD says'? [14]Now I am going back to my people, but come, let me warn you of what this people will do to your people in days to come."

BALAAM'S THIRD ORACLE (23:27–24:14). With the second attempt at cursing Israel through means of divination at Sedeh Zophim on Mount Pisgah having ended in greater failure than the first, the persistent Balak again ascertained that perhaps the location was inappropriate for accomplishing the goal of gaining an upper hand against Israel. Only this time no mention is made of the worship locale being within sight of any portion of Israel until after the sacrifices have been performed. Another alternative locale might bring them into closer proximity to the gods or goddesses who often were understood to have some topographical preferences or even geographical limitations. The Moabite king does not yet fully understand that the blessing of Yahweh upon Israel has no limitations by physical geography or prophetic manipulation; place does not matter if the intent is contrary to the will of God. The structure of the introduction to the third oracle is patterned after that of the first but with some abbreviated elements. Balaam did not instruct Balak to stand by his sacrificial altars and then journey off on his own to perform any additional acts of sorcery. Instead the Lord dynamically appears to him as he was empowered by his Spirit to proclaim the oracle.

*Balak Leads Balaam to Bamoth Baal (23:27–28).* **23:27–28** The site chosen for this third attempt at divine manipulation was "the top of the Peor" *(rōʾš happĕʿôr)*, known also in Num 25:18; 31:16; Josh 22:17 as the place where Balaam later counseled the Moabites to entice many Israelites into idolatrous activities.[594] The locale is also known as Baal Peor, at which the familiar northwestern Semitic deity Baal was worshiped, probably as a result of some perceived theophany of Baal in earlier antiquity (Num 25:3; Deut 4:3; Ps 106:28; Hos 9:10). Though the precise whereabouts of the cultic site remains unidentified, it was no doubt located in the same Abarim range of mountains in which Bamoth Baal and Sedeh Zophim were situated.[595] The mountain overlooked "the wasteland" *(hayĕšîmōn)*, a descriptive toponym for an arid region just south of the Israelite camp but just north of Maon. Jeshimon occasionally is translated as a proper name.[596]

*Balaam Instructs Balak to Prepare Sacrifices (23:29).*[597] **23:29** Balaam again provided the instructions for Balak to construct seven altars to carry out the sacrifices of a bull and a ram on each altar as preparation for another encounter with God. See commentary on 23:1 above for discussion of the significance of the number seven.

*Balak Obeys Balaam (23:30).* **23:30** The Moabite repeated dutifully his mediator role as a faithful servant of Balaam in this cultic process. See commentary above on 23:2.

*God Manifests Himself to Balaam (24:1-2).* **24:1-2** The narrative now takes an unusual turn, for Balaam does not depart from Balak and the altars to a place of solitude. He does not perform any divination rituals to prepare for the encounter with the divine, nor does he receive the revelation in the same manner of Yahweh putting the words into his mouth. In this case the Spirit of God came upon the prophet, and he may have entered into an ecstatic trance in the manner of Saul (1 Sam 10:6) or Micaiah (1 Kgs 22:10–23). The process transpired as Balaam lifted up his eyes and saw *(wayyiśśā᾽ bilʿām ᾽et-ʿênāyw wayyar᾽*, i.e., fully focused his attention). The preterite form of the verb *rā᾽â* ("he saw") here and elsewhere is used to denote an individual seeing or observing perceptively. In this case Balaam is endowed with divine insight as he observed the Israelites below him in the wilderness of Moab.

*Balaam Obeys Yahweh: Speaks the Third Oracle (24:3-9).* **24:3a** The third oracle of Balaam enlarges upon the central themes of the first and second, that of the divine blessing upon Israel that has rendered them invincible before their enemies. Attention now begins to turn toward the future as Israel prepares for the fulfillment of the Exodus in the dramatic entry into the Promised Land. The introduction to the oracle in v. 18a is the same as that of the first oracle. See the commentary above on 23:7. Again the oracle type denoted by the Hebrew

---

[594] Cf. NT references to Balaam's role in leading Israel astray at this site in 2 Pet 2:15; Jude 11; Rev 2:14, though the site name Peor is lacking in each case.

[595] Num 22:41; 23:14; cf. 21:11; 33:47–48.

[596] Num 33:49—Beth Jeshimoth; also 1 Sam 23:19,24; 26:1–3; Ps 78:40.

[597] See the above outline in the introduction to the first oracle of Balaam.

*māšāl* is a prophetic figurative discourse in poetic form.

In the literary structure of the third oracle as outlined below one can observe the general chiastic structure that focuses on the unique relationship between Yahweh and his people Israel. Working from the focal point of the chiasmus outward, one can observe that at the center of that relationship was the most miraculous and irrefutable demonstration of God's deliverance of the nation from bondage in Egypt (v. 8a). God's blessing has been Israel's destiny, so their kingdom will be incomparable (v. 7b) and thus unconquerable (v. 8b) since they were to live out their destiny in a faithful and obedient relationship to Yahweh. With God's blessing they became a creation of beauty by Yahweh that was beyond compare, a luxurious oasis in a world of desert and despair (vv. 5–7a). Likewise the land that God was giving them was as beautiful and productive, a land so described in the recurrent phrase "flowing with milk and honey." But their splendor is complemented by their prowess, which none dare provoke (v. 9a). In the A – A′ sections that bracket the oracle, the role of Balaam as God's instrument for revelation of this blessing, is magnified, but the prophet had to be subdued by the revelations of a female donkey before he would willingly submit to Yahweh's sovereign control over his life (vv. 3b–4). In the end he could only echo what God had said to Abraham at the beginning of this new creation from and for humanity—those who bless you will be blessed; those who curse you will be cursed (Gen 12:3).

### Literary Structure of the Third Oracle of Balaam

**A  Balaam God's Seer (24:3–4)**

Intro: Then he took up his discourse and said,
"Oracle of Balaam, son of Beor,

|  |  |  |
|---|---|---|
| (a) Oracle of the man | [with] unveiled | eyes |
| (b) Oracle of him | who hears | the words of God (El) |
|  | who | the vision of Shaddai he beholds |
| (a′) Who falls down | but with uncovered | eyes. |

**B  Beauty of Israel (24:5–7a)**

|  |  |  |
|---|---|---|
| How beautiful | your tents | O Jacob |
|  | your dwelling places | O Israel |
| Like | river valleys | they spread out |
| Like | gardens | beside a river |
| Like | aloes | planted by Yahweh |
| Like | cedars | beside [the] waters |
| Flows | water | from its buckets |
| Its seed | with abundant water |  |

**C  Israel's King and Kingdom Exalted (24:7b)**

|  |  |  |
|---|---|---|
| He will be exalted | greater than Agag | his king |
| and it shall be lifted up |  | his kingdom |

**D  God Delivers from Egypt (24:8a)**

|  |  |  |
|---|---|---|
| God (El) | brings them out | from Egypt |

Like the towering horns      of a wild ox                          is [He] for him!

**C′ Israel's Power to Defeat Nations (24:8b)**

He shall devour         nations                          his enemies
Their bones             he will break
His arrows              he will shatter

**B′ Israel Is Like a Lion (24:9a)**

He crouches             he lay down         like a lion
Like a lioness          who would arouse her

A Balaam's Benediction: Blessing and Cursing (24:9b)

Those who bless you     shall be blessed
Those who curse you     shall be cursed

**24:3b–4** Whereas the first and second oracles commence with references to Balak, king of Moab, the third oracle begins with an extended description of the person and purpose of Balaam in this whole affair. Seeing and hearing rightly before God must come as the result of divine inspiration and human submission in order for the revelatory process to be effective. The vision he saw was one of an unfolding future for Israel as they were on the verge of completing the Exodus event by entering and conquering the Promised Land, fulfilling the promise originally made to Abram and reiterated to Isaac, Jacob, and Moses.[598] The phraseology Balaam used in this self-revelation, namely *nĕʾūm haggeber* ("oracle of the [mighty] man"), one who is used by *ʾēl* ("God")[599] and upon whom the *rûaḥ ʾĕlōhîm* ("Spirit of God") comes to empower an individual to speak, is used by the great King David in 2 Sam 23:1–2. In the context of the future kingship in Israel (vv. 7–8), these words of Balaam provide a precursive pattern for the coming fulfillment of the anointed deliver for the kingdom.

The parallelism of these verses set in chiastic structure (see above) is also quite revealing. The threefold use of the oracular term *nĕʾūm* is remarkable here, introducing three statements concerning Balaam's role as a recipient of the Lord's handiwork.[600] The overwhelming number of occurrences have *nĕʾūm* in the construct state to *YHWH*, and only here and in 1 Sam 23:1; Prov 30:1; and Ps 36:1 is the object of the construct someone other than God. On the other hand, the origin of these words was not Balaam but the Spirit of God working on the mind, heart, and mouth of the prophet. Harrison described the *nĕʾūm YHWH* as "the most solemn asseveration of divine truth that a human being can utter in the Lord's name."[601] The mighty Bal-

---

[598] Gen 12:1–3; 15:18–2; 17:1–1–8; 26:2–6; 28:10–15; 46:3–4; Exod 3:5–17; Num 10:29; 15:2; etc.

[599] See commentary on 23:19 above.

[600] Outside of the prophets, esp. Isaiah and Jeremiah (who uses the phrase נְאֻם־יְהֹוָה 175 times, and seventeen times in chap. 23 alone!), seldom does one find three uses of the term in such close proximity. Other examples would include Isa 14:22–23; Jer 3:10–16 (6x); Jer 31 (14x); etc.

[601] Harrison, *Numbers*, 317.

aam *(haggeber)* must fall down prostrate *(nōpēl)* before God in submissive obedience in order be in the right physical and spiritual posture to receive a revelation from God. Hearing and seeing (both participle forms) are the two modes by which the dynamic of revelation takes place. Balaam had heard God speak in a variety of ways at night in his home and through a donkey on the road to Moab. Though unseeing at first, his eyes had been uncovered by Yahweh to see his emissary in 22:31.[602] Many scholars interpret Balaam's words as indicating that he entered into some kind of trance or ecstatic state as the Spirit of God came upon him, as with Saul in 1 Sam 10:6–13, but the precise nature of this activity remains unclear.

The terms for God, *ʾēl* and *šadday*, are juxtaposed at the center of the chiasmus, emphasizing that it was not the great divination prophet Balaam who was the revealer of mysteries but the great and mighty *ʾēl šadday*[603] who enabled the prophet to become such a spokesman. The two names are archaic forms, El being derived etymologically from *ilu*, the basic Semitic word for God, and Shaddai from perhaps *šadû*, an Akkadian word meaning "mountain" or "steppe-land." Albright noted that the gods Asshur and Bel of northern Mesopotamian provenance were called by the epithet *šadû rabû*, or "great mountain."[604] Notable is the occurrence of the same divine name *šaddayin* along with *ʾēl* in the Balaam texts from Deir ʿAlla, which in the Aramaic plural form refers to the part of the divine council of deities.[605]

**24:5–7a** Four phrases or clauses, each introduced by the comparative *k-* ("like"), qualify the introductory declaration that Israel was an entity of divine handiwork, a historical work of art that was about to flower in its full glory in the Promised Land. In a crescendo of phrases, the geographical and floral aspects begin and end with references to the highly prized bodies of

---

[602] Both cases use forms of the verb גלה (וַיְגַל) in 22:31 and וּגְלוּי here and in 24:16. This verb is often used in revelatory contexts; e.g., 1 Sam 9:15; Amos 3:7.

[603] Gen 17:1; 28:13; 35:11; 43:14; Exod 6:3; Ezek 10:5.

[604] W. F. Albright, "The Names Shaddai and Abram," *JBL* 54 (1935): 180–87. Note also V. P. Hamilton, *TWOT,* "שַׁדַּי" 2:907; J. Hehn, *Babylonische und Israelitische Gottesidee,* 265ff., M. Walker, "A New Interpretation of the Divine Name 'Shaddai,'" *ZAW* 72 (1960): 64–66; Ashley, *Numbers,* 488–89; M. Weippert, *THAT,* 2:873–81; and F. M. Cross, *Canaanite Myth and Hebrew Epic* (Cambridge: Harvard University Press, 1973), 52–66. Others appeal to the Hb. root שׁדד, meaning "destroy" or "devastate," for the origin of the divine epithet.

[605] See discussion of *šaddayin* in the Balaam texts (Comb I, 5–6; Comb II, 2) in above "Introduction to the Book of Balaam," as well as M. S. Moore, *The Balaam Traditions,* 84–95,101; F. M. Cross, "Notes on the Ammonite Inscription from Tell Sīrān," *BASOR* 212 (1973): 12–15; H. J. Franken, "Texts from the Persian Period from Tell Deir ʿAllā," *VT* 17 (1967): 480–81; J. Hackett, The Balaam Text from Deir ʿAllā," HSM 31 (Chico, Cal.: Scholars Press, 1984), 1–19. Note also P. K. McCarter, "The Balaam Texts from Deir ʿAllā: The First Combination," *BASOR* 239 (1980): 49–60; Milgrom, *Numbers,* Excursus 60, "Balaam and the Deir ʿAlla Inscription," 473–74, and linguistic issues addressed by J. Naveh, "The Date of the Deir ʿAlla Inscriptions in Aramaic Script," *IEJ* 17 (1967): 256–58.

water Israel would possess in great abundance in the land. The river valleys would include the Jordan and its tributaries such as the Yarmuk, Jabesh, Jabbok, Harod, and the Farah, as well as the coastal streams of the Besor, Lachish, Elah, Sorek, Yarqon, and Qishon. These would be fed by the rains brought by the Lord upon the land and the resplendent aquifers beneath the hill country and mountainous regions of Hermon. Gardens could even be found along the Dead Sea in such well-watered places as En Gedi and En Boqeq. The allusion to water flowing from buckets may refer to irrigation practices they would have learned from the Egyptians while living in Goshen and applicable to their new setting. The buckets *(dālyāw)* were of the type borne in pairs upon a yoke across the shoulders.[606]

**24:7b** Patriarchal texts in the Book of Genesis bespeak the coming of kingship from the lineage of Abram and Sarai that would come forth and rule over the land then belonging to the Canaanites but promised to the future generations of Jacob (Gen 17:6–8, 16; 35:11). The king that would one day be anointed and lead Israel in its glory would be superior to the great king Agag. The structural counterpart to this portion of the verse is 24:8b, which describes the kingdom of Israel as devouring nations, as would one day come to fruition in the expansion of the kingdom under David (1 Sam 5:6–25; 8:1–14; 10:1–19).

The reference to the name Agag, known best as the name belonging to one of the kings of the Amalekites defeated by Saul and executed by Samuel (1 Sam 15:7–9,32–33), has caused considerable consternation among interpreters dating back at least to the second century B.C. The interpretation of this king named Agag can be categorized into four approaches: (1) emend the text to read "Gog" or "Og," (2) source-critical in which the Elohist included the name Agag as a reference to the setting of Saul's day, (3) predictive prophecy concerning the Agag of Saul's day; or (4) Agag is to be read as a dynastic name among the Amalekites, including a hitherto unknown king of the Late Bronze Age, the time frame represented by the text itself. (1) In the Septuagint and the Samaritan Pentateuch, the text is emended to read "greater than Gog," which would be a reference to the region of northeastern Asia Minor, well to the north of the region from which Balaam came. (2) For source-critical scholars the association of Agag here with the Agag of Saul's day simply supports their theory that the texts as we know them were composed many centuries after the purported historical events recounted within and in many cases reflect real political and historical issues in the later periods of Israel's divided monarchies. Besides taking the accounts out of their explicit historical and canonical literary contexts, Gray suggested that Agag of Saul's day was "scarcely so formidable

---

[606] Ashley, *Numbers,* 491; Harrison, *Numbers,* 318.

king to justify such an allusion."[607] (3) Wenham and Allen have suggested
that what we have is the prediction that Israel will one day defeat its earliest
archrival the Amalekites.[608] Reference to the Amalekites in Balaam's final
oracles as "first among the nations" but who "will come to ruin at last"
(24:20) may support this argument. If the passage is meant to be predictive
prophecy, however, it is at best implicit in the general tenor of the structure
of the passage. (4) The more likely conclusion is that Agag was a dynastic
name among the Amalekites, one of the early foes of Israel (Exod 17:8–13)
whose downfall is predicted in 24:20.[609]

**24:8a**[610]   This portion of the verse is a stock duplicate of the central
structure of the second oracle (cf. 23:21). What set Israel apart was not their
population, power, or perseverance in the wilderness over the past forty
years; what set Israel apart was their God. The statement that Yahweh God
is with his people means that no form of opposition can overcome them. He
was their invincible King and Warrior, who demonstrated his royal nature by
delivering his people from bondage to one of the most powerful nations in
the ancient Near East. God was and still is in the process of bringing his
people out of bondage.[611] This is the central theme of Israel's salvation history, as repeated numerous times throughout the Hebrew Bible.[612] Again the
power of Yahweh is compared to the wild ox.[613]

**24:8b**   Israel's strength as a kingdom derived solely from their relationship with Yahweh their God who delivered them from bondage in Egypt.
Their kingship and kingdom were incomparable and spoken of in exalted
fashion by the nations. The narrator of the story, Balaam, and even Balak
himself in his initial communication with Balaam echoed this grave concern
as to whether they could survive against the overwhelming people of Yahweh (22:2–6,11). The Lord had said from the beginning, however, "You
must not put a curse on those people, because they are blessed" (22:12). If
Balak had learned the basic principle of blessing, he and his people would
not only have survived but would have been successful and prosperous in

---

[607] Gray, *Numbers,* 366; Noth, *Numbers,* 191. Note though that scholars as recent as Budd
(*Numbers,* 269) have maintained this identification.

[608] Wenham, *Numbers,* 178. Allen describes this passage as "something wondrous: a specific
predictive prophecy of a victory of a king of Israel over a great enemy. ... we may have a heilsge-
schichtliche continuity that begins in the desert with the attacks of Amalek in Israel's recent past,
that leads to the future victory of Saul over his nemesis, Agag (1 Sam 15:32–33), and that culminates in the final victory of Israel's greatest King (Y'shua) over all her enemies" ("Numbers," 906).

[609] See Keil, *Numbers,* 189; W. Kaiser, Jr., "Agag," *ZPEB,* 1:68; Harrison, *Numbers,* 319;
D. Christensen, "Agag," *ABD,* 1:88–89.

[610] See commentary on 23:22 above.

[611] Cf. Pss 115:9–14; 118:1–29; Judg 3:10,30; Isa 61:1; Amos 9:11–15; Luke 4:16–21; etc.

[612] E.g., Ps 105:23–45; Jer 2:6; 23:1–8; Hos 11:1.

[613] See commentary on 23:22 above.

their national endeavors. Instead they would face destruction, vividly portrayed in the sharp and crackling sound of bones breaking and arrows splintering. This imagery leads into the following portrayal of the lion, which is able to crush the bones of its prey with its powerful paws and toothy jaw.

**24:9a** Imagery of forcefulness and brute strength are conveyed through the use of terms for "lion" in the Old Testament. The lion represents raging power when it is on the hunt for prey, but it can also denote a firm but quiet force when pictured in a posture of repose. Iconographic forms of lions are prolific throughout the ancient Near East, from Ethiopia and Egypt to Hazor and Ugarit and from Assyria and Babylon. The distinction between the pair of Hebrew words for lion in this text and again in 24:6 *(ʾărî // lābîʾ)* probably is minimal due to their use in synonymous parallelism.[614] See commentary above on 23:24. In the present context the lion is depicted in the quietude of repose, but if aroused or provoked it could easily spring into action with its terrifying swiftness and brute power. Nations beware if they should provoke the Lord to anger by attempting to destroy the divinely chosen Israel.

**24:9b** When Israel lived faithfully under Yahweh's incomparable and indomitable dominion, its armies were invincible before its enemies. Calamity and/or destruction could bring deleterious affect on them if they rebelled against their God, as they had so often experienced in the desert after departing Sinai. The recurrent theme of the Book of Balaam, that God has and will continue to bless Israel,[615] now reverberates through the mouth of the prophet. God's blessing is so powerful and irrevocable that even the most renowned divination expert of the day could not counter its effectiveness. Only God could rescind his blessing upon Israel, and he would not because such an act would defile his inviolable character.

*Balak's Angry Response (24:10–11).*     **24:10–11**    For Balak the third strike against Balaam was enough to send him packing on that long journey back to Pethor (Pitru) in the upper Euphrates region. His anger was expressed in the clapping of the hands, a sign of derision or defiance.[616] The expression that Balak's "anger burned" *(wayyiḥar-ʾap)* is used earlier in the Book of Balaam of God's anger with Balaam (22:22) and of Balaam's anger with his donkey (22:27).[617] Anger had come full circle in that the one who

---

[614] For a comprehensive study of the seven terms for 'lion' in the OT, see G. J. Botterweck, "אֲרִי," *TDOT*, 374–88. אֲרִי is one of the most common words for lion and occurs thirty-five times in the OT, whereas לָבִיא is found only eleven times. Botterweck has suggested that the latter term may refer to the Asian lion as opposed to the African lion, but this is somewhat conjectural.

[615] Num 22:12; 23:8–10 (neg. implication),20; 24:5,11.

[616] Job 27:23; 34:37; Lam 2:15.

[617] Note also in Numbers the use of the phrase to express God's anger with the rebellious Israelites (11:1,10,33;12:9; 25:3; 32:10,13).

instigated this whole affair was now enraged against the one whom he had tried so hard to get to help him. Balak was furious because the best opportunity the world afforded to overcome this perceived enemy had turned, or been turned, against him. Then came the added response that raised the prophet's ire; he was to receive no honorarium for his concerted attempts to fulfill Balak's wishes. He was saying, in effect, that since Balaam had blessed Israel as the prophetic instrument of Yahweh, it was then Yahweh's fault that he must return home empty handed.

*Balaam's Retort (24:12–14).* **24:12–14** Balaam reminded Balak of that which had been saying all along, ever since the first messengers had approached him on behalf of the Moabite and Midianite leaders. He could only speak what Yahweh revealed to him, no matter what methods of sorcery, divination, or magic he might try to employ in the process. The words of Balaam, set in simple chiastic form as outlined below, echoed those of 22:18:

    (a) I would not be able to disobey the word of Yahweh

      (b) By doing good or evil on my own.

    (a') That which Yahweh speaks I will speak.

The Hebrew text of 24:13a exactly duplicates 22:18a, then the text diverges from the former in that Balaam stated that he could not do "good or evil" such that it would countermand the word of God, versus the terminology "great or small" in the earlier verse. One recalls what Moses had said to Hobab before the cycle of rebelliousness had begun, "The Lord has promised good things for us." So then if God be for Israel, who could stand against them? Balaam had pronounced good over Israel by blessing them three times at God's bidding. He was Yahweh's instrument for the revelation of blessing, and no form of divination could contend with the power of the One True God. For a moment Balak thought the whole dreaded affair was over and Balaam was about to embark on the two-week-long journey home. But God was not finished yet with his prophetic agent in revealing some ominous words to this enemy of Israel. What then would issue forth from the mouth of Balaam was a pronouncement that Olson notes "unleashes all the power of the preceding heavenly visions onto the stage of earthly history."[618]

<sup></sup>**¹⁵Then he uttered his oracle:**
**"The oracle of Balaam son of Beor,**
   **the oracle of one whose eye sees clearly,**
**¹⁶the oracle of one who hears the words of God,**
   **who has knowledge from the Most High,**
**who sees a vision from the Almighty,**

---

[618] Olson, *Numbers,* 150.

**who falls prostrate, and whose eyes are opened:**

[17]"**I see him, but not now;**
 **I behold him, but not near.**
**A star will come out of Jacob;**
 **a scepter will rise out of Israel.**
**He will crush the foreheads of Moab,**
 **the skulls**
**of all the sons of Sheth.**
[18]**Edom will be conquered;**
 **Seir, his enemy, will be conquered,**
 **but Israel will grow strong.**
[19]**A ruler will come out of Jacob**
 **and destroy the survivors of the city."**

BALAAM'S FOURTH ORACLE (24:15–19).   The fourth oracle required no journey to a sacred observation point, no sacrificial preparations, no standing by the sacrificial altars, and no performing of special rituals of divination. The Lord spontaneously prompted the prophet to commence his utterance against his former employer, from whom he never would receive his due compensation. The introduction to the oracle in v. 15a is the same as that of the first oracle. See the commentary above on 23:7. Again the oracle type denoted by the Hebrew *māšāl* is a prophetic figurative discourse in poetic form. The structure of the oracle is outlined as follows.

**Introduction:** "Then he took up his discourse and said,
**A Balaam, God's Visionary (24:15b–16)**
 "Oracle of Balaam, son of Beor,

| | | |
|---|---|---|
| (a) Oracle of the man | with] unveiled | eyes |
| (b) Oracle of him | who hears | the words of **God (El)** |
| | who knows | the knowledge of **Elyon**, |
| | who | the vision of Shaddai     he beholds |
| (a') Who falls down | but with uncovered | eyes. |

**B Balaam's Vision          (24:17–19)**
 (a) Balaam Sees into the Future (24:17a)

| | |
|---|---|
| I see him | but not now |
| I behold him | but not near |

  (b) Balaam Sees a Future King of Israel (24:17b)

| | | |
|---|---|---|
| He shall march | a star | from Jacob |
| He shall arise | a scepter | from Israel |

    (c) Balaam Sees the Destruction of Moab and Edom (24:17c–18a)

| | | |
|---|---|---|
| He shall crush | the foreheads | of Moab |
| | the scalps | of all the children of Seth |
| It shall be    Edom | dispossessed | |
| It shall be    dispossessed | Seir | his enemies |

  (b') Balaam Sees Israel's Triumph (24:18b–19)

| | | |
|---|---|---|
| So Israel | shall contend | valiantly |

| He shall trample them | Jacob |  |
|---|---|---|
| He shall destroy | the remnant | from the city |

**24:15b–16** The beginning of the fourth oracle is almost identical to that of the third (24:3–4), except for the addition of a third reference to the source of his revelation. Not only does he hear the words of El and see the vision of Shaddai, but he also knows the knowledge of Elyon. Now the two senses of seeing and hearing are supplemented by an intimate knowledge (*wĕyōdēaʿ daʿat*, "who knows knowledge") of the Most High that can only come as the result of divine inspiration and human receptiveness. Balaam had acquired knowledge by prophetic revelation that transcends the human sphere. The name and epithet *ʿelyôn*, derived from an adjectival form meaning "high, highest,"[619] is found most commonly in the Pentateuch and the Psalms[620] and often in combination with other divine names.[621] This time the vision he sees is exclusively one of a promising future for Israel in the Promised Land, when their archenemies Moab and Edom would be once and for all subdued and destroyed. The structure of the focal point of the chiastic structure of v. 16 with the divine names in the middle, follows the a b c d / b' c d' /c" d" a" pattern found in Ugaritic literature. This pattern recurs in vv. 17c–18a. For additional insights on the meaning and use of the terms in this section, see commentary on 24:3–4 above.

One of the most remarkable prophecies of the Hebrew Bible, interpreted for centuries before the Christian era as portending and heralding the great Messianic king and kingdom, is here uttered by a pagan divination expert. Allen remarked, "That this prophecy should come from one who was unworthy makes the prophecy all the more dramatic and startling."[622] As noted earlier, the Book of Balaam presents an amazing picture of God in his sovereign desire to bless his people Israel. He will utilize whatever means he chooses to reveal himself and his will for his people, even if it means divinely drafting for service one who would seem the ultimate antithesis of what the world would envision for a leader and spokesman—but his thoughts are not our thoughts (Isa 55:8).

**24:17a** These synonymous parallel cola translate the hearer into the distant future. The three previous oracles have moved progressively toward the future. Beginning with the theme of blessing and cursing (23:8) and

---

[619] The term עֶלְיוֹן as adjective meaning "high" or "highest" occurs some twenty-two times in the Hebrew Bible, such as in Deut 26:19; 28:1; 2 Kgs 15:35; 18:17; Isa 7:3; etc.

[620] Of the twenty-nine usages of עֶלְיוֹן as a divine name, only four occur outside the Pentateuch and the Psalms (2 Sam 22:14; Isa 14:14; Lam 3:35,38). Cf. Deut 32:8; Pss 9:3; 18:14; 21:8; 46:5; 50:14; 73:11; 77:11; 78:17; 83:19; 91:1,9; 92:2; 107:11.

[621] Cf. combinations with El in Gen 14:18–22 (4x); with Yahweh in Pss 7:18; 47:3; with Elohim in Pss 57:3; 78:56.

[622] Allen, "Numbers," 909.

moving to the deliverance from Egypt (the focal point of the first oracles two and three; 23:22; 24:8) which demonstrated God's blessing upon Israel, the divine message progressed to the future hope of a mighty kingdom (23:7b,8b). Now in the fourth oracle the contents project the reader/hearer immediately into the future; the knowledge Balaam has received from Yahweh applies not to the now, for the time is not yet at hand for this glorious kingdom.

**24:17b**  The glory of this King is portrayed using two metaphors, the "star" *(kôkāb)* and the "scepter" *(šēbeṭ)*. Isaiah used the star imagery in the context of royalty in describing the coming fall of the king of Babylon (Isa 14:12–13), and in the New Testament Jesus Christ is referred to as the royal "Root and Offspring of David, the Bright Morning Star" (Rev 22:16). His birth as the incarnate King was declared by the heavens in the appearance of a star over Bethlehem (Matt 2:1–10). The Qumran sectarians interpreted this passage as having Messianic import, as did other Jewish sources of the period between the mid-second century B.C. and the first century A.D.[623] Around 100 B.C., the Hasmonean king Alexander Janneus had the star imprinted upon some of the royal coins, thereby implicating him as the conquering star of Num 24:17. Rabbi Akiba understood the Messianic significance of this passage when he proclaimed Simon bar Kosiba to be "Bar Kochba" ("Son of the Star"), thereby consecrating him as the messiah.[624]

The royal scepter or staff represented the position of a ruler, a symbol of authority and power.[625] In the blessing of Jacob upon his son Judah, the patriarch stated that the scepter would not depart from Judah (Gen 49:9–10), meaning that Judah's royal lineage would be everlasting. Moses and Aaron carried staffs (same Hb. word), which symbolized their divinely granted authority and power over nature.[626] Scepters or staffs were thin wooden or metal poles, sometimes capped by a mace head of copper or bronze and shaped in various forms. In Bronze Age Egyptian murals, the pharaoh is depicted smiting his foes with his glorious scepter, as the future king of Israel is portrayed in the next section.[627]

**24:17c–18a**  As featured in the above structural outline of this oracle, the versification divisions have been altered to reflect the structure of the

---

[623] J. J. Collins, *The Scepter and the Star: The Messiahs of the Dead Sea Scrolls and Other Ancient Literature* (New York: Doubleday, 1995), esp. 24, 63–70. See also J. A. Fitzmyer, *The Dead Sea Scrolls and Christian Origins* (Grand Rapids: Eerdmans, 2000), 75, 86, 98; C. G. Boyles, "The Redeeming King: Psalm 72's Contribution to the Messianic Ideal," in *Eschatology, Messianism, and the Dead Sea Scrolls*, ed. C. A. Evans and P. W. Flint (Grand Rapids: Eerdmans, 1997), 23.

[624] Collins, *The Scepter and the Star,* 202.

[625] Gen 49:10; Ps 45:6; Amos 1:5,8. Cf. also Esth 5:2.

[626] Exod 4:2–5; 7:8–13; 17:5–6; 17:1–10 (Eng).

[627] *ANEP,* 317.

Hebrew parallelism. In the third oracle the coming king was portrayed as having the power to devour hostile nations and crush the bones of the enemies of Israel (24:7b,8b). The future ideal king will vanquish once and for all those enemies of Israel who have most recently caused them harm or distress. The Moabite king had enlisted Balaam's help in an attempt to curse and therefore overthrow Israel. The Edomites not only refused safe passage to the Israelites who were traveling through the southern Transjordan region but also dispatched their armies against them as they drew near (Num 20:14–21). In the distant future both peoples would be conquered, captured, and eventually disappear from being distinctive ethnic groups. The phraseology of "crushing of the head" is a symbol of defeating one's enemies in Egyptian, Ugaritic, and Hebrew literature. The term translated "skulls" (*qarqar*, "tear down") requires an emendation to *qodqōd* ("crown of the head") that is based on comparison with the Samaritan Pentateuch and the use of the same phrase in Jer 48:45.[628]

The "children of Seth" are probably not the Sethites of Adamic ancestral lineage, for that would imply the annihilation of a major portion of the human race. But if instead one takes the bicola as synonymous Hebrew parallelism, the phrase "children of Seth" would be the equivalent of the phrase "of Moab," hence described as one of the people groups from the lineage of Seth.[629] Such parallelism is reinforced by the common word pair found in the succeeding bicola, that of Edom and Seir.[630] Others suggest these Sethites to be the nomadic Shutu (or Shosu) tribe known from nineteenth and eighteenth century B.C. Egyptian execration texts.[631]

**24:18b–19** As featured in the above structural outline of this oracle, the versification divisions have been altered to reflect the structure of the Hebrew parallelism. Keeping the common word pair of Israel // Jacob intact yields a tricolon of 3:2:3 meter, with the first two in chiastic parallel and the final colon expanding upon the second. Numerous variations from the translation have been proffered by scholars due to the arrangement of the Hebrew

---

[628] Most scholars, almost without exception, adopt this emendation based upon the comparative textual evidence.

[629] Ashley, *Numbers,* 501.

[630] This identification of the Edomites (a people) with [Mount] Seir is based upon the movement of Esau to the Mount Seir region (Gen 32:4; 36:1–9) following the blessing of Jacob by Isaac. Henceforth, the trio of terms (Seir – Edom – Mount Seir) become somewhat synonymous, though not necessarily equivalents.

[631] *ANET,* 329. In his textual notes the translator J. A. Wilson took the Shutu to be the equivalent of the "children of Seth" and Moab in Num 24:17. If so, the Shutu could have been the Semitic forerunners of the classical Iron Age Moabites. See also Milgrom, *Numbers,* 208; Wenham, *Numbers,* 179. In another alternative Noordzij translates the term "sons of Seth" as "sons of tumult" or "war-minded," referring to the prideful character of the Moabites confronted by the latter prophets (Isa 16:6; 25:11; Zeph 2:10).

text and the corruptions evident in the text. Wenham suggested a rearrangement of the text in which the word "his enemies" (*ʾōybāyw*) is transposed from v. 18 to the first colon in v. 19. This would yield the following translation: "Jacob shall rule his enemies and destroy the survivors from Ir."[632] This emended composition is inviting but unnecessary because the term "his enemies" stands in apposition to Seir. The translation I have offered above in the structural outline works with the canonical text as it stands.

The meaning of the NIV clause in v. 19, "A ruler will come out of Jacob" closely parallels the translation in the NKJV, "Out of Jacob One shall have dominion." Both of these take the Hebrew verb form *wĕyērd* as derived from the root *rādâ*, "to rule, have dominion."[633] That the MT is corrupt here is quite evident in the BHS. Wenham and others take the *m-* that is prefixed to "Jacob" in the MT (*miyyaʿăqōb*, "from Jacob") to be an enclitic *mem* that should have been attached to *wĕyērd*. Thus the translation is derived: "Jacob shall rule his enemies and destroy the survivors from Ir."[634] Another possibility would be to take the *mem* as a pronominal suffix, whereby yielding the translation, "Jacob shall rule them." But as Balaam continued to envision Israel launching forth in a military campaign that would obliterate even the last remnant of the people from the city, a translation of *rādâ* as meaning "tread" or "trample" might be more appropriate in the context. Taking each of these suggestions into account, the translation offered above seems to do the least manipulation of the text and still preserve the context. The final word of the oracle "of the city" (*mēʿîr*) may be a reference to an actual city known as Ir Moab, mentioned in Num 22:36, or even Ar of Moab of 21:28.[635] In conclusion Wenham remarks, "With bone-chilling drama he declares that every inhabitant of Ir will perish. This prediction of Moab's total defeat at the hand of a future Israelite king is an appropriate point for Balaam to end."[636]

**[20]Then Balaam saw Amalek and uttered his oracle:**
**"Amalek was first among the nations,**
**but he will come to ruin at last."**
**[21]Then he saw the Kenites and uttered his oracle:**
**"Your dwelling place is secure,**
**your nest is set in a rock;**
**[22]yet you Kenites will be destroyed**
**when Asshur takes you captive."**

---

[632] Wenham, *Numbers,* 180; also followed by Milgrom, *Numbers,* 208.

[633] Cf. the same form in Ps 72:8.

[634] Wenham, *Numbers,* 180. Cf. Budd, *Numbers,* 253, 256; Albright, "The Oracles of Balaam," *JBL* 63 (1944): 207-33.

[635] See Milgrom, *Numbers,* 208; Wenham, *Numbers,* 180.

[636] Wenham, *Numbers,* 180.

²³Then he uttered his oracle:
"Ah, who can live when God does this?

²⁴Ships will come from the shores of Kittim;
they will subdue Asshur and Eber,
but they too will come to ruin."

BALAAM'S FINAL THREE ORACLES (24:20–24). Each of the final
three oracles of Balaam commences with the standard oracular formula used
in each of the four previous prophetic pronouncements. The three oracles
together form a literary unit shaped by an inclusio using the clause *ʿădê
ʾōbēd* (lit, "until he perishes"), the central theme of the collection. The
theme of the destruction of the enemies of Israel extends that which was
begun in the third oracle (24:8) and continued in the fourth (24:17–19).[637]
Each of the first two oracles begins with a brief introductory clause citing
Balaam's role as a seer *(wayyarʾ ʾet-),* one who does more than look with
the eyes but one who examines the situation with divinely aided perception.
One might translate each of these as "then he keenly observed X, and so he
took up his discourse and said." Balaam might have been able to observe
each of these three peoples from the vantage point in the Abarim mountains,
looking southward toward the Amalekites, Kenites, and the Asshurites.[638]
Each of these oracles is very brief, though the textual difficulties abound.
This collection of successive oracles against the nations that surrounded
Israel was the first of a genre of prophetic pronouncements, later exemplified
by Amos (1–2), Isaiah (13–23), Jeremiah (46–51), and Ezekiel (25–32); and
Zephaniah (2:4–3:7).

*Balaam's Fifth Oracle: Against the Amalekites (24:20).* **24:20** The
theme of the oracle against the Amalekites is that though they considered
themselves among the preeminent of the nations, they will be destroyed. The
bicolon contains antithetic parallelism using the bookend terms *rēʾšît* ("first,
beginning") and *ʾaḥărît* ("end, last").

| Beginning | of nations | [was] Amalek |
| But its end | [will be] unto destruction. | |

Though several scholars have suggested emending the text by rearranging the
characters,[639] the text can stand on its own in its typically oblique Hebrew
poetic character. The Amalekites, who seem to have originated in the Sinai

---

[637] Contra the view that there is little or no connection between these three oracles and the previous Balaam material, such as presented by Noordzij, *Numbers,* 233; Gray, *Numbers,* 373; Noth,
*Numbers,* 193; deVaulx, *Numbers,* 295.

[638] Many scholars believe that the prophet is referring not to the Assyrians but to the Asshurites
(Asshurim), a nomadic group known from Gen 25:3,18 and Ps 83:9.

[639] Albright realigns the Hb. consonants to read עד יאבד and translates the clause as "his end
is to perish forever."

region in the third millennium B.C., were the first enemies Israel encountered after the Exodus from Egypt (Exod 17:8–16). The Amalekites were defeated at Rephidim in the west central Sinai peninsula as Moses held up his hands (with the help of Aaron and Hur) during the lengthy battle. The Exodus passage concludes with a statement that is apropos in the present context, "The LORD will be at war against the Amalekites from generation to generation." The Amalekites with help from the Canaanites defeated the Israelites when they first tried to enter the Promised Land after they had rejected it at Kadesh in the Wilderness of Zin (Num 14:43–45). Several centuries later both Saul and David conquered the Amalekites in the tenth century B.C. (1 Sam 15:1–33; 30:1–19) followed by Hezekiah's victories in the late eighth century (1 Chr 4:43).

*Balaam's Sixth Oracle: Against the Kenites (24:21–22).* **24:21–22** The Kenites (*haqqênî*, or *qayin* = "smith") by name seem to have originated in the southern Negev or northeastern Sinai regions, areas that were also inhabited by the Midianites and Amalekites (Exod 2:16; Num 10:29; Judg 1:16; 4:11; 1 Sam 15:6; 27:10). In the reiteration of God's promise of the land to Abram in Gen 15:18–21, the Kenites were among those occupying the land at that time but who were to be dispossessed. The structure of this brief oracle is that of an antithetical chiasmus, as noted below.

+A "Enduring is      your dwelling place,
  +B Set in the rock   is your nest.
 -B Nevertheless   he shall be for burning     Kain
-A Until Asshur     takes you captive."

The Kenites put their faith in the security afforded them by their geographical positioning, nestled in the rocky highlands of southern Canaan or the northeastern quadrant of the Sinai region. Though they felt as though their settlements were impregnable, Balaam boldly described their homes as "nests" *(qinnekā)*, a prophetic pun based on the name of the people group. Such nests of straw and twigs could easily be destroyed by fire, so their faith was in vain.

The terminology of the final line of the oracle is difficult, if the name Asshur is taken to mean the Assyrians (=Asshur) of the ninth to seventh centuries B.C. Even if the name implicates the Assyrians, the dating or the oracle need not be moved to the Iron II period, for the Assyrians were a major ethnic entity under its kings of the early second millennium B.C. As noted above in the introduction to these final oracles, however, the term Asshur probably refers to the Asshurites of the Negev regions, the nomadic group known from Gen 25:3,18 and Ps 83:9.[640]

---

[640] The conquering Asshurim of this passage might also refer to the Assyrians of the Middle Assyrian period, who began their deportation practices in the late fourteenth to early thirteenth centuries B.C.

*Balaam's Seventh Oracle: Against Assyria (24:23–24).* **24:23–24** The final oracle does not begin with Balaam keenly observing a people group but goes right into the introductory discourse formula, "Then he took up his discourse and said," found in all seven oracles.[641] The initial proclamation of the oracle seems elliptical and hence difficult to translate.[642] A translation, as close to literal as possible, is presented in the structural outline of the oracle below.

(a) "Alas who shall live when God establishes it!
  (b) Ships from the coast of Kittim,
      They shall subdue Asshur,
      They shall subdue Eber,
(a') So even he will be unto destruction."[643]

Even the mighty Asshurim, whom Balaam proclaimed would subdue and take captive the Kenites, were destined by God for destruction.[644] Ships (ṣîm)[645] would sail from the coastlands and islands (lit, "from the hand of the Kittim") of the Mediterranean. Ugaritic sailors and those from other coastal peoples traversed the often formidable seas from the Levantine seashores to the Iberian peninsula throughout the second millennium B.C. The Philistines of the period of the judges came in the massive migrations that took place toward the end of the Late Bronze Age, along with other Sea Peoples such as the Sherden, Tekelet, and Danoi. The name Kittim probably derived from the name of the prominent city on Cyprus known as Kition.[646] In the Qumran literature the term "Kittim" became a byword for the archenemies of God and his kingdom, who would finally be defeated in the future great eschatological battle. Eber also would be subdued by the noble Israelite kingdom. The meaning of the reference to Eber has puzzled scholars for centuries. In the Septuagint the name is translated as "Hebrews" though this is historically and politically untenable. The name Eber occurs in the genealogy of Shem in Gen 11:14–17 and perhaps could be associated with the king known as Ibrim in the Ebla tablets of northern Syria of the third millennium B.C. Such an identification remains quite tentative.

---

[641] See commentary on 23:7 above.

[642] Milgrom simply states, "A literal rendering is incomprehensible" (*Numbers,* 210). Scholars have proposed a variety of reconstructions of the Hb. text of v. 24, ranging from Wenham, who translates the line as "the isles shall assemble in the North, ships from the farthest sea" (*Numbers,* 182).

[643] For discussion of the final phrase אֹבֵד עֲדֵי, "unto destruction," see above commentary on 24:20.

[644] See discussion notes on "Asshur" in the commentary on 24:22 above.

[645] The Hb. plural צִים derives from an Egyptian loan word ṯꜣi (BDB, 851) and occurs also in Isa 33:21; Ezek 30:9; and Dan 11:30.

[646] Phoenician Kiti, whose tel is in modern Larnaca, Cyprus.

God had decreed the destruction of the enemies of Israel, who were thus by definition enemies of Yahweh himself. The defeat of the enemies of Israel would be accomplished in part during the reign of David, during which the Philistines (who had come from the islands of Crete, Cyprus, and Mycenaean Greece), Canaanites, Amalekites, Edomites, Arameans, and others were subdued and subject to Israelite hegemony. But the model of the exploits of the Davidic kingdom would serve only as a meager example of the glory of the great Messianic kingdom to come off in the more distant future. The final chapter of the kingdom story is delineated in the Book of Revelation, when Jesus the One True Messiah would be crowned as King of Kings and Lord of Lords (Rev 19:16; 22:13,16).

**[25]Then Balaam got up and returned home and Balak went his own way.**

BALAAM DEPARTS HOMEWARD (24:25).    **24:25**    The Book of Balaam has now completed its full cycle with Balaam and Balak returning toward their respective homes. The verb sequence "arose and went" is a common narrative idiom, found also in the patriarchal materials.[647] Likewise the statements that "he returned to his place" or "he returned on his way" are a common means of completing a narrative cycle.[648] Before he departed for his hometown of Pethor (Pitru), however, he provided some additional advice to the Midianite and Moabite leaders concerning an alternate way to influence the Israelites in a harmful manner. According to Num 31:8,16 and Josh 13:22, Balaam counseled them to try seduction via the sexual activities of their religious cult at Baal Peor near Abel Shittim. Unfortunately this advice proved successful in captivating the attention of the Israelites and provoking the Lord to anger against his chosen people. This event would serve as a reminder, as would their previous rebellions, that God will not tolerate outright sinfulness in rebellion against him. What could not be accomplished via direct confrontation was realized through indirect means. The power of evil and Satan to bring down the otherwise godly person is often done through subtle, backdoor methods. Giving such advice would also seal Balaam's fate; he would be killed in the reprisal against the Midianites for their part in the idolatrous corruption of the Israelites.

*(7)  The Final Rebellion: Idolatry at Baal Peor (25:1–18)*

**[1]While Israel was staying in Shittim, the men began to indulge in sexual immorality with Moabite women, [2]who invited them to the sacrifices to their**

---

[647] Cf. Gen 22:3; 24:10; 28:2 (as imperatives); 38:19; etc. The verb קוּם is also used in conjunction with other verbs such as עלה ("he arose and ascended") Gen 35:1; with עבר (Gen 31:21); and many others.

[648] Cf. Gen 18:33; 32:1–2.

gods. The people ate and bowed down before these gods. [3]So Israel joined in worshiping the Baal of Peor. And the LORD's anger burned against them.

[4]The LORD said to Moses, "Take all the leaders of these people, kill them and expose them in broad daylight before the LORD, so that the LORD's fierce anger may turn away from Israel."

[5]So Moses said to Israel's judges, "Each of you must put to death those of your men who have joined in worshiping the Baal of Peor."

[6]Then an Israelite man brought to his family a Midianite woman right before the eyes of Moses and the whole assembly of Israel while they were weeping at the entrance to the Tent of Meeting. [7]When Phinehas son of Eleazar, the son of Aaron, the priest, saw this, he left the assembly, took a spear in his hand [8]and followed the Israelite into the tent. He drove the spear through both of them—through the Israelite and into the woman's body. Then the plague against the Israelites was stopped; [9]but those who died in the plague numbered 24,000.

[10]The LORD said to Moses, [11]"Phinehas son of Eleazar, the son of Aaron, the priest, has turned my anger away from the Israelites; for he was as zealous as I am for my honor among them, so that in my zeal I did not put an end to them. [12]Therefore tell him I am making my covenant of peace with him. [13]He and his descendants will have a covenant of a lasting priesthood, because he was zealous for the honor of his God and made atonement for the Israelites."

[14]The name of the Israelite who was killed with the Midianite woman was Zimri son of Salu, the leader of a Simeonite family. [15]And the name of the Midianite woman who was put to death was Cozbi daughter of Zur, a tribal chief of a Midianite family.

[16]The LORD said to Moses, [17]"Treat the Midianites as enemies and kill them, [18]because they treated you as enemies when they deceived you in the affair of Peor and their sister Cozbi, the daughter of a Midianite leader, the woman who was killed when the plague came as a result of Peor."

The human tendency to lapse into unfaithfulness, even after some of the most dramatic demonstrations of God's love and power, is underscored by the positioning of the Baal Peor incident immediately after accounts of the successful victories of the Israelites over Sihon and Og of the Amorites in Transjordan and the climactic work of God in using the pagan prophet Balaam to pronounce blessing upon his people. Wenham remarks: "The Bible startles its readers by the way it juxtapositions the brightest of revelations and the darkest of sins. ... In this way Scripture tries to bring home to us the full wonder of God's grace in the face of man's incorrigible propensity to sin."[649]

The rebellious idolatry incident at Baal Peor serves several purposes in the Book of Numbers. First, the account concludes the third cycle of rebellion and completes the larger sequence of defiant acts against God's deliv-

---

[649] Wenham, *Numbers,* 184.

erance of his people from Egypt and his faithful provision for their needs in the desert. The three rebellion cycles end on a deeply somber note, and yet in the structure of this cycle the verb usage indicates that Moses experiences a restoration of his relationship with God. Second, it serves as a reminder to the new generation and its successive descendants concerning the grave consequences of rejecting God's sovereign rule over their lives through the worship of other deities. Idolatry would become the thorn in the flesh for Israel from the days of the judges to the united kingdom under Solomon and continuing until the destruction of both kingdoms in 722 and 586 B.C., functioning as a major component of the prophetic Deuteronomic history. Third, this chapter adds an additional Levitical/priestly element to the conclusion of the third rebellion cycle, when the high priest Eleazar's son Phinehas becomes the exemplar of one defending the sanctity of Israel and the Tent of Meeting.

This account parallels the Levites' response to the Israelites' sinfulness at Mount Sinai in the golden calf incident, where they as a tribe became the exemplars of defending the faith. Both followed periods when the people were unaware of what events were transpiring beyond their view, Moses on Mount Sinai and Balaam in Moab. Wenham and Milgrom have highlighted two additional parallels between the accounts: both involve the worship of other gods (Exod 32:8), and both accentuate the allaying of God's wrath via the punishment of the guilty participants (Exod 32:26–28). Milgrom goes as far as to say that the Baal Peor punishment was the fulfillment of the promise in Exod 32:34, "However, when the time comes for me to punish, I will punish them for their sins."[650] Like the former generation that died in the wilderness, the new generation had to learn the most important lesson concerning God and their relationship to him—that he is and always will be holy, and he will not allow idolatry to go unreproved.

SETTING OF IMMORALITY (25:1–3). **25:1a** The incident is set forth in chiastic structure as outlined below, with the focal point being the sacrificial activities in which the Israelite men were participating. A minor inclusio is formed by the use of the name "Israel" in vv. 1b and 3. The geographical link to the previous and later material is derived from the references to Shittim (full name as in Num 33:49, "Abel Shittim; Josh 2:1; 3:1), Baal (22:41, "Bamoth Baal), and Peor (Deut 3:29). The name Shittim is an example of a floral toponym, derived from the word for "acacia tree" that is so prominent in these arid regions. Glueck identified Abel Shittim with Tell el-Khefrein, though Tell el-Hamman, a site located at the mouth of the Wadi Kefrein, has also been suggested.[651] Josephus identified the

---

[650] Wenham, *Numbers,* 184; Milgrom, *Numbers,* 211.
[651] N. Glueck, *Explorations in Eastern Palestine,* AASOR 25–28 (1945–48): 221, 371–82.

site with Abila of his day, a site located seven miles east of the Jordan and
about five miles north of the Dead Sea.[652] This general area just a few
miles northeast of the Dead Sea, also referred to several times by the
description "on the plains of Moab by the Jordan across from Jericho,"[653]
was to be the geographical setting for the remainder of the Israelite
sojourn prior to entering the Promised Land. The text transitions into the
final two cycles of material that focus on preparation for entry into the
Promised Land. The Israelites were poised for entry but had a very difficult lesson to learn. The reference to Baal Peor would be remembered
throughout biblical history, even into the early Christian church. The worship style related to the Baal cult would from this point on be a constant
temptation to the Israelites, eventually becoming one of the key reasons
for the subjugation, destruction, and captivity of Jerusalem, Judah, and
Israel in the eighth to sixth centuries B.C.

(a) When **Israel** was dwelling in Shittim,    (25:1a)
   (b) The *people* profaned themselves by fornicating with the daughters
      of Moab.    (25:1b)
      They called the *people* to the sacrifices of their gods,    (25:2)
      And the *people* ate and drank to their gods.
(a') Thus **Israel** joined themselves to Baal Peor,    (25:3)
      So the anger of Yahweh burned against Israel.

**25:1b–2** The moral and ethical transgression of the Israelites is
described in emphatic fashion. The threefold repetition of "people"
*(hā'ām)* following preterit forms in consecutive clauses produces a hammering staccato effect, accentuating the matter of the people's downfall. In
the first line the issue was uncleanness by means of sexual immorality. The
NIV phraseology, "The men began to indulge in sexual immorality," translates the more emphatically worded Hebrew text, which literally reads,
"Then they committed profanity by fornicating" with Moabite women
residing in the area. The Moabites of this region had been under the
dominion of Sihon prior to his defeat at the hands of the Israelites (Num
21:26), but now were in Balak's control. The word "profane" *(wayyāḥel)*
means "to render something unclean by an immoral or unethical act" or
"to remove from sacred usage into the realm of the common." It is used of
the defiling of the Sabbath (Exod 31:14) or the defamation of God's name
(Ezek 20:9). The "sexual immorality" of the NIV (Hb. *liznôt* from *zānâ*) in
the context of the following clauses denotes the beginning of a process

---

[652] Josephus, *Antiquities,* 4.8.1; 5.1.1. Cf. Ashley, *Numbers,* 516; Harrison, *Numbers,* 335; Milgrom, *Numbers,* 212; Wenham, *Numbers,* 184.

[653] Num 22:1; 26:63; 31:12; 33:48,50; 36:13.

that led from general sexual immorality with the Moabite women to full-scale idolatry that probably included ritual prostitution in the Baal Peor cult. In the second line the Moabite women are described as having seduced the Israelite men, literally inviting them by "calling" *(wattiqre'nā)* them to the sacrificial feast. The feasts themselves were probably somewhat like the Israelite communion offering ceremonies in which the offerer (individual or group) consumed portions of the offerings after the ritual slaughtering of the animals (Lev 3:1–17; 7:11–21,28–34). Certain portions were rendered unto God, other portions provided for the priests, and the remainder was to be eaten in a ceremonial manner in the tabernacle. So at the Baal Peor worship center Israelite men were invited in to the festival banquet, at the meat offered to the famous northwest Semitic deity, and then completed the ritual process by bowing down *(wayyištaḥwû,* "they prostrated themselves, worshiped") to Baal or Peor, and perhaps others of the various deities of the Moabite pantheon.[654]

The sequencing parallels the prediction of Exod 34:15–16 as to the natural results from entering into treaties with the peoples of the land: "Be careful not to make a treaty with those who live in the land; for when they prostitute themselves to their gods and sacrifice to them, they will invite you and you will eat their sacrifices. And when you choose some of their daughters as wives for your sons and those daughters prostitute themselves to their gods, they will lead your sons to do the same."[655] The great tragic exemplar of this tendency was King Solomon, who loved numerous foreign women, many of whom he had acquired via treaties with Egypt, Phoenicia, Ammon, and even these same Moabites. He would even go so far as to build temples to the gods his wives worshiped, on the hill east of the city, directly opposite the glorious Temple of Yahweh (1 Kgs 11:1–10). The result was a collapse of his kingdom, which was then split apart under the reign of his son Rehoboam (1 Kgs 11:14–25; 12:1–24).

**25:3** The idolatrous sin of the Israelites at Baal Peor is summarized by the verbal phrase "joined in worshiping," which translates the single Hebrew term *wayyiṣṣāmed,* thus "he yoked himself to." As to verbal usage this term is rare in biblical Hebrew, found elsewhere only in v. 5 and Ps 106:28,[656] the latter being a summary of this incident. The noun form *ṣemed* is usually translated "yoke." Milgrom suggests some kind of covenant agreement was enacted in the process by which the Israelites were

---

[654] The plural term for gods is here used, לֵאלֹהֵיהֶן, but this could be taken as a singular reference to the "great god Baal." Cf. singular meaning view of Milgrom, *Numbers,* 212; Ashley, *Numbers,* 516–17; contra plural of Harrison, *Numbers,* 336.

[655] See Deut 7:3–4; Judg 3:6; Ezra 9:9,12; Neh 10:30; 13:25.

[656] Only three occurrences in the *niphal* form. Also the *pual* participle מְצֻמֶּדֶת in 2 Sam 20:8 and in the *hiphil* imperfect form תַּצְמִיד in Ps 50:19.

permitted (after being invited) to engage in the various forms of debauchery associated with the Baal cult. The Israelites yoked themselves together in the formal cultic ritual with the Moabites and Midianites in the worship of Baal and Beth Peor ("house/temple of Peor"). Milgrom suggests some kind of covenant agreement was enacted in the process by which the Israelites were permitted (after being invited) to engage in the various forms of debauchery associated with the Baal cult.[657] By engaging in such worship practices, the Israelites had violated both the first and second Commandments—to have no other gods and to worship no other deities by bowing down and serving them in the cult (Exod 20:2-5; Deut 5:7-9). Abrogation of any one of the Ten Commandments was punishable by death, and hence the punishment to be meted out against the idolatrous Israelites was severe.

This is the first occurrence of Baal in the Hebrew Bible, and he would become the primary antagonist to Yahweh for the hearts of the people of Israel from this setting to the end of the two Israelite kingdoms. The historical setting is the latter half of the Late Bronze Age, when the deity Baal was emerging as one of the major operative deities in the land of Canaan. He is best known from the texts of Ugarit as the agent of the creative order, who with his consort Anath defeated the forces of evil, namely the deities Yammu (Sea), Mot (Death), and Lotan (Leviathan, Sea Monster), thereby bringing order to the chaos. Baal was a lesser known deity in Mesopotamia during the Early Bronze Age and in the beginning of the Middle Bronze (patriarchal) period. Milgrom simply states that "the patriarchs did not know him."[658] The first appearance of Baal as a prominent deity in the land of Canaan is evidenced in the Hyksos period texts from Egypt in the latter half of the Middle Bronze Age. The Egyptians bemoaned the fact that the "foreign rulers" from the land of the Hurru and Retenu were not worshipers of Amon-Re but of a god called Baal Hazor, which they associated with their god Seth.[659] With the emergence of the classical Canaanites in the land of the southern Levant, apparently an amalgam of northwest Semitic peoples and some non-Semitic elements such as the Hurrians and Hittites, came the emergence of Baal as a primary operative deity in the cults of the land.

MOSES RECEIVES INSTRUCTION FROM YAHWEH (25:4). **25:4** The secondary means of introducing divine instruction in the Book of Numbers is employed here, "So Yahweh said to Moses" *(wayyō'mer YHWH 'el-*

---

[657] Milgrom, *Numbers,* 212.

[658] Ibid., 213.

[659] *ANET,* 179.

*mōšeh)* instead of the primary phraseology, "Thus Yahweh spoke/instructed Moses" *(wayyĕdabbēr YHWH ᵓel-mōšeh lēᵓmōr)*.[660] As noted in the "Introduction to the Balaam Oracles," the secondary phraseology has been employed in the context of Moses receiving revelation from the Lord ever since he sinned at Meribah Kadesh (20:1–13). The primary means of introducing divine instruction will be employed again after the sin at Baal Peor has been dealt with properly under Moses' leadership, as seen in the shift of verbal usage in v. 10.

The instructions given to Moses were severe but necessary to accomplish the purging of the sins of the people. Moses was charged to literally "take *[qaḥ]* all the leaders of the people *[roᵓšê hāᶜām]* and impale them to Yahweh *[laYHWH]* before the sun *[neged haššāmeš]*." Moses was to round up all the tribal leaders, those representatives of the people who presumably should have either prevented the idolatrous activities or carried out the punishment of the guilty members of their tribes, and execute them by impaling them on poles such that their bodies would hang out in the open in broad daylight ("before the sun").[661] The term "impale" *(hôqaᶜ)* is a rare Hebrew verb that has been variously translated as "kill," "execute," "impale," or "dismember."[662] Exposure to the elements usually followed this form of execution, as in the case of Saul's sons (2 Sam 21:8–13). Such public exposure was reserved for only the most heinous of crimes in ancient Israel and Mesopotamia. Later Assyrian bas relief murals, such as those of Sennacherib's palace at Nineveh, depict rebellious vassals impaled upon poles and left for public viewing, presumably to act as a deterrent to further insurrection. Such seems to be the intended result of this form of execution and public display.[663] That the guilty parties were to be executed as "unto Yahweh" means that they were rendered unto the Lord in order to expiate the divine wrath as evidenced in the plague.

A second interpretive question is that of exactly who was to be executed

---

[660] Note the shift in revelatory terminology in the Book of Numbers in the following verses:

20:7–8a וַיְדַבֵּר יְהוָה אֶל־מֹשֶׁה לֵּאמֹר: קַח אֶת־הַמַּטֶּה

20:12 וַיֹּאמֶר יְהוָה אֶל־מֹשֶׁה וְאֶל־אַהֲרֹן

25:4 וַיֹּאמֶר יְהוָה אֶל־מֹשֶׁה קַח אֶת־כָּל־רָאשֵׁי הָעָם

25:10 וַיְדַבֵּר יְהוָה אֶל־מֹשֶׁה לֵּאמֹר

[661] Cf. the use of the phrase נֶגֶד הַשָּׁמֶשׁ in 2 Sam 12:12.

[662] NIV, "kill," with NKJV; "execute" in NASB; "impale" in NRSV, "hang" in RSV. R. Polzin has suggested the meaning of "dismember" in "'HWQY' and Covenantal Institutions in Early Israel," *HTR* 62 (1969): 227–40. The *qal* form of the verb יקע means "dislocate, sprain" as happened to Jacob's hip when he wrestled with the angel at Penuel (Gen 32:26). Cf. also the Code of Hammurabi, 153.

[663] Cf. Joshua and the Israelites' treatment of the five kings of the coalition of southern Canaanite cities who attacked the city of Gibeon, which incident precipitated the southern campaign of the conquest (Josh 10:1–27).

by this methodology. Was it all of the tribal and clan leaders or just the actual offenders? What was the difference between the "leaders" and the "judges" of v. 5. The question has puzzled translators and interpreters throughout history. The Samaritan Pentateuch reads interpretively "command that they slay all the men who have attached themselves to Baal-peor," thereby limiting the execution to only those who joined themselves to Baal Peor. The same limitation is evidenced in *Targum Onkelos*. Modern interpreters such as Keil have taken a similar stance, reading the "them" object of the verb "kill" as referring to the offenders of v. 5 and not to all the leaders.[664] On the other hand Ashley, who describes the present chapter as combining and summarizing two stories, sees this interpretation as untenable from the text, since as he notes, "Neither God's nor Moses' sentence was carried out."[665] He suggested that the original command to Moses extended to all the leaders of Israel, taking the "them" to refer to the nearest antecedent, the *ro'šê hā'ām*, but this was a different command than that actually carried out by Moses, who acted on the side of pragmatism by ordering the judges to execute only the actual idolaters.

An alternative approach would be to see the Hebrew narrative in a typical fashion as moving deliberately from the broad perspective to the narrow. In the literary rhetorical outline of the chapter, the text moves judiciously from the broad instructions to Moses (v. 4), to the more specific instruction of Moses (v. 5), and then to the specific exemplar of Phinehas, who executed the couple who acted with such blatant depravity at the entrance to the Tent of Meeting. Note the broad chiastic outline of the narrative below.

A  Setting of Immorality: Worship of Baal of Peor (25:1–3)
   B  Moses' Instruction from Yahweh: Take, Execute, and So Allay Wrath (25:4)
     C  Moses Instructs the Leaders of Israel: Kill the Offenders (25:5)
     C'  Phinehas Follows Moses' Instruction: Kills Zimri and Cozbi (25:6–8a)
   B'  Wrath of Yahweh Allayed: Plague Halted (25:8b)
A'  Results of Israel's Immorality: 24,000 Died in Plague (25:9)

With the execution of Zimri, described as a leader *(nāśî')* of the Simeonites

---

[664] Keil, *Numbers*. 204–5. Cf. also F. C. Cook, *The Fourth Book of Moses Called Numbers* (London: Murray, 1871), 750; A. Dillmann, *Das Bücheri Numeri, Deuteronomium und Joshua* (Leipzig: Hirzel, 1886), 169.

[665] Ashley, *Numbers*, 514–15, 518–19. Ashley states: "This execution of the whole corps of Israelite leaders may seem unjust to a modern Western individualism. It must be remembered, however, that these men were the divinely appointed representatives of the people. In v. 3 it was Israel (as a whole group) that bound itself to Baal-peor, so that either the whole group must pay the price of God's wrath, or a representative group must. It is a serious thing to be a leader" (p. 518).

(and thereby utilizing all the major terms for Israelite leadership), Yahweh's anger was satisfied and the plague ended. That Moses faltered in his leadership responsibility, as Ashley suggests, is in contradistinction to the restoration of the relationship between Yahweh and Moses as indicated by the use of the revelatory terminology of v. 10, which was last used in Num 20:7.[666] The narrative intent is to highlight the role of Phinehas, a priest of the direct lineage of the high priest Aaron, in allaying the fury of God's wrath. As in the manner that the Levites defended the faith in slaying the idolatrous Israelites in the incident involving the golden calf (Exod 32:1–35) and as the actions of Aaron and Eleazar helped halt the plague that resulted from the Korah rebellion (Num 16:31–50), so the haste of Phinehas in faithfully fulfilling God's and Moses' instructions brought an end to the divine punishment and atoned for the sins of the people.

MOSES INSTRUCTS THE LEADERS OF ISRAEL (25:5). **25:5** The "judges of Israel" *(šōpṭê yiśrāʾēl)* probably were those appointed by Moses over the Israelite divisions of the thousands, hundreds, fifties, and tens and who settled disputes among the Israelites (Exod 18:13–26).[667] They were given instruction to execute only those who had participated in the ritual activities and thereby had committed themselves to the worship of Baal Peor.

PHINEHAS FOLLOWS MOSES' INSTRUCTION (25:6–8a). **25:6–8a** The scene quickly shifts to the exemplary action by Phinehas in defending the sanctuary of Yahweh against a couple whose illicit actions were about to defile the holy place. The introductory phraseology of the verse, *wĕhinnēh ... bāʾ ...* ("and behold ... he came forth"), indicates simultaneous action[668] to Moses' charge to the judges to execute all participants in the idolatry. Just as the words had been spoken by Moses, an Israelite man[669] presented one of the seductive Midianite women to his brother for whatever use he deemed fit, directly in front of Moses and the people who had gathered at the entrance to the Tent of Meeting for at time of penitent mourning. As Moses and other people had assembled themselves at the place where so often the Lord had manifested and revealed himself to his faithful servants, the insolent man flaunted his wantonness before the nation's leadership. Though some have interpreted the actions of the man and woman as cultic prostitution, the terminology used here is not that specific. The argument of Milgrom is convincing here, for he observes that "sacrificing following whoring makes sense. Sexual attraction led to participation in the sacrificial feasts at

---

[666] See above comment.

[667] M. Weinfeld, "Judge and Officer in Ancient Israel and in the Ancient Near East," *IOS* 8 (1977): 65–88.

[668] Milgrom, *Numbers,* 324, n. 32.

[669] A minor inclusio is formed by the use of אִישׁ מִבְּנֵי יִשְׂרָאֵל in v. 6 and אִישׁ יִשְׂרָאֵל in v. 8.

the shrine of Baal-peor and, ultimately, to intermarriage."[670] Either way the Israelite man in conjoining himself with the worship of Baal was challenging the cult of Yahweh by committing such an act of political and religious treason in close proximity to the place that symbolized God's presence, power, and personhood. According to the outlay of the tribes in camping around the sanctuary, the Simeonites were supposed to be camped on the South side of the Tent of Meeting along with the Reubenites and Gadites, so their activities would have had to have been outwardly flagrant for them to have been seen from the tabernacle entrance. At the entrance to the Tent of Meeting revelation took place, anointment rituals commenced, and atonement processes began.[671] Nearby an unfaithful Israelite attempted to complete a sacred union with a Baal worshiper, but to his mortal detriment.

Phinehas was of a royal priestly bloodline, having been born to Aaron's son Eleazar and one of the daughters of Putiel (Exod 6:25). His name was of Egyptian derivation (*piʾ-n-ḥaś*, meaning "dark-skinned one") and he served the Lord and the Israelites faithfully throughout his life. On the basis of his righteous indignation in defense of the sanctuary of Yahweh, he was asked to accompany the Israelite armies in the campaign against Midian, during which Balaam, who was the instigator of this whole affair, was slain (Num 31:6–8). He was sent to arbitrate on behalf of the priesthood the dispute over the altar—later called the "Witness"—built by the Transjordan tribes near the Jordan River following the conquest (Josh 22:13–34). It was Phinehas who sought direction from the Lord in the context of war with the Benjamites during the days of the Judges (Judg 20:27–28). In comparing the role of Phinehas in this incident to that of the Levites in the case of the gold calf (Exod 32:19–20), Milgrom remarks that "both had to slay 'each his brother,' for which both received ordination to the priesthood."[672] He would later serve as the high priest during the days of Joshua and the judges period.

Phinehas abruptly left the assembly of mourners, took a short spear, and pursued the insolent idolaters into the tent shrine where the two were about to engage in their cultic ritual. The positioning and the ability to thrust the spear through both bodies, the man's first and then the woman's, suggests that they had involved themselves immediately in sexual intercourse upon entering the tent. They were impaled on the spear from the middle of his back through the woman's stomach (*ʾel-qŏbātāh*) while in the tent shrine (*ʾel-haqqŭbbâ*), a sarcastic Hebrew pun. The term for "tent" here is a

---

[670] Milgrom, *Numbers*, 212.

[671] Cf. Lev 8:1–4; 12:6; 16:7; Num 6:13; 12:5; 16:18–19; etc.

[672] Milgrom, *Numbers*, 214.

Hebrew hapax legomenon, sometimes translated "woman's quarters,"[673] is thought to be related to an Arabic term for a domed tent shrine.[674]

WRATH OF YAHWEH ALLAYED (25:8b). **25:8b** The actions of Phinehas in accomplishing the abatement of Yahweh's fierce anger against the idolatrous Israelites was a role he had learned from observing the exemplary actions of his priestly ancestors.[675] The redemptive and atoning role of a priestly intermediary was evidenced previously when Phinehas's father Eleazar and grandfather Aaron literally stood in the gap between the living and the dying in the punishment that resulted from Korah's rebellion (Num 16:46–50). He learned his lesson well and saved the lives of countless thousands of Israelites who might otherwise have died in the plague, which still took the lives of some twenty-four thousand before Phinehas stepped into the limelight.

THE RESULTS OF ISRAEL'S IMMORALITY (25:9). **25:9** The verse both completes the chiastic structure of the first section of the chapter (vv. 1–9) and functions as a hinge verse introducing the final chiastic cycle of material. Thus the plural preterit form *wayyihyû* functions as a summarizing element in the narrative. In typical Hebrew narrative style, the text moves from the broad context to the narrow, for the second section has as its focus the special relationship and privileges the Lord affords to Phinehas and his descendants. A covenant of peace and an eternal priesthood was granted to this priestly paragon of virtue and righteous indignation, whose actions limited the effect of the plague to some twenty-four thousand. Milgrom notes, "Presumably, this number included the rest of the older generation who were doomed to die in the wilderness (14:29), since the census that follows this incident expressly certifies this (26:64–65)."[676]

MOSES RECEIVES FURTHER INSTRUCTION FROM THE LORD (25:10– 18). The narrative progresses toward the narrower context in providing certain details concerning the two people Phinehas executed, which then provides impetus for the Midianite reprisal campaign of chap. 31. This section contains two sets of instructions for Moses, one delineating the honor of Phinehas for his zealous defense of the faith (vv. 10–15), and the second presenting the challenge to take vengeance against the Midianites

---

[673] Noordzij, *Numbers,* 241; Noth took the term to mean "bridal chamber" (*Numbers,* 198); S. C. Reif translated the term as "cult shrine" in "What Enraged Phinehas?" *JBL* 90 (1971): 200–206.

[674] For a discussion of the Arabic *qubbah* see R. de Vaux, *Ancient Israel: Its Life and Institutions,* 2 vols. (New York: McGraw-Hill, 1961), II:296–97. Cf. Milgrom, *Numbers,* 214–15; "Excursus 61: The Apostasy of Baal-peor (25:1–18)," 476–80.

[675] In contrast to the antithetical examples of his uncles Nadab and Abihu (Lev 10:1–7; Num 3:2–4.

[676] Milgrom, *Numbers,* 215.

who with Balaam had instigated this sordid affair (vv. 16–18). The two sections are linked by the reference to Cozbi, the daughter of one of the Midianite leaders who was executed along with Zimri, the Israelite from the tribe of Simeon.

**25:10** The verse commences in marvelous fashion, pregnant with implications regarding the restoration of Moses in his relationship to the Lord. As noted in v. 4, after Phinehas follows Moses' instruction, the narrator shifts back to the use of the primary phraseology of divine revelation to Moses, *wayyĕdabbēr YHWH ʾel-mōšeh lēʾmōr* ("Then the Lord spoke to Moses, saying ..."). In v. 4 the secondary phraseology, *wayyōʾmer YHWH ʾel-mōšeh* ("Then Yahweh said to Moses, saying ..."), was used in the manner consistent with the revelatory phraseology utilized since Moses' sin.[677] Now that restoration has taken place, the primary phraseology will continue to be used through the remainder of the Book of Numbers, including a recurrence in v. 16.[678]

**25:11** The basis for the rewarding of Phinehas is set forth initially. Phinehas's prompt dispatch of the amorous couple in the tent near the entrance to the Tent of Meeting is described as acting in the interest of the Israelite cult of Yahweh, as he "turned back" *(hēšîb)* God's wrath. The cognate terminology emphasizes the likemindedness of Phinehas with that of Yahweh, since the text reads literally, "When he acted zealously with my zeal among them" *(bĕqanʾô ʾet-qinʾātî bĕtôkām)*, followed by a repetition at the end of the verse of the phrase "my zeal." The verb *qānāʾ* can be translated as "to become deeply impassioned" or "to be come furiously jealous," and it is used in the Book of Numbers in the case of the husband who becomes passionately jealous when he thinks his wife is guilty of adultery (Num 5:11–31). In the Decalogue the same term is used of Yahweh's jealousy in being the focal point of Israel's covenant loyalty and worship (Exod 20:4–5). The grace exacted in this situation must be seen in the contrast to the potentiality of the divine wrath to wipe out the entire nation of Israel.

**25:12–13** The "covenant of peace" *(bĕrîtî šālôm)* Yahweh was "making" (lit., "giving," *nōtēn*) with Phinehas in v. 12 is further explicated in the following verse by the "covenant of a lasting priesthood" *(bĕrît kĕhūnnat ʿôlām)*. Similar phraseology as to the giving of a covenant is found in Gen 17:2, which recounts the unilateral covenant with Abram that was confirmed by the Lord after the birth of Ishmael to Hagar. The covenant of peace or well-being, also known from Isa 54:10 and Ezek 34:25, provided assurance to the beneficiaries that God was with them to will and to work to his good pleasure. The benefits that would accrue to the covenant recipients were safe

---

[677] See n. 660 above.
[678] See "Introduction to the Book of Numbers."

dwelling and abundant blessing. As with the Abrahamic and Davidic covenants, this one originated with Yahweh and was as dependable and trustworthy as God himself. The covenant relationship would be constantly remembered by the Lord proactively to the benefit of Israel. The binding obligation to Phinehas confirmed his anointment as a priest, which had come via his family lineage and had assured him and his descendants of a special place in the future service of the God of Israel. Allen summarized the progression of the covenant confirmation upon Phinehas as follows: "He was a priest by divine right, being descended from the right family in an immediate line. He showed himself to be the rightful priest by his interest in divine righteousness. He is now confirmed priest by the rite of divine covenant."[679]

The righteous act of Phinehas in executing the two defiant Baal worshipers also brought about atonement *(kipper)* for the children of Israel.[680] Again this act of grace by vigilant defense of the faith resulted in the survival of the majority of the Israelites, and the nation was restored on account of God's grace. Milgrom remarks, "Phinehas provided a ransom for Israel, and God's wrath was assuaged. So too, when the Levitical guard cuts down the encroacher on God's sancta, he also provides a ransom that stays God's wrath from venting itself upon Israel."[681] By virtue of Phinehas's priestly role in being a mediator between God and man, the covenant of peace extended well beyond him and his priestly descendants; it included the entire nation that survived the plague. Now in the third generation of the lineage of Aaron, the first high priest, the priesthood is reconfirmed as everlasting (1 Chr 6:4–15). Phinehas demonstrated through his defense of the sanctum that he was a worthy mediator between God and man in the Israelite cult.

**25:14–15** The final details provided for the narrative were the names and backgrounds of the two defiant worshipers of Baal whom Phinehas executed. The Israelite was named Zimri, a chieftain *(něśîʾ,* "prince") of the patriarchal clan *(bêt-ʾāb,* "father's household") of Salu, which belonged to the tribe of Simeon. This Zimri is not otherwise known in the Hebrew Bible.[682] The paramour of Zimri was named Cozbi, a daughter of Zur *(ṣûr),* who is described as a "tribal chief" *(rōʾš ʾummôt,* lit, "head of the peoples") here in v. 15, and a "leader" *(něśîʾ)* in v. 18.[683] Later in the account of the reprisal against the Midianites (Num 31:8), Zur is called one of the "kings of the Midianites" *(malkê midyān).*

---

[679] Allen, "Numbers," 922.

[680] The preterit form of the verb here (וַיְכַפֵּר) evidences the sequencing of the narrative account, whereby the act of one priest accomplished atonement for the sins of many Israelites.

[681] Milgrom, *Numbers,* 217.

[682] Other Zimris in the Hebrew Bible include the Northern Kingdom king (1 Kgs 16:9–20) and a grandson of Judah and Tamar (1 Chr 2:6).

[683] Note the latter term נָשִׂיא is used of Zimri in v. 14.

The combined references implies that the term "king" was often used to denote a political leader rather than a national monarch.

**25:16–18** The final section of this chapter commences with the repetition of the divine revelatory phraseology used immediately above in v. 10, "Then the Lord spoke to Moses, saying …" *(wayyĕdabbēr YHWH ʾel-mōšeh lēʾmōr)*. The text rehearses the events of Baal Peor, highlighting the crafty nature of the Midianite seduction of Israel, exemplified by the actions of Cozbi in enticing Zimri to sin against Yahweh. Because of their role in the seduction of the Israelites at Baal Peor, the Midianites were to be avenged by them in a military campaign following the reorganization of the army in this new generation of fighting men. The initial verb *ṣārôr*, translated "Treat … as enemies" in the NIV, means "to be hostile toward" or "to oppress." The form is an infinitive absolute used in an imperatival sense.[684] Thus the Israelites were given a directive by the Lord to assail the Midianites because of their role in leading the people of God to abandon their covenant relationship. This section functions also as a precursor to the directive of Num 33:50–56, in which the Lord instructed the Israelites to drive out the idolatrous Canaanites lest these inhabitants of the Promised Land lead Israel into idolatry. The reprisal against the Midianites would first be exacted soon after these directions were given, and that would be the last military leadership role carried out by Moses prior to his death (Num 31:2). In that campaign the trumpets, which were made according to the Lord's instructions (Num 10:1–10), would be sounded under the direction of the inimitable Phinehas. In Numbers 10 the very same verb *ṣārar* is used in describing the oppressive enemies of Israel. During the Midianite campaign the prophet-diviner Balaam, who had counseled Balak with regard to this means of deterring Israel's advance, would be killed along with all of the major Midianite chieftains (31:8). A later campaign against the Midianites would be led by Gideon during the period of the Judges (Judg 7:9–8:21).

CONCLUSION: THE END OF THE FORMER GENERATION AND SETTING FOR THE NEW (25:19). **25:19** The Baal Peor incident would provide a reminder to the Israelites throughout their history of the dangers of intermarriage with the women of the nations whose strong religious influence could lead men astray to worship other gods. This incident served as a case study in understanding the inviolability of God's holiness and righteousness. The prophet Micah would use the sequence of the Exodus and Baal Peor to challenge the Israelites with the need to remember God's faithfulness in redemption so that they might not succumb to the world's influences and that they "may know the righteousness of the Lord." By this they would understand the will of God for their lives, to be a distinctive people

---

[684] *IBHS,* 279.

for whom Yahweh meant the greatest good and by whom the world would see the fullness of God's grace and mercy. Micah then summarized the essential issues of man's response to God in this special relationship, "He has shown you, O man, what is good; and what does the Lord require of you, but to act justly, to love mercy, and to walk humbly with your God" (Mic 6:5–8).

"Then it came about after the plague." This brief verse of three Hebrew words functions as a hinge verse in the narrative flow of the Book of Numbers. The verse ends abruptly in the Masoretic Text with the major disjunctive accent, the atnach. Under normal grammatical circumstances the verse would be conjoined with 26:1, as many modern editors and interpreters have suggested. But the early textual editors apparently sought to make the distinction at this point by commencing the text of the second census in the same manner as the first, with the primary divine revelatory phraseology, "Then the LORD spoke to Moses, saying ..." *(wayyĕdabbēr YHWH ʾel-mōšeh lēʾmōr).*[685] This verse concludes the drama of the story of the first generation that God liberated from bondage in Egypt, brought through the Red Sea and the desert wilderness, provided for their every need, led to Mount Sinai, and gave them the Torah to seal that special relationship between God and his people. The covenant stipulations revealed the essential nature of God and how humanity was to respond by being solely devoted and obedient to him. By their faithful submission to his revelation, they would evidence to the nations the magnitude of God's love for his creation and the nature of his grace. There was another side to this God-man relationship, however: the consequences of disobedience. Following the departure from the mountain of God, that first generation began a downward spiral of rebellion against Yahweh that led to disastrous consequences, the most dramatic being the rejection of the Promised Land by the people and God's rejection of that generation from inheriting it. Out of those thousands who were numbered in the first census of Israel's fighting forces, only two men, Joshua and Caleb, survived to see the wondrous fulfillment of the promise of a homeland in Canaan.

With the plague of Baal Peor the punishment of the first generation was complete, and the process of preparing the second generation to enter the Promised Land was at hand. This process would commence in the manner of the previous cycle of events with a military conscription census, those men who, under both the divine leadership of Yahweh God of Israel and the human servant-leader Joshua, would lead the nation to experience the fulfillment of a promise made centuries before to Abraham, Isaac, and Jacob: "I will make you a great nation; I will bless you and make your name great, and you shall be a blessing"; and, "To your descendants I will give this land" (Gen 12:2,7).

---

[685] Taking the alternate reading of the Samaritan Pentateuch, וידבר over the MT's ויּאמֶר, as the preferred text. This emendation of the MT best suits the usage of the two revelatory phrases through the Book of Numbers. See "Introduction to the Book of Numbers: Structural Outline."

BOOK TWO:  THE NEW GENERATION AND THE PROSPECTS OF THE
            PROMISED LAND (26:1–36:13)
III.  PREPARATION OF THE NEW GENERATION OF ISRAEL
    (26:1–30:16)
    1.  The Second Census in the Plains of Moab (26:1–65)
        (1)  Census Instructions (26:1–4)
        (2)  Reuben's descendants (26:5–11)
        (3)  Simeon's Descendants (26:12–14)
        (4)  Gad's Descendants (26:15–18)
        (5)  Judah's Descendants (26:19–22)
        (6)  Issachar's Descendants (26:23–25)
        (7)  Zebulun's Descendants (26:26–27)
        (8)  Sons of Joseph: Manasseh's Descendants (26:28–34)
        (9)  Sons of Joseph: Ephraim's Descendants (26:35–37)
     (10)  Benjamin's Descendants (26:38–41)
     (11)  Dan's Descendants (26:42–43)
     (12)  Asher's Descendants (26:44–47)
     (13)  Naphtali's Descendants (26:48–50)
     (14)  Total Population of the Second Generation (26:51)
     (15)  Instructions for Division of the Land (26:52–56)
     (16)  Levi's Descendants (26:57–62)
     (17)  Conclusion of the Second Census (26:63–65)
    2.  Land Inheritance Laws: The Case of Zelophehad's Daughters
        (27:1–11)
        (1)  The Case of Zelophehad's Daughters (27:1–5)
        (2)  Case Decision and Derived Principles (27:6–11)
    3.  Joshua Heir to Moses (27:12–23)
        (1)  Moses' Sin Recapitulated (27:12–14)
        (2)  Moses' Entreaty for a New Leader (27:15–17)
        (3)  Moses' Instruction from the Lord (27:18–21)
        (4)  Moses Commissions Joshua (27:22–23)
    4.  The Appointed Times and Offerings (28:1–29:40)
        (1)  Introduction (28:1–2)
        (2)  Daily Offerings (28:3–8)
        (3)  Weekly (Sabbath) Offerings (28:9–10)
        (4)  Monthly (Rosh Chodesh) Offerings (28:11–15)
        (5)  Passover (Pesach) and Unleavened Bread Offerings (28:16–25)
        (6)  Feast of Weeks (Shavuoth / Pentecost) Offerings (28:26–31)

(7)  Feast of the Blowing Trumpets Offerings (29:1–6)
(8)  Day of Atonement (Yom Kippur) Offerings (29:7–11)
(9)  Feast of Booths (Sukkoth) Offerings (29:16–38)
(10)  Summary (29:39–40)
5. Women's Vows (30:1–16)
  (1)  Introduction: General Principle for Vows (30:1–2)
  (2)  Vows of Unmarried Women (30:3–5)
  (3)  Vows of Newly Married Women (30:6–8)
  (4)  Vows of Widowed or Divorced Women (30:9)
  (5)  Vows of Married Women (30:10–15)
  (6)  Summary (30:16)

## ──── III. PREPARATION OF THE NEW GENERATION ──── OF ISRAEL (26:1–30:16)

### 1. The Second Census in the Plains of Moab (26:1–65)

The second census of Israelite men stands at a pivotal point in the Book of Numbers, in the Pentateuch, indeed in the entire Old Testament. As D. Olson has pointed out, "The theme of the death of the old generation and the birth of the new generation of hope is one which continues far beyond Numbers and the Pentateuch."[1] The two enumerations of tribes and clans provide reference points to the two epochs in the history of God's forming a distinct people for himself. The first list marks the summation and conclusion of the first generation which began with the patriarchs in Genesis and concluded with the idolatrous rebellion at Shittim and the Baal Peor. The glorious organizational unity and solemn ritual sanctification in preparation for the march from Sinai (1:1–10:10) are followed by three cycles of rebellion in 11–25. The second census marks the commencement of the second generation which is about to enter the Canaanite territory and begin the process of inheriting the land of promise. Additional laws of sanctification and pertinent guidelines related to the inheritance and settlement of the land are outlined.

The first generation possessed an inheritance of unfulfilled hope as promised to Abram (Gen 15:7–21; Heb 11:8–10), but never realized by his descendants; the second would possess inheritance instructions (Num 33:50–56) as they proceeded under the direction of the Lord. God challenges his new people to advance by faith and claim their rightful heritage.

Chronological and geographical notes, which have been utilized by a

---

[1] D. T. Olson, *The Death of the Old and the Birth of the New: The Framework of the Book of Numbers and the Pentateuch,* BJS 71 (Chico, Cal.: Scholars Press, 1985), 191.

majority of earlier writers and commentators (see "Introduction: Outline") in subdividing the Book of Numbers, are scant and problematic. Such difficulties were cited earlier in the varying analyses of Budd, Gray, and de Vaulx in basing divisions on geographical markers. The dilemma lay in where to distinguish the beginning of the third movement, in the Desert of Zin, the Arabah, or the Plains of Moab. Furthermore, the sections of material are not fully in chronological sequence, the basis of organization being thematic and holistic rather than linear time sequence.

The texts have a long history of transmission, even a prehistory. How ancient some of the genealogies of Genesis and Numbers are is unknown. They may date to the period of Egyptian sojourn prior to the time of Moses. Genealogies were maintained in oral history and tradition for religious, political and familial reasons and were later edited to trace particular lines of development and to justify claims to inheritance or leadership. The genealogical census lists of Numbers serve historical purposes as well.

The new generation of Israel, guided by Yahweh under the leadership of Joshua and Eleazar, must, like the first generation, encounter obstacles. The anticipatory element of the book for the second Israel is one of positive but cautious expectation. The structure of the Book of Numbers poses a decisive question for the generations to come: Can this new generation, including its successive descendants, enter and claim the land of promise, remain faithful and reap the benefits of God's blessing, and reach out and fulfill its calling to be a source of light and blessing to the nations? Or will the newborn community succumb to the same pressures, fears, and temptations of her forefathers? May it never be! The challenge remains the same for all generations of the people of God.

### (1) Census Instructions (26:1–4)

[1]After the plague the LORD said to Moses and Eleazar son of Aaron, the priest, [2]"Take a census of the whole Israelite community by families—all those twenty years old or more who are able to serve in the army of Israel." [3]So on the plains of Moab by the Jordan across from Jericho, Moses and Eleazar the priest spoke with them and said, [4]"Take a census of the men twenty years old or more, as the LORD commanded Moses."

These were the Israelites who came out of Egypt:

**26:1–4** The initial phraseology of 26:1 in the NIV is actually 25:19 in the Hebrew text of the MT, an incomplete sentence which reads *wayĕhî ʾaḥărê hammaggēpâ*, translated literally in the NKVJ as "And it came to pass, after the plague." This clause functions as a transitional element in conjoining the account of the plague at Baal Peor with the military conscription census of the second generation in 26:1–51. The plague of chap. 25 concluded the judgment that befell the first generation of Israelites whom the Lord had delivered from bondage in Egypt. After the three cycles of rebellion and judgment of 11:1–25:18, 25:19 functions as a literary hinge that links the previous narrative with the final two cycles of the Book of Numbers, which looks forward to the completion of the journey to the Promised Land. The transition is made complete with the introduction of the divine message formula, "the LORD said" *(wayyō'mer YHWH 'el . . . lē'mōr)*, which has been shown to function as a major dividing marker in the Book of Numbers for organizational and mnemonic purposes (see Introduction: Outline).[2] The census instructions come as divine command and are parallel in stipulation and purpose to the original command of 1:2–3.

Nearly thirty-eight and a half years had transpired since the first census, which was ordered to enumerate for military purposes the Israelite men over twenty years of age who were able to serve in the army. The upcoming battles against the Midianites, announced in 25:16–18, and the advance of the nation into the land of Canaan serve as ample reasoning for the census. Furthermore, the census would provide the relative size guidelines for the division of the Promised Land among the tribes, a process governed by proportion and by lot (26:52–56). The first generation had failed to live up to its name as the people of Yahweh by rejecting the land of promise; the new generation must claim its inheritance, moving forward by faith under her new leaders.

Moses had watched a generation of men over twenty pass away. This was, no doubt, a remorseful and bittersweet time, for he knew that this new generation would commence on a journey he so longed to have made with his generation. Miriam (20:1) and Aaron (20:25–28) had died, and Moses' time was near. Aaron's son Eleazar had received the royal priestly garments on Mount Hor. Together Moses and Eleazar, the first generation and the second united under divine direction, proceed with the task at hand in the plains of Moab, overlooking the Jordan toward Jericho.[3]

---

[2] The three words of the BHS, הַמַּגֵּפָה אַחֲרֵי וַיְהִי, "And it came about after the plague," end with the major disjunctive accent, the Athnach, giving the phrase the function of half of a sentence, a temporal clause in MT 25:19 that provides the historical context of the material in the main clause MT 26:1. The placement of the Hebrew letter Pe, a section or paragraph marker, after the phrase adds further difficulty. Perhaps the Masoretes made the division in the middle of the original continuous verse in order to maintain the sequence of using the divine messenger formula for sectional markers. The Samaritan Pentateuch probably retains the original text here, utilizing the more commonly used divine formula, מֹשֶׁה אֶל־יְהוָה וַיְדַבֵּר, adding additional support to the integrity and continuity of the text and the contention that the phraseology functions vitally in the organization of the text.

[3] The phrase "by the Jordan across from Jericho," or perhaps more literally "by, or opposite, the Jordan of (from) Jericho," may "be an older way of speaking of the region of the Jordan River that is across from the city of Jericho," according to R. B. Allen, "Numbers," EBC, vol. 2 (Grand Rapids: Zondervan, 1986), 926.

The introductory phrase of v. 4b serves as the heading for the delineation of the tribes and clans, reminding the reader that the new generation is numbered according to the tribes and clans of the first generation. Identification with the past is paralleled by the yearly Passover celebration, which calls each participant in every generation to act as if he or she were present among the original Exodus families. The new generation had indeed been delivered from the bondage of Egypt, as had the first. That this new generation is to be perceived as if the previous had not existed or rebelled may be an implicit connotation in the heading phraseology.[4]

The order of the tribal enumeration in the MT follows that of Num 1:20–43, with the exception that the sons of Joseph are reversed. The Septuagint retains the order of the earlier list in Gen 46:8–27, which places Gad and Asher in succession after Zebulun and Levi after Simeon. The individual clans of the tribes comply largely with Genesis 46 as well, with notable differences cited below under individual tribal discussion. The general pattern of sequential listing is broken three times for explanatory purposes. Twice (8–11 and 19) the excurses are retrogressions into past rebellions in Numbers and Genesis. The third anticipates the issue of Zelophehad's daughters' land inheritance in 27:1–11 and 36:1–12, with implications that carry over into preexilic and postexilic periods. Together these excurses provide further support to the pivotal character of this chapter in the overarching design of the Book of Numbers, as well as the entire Old Testament.

### Census Results by Ancestral Tribes and Clans (26:5–50)

| Tribe | First Census | Second Census | Change | Variants |
|---|---|---|---|---|
| Reuben | 46,500 | 43,730 | -2,770 | 43,750 G$^s$ |
| Simeon | 59,300 | 22,200 | -37,100 | |
| Gad | 45,650 | 40,500 | -5,150 | 44,500 G$^s$ |
| Judah | 74,600 | 76,500 | +1,900 | |
| Issachar | 54,400 | 64,300 | +9,900 | |
| Zebulun | 57,400 | 60,500 | +3,100 | |
| Manasseh | 32,200 | 52,700 | +20,500 | 62,500 G$^s$ |
| Ephraim | 40,500 | 32,500 | -8,000 | |
| Benjamin | 35,400 | 45,600 | +10,200 | 35,500 G$^s$ |
| Dan | 62,700 | 64,400 | +1,700 | 64,600 G$^s$ |
| Asher | 41,500 | 53,400 | +11,900 | |
| Naphtali | 53,400 | 45,400 | -8,000 | 30,300 G$^s$ |
| Total | 603,550 | 601,730 | -1820 | |

*G$^s$ = some Greek manuscripts read

---

[4] Cf. P. Budd, *Numbers*, WBC (Waco: Word), 286; Allen, "Numbers," 926. An explicit meaning is belied by the reference to the Korah rebellion in 26:8–11.

## (2) Reuben's Descendants (26:5-11)

⁵The descendants of Reuben, the firstborn son of Israel, were:
   through Hanoch, the Hanochite clan; through Pallu, the Palluite clan;
   ⁶through Hezron, the Hezronite clan; through Carmi, the Carmite clan.
⁷These were the clans of Reuben; those numbered were 43,730.
⁸The son of Pallu was Eliab, ⁹and the sons of Eliab were Nemuel, Dathan and Abiram. The same Dathan and Abiram were the community officials who rebelled against Moses and Aaron and were among Korah's followers when they rebelled against the LORD. ¹⁰The earth opened its mouth and swallowed them along with Korah, whose followers died when the fire devoured the 250 men. And they served as a warning sign. ¹¹The line of Korah, however, did not die out.

**26:5-11** Rights of primogeniture are retained by Reuben in the tribal listings. The four clans descended from Reuben—Hanoch, Pallu, Hezron, and Carmi—are identical with those recorded in Gen 46:9. The slight variation in the census of Reubenite clans in the Aquila recension of the Septuagint seems insignificant.

The retrospective excursus regarding the relationship of the Pallu clan to the Korah rebellion yields several important aspects. Two of the descendants, namely Dathan and Abiram, were among the 250 leaders of Israel who joined in the revolt against Moses and Aaron. The demonstrative nature of this insurrection would serve for many generations as a dark reminder, a "warning sign" of the future consequences of such an uprising against not only God's ordained leaders but against God himself. The term employed for "sign," the Hebrew *nēs*, typically is used to denote an ensign or banner around which people rally (Jer 50:2) or soldiers muster for battle (Jer 50:2). In Isa 11:10 the root of Jesse stands as a banner *(nēs)* for the nations to seek. But like Sodom and Gomorrah, or Nadab and Abihu, Dathan and Abiram, or Korah, these individuals would serve as historical bywords for how God deals with revolutionaries. Heaven (fire) and earth (pit), God's creation and witnesses, were called upon to execute his judgment against his own people.

## (3) Simeon's Descendants (26:12-14)

¹²The descendants of Simeon by their clans were:
   through Nemuel, the Nemuelite clan;
   through Jamin, the Jaminite clan;
   through Jakin, the Jakinite clan;
   ¹³through Zerah, the Zerahite clan;
   through Shaul, the Shaulite clan.
¹⁴These were the clans of Simeon; there were 22,200 men.

**26:12-14** The five clans of the tribe of Simeon are delineated as Nemuel, Jamin, Jakin, Zerah, and Shaul. Several variations from this list from the MT are notable. "Nemuel" occurs as "Jemuel" in the Syriac text of Numbers, in agreement with Gen 46:1 and Exod 6:15; whereas in 1 Chr 4:24 the MT reading finds support. "Jamin" does not occur in Gen 46:10 and Exod 6:15, which both contain "Ohad" as an additional clan name. Allen suggests that perhaps Ohad died childless or for some unknown reason did not generate a clan. Instead of "Zerah," Gen 46:10 and Exod 6:15 contain the reading "Zohar," a consonantal metathesis in the history of transmission of the text. That Shaul was the son of a Canaanite woman finds notation in Gen 46:10, but not in the present text (cf. Gen 38).

The tribe of Simeon suffered the greatest decline in population since the first census, a net loss of 37,100 or more than 62 percent. Much of the loss was due perhaps to the participation of many Simeonites, along with Zimri, "the leader of a Simeonite family" in Num 25:14. Zimri was killed by Phinehas because of his leadership in the aberrant cultic activities of Baal Peor. The unexplained disappearance of the clan of Ohad also could have contributed to the decrease.

### (4) Gad's Descendants (26:15–18)

**15The descendants of Gad by their clans were:**
**through Zephon, the Zephonite clan;**
**through Haggi, the Haggite clan;**
**through Shuni, the Shunite clan;**
**16through Ozni, the Oznite clan; through Eri, the Erite clan;**
**17through Arodi, the Arodite clan; through Areli, the Arelite clan.**
**18These were the clans of Gad; those numbered were 40,500.**

**26:15–18** The order of the tribal enumerations varies in the Septuagint, which lists Gad after Zebulun, following the tradition of Gen 46:16, which adheres to the matriarchal order of the sons of Leah, Zilpah, Rachel, and Bilhah. Gad was born to Zilpah, a servant of Leah, as was Asher. Levi, who also was born to Leah, follows Simeon in Genesis 46, but in keeping with the Numbers 1 census stands at the end of the twelve-tribe listing in the present text.

Several orthographic variations from Numbers occur in the Gadite clan lists of Gen 46:16–17 (MT) and the texts of the Samaritan Pentateuch and the Septuagint. Zephon reads as Ziphion in the MT of Gen 46:16, in which text the LXX and SamPen agree with the present reading. Zephon should be preferred in all texts, though the reading of Ziphion may attest to a very early spelling in the Gadite genealogy. Similarly, Ozni reads as Ezbon in Gen 46:16, a more difficult variant. Eri, here as in Gen 46:16, is Adi in Sam-Pent, the LXX, and the Syriac. This variation is easily explained by the visual confusion of the Hebrew consonants *dālet* and *rêš*. Arod obtains as Arodi, which probably is an ancient Gentilic spelling supported by the Sam-Pent, LXX, and Syriac. Areli is Aroli in the SamPent, Adil in the Syriac, and

Ariel in the LXX and Vulgate. The latter reading comes as a result of scribal metathesis at some point in the history of transmission, by which the two letters ʾaleph and lamedh were transposed.

The retention of these variants among the five textual traditions evidence the integrity maintained by the respective scribal circles in adhering to the texts from which they copied. Though the precise historical origins of these variants are untraceable, several general explanations can be posited: (1) varied spellings of the same name at the same or different points in history, keeping in mind the internal orthographic developments in the history of the Hebrew language, (2) scribal transmission errors such as metathesis, (3) scribal editing from variant manuscripts available, or (4) different names for the same person. Allen notes that "the very problems we find in these parallel listings of names may be a strong indicator of the tradition of textual integrity."[5]

The total of 40,500 men of age for military conscription represents a net loss of 5,150, or 11.3 percent. A textual variant also occurs in a few LXX texts, yielding a total of 44,500.

### (5) Judah's Descendants (26:19–22)

[19]Er and Onan were sons of Judah, but they died in Canaan.
[20]The descendants of Judah by their clans were:
  through Shelah, the Shelanite clan;
  through Perez, the Perezite clan;
  through Zerah, the Zerahite clan.
[21]The descendants of Perez were:
  through Hezron, the Hezronite clan;
  through Hamul, the Hamulite clan.
[22]These were the clans of Judah; those numbered were 76,500.

**26:19–22** The register of the clans of Judah commences with the despicable Er and Onan, the first two sons of Judah via the daughter of the Canaanite man Shua. Both sons were deemed "wicked in the LORD's sight" and died at the hand of the Lord in Canaan (Gen 38:1–10). The daughter of Shua later gave birth to a third son, Shelah, who would survive to father a clan of Israel. Like Simeon's sons Dathan and Abiram, Er and Onan would serve as reminders of God's judgment upon disobedience in the previous generation, providing a referential link of the second census to the flaws of the forefathers. The purpose of the historical allusions was to challenge the new generation to renounce the past and heed the word of the Lord by faith

---

[5] Allen, *Numbers*, 930. The MT evidences the careful work of the ancient Hebrew scribes in maintaining the textual variants through the history of transmission, without necessarily attempting to standardize the names.

as they advance into the Promised Land.

The three clans of Judah are recorded as Shelah, Perez, and Zerah, the latter two being the twin sons of Tamar. The preeminence of Perez is noted via the unusual listing of his second generation sons Hezron and Hamul (cf. Gen 46:12). Through Perez would come the greatest heirs of the line of Judah and indeed of Israel (Ruth 4:18–21; 1 Chr 2:4–17). Their descendants would be chosen for the kingship of Israel commencing with David and culminating with the greatest Son of David, Jesus of Nazareth (Luke 3:23–33; Matt 1:3–16).

The three clans of Judah would sire the largest of the tribes of Israel, 76,500 in the second census, or a net increase of 1,900, or 2.6 percent. The lone textual variant in the Judahite clan list is for that of Hamul, which reads as Hamuel in SamPent and the LXX.

### (6) Issachar's Descendants (26:23–25)

**23The descendants of Issachar by their clans were:**
   **through Tola, the Tolaite clan;**
   **through Puah, the Puite clan;**
   **24through Jashub, the Jashubite clan;**
   **through Shimron, the Shimronite clan.**
**25These were the clans of Issachar; those numbered were 64,300.**

**26:23–25** The listing of the clans of Issachar through Tola, Puah, Jashub, and Shimron follows standard form. Two names reflect significant textual variation, that of Puah and Jashub. The NIV form *pûʾâ* concurs with the *pûʾâ* of 1 Chr 7:1, SamPent, LXX, Syriac, and Vulgate, a possible influence of Aramaic orthography. The MT reads Puvah *(pūwâ)*, and some Hebrew MSS have *pūwwâ*. Jashub is errantly spelled Iob in the MT of Gen 46:13, in which text the NIV contains the preferred reading Jashub of SamPent and LXX. The total of 64,300 reveals an increase of 9,900 (+18.2 percent) in potential military service.

### (7) Zebulun's Descendants (26:26–27)

**26The descendants of Zebulun by their clans were:**
   **through Sered, the Seredite clan;**
   **through Elon, the Elonite clan;**
   **through Jahleel, the Jahleelite clan.**
**27These were the clans of Zebulun; those numbered were 60,500.**

**26:26–27** The three clans enumerated of the Zebulunites were through Sered, Elon, and Jahleel. Hebrew and Greek textual traditions are in complete agreement on the names and orthography. Unlike the other descendants of the sons of Jacob and Joseph, the history of the Zebulunite clan is not outlined in 1 Chronicles 2–8. Only in the list of the sons of Jacob in 2:1 does the name Zebulun occur. The counting of 60,500 Zebulunite men represents an increase of 3,100, or 5.4 percent.

### (8) Sons of Joseph: Manasseh's Descendants (26:28–34)

[28]The descendants of Joseph by their clans through Manasseh and Ephraim were:

[29]The descendants of Manasseh:
    through Makir, the Makirite clan (Makir was the father of Gilead);
    through Gilead, the Gileadite clan.
[30]These were the descendants of Gilead:
    through Iezer, the Iezerite clan;
    through Helek, the Helekite clan;
    [31]through Asriel, the Asrielite clan;
    through Shechem, the Shechemite clan;
    [32]through Shemida, the Shemidaite clan;
    through Hepher, the Hepherite clan.
[33](Zelophehad son of Hepher had no sons; he had only daughters, whose names were Mahlah, Noah, Hoglah, Milcah and Tirzah.)
[34]These were the clans of Manasseh; those numbered were 52,700.

**26:28–34** Verses 27 and 38b form an inclusio under the subject heading of "the descendants of Joseph by their clans," subdivided according to his two sons Manasseh and Ephraim. The order of this pair is the reverse of the original census of chap. 1. The transposing of the two may reflect the second generation population inversion; Manasseh experienced the most substantial increase of all the tribes, 20,500 (+63.7 percent) to 52,700, whereas Ephraim decreased by 8,000 to 32,500 (-24.9 percent). Note the even larger LXX census figure of 62,500, a potential increase of 94 percent. Yet in the Divided Kingdom period Ephraim became the paradigm for the Northern Kingdom in the writings of the Latter Prophets (Hos 7:1; Isa 28:1).[6] Manasseh and Ephraim were born to Joseph through his Egyptian wife Asenath, the daughter of a priest of the god On. The expanded clan history of the tribe of Manasseh is found in 1 Chr 7:14–19.

Not until the fourth generation are the sons of Joseph subdivided into individual clans under the heading of Gilead, the son of Makir, the son of Manasseh. Six families are listed, namely those descended from Iezer, Helek, Asriel, Shechem, Shemida, and Hepher. The later expansion of the

---

[6] Allen suggests: "This datum seems to argue against the critical theory ... that the lists in these chapters of Numbers were projections backwards from late in Israel's history, based on their conceptions of the ideal state of affairs during the times of David and Solomon. Yet these numbers do not accord with any later period of Israel's history" ("Numbers," 933).

clans of Gilead is delineated in 1 Chr 7:14–19. There the passage reveals that Makir's mother was an Aramean concubine, another instance of the inclusiveness of the lineage of the Israelites. In the military conscription census of the second generation, no family of the clans of the Israelite tribes was lost from the first generation the Lord brought forth from Egypt. God's faithfulness is evident in the preserving of at least some remnant of each of the first generation of patriarchal clans.

The third excursus in the text relates to the clan of Hepher, whose son Zelophehad fathered only daughters. The mere mention of women is remarkable in a text designed to calculate potential numbers of men for war. This digression foreshadows the legal issues of land inheritance of chaps. 27 and 36, with further implications for the history of Israel.[7] Together these form an inclusio for the second major division of the Book of Numbers, with its focus upon the new generation moving toward the Promised Land of Canaan. The five daughters of Zelophehad form the rare fifth generation genealogy, adding further emphasis to the unique character of this chapter and section.

### (9) Sons of Joseph: Ephraim's Descendants (26:35–37)

**35These were the descendants of Ephraim by their clans:**
    **through Shuthelah, the Shuthelahite clan;**
    **through Beker, the Bekerite clan;**
    **through Tahan, the Tahanite clan.**
**36These were the descendants of Shuthelah:**
    **through Eran, the Eranite clan.**
**37These were the clans of Ephraim; those numbered were 32,500.**
**These were the descendants of Joseph by their clans.**

**26:35–37** Three clans and one subclan are found in the census list of the tribe of Ephraim. Ephraim has been supplanted by the more populous Manasseh in the order of the sons of Joseph. Minor textual variants occur: (1) Beker is missing in the LXX original; (2) Tahan in the MT is Taham in the SamPent and Tanak (metathesis) in the LXX; (3) Eran is Edan (confusion of Hebrew *d* and *r*) in some MSS of the SamPent, LXX, and Syriac. The decrease in population will play a role in the proportional land distributions of Josh 16:5–10. Further accounts of the clans of Ephraim and their territory are developed in 1 Chr 7:20–29.

### (10) Benjamin's Descendants (26:38–41)

**38The descendants of Benjamin by their clans were:**
    **through Bela, the Belaite clan;**

---

[7] These legal implications find fruition first in Josh 17:3–6, and then in the such diverse settings as the life of Ruth (Ruth 2:1–20) and the reign of Ahab and Jezebel (1 Kgs 21:1–19).

through Ashbel, the Ashbelite clan;
through Ahiram, the Ahiramite clan;
[39]through Shupham, the Shuphamite clan;
through Hupham, the Huphamite clan.
[40]The descendants of Bela through Ard and Naaman were: through Ard, the
Ardite clan; through Naaman, the Naamite clan. [41]These were the clans of
Benjamin; those numbered were 45,600.

**26:38–41** Numerous significant textual variants occur in the several
clan lists for the tribe of Benjamin. The following comparative list ensues:

| Gen 46:21 | Num 26:38–40 | 1 Chr 7:6 | 1 Chr 8:1–2 |
|---|---|---|---|
| Bela | Bela* | Bela | Bela (1) |
| Beker | ***** | Beker | |
| Ashbel | Ashbel | | Ashbel (2) |
| Gera | ***** | (no | |
| Naaman | *Naaman b. Bela | others | |
| Ehi | Ahiram (?=Ehi) | listed— | Aharah (3) |
| Rosh | ***** | only | |
| Muppim | Shupham (?=Muppim) | subclans) | |
| Huppim | Hupham | | |
| Ard | *Ard b. Bela | | Addar b. Bela |
| | | | Nohah |
| | | | Rapha |

*Ard and Naaman given as sons of Bela.

Several aspects of text and genealogical history are notable: (1) the list of clans
for the youngest son of Jacob seems to be rather fluid; (2) grandsons such as
Naaman and Ard are often listed as sons in genealogical reckoning;[8] (3) the
loss of 25,100 from the tribe of Benjamin in the civil war during the period of
the Judges (Judg 20) may have resulted in the loss of entire clans, hence the
significant differences in the later record of 1 Chronicles; yet the clan of Beker
unexplainably returns in 1 Chr 7:6; (4) scribal error and orthographic variations probably contributed to differences such as in Hupham / Huppim; and (5)
variants among the versions in the history of transmission—Ashbel in the MT
is Ashbeel in SamPent and Ashuber in LXX, both possibly as a result of the
influence of Aramaic orthography. Naaman is lacking in the SamPent version
of Num 26:40.

The population census of 45,600 reflects a considerable increase of
10,200 (+28.8 percent) in the MT, though some LXX manuscripts have
35,500. No doubt the later turmoil involving the tribe of Benjamin and the
Levite concubine contributed greatly to the difficulties in the keeping of clan
and family genealogies, resulting in the textual dilemmas observed above.
The loss of perhaps more than one-half of the males of the tribe, and a major

---

[8] Compare the genealogies of Esau in Genesis 36.

proportion of the women, in the incident had disastrous effects on the Benjamite families, necessitating the provision of wives for them in the dance of the maidens at Shiloh (Judg 21) and the restructuring of many clans. Yet from the smallest of the tribes would come the first king of Israel, Saul of Gibeah (1 Chr 8:1–33).

## (11) Dan's Descendants (26:42–43)

**⁴²These were the descendants of Dan by their clans:**
**through Shuham, the Shuhamite clan.**
**These were the clans of Dan: ⁴³All of them were Shuhamite clans; and those numbered were 64,400.**

**26:42–43** The populous tribe of Dan ranks second only to Judah in both lists of Numbers 1 and 26, remarkable in that only one clan is registered. The phrase "all of them" (*kol-mišpĕḥōt*, "all the clans") occurs only here in the census lists, accounting for the fact that all clans were descendants of the one son of Dan, Shuham. Yet unexplained is why subclans are not mentioned as with such tribes as Manasseh, Benjamin, and Asher. Neither does Dan find mention in the tribal genealogies of 1 Chronicles 1–8, an argument against the critical view that this material has origin in the priestly circles responsible for the Book of Chronicles. Shuham is recorded as Hushim in Gen 46:23, a possible metathesis in the early history of transmission. The total population of 64,400[9] represents a modest increase of 1,700 men for potential war conscription, or 2.7 percent.

## (12) Asher's Descendants (26:44–47)

**⁴⁴The descendants of Asher by their clans were:**
**through Imnah, the Imnite clan;**
**through Ishvi, the Ishvite clan;**
**through Beriah, the Beriite clan;**
**⁴⁵and through the descendants of Beriah:**
**through Heber, the Heberite clan;**
**through Malkiel, the Malkielite clan.**
**⁴⁶(Asher had a daughter named Serah.)**
**⁴⁷These were the clans of Asher; those numbered were 53,400.**

**26:44–47** The clans of Asher are located after Zebulun and Gad in the LXX beginning with v. 28. Ishvah of Gen 46:17 is lacking here but recorded in 1 Chr 7:30, though the Chronicler lists no clan history. Apparently he died without producing offspring. Three clans and two subclans are delineated: Imnah, Ishvi, and Beriah, with Beriah's sons Heber and Malkiel founding

---

[9] Some manuscripts of the LXX read 64,600.

subclans. The sons of Beriah are lacking in the SamPent and LXX but derive from Gen 46:17. The names recur in 1 Chr 8:31–32 along with the further descendants of Heber.

The historical occasion for the inclusion of one daughter of Asher, Serah, following Gen 46:17 (cf. 1 Chr 7:30) is uncertain. The placement of the names of women in a census dedicated to the calculation of men of military potential heightens the importance of their notation and the role of women in general. But unlike the mention of Shua and the daughters of Zelophehad, the purpose of the allusion to Serah remains a mystery.

The population of Asher experienced considerable growth during the wilderness sojourn, an increase of 11,900 to 53,400 (+29 percent). By the time of the Chronicler's work, however, the number had declined to 26,000 (7:40).

### (13) Naphtali's Descendants (26:48–50)

48The descendants of Naphtali by their clans were:
    through Jahzeel, the Jahzeelite clan;
    through Guni, the Gunite clan;
  49through Jezer, the Jezerite clan;
    through Shillem, the Shillemite clan.
50These were the clans of Naphtali; those numbered were 45,400.

**26:48–50** Naphtali's descendants originated through the four families of Jahzeel, Guni, Jezer, and Shillem who went down to Egypt. The LXX has Shillom instead of Shillem. The tribe suffered a moderate loss during the wilderness sojourn, declining by 8,000 to 45,400 (-15 percent). The LXX records an even greater 44 percent drop to 30,300. Only the listing of the same four sons of Naphtali is recounted in 1 Chr 7:13, but no further subclans or descendants are given.

### (14) Total Population of the Second Generation (26:51)

51 The total number of the men of Israel was 601,730.

**26:51** The total population census of 601,730 demonstrates the providence of God in preserving his people through nearly forty difficult years in a formidable wilderness. An inconsequential net decline of only 1,820 (0.3 percent), in spite of physical obstacles, spiritual failures, and harsh judgment from the Lord, confirms that the promise to Abraham of innumerable descendants remains in effect. Only Moses, Joshua, and Caleb are known to have survived of those over twenty years of age when the people revolted at the spies' report (Num 13:26–14:35). The number represents an accurate sum of the census figures for each tribe. The new generation of Israel would become heirs to the challenge to enter the very promised land that their fore-fathers had rejected.[10]

### (15) Instructions for Division of the Land (26:52–56)

**[52]The LORD said to Moses, [53]"The land is to be allotted to them as an inheritance based on the number of names. [54]To a larger group give a larger inheritance, and to a smaller group a smaller one; each is to receive its inheritance according to the number of those listed. [55]Be sure that the land is distributed by lot. What each group inherits will be according to the names for its ancestral tribe. [56]Each inheritance is to be distributed by lot among the larger and smaller groups."**

**26:52–56** The conclusion to the second census sets forth an additional purpose beyond that of potential military conscription. The material takes on a proleptic character in the setting forth of two principles governing the distribution of land as the new generation of the tribes of Israel march onward by faith and claim their inheritance. Based on the populations derived from the census of tribal clans, "the land is to be allotted to them as an inheritance." The principle of proportion is described in explicit terms—greater territory for larger tribes, smaller portions for the less populated. Clan apportionment would be assumed under the aegis of their ancestral tribe. The proportional distribution would take into consideration the percentage of arable land available or accessible by clearing or irrigation. Joshua later would challenge tribes to harvest forested areas within their allotments for ample farming acreage (Josh 17:17–18).

The second principle governing land allocation was that of providential probability. Casting of lots was the common means of determining the will of the Lord for the division of spoils of war, for distinguishing the scapegoat on the Day of Atonement, or for settling political issues. The Lord was presumed to oversee the tossing of the lots and to bring his decision to pass. Distribution of tracts of land for tribal inheritance would follow this method, and that inheritance was to remain within the tribal family for posterity.[11] Harrison notes three discernible precepts in the outline of the process: the entire land belongs to God alone, allocation methods constituted God's gift to his people, and the procedure would be equitable and avert potential jealousy and dissension.[12]

---

[10] For an expanded discussion of the large numbers of both censuses in Num 1 and 26, see the "Introduction: The Large Numbers of the Book of Numbers."

[11] Fulfillment of this passage is found in Josh 15:1; 16:1; 17:1; 18:6,10,11; 19:1,10,17,24, 32, 40. Lots were cast first at Gilgal and then at Shiloh. Levitical cities would likewise be apportioned by casting lots (Josh 21).

[12] Harrison, *Numbers: An Exegetical Commentary,* (Grand Rapids: Baker, 1992), 350.

*(16) Levi's Descendants (26:57–62)*

⁵⁷These were the Levites who were counted by their clans:
    through Gershon, the Gershonite clan;
    through Kohath, the Kohathite clan;
    through Merari, the Merarite clan.
⁵⁸These also were Levite clans: the Libnite clan, the Hebronite clan, the Mahlite clan, the Mushite clan, the Korahite clan. (Kohath was the forefather of Amram; ⁵⁹the name of Amram's wife was Jochebed, a descendant of Levi, who was born to the Levites in Egypt. To Amram she bore Aaron, Moses and their sister Miriam. ⁶⁰Aaron was the father of Nadab and Abihu, Eleazar and Ithamar. ⁶¹But Nadab and Abihu died when they made an offering before the LORD with unauthorized fire.)

⁶²All the male Levites a month old or more numbered 23,000. They were not counted along with the other Israelites because they received no inheritance among them.

**26:57–62**    The census of the Levite clans parallels the position afforded to the Levites in the first cycle of material in Num 3:17–43, following the enumeration of the twelve tribes and their clans. The structure varies in that only a few of the subclans are included here in a separate list. The whereabouts of Shimei, Amram, Uzziel, and Mushi is unknown, for they continue to be omitted in 1 Chr 6:1–29. Numbers 3 follows the listing in Exod 6:16–19 of the sons and grandsons of Levi. Note the following comparative chart:

| Gen 46:11 | Num 3:17–20 | Num 26:57–58 | 1 Chr 6:1–29 |
|---|---|---|---|
| Gershon | Gershon | Gershon | Gershon |
|  | Libni | Libnite | Libni and sons … |
|  | Shimei |  |  |
| Kohath | Kohath | Kohath | Kohath |
|  | Amram |  | Amminadab and sons … |
|  | Izhar | Korahite | (incl. a Korah) |
|  | Hebron | Hebronite |  |
|  | Uzziel |  |  |
| Merari | Merari | Merari | Merari |
|  | Mahli | Mahlite | Mahli and sons … |
|  | Mushi | Mushite |  |

The Levites were not required to serve in the Israelite army, nor were they eligible for territorial land distribution. Instead they were supplied parcels of land near a number of prominent cities throughout the country, wherein they could supply their families and serve the local communities in priestly capacities. Levitical priestly families would continue to trace their lineage through the three sons of Levi, though few of the subclans that first entered the land would retain their identity.

    The excursus of vv. 58b–61 relates particulars of the Kohathite clan of

Amram through whom Moses, Aaron, and Miriam descended. The preeminence of the Moses-Aaron leadership is reasserted, despite the tragedy of the death of Nadab and Abihu, who improperly offered a sacrifice (Lev 10:1–2). The placement of the lineage at the conclusion of the second census would ensure the priority of the Aaronic priesthood for the new generation as was the case in the former. Furthermore, Aaron's son Eleazar is listed as Moses' assistant (v. 63) in the census taking.

The NIV properly translates the Hebrew *hôlid* ("gave birth, begat") as "forefather," since the time span between Kohath and Amram was perhaps three hundred years or more. That Moses was the true son of Amram and Jochebed remains uncertain since the names are not recounted in Exod 2:1–10. They may have been important ancestors within the Kohathite clan history. If one reads Exodus 2, Numbers 3 and 6, and 1 Chronicles 6 literally, then the time span between Levi son of Jacob and Moses, Aaron, and Miriam, hence the length of the Egyptian sojourn, would be about 160 years or less. Yet according to 1 Chr 7:14–27, ten generations elapsed between Joseph and Joshua. The purity of lineage is noted in that Amram's wife Jochebed was also of Levite lineage.

The reckoned population of male Levites over one month of age is listed as 23,000, an increase of less than 5 percent. The original figure of 22,000 (3:39) is given more precisely as 22,273 in 3:42 (meaning a net increase of 3.3 percent).

## *(17) Conclusion of the Second Census (26:63–65)*

**[63]These are the ones counted by Moses and Eleazar the priest when they counted the Israelites on the plains of Moab by the Jordan across from Jericho. [64]Not one of them was among those counted by Moses and Aaron the priest when they counted the Israelites in the Desert of Sinai. [65]For the LORD had told those Israelites they would surely die in the desert, and not one of them was left except Caleb son of Jephunneh and Joshua son of Nun.**

**26:63–65** The conclusion to this pivotal chapter in the Book of Numbers befits its character, design, and purpose. Retrospective and prospective elements are furnished. The census takers, Moses and Eleazar, bridge the generations. Moses has led the people of Israel mightily and valiantly through the Sinai and wilderness experiences, but he will not enter the Promised Land. Instead Eleazar will assume the responsibility of priestly leadership for the new generation. The census was conducted "on the plains of Moab by the Jordan [of] across from Jericho," the first city of the coming campaign into Canaan. Hence the prospects of fulfillment of the promise to the patriarchs and their descendants are bright. The text reminds the reader of the consequences of disobedience and rebellion that befell the original Exodus participants; they would not inherit the promises of God.

Only the two faithful spies of the twelve sent forth to survey the land, who spoke favorably and faithfully of the opportunities and blessings that lay ahead, would survive to experience the richness and abundance of God's steadfast love.

## 2. Land Inheritance Laws: The Case of Zelophehad's Daughters (27:1-11)

Principles regarding the allotment and apportionment of the land of promise had been set forth in terms of the clans of the twelve tribes of Israel, of which only male descendants are registered. Such practice bespeaks the patriarchal social and cultural milieu of the period among most Semitic peoples. The case of Zelophehad's daughters raises the issue of the status of women in Israelite society, particularly as rightful heirs in the Promised Land. The structure of the story contributes to our understanding of the development of casuistic legislation in Israelite history: specific case presentation and appeal to legislative authority (27:1-5) and precedent-setting decision and derived principles (27:6-11). The epilogue to the case is presented at the conclusion of the Book of Numbers, where additional case issues are raised and further legal implications are delineated (36:1-12).

### (1) The Case of Zelophehad's Daughters (27:1-5)

**[1]The daughters of Zelophehad son of Hepher, the son of Gilead, the son of Makir, the son of Manasseh, belonged to the clans of Manasseh son of Joseph. The names of the daughters were Mahlah, Noah, Hoglah, Milcah and Tirzah. They approached [2]the entrance to the Tent of Meeting and stood before Moses, Eleazar the priest, the leaders and the whole assembly, and said, [3]"Our father died in the desert. He was not among Korah's followers, who banded together against the LORD, but he died for his own sin and left no sons. [4]Why should our father's name disappear from his clan because he had no son? Give us property among our father's relatives."**
**[5]So Moses brought their case before the LORD**

**27:1-5** The Manasseh tribe descendant fathered only daughters prior to his death in the wilderness. One of the old generation who had rebelled against God and Moses and suffered the mortal consequences, Zelophehad perished ("he died for his own sins") without a rightful male heir through which his family would receive its share in the allotment of the land. The concern shared by Mahlah, Noah, Hoglah, Milcah, and Tirzah was that their family would be passed over in the apportionment and that name be forgotten in posterity. The second census had been outlined in terms of patriarchal clans, without reference to the status of women within the system. This issue is foreshadowed in 26:33, where the female progeny are first listed.

The five women approached (*tiqrabnâ*, "come near")[13] with an attitude of supplication to the Tent of Meeting to present before the proper religious authorities (Moses, Eleazar, et al.). Matters of land and inheritance were sacred in Semitic culture, and two facets of the request are offered. The disclaimer that their father had not participated in Korah's rebellion assured the priestly leaders of the general faithfulness of the family and provided requisite qualification for their petition. The perception that one would "die for his own sin" is notable in a passage having community responsibility as its focus. Both individual and corporate accountability are evidenced here. With regard to the perceptiveness of the women, Allen notes: "These were pious women with a sound understanding of the nature of the desert experience and a just claim for their family."[14] The request anticipates the fulfillment of divine blessing in the inheritance of the land.

Second, the potential disappearance of one's family name was a matter of grave concern, often associated with divine judgment and eventuating in societal abandonment. The entreaty for property within the clan allotment bespeaks comprehension of and derives from the principles set forth in 26:52–56. Thus the daughters of Zelophehad desire status and inheritance rights within the Makirite clan of the tribe of Manasseh. Later, in Num 32:39–42, the Makirites receive an inheritance in the Gilead region of Transjordan.

Moses does not reply immediately because of a lack of legal precedent related to the women's petition. As a quality spiritual leader he seeks the Lord for an answer to the matter of women and land inheritance. The feminine emphasis in this unusual request was heightened in the Masoretic Text by means of an enlarged feminine plural suffix, the Hebrew letter *nûn*. The NIV text breaks the paragraphing between vv. 4 and 5, whereas the MT division appears after v. 5.

### (2) Case Decision and Derived Principles (27:6–11)

**[6]and the LORD said to him, [7]"What Zelophehad's daughters are saying is right. You must certainly give them property as an inheritance among their father's relatives and turn their father's inheritance over to them.**

**[8]"Say to the Israelites, 'If a man dies and leaves no son, turn his inheritance over to his daughter. [9]If he has no daughter, give his inheritance to his brothers. [10]If he has no brothers, give his inheritance to his father's brothers. [11]If his father had no brothers, give his inheritance to the nearest relative in his clan, that he may possess it. This is to be a legal requirement for the Israelites, as the LORD commanded Moses.'"**

---

[13] The Hb. תִּקְרַבְנָה (2fp) from קרב, which often carries a cultic sense, especially in the *hiphil* form, which is generally used when a person "brings near" a sacrifice or offering.

[14] Allen, "Numbers," 942.

**27:6–11** The response begins with the precedent-setting divine formula, "And the LORD said to him," lit., "And the LORD said to him saying" *(wayyōʾmer YHWH ʾel-mōšeh lēʾmōr)*, thus utilizing an important thematic element of the Book of Numbers.[15] The structure provides a precursor to the midrashic process whereby matters of legal consequence not explicitly addressed in Torah would be posed to the council of religious elders for dialogue and decision. Applicable Torah precedents were brought to bear on the discussion, then the council ruling was disseminated to the Jewish communities.

The divine response was favorable on behalf of the women. The technical terminology of v. 11, "legal requirement" *(lĕḥūqqat mišpāt*, "for enactment of justice"), is suitably translated "legal precedent" in the NEB. Budd noted: "Theologically the section presses the rights of women to a clear and recognized legal position within the sphere of property law. They are seen as a proper channel through which the threads of possession and inheritance may properly be traced."[16] Thus the children of Zelophehad's daughters, as well as future generations of women, could receive landed property via familial inheritance, whether male or female.

Additional clarifications are set forth in vv. 8–11. The sequence of familial property inheritance was as follows: (1) if no son, the land reverts to a daughter, (2) if no daughter, then to the man's brothers, (3) if no brothers, then to his father's brothers, (4) if no father's brothers, then to the nearest relative within the clan. These specific delineations supplement the laws pertaining to the Year of Jubilee (Lev 25:23–28), in which the principle of divine ownership of the land reigns supreme. Marital implications are presented in Deut 25:5–10. Land inheritance and family preservation are inextricably intertwined.

## 3. Joshua: Heir to Moses (27:12–23)

The editorial juxtapositioning of the case of land inheritance for Zelophehad's daughters with the directive for Moses to view the land from a distance and announce his successor serves several functions. In retrospect the restriction of Moses from entering the Promised Land served as a poignant reminder of the disastrous results described in the rebellion cycles of Numbers 11–25. This section climaxed with Moses the righteous lawgiver obstinately defying God and being informed he would suffer the same consequence of his generation—to die before experiencing the fullness of

---

[15] See "Introduction: Structure and Outline" for an analysis of the use of this divine speech formula.

[16] Budd, *Numbers*, 302–3.

God's blessing. In prospect Moses was called upon to commission the faithful visionary Joshua as heir to his leadership of the nation. The fulfillment of the promise of land would fall under his administration and be subordinate to the direction of God himself.

The pericope adheres to an orderly progression, outlining the transition of leadership: (1) Moses' sin recapitulated (27:12–14), (2) Moses' entreaty for a new leader (27:15–17), (3) Moses' instruction from the Lord (27:18–21), (4) Moses commissions Joshua (27:22–23). The first section is recounted in Deut 3:21–29; 32:48–52, and the fulfillment is in Deut 34:1–8. Joshua's empowerment and guidance come to fruition in Deut 34:9 and throughout the Book of Joshua.

### (1) Moses' Sin Recapitulated (27:12–14)

**¹²Then the LORD said to Moses, "Go up this mountain in the Abarim range and see the land I have given the Israelites. ¹³After you have seen it, you too will be gathered to your people, as your brother Aaron was, ¹⁴for when the community rebelled at the waters in the Desert of Zin, both of you disobeyed my command to honor me as holy before their eyes." (These were the waters of Meribah Kadesh, in the Desert of Zin.)**

**27:12–14**   The elderly Israelite lawgiver was directed to journey about ten miles to the mountainous region of northwestern Moab, called Mount Abarim, where from the vantage point of Mount Nebo (Deut 32:49) he could see the Promised Land. After previewing what the new generation would inherit, he would die like his older brother Aaron and be buried at this place of visionary hope. The expression "gathered to your people" describes the Hebrew concept of unity and identity with the faithful forefathers (Gen 15:15; 25:8; 35:29; 47:30), with whom they would rest and find peace. The concept of ancestral continuity may relate an early view of immortality, though as Harrison notes, "Wherever the phrase occurs it carries with it an intimation of immortality, but it should not be understood in a purely literal sense."[17]

The reminder of the rebellion of Moses and Aaron at the waters of Meribah (Num 20:1–13) served to instruct future generations that no follower of the Lord is immune from sin and its judgment. Those called to lead the people of God must maintain the highest standards of holiness in obedience and faith or reap the results of their transgressions. Moses pleaded urgently for the Lord to allow him to tour the Land his people would possess and eat its fruit, but his request was cut short by a divine demand to refrain from pursuing the issue any further (Deut 3:23–27).

---

[17] Harrison, *Numbers,* 357.

## (2) Moses' Entreaty for a New Leader (27:15–17)

[15]Moses said to the LORD, [16]"May the LORD, the God of the spirits of all mankind, appoint a man over this community [17]to go out and come in before them, one who will lead them out and bring them in, so the LORD's people will not be like sheep without a shepherd."

**27:15–17** The response of the elder statesman of Israel reflected the true character of a spiritual leader, prayerful submission to the will of God, and concern for the future welfare of the people whom God had called him to guide. The expression "the Lord, the God of the spirits of all mankind," is rare phraseology (here and Num 26:22) that bespeaks the sovereignty of God over all humankind. That God would raise anew a righteous commander-in-chief demonstrates his sovereign concern for the welfare of his people. Moses likewise does not bemoan here his being hindered from entering the land of promise and hope.

The request of divine appointment for the new leader parallels Moses' own method of calling; he was not of royal lineage nor elected by the common populace. One who would march forth into the land of Canaan and face the challenges and perils that lay ahead must possess a divine commission, blessed with a sovereign hand of guidance and strength. Without such direction the often recalcitrant Israel might spend another forty years aimlessly wandering in a wilderness of spiritual darkness, "like sheep without a shepherd." The phraseology "to go out and come in ... lead them out and bring them in" (v. 17) reflects a verbal device designed to convey leadership potential parallel to that of Moses himself.

## (3) Moses' Instruction from the Lord (27:18–21)

[18]So the LORD said to Moses, "Take Joshua son of Nun, a man in whom is the spirit, and lay your hand on him. [19]Have him stand before Eleazar the priest and the entire assembly and commission him in their presence. [20]Give him some of your authority so the whole Israelite community will obey him. [21]He is to stand before Eleazar the priest, who will obtain decisions for him by inquiring of the Urim before the LORD. At his command he and the entire community of the Israelites will go out, and at his command they will come in."

**27:18–21** The selection of a new leader to succeed an individual of the spiritual and charismatic character of Moses should come from among those of proven character and integrity. Few among Israel had the necessary elder status and demonstrated spiritual leadership quality. None but Joshua ben Nun and Caleb ben Jephunneh of the earlier generation had survived the desert sojourn, and so a choice from these two men who had given a good report of the land and implored Israel to advance by faith into the land was most appropriate (Num 13:30–14:38). Joshua ben Nun of the tribe of

Ephraim, who had directed the army of Israel against the Amalekites (Exod 17:8–16) and who had aided Moses in the administration of the Tent of Meeting soon after the golden calf incident (Exod 33:7–11; cf. Num 11:28), was chosen as the individual best suited to assume the role of Moses. Joshua is described here as "a man in whom is the spirit." The NIV marginal reading, "Spirit," reflects a preferable interpretive translation, paralleling the personal trait described in Deut 34:9, "Now Joshua son on Nun was filled with the spirit (or Spirit) of wisdom because Moses had laid his hands on him." The lower case rendering would imply a general spirit of leadership. Whether the term spirit connotes a reference to the Holy Spirit, the Spirit of God, or a spirit of leadership is indefinite by terminology alone, but the life of Joshua evidenced that the [Holy] Spirit of God controlled his life. At Joshua's command the people would "go out, and ... come in," terminology that bespeaks full obedient response and also echoes (inclusio) the words of Moses' request.

The conferring of command was accomplished by the laying on of the [right] hands, symbol of power and authority, in the people's presence and under the supervision of Eleazar, the high priest who was also Moses' nephew. A portion of Moses' authority was to be bestowed immediately so that the transition would be smooth, and the obedient consent of the people would be harmonious. Unlike Moses, who enjoyed direct access to Yahweh in seeking his will, Joshua's authority was complemented by Eleazar, who would assist in decision making by inquiring of the Lord via the Urim, the sacred lots. The Urim, usually listed in conjunction with the Thummim, were among the stones placed in the high priest's breastplate, and probably were in addition to the twelve stones representing the tribes of Israel (Exod 28:30; Lev 8:8). The Urim and Thummim were instruments of divine illumination via a priestly intermediary, though the physical shape and the methodology of utilization are not revealed in Scripture. Harrison notes concerning these two words, which begin with the first *(ʾālep)* and last *(tāw)* letters of the Hebrew alphabet, "If this is the *merismus* motif, in which opposites are paired to denote totality, it could be interpreted to mean 'complete truth in revelation.'"[18] Later in Israelite history the prophets, as spokesmen for the Lord, superseded the Urim and Thummim as instruments of divine revelation (1 Sam 28:6; 1 Kgs 22:7–8).

### (4) Moses Commissions Joshua (27:22–23)

**[22]Moses did as the LORD commanded him. He took Joshua and had him stand before Eleazar the priest and the whole assembly. [23]Then he laid his hands on him and commissioned him, as the LORD instructed through Moses.**

---

[18] Ibid., 359.

**27:22–23**  The faithful servant Moses performed the task in full obedience to the command of the Lord. The MT indicates that Moses used both hands in a paramount manner of blessing, though some manuscripts of SamPent and Syriac contain the singular as in v. 18 and v. 23b. Joshua, whose name means "Yahweh is salvation," would carry the dual responsibilities of military and political leadership for the new generation of Israel. Beside him to assist and support him would be the priestly intermediary Eleazar, son of Aaron.

## 4. The Appointed Times and Offerings (28:1–29:40)

### (1) Introduction (28:1–2)

**[1]The LORD said to Moses, [2]"Give this command to the Israelites and say to them: 'See that you present to me at the appointed time the food for my offerings made by fire, as an aroma pleasing to me.'**

**28:1–2**  The second section of the first cycle of Part II of the Book of Numbers contains a series of offerings connected to each of the major divisions of the Israelite calendar. Structurally this pericope corresponds to Numbers 5–6 of cycle one of the first section. In the former section laws of purification complete the groundwork for sanctification of the nation prior to the presentation of tribal offerings and the dedication of the Tent of Meeting. In the present section the delineation of offerings for each of the calendrical commemorations and celebrations demonstrates the lavishness involved in sacrificial worship and anticipates the period of blessing from the Lord in the land, when abundant animal, grain, and drink elements would be available. G. Wenham noted: "Here again the giving of these laws acts as a strong affirmation of the promise to Joshua and the rest of the people. Every year in the future the priests will have to sacrifice 113 bulls, 32 rams and 1,086 lambs and offer more than a ton of flour and a thousand bottles of oil and wine."[19] The listed offerings were cumulative, such that during the annual Feast of Weeks the offerings listed were in addition to the regular daily sacrifices. Hence on the day of firstfruits at the beginning of the Feast of Weeks, the total would have been burnt offerings of nine lambs, two young bulls, and one ram, one and three-fifths ephah (twenty-six liters) fine flour mixed with three hin (twelve liters) of olive oil, and one and one-half hin (six liters) of fermented drink, plus one male goat for a sin offering.

The order of presentation closely parallels Leviticus 23, where the emphasis is upon (1) the participation of the worshipers in the celebration or commemoration, and (2) notable offerings particular to the given holy day.

---

[19] Wenham, *Numbers,* 197. Cf. A. F. Rainey, "The Order of Sacrifices in the Old Testament Ritual Texts," *Bib* 51 (1970): 495–98.

In Numbers 28–29 the priestly considerations are of primary concern, providing supplemental material to that of Leviticus 23. The species, methods, and amounts that are to be offered by the priests on behalf of the nation of worshipers are delineated. L. R. Fisher has suggested that this section is of great antiquity since it is analogous to a Ugaritic ritual calendar from circa fourteenth century B.C.[20] These texts instructed the priests as to the necessary time sequence and measure of given sacrifices to be offered during the seasonal cycles of the agricultural calendar year. One of the earliest Hebrew inscriptions unearthed in Palestine was the so-called Gezer calendar of the late tenth or early ninth century B.C., a text that outlines the agricultural seasons of early Israel.

The section is introduced by the standard divine message formula that functions throughout the Book of Numbers as a key sectional divider.[21] Stress is placed upon the ownership of Yahweh of the gifts and the demands placed by Yahweh upon the givers. Allen's translation of vv. 1–2 highlights this aspect:

Then Yahweh spoke to Moses saying:
"Command the Israelites, and say to them,
'You must be careful to present to **me my** offering
**my** food of **my** offerings by fire, **my** soothing
aroma, at the appointed time for each.'
"And you will say to them,
'This is the offering by fire that you shall
present to Yahweh.' "[22]

The life of the offering (animal) and the life of the offerer were gifts from God, and the return of the life of the offering was in celebration for the life given to the offerer.

The "appointed time" *(môʿēd)* denotes a designated time for religious assembly or may refer to the worshiping assembly itself (e.g., "Tent of Meeting" = *ʾōhel môʿēd*). Collectively the three annual pilgrimage assemblies are called the "appointed feasts of the LORD" (Lev 23:2). The sacrifices were prescribed according to the cycles of time and agricultural seasons, which were designed to honor and praise God for his beneficence in nature and history. Observances during several of the holy days combined elements of the agricultural calendar with salvation events in the history of

---

[20] L. R. Fisher, "A New Ritual Calendar from Ugarit," *HTR* 63 (1970): 485–501; *Ras Shamra Parallels,* II (Rome: Pontifical Biblical Institute, 1975): 143f. Cf. also B. A. Levine, "The Descriptive Tabernacle of the Pentateuch," *JAOS* 85 (1965): 315–18.

[21] See "Introduction: Structure and Outline" for a detailed analysis of the use of the divine message formula.

[22] Allen, "Numbers," 948.

the nation. The Feast of Booths integrated the providential protection of God during the wilderness experience with the fall fruit harvest. The Feast of Weeks combined elements of the wheat harvest with the gift of the law at Sinai. The second major division of the Mishnah, the late second century A.D. commentary on Jewish law, is called the Mo'ed and provided detailed interpretations and descriptions of Jewish law and practices relative to the biblical festivals from that time and earlier.

The prescribed offerings of Numbers 28–29 are largely burnt offerings *('ōlâ)*, which are consumed entirely on the altar by fire (cf. Lev 1). Each of the bulls, rams, and lambs had a prescribed amount of flour and oil to accompany the animal sacrifice, and wine or other ferment drink supplemented several. Sacrifices of this type (described in greater detail in Lev 1) reflect several important theological aspects: (1) a total burnt offering is a method by which the physical sacrifice is rendered fully to the Lord, the visible is rendered into the world of the invisible, and the smoke enters symbolically the nostrils of God with a sweet aroma such that he is pleased; (2) the animal must be perfect and unblemished because God requires nothing short of absolute purity; (3) nothing is returned to the offerer, signifying God's complete ownership; (4) offerings are made publicly as expressions of faith and obedience by those who must be ritually pure before presentation of the object; and (5) blood, the symbol of life of the sacrifice, was poured out on the altar as a means of returning life to the giver of all life.[23] Some were expiatory or propitiatory in nature, effecting atonement for the offerer, while others were celebrative, honoring God for the blessings of life. The New Testament supports this interpretation by describing the sacrifice of Christ as "a fragrant offering and sacrifice to God" (Eph 5:2), and the faithful and righteous life of the Christian as "living sacrifices, holy and pleasing to God—this is your spiritual act of worship" (Rom 12:1).

### *(2) Daily Offerings (28:3–8)*

**³Say to them: 'This is the offering made by fire that you are to present to the LORD: two lambs a year old without defect, as a regular burnt offering each day. ⁴Prepare one lamb in the morning and the other at twilight, ⁵together with a grain offering of a tenth of an ephah of fine flour mixed with a quarter of a hin of oil from pressed olives. ⁶This is the regular burnt offering instituted at Mount Sinai as a pleasing aroma, an offering made to the LORD by fire. ⁷The accompanying drink offering is to be a quarter of a hin of fermented drink with each lamb. Pour out the drink offering to the LORD at the sanctuary. ⁸Prepare the second lamb at twilight, along with the same kind of grain offering and drink offering that you prepare in the morning. This is an offering made by fire, an aroma pleasing to the LORD.**

---

[23] See also R. de Vaux, *Ancient Israel* (New York: McGraw-Hill, 1961), 415–17, 451–54. Cf. G. Wenham, *Leviticus,* 55–66.

**28:3-8**  Each morning after daybreak and each evening before sunset, a one-year-old lamb was prepared and sacrificed along with one-tenth ephah (about two liters) of finely ground flour and one-fourth hin (about one liter) of olive oil. This offering was one of those originally decreed on Mount Sinai (Exod 20:24; 29:38–43) for the purpose of consecration of the Tent of Meeting and the community that met God there. The more detailed cereal offerings of Num 15:1–21, which have the future life in the land in view, are presumed in this section. The addition of one-fourth hin of strong drink (šēkār, "beer, strong fermented or distilled drink," or more specifically yayin, "wine" in Exod 29:40) completes the collection of agricultural products that combined to produce a savory smell when consumed by fire. Šēkār derives from the Akkadian šikāru, the common word in Mesopotamia for prominent barley beer. Recently, however, Stager has suggested that šēkār may have actually been a kind of brewed and distilled grape beverage made from a variety of vineyard products.[24] Wine and other fermented liquids were considered special gifts from God (or the gods) in the ancient Near East and thus were to be reciprocated in kind as part of the array of sacrifices.[25]

The chronological setting of offering morning and evening sacrifices reflects upon the evening-morning sequence of the creation account in Genesis 1. This merismus intimates that God was to be worshiped continuously because of his creative power in ordering the universe, his providential power in nature whereby humankind's needs are provided, and his bestowing of power and dominion upon the pinnacle of his creation, humanity as male and female. Daily repetition would provide an endless picture of the dual (and often paradoxical) aspects of God's beneficent sovereignty and mankind's faithful responsibility to him.

### (3) Weekly (Sabbath) Offerings (28:9–10)

**[9]"'On the Sabbath day, make an offering of two lambs a year old without defect, together with its drink offering and a grain offering of two-tenths of an ephah of fine flour mixed with oil. [10]This is the burnt offering for every Sabbath, in addition to the regular burnt offering and its drink offering.**

**28:9-10**  Double portions of the daily offerings were called for on the Sabbath. As one of the unique contributions of Israelite religion to the world, the Sabbath observance centered on three facets: (1) the imitation of

---

[24] L. Stager, "The Impact of the Early Philistines of Ashkelon," SBL Annual Meeting, Orlando, FL, Nov 1998.

[25] For an extensive analysis of wine as a divine fluid in ANE and Mediterranean cult and culture, see E. R. Goodenough, *Jewish Symbols in the Greco-Roman Period* (New York: Pantheon, 1953–68), 5:99–197; 6:126–217.

God's resting from creative activity on the seventh day of creation (Gen 2:2), (2) the remembrance of the covenant relationship between God and Israel (Exod 20:8–11), and (3) recalling the foundation of the nation in the deliverance from Egypt (Deut 5:12–15). The Sabbath would emerge as a special day of worship activity during the postexilic era.

### (4) Monthly (Rosh Chodesh) Offerings (28:11–15)

[11]"'On the first of every month, present to the LORD a burnt offering of two young bulls, one ram and seven male lambs a year old, all without defect. [12]With each bull there is to be a grain offering of three-tenths of an ephah of fine flour mixed with oil; with the ram, a grain offering of two-tenths of an ephah of fine flour mixed with oil; [13]and with each lamb, a grain offering of a tenth of an ephah of fine flour mixed with oil. This is for a burnt offering, a pleasing aroma, an offering made to the LORD by fire. [14]With each bull there is to be a drink offering of half a hin of wine; with the ram, a third of a hin; and with each lamb, a quarter of a hin. This is the monthly burnt offering to be made at each new moon during the year. [15]Besides the regular burnt offering with its drink offering, one male goat is to be presented to the LORD as a sin offering.

**28:11–15** This passage contains the most extensive discussion of the monthly new moon festival (ro'šê ḥodĕšîm, the firsts of the months, or the new moons). Though the significance of this holy day for Jewish life waned following the destruction of the Jerusalem temple in A.D. 70, the new moon festival held an important place in the cycle of religious observances. Ram's horns and/or trumpets were sounded over the burnt offerings (Num 10:10; Ps 81:3) on Rosh Chodesh, and commerce was suspended (Amos 8:5). David's absence from Saul's festival table (1 Sam 20:5) was cause for concern. But during the eighth century B.C., the celebration had become contemptible in the eyes of the Lord because of social injustice and religious idolatry in the nation (Isa 1:13; Hos 2:11).

The lunar month, which commenced at the first official sighting of the smallest crescent of the new moon, was the basis for setting the sequence of the annual holy days and festivals ("on the first day of the seventh month," Lev 23:23). In the Mishnah regulations and requirements for witnesses are outlined, which were in effect during the late Second Temple period (Rosh Ha-Shanah 1.3–3.1). The lunar calendar is reflected throughout the Pentateuch, though the Qumran-Dead Sea Scroll community contended that the proper chronological reckoning should be the solar calendar, the lunar being considered of satanic origin.

The sizable quantity of sacrificial elements offered on this day bespeaks the status of the holiday for the Israelite community. In addition to the daily sacrifices, the following animals and accompanying grain, oil, and wine were rendered:

| Animal | Fine flour (ea) | Liquid | Wine Libation |
|---|---|---|---|
| 2 young bulls | 3/10 ephah | oil | 1/2 hin |
| 1 ram | 2/10 ephah | oil | 1/3 hin |
| 7 yearling lambs | 1/10 ephah | oil | 1/4 hin |
| 1 male goat (sin) | | | |

Together these constituted a grand rite through which the nation paid homage to its Creator and Sustainer.

### (5) Passover (Pesach) and Unleavened Bread Offerings (28:16–25)

[16]" 'On the fourteenth day of the first month the LORD's Passover is to be held. [17]On the fifteenth day of this month there is to be a festival; for seven days eat bread made without yeast. [18]On the first day hold a sacred assembly and do no regular work. [19]Present to the LORD an offering made by fire, a burnt offering of two young bulls, one ram and seven male lambs a year old, all without defect. [20]With each bull prepare a grain offering of three-tenths of an ephah of fine flour mixed with oil; with the ram, two-tenths; [21]and with each of the seven lambs, one-tenth. [22]Include one male goat as a sin offering to make atonement for you. [23]Prepare these in addition to the regular morning burnt offering. [24]In this way prepare the food for the offering made by fire every day for seven days as an aroma pleasing to the LORD; it is to be prepared in addition to the regular burnt offering and its drink offering. [25]On the seventh day hold a sacred assembly and do no regular work.

**28:16–25** The Passover begins the annual cycle of agricultural and religio-historical festivals, commencing on the fourteenth of the first month, called Abib in the Hebrew calendar and Nisan in the Babylonian. Pesach initiated the Feast of Unleavened Bread, a week-long celebration. The dual commemoration of Passover and Unleavened Bread reflect the dual aspects of the annual fetes, God's paramount salvation event in the deliverance of Israel from Egypt and his sustaining blessing in the spring barley harvest. Passover was the most important festival of the year, whereas Yom Kippur and Rosh Ha-Shanah were considered the two most holy days.

The general rites and regulations for Passover are outlined in Exod 12:1–20; Lev 23:4–8; and Deut 16:1–8. The focus of the present pericope is the priestly responsibility in the sacrificial system for burnt offerings and the sin offering. The pesach itself on the fourteenth of the first month just prior to sundown was an individual freewill offering exalting God for the deliverance from the bondage of slavery and oppression in Egypt. The yearling lamb was slaughtered and consumed by the family members along with the required unleavened bread and bitter herbs.

On each of the seven days of the Feast of Unleavened Bread, burnt offerings, in the equivalent amounts to the monthly offerings above (vv. 11–15), were sacrificed, except that drink offerings of wine were not included. Red wine would later be prescribed for participant consumption during the Passover meal.[26] The two bulls, one ram, seven lambs, and their concomitant grain, oil, and wine, plus a male goat for a sin offering, were presented along with the daily offerings (which included wine). The first and seventh days were set aside as Sabbaths for sacred assembly as the community of faith gathered for worship. During the eight days of celebration, a total of sixty-six lambs, fourteen bulls, seven rams, seven goats, seven and a half bushels of fine flour, over twenty-five gallons of olive oil, and at least one-half gallon of wine were expended.

The testimony of the New Testament that Christ's death, burial, and resurrection took place during the Jewish celebration of Passover and Unleavened Bread attests to the importance of the holy season (Matt 26:17–19; Luke 22:1–7). The Christ event was the fulfillment of Passover, the salvation event for Christians as the Exodus was for the Israelites in the days of Moses (1 Cor 5:7).

### (6) Feast of Weeks (Shavuoth / Pentecost) Offerings (28:26–31)

**[26]"'On the day of firstfruits, when you present to the LORD an offering of new grain during the Feast of Weeks, hold a sacred assembly and do no regular work. [27]Present a burnt offering of two young bulls, one ram and seven male lambs a year old as an aroma pleasing to the LORD. [28]With each bull there is to be a grain offering of three-tenths of an ephah of fine flour mixed with oil; with the ram, two-tenths; [29]and with each of the seven lambs, one-tenth. [30]Include one male goat to make atonement for you. [31]Prepare these together with their drink offerings, in addition to the regular burnt offering and its grain offering. Be sure the animals are without defect.**

**28:26–31** The Feast of Weeks, also called the day of firstfruits of the wheat harvest (Exod 34:22), marked the end of the Passover season, coming seven weeks and a day afterward.[27] The New Testament name Pentecost derives from this chronological reckoning and the Greek word *pentēkostos*, "fiftieth." The wheat harvest was one of the principal periods in the agricultural calendar, according to the Gezer calendar as well as Scripture (Gen 30:14; Judg 15:1; 1 Sam 6:13). The highlight of the festival was the priest's waving of the two bread loaves of new grain and the two lambs of the fellowship offering (Lev 23:15–21).

Later in Jewish history, Shavuoth was embellished with the celebration of the giving of the law at Sinai and with rites of Messianic hope. These elements were based upon the chronological sequence of the Exodus-Sinai events ("in the third month," Exod 19:1) and the wheat harvest background

---

[26] Mishnah, Pesachim 10.1–7.

[27] According to the prevailing view of the Pharisees, the day was established as the sixth of Sivan, the third month.

of the story of Boaz and Ruth, David's great-grandmother (1 Chr 2:12–15). For the Messianic community at Qumran, this festival was the most important of their solar calendar year.[28] The founding of the church in Acts 1 occurred during this pilgrimage festival, infusing a Christo-centric Messianic hope and fulfillment into the holy day.

The priestly sacrificial requirements were equivalent to those required for the new moon celebration. Leviticus 23:18, however, called for two rams and one bull versus the opposite amounts, an unexplained divergence. The Day of Firstfruits was also a Sabbath set aside for the community to rest from their labors and exalt Yahweh for the abundant harvest of barley and wheat. The concluding reminder that the animals presented for slaughter must be without blemish or defect, provides an allusion for the Christian reader to the words of Heb 9:14:

> How much more then will the blood of Christ, who through the eternal Spirit, offered himself unblemished to God, cleanse our consciences from acts that lead to death, so that we may serve the living God.

Paul called Christ the firstfruits, through whom all will be made alive (1 Cor 15:22–23).

### (7) Feast of the Blowing Trumpets Offerings (29:1–6)

**¹"'On the first day of the seventh month hold a sacred assembly and do no regular work. It is a day for you to sound the trumpets. ²As an aroma pleasing to the LORD, prepare a burnt offering of one young bull, one ram and seven male lambs a year old, all without defect. ³With the bull prepare a grain offering of three-tenths of an ephah of fine flour mixed with oil; with the ram, two-tenths; ⁴and with each of the seven lambs, one-tenth. ⁵Include one male goat as a sin offering to make atonement for you. ⁶These are in addition to the monthly and daily burnt offerings with their grain offerings and drink offerings as specified. They are offerings made to the LORD by fire—a pleasing aroma.**

**29:1–6** The fall season of festivals commenced with the Day of the Blowing [of Trumpets], later called Rosh Ha-Shanah—The New Year. This instrument was the ram's horn *(šôpār)* rather than the silver trumpets blown over the burnt and fellowship offerings at other festivals (Num 10:1–10). Ethanim, the seventh month of the Hebrew calendar (Teshritu or Tishri of Babylonian derivation), accommodated two other important holy days, the Day of Atonement and the Feast of Booths, making it the most festive (or commemorative) time of the year. In late postexilic times the ten days through Yom Kippur were set apart for penitence and personal remorse, fol-

---

[28] On this day the community held a sacred assembly for worship, assessment of members and initiates, and recitation of oaths of allegiance to God, to their community, and to their tenets of faith (1 QS 3.7, etc.).

lowed by the week-long Feast of Booths beginning on the fifteenth, a total of eighteen days of remembrance and celebration. Rosh Ha-Shanah today is considered the second most holy day of the Jewish calendar.

As in the previous chapter, this section accentuates the role of the priests in sacrificial worship. The inclusio formed by the use of the phrase "pleasing aroma" highlights the anthropomorphic soothing aspect of the sacrifices by which God is heartened and satisfied with the act of the worshiper. The priests performed their duties as intermediaries for the community, and in concert the special relationship between God and man is fulfilled. The former and latter prophets alike heralded God's demand for faithfulness and obedience on the part of the priests and the people. Apart from these traits their sacrifices were detestable and could never achieve their purpose (Judg 2:10–19; Amos 5:21–27; Jer 5:20–31; Zeph 4:1–8).

The burnt and sin offerings parallel those of the new moon, Passover, and Weeks, except that only one bull was slaughtered instead of two. Three sets of sacrifices were offered on the first of Ethanim: daily, new moon, and trumpets, for a total of three bulls, two rams, sixteen male lambs, one and six-tenths bushels of fine flour, and six gallons each of oil and wine.

### (8) Day of Atonement (Yom Kippur) Offerings (29:7–15)

[7]"'On the tenth day of this seventh month hold a sacred assembly. You must deny yourselves and do no work. [8]Present as an aroma pleasing to the LORD a burnt offering of one young bull, one ram and seven male lambs a year old, all without defect. [9]With the bull prepare a grain offering of three-tenths of an ephah of fine flour mixed with oil; with the ram, two-tenths; [10]and with each of the seven lambs, one-tenth. [11]Include one male goat as a sin offering, in addition to the sin offering for atonement and the regular burnt offering with its grain offering, and their drink offerings.

[12]"'On the fifteenth day of the seventh month, hold a sacred assembly and do no regular work. Celebrate a festival to the LORD for seven days. [13]Present an offering made by fire as an aroma pleasing to the LORD, a burnt offering of thirteen young bulls, two rams and fourteen male lambs a year old, all without defect. [14]With each of the thirteen bulls prepare a grain offering of three-tenths of an ephah of fine flour mixed with oil; with each of the two rams, two-tenths; [15]and with each of the fourteen lambs, one-tenth.

**29:7–15** The tenth of Ethanim (Tishri) was the holiest day of the Israelite / Jewish calendar, the time when the people gathered in solemn assembly to humble themselves before the Lord (Lev 16:29–31; 23:26–28). The term translated "deny" (ʿānâ) means "to afflict, oppress, be humble, or be lowly" and is used occasionally in the context of fasting (Ezra 8:21). This latter means of self-denial became the principal means of individual participation during the late postexilic period, when the day became known as "The Fast." Yom Kippur also was called "The Day," a title echoed in the Mishnah tractate (Yoma) dedicated to its discussion.

The descriptive title of the day, *yôm hakippūrîm* (or simply *hakappōret*), has been translated variously as Day of Atonement, Atonings, Day of Expiations, Propitiations, or Coverings, but it is not found in the present pericope. And whereas the detailed rites of the high priest and his attendants are outlined in Leviticus 16, with additional stipulations in 23:26–32, this section is concerned only with the required burnt and sin offerings and with the concomitant grain and oil components. The numbers of animals and amounts of flour and oil are equivalent to those for the Feast of Trumpets, but no wine is prescribed in the ritual.

The work of Christ on the cross as "a lamb without blemish or defect" (1 Pet 1:19) brought ultimate fulfillment to the ritual of Yom Kippur. Functioning as a superior high priest (Heb 7:22–28), he offered himself as a once-for-all, eternal sacrifice (Heb 9:11–28). His work accomplished our redemption from sin and cleansed our guilty consciences (Heb 10:19–22).

### (9)  Feast of Booths (Sukkoth) Offerings (29:16–38)

[16]Include one male goat as a sin offering, in addition to the regular burnt offering with its grain offering and drink offering.

[17]"'On the second day prepare twelve young bulls, two rams and fourteen male lambs a year old, all without defect. [18]With the bulls, rams and lambs, prepare their grain offerings and drink offerings according to the number specified. [19]Include one male goat as a sin offering, in addition to the regular burnt offering with its grain offering, and their drink offerings.

[20]"'On the third day prepare eleven bulls, two rams and fourteen male lambs a year old, all without defect. [21]With the bulls, rams and lambs, prepare their grain offerings and drink offerings according to the number specified. [22]Include one male goat as a sin offering, in addition to the regular burnt offering with its grain offering and drink offering.

[23]"'On the fourth day prepare ten bulls, two rams and fourteen male lambs a year old, all without defect. [24]With the bulls, rams and lambs, prepare their grain offerings and drink offerings according to the number specified. [25]Include one male goat as a sin offering, in addition to the regular burnt offering with its grain offering and drink offering.

[26]"'On the fifth day prepare nine bulls, two rams and fourteen male lambs a year old, all without defect. [27]With the bulls, rams and lambs, prepare their grain offerings and drink offerings according to the number specified. [28]Include one male goat as a sin offering, in addition to the regular burnt offering with its grain offering and drink offering.

[29]"'On the sixth day prepare eight bulls, two rams and fourteen male lambs a year old, all without defect. [30]With the bulls, rams and lambs, prepare their grain offerings and drink offerings according to the number specified. [31]Include one male goat as a sin offering, in addition to the regular burnt offering with its grain offering and drink offering.

32"'On the seventh day prepare seven bulls, two rams and fourteen male lambs a year old, all without defect. 33With the bulls, rams and lambs, prepare their grain offerings and drink offerings according to the number specified. 34Include one male goat as a sin offering, in addition to the regular burnt offering with its grain offering and drink offering.

35"'On the eighth day hold an assembly and do no regular work. 36Present an offering made by fire as an aroma pleasing to the LORD, a burnt offering of one bull, one ram and seven male lambs a year old, all without defect. 37With the bull, the ram and the lambs, prepare their grain offerings and drink offerings according to the number specified. 38Include one male goat as a sin offering, in addition to the regular burnt offering with its grain offering and drink offering.

**29:16–38** The third in the series of seventh month holy days is the Feast of Booths, an eight-day celebration concluding the agricultural season that began with Passover. The fall harvest of the vineyard, olive orchards, and vegetable crops, the fruit of God's abundant blessing upon the community, was celebrated in concert with the remembrance of God's special provision of dwelling places (*sūkkôt*, "tents, booths") in the wilderness. When the people entered and settled the Promised Land, they were to actively imitate their forefathers by building *sūkkôt* adjacent to their homes and living in them during the seven days of the feast (Lev 23:39–43). Branches from four green leafy trees were utilized in the celebration, perhaps in a ritual procession in the temple courts, a tradition known from Second Temple times and modern synagogue custom. The association of Sukkoth with the Exodus from Egypt provided a continuation of the salvation-redemption and providence-preservation motifs of Passover, Unleavened Bread, and Pentecost.

The large quantities of offerings enumerated in this section confirm the agricultural nature of the festival. The total number of animals slaughtered was seventy-one bulls, fifteen rams, and one hundred and twenty-two lambs for burnt offerings (including the daily burnt offerings and at least one for the Sabbath). The number seven was featured in the double portion of the seven lambs offered (an additional sign of blessing) and the decreasing numbers of bulls daily whereby seven bulls were sacrificed on the seventh day, for a total of seventy (plus one on the eighth day). The accompanying grain and oil added up to approximately twenty-two bushels of fine flour and sixty-five gallons of olive oil. In honoring Yahweh for the fullness of blessing, the number of fullness of community offerings from the flock and the field were returned to God via the holocaust upon the altar.

The first and eighth days of Sukkoth were Sabbaths for sacred assembly. Days of rest were for remembrance of creation, covenant, and deliverance, fundamental aspects of the unique relationship between God and his people. The day-by-day delineation draws a resounding conclusion to the ceremonies that reflect upon essential elements for the livelihood of Israelite agrarian society. By giving back to God the life of a portion of that which he has given to sustain life, the people would acknowledge his sovereignty and ownership of all. In like manner, Jesus' pronouncement on the last day of the Feast of tabernacles in Jerusalem emphasized the essential aspect of life in submission to God, "If anyone is thirsty, let him come to me and drink. Whoever believes in me as the Scripture has said, streams of living water will flow from him" (John 7:37–38). In the first century A.D. the Pharisees practiced a ritual of carrying a large golden flagon of fresh spring water, drawn from the Pool of Siloam, paraded ceremonially through the city to the Temple, and where it was then poured out as a libation offering to God upon the sacrificial altar. In this ritual, water, which was a symbol of life throughout the ancient world, would be poured out unto God in thanksgiving for the rains of the past year and in prayerful anticipation of that with which he would bless the people. Jesus utilized the imagery conveyed in this ceremony to teach an amazing lesson regarding himself. He was the true source of life symbolized in the living water.[29]

### *(10) Summary (29:39–40)*

[39]"'In addition to what you vow and your freewill offerings, prepare these for the LORD at your appointed feasts: your burnt offerings, grain offerings, drink offerings and fellowship offerings.'"
[40]Moses told the Israelites all that the LORD commanded him.

**29:39–40** The final verses recapitulate the essential sacrificial elements for the holy days outlined in chaps. 28 and 29. The animal, grain and oil, and wine offerings were to be submitted in addition to any other vow, freewill or thanksgiving offerings brought by individuals, families, or the community (Lev 7:11–21; 22:17–25; Num 15:1–21).

In preparation for entry and settlement of the land flowing with milk and honey, the priests of the people of God were called upon to render to him the sacrifices of field and flock that were so important to their survival. Allen concludes: "The restatement of these various offerings is a mark of faith and trust in the Lord, that at last he will complete his promise to bring his people into the land that is his gift for them."[30]

The reference to vows provides a structural preview to the material in the following chapter. The final verse (29:40 Eng., 30:1 Hb. MT) completes the inclusio of divine command concerning appointed times begun in 28:1–2. These instructions have been given by special divine revelation.

---

[29] Cf. G. Borchert, *John 1–11*, NAC (Nashville: Broadman & Holman, 1996), 289–91; R Brown, *The Gospel according to John*, I–XII, AB (Garden City: Doubleday, 1966), 320–29.
[30] Allen, "Numbers," 955.

## 5. Women's Vows (30:1–16)[31]

Vows for women provide a structural parallel to the special vows for Nazirites in 6:1–21.[32] This section is anticipated by the mention of vows (votive offerings) at the end of the cultic discussion of the previous chapter. The occasion for this material is unknown, though perhaps the issue of women's inheritance raised by Zelophehad's daughters provided the impetus. The primary focus of the treatise is the binding character of vows for all community members, with exceptions made for women of special status. The serious nature of vows is reflected in Eccl 5:4: "When you make a vow to God, do not delay in fulfilling it. He has no pleasure in fools; fulfill your vow." Proverbs 20:15 warns against rash or hastily made vows.

The internal bifid structure observed by Wenham groups the two triads of statutes as follows:[33]

| Verses | Material | Verses | Material |
| --- | --- | --- | --- |
| 2 | Men's vows unbreakable | 9 | Widow's and divorcees unbreakable |
| 3–5 | Girls' vows voidable by father | 10–12 | Wives' vows voidable by husband w/o penalty |
| 6–8 | Girls' vows voidable by fiance' | 13–15 | Wives' vows voidable w/ penalty |

Such arrangements were common to ancient Near Eastern law and the Old Testament.

### (1) Introduction: General Principle for Vows (30:1–2)

**[1]Moses said to the heads of the tribes of Israel: "This is what the LORD commands: [2]When a man makes a vow to the LORD or takes an oath to obligate himself by a pledge, he must not break his word but must do everything he said.**

**30:1–2** The making of vows was strictly voluntary, but any person who made a vow to the Lord, or by oath entered into an obligatory relationship, must fulfill that commitment. The term "vow" *(neder)* carries connotations of the verbal act of commitment to a task or to consecration of self or property to the Lord, sacrificial offerings (votive) as part of the obligation, or an oath of abstinence (e.g., Nazirite). A parallel term "pledge" *(neder)* occurs together with "vow" fourteen times in this chapter. T. W. Cartledge distinguishes between "vows" and "obligations" (NIV "oath to obligate"), defining the former as "a conditional promise, made in the context of petitionary

---

[31] The versification of the English text varies slightly from the MT; 30:1–16 in the English is 30:2–17 in the Hebrew.

[32] See "Introduction: Outline and Structure" for a more detailed study on the cycles and structural parallels in the Book of Numbers.

[33] Wenham, *Numbers,* 206.

prayer," and the latter as "an oath of abnegation."[34] Terms of swearing and oath taking are not precise synonyms because they derived from a different *Sitz im Leben* and can have as its indirect object something or someone other than God. Biblical vows were made only to deity, intensifying the solemnity of the pledge.

The reference to "a man" (*ʾîš,* man, mankind) in v. 2 may be interpreted in one of two ways: (1) the word may refer simply to the general category of men, with women being addressed in the following sections, or (2) the word in the verse context may set forth the general principle (or precedent) for men's vows, which are to be interpreted and applied to specific case needs for vows made by women. The latter function is preferred in that particular men's issues are not dealt with, and many of the women's issues are prescribed with the male-female relationship in view (30:16). For example, vows by boys under their father's household dominion are not addressed. In cases where women were under male authority, exception clauses were afforded.

### (2) Vows of Unmarried Women (30:3–5)

**³"When a young woman still living in her father's house makes a vow to the LORD or obligates herself by a pledge ⁴and her father hears about her vow or pledge but says nothing to her, then all her vows and every pledge by which she obligated herself will stand. ⁵But if her father forbids her when he hears about it, none of her vows or the pledges by which she obligated herself will stand; the LORD will release her because her father has forbidden her.**

**30:3–5** Casuistic law was delineated concerning the binding nature of vows and/or pledges made by women while still living under the patriarchal headship of her father. Cartledge noted: "Male dominance becomes the controlling rule: any dependent woman may make vows, but such vows are subject to cancellation on first hearing by the male authority figure on whom the woman is dependent, whether father or husband."[35] The young female lived under her father's watchcare and authority until she married (usually in the late teenage years), at which time her husband would assume that responsibility.

If the young woman entered into a vow or took an oath that she might not be able to fulfill or one that might cause hardship or embarrassment to the family, the patriarch could cancel the obligation. If he rescinded the vow,

---

[34] T. W. Cartledge, *Vows in the Hebrew Bible and the Ancient Near East,* JSOTSup 147 (Sheffield: Sheffield Academic Press), 25. He suggests furthermore that "when Numbers 30 was codified, אָסָר did not refer to a vow of abstinence. The verbal form נָדַר occurs 31 times in the Hebrew Bible, and in 19 of 22 transitive uses, the object is the cognate accusative נֶדֶר, hence "to vow a vow."

[35] Ibid., 34.

then she was released by God from her promise (*sālaḥ*, "forgive, pardon").[36]
This stipulation also allows that a father may confirm such a vow or simply
permit it to remain in effect by choosing no course of action.

### (3) Vows of Newly Married Women (30:6–8)

**6"If she marries after she makes a vow or after her lips utter a rash promise
by which she obligates herself [7]and her husband hears about it but says nothing
to her, then her vows or the pledges by which she obligated herself will stand.
[8]But if her husband forbids her when he hears about it, he nullifies the vow that
obligates her or the rash promise by which she obligates herself, and the LORD
will release her.**

**30:6–8** The case law of this chapter is formulated in progressive stages
of marital relationship. The second category of women's vows relates to a
previous commitment that was carried over into the marriage relationship.
The terminology of v. 6, "utter a rash promise" (*mibtā᾿ šĕpāteyhā*, "rashness
of her lips"), implies the possible immature vow that might be made by a
young woman or girl. Leviticus 5:4 recounts the culpability of a person who
thoughtlessly takes an oath of action. That person was required to make a sin
offering. Taking a beneficent view of this law, Allen noted:

> That she might be released from such a vow is greatly liberating both to her
> and her husband. ... This is a protective clause. It also works for her in that she
> might have been pressured into making a vow that was not at all in her best
> interests to keep. This frees her from unnecessary complications to her life as
> well.[37]

The same guidelines ensue for the husband in this setting as for the father
in the previous section. The husband, as the male authority figure in the relationship, may choose from several courses of action: (1) permit the vow or
oath to remain in effect by default—no action, (2) negate the obligation, or
(3) affirm the commitment by word or deed. Again, if the preference of the
husband was cancellation, the woman was assured of the forgiveness and
pardon from the Lord with regard to her vow and its concomitant offerings.

### (4) Vows of Widowed or Divorced Women (30:9)

**9"Any vow or obligation taken by a widow or divorced woman will be binding
on her.**

**30:9** A woman who was no longer under the patriarchal authority of her
father or her husband, whether by his death or by divorce, possessed the

---

[36] The term סלח is used only of God in the OT. The common usage relates to the pardon or
forgiveness of sinners, whether an individual or a community.

[37] Allen, "Numbers," 960.

same status and responsibility of a man with regard to vows and obligations. Women were afforded a significant position in Israelite society, for they were permitted to buy and sell property, negotiate contracts, operate businesses, and make vows and pledges (Num 27:7; 36:8). That widows and divorcees are classified together implies that in the functional relationship, the former husband of the latter was viewed as if he were dead, like the late husband of the widow.

### (5) Vows of Married Women (30:10–15)

[10]"If a woman living with her husband makes a vow or obligates herself by a pledge under oath [11]and her husband hears about it but says nothing to her and does not forbid her, then all her vows or the pledges by which she obligated herself will stand. [12]But if her husband nullifies them when he hears about them, then none of the vows or pledges that came from her lips will stand. Her husband has nullified them, and the LORD will release her. [13]Her husband may confirm or nullify any vow she makes or any sworn pledge to deny herself. [14]But if her husband says nothing to her about it from day to day, then he confirms all her vows or the pledges binding on her. He confirms them by saying nothing to her when he hears about them. [15]If, however, he nullifies them some time after he hears about them, then he is responsible for her guilt."

**30:10–15** The concluding and most detailed case relates to married women who make vows or oaths. In the patriarchal society of ancient Israel, vows that might have been detrimental to the woman, her husband, or the husband-wife relationship could be annulled by the husband. Special considerations were given to the circumstances and time sequence of when the wife took a vow or oath, when the husband was apprised of the commitment, and when and how he responded to the information.

First, the general principles that were outlined for the unmarried and newly married women applied also to married women. The husband may confirm by action or inaction or nullify his wife's vow or oath. Annulment by the husband frees the woman from fulfilling her commitment, and pardon is afforded her from the Lord. Second, if the husband deliberately delayed[38] in responding to the statement of his wife's vow, his inaction confirmed her action. If he should decide after that extended period to annul the commitments of his wife, however, he would incur the guilt of a broken vow. The husband must not delay or waver in addressing the issue of his wife's vow, especially if disallowance were a possibility.

A third differentiation in this section is the inclusion of the particular lan-

---

[38] The language here is intensified. The Hb. reads וֹם וְאִם־הַחֲרֵשׁ יַחֲרִישׁ לָהּ אִישָׁהּ מִיּוֹם אֶל־יֹ, "keeps silent ... from day to day (= for days?)," indicating an intentional silence for an extended period of time

guage of self-denial. The phraseology *ʾissār lĕʿannōt nāpeš*, "oath to deny self," is used in the context of fasting in Lev 16:29,31; Num 29:7; Ezra 8:21; Ps 35:13 or may refer to any other manner of self-abnegation (Gen 16:9; Dan 10:12). Hannah, Samuel's mother, provides a classic example of a woman who took upon herself a Nazirite vow of dedication and self-denial, which Elkanah her husband allowed to come to fulfillment by taking no action. Her vow was completed when she presented her son to Eli the priest for service of the Lord and offered sacrifices of bull, flour, and wine (1 Sam 1:3–28). In the New Testament, Jesus disparaged oaths that were detrimental to the well-being of others (Matt 15:3–9) and encouraged his followers to speak in resolute manner and avoid ambiguity (Matt 5:33–37; cf. Jas 5:12).

*(6) Summary (30:16)*

¹⁶**These are the regulations the LORD gave Moses concerning relationships between a man and his wife, and between a father and his young daughter still living in his house.**

**30:16** The concluding summary indicates the central issue of the chapter, women's vows within the familial context. Together, Numbers 27 and 30 elevate the status of women within the patriarchal society of ancient Israel. Intermittent examples throughout the Old Testament advance a progressive development of laws regarding women in society and female-male relationships. Jesus would further elevate women by his close associations with those such as Mary the Magdalene and Martha and by his freedom in discussing vital theological issues with one such as the Samaritan woman at Jacob's well (John 4:1–26).

------ IV. ADVENT CYCLE B: PREPARATIN FOR WAR  ------
AND ENTRY INTO THE PROMISED LAND (31:1–36:13)

### Introduction to the Second Advent Cycle

After the chronological interlude of chaps. 26–30 the final cycle of the
Book of Numbers draws the reader's attention to the preparation for entry
into the Promised Land in fulfillment of the covenantal promise made to
Abraham, Isaac, Jacob, and Moses. According to the cyclical outline delineated in the introduction to this commentary, the theme develops as follows:

1. Historical setting: Lord's vengeance versus Midianites and Balaam,
Num 25:16–18 (chap. 31);

2. Twelve tribe listing: "thousand men from each of the tribes of Israel"
(3x in 31:4–6);

   ten leaders to divide land of Canaan, two and one-half tribes in Transjordan (Num 34:13–29);

3. Thematic development: journey and land motifs combined (Num 32–34);

4. Matters related to the priests and Levites: provision of Levitical cities
in 35:1–8;

5. Laws governing the community of faith: cities of refuge and property
rights for the daughters of Zelophehad in 35:9–36:12.

The final verse of the book, cycle, and chapter returns to the geographical
setting from which the entry into the Promised Land will be launched, with
the reminder that the Book of Numbers is ultimately a book of instruction
for faith and practice, with numerous examples concerning life lived in the
world in relationship to the Lord.

### 1. The Midianite Campaign (31:1–54)

Chapter 31 picks up where chap. 25 left off, namely with a reprisal attack
against the Midianites who with Balaam had instigated a plot to induce
Israel toward idolatry and adulterous immorality. After the expurgation of
the sinful elements of their people, the second generation of Israel, now
poised in the plains of Moab opposite Jericho, was facing the same moral,
ethical, and spiritual dilemma that the first generation had faced in the wilderness. Would they be faithful to their unique covenant relationship with
Yahweh their God or succumb to the temptations that lay ever before them?
The seriousness of the Midianite sinfulness reverberates through the text,
which recounts the Lord's vengeance against them. In reality the content of
this passage is much more concerned with matters related to the process of

holy war than with matters of warfare; the material reflects more concern for
the cult than for the waging of warfare. T. Ashley has rightly outlined chap.
31 with respect to four aspects of holy war methodology, which follow the
brief section on the battle against the Midianites (vv. 1–12): (1) inflicting the
ban or *ḥērem*, vv. 13–18, (2) cleansing the soldiers, vv. 19–24, (3) dividing
the booty, vv. 25–47, and (4) bringing an offering to Yahweh, vv. 48–54.[1]
The *BHS* further subdivides vv. 25–47 into two sections, with vv. 25–30
containing the method of distribution under the leadership of Eleazar the
priest and vv. 31–47 the summary count of all the booty. Thus this chapter
has provided a case study for the postcombat concerns for the upcoming
campaigns in the land of Canaan. As such it would be natural to include the
application of other laws and statutes from the Book of Numbers, such as
the purification of soldiers who had come in contact with the dead (vv. 19–
24 from 19:14–19), provisions for the priests and Levites from the tithes and
offerings of the people (vv. 28–41,47,50–54 from 18:2,8–16), the gathering
of Moses to his people in his upcoming death (v. 2 from 20:12,24), and the
obedience of Moses and the people to the Lord's commands (vv. 7,21,41
from 20:9,27).[2]

### Critical Issues in Numbers 31

Source critical scholars have generally assigned this passage to the supposed priestly editor / composer due to the role of Phinehas the priest, son
of Eleazar, the delineation of provisions for the priests and Levites, several
'late' Hebrew words, and the extensive onomastic listing of numerous animals. G. B. Gray described this chapter as "not history, but Midrash" which
belonged to "the age which saw the rise of Midrashic literature; it clearly
belongs to the secondary strata of the Priestly Code (Ps)."[3] Budd suggested

---

[1] T. Ashley closely followed the divisions in the MT (*The Book of Numbers*, NICOT [Grand Rapids: Eerdmans, 1993], 587).

[2] See also 1:19,54; 2:33–34; 3:16,39,42,51; 4:37,41,45,49(2X); 5:4; 8:3,4,20,22 in the first two cycles. Only in 10:13; 17:11 (MT 17:26), and 20:9,27 does this phraseology occur in the three rebellion cycles. Then in the advent cycles the theme recurs in 26:4; 27:11,22–23; 31:7,31,41,47; 32:25; 36:5,10. An alternate expression עַל־פִּי יְהוָה occurs in 3:16,39,51; 4:37,41,45,49; 9:18,20,23; 10:13; 13:3; 33:2,38; 36:5.

[3] G. B. Gray, *A Critical and Exegetical Commentary on Numbers*, ICC (Edinburgh: T & T Clark, 1903), 419. His view has been adopted recently by P. Budd, *Numbers*, WBC 5 (Waco: Word, 1984), 333. M. Noth called this chapter "one of the very late sections of the Pentateuch" that was added to the Pentateuch after its priestly compilation (*Numbers: A Commentary*, OTL [Philadelphia: Westminster, 1968], 229). Cf. also A. Dillmann, *Das Bücheri Numeri, Deuteronomium und Joshua* (Leipzig: Hirzel, 1886), 187–92; N. Snaith, *Leviticus and Numbers*, The Century Bible (London: Thomas Nelson, 1967), 193; J. Sturdy, *Numbers*, CBSC (New York: Cambridge University Press, 1976), 214–16.

that "the story has little 'realism,' and is best understood as a midrashic construction, celebrating the power of Yahweh to defeat enemies, emphasizing
the need in all circumstances to support the priests and Levites."[4] Yet the
passage contains substantial portions that relate to the priests and Levites
and their support primarily as managerial accountants and guardians of the
purity of the community and its sanctuary. The priests, under the auspices of
their leader Eleazar, would oversee the counting and distribution of the
booty, but their share was but a very small portion when compared to that
received by the soldiers and the rest of the community. That maintaining of
the purity of the sancta was an important role of priesthood among the religious cultures throughout the ancient Near East is evidenced from the very
earliest cultic or priestly literature of the third millennium B.C., an argument
for early antiquity as much as late antiquity. The priests also served as the
trumpeting signal corps for the dispatching of the Israelite militia.

Numbers 31 is said to be dependent on Deuteronomy 20, Judges 8, and
1 Samuel 30. Yet, as Wenham and Ashley have so astutely pointed out, none
of these arguments is conclusive; and in fact if one hypothesizes that the
chapter derives from the Mosaic era, the three passages above derive from
Numbers 25 and 31 sequentially and logically. In a general sense Gray may
have been correct in describing Numbers 31 as midrashic (a literary tool for
teaching certain lessons or principles) in its literary structure, but that need
not imply that it should be associated with midrashic exegesis of the late
postexilic era (second century B.C. and later). The basis of the passage is
material that should be taken as historically reliable, which was fashioned
into a literary composition that had the function of providing case law precedents for future holy war endeavors for this generation that would enter
the land and for generations to come.[5] J. Milgrom concluded that "the
assembled evidence clearly points to the historic reality that Midian was the
most powerful and menacing enemy that Israel had to encounter during its
migration into Canaan."[6]

Critics have observed that several components in the account seem
incredulous, including the annihilation of all the males of Midian, the enormous numbers of various animals seized in the plunder, and that none was

---

[4] Budd, *Numbers*, 333.

[5] Cf. also the views of G. Wenham (*Numbers: An Introduction and Commentary*, TOTC
[Downers Grove: InterVarsity Press, 1981], 209–10), and C. F. Keil (*The Book of Numbers* [Edin-
burgh: T & T Clark, 1869], 226), who argue for the historical and / or literary priority of Numbers
31. J. Milgrom (*Numbers*, JPS Torah Commentary [Philadelphia: Jewish Publication Society,
1990]) attests to "a verifiable historical nucleus" of such elements as the antiquity of the names of
the Moabite kings (v. 8), Moses' allowing marriage to virgin Midianite women (which would have
been vehemently opposed by the postexilic priest Ezra), the political parallels with the account of
the judgeship of Gideon, and the use of 'hand-picked shock troops' as a preface to major battle.

[6] See Milgrom, "Excursus 67: The War Against Midian," 490–91.

missing or lost from Israel's battalions. G. Wenham and Ashley have provided answers to these and other questions regarding the content and character of the narrative.[7] First, it is an overstatement of the data in the narrative to suggest that the report of vv. 7–8, that Israelites "killed all the males of Midian" including the kings (or tribal chiefs), implies that every male of every Midianite tribe from the Transjordan to Arabia to Sinai was exterminated in this one campaign. Obviously this was not the case since the Midianites are well attested in the biblical and ancient Near Eastern texts.[8] Taken in the historical context of this being a divinely directed follow-up campaign after the sinful Baal Peor incident (25:16–18; 31:3–8), this crusade was directed at the tribes or clans of Midianites who dwelled in the central and northern Transjordan highlands, in the vicinity of the lands of the Moabites, Ammonites, and Amorites. The Midianites of the southern regions, such as those of Moses in-laws, were on better terms with the Israelites or were not involved on this occasion.

Second, the large numbers of animals taken as spoils of war seem incredulous. The totals are much higher by comparison with those confiscated in the campaign of Thutmose III of Egypt ca. 1460 B.C. during his campaign against Megiddo and other northern Canaanite cities. The Karnak temple account lists booty of 1,929 cattle, 2,000 goats, 20,500 sheep, and 2,503 slaves (men, women, and children), along with a variety of physical objects such as gold bowls and ebony statues.[9] G. Wenham suggests an adjustment should be made to the numbers by analogy with the two census summaries of 1:1–46 and 26:1–51. Taking the alternative meaning of the word for thousand *(ʾelep)*, that of "clans" or "battalions of troops," as perhaps herds or flocks in this analogy, the totals of the animals might be interpreted as 67,500 or even fewer sheep (vs. 675,00 in v. 32), 3,600 or fewer cattle taken by the men of war as their share (vs. 36,000 in v. 38), et cetera.[10] Yet within the text there is consistency in the resultant numbers of animals and persons provided as gifts to the Lord (and hence the priests) on the basis of the 1:500 ratio delineated in v. 28. Of 32,000 persons captured, 32 (1/500 of the warriors' half=16,000) were presented as the Lord's tribute (v. 40).

The testimony that not a man was missing from those who went out to war against the Midianites (v. 49) seems exaggerated on the surface, yet such claims are not unknown from the Bible or the texts of the ancient Near East. The account of Gideon's night raid against the Midianites suggests that all three hundred men survived the initial confrontation and continued their

---

[7] G. Wenham, *Numbers*, 209–10; Ashley, *Numbers*, 598.

[8] As in the judgeship of Gideon (Judg 6–8).

[9] J. Wilson, trans., "The Asiatic Campaigns of Thut-mose III," *ANET*, 237.

[10] G. Wenham, *Numbers*, 60, 209. Ashley simply suggested that "perhaps some adjustment in our understanding of these figures is necessary" (*Numbers*, 589).

efforts by pursuing their enemies down into the Jordan Valley and beyond (Judg 7:7,16,19–22; 8:4). The Persian King Cyrus, for example, who captured the city of Babylon only after conquering the rest of the Babylonian kingdom, claims to have captured this seemingly impregnable city "without any battle" in 539/538 B.C.[11] The victory over the Midianites was a remarkable one indeed, but with the providential direction and protection of the armies of Israel, such was definitely not out of the realm of possibility.

Finally, a word should be mentioned about the moral and ethical concerns of holy war. The goal of holy war was to drive out human populations (Num 33:50–53). In some cases it included the total annihilation of human life in a given area to purge idolatry and remove its temptations (Deut 20:16–19), the subjugation of women who were not killed (Deut 10–14), and the banning of certain objects and materials from the public usage (Deut 7:5,24–26; Josh 6:18–19). But these requirements were intended for Israel during the period of the late second and first millennia B.C. As D. Howard has aptly observed: "We should note that the instructions to Israel to annihilate the Canaanites were specific in time, intent, and geography. ... While God abhors evil of every kind and Christians are to oppose it vigorously, the extremes of the *ḥerem* are not enjoined upon Christians to practice today."[12] By the principles and standards set forth by Jesus Christ, the law of holy war has been superseded by the law of love. There is no successor to Israel as the theocratic kingdom in the Bible or in subsequent human history, no realm defined by ethnicity or national boundaries. The kingdom of God is still a theocracy, but it is defined by the Christian community of faith, those who have believed in Jesus as the Christ.

For Christians the kingdom of God, which has been established in and through the person and work Christ, transcends nationalism, definable geographical parameters, and man-made religious codes. It is not defined by ethnicity but by the ethical and moral demands that God has revealed to humanity through his word. This kingdom is ever moving toward the goal of the transformation of all peoples and nations into a kingdom that evinces Christlikeness. Thus no nation can now claim to be heirs of the law of holy war, but each Christian who is a citizen of a given state, nation, or ethnic group should work diligently in exerting influence on the state so that its laws and statutes might reflect the fullness of justice, righteousness, and ethical quality that derive from the very nature of God. In an imperfect world so deeply affected by the sin of humanity, however, any just state must by necessity participate in means of violence to maintain order and quality of

---

[11] "Cyrus Cylinder," *ANET*, 315–16.

[12] D. Howard, *Joshua*, NAC (Nashville: Broadman & Holman, 1998), 186–87.

life for its citizens. As for the Christian who participates in this world system, P. Craigie aptly states:

> The human state to which he [the Christian] belongs is bound by the order of necessity, of violence; it is caught in the same dilemma which characterized the existence of the ancient state of Israel, and the Old Testament has made it clear that such is an inevitable dilemma. No state can exist free from the necessity of violence or liberated from the possibility of war. And the dilemma for the Christian will be in determining how to understand the relationship between his two citizenships.[13]

### The Midianites

The Midianites are an enigmatic people in biblical, historical, and archaeological research. According to the ancestral genealogies of Gen 25:1–4, Midian was one of the sons of Abraham through his concubine Keturah. Midianites are depicted as having close associations with the Moabites (Gen 36:35; Num 22:7; 25:6,14–18), with the Amalekites (Judg 6:3; 7:12), and with the Ishmaelites in the sale of Joseph to a caravan headed to Egypt (Gen 37:28). The Midianites seem to have been a large yet loosely associated confederation of nomadic and seminomadic tribes who traveled the regions of the Sinai peninsula, the Negev of southern Israel, southern Jordan and the Arabah, and southeastward into the northwestern part of the Saudi Arabian peninsula. From the variety of biblical examples some of the Midianite clans seem to have been more amiable, as in the case of the family of Jethro, Reuel, and Hobab (Exod 2:15–3:1; 4:18–20),[14] while others were marauding nomads taking opportunity for personal gain by raiding towns and crops (Judg 6:1–8:21). Moses fled to the region of Midian from Egypt, labored in the Midianite household of Jethro (Reuel), married one of his seven daughters (Zipporah), and there first encountered the Lord in the theophany at the burning bush (Exod 2:15–3:4). Some have even suggested that Moses derived some of his monotheistic theology from his association with Jethro, who was a priest of Midian.

### *(1) Israelite Armies Battle the Midianites (31:1–12)*

**¹The LORD said to Moses, ²"Take vengeance on the Midianites for the Israelites. After that, you will be gathered to your people."**

**³So Moses said to the people, "Arm some of your men to go to war against the Midianites and to carry out the LORD's vengeance on them. ⁴Send into battle a thousand men from each of the tribes of Israel." ⁵So twelve thousand men armed for battle, a thousand from each tribe, were supplied from the clans of Israel. ⁶Moses sent them into battle, a thousand from each tribe, along with Phinehas**

---

[13] P. Craigie, *The Problem of War in the Old Testament* (Grand Rapids: Eerdmans, 1978), 102.

[14] See discussion of the family of Hobab in commentary on Num 10:29.

son of Eleazar, the priest, who took with him articles from the sanctuary and the trumpets for signaling.

⁷They fought against Midian, as the LORD commanded Moses, and killed every man. ⁸Among their victims were Evi, Rekem, Zur, Hur and Reba—the five kings of Midian. They also killed Balaam son of Beor with the sword. ⁹The Israelites captured the Midianite women and children and took all the Midianite herds, flocks and goods as plunder. ¹⁰They burned all the towns where the Midianites had settled, as well as all their camps. ¹¹They took all the plunder and spoils, including the people and animals, ¹²and brought the captives, spoils and plunder to Moses and Eleazar the priest and the Israelite assembly at their camp on the plains of Moab, by the Jordan across from Jericho.

**31:1–2** The cycle begins with the standard introductory formula for divine instruction, *wayĕdabbēr YHWH ʾel-mōšeh lēʾmōr*, "Then Yahweh instructed Moses saying"—used as a major organizational element throughout the Book of Numbers.[15] This would be the final exercise of leadership carried out by Moses before his death, his final act of faithful obedience before he would be "gathered to his people" like his brother Aaron.[16] That Moses was directed by God to "take vengeance" (NIV, NKJV) on the Midianites reflects one side of the Hebrew verb *nqm*, which can also mean "vindication." God directs his vengeance against the immoral, idolatrous, and unjust; and yet his vengeance is often self-limiting according to his great mercy. Smick notes, "The Bible balances the fury of God's vengeance against the sinner with the greatness of his mercy on those whom he redeems from sin."[17] G. Mendenhall has defined the content of this instruction as "punitive vindication."[18] Mendenhall is right in suggesting that the use of the words "avenge" or "revenge" with God as the subject reflects an improper theology based on a low view of God. Rather God vindicates the righteous and punishes the sinner as an essential part of his ethical, moral, and just character. God is not out for retaliatory revenge but for vindication of the honor of his people and himself and ultimately for restoration of the well-being of humanity.

**31:3–5** The battle instructions are given in terms of the size of the army to be mustered for the campaign and the involvement of the priestly leadership under Phinehas, the son of the high priest Eleazar son of Aaron. The

---

[15] For discussion of the phraseology וַיְדַבֵּר יְהוָה אֶל־מֹשֶׁה לֵּאמֹר and its use in the Book of Numbers, see "Introduction: Structure and Outline of the Book of Numbers" and commentary on Num 1:1.

[16] See commentary and notes on the phrase תֵּאָסֵף אֶל־עַמֶּיךָ above on 20:24–28 and 27:13.

[17] E. B. Smick, "נקם (nāqam)," *TWOT* 2:598–99.

[18] Following the translation of G. Mendenhall, "The 'Vengeance' of Yahweh," in *The Tenth Generation* (Baltimore: Johns Hopkins University, 1973), 99.

equal enlistment of one thousand from each of the twelve tribes[19] recalls the corporate community's equal participation in the bringing of gifts to the sanctuary when it had been dedicated in the valley below Mount Sinai (7:1–89). This was to be a unified effort in carrying out the instructions from the Lord. Unity and wholesome structure of the community of faith was a major theme of Numbers 1–7, and as noted above in the introduction to this chapter, it supplies the needed cyclical element with a statement regarding the twelve Israelite tribes. This theme will be evidenced throughout the chapter.

**31:6** Moses responded faithfully by mustering the required contingent of one thousand men from each of the twelve tribes. Phinehas was dispatched along with the troops as the priest who would serve the military in his necessary cultic capacities with the "articles from the sanctuary"[20] and the trumpets that had been made for directing the movements of the camps along their journey from Mount Sinai and rallying the troops for war (Num 10:1–10). Eleazar the high priest was not sent so as to preserve his sanctity from the potential contamination that would be brought on by exposure to the dead in battle.[21] The connection with 25:16–18 is evidenced again in the role played by Phinehas, to which Milgrom remarked: "Here we see Phinehas once again acting as the antidote to Balaam. Just as he countered Balaam's plan to seduce the Israelites at Baal-peor (25:7–13), so now he serves as the spiritual leader of Israel's forces as they seek retribution from the Midianites, in whose midst Balaam was also active (v. 8)."[22]

Scholars have debated which holy implements might have been taken from the sanctuary into battle. Some have suggested that the ark of the covenant was included among these items, while others disagree.[23] It seems, however, that if the ark of the covenant was intended by this phrase it would have been mentioned as when the Israelites tried to use it against the Philistines in the Battle of Aphek-Ebenezer (1 Sam 4:3–11). Noordzij and Milgrom suggested these vessels were the Urim and Thummim, but Ashley argues that this was unlikely since they were kept in the possession of the

---

[19] The common syntactical means of expressing equal distribution in Hb. phraseology by means of repetition is utilized here— אֶלֶף לַמַּטֶּה אֶלֶף לַמַּטֶּה לְכֹל מַטּוֹת יִשְׂרָאֵל —lit. translated as "1,000 for the tribe, 1,000 for the tribe, for all the tribes of Israel."

[20] The כְּלִי הַקֹּדֶשׁ, better translated "holy vessels" or "holy implements."

[21] Note that in Lev 21:10–12 the high priest was to avoid ritual defilement at all costs. Cf. also Eleazar, who served in a similar capacity by picking up the censers left by the dead rebels in the Korah incident (16:37–40; Hb. 17:2–5). Presumably they had been purified by the fire from the Lord, but other impurity might have been contracted through exposure to the dead.

[22] Milgrom, *Numbers,* 256–57.

[23] Those favoring the use of the ark include Snaith, *Leviticus–Numbers,* 194–95; Ashley, *Numbers,* 592. Those against its use in this kind of operation include Budd, who suggested that "these objects appear to take the place of the ark" (*Numbers,* 330). Noth stated that the ark would have been taken automatically and thus would not be categorized among these items (*Numbers,* 229).

high priest.[24] R. K. Harrison interpreted the conjunction between "articles of the sanctuary" and "trumpets for signaling" as a *waw explicitum*," so the signal trumpets explain what the articles were—"the implements of the sanctuary, namely the signal trumpets." Milgrom disagreed, suggesting that the trumpets could not have been named among the vessels because they were not anointed items like the other furnishings.[25] Yet this factor is not mentioned in either the present text or in Num 10:1–10, and Milgrom's argument derives from silence. The trumpets probably were kept in the sanctuary for their regular cultic usage, such as during festivals and holy days, during sacrificial activity, and during their wilderness journeys.

**31:7** That the Israelites attacked the Midianites "as Yahweh commanded Moses" recalls one of the key themes of chaps. 1–10, that when the nation acts in obedience to their God, victory, blessing, and fullness of life were theirs.[26] This expression of faithful conformity to the revealed will of God finds a rare fourfold repetition in this chapter (vv. 7,31,41,47)[27] in the present context and in that of the distribution of the spoils of war among the Israelite warriors, common populace, priests, and Levites. The new generation of the Israelite community faced the challenge of faithful obedience with success against the Midianites, and the challenge would be repeated numerous times in the months and years to come.

**31:8–12** Information concerning the victorious battle over the Midianites is summarized succinctly, as is often the historiographic style of ancient Israelite historians, who were more concerned with declaring matters related to their faith in God and the implications for the community. Yet this portion is vital in presenting the historical foundation for matters of faith and practice. Thus Ashley noted: "This admittedly vague battle report is the historical peg on which three related narratives are hung: the carrying out of the ban (vv. 13–18), the cleansing of the warriors (vv. 19–24), and the division (and annotation) of booty (vv. 25–54)."[28] All the males, including the kings (or chieftains) of the Midianites, were killed according to the guidelines of holy war.

The names of the five kings (Evi, Rekem, Zur, Hur, Reba) are recounted again in the same order as in the battle summary of Josh 13:21, where they are called princes of Sihon. The precise political relationships among the Amorites, Moabites, and Midianites remains somewhat nebulous. These

---

[24] A. Noordzij, *Numbers,* BSC (Grand Rapids: Zondervan, 1983), 271; also *Targum Pseudo-Jonathan;* Milgrom, *Numbers,* 257; contra Ashley, *Numbers,* 592; Harrison, *Numbers,* 383.

[25] Milgrom, *Numbers,* 257; *Studies in Levitical Terminology,* I:49.

[26] On the occurrences of the clause כַּאֲשֶׁר צִוָּה יְהוָה אֶת־מֹשֶׁה see n. 2 in introduction to chap. 31 above.

[27] Here and in chap. 8 are the two examples.

[28] Ashley, *Numbers,* 594.

Midianite chieftains may have been subject to Sihon prior to the defeat of the Amorites, and then gained their independence through the earlier Israelite victory. One of these leaders, Zur, was the father of Cozbi, the Midianite woman who was killed by Phinehas along with her Israelite paramour Zimri ben Salu (25:14–18). Zur and Zimri are both regarded as patriarchal clan leaders,[29] as is evidenced by the use of the phrase *bêt-ʾāb*, "house of a father" in 25:14,15. Hence the title "king" *(melek)* has a broad semantic domain in Hebrew usage, and the use of the term in reference to the king of Edom in Num 20:14 need not imply that the Edomites were a well-organized nation during the days of the Israelite wilderness sojourn.

In addition to the five chieftains and all the males of the Midianite forces, the Israelite army executed Balaam ben Beor of Pethor in Mesopotamia. Balaam was perhaps one of the counselors of the Moabites and Midianites in the Baal Peor incident, as well as having the role as the prophet-diviner called by the Moabite-Midianite coalition under Balak to pronounce a debilitating curse upon Israel. In Num 24:25 Balaam is said to have returned to his place, yet it seems on his way he lodged for a time among the Midianites, during which time he met his demise.

Women and children were taken as captives along with the flocks, herds, and other material goods that belonged to the Midian clans. This collective "war booty" that was confiscated from the often seminomadic Midianites included substantial quantities of animals, as listed in the ensuing vv. 32–47. Midianite dwelling places were reduced to rubble and ash by the scorched-earth policy of holy war. That which could be retained as booty was then brought back to the Israelite encampment on the plains of Moab, where the goods were presented to Moses their leader and Eleazar their high priest in view of the assembled Israelite community.

## (2) Preserving the Sanctity of the Camp (31:13–24)

**[13]Moses, Eleazar the priest and all the leaders of the community went to meet them outside the camp. [14]Moses was angry with the officers of the army—the commanders of thousands and commanders of hundreds—who returned from the battle.**

**[15]"Have you allowed all the women to live?" he asked them. [16]"They were the ones who followed Balaam's advice and were the means of turning the Israelites away from the LORD in what happened at Peor, so that a plague struck the LORD's people. [17]Now kill all the boys. And kill every woman who has slept with a man, [18]but save for yourselves every girl who has never slept with a man.**

**[19]"All of you who have killed anyone or touched anyone who was killed must**

---

[29] Similar phrases are used for Zur the Midianite, who was called a רֹאשׁ אֻמּוֹת בֵּית־אָב בְּמִדְיָן —"chief [head] of a Midianite family" (25:15), compared to Zimri the Israelite, who was called a נְשִׂיא בֵית־אָב לַשִּׁמְעֹנִי – "a leader of a Simeonite family" (25:14).

stay outside the camp seven days. On the third and seventh days you must purify yourselves and your captives. [20]Purify every garment as well as everything made of leather, goat hair or wood."

[21]Then Eleazar the priest said to the soldiers who had gone into battle, "This is the requirement of the law that the LORD gave Moses: [22]Gold, silver, bronze, iron, tin, lead [23]and anything else that can withstand fire must be put through the fire, and then it will be clean. But it must also be purified with the water of cleansing. And whatever cannot withstand fire must be put through that water. [24]On the seventh day wash your clothes and you will be clean. Then you may come into the camp."

**31:13–18**   Holy war had as its purpose the eradication of all impure elements from the geographical region or ethnic territory placed under the ban. Coming on the heels of an idolatrous and adulterous affair at Baal Peor involving Israelite and non-Israelite participants, a cleansing of the camp was in order so that the sanctity and purity of the community might be maintained (5:1–4). The violence of war brings death in its most heinous and comprehensive forms, rendering the combatants in a state of ritual impurity. Therefore anyone who comes in contact with the dead in an open field of battle, or within the tent of one's enemies in the pursuit of fleeing armies, must endure the process of ritual purification for the dead as outlined in 19:11–19.[30] The impurity of death was a serious issue in ancient Israel, for anyone who failed to be cleansed was subject to the penalty of death, that of being totally cut off from the community of faith (19:11,20). Such impurity made it necessary for Moses, Eleazar, and those clean persons who were dwelling within the holy camp to exit the encampment and meet the warriors and officers outside the camp so that any contaminants they might have been exposed to during the campaign would not be brought into the camp.

Deuteronomy 20:13–14 prescribed the killing of all the males in an attack on a city but allowed women, children, livestock, and various commodities to be plundered by the warriors. Moses, however, was angry with his military leaders and dismayed that the Israelite warriors returned with so many women among the spoils of war. He protested their actions, decrying the fact that it was primarily the Midianite women who had followed Balaam's counsel by leading the Israelite men into idolatry and adultery, both of which were punishable by death. So he gave orders to slay all of the males, even the young boys, and any of the women who had engaged in sexual relations with a man. Ashley suggested that God ordered the young men to be executed "in order to destroy the means of future rebellion in Midian, and that all the women who were capable of sexual intercourse be killed in order to cut off the future population and to emphasize the nature of the sin of

---

[30] Numbers 19 allows persons to remain in the camp when they had been contaminated by the death of a family member or other person in their tent.

Baal-Peor."[31] Women who had known men sexually, whether Midianite or sinful Israelite men, were to be considered unclean, since they were the main instrument of Israel's demise at Baal Peor. Only the young girls would be allowed to live so that they may be taken as wives or slaves by the Israelite men, according to the principles of holy war (Deut 20:13–14; 21:10–14). By this they could be brought under the umbrella of the covenant community of faith.

**31:19–20** The application of the law related to uncleanness derived through contact or exposure to the dead is an extension of the statute delineated in Num 19:16–19. In that context exclusion from the camp was not required, perhaps because the exposure was often inadvertent and happened within the camp. By application the purification of the warriors on the third and seventh days was accomplished by a ritually clean person sprinkling the waters of purification, made from pure water and the ashes of the red cow, upon the unclean person utilizing a bunch of hyssop (or marjoram) as an applicator.[32] Afterward they would wash their garments, no matter what material was used in the making of their clothing, and then bathe their bodies to complete the required cleansing process.

**31:21–24** Additional instructions were given through Eleazar concerning the purification of certain material goods taken as booty in the battle. Since warfare exposed all persons, animals, and material goods to various forms of uncleanness, especially that of death and blood, they must be cleansed. That this is a new statute of *halakhah* is evidenced by the use of the phrase "this is the statute of law which Yahweh commanded Moses."[33] This law would be most applicable in the coming campaigns in the conquest of the land of Canaan. The new ordinance had to do with the purification of metallic products by means of fire because of their ability to withstand the high temperatures. Perishable goods such as glass beads, clothing, wood, leather, animals, and other organic commodities would be purified with water, probably through washing, like the garments of the soldiers (v. 20), and then applying the waters of purification made from fresh water and the ashes of the red cow.[34] After the total cleansing effort had been completed,

---

[31] Ashley, *Numbers,* 595

[32] Cf. also applications of the seven-day purification rule for women after childbirth (Lev 12:1), persons with skin diseases (Lev 13:5–6,26,31; 14:8–9), exposure to mildew (Lev 13:50–52), etc. Various applications of this type of ritual purification are nuanced based on the derived principles of cleansing from existing statutes of Torah. Thus not every possible case law application is detailed in the Scriptures to the degree reflected in the Mishnah or Talmud.

[33] Cf. other examples of this phraseology of legislation, most often as לְחֻקַּת עוֹלָם — "for a perpetual statute," in Exod 12:14,17; 27:21; 29:9; Lev 3:17; 7:36; 10:9; 16:29,31,34; 17:7; 23:14, 21,41; 24:3; Num 10:8; 15:15; 18:23; 19:2,10,21; 30:16; 35:29.

[34] The same terminology is used in v. 23 as in Num 19:9,13,17–20, namely בְּמֵי נִדָּה, "with waters of purification/cleansing."

the ceremonially clean warriors could enter the camp, bringing the purified spoils of war with them for the tabulation and distribution process that would be overseen by Eleazar the high priest and his assistants.

### (3) Division of the War Booty among the Israelites (31:25–54)

[25]The LORD said to Moses, [26]"You and Eleazar the priest and the family heads of the community are to count all the people and animals that were captured. [27]Divide the spoils between the soldiers who took part in the battle and the rest of the community. [28]From the soldiers who fought in the battle, set apart as tribute for the LORD one out of every five hundred, whether persons, cattle, donkeys, sheep or goats. [29]Take this tribute from their half share and give it to Eleazar the priest as the LORD's part. [30]From the Israelites' half, select one out of every fifty, whether persons, cattle, donkeys, sheep, goats or other animals. Give them to the Levites, who are responsible for the care of the LORD's tabernacle." [31]So Moses and Eleazar the priest did as the LORD commanded Moses.

[32]The plunder remaining from the spoils that the soldiers took was 675,000 sheep, [33]72,000 cattle, [34]61,000 donkeys [35]and 32,000 women who had never slept with a man.

[36]The half share of those who fought in the battle was:

337,500 sheep, [37]of which the tribute for the LORD was 675;
[38]36,000 cattle, of which the tribute for the LORD was 72;
[39]30,500 donkeys, of which the tribute for the LORD was 61;
[40]16,000 people, of which the tribute for the LORD was 32.

[41]Moses gave the tribute to Eleazar the priest as the LORD's part, as the LORD commanded Moses.

[42]The half belonging to the Israelites, which Moses set apart from that of the fighting men— [43]the community's half—was 337,500 sheep, [44]36,000 cattle, [45]30,500 donkeys [46]and 16,000 people. [47]From the Israelites' half, Moses selected one out of every fifty persons and animals, as the LORD commanded him, and gave them to the Levites, who were responsible for the care of the LORD's tabernacle.

[48]Then the officers who were over the units of the army—the commanders of thousands and commanders of hundreds—went to Moses [49]and said to him, "Your servants have counted the soldiers under our command, and not one is missing. [50]So we have brought as an offering to the LORD the gold articles each of us acquired—armlets, bracelets, signet rings, earrings and necklaces—to make atonement for ourselves before the LORD."

[51]Moses and Eleazar the priest accepted from them the gold—all the crafted articles. [52]All the gold from the commanders of thousands and commanders of hundreds that Moses and Eleazar presented as a gift to the LORD weighed 16,750 shekels. [53]Each soldier had taken plunder for himself. [54]Moses and Eleazar the priest accepted the gold from the commanders of thousands and commanders of hundreds and brought it into the Tent of Meeting as a memorial for the Israelites before the LORD.

This instruction for the distribution of the spoils of war among the community members would set the standard for the coming campaigns in the Promised Land in the months and years to come. In many other imperial and marauding cultures of the ancient Near East, the warriors would retain whatever goods or persons they captured during and after battle, with certain portions being allocated to the king and his court and other portions rewarded to the priesthoods of the patron deity of that people. In Israelite holy war, a broader-based distribution was achieved through this legislation, so that the community as a whole could benefit from the proceeds of a war that was won in the name of Yahweh, the God of the nation. This expression of corporate solidarity envisioned the priests, Levites, and other community members as the support personnel for the soldiers in combat and would thus benefit fully from the conquest. By application the Christian community must act in concert in the struggle in this world against all of the forces of evil, for spiritual warfare is an everyday reality for the community of faith.

**31:25–26** This section is introduced by the secondary phrase used for introducing divine instruction throughout the Book of Numbers.[35] The directions for counting the human and animal portions of the war spoils were essentially the same as those given for the taking of the initial census in Num 1:2–4. A committee of Moses, the high priest (here Eleazar instead of Aaron), and leaders from each of the twelve tribes would assess and compute by counting the heads, literally "lift up the head of the booty captured among the human and animal."[36] Counting heads was a common means of taking a census whether in human or animal assessments. The persons and goods were then to be divided equally among the warriors and the community members.

**31:27–30** The booty captured in the war against the Midianites was to be equally divided between those who had gone out to war and those of the congregation who had remained in the camp. A tribute tax was to be levied against each of the halves of the booty, but at varying rates. The tribute exacted from the soldier's portion for the priesthood was 1/500 of each of the human and animal captives, whereas the duty levied against the congregation's portion was 1/50. Thus out of every 1,000 animals seized in the conflict the soldiers would keep 499 and the people would

---

[35] For discussion of the phraseology וַיֹּאמֶר יְהוָה אֶל־מֹשֶׁה לֵּאמֹר and its use in the Book of Numbers, see "Introduction: Structure and Outline of the Book of Numbers."

[36] Cf. the phraseology here שָׂא אֵת רֹאשׁ מַלְקוֹחַ הַשְּׁבִי בָּאָדָם וּבַבְּהֵמָה with that of Num 1:2, which reads שְׂאוּ אֶת־רֹאשׁ כָּל־עֲדַת בְּנֵי־יִשְׂרָאֵל—"Lift up the head of all the congregation of the children of Israel." Presumably the description for the leaders in this verse, רָאשֵׁי אֲבוֹת הָעֵדָה, "patriarchal heads of the congregation," is a short form for אִישׁ אֶחָד אִישׁ לַמַּטֶּה אִישׁ רֹאשׁ לְבֵית־אֲבֹתָיו — "one man per tribe, each man a leader from his patriarchal household" in Num 1:4.

keep 490. The term for the tribute is *mekes*, found only three times in this chapter but nowhere else in the Hebrew Bible. The term is attested in Ugaritic *(mekes)* and in Akkadian *(miksu)* and occurs often in later rabbinical sources.[37]

The tradition in Abraham's day that a tithe of ten percent was presented to the temple priesthood, as he did with the spoils of war confiscated from the battle against the four kings of Mesopotamia who had attacked the five cities of the plain (Gen 14:1–24). After presenting the tithe to the regional high priest Melchizedek in Jerusalem, he acted virtuously and went beyond the tradition of the day by returning the other ninety percent to the former owners. Later in Israelite history David likewise prescribed equal distribution of war booty for the armed forces who participated in the conflict and those who remained with the supplies during the battle against the Amalekites in the western Negev near Ziklag (1 Sam 30:21–25). The offering from the warriors to the priests is called a *těrûmat YHWH*, "the contribution offering of Yahweh," which was elevated before the Lord in a dedicatory ceremony before being presented to the priests for their consumption.[38]

**31:31** This verse functions as a transitional colophon between the giving of the instructions (vv. 25–30) and the carrying out of each step of the process (vv. 31–40), with repetition of the clause at the end of the distribution for the priests (v. 41) and at the conclusion of the accounting and distribution of that which was apportioned for the Levites from the people. Moses, Eleazar, and the patriarchal leaders of the Israelite tribes faithfully followed the instructions from the Lord regarding the counting and distribution of the spoils of war. Again this principle of faithful obedience to the instructions from the Lord was a key to the success and well-being of the Israelite community.

**31:32–47** According to the methods for counting and principles for distribution, the war booty was meted out proportionately to the warriors and the Levites and to the people and the Levites. The following chart delineates the resultant distribution.

---

[37] In Ug. *mekes* (C. Gordon, UT, XX); Akk. *miksu* (*CAD*, x:XX); and for rabbinical sources see M. Sokoloff, *A Dictionary of Jewish Palestinian Aramaic of the Byzantine Period* (Ramat-Gan, Israel: Bar Ilan University, 1920), 308.

[38] Cf. the use of תְּרוּמַת יְהֹוָה in the sacrifice by the Nazirite at the conclusion of the period of the vow (Num 6:20); the first dough offering of the Israelites (15:19–20); the larger body of such offerings, which provided the regular food supply of the priests (18:8–19); and likewise for the Levites (18:21–30). It is repeated in 31:41,52 in relation to the dedicatory gifts given to the Lord by the warriors. Cf. also portions of the peace/fellowship offering (Lev 7:14,32,34; 10:14.15).

**Spoils of War Shared among the Israelite Community (31:32–47)**

| Animal / Human Commodity | Quantity of Booty | Quantity – Split Warriors / People | Lord's Tribute (0.2%) Priests from Warriors | Levites' Portion (1.0%) from the People |
|---|---|---|---|---|
| Sheep | 675,000 | 337,500 | 675 | 6,750 |
| Cattle | 72,000 | 36,000 | 72 | 720 |
| Donkeys | 61,000 | 30,500 | 61 | 610 |
| Women | 32,000 | 16,000 | 32 | 320 |

The priests and Levites, who by the nature of their service to the tabernacle and to the Lord, were not permitted to participate in combat and thus would have otherwise not been able to benefit from the spoils of war. As noted previously in vv. 7, 31, and 41, the Israelites carried out their instructions faithfully and diligently.

**31:48–54**  Then all of commanders of the Israelite armed forces, from each level of the battalion divisions that were over the thousands and the hundreds, approached Moses with proper submissive demeanor heralding a remarkable report. Not one of the twelve thousand who were dispatched for combat had been killed or were missing in action, in what R. K. Harrison aptly called "a divine act of magnificent proportions, a miraculous victory, considering the strength of the opposing forces."[39] This wondrous indication of Yahweh's providence and protection would provide the armies of Israel with assurance and confidence for the coming campaigns in the land of Canaan.

On the heels of this marvelous message was their announcement that they were presenting to the Lord offerings of gold from the war booty for the purpose of making atonement before the Lord. Most scholars, from source critical to evangelical interpretation, have taken this statement of atonement (*lĕkappēr ʿal-napšōtênû lipnê YHWH*, "to make atonement/to pay a ransom on behalf of themselves before Yahweh") as something the commanders did voluntarily because of their taking a census, something considered somewhat of a taboo among Israelites.[40] The rationale for this "ransom" payment generally has been derived from Exod 30:11–16, which states that if Israel

---

[39] Harrison, *Numbers*, 390.
[40] So interpret Noth, *Numbers*, 232; Budd, *Numbers*, 332; Wenham, *Numbers*, 212; Ashley, *Numbers*, 599–600; Harrison, *Numbers*, 390–91. On the other hand Noordzij disavows any connection between Num 31:50 and Exod 30:11–16 (*Numbers*, 276).

should take a census (lit. "lift up the head" as in Num 31:49) of their men, then each man was to present a ransom *(kōper)* to the Lord in the amount of one-half shekel, by the sanctuary shekel weight of twenty gerahs (or 0.4 ounce). In doing so they would prevent a plague from the Lord that would have brought death to many of the troops who had survived the amazing battle. An example in biblical history of an improper census was that in which David counted valiant warriors of Israel and Judah, which resulted in a one-day plague that left seventy thousand dead in its wake (2 Sam 24:15–17). With regard to the seeming taboo on human-initiated census taking, Milgrom noted the suggestion of A. Schenker that "as the shepherd counts his sheep so the counter of persons must be their owner, a title belonging solely to God and not to man."[41] Only census taking that was done in response to direct instruction from God was permissible, as were those described in chaps. 1 and 26.

The total amount of the gold offered by Israel's commanders on behalf of their enumerated troops far exceeded the minimal requirement of one-half shekel per person, a ransom of some 6,000 shekels, or about 2,500 ounces = 158 pounds of gold. Instead they presented almost 2.8 times the minimal amount, with a combined weight of the armlets *(ʾeṣʿādâ),* bracelets *(ṣāmîd),* signet rings *(ṭabaʿat),* earrings *(ʿāgîl),* and necklaces *(kûmāz)* totaling 16,750 shekels, or about 7,000 ounces = 440 pounds of gold. The amount of gold seems phenomenal considering the seminomadic nature of the Midianites. Yet they traveled the caravan routes into Arabia and beyond by which such wealth could have come, and adornment in gold is still prized today among bedouins, and samples of such wealth will occasionally find its way into burials. A personal experience of some relevance came in 1996 while participating in the excavation of Tel Beth Shean (Tel el-Husn). In the removal of material from a child burial from the MBII "Hyksos" period, we uncovered among the burial goods an ornate white alabaster vase, four gold earrings, and a gold ring with a beautifully etched amethyst mounted on it with gold thread.

Perhaps out of thanksgiving for their protection in battle as well as the adherence to the ordinance regarding the census payment, the faithful armies of Israel exceeded that which was demanded of them by giving sacrificially of that which would have been of great benefit to themselves personally. This account of the bounteous response of the Israelite army commanders was another example of the second generation community acting in concert with the will of God, in contrast to the actions of the first generation. Another parallel with Exodus 30 is that the census ransom payment

---

[41] Milgrom, *Numbers,* 264 (nn. 69, 328), from A. Schenker, *Versöhnung und Sühne* (Freiburg: Swiss Catholic Bible Society, 1981), 100.

was to provide for the service of the sanctuary as a memorial for the Israelites before Lord.[42] That which would be produced from this abundance of gold would provide a memorial to future generations of God's providential protection in the battle against the Midianites, a memorial to challenge future generations to faithfulness to the Lord and benevolence in his service.

## 2. Settlement of the Transjordan Tribes (32:1–42)

Unexpectedly the abundant gains in livestock resulting from successive victories over the Amorites Sihon of Heshbon and Og of Bashan, as well as the miraculous defeat of the Midianites, precipitated a crisis for the Israelites. Satisfied with the gains of the present and not having the vision for the even greater opportunities that lay ahead in the Promised Land, two and a half tribes from the twelve-tribe confederation presented a request to Moses that would shake the foundation of the tribal unity, threatening potentially the very structural fiber of the nation. Reuben, Gad, and part of the tribe of Manasseh desired to take their cattle and flocks and settle in the recently conquered territory of Transjordan.[43] This seemed on the surface quite normative for in fact land grants from conquering kings to his servants and troops were a common means of rewarding faithful subjects. If one examines closely the territorial boundaries described for the twelve Israelite tribes in Num 34:1–15, however, the eastern boundary in this region extends only to the Jordan River system, including the Sea of Galilee (Chinnereth) and the Dead Sea (Salt Sea). Moses expressed legitimate concerns and argued on the basis of past history in dealing with such a sensitive and serious issue. Would these brothers in the community of faith now abandon their comrades and not participate in the fulfillment of the promise of the gift of land by Yahweh to his children? Negotiations ensued and a compromise was reached, but the seeds of disharmony and discontent were planted. This passage would portend future divisions among the tribes that would transpire during the period of the judges and again near the conclusion of Solomon's reign.

Milgrom has discerned the chiastic literary structure of chap. 32, and it has been revised below in a simplified form.[44] The literary fiber that lends cohesiveness to the chapter is the "sevenfold recurrence of five key terms" or phrases, (1) Gad and Reuben, (2) possession/inheritance, (3) cross/across the Jordan, (4) armed troops, and (5) before the Lord.

---

[42] Note the parallel phraseology of Exod 30:16– לְזִכָּרוֹן לִפְנֵי יְהוָה – "for a memorial before Yahweh," and that of v. 54 – זִכָּרוֹן לִבְנֵי־יִשְׂרָאֵל לִפְנֵי יְהוָה – "a memorial for the Israelites before Yahweh.

[43] D. T. Olson aptly entitled chaps. 32–33 "A Crisis Averted, a Journey Remembered: Warning and Encouragement from a Generation Past" (*Numbers*, INT [Louisville: John Knox, 1996], 181).

[44] Milgrom, *Numbers*, "Excursus 69: The Literary Structure of Chapter 32," 492–93.

A Gad and Reuben Request Land in Transjordan (1–5)
  B Moses Rejects the Request (6–15)
    C Gad and Reuben Propose a Compromise (16–19)
      D Moses Revises the Proposal (20–24)
    C' Gad and Reuben Accept Moses' Revisions (25–27)
    B' Moses' Revised Proposal Is Offered the Leaders (28–32)
A' Moses Provisionally Grants Land in Transjordan to Gad, Reuben, Manasseh (33–42)

### (1) Reubenite and Gadite Request (32:1–5)

[1]The Reubenites and Gadites, who had very large herds and flocks, saw that the lands of Jazer and Gilead were suitable for livestock. [2]So they came to Moses and Eleazar the priest and to the leaders of the community, and said, [3]"Ataroth, Dibon, Jazer, Nimrah, Heshbon, Elealeh, Sebam, Nebo and Beon— [4]the land the LORD subdued before the people of Israel—are suitable for livestock, and your servants have livestock. [5]If we have found favor in your eyes," they said, "let this land be given to your servants as our possession. Do not make us cross the Jordan."

**32:1–3** This chapter begins with an issue and an incident rather than instruction from the Lord. The first word in the Hebrew text, *ûmiqneh* ("so livestock"), establishes the context for the discussion, the enormous quantity of livestock owned by the Reubenites and Gadites and the need for adequate pasturage for these animals. The term is used broadly to refer not only to cattle but also to donkeys, camels, sheep, and goats. An inclusio using the term *miqneh* provides a bracketing framework for the request section, highlighting further the subject matter. The term also provides a verbal link between this chapter and the previous one (31:9). The name Reuben, the firstborn of Jacob by Leah (Gen 29:32; 35:23), is mentioned first only here in the account, perhaps because of his status as primogenitor; but throughout this chapter and in Josh 18:7 and 2 Kgs 10:33, Gad precedes Reuben in listing of the Transjordan tribes.

Having journeyed through the more arid regions south of the Arnon, such as Edom and Moab, the Gadites and Reubenites had observed that the region of Gilead northward was more fertile with highland grassy regions for grazing and with valleys and hillsides suitable for grain crops and fruit orchards. The several rivers, such as the Yarmuk, Jabesh, and Jabbok and their tributaries, as well as the numerous springs in the region, would provide ample water supply for humans and animals alike. The "land of Jazer" was an arable area west-northwest of Amman, generally associated with the region around Kh. Jazzir, which is located about ten miles from the modern Jordanian capital. Jazer is listed among the Levitical cities in Josh 21:39.

**32:4–5** The proposal was presented to the combined leadership of

Moses, Eleazar, and the leaders of the congregation (*něśî᾽ê hā᾽ēdâ*, "princes of the assembly"), the same group as in Num 31:13 who went out of the camp to meet the military leaders as they returned from war. The elocution of the entreaty was in proper protocol format, as the language reveals: "If we find favor in your eyes, may this land be granted to your servants." Such rhetoric of entreaty occurs often in diplomatic correspondence of the ancient Near East, including the basic letter writing language such as has been found in the Lachish and Arad ostraca.[45] The preface to their request included a list of the cities that had been conquered from the Amorites and an acclamation that it was Yahweh their God who had been responsible for granting them the victory. The content of their request, however, was a bit disconcerting to Moses, especially on two counts: that they would desire land east of the Jordan River, which had not been included within previous Promised Land boundary descriptions, and that they did not desire to be led across the Jordan and into the Promised Land.

### (2) Moses' Response (32:6–15)

**⁶Moses said to the Gadites and Reubenites, "Shall your countrymen go to war while you sit here? ⁷Why do you discourage the Israelites from going over into the land the LORD has given them? ⁸This is what your fathers did when I sent them from Kadesh Barnea to look over the land. ⁹After they went up to the Valley of Eshcol and viewed the land, they discouraged the Israelites from entering the land the LORD had given them. ¹⁰The LORD's anger was aroused that day and he swore this oath: ¹¹'Because they have not followed me wholeheartedly, not one of the men twenty years old or more who came up out of Egypt will see the land I promised on oath to Abraham, Isaac and Jacob— ¹²not one except Caleb son of Jephunneh the Kenizzite and Joshua son of Nun, for they followed the LORD wholeheartedly.' ¹³The LORD's anger burned against Israel and he made them wander in the desert forty years, until the whole generation of those who had done evil in his sight was gone.**

**¹⁴"And here you are, a brood of sinners, standing in the place of your fathers and making the LORD even more angry with Israel. ¹⁵If you turn away from following him, he will again leave all this people in the desert, and you will be the cause of their destruction."**

**32:6–15** Moses responded promptly and poignantly with a rhetorical retort, advancing two contrasting issues, unity in participation and discouragement from mobilization. When Moses asked whether they would remain back on the east side of the Jordan, he may have implied both parallel concepts in the semantic field of the Hebrew verb *yāšab*, meaning "to sit or to dwell," a double entendre. Would they simply *sit* back and watch their broth-

---

[45] See examples in *ANET,* 322; J. C. L. Gibson, *Textbook of Syrian Semitic Inscriptions,* 3 vols. (Oxford: Clarendon Press, 1971, 1975, 1982), 49–54; cf. Dan 2:4; Ezra 5:7–17.

ers go to war against the Canaanites on the other side of the Jordan? Would they simply remain in this lush and secure region of Gilead and *dwell* there in relative security? The unity of the twelve tribes was threatened, so the possible failure of their mission to conquer the land of Canaan and to see the fulfillment of the promised inheritance was at stake. Would Moses' acquiescing to their request bring discouragement to the other nine and one-half tribes and prevent them from completing the final step of the journey? The word "discourage" in the NIV translates the Hebrew phrase *tĕnî'ûn*[46] *'et-lēb*, meaning "you restrain the heart." The fear was that the Israelites would lose heart if these tribes broke rank and settled in the Transjordan region. The phraseology referencing the Promised Land as "the land the Lord has given them," used here and in v. 9, recalls the language of Num 13:1; 14:8,16,30, as well as the other numerous promises of the land throughout the Pentateuch. Note the emphases in the short chiastic structures in the following outline of vv. 6–15.

**Intro**: Moses Questions Gadites and Reubenites: (6)
      Shall your brethren go to war while your sit here?
**A** Will you discourage the heart of Israelites (7)
   From going into the land which YHWH has given to them?
   **B** Thus your fathers did when I sent them from Kadesh Barnea to see the land (8)
   **B'** For when they went up to the Valley Eshcol and saw the land (9a)
**A'** They discouraged the heart of the Israelites (9b)
   So they did not go into the land which YHWH had given to them.
**C** YHWH's anger burned that day (10)
   He swore and oath saying:
   **B** None who came up from Egypt twenty yrs + shall see the land (11)
      That I swore to Abraham, Isaac, and Jacob
      **D** Because they have not followed me wholly
      **D'** Except Caleb and Joshua who followed YHWH wholly (12)
**C'** YHWH's anger burned vs. Israel (13)
   He made them wander in the wilderness 40 years
      **D''** All that generation that did evil in the eyes of YHWH
      **D'''** Look! You have risen in your fathers' place – a brood of sinners (14)
**C''** To increase more the fierce anger of YHWH vs. Israel
**Conclusion**: If **YOU** turn away from following **him** (15)
      **He** will leave them in the wilderness
    And **YOU** will destroy all these people.

---

[46] Taking the *qere* reading here, attested without the epenthetic *nûn* in the Samaritan Pentateuch, hence a *hiphil* form as in all other occurrences of בוא.

The setting parallels that of Numbers 10–14, in which the Israelites had moved out from Mount Sinai in a unified march toward the Promised Land but then soon fell into a mind-set of unrest, discouragement, and rebellion that eventually led to the rejection of the land on the basis of the divided report of the scouts (13:26–14:9). Note below the chart of parallels between Num 32:7–13 and 11:1–14:40. In the present setting the Israelites had been united in the campaign against the Midianites, and the spoils of war had been appropriately apportioned among the twelve tribes, the Levites, and the priests. Now in the midst of prosperity rather than the destitute conditions of their earlier wilderness experience, that harmony and solidarity of the nation was in jeopardy once again. The first generation, which rejected the land Yahweh had given them, had died in the desert, and Moses feared the same consequences might accrue to the new generation if they likewise lost heart in the face of opportunity. Only a nation unified in form (the twelve tribes), focus (upon the Lord), and function (the possession of the land) would be victorious in the coming conquest. If they were divided in form and focus, that is, if they were not together as a people who were wholly devoted to the Lord, they would be doomed to failure and destruction just as their forefathers had been.

Parallels Between Numbers 11:1–14:40 and 32:7–15

| Parallel Phraseology | Num 11:1–14:40 | Num 32:7–15 |
| --- | --- | --- |
| "land YHWH has given them" | 13:1; 14:8,16,30 | 32:7,9 |
| "I (Moses) sent men to scout/see the land" | 13:2 | 32:8 |
| "Valley Eshcol" | 13:23,24 | 32:9 |
| "YHWH's anger burned" | 11:1; 12:9 | 32:10,13 (14) |
| "not one of the men 20 yrs" | 14:29 | 32:11 |
| "wander in the desert 40 yrs" | 14:33[47] | 32:13 |
| death/destruction "in the desert" | 14:33,35 | 32:15 |

## (3) Promise of Support (32:16–19)

[16]Then they came up to him and said, "We would like to build pens here for our livestock and cities for our women and children. [17]But we are ready to arm ourselves and go ahead of the Israelites until we have brought them to their place. Meanwhile our women and children will live in fortified cities, for protection from the inhabitants of the land. [18]We will not return to our homes until every Israelite has received his inheritance. [19]We will not receive any inheritance with them on the other side of the Jordan, because our inheritance has come to us on the east side of the Jordan."

The Gadites and Reubenites countered Moses' fervent retort with a counterproposal in order to achieve their own goals of land grant and own-

---

[47] The Vg. reads "wanderers" in 14:33 rather than "shepherds."

ership. They "drew near" to Moses in a proper protocol of submissiveness[48] to enter into negotiations they believed would benefit both parties. The men of war would prepare the necessary dwellings and pens for their wives, children, and animals, but they themselves would not reside in the Transjordan region until the conquest of the land was complete and all the other Israelite tribes had been allotted their inheritances.

**32:16–17** The "pens" (*gidrōt ṣiʾōn*, "stone pens for sheep" or "sheepfolds") were perhaps the V-shaped stone enclosures found in Transjordan and in the Arabah for protecting sheep, goats, and cattle during times of danger.[49] The NIV phrase "women and children" translates the single Hebrew term *ṭappênû*, meaning "dependants," which would include wives, other women, and children who would remain in the grated land allocations of Transjordan. The Transjordan tribes promised to send forth their speediest troops[50] into the coming foray into Canaan until the other Israelite tribes were successful in entering their territories. According to Josh 4:13, about 40,000 troops from Gad, Reuben, and half of Manasseh crossed over the Jordan River to participate in the conquest of the land of Canaan, or about one-third of the approximately 110,580 numbered in the second military conscription census (Num 26:7,18,34). The other two-thirds would remain behind to protect the otherwise defenseless women and children against possible reprisal attacks from other Amorites, Ammonites, and Moabites dwelling in the region.

**32:18–19** The two positive statements of building and contributing troops for the upcoming conquest are balanced by two negative statements that confirm their intent to aid their fellow tribesmen. They would not return home to their newly allotted Transjordan inheritance until the conquest was complete, and they would not expect to receive an inheritance in the land of Canaan, though its territory proper was the Promised Land. The eastern border of the Israelite inheritance, as delineated clearly in 34:11–12, was the Jordan River and the eastern shorelines of the Sea of Galilee and the Dead Sea. The land they desired and eventually occupied was across the Jordan from "the land that the LORD had given to them" (vv. 7,9).

---

[48] Ashley rightly notes that וַיִּגְּשׁוּ אֵלָיו implies that they came to Moses as "a lesser party coming into the presence of a greater" in order to argue their case before Moses (*Numbers*, 611). Cf. Gen 43:19; 44:18; 45:4; Deut 25:1; Josh 3:9; 14:6; Isa 41:1,21; 45:20–21.

[49] Milgrom, *Numbers*, 270. Cf. G. L. Harding, "The Cairn of Hani," in *Annual of the Dept. of Antiquities of Jordan* 2 (1953): 8–56. The Hb. צֹאן may refer to sheep or goats or both, which are often herded together.

[50] Milgrom perhaps rightly translates the Hb. phrase נֶחָלֵץ חֻשִׁים (lit. "those picked as fast ones") as "shock troops."

*(4) Moses' Response to the Promise (32:20–24)*

<sup>20</sup>Then Moses said to them, "If you will do this—if you will arm yourselves before the LORD for battle, <sup>21</sup>and if all of you will go armed over the Jordan before the LORD until he has driven his enemies out before him— <sup>22</sup>then when the land is subdued before the LORD, you may return and be free from your obligation to the LORD and to Israel. And this land will be your possession before the LORD.

<sup>23</sup>"But if you fail to do this, you will be sinning against the LORD; and you may be sure that your sin will find you out. <sup>24</sup>Build cities for your women and children, and pens for your flocks, but do what you have promised."

**32:20–24** Moses' direct response to the compromise proposal proffered by the Gadites and Reubenites was structured as a repetition of the suggested stipulations in the formula of blessing and curse: "if you do *X*, then you will have *Y* blessing; but if you do **not** do *X,* then *Z* curse will come to you." Noordzij has pointed out the covenant nature of this agreement reached between the two tribes of Gad and Reuben and the other ten tribes with Moses as the mediator and Yahweh as the divine witness and guarantor of the commitment made by the two tribes.[51]

The basic stipulation for Gad and Reuben was that they be faithful participants in the Lord's plan for the nation in the foray into the Promised Land, and as a result they would be blessed with their requested inheritance in Transjordan. Ultimately the Lord was responsible for bringing the victory over the enemies of God and Israel, for he was the one who would fight for Israel. The phrase *lipnê YHWH* ("before Yahweh") occurs four times in vv. 20–22 and is highlighted in the following parallel pattern:

A **IF** you will carry out this instruction: (20)
　　If you will arm yourselves *before the Lord* for battle,
　　If you yourselves will cross all armed across the Jordan *before the Lord*, (21)
　　　　Until he has driven out his enemies from *before him,*[52]
　　　　And the land is subdued *before the Lord;* (22)
　　　　**B** Then you may return,
　　　　And you will be blameless from the Lord and from Israel,
　　　　And this land will be for your possession *before the Lord.*
A′ **BUT IF** you do not carry *it* out, (23)
　　　　**B′** Then Behold you will have sinned *against the Lord,*[53]
　　　　And know that your sin is that which will find you out.

---

[51] Noordzij, *Numbers,* 281.

[52] Syntactically this is a fifth occurrence using the pronominal suffixed form מִפָּנָיו. The phrase לִפְנֵי יְהוָה often carries with it the connotation of faithful service to the Lord as one walks through life in his presence.

[53] The phrase לַיהוָה functions as a contrastive element to the previous usage of לִפְנֵי יְהוָה.

The Israelites, including now Gad and Reuben, were to drive out or dispossess the enemies of God by his power and strength. If they were unfaithful, however, they would reap the results of their sinfulness. Though the stipulations are clearly delineated for the participation of the Transjordan tribes in the conquest, the particular curse for failure to do so is implicit in the larger context of this pericope. One must refer to vv. 14–15 for the judgment described for the failure to follow through with the conquest. The Gadites and Reubenites are called by Moses a "brood of sinners" (*tarbût ʾanošîm ḥaṭṭāʾîm,* "large group of sinful men"), who if they "turned away" *(tĕšûbūn)* from following the Lord would all die in the wilderness. Rebellion against God ultimately leads to abandonment and destruction.

After the conditions of the covenant had been established and ratified, the Gadites and Reubenites received permission to take care of their flocks and families. The language echoes that of v. 16 in variant order, A B C::B C A (see below), with an inclusio using the words for "sheep pens" at this pivotal point in the narrative:

**v. 16 A** Sheepfolds    **B** we shall build for our livestock here    **C** and cities for our families
**v. 24 B'** Build for yourselves    **C'** Cities for your families    **A'** and pens for your sheep.

The section concludes with the repetition here in the epilogue to the apodosis of *taʿăśû(n)* from the initial protasis of v. 20. What they have agreed to in this oral contract, by those stipulations that proceeded out of their mouths, they should carry out dutifully.

### (5) Gad and Reuben Ratify the Agreement (32:25–27)

**<sup>25</sup>The Gadites and Reubenites said to Moses, "We your servants will do as our lord commands. <sup>26</sup>Our children and wives, our flocks and herds will remain here in the cities of Gilead. <sup>27</sup>But your servants, every man armed for battle, will cross over to fight before the LORD, just as our lord says."**

**32:25–27** Gad and Reuben once again address Moses in the protocol of submissive servants, echoing their willingness to adhere faithfully to their agreed upon stipulations for receiving their desired inheritance in Transjordan. The passage is introduced by the secondary formula for instruction, utilizing the preterit form *wayyōʾmer,* of which usually Yahweh is the speaker. Here it introduces the formal speech in which the oral covenant is ratified. Verses 25b and 27 evidence close parallels in vocabulary and structure. In both, the Gadites and Reubenites present themselves as "your servants" before Moses, whom they address as "my lord" or "my master." The language generally would be used in the context of covenant relations in addressing royalty or a sovereign leader (Deut 9:27; Josh 9:8–9). The singular is used severally here for the collective single voice of the combined tribes. Note the following parallels:

**25b**  Your servants will do (impf)
    according to that which my lord commands (ptc)
**27**  Your servants will cross over (impf), all armed for war before the
    Lord for battle
    according to that which my lord instructs (speaks)(ptc).[54]

At the center of the passage (v. 26) is the restated intent of the Gadites and
Reubenites to prepare facilities for housing their families and their abundant
livestock during the period of conquest across the Jordan River.

### (6) Moses Informs Eleazar and Joshua of the Decision (32:28–30)

[28]**Then Moses gave orders about them to Eleazar the priest and Joshua son of
Nun and to the family heads of the Israelite tribes.** [29]**He said to them, "If the
Gadites and Reubenites, every man armed for battle, cross over the Jordan with
you before the LORD, then when the land is subdued before you, give them the
land of Gilead as their possession.** [30]**But if they do not cross over with you armed,
they must accept their possession with you in Canaan."**

**32:28–30**  With the covenantal arrangements drawn to a conclusion,
Moses gathered together the most important witnesses, those whose responsibility it would be to oversee the implementation of the accord. The great
prophet and leader knew he would soon vanish from the scene and thus
would not be there to ensure the participation of these tribes. Eleazar the
high priest was now the cultic leader and spiritual overseer for the nation
since the death of his father Aaron, and Joshua ben Nun was the appointed
heir apparent to the leadership role Moses had held since he led the Israelites
out of Egypt.[55] In addition, the patriarchal heads from the other tribes were
called as witnesses to the basic specifications of the agreement so that they
might be informed as to its content and work to ensure compliance on the
part of the Transjordan tribes in the conquest.

    As in vv. 20–24 the propositions are set forth in vv. 29b and 30 in cove-
nantal language of blessing and curse, in the "if X … then Y; but if not X …
then Z" form, only here they are presented in the third person to the group
of witnesses rather than to the tribes themselves.[56] The question arises as to
the particular consequences that would accrue to these tribes for failure to
cross over the Jordan armed for holy war. If they later refused to cross the

---

[54] 25b עֲבָדֶיךָ יַעֲשׂוּ כַּאֲשֶׁר אֲדֹנִי מְצַוֶּה

27 וַעֲבָדֶיךָ יַעַבְרוּ כָל־חֲלוּץ צָבָא לִפְנֵי יְהוָה לַמִּלְחָמָה כַּאֲשֶׁר אֲדֹנִי דֹּבֵר

[55] Cf. Num 11:28.

[56] Note again the parallel structure between vv. 29b and 30:

(29) אִם־יַעַבְרוּ בְנֵי־גָד וּבְנֵי־רְאוּבֵן אִתְּכֶם אֶת־הַיַּרְדֵּן כָּל־חָלוּץ לַמִּלְחָמָה לִפְנֵי יְהוָה
וְנִכְבְּשָׁה הָאָרֶץ לִפְנֵיכֶם וּנְתַתֶּם לָהֶם אֶת־אֶרֶץ הַגִּלְעָד לַאֲחֻזָּה:
(30) וְאִם־לֹא יַעַבְרוּ חֲלוּצִים אִתְּכֶם
וְנֹאחֲזוּ בְתֹכְכֶם בְּאֶרֶץ כְּנָעַן:

Jordan with the rest of the Israelites, how would they be forced to bring their families and belongings into Canaan, where they were to receive allotments like the other tribes? The text seems to imply that if such were to have come to pass, the combined efforts of Joshua, Eleazar, and the patriarchal heads of the other tribes would have been needed to compel their obedience. Fortunately, the Transjordan tribes of Gad, Reuben, and one-half of Manasseh did cross the Jordan and fully participated in the campaigns in the land of Canaan, sending across 40,000 troops armed for battle who then remained until apportioning of the land at Shiloh (Josh 4:12–13; 22:1–9).[57]

## (7) Gad and Reubenite Reiterate the Promise (32:31–32)

**[31]The Gadites and Reubenites answered, "Your servants will do what the LORD has said. [32]We will cross over before the LORD into Canaan armed, but the property we inherit will be on this side of the Jordan."**

**32:31–32** What the Gadites and Reubenites had pledged to Moses and the Lord in the previously private negotiations, they now committed themselves to do before the remainder of the witnesses. Again the language of covenant oath taking is in view as the two tribes take on the identity of vassal-servants before Moses, acting as the sovereign representative of Yahweh in this covenant ceremony. The Lord is also called upon to testify to the oath taking, as the Gadites and Reubenites swear to faithfully obey all of the stipulations of the agreement. The language is reminiscent of the numerous times in the Book of Numbers where the faithful obedience of the nation of Israel is described by the phrase, "They did according to everything which Yahweh commanded."[58]

## (8) Moses Grants Transjordan Tribal Territory (32:33–42)

**[33]Then Moses gave to the Gadites, the Reubenites and the half-tribe of Manasseh son of Joseph the kingdom of Sihon king of the Amorites and the kingdom of Og king of Bashan—the whole land with its cities and the territory around them.**
**[34]The Gadites built up Dibon, Ataroth, Aroer, [35]Atroth Shophan, Jazer, Jogbehah, [36]Beth Nimrah and Beth Haran as fortified cities, and built pens for their flocks. [37]And the Reubenites rebuilt Heshbon, Elealeh and Kiriathaim, [38]as well as Nebo and Baal Meon (these names were changed) and Sibmah. They gave names to the cities they rebuilt.**
**[39]The descendants of Makir son of Manasseh went to Gilead, captured it and drove out the Amorites who were there. [40]So Moses gave Gilead to the Makirites,**

---

[57] Cf. Deut 3:18–20. See also Howard, *Joshua,* 138, 402–5.
[58] Cf. phraseology in 1:54; 2:34; 3:16,39,42,49; 4:49; 5:4; 8:3,20,22; 9:5,8; 15:23,36; 17:26; 20:9,27; 26:4; 27:11,22; 31:7,21; etc.

the descendants of Manasseh, and they settled there. [41]Jair, a descendant of Manasseh, captured their settlements and called them Havvoth Jair. [42]And Nobah captured Kenath and its surrounding settlements and called it Nobah after himself.

**32:33–42** Following negotiations between Moses and the two and one-half tribes desiring territory east of the Jordan, and the giving of instructions to Eleazar and Joshua concerning their compliance in the conquest, Moses granted the Gadites, Reubenites, and Manassites the agreed upon land distribution. The Manassites are included in the discussion for the first time in v. 33, and the rationale for their inclusion in the deal is provided in vv. 39–42. The explanation provides additional information as to the role of the clan of the Machirites from the tribe of Manasseh in the conquest of Gilead. The citation that this region had been part of the kingdom of the Amorite kings Sihon and Og serves to draw the reader back to the earlier victories over the Amorites recounted in 21:21–35.

The historical background and rationale as to why the Manassites were a divided tribe is not provided, though it has been suggested that there were differences based upon occupations and family practices. More likely the rationale is provided implicitly in the text of vv. 39–40, which recounts the role of the Machirites of the tribe of Manasseh as the key combatants in the Transjordan campaigns in the regions of Gilead. The Machirites had conquered Gilead and driven out the Amorites, and the other Manassites, Jair and Nobah, had likewise made forays into this region. These clans desired to settle in and provide pasturage for their livestock in the areas they had personally conquered. Beyond the territory and cities mentioned in connection with the two conquering clans of Jair and Nobah of Manasseh, the list is delineated further in Josh 17:1–6. The remnants of the early settlement whose clans were still remaining during the Assyrian conquests in this region were defeated and deported by the Assyrians under Tiglath Pileser III in his second campaign of 733 B.C. (1 Chr 5:23–26).

The Gadites were allocated the land grants in the central part of the former kingdom of Sihon of the Amorites, specifically in the areas of Dibon, Atharoth, Aroer, Atroth, Shophan, Jazer, Jogbehah, Beth-Nimrah, and Beth-haran. Gad shared a border with the half-tribe of Manasseh to the north, though the cities listed for Gad in various Old Testament passages suggest a narrow strip of land extending from the Jabbok River to the Sea of Galilee was to be included in the allocation. The Aroer listed for Gad, as opposed to the city of like name listed in Reuben, is said to have been located "before Rabbah" (of the Ammonites), from the direction of Jazer and Jogbethah, which have traditionally been located northwest of Amman. Hence the location would be just northwest of Amman. Beth-nimrah has been identified tentatively with Tel Bleibil, west-southwest of Amman near the edge of the

Jordan Valley, though the original name survives in a Roman–Byzantine site about one mile south-southwest, named Tel Nimrin. The Gadites constructed fortified cities and sheep pens for the enormous flocks they had amassed. The cities of the Gadites are detailed further in Josh 13:24–28.[59]

The area and cities allocated to the tribe of Reuben were generally on the south of those of the tribe of Gad. Among the cities were Heshbon, the former capital of Sihon's Amorite kingdom,[60] Elealeh, Kiriathaim ("twin cities"?), Nebo and Baal-meon. Additional cities and territories are delineated in Josh 13:15–23, including Dibon and Aroer, which were located on the highland plateau just north of the Arnon River valley.[61] J. Simons identified Kiriathaim with Khirbet el-Qureiyat, six miles northwest of Dibon, though Aharoni's suggestion of Kh. el-Mekhaiyet, northwest of Madaba, seems more likely.[62]

The area and cities which Moses then allocated to the tribe of Manassite were generally to the north of the tribe of Gad, extending from the region of Gilead into Bashan and the Golan. Only the cities of Havoth Jair ("settlements of Jair") and Kenath-Nobah are mentioned here, but "sixty cities" in the region of Jair are noted (but not listed), along with "all of Bashan" and "half of Gilead" in Josh 13:29–32.[63] However, the Israelites of the half-tribe of Manasseh did not drive out the Geshurites or Maacathites who were dwelling in the region east and northeast of the Sea of Galilee (Josh 13:12–13).[64]

### 3. The Israelite Victory March: From Ramses to the Plains of Moab (33:1–49

**[1]Here are the stages in the journey of the Israelites when they came out of Egypt by divisions under the leadership of Moses and Aaron. [2]At the LORD's command Moses recorded the stages in their journey. This is their journey by stages:**

**[3]The Israelites set out from Rameses on the fifteenth day of the first month, the day after the Passover. They marched out boldly in full view of all the Egyptians, [4]who were burying all their firstborn, whom the LORD had struck down among them; for the LORD had brought judgment on their gods.**

---

[59] Note also the discussion of the Gadite territory and cities in Simons, *GTTOT,* 119–23; Y. Aharoni, *Land of the Bible* (Philadelphia: Westminster, 1971), 207. See also Howard, *Joshua,* 313–14.

[60] For a discussion as to the location of Heshbon and matters related to the historicity of these accounts, see commentary on 21:25–28.

[61] Note also the discussion of the territory of Reuben and its cities in Simons, *GTTOT,* 115–19; Aharoni, *Land of the Bible,* 207–8.

[62] Simons, *GTTOT,* 118; Aharoni, *Land of the Bible,* 142, 337, 438.

[63] Simons, *GTTOT,* 123–25; Aharoni, *Land of the Bible,* 314; also Howard, *Joshua,* 314–15.

[64] Howard, *Joshua,* 308–9

[5]The Israelites left Rameses and camped at Succoth.

[6]They left Succoth and camped at Etham, on the edge of the desert.

[7]They left Etham, turned back to Pi Hahiroth, to the east of Baal Zephon, and camped near Migdol.

[8]They left Pi Hahiroth and passed through the sea into the desert, and when they had traveled for three days in the Desert of Etham, they camped at Marah.

[9]They left Marah and went to Elim, where there were twelve springs and seventy palm trees, and they camped there.

[10]They left Elim and camped by the Red Sea.

[11]They left the Red Sea and camped in the Desert of Sin.

[12]They left the Desert of Sin and camped at Dophkah.

[13]They left Dophkah and camped at Alush.

[14]They left Alush and camped at Rephidim, where there was no water for the people to drink.

[15]They left Rephidim and camped in the Desert of Sinai.

[16]They left the Desert of Sinai and camped at Kibroth Hattaavah.

[17]They left Kibroth Hattaavah and camped at Hazeroth.

[18]They left Hazeroth and camped at Rithmah.

[19]They left Rithmah and camped at Rimmon Perez.

[20]They left Rimmon Perez and camped at Libnah.

[21]They left Libnah and camped at Rissah.

[22]They left Rissah and camped at Kehelathah.

[23]They left Kehelathah and camped at Mount Shepher.

[24]They left Mount Shepher and camped at Haradah.

[25]They left Haradah and camped at Makheloth.

[26]They left Makheloth and camped at Tahath.

[27]They left Tahath and camped at Terah.

[28]They left Terah and camped at Mithcah.

[29]They left Mithcah and camped at Hashmonah.

[30]They left Hashmonah and camped at Moseroth.

[31]They left Moseroth and camped at Bene Jaakan.

[32]They left Bene Jaakan and camped at Hor Haggidgad.

[33]They left Hor Haggidgad and camped at Jotbathah.

[34]They left Jotbathah and camped at Abronah.

[35]They left Abronah and camped at Ezion Geber.

[36]They left Ezion Geber and camped at Kadesh, in the Desert of Zin.

[37]They left Kadesh and camped at Mount Hor, on the border of Edom.

[38]At the LORD's command Aaron the priest went up Mount Hor, where he died on the first day of the fifth month of the fortieth year after the Israelites came out of Egypt. [39]Aaron was a hundred and twenty-three years old when he died on Mount Hor.

[40]The Canaanite king of Arad, who lived in the Negev of Canaan, heard that the Israelites were coming.

[41]They left Mount Hor and camped at Zalmonah.

[42]They left Zalmonah and camped at Punon.

⁴³They left Punon and camped at Oboth.

⁴⁴They left Oboth and camped at Iye Abarim, on the border of Moab.

⁴⁵They left Iyim and camped at Dibon Gad.

⁴⁶They left Dibon Gad and camped at Almon Diblathaim.

⁴⁷They left Almon Diblathaim and camped in the mountains of Abarim, near Nebo.

⁴⁸They left the mountains of Abarim and camped on the plains of Moab by the Jordan across from Jericho. ⁴⁹There on the plains of Moab they camped along the Jordan from Beth Jeshimoth to Abel Shittim.

**33:1–49** The onomasticon of the stages of Israel's journey and encampment from Pithom and Ramses in Egypt to the plains of Moab opposite Jericho stands in the tradition of the lists of cities recounting the victorious campaigns of such pharaohs as Thutmose III, Seti I, Ramses II, and Shishak (Sheshonq).[65] Their triumphant crusades of the Late Bronze Age extended from Egypt through Cisjordan and Transjordan into Lebanon and Syria, bringing numerous peoples under their imperial dominion. The biblical text recounts the sequence of the Israelites breaking of camp[66] some forty-one times along their forty-two station journey from Ramses in Egypt to the edge of the promised land, just across the Jordan River from Jericho. The ancient kings recorded in geographical sequence those towns, villages, and cities they conquered on their crusade to expand their territorial dominion, often including the quantity of booty acquired by their exploits. Moses recounts the steps by which Yahweh God of Israel has led his people victoriously, even in light of their rebellious tendencies, from bondage and oppression in Egypt to freedom and prosperity, to the brink of great blessing in the fulfillment of his ancient promise to Abraham, "To your offspring I will give this land."[67]

Within the theological structure of the Book of Numbers, this chapter stands conspicuously between the granting of tribal inheritance in Transjordan to the two and one-half tribes and the defining of the boundaries of the promised land which will be divided among the other nine and one-half tribes. Remarkable in the border delineations of 34:1–12 is that the Transjordan territories are not included within the inheritance. The inclusive commentaries on the itinerary in 33:3–4 and 33:50–56 served to remind the people of their God's victory over the Egyptians in the Exodus and to chal-

---

[65] See the combined lists of these and other Egyptian kings in *ANET,* 242–43. The records of the campaigns of these pharaohs (*ANET,* 234–58) focus upon the military prowess of the given leader and the granting of dominion and power to them by the combined deities of the Horus, Amon, Re, and the Apis Bull.

[66] The Hb. מַסְעֵי, often translated "stages" or "stations," refers to the "breaking of camp" or "departures" from each of the locations of the Israelite encampment.

[67] Gen 12:7; 13:14–17; 15:7,18–21; 17:8; 24:7; etc.

lenge them to possess the land which he had given to them as an inheritance.

The interpretation of Numbers 33 and its composition has varied widely, even among source critical and literary scholars. J. de Vaulx, as an example of a source critical approach, subdivided the itinerary into the following source-based divisions:[68]

| Verses | Source | Verses | Source |
|--------|--------|--------|--------|
| 1–4 | JE or Editorial Gloss | 30–33 | Deuteronomist |
| 5–8 | Priestly | 34–35 | Separate Document |
| 8–9 | Yahwist / Gloss | 36–37 | Priestly |
| 10–11 | Priestly | 38–40 | Editorial Gloss |
| 12–14 | E,P,R or Separate Document | 41–42 | Separate Document |
| 15–17 | Priestly | 43–44 | Priestly |
| 17–18 | JE — Yahwist/Elohist | 45–49 | Conflation of Ps |
| 18–30 | Separate Document | 50–51a | Priestly |

However, positing divisions between groups of verses, such as between 10–11 and 12–14 or between 18–30 and 30–33, seems extremely arbitrary when viewed from the context of literary structure, and are based on very hypothetical source theory. These verses are structured exactly alike, and divisions by source seem based solely on the mention of names in Exodus (some Yahwist, but primarily priestly) and Deuteronomy (Deuteronomic). Dillmann countered this type of approach with the theory that Numbers 33 represents a master list for the other itinerary portions in the various narratives rather than a conflation of sources.[69] Yet the master list does not contain all of the collective sites mentioned in those narratives, such as the encampments in the Wadi Zered and Nahal Arnon, and those of Mattanah, Nahaliel, and Bamoth, mentioned in Num 21:12–20, and more than one-third of the sites are never used elsewhere. It may have served a number of texts as a master list, but this was not its primary function.

Each of these approaches has neglected the internal literary evidence of this section and its homogeneity as a literary unit, which probably functioned as an example of what Ashley called "the journey of life" motif in the Bible.[70] This wilderness itinerary was recorded by Moses for the second generation of Israel as a recitation for remembering the stages of God's leading his people from the point of great deliverance in Egypt to the staging point of a new victory campaign in the land of Canaan. The critical

---

[68] The table reflects a combination of the approaches of de Vaulx, *Les Nombres,* 372–81; Gray, *Numbers,* 442–52.

[69] Dillmann, *Das Bücher Numerii, Deuteronomium, und Josua;* cf. Milgrom, *Numbers,* "Excursus 72: The Integrity of the Wilderness Itinerary," 497–99.

[70] Ashley, *Numbers,* 625. Ashley suggests this kind of journey motif is later paralleled in the Book of Hebrews in 3:7–4:16. The exemplars of the faithful in Hebrews 11 represent another form of this motif using people rather than places.

approaches also have overlooked the literary and thematic ties with the marching song included in Num 9:15–23, which contains the pattern:

"At the Lord's command they departed
and at the Lord's command they encamped. " (9:18)

In this passage stages of the movement of the Israelites were recorded by Moses using the similar terminology. The record begins with the same phraseology for divine instruction, with Moses writing

"Their beginnings of their departures the Lord's command,
and these are their departures by their beginnings."[71] (33:2)

Then each stage is delineated with the following pattern, as exemplified by 33:13,

"They departed from Dophkah
And they encamped at Alush

Wenham has rightly observed that the departure / encampment sites are organized into six groups or stages of seven sites. The conclusion to the recitation is found in the instructions for the conquest of the land of Canaan, their Promised Land, in 33:50–56. This challenge to assume ownership of their inheritance is the open-ended seventh stage of the journey motif, that which remains to be written under the leadership of Joshua in the coming months and years.

### THE ISRAELITE VICTORY MARCH

#### Cycle I: From Ramses to the Red Sea

| Numbers 33 | Exodus 12–17 Numbers 1–21 Deuteronomy 1–4; 10 | Variant Readings Additional Sites Location |
|---|---|---|
| RAMSES (3,5) | Ramses (Exod 12:37) | Pi-Ramses = Qantir (not = Tanis; Avaris = Tel Daba). Named Ramses after Egyptian pharaoh. Gen 47:11 Israelites lived in District of Ramses.[a] |

---

[71] Note the simple chiasm in the structure of the terms for "departures" and "beginnings."

## Cycle I: From Ramses to the Red Sea

| Numbers 33 | Exodus 12–17 Numbers 1–21 Deuteronomy 1–4; 10 | Variant Readings Additional Sites Location |
|---|---|---|
| SUKKOTH (5,6) | Sukkoth (Exod 12:37; 13:20) | W of Sea of Reeds; Sukkoth = "Booths" in Hb.; *Tjeku* in Egyptian; recently identified with Tell el-Maskhutah in Wadi Tumilat, ca. 40 miles SE of Pi-Ramses[b] |
| ETHAM WILDERNESS (6,7) | Etham (Exod 13:20) | Part of or equal to Shur Wilderness; Hb. *šûr*= "wall" and Egyptian *htm* = "wall, fortress" |
| (PI-)HAHIROTH (7,8) | Pi-Hahiroth (Exod 14:2); between Migdol & Sea, opp Baal Zephon Yam Suph crossing (Exod 14:21–31) Shur Wilderness (Exod 15:22) | MT - *miphney-hahiroth* — "from facing the gorge"; SP, Syriac, Vulgate, Sebourin = *Pi*- "Mouth of the canals" that empty into Sea of Reeds, near location of Sea crossing[c] – Probably in Bitter Lakes or Lake Timsah area. |
| MARAH (8,9) | Marah (Exod 15:23) Bitter waters made sweet | Traditionally located at ʿAin Hawara (Bir el-Muwarah), just inland 8 miles E from city of Suez; alt. perhaps ʿUyun Musa. |
| ELIM (9,10) with 12 springs, 70 palms | Elim (Exod 15:27) 12 springs, 70 palms, water | Trad. JM[d] - Oasis in Wadi Gharandel, 75 miles south of Bitter Lakes. JSB - area of ʿUyun Musa or Wadi Riyanah |
| YAM SUPH (10,11) | Yam (Sea) – Sea crossing site - Exod 14:21–31, but here camp by Yam Suph | Sea of Reeds / Red Sea (see comment on Num 21:4).[e] JSB or JM – Somewhere along the E shoreline of Suez Gulf. |

a. N. Bietak, *Tell el-Dabʿa*, 2 (Untersuchungen der Zweigstelle Kairo des Osterreichischen Archäologischen Instituts, 1975), 179–221.

b. J. Hoffmeier, *Israel in Egypt*, 120.

c. Ibid., 170–71; 188–89.

d. For Cycles I–IV sites suggested relative to locating Mount Sinai at either Jebel Sin Bisher (JSB) or Jebel Musa (JM).

e. Hoffmeier, *Israel in Egypt,* 182–83, 199–222.

### Cycle II: The Deserts of Sinai, Sin, and Paran

| Numbers 33 | Exodus 12–17<br>Numbers 1–21<br>Deuteronomy 1–4; 10 | Variant Readings<br>Additional Sites,<br>Location |
|---|---|---|
| Sin Wilderness (11,12) | Sin Wilderness (Exod 16:1–15) – between Elim and Sinai on 15th day of 2nd month. Complaint of food, God gives manna and quail. | Probably coastal area of NW Sinai along Suez Gulf since quail generally do not migrate into the mountains.[a]<br>JM – Dibbet el-Rammleh or JSB – SE of Bitter Lakes, E of city of Suez |
| DOPHKAH (12,13) | | LXX - Raphaka<br>Trad. Serabit el-Khadim & Wadi el-ʿEšš uncertain[b] – remains unknown. |
| ALUSH (13,14) | | SP - Alish<br>Unknown location. |
| REPHIDIM (14,15)<br>no water for people to drink | Rephidim (Exod 17:1) No water quarrel; Massah & Meribah Amalekite attack, Israel's Victory | Trad. Wadi Refayid (30 miles NNW) of south tip of Sinai Peninsula – Too far South. Site still unknown. JM - Wadi Feiran preferred.<br>JSM - Prob. Wadi es-Sudr if Israel moved south; or Refidim if E, 35 miles E of Bitter Lakes (neg - in Shur Wilderness (to JSB = 55 miles) |

## Cycle II: The Deserts of Sinai, Sin, and Paran

| Numbers 33 | Exodus 12–17 Numbers 1–21 Deuteronomy 1–4; 10 | Variant Readings Additional Sites, Location |
|---|---|---|
| SINAI WILDERNESS (15,16) | Sinai Wilderness (Exod 19:1f. – Moses w/God, Mount Sinai | JSB - Jebel Sin Bisher (618m elev.) vicinity & Wadi es-Sudr JM - Central S. Sinai region, mt. 2285m elev. Other suggestions for Mount Sinai are numerous, including more recently Har Karkom in the southern Negev, 23 miles S of Mizpe Ramon. |
| KIBROTH HATTAAVAH (16,17) | Paran Desert (Num 10:12;) Kibroth Hattaavah (Num 11:34) | JM - between Jebel Musa and Ein Hudrah JSB - Suggest upper Wadi es-Sudr or upper Wadi Gheidara |
| HAZEROTH (17,18) | Hazeroth (Num 11:35) Paran Desert (Num 12:16) | JM - Wadi Hudeirat region & Ein Hudrah, 35 miles NE of Jebel Musa (oasis area) JSB - Region of Wadi Gheidara |

a. Simons, *GTTOT,* §428–29.
b. Davies, *Way of the Wilderness,* 84.

One of the key issues for locating sites in the second through fifth cycles is the location of Mount Sinai. No less than twenty different suggestions have been tendered through the centuries, ranging from Jebel Helal in the northeastern Sinai peninsula, to Jebel Sin Bisher in the western central region, to Jebel Serbal and Jebel Musa in southern Sinai region, to Har Karkom in northeastern Sinai, southern Negev region, to several mountains in the northwestern Arabian peninsula, southeast of Aqaba. If Moses' request before the pharaoh to journey three days into the wilderness to celebrate a festival to the Lord (Exod 8:3) is to be applied to the quest for the mountain's locale, then the sacred summit must be closer to the Egyptian border fortresses than most of the mountains except Jebel Sin Bisher or another mountain in western Sinai. The most explicit passage bearing on this question is the statement in Deut 1:2 that the distance from Horeb (=Sinai) to Kedesh Barnea, via Ezion Geber, is a distance of eleven days' journey or about 150 to 165 miles.

**Cycle III: Spies Sent from Desert Paran (13:3); Return to Kadesh (13:3)**

| Numbers 33 | Exodus 12–17 Numbers 1–21 Deuteronomy 1–4; 10 | Variant Readings Additional Sites Location |
|---|---|---|
| RITHMAH (18,19) | | Location Unknown |
| RIMMON-PEREZ (19,20) | | Location Unknown |
| LIBNAH (20,21) | | SP (Gk.) - Lebonah Location unknown. |
| RISSAH (22,23) | | Location Unknown |
| KEHELATHAH (22,23) | | LXX - Makellath (w/ v. 25), thus some scholars suggest that Kehelathah may be an alt form of Macheloth Location unknown. |
| MOUNT SHEPHER (23,24) | | Location Unknown |
| HARADAH (24,25) | | Location Unknown |

**Cycle IV: Kadesh to Arabah**

| Numbers 33 | Exodus 12–17 Numbers 1–21 Deuteronomy 1–4; 10 | Variant Readings Additional Sites Location |
|---|---|---|
| MAKHELOTH (25,26) | Kadesh in Zin Wilderness Meribah | Location Unknown |
| TAHATH (26,27) | | LXX – Kataath Location Unknown |
| TERAH (27,28) | | SP – *Mĕtikah* Location Unknown |
| MITHKAH (28,29) | | Location Unknown |

## Cycle IV: Kadesh to Arabah

| Numbers 33 | Exodus 12–17 Numbers 1–21 Deuteronomy 1–4; 10 | Variant Readings Additional Sites Location |
|---|---|---|
| HASHMONAH (29,30) | | LXX – Selmona Location Unknown |
| MOSEROTH (30,31) | Moserah in Deut 10:6 | Location Unknown |
| BENE-YAʿAKAN (31,32) | Deut 10:6 | Location Unknown |

## Cycle V: Desert Journeys to Edom and the Death of Aaron

| Numbers 3 | Exodus 12–17 Numbers 1–21 Deuteronomy 1–4; 10 | Variant Readings Additional Sites Location |
|---|---|---|
| HOR-HAGGIDGAD (32,33) | Gudgodah in Deut 10:7 | Few MSS, LXX, Vg – *Har*-Haggidgad SP - Haggidgadah |
| YOTBATHAH (33,34) | Deut 10:7 | JM - ʿAin Tabah and et-Tabah, 6 miles S of Elat (etymologically weak) Modern Yotvata in southern Arabah |
| ABRONAH (34,35) | Lacking | Suggestion: ʿAin Defiyeh?? |
| EZION-GEBER (35,36) | Lacking, but "Way of Red Sea" mentioned in Num 21:4 | Trad. Tell el-Kheleifeh, just NE of Elat. Alt. site Jezirat Faroun island in northern Gulf of Aqaba |
| KADESH (36,37) in Zin Wilderness | Kadesh (Num 20:1) – Miriam dies; Waters of Meribah | Trad. ʿAin Qudeirat |

## Cycle V: Desert Journeys to Edom and the Death of Aaron

| Numbers 3 | Exodus 12–17 Numbers 1–21 Deuteronomy 1–4; 10 | Variant Readings Additional Sites Location |
|---|---|---|
| MOUNT HOR (37–41) | Mount Hor (Num 20:22) nr. border of Edom; Aaron dies at age 123, 40 yrs after Exodus | Others: Hormah (& Arad) Deut 10:6 – Aaron dies at Moserah. On the border of Edom. Traditional - Jebel Madeirah just S of Petra, too far East. Possible mountain in N. Zin region such as Hor Hahar[a] |
| ZALMONAH (41,42) | Lacking | Unknown elsewhere in OT. Perhaps in region of Wadi Salmana, E of ʿEin Hazeva |

a. See commentary on 20:22–29.

## Cycle VI: Punon to the Plains of Moab

| Numbers 3 | Exodus 12–17 Numbers 1–21 Deuteronomy 1–4; 10 | Variant Readings Additional Sites Location |
|---|---|---|
| PUNON (42,43) | Lacking | Trad. Feinan, 31 miles S of Dead Sea on E side of Arabah (ancient copper mining center)[a] Roman – Phaenon |
| OBOTH (43,44) | Oboth (Num 21:10) | Suggestions: ʿAin el-Weibeh (Simons) Alt. site N of Kh. Feinan toward Kh. Ay[b] |
| IJE ABARIM (44) IYIM (45) | Iye Abarim – E of Moab, then to Zered, Mattanah, Nahaliel, Bamoth, Pisgah (Num 21:11 | Add'l sites: Wadi Zered, Mattanah, Nahaliel, Bamoth, Pisgah (Num 21:18b–20). Iye Abarim = "ruins of Abarim (Mts.)" Thutmose III – "Iyyin" |

## Cycle VI: Punon to the Plains of Moab

| Numbers 3 | Exodus 12–17 Numbers 1–21 Deuteronomy 1–4; 10 | Variant Readings Additional Sites Location |
|---|---|---|
| DIBON-GAD (45,46) | Dibon in Num 21:30 proverb | Add'l sites: Heshbon, Jazer Egyptian *t-b-n-i*; modern Dhiban – 3 miles N of Arnon River gorge Ramses II – "Qarho (Dibon)" |
| ALMON-DIBLATHAIM (46,47) | | = Beth-diblathaim? (Jer 48:22 mentioned w/ Dibon and Nebo), Mesha stela, line 30.[c] Near Baal-meon & Madaba. Suggestion: Deleilat el-Ghar-biyeh[d] |
| MTS. ABARIM (47,48) before Nebo | cf. Iye Abarim above (Num 21:11) – Mount Nebo in Abarim Mts. in Deut 32:49 | Abarim = Ridge of mountains separating Trans-jordan plateau from Jordan Valley, W of Mad-aba and Heshbon. Mt. Nebo traditionally identi-fied w/ mountain of 802 meters elev., 5 miles NW of Madaba |
| PLAINS OF MOAB (48–49) by Jordan from Beth Jeshimoth up to Abel Shittim | Plains of Moab (22:1) Balaam encounters | Beth Jeshimoth = Tel ʿAzeimah, 12 miles SE of Jericho near Dead Sea.[e] Abel-shittim = Tell Kefrein, 5 miles E of Jor-dan & 7 miles N of Dead Sea (Josephus)[f] – or Tel Hammam Thutmoses III, Ramses II – "Abel" |

a. Simons, *GTTOT*, §439.
b. Davies, "The Way of the Wilderness," 90.
c. *ANET*, 320.
d. Simons suggested the existence of twin cities of Almon Diblathaim and Beth Diblathaim to be identified with the mounds of Keleilat el-Gharbiyeh and Deleilat esh-Sherqiyeh respectively, due north of Dhiban (*GTTOT*, §440).
e. Near Dead Sea, ten miles south of Jericho according to Eusebius, *Onomasticon*.

f. Following Milgrom and Rabba bar Bar Hana, estimates are that the Israelite encampment would have covered about 4,020 yards square = 2.28 x 2.28 miles = 5.2 square miles (3 x 3 Persian parsangs; 1 parsang = 1,219 meters).

For the completion of the victory march, Cycle VII lay ahead for the Israelites as the challenge of vv. 50–56 implies.

## 4. Instructions for the Conquest of the Land (33:50–56)

[50]On the plains of Moab by the Jordan across from Jericho the LORD said to Moses, [51]"Speak to the Israelites and say to them: 'When you cross the Jordan into Canaan, [52]drive out all the inhabitants of the land before you. Destroy all their carved images and their cast idols, and demolish all their high places. [53]Take possession of the land and settle in it, for I have given you the land to possess. [54]Distribute the land by lot, according to your clans. To a larger group give a larger inheritance, and to a smaller group a smaller one. Whatever falls to them by lot will be theirs. Distribute it according to your ancestral tribes.
[55]"'But if you do not drive out the inhabitants of the land, those you allow to remain will become barbs in your eyes and thorns in your sides. They will give you trouble in the land where you will live. [56]And then I will do to you what I plan to do to them.'"

The seventh and final cycle of the victory march from Egypt to the Land of Canaan comes in the form of a challenge, the list that remains to be written by Joshua, Moses' successor. The chiastic structure of the future and final stage of the Israelite victory march from Egypt to the Promised Land has been duly noted by Milgrom.[72] As they departed the plains of Moab, led by the Lord and the symbol of his presence in the ark of the covenant in crossing the Jordan River, they would make their encampment at Gilgal from which their task would be to carry out the enclosed instructions for taking possession of their inheritance. The following outline is based on Milgrom, with my own modifications:

Introduction: Instructions from the Lord for the Israelites (50–51)
Setting Protasis: When you cross over the Jordan into the Land of Canaan
A **Possession** of the Promised Land (two apodoses with *wĕhôraštem*) (52–53)
1 Possessing by Dispossessing *(wĕhôraštem)* the Inhabitants of the Land(52)
a Dispossess all the inhabitants of the land from before you
b Destroy all their carved images
b' All their molten images you shall destroy

---

[72] Milgrom, "Excursus 72: The Literary Structure of 33:50–56," *Numbers,* 500–501.

a′ All their high places you shall demolish

2 Possessing *(wĕhôraštem)* by Inhabiting the Land (53)

a You shall possess the land and dwell in it

b For You I have given the land to possess it.

B **Inheritance** To Be Divided among the Tribes (54)

1 You shall receive the inheritance of the land by lot for your clans

a For the large you shall make large its inheritance

a′ For the small you shall make small its inheritance

1′ Toward whatever comes out to him there by lot is his

By your patriarchal tribes you shall inherit.

A′ **Dispossession** Warning (two apodoses *wĕhāyâ*) (55–56)

1 Protasis: If you do not dispossess the inhabitants of the land from before you

a Then it will be *(wĕhāyâ)* that those you allow to remain from them [will be]

Splinters in your eyes and thorns in your sides

They shall trouble you in the land where you dwell

b Then it will be *(wĕhāyâ)*

According to what I intended to do to them

I will do to you!

**33:50–51** In the standard introduction to didactic material throughout the Book of Numbers, this pericope begins with the full Hebrew version of the familiar revelatory phraseology *wayĕdabbēr YHWH ʾel-mošeh ... lēʾmōr ... dabbēr ʾel-bĕnê yiśrāʾēl wĕʾāmartā ʾălēhem*, "Then Yahweh instructed Moses, saying: 'Instruct the children of Israel, and thus you shall say to them.' "[73] Typically this extended formal introduction is found in specific priestly legislation,[74] though it also occurs in the introductions to the two challenges to enter the Promised Land and drive out its inhabitants.[75] The proper conclusion to the Israelites' following these instructions faithfully would be the phraseology of obedience found throughout the Book of Numbers, that Israel did "according all that the LORD commanded Moses."[76] This would be recorded in Josh 11:20,23, that "he [the Lord]

---

[73] See the three sections of Lev 6:1–11, 12–16; and 17–23, each with וַיְדַבֵּר יְהוָה אֶל־מֹשֶׁה לֵּאמֹר, and Num 15:1,17,37. For further discussion of this phraseology and its use in the Book of Numbers, see "Introduction: Structure and Outline of the Book of Numbers" and commentary on Num 1:1.

[74] Num 5:11–12; 6:1–2; 8:1–2; 9:9–10; 16:23–24; 18:25–26; 29:1–2; 35:9–10.

[75] Here and in Num 34:1–2.

[76] The phraseology such as כְּכֹל אֲשֶׁר צִוָּה יְהוָה אֶת־מֹשֶׁה כֵּן עָשׂוּ (1:54) is found in 1:19,54; 2:33–34; 3:16,39,42,51; 4:37,41,45,49(2x); 5:4; 8:3–4,20–22; 9:5,8,18,20,23. Only in 10:13; 17:11 (MT 17:26) and 20:9,27 does this phraseology occur in the three rebellion cycles. Then in the advent cycles the theme recurs in 26:4; 27:11,22–23; 31:7,31,41,47; 32:25; 36:5,10.

might destroy them as the Lord had commanded Moses. ... So Joshua took the whole land according to all that the Lord had said to Moses, and Joshua gave it as an inheritance to Israel according to their divisions by their tribes" (NKJV). The introduction also includes a reference to the geographical setting for receiving the instructions from the Lord, "on the plains of Moab by the Jordan across from Jericho," Jericho being the place where the conquest would begin in the near future.

**33:52–53** The Lord's instructions are set forth using the two parallel meanings of the *hiphil* form of the Hebrew verb *yāraš (hôraštem)*, which can mean either "possess" or "dispossess" depending on one's perspective. For the Israelites to possess the land would mean dispossessing the Canaanite inhabitants, driving the Canaanite inhabitants out of the land so that they might inhabit it. The instructions concerning the dispossessing of the Canaanites were deliberately expanded to include that which would be the most problematic aspect of the Canaanite culture to Israel, the various forms of aberrant worship practiced by the land's inhabitants. They were to demolish (*ʾibbadtem / tĕʾabbĕdû*, "you shall demolish / exterminate") their sculpted or carved images *(maśkiyōtām)* and their molten images *(ṣalmê massēkotām)*, and they were to obliterate all their high places *(bāmōtām)* throughout the land. In the Ten Commandments Israel had been prohibited explicitly from making any form of image of Yahweh their God or worshiping any other gods (Exod 20:3–5), and now they were commanded to demolish all forms and locales where the idolatrous activities took place. Pluralism in the form of peaceful coexistence with idolatry would be impossible, both for the well-being of the people and the sanctity of the land Yahweh had given as a gift to his people. That gift was to be purified by the expurgation of idolatry and by remaining pure and holy before the Lord. Otherwise those various forms and accompanying practices would ensnare Israel and turn their hearts from their God. The tragedy of Israel's history was that they failed to follow faithfully these commands from the Lord, so their demise at the hands of the Assyrians and Babylonians was largely due to their tendency toward idolatry.[77]

**33:54** The land belonged to the Lord, and it was his to grant to whom he desired. By his love, grace, and mercy he had promised and was now presenting the gift of the land to his people Israel. The distribution of the land among the tribes was to be proportionate based on the size of the tribe and

---

[77] The prophetic voices of Isaiah and Hosea of the eighth century B.C. and Jeremiah, Ezekiel, and Zephaniah of the seventh to sixth centuries B.C. all echoed the refrain that Israel's exile was due largely to their stubbornness of heart and persistence of spirit in pursuing the "other gods" of the nations that surrounded Israel. Cf. Isa 2:5–22; Jer 7:1–34; 9:12–16; 10:11–18; Ezek 5:5–6:14; Hos 4:11–5:15; Zeph 1:2–18.

through the casting of lots.[78] Lots were cast with the confidence in the providence of God to apportion justly and fairly among the tribal components of the people of Israel.[79]

**33:55–56** The words of blessing in v. 24 that would result from the Israelites faithfully following the commands of the Lord are now contrasted with a stern warning and potential curse that would accrue to the nation if it were not steadfast in cleaving to Yahweh alone. The antithesis to the Israelites dispossessing the inhabitants of the land would be that of being dispossessed themselves by the hand of the one who had given it to them. Joshua issued a similar warning to Israel in his farewell address to the nation before his death (Josh 23:11–13).

> Therefore take diligent heed to yourselves, that you love the Lord your God.
> (11)
> Or else, if indeed you do go back, and cling to the remnant among you
> –and make marriages with them, and go in to them and they to you, (12)
> know for certain that the Lord your God will no longer drive out these nations
> from before you.
> But they shall be snares and traps to you, and scourges on your sides, and
> thorns in your eyes,
> until you perish from this good land which the Lord your God has given
> you. (13)

The language of the curse was very foreboding. Allowing the peoples of the land who were the source of idolatry to remain in the land would eventually lead to an infectious disease that would gradually consume the nation like leprosy.

What lay ahead for the nation on this last stage of the journey on the victory march to the Promised Land was a challenge of faith. Faithfulness like that which was depicted of the nation in Numbers 1–10 would result in their experiencing the fullness of God's blessing in the land flowing with milk and honey. Unity and harmony, celebration and worship, would be theirs. But if they rebelled against God as that first generation did in Numbers 11–25, then discord and disparagement would be their woeful conclusion to the story. The words were ominously prophetic.

---

[78] The two terms for referring to the familial subgroups within Israel, "your clans" (מִשְׁפְּחֹתֵיכֶם) and "your ancestral tribes" (מַטּוֹת אֲבֹתֵיכֶם) are used synonymously in this verse. In the Hb. structure these two phrases and a *hithpael* form of the verb נחל provide a chiastically structured inclusio to the verse, rendering a literary artistry to the verse's emphases. See below:
לְמַטּוֹת אֲבֹתֵיכֶם תִּתְנֶחָלוּ (A) and (A') וְהִתְנַחַלְתֶּם אֶת־הָאָרֶץ בְּגוֹרָל לְמִשְׁפְּחֹתֵיכֶם.
[79] Cf. Prov 16:33.

## 5. Preparation for Allocation of the Promised Land (34:1–29)

Following the recitation of the victory march from Egypt to the doorstep of the Promised Land (33:1–49) and the provision of instructions for the appropriation of the land of Canaan (33:50–56), the borders of their long-awaited inheritance are delineated. The chapter concludes with a listing of the leaders of the ten remaining tribes who would carry out the land distribution, the other two and one-half tribes having received their allocation in Transjordan. As Harrison vividly noted, "This chapter and the next look forward to the occupation of Canaan, which lay tantalizingly just across the River Jordan to the West of the Israelite encampment. Although God had promised victory to His people if they continued to obey His commands, nothing was left to chance in the organization of their new life in their own land."[80]

The outline of Israel's territorial inheritance on the North and the South closely follows that of the region scouted by the Israelite spies during the first attempt to enter the Promised Land (13:21–29). On the southern side, the Zin Wilderness (v. 3) is the point from which the scouts were sent. As to the northern extent, Lebo Hamath is cited in both 13:21 and 34:8. The Great Sea on the West was the natural boundary, and on the East side the Jordan River is mentioned in both 13:29 and 34:10–12. A number of other lists defining the Promised Land or the Land of Canaan are interspersed throughout the Books of Genesis, Numbers, Joshua, and Ezekiel. Note the comparison of the various lists below.

A subtle tension exists in this section in that the borders specified in vv. 3–12 do not include the territories recently granted to the two and one-half tribes who desired to live in Transjordan region. According to Num 32:30 it is evident that these tribes were intended to have received allotments in Cisjordan along with the other nine and one-half tribes. The tribal dissonance which arose due to their choosing this region for an inheritance (32:1–19) will remain alive for generations to come. By the time of the division of the kingdoms of Israel and Judah, the distinctive regions of the Reubenites, Gadites, and eastern Manassites will have all but disappeared as the kingdoms of Ammon and Moab emerged at the end of the tenth and beginning of the ninth centuries B.C.

### COMPARISON OF BOUNDARY AND TERRITORIAL LISTS

|       | Num 34:1–12 | Josh 14:1–19:51 | Ezek 47:13–20 |
|-------|-------------|-----------------|---------------|
| South | Zin Wilderness border | Zin Wilderness border | Dead Sea toward Negeb, |
|       | w/Edom; Salt Sea to | w/Edom, Salt Sea, S. | Tamar to Waters of Meribah |
|       | Scorpion Pass N. Zin, | of Kadesh Barnea, Hezron | dr. Kedesh, Brook of Egypt |

---

[80] Harrison, *Numbers*, 411–12.

| | | | |
|---|---|---|---|
| | S. of Kadesh Barnea<br>Hazar Addar, Azmon<br>Brook of Egypt to<br>Great Sea | Addar, Karka, Azmon<br>Brook of Egypt to Great Sea | to Great Sea |
| **West** | Great Sea | Great Sea | Great Sea |
| **North** | Great Sea to Mt. Hor<br>Lebo Hamath, Zedad,<br>Ziphron, Hazar Enan | Abdon, Rehob, Hammon<br>Kanah, Greater Sidon, back<br>to Ramah, Tyre, Hosah,<br>Great Sea | Great Sea along Helon Rd.<br>to Zedad, Hamath,<br>Berothah, Sibraim (between<br>Damascus and Hamath),<br>Hazar Hatticon; Sea to<br>Hazar Enan, on Damascus<br>border |
| **East** | Hazar Enan, Shepham,<br>Riblah, East of Ain,<br>Slopes E. of Kinnereth<br>Sea, Along Jordan to<br>Salt Sea | Jordon River and Sea of<br>Kinnereth (Naphtali,<br>Issachar, Manasseh,<br>Ephraim) Except for<br>Transjordan allocations | Hauran / Damascus, to<br>between Gilead and Israel,<br>along Jordan River, E side<br>of [Dead] Sea |
| | **Transjordan Tribes**<br>**Num 32:33–42** | **Transjordan Tribes**<br>**Josh 13:8–33; 17:1–6** | |
| Gad | Dibon, Ataroth, Aror,<br>Atroth Shophan, Jazar<br>Jogbehah, Beth<br>Nimrah, Beth Haran | Jazar territory, all Gilead towns<br>half of Ammon, Aror nr. Rabbah<br>Mizpah and Betonim, Mahanaim,<br>Debir territory, Beth Haram, Beth<br>Nimrah, Succoth, Zaphon,<br>Remainder of Sihon's territory<br>E. side of Jordan to Kinnereth Sea | |
| Reuben | Heshbon, Elealeh,<br>Kiriathaim, Nebo,<br>Baal Meon, Sibmah | Aror (Arnon gorge), Medeba plateau<br>to Heshbon<Dibon, Bamoth Baal,<br>Beth Baal Meon, Jahaz, Kedemoth,<br>Mephaath, Kiriathaim, Sibmah,<br>Zereth Shahar, Beth Peor, Pisgah<br>slopes, Beth Jeshimoth (and the<br>entire realm of Sihon of Amorites) | |
| Manasseh | Gilead (Makirites) | Territory of Mahanaim, Bashan<br>(including all of Makir, Havoth<br>Jair, Nobah (Kenath), Og of<br>Bashan's kingdom), Jair towns<br>in Bashan (60), half of Gilead,<br>Ashtaroth, Edrei | |
| **Genesis 15:18–21** | | **Genesis 17:8** | |
| | River of Egypt to the<br>Great River (Euphrates) | Whole Land of Canaan | |

Land of Kenites, Kenizzites,
Kadmonites, Hittites, Perizzites
Rephaites, Amorites, Canaanites,
Girgashites, Jebusites

## (1) Boundaries of the Promised Land Delineated (34:1–15)

[1]The LORD said to Moses, [2]"Command the Israelites and say to them: 'When you enter Canaan, the land that will be allotted to you as an inheritance will have these boundaries:

[3]"'Your southern side will include some of the Desert of Zin along the border of Edom. On the east, your southern boundary will start from the end of the Salt Sea, [4]cross south of Scorpion Pass, continue on to Zin and go south of Kadesh Barnea. Then it will go to Hazar Addar and over to Azmon, [5]where it will turn, join the Wadi of Egypt and end at the Sea.

[6]"'Your western boundary will be the coast of the Great Sea. This will be your boundary on the west.

[7]"'For your northern boundary, run a line from the Great Sea to Mount Hor [8]and from Mount Hor to Lebo Hamath. Then the boundary will go to Zedad, [9]continue to Ziphron and end at Hazar Enan. This will be your boundary on the north.

[10]"'For your eastern boundary, run a line from Hazar Enan to Shepham. [11]The boundary will go down from Shepham to Riblah on the east side of Ain and continue along the slopes east of the Sea of Kinnereth. [12]Then the boundary will go down along the Jordan and end at the Salt Sea.

"'This will be your land, with its boundaries on every side.'"

[13]Moses commanded the Israelites: "Assign this land by lot as an inheritance. The LORD has ordered that it be given to the nine and a half tribes, [14]because the families of the tribe of Reuben, the tribe of Gad and the half-tribe of Manasseh have received their inheritance. [15]These two and a half tribes have received their inheritance on the east side of the Jordan of Jericho, toward the sunrise."

**34:1–2**   The divine instruction formula introduces appropriately at this point the delineation of the boundaries of Canaan, which was promised to Abraham (Gen 15:18–21), Isaac (Gen 26:4), and Jacob (Gen 28:13–14). The descriptions and lists in Numbers 34 anticipate the division of the land among the tribes as described in Joshua 15–19. Moses in turn gave the explicit instructions from the Lord to the Israelites as they were poised to enter the land of their inheritance, the Promised Land, the land Yahweh himself had granted to his chosen people.

Reference to "the land of Canaan" is in the explicative form with the articular *haʾareṣ* (the land).[81] In addition, the utilization of the twin references to "the

---

[81] R. J. Williams, *Hebrew Syntax: An Outline,* 2nd ed. (Toronto: University of Toronto Press, 1976), 17, §20.

land of Canaan" in v. 2 and at the conclusion of v. 29 form an inclusio encompassing the entire chapter in which the theme is the land of Canaan as the inheritance of the Israelites.[82] Canaan was a definable geographical entity in Egyptian onomastica as early as the fifteenth century B.C., for Egypt controlled much of Canaan during the reigns of the pharaohs of the eighteenth and nineteenth dynasties. Though the detailed borders are not as explicitly demarcated in the Egyptian records of the Late Bronze and Early Iron Ages, the cities and towns listed in both sets of documents encompass substantially the same region. The boundaries are detailed in the following verses.

**34:3–5** The southern boundary is described from the reference point of the Wilderness of Zin from which the original scouts had been sent forty years previously. From that point the line of the border is extended first east-northeast to the southern end of the Dead Sea (*yām hammelaḥ*, Salt Sea), circumventing the Edomite territory that was on the west side of the Arabah. The boundary was then delineated from the Wilderness of Zin westward and then northwestard toward the Great Sea, the Mediterranean. Though many would confine the Edomites to the east side of the Arabah, the geographical patterns both in the present context and in Num 20:14–21:12 would suggest otherwise. When the Israelites were ready to depart from Kadesh in the Zin Wilderness where Miriam had died and which is described as "on the edge of your territory" (Num 20:16),[83] they requested safe passage from the Edomites through their territory. After being refused passage, the Israelites journeyed from Kadesh in the Wilderness of Zin, around the Edomite territory and along its border, and then into the wilderness just east of Moab (Num 20:22; 21:1,4,10–12). This itinerary can also be interpreted as following a line on the north side of the Zin Wilderness, with the Edomites occupying the hilly region south of the Nahal Zin, southwest and west of Ein Khasteva and Ein Yahav, and in the basin of the Nahal Nekarot. The Edomites are now known to have moved even further north into the area just south of Arad by the early Israelite kingdom period, and certainly no later than by the seventh century B.C.[84]

---

[82] Note the parallel Hb. phraseology in the verses below:

v. 2 בְּנַחֲלָה אֶרֶץ כְּנַעַן and הָאָרֶץ כְּנָעַן

v. 29 צִוָּה יְהוָה לְנַחֵל אֶת־בְּנֵי־יִשְׂרָאֵל בְּאֶרֶץ כְּנָעַן

[83] Note the Hb. in Num 20:17, בְּקָדֵשׁ עִיר קָצֶה גְבוּלֶךָ – the Israelites were "in Kadesh, a town (city) on the edge of your border."

[84] I. Beit-Arieh, "Edomites Advance into Judah: Israelite Defensive Fortresses Inadequate," *BAR* 22/6 (1996): 28–36. Fortresses built by the Israelites throughout the southern Negeb region during the ninth and eighth centuries B.C., and possibly even earlier, may have been constructed with this potential threat in mind from Edomites who lived in not only east of the Arabah but quite possibly in the extreme SE Negeb south of the Nahal Zin. Iron IIB Edomite pottery is very distinctive, but Iron I Edomite pottery may be as nondistinctive as Israelite ware from the same period since both were probably fledgling tribal groups in the twelfth century B.C.

The southern border passed just south of the famous "Scorpion Pass,"[85] a winding road from the Nahal Zin basin into the Negeb south of Mampsis, that continued to be known by that name through the Roman period[86] and is so even until today. Kadesh Barnea generally has been identified with either of the oases of Ain Qedeis or Ain el-Qudeirat or the region surrounding the two. The border continued on to Hazar Addar and Azmon, which are mentioned in Josh 15:3 as the southern border of Judah, with the variations that Hazar Addar is separated into Hezron and Addar and an additional site Karka is supplied. The locations of Hazar Addar and Azmon are unknown, though they probably were along a natural geographical and topographical line between Kadesh Barnea and the Brook of Egypt, now know as the Wadi el-ʿArish, the natural boundary between the southwestern Negev and the northeastern Sinai peninsula regions. Aharoni suggested the identification of Hazar Addar with Ain Qedeis, Azmon with Ain Muweilih, and Karka of Josh 15:3 with Qetseimeh.[87] The Wadi el-ʿArish and its tributaries drain a large basin of the northeastern Sinai, and the three sites above probably were along the watershed between the Wadi el~Arish on the west and northwest and the smaller Nahal Zin basin to the east and northeast.

**34:6** The natural western boundary (*gĕbûl yām*, "sea border")[88] was of course the formidable expanse of the Mediterranean Sea, known to Hebrews, Phoenicians, and before them the seafarers of Ugarit as the Great Sea. A stormy body of water in the fall, winter, and into the spring, and often unpredictable even in the summer, it was feared and respected by all ancient peoples. Hence it was believed to be the abode of an often malevolent deity Yammu and his associate the great sea serpent Lotan (Leviathan of the OT). The western border extended along the shoreline from the Brook of Egypt (modern Wadi el-ʿArish) in the south to a point west of Mount Hor and Lebo Hamath, with Ezek 47:15 adding "the Way of Hethlon." These coastal plain regions were occupied by the Philistines (south of the Yarkon River) and various Sea Peoples and Phoenicians during the Iron I and Iron II periods, and they were under Israelite control only briefly during the reigns of David and Solomon.[89] These peoples, along with the Canaanites, would be a continual source of temptation to the Israelites to abandon their sole allegiance

---

[85] מִנֶּגֶב לְמַעֲלֵה עַקְרַבִּים is better translated "from the south of the Ascent of the Scorpions."

[86] Portions of the Roman Maʿale Aqrabbim can be seen today at several points just west of the modern road by the same name.

[87] Aharoni, *Land of the Bible*, 72.

[88] Milgrom translates יָם גְּבוּל as "sea coast," taking גְּבוּל as "land's edge" (*Numbers*, 286). Cf. Deut 3:16,17; Josh 13:23,27; 15:12,47.

[89] Cf. Josh 13:2–6; Judg 1:19,27,29,31; 3:3 for the unconquered lands of the early Israelite emergence in Canaan. See also 2 Sam 5:17–25; 8:1–14; 2 Chr 2:1–16 for the Israelite relations with Hiram, king of Tyre of the Phoenicians.

to Yahweh and the stipulations of their covenant relationship to him, and such would be the eventual cause of the nation's downfall and deportation.

**34:7-9** The northern boundary of the Promised Land extended on a line from the Great Sea toward Mount Hor, another mountain by the same name as that on which Aaron died and was buried (Num 20:22-29). Based on the relative location of the succeeding sites, this Mount Hor is likely to be associated with one of the Lebanon mountain peaks just north of Byblos, perhaps Jebel Akkar.[90] The northern border town of Hethlon (Ezek 47:15) is identified with modern Heitela on the lower slope of Jebel Akkar. The border is also marked by Lebo Hamath ("the entrance to Hamath"), perhaps named so because of its geographical location as a southern access route to the territory of the city state of Hamath. Lebo Hamath is generally identified with modern Lebweh near one of the sources of the Orontes River. This city was the northernmost extent of the land surveyed by the twelve Israelite scouts, according to Num 13:21. Lebo Hamath is also the northern boundary of the Israelite kingdom during the monarchy of David and Solomon (1 Kgs 8:65), from which the people were summoned to celebrate the great feast during the dedication of the Temple to the Lord in Jerusalem. Joshua 13:4 contains the additional site of Aphek, identified with modern Afqa, about fifteen miles east of Byblos.

Zedad is associated with the modern town of Tsada (Tsadad), about thirty-five miles northeast of Lebweh, but Ziphron remains unknown. Milgrom has suggested that Ziphron and Hazar Enan be identified with two oases east of Zedad, namely Hawwarin[91] and Qaryatein. Harrison has suggested locating Hazar Enan at modern Hadr on the lower slopes of Mount Hermon. Ezekiel 47:17 places Hazar Enan on the northwestern border of the territory of Damascus.

**34:10-12** The eastern border of the Israelite inheritance picks up where the northern boundary left off in v. 9, namely at the site of Hazar Enan, which as noted above has been associated with either the oasis of Qaryatein or modern Hadr in the vicinity of Mount Hermon. The border continued from Hazar Enan toward Shepham and then southward toward Riblah, then around the east side of Ain and onward to the eastern edge of the Sea of Galilee, known as the Sea of Chinnereth. Shepham, Riblah, and Ain have not been identified, though several suggestions have been tendered and several sites of the same name can be excluded. Shepham is completely unknown; The Riblah here is not the Riblah on the Orontes River, mentioned in 2 Kgs 25:6 as the place where the captive king Zedekiah was taken to meet with Nebuchadnezzar and face punishment. The name in the Hebrew text con-

---

[90] Cf. Milgrom, *Numbers*, 286; Aharoni, *Land of the Bible*, 72-73.

[91] So also Aharoni, *The Land of the Bible*, 73.

tains the definite article *(hāriblâ),* and the LXX has "Arbela." The mountain and town of that name on the prominent escarpment on the western side of the Sea of Galilee are not to be associated with this northern boundary location, since they are too distant from any logical geographical line between the Lebanese mountains east of Lebweh and Tsadad and continuing to the eastern slopes of the Sea of Galilee. Gray postulated a conflated form Harbelah, for which he suggested two alternatives of Harmel at the source of the Orontes River or at Arbin near Damascus.[92] The town Ain, whose name simply means "spring," could be associated with one of the springs that serve as the sources of the Jordan River. These would include the possibilities of the springs at Iyyon (Ijon)[93] near Tel ed-Dibbin, the springs at the base of Tel Dan, or the springs at Banias (NT Caesarea Philippi). The border then followed the eastern side of the Upper Jordan Valley, descending toward the eastern slopes of the Sea of Galilee, the *ketep yām-cinneret.* The term *ketep,* meaning "shoulder," is used to describe hill or mountain slopes or even some escarpments, such as in the Ketef Hinnom on the southwestern side of Jerusalem. Hence the border may have extended along the upper slopes of the ridge that extends from Banias / Caesarea Philippi southward along the western edge of the Golan Heights, overlooking the Upper Jordan Valley and the Sea of Galilee. The sea was originally named Chinnereth, presumably because the heart-shaped eight-mile-wide by thirteen-mile-long lake looked like a harp from distant vistas such as Mount Arbel, Mount Meiron, Gamla, or Hippos. From the Sea of Galilee the eastern border then followed the Jordan River down to the Dead Sea, a direct distance of about sixty miles, though the river itself meanders back and forth over a distance of about eighty-five miles.

The borders outlined reflect the ideal territorial limits for the land of Israel as outlined by divine instruction, but not fully realized until the time of the United Monarchy of Kings David and Solomon (2 Sam 8:1–18; 10:1–19; 2 Chr 18:1–20:3). The challenge set forth in Num 33:50–56 and Deut 7:1–5 was for Israel to drive out the various peoples from the land of their inheritance so that these nations might not be a stumbling block to Israel's sole faithfulness to Yahweh their God and the special covenant he had established with them. Socially, politically, and religiously Israel was to be a holy people to the Lord, distinctive in character and practice, so that they might be a light to the nations and a source of salvation to the Gentiles.

### (2) Leaders Appointed to Divide the Promised Land (34:16–29)

**[16]The LORD said to Moses, [17]"These are the names of the men who are to assign the land for you as an inheritance: Eleazar the priest and Joshua son of**

---

[92] Gray, *Numbers,* 461; note also the discussion in Ashley, *Numbers,* 638, 641.
[93] See Gray, *Numbers,* 461.

Nun. ¹⁸And appoint one leader from each tribe to help assign the land. ¹⁹These are their names:

Caleb son of Jephunneh, from the tribe of Judah;
²⁰Shemuel son of Ammihud, from the tribe of Simeon;
²¹Elidad son of Kislon, from the tribe of Benjamin;
²²Bukki son of Jogli, the leader from the tribe of Dan;
²³Hanniel son of Ephod, the leader from the tribe of Manasseh son of Joseph;
²⁴Kemuel son of Shiphtan, the leader from the tribe of Ephraim son of Joseph;
²⁵Elizaphan son of Parnach, the leader from the tribe of Zebulun;
²⁶Paltiel son of Azzan, the leader from the tribe of Issachar;
²⁷Ahihud son of Shelomi, the leader from the tribe of Asher;
²⁸Pedahel son of Ammihud, the leader from the tribe of Naphtali."
²⁹These are the men the LORD commanded to assign the inheritance to the Israelites in the land of Canaan.

**34:16–29** The divine instruction formula (*wayĕdabbēr YHWH ʾel–Mōšeh lēʾmōr*, "then Yahweh spoke/instructed Moses, saying") introduces appropriately at this point the delineation of the leaders of the nine and one-half tribes who would inherit the land west of the Jordan River Valley. Of the ten divinely appointed tribal representatives mentioned in this context, only Caleb is mentioned elsewhere in the Old Testament. Yet we presume the selection was based upon the quality of life they lived in faithfulness to the Lord and his commands, since this is such a major theme in the Book of Numbers, as well as the level of leadership skills they possessed and demonstrated. With the results of the distribution having the potential for lasting innumerable centuries, their assigned task was an awesome one. Harrison also notes that "the fact that they were chosen by God for their particular task guaranteed their survival during the period when Canaan was being conquered."[94]

The structure of the present pericope is defined by the inclusio in vv. 17 and 29 using the demonstrative pronoun *ʾelleh* as in *ʾelleh šĕmōt* ("these are the names") and simply *ʾelleh* ("these are [the ones]").[95] The basic formula for introducing each of the tribal representatives is "for the tribe of the children of X, a leader, Y ben Z (Y son of Z)." An abbreviated variation of the form is found with the first representative, Caleb son of Jephunneh, perhaps because he was very familiar to the reader and the audience as a result of his demonstrated faithfulness to the Lord as a scout during the initial process of preparation for entry (13:30–14:9). Only he and Joshua, the other faithful scout who was about to assume Moses' role of leadership over the nation, had survived from those who were first counted in the military conscription

---

[94] Harrison, *Numbers,* 415.
[95] The Hb. text of 34:16 reads אֵלֶּה שְׁמוֹת הָאֲנָשִׁים אֲשֶׁר־יִנְחֲלוּ לָכֶם אֶת־הָאָרֶץ, and for 34:29 אֵלֶּה אֲשֶׁר צִוָּה יְהוָה לְנַחֵל אֶת־בְּנֵי־יִשְׂרָאֵל בְּאֶרֶץ כְּנָעַן.

census performed in the Sinai Wilderness. Only they would experience God's blessing in the Promised Land from that first generation. The citation of the leader from Simeon, Shemuel son of Ammihud, does not contain the term $n\bar{a}\hat{s}\hat{\imath}$ (leader, prince, chieftain[96]). All others follow true to the form. The list according to the representative tribe is provided below.

| Tribe | Tribal Leader |
|---|---|
| Judah | Caleb ben Jephunneh |
| Simeon | Shmemuel ben Ammihud |
| Benjamin | Elidad ben Chislon |
| Dan | Bukki ben Jogli |
| Manasseh (1/2) | Hanniel ben Ephod |
| Ephraim | Kemuel ben Shiphtan |
| Zebulun | Elizaphan ben Parnach |
| Issachar | Paltiel ben Azzan |
| Asher | Ahihud ben Shelomi |
| Naphtali | Pedahel ben Ammihud |

These were the men the Lord had appointed to apportion the inheritance of the land. Some have argued that the absence of the theophoric elements -*yah* or -*iah* from the names is an indicator of their antiquity, but this is as yet inconclusive. On the other hand the relative lack of occurrences of these names in texts that can be definitely assigned to the end of the Israelite kingdom or into the postexilic period (seventh to sixth centuries B.C.) would support this contention.

The order of the list is quite different from previous tribal lists, which Ashley deemed as "fitting for the new beginning."[97] In general it outlines a south-to-north orientation in stages by pairs of tribes, beginning with Judah and Simeon in the south (Simeon was contained within Judah; Josh 19:1–9), Benjamin and Dan flanking Judah on the north (Josh 18:11–28; 19:40–48 respectively), followed by Manasseh and Ephraim (though Ephraim's territory was allotted on the south side of Manasseh's; Josh 16:1–10),[98] Zebulun and Issachar in the Jezreel Valley region (Josh 19:10–23), and then Asher and Naphtali to the northwest and northeast respectively (Josh 19:24–39).[99] Variations in the present passage from other tribal lists would imply that this was an independent narrative, not dependent on Joshua or later materials compiled by the Chronicler but in keeping with the situation in the Book of

---

[96] Translation of Milgrom, *Numbers,* 289–90.

[97] Ashley, *Numbers,* 644.

[98] Ephraim precedes Manasseh in lists from Num 1:32–35; 2:18–21; 7:48–59; 10:22–23; 13:8–11; whereas Manasseh precedes Ephraim in Num 26:28–37 and the present context.

[99] Ashley's suggestion that the present tribal order "is basically the same as the order of Josh 13–19" is somewhat of an overgeneralization due to the several variations from it (*Numbers,* 644).

Numbers. The tribal list, now truncated because of the choice of two and one-half tribes to seek an inheritance on the east side of the Jordan River, perhaps reflects the situation as envisioned by Moses from Mount Nebo in Transjordan.

The chapter concludes with the restatement of the divine appointment of the tribal leaders to apportion the land among the Israelite tribes. Their function would be exercised when, after the northern and southern campaigns were concluded (Josh 6–12), they would again scout out the land so they could carry out with due process their duties of allotment. The fulfillment of that process of possessing the Promised Land would be the goal of the Israelite armies under Joshua after they had crossed the Jordan River. According to Num 34:50–56, they were to drive out the inhabitants of the land as they followed the Lord's instructions faithfully. If they proved to be disloyal or deceitful, dishonest or idolatrous, however, Yahweh would have them removed from the land as well (33:50–56). The basic challenge lay before them: Be faithful to the Lord's commands and he will bring abundant blessing. But if they rebelled as the previous generation in the wilderness did, they would likewise not inherit the Promised Land.

## 6. Levitical Cities and the Cities of Refuge (35:1–34)

Chapter 35 contains two blocks of halakhic material that provide the Levitical-Priestly portion of the final cycle of the Book of Numbers. This cycle focuses on matters pertaining to land in preparation for entry into the land of Canaan. The placement of this chapter is fitting in that in chap. 32 inheritances for the two and one-half tribes in Transjordan were delineated, and both Levitical and refuge cities were established for those living on both sides of the Jordan, Further, in chap. 33 the journey march rehearsed the itinerary of God's program in leading his people from bondage and oppression in the land Egypt to the doorstep of freedom and prosperity in the Promised Land. Finally, in chap. 34 the boundaries of the land were delineated, and representative leaders from each of the remaining nine and one-half tribes were divinely appointed to carry out the responsibility of apportioning the land among the tribes. Now an infrastructure for the religious and social well-being of the nation is set forth.

The first pericope defines the provision of cities for the Levites since they were not to be assigned a territorial allotment in the Promised Land in the manner of the other tribes. Circumscribed sections of land on the perimeter of forty-eight cities were prescribed for their utilization in pasturage and farming, including six cities that also functioned as cities of refuge. The second pericope sets forth the case law regarding the function of the cities of refuge, a means by which order would be maintained for the community of faith in the cases of accidental death or manslaughter. Structurally, this chapter parallels the material of Num 15:22–36, in which statutes were outlined for Israelites to gain expiation for the sins they had committed unintentionally. As sacrificial atonement rituals were delineated in such cases in 15:22–29, so also protection in the cities of refuge was afforded one who had committed manslaughter or unintentionally caused the death of another human being. If a person committed the intentional "sin of a high hand" and thus despised the word of the Lord, that person was to be cut off from his people. In like manner the intentional murderer was afforded no refuge or protection under the law.

Source critical scholars have readily assigned this chapter to the alleged priestly source.[100] Gray went so far as to claim that this kind of distribution is historical fiction, suggesting that "Levitical cities in the meaning of the law never existed; they were merely the objects of desire in certain circles."[101] Noth suggested this section was the result of "the redactional unification of Pentateuchal narrative and deuteronomistic historical work."[102] Yet an obviously exilic/postexilic and priestly oriented (due to its author's background) Book of Ezekiel knows nothing of this territorial allotment of cities to the Levites, but rather apportions them territory opposite the priests from the sanctuary in a manner somewhat similar to their proximus position adjacent to the sanctuary in Num 2:17; 3:5–38.[103] Note that in addition to Ezekiel, none of the prophets Haggai, Zechariah, or Malachi know of what Gray suggested were the objects of desire of the Levites that were simply never fulfilled. If the Levitical cities were a late invention of the postexilic priests, as is often presupposed, their redactions of the material outside the Pentateuch should have been brought into conformity with its contents. Such projections instead are superfluous speculation. Instead the Levitical city distribution was appropriate to the theological purposes for the people of God for the reasons noted above.

The organization of the ideal theocratic state as presented here in Numbers 35 was such that the Levites were to provide a constant visible presence whereby the peoples of the twelve tribes would be reminded actively and passively of the need for holiness and righteousness as the people of God before the nations of the world. Along the wilderness journey the three clans of the Levites and the Aaronic priests camped adjacent to the Tent of Meeting, one group on each of the four sides to provide a buffer zone of protec-

---

[100] Dillmann, *Numeri, Deuteronomium, und Josua*, 214–27; Gray, *Numbers*, 464–67; J. Wellhausen, *Die Composition des Hexateuchs und der historischer Bücher des Alten Testaments* (Berlin: Reimer, 1889), 183–84; etc.

[101] Gray, *Numbers*, 465.

[102] Noth, *Numbers*, 253.

[103] This incongruence was also noted by de Vaulx, *Les Nombres*, 393–95.

tion so that the Holy Place might not be defiled and so they may protect their fellow Israelites from death due to encroachment. As Olson notes: "The Levites both protect the boundary and cross the boundary between the divine and human, between God's holy love and the people's sinful rebellion. The scattered presence of the Levites throughout the land of Israel suggests that the presence and holiness of God will likewise be distributed over the entire land. ... but the presence of God eludes capture in any fixed structure or place. God is greater than any house in which God's presence dwells."[104]

Jesus likewise spoke these words to the woman at the well in central Samaria who had raised the issue of the proper place to worship the Lord: "Woman, believe Me, the hour is coming when you will neither on this mountain nor in Jerusalem, worship the Father. ... But the hour is coming and now is, when the true worshipers will worship the Father in spirit and in truth; for the Father is seeking such to worship Him" (John 4:21,23, NKJV)

### (1) The Levitical Cities (35:1–8)

**[1]On the plains of Moab by the Jordan across from Jericho, the LORD said to Moses, [2]"Command the Israelites to give the Levites towns to live in from the inheritance the Israelites will possess. And give them pasturelands around the towns. [3]Then they will have towns to live in and pasturelands for their cattle, flocks and all their other livestock.**

**[4] "The pasturelands around the towns that you give the Levites will extend out fifteen hundred feet from the town wall. [5]Outside the town, measure three thousand feet on the east side, three thousand on the south side, three thousand on the west and three thousand on the north, with the town in the center. They will have this area as pastureland for the towns.**

**[6] "Six of the towns you give the Levites will be cities of refuge, to which a person who has killed someone may flee. In addition, give them forty-two other towns. [7]In all you must give the Levites forty-eight towns, together with their pasturelands. [8]The towns you give the Levites from the land the Israelites possess are to be given in proportion to the inheritance of each tribe: Take many towns from a tribe that has many, but few from one that has few."**

The structural outline of vv. 1–8 is as follows.

Introduction: Divine Instruction Formula and Geographical Setting (v. 1)
   A   Instruction: Give the Levites Cities for Dwelling[105] (v. 2)
     B   Purpose: Lands for Cattle and Flocks (v. 3)
       C   Dimensions of Land Grants around Cities (vv. 4–5)

---

[104] Olson, *Numbers,* 189–90.

[105] Note the internal chiasm in this verse based upon the use of לַלְוִיִּם מִנַּחֲלַת אֲחֻזָּתָם עָרִים (2a) and וּמִגְרָשׁ לֶעָרִים סְבִיבֹתֵיהֶם תִּתְּנוּ לַלְוִיִּם וְנָתְנוּ.

B' Purpose: Six Cities of Refuge Plus 42 Others (vv. 6–7)
A' Cities Given Levites Based Upon Proportionate Size of the Tribe (v. 8)

**35:1–2** The chapter and pericope commence with the standard formula for divine revelatory instruction used throughout the Book of Numbers, *wayĕdabbēr YHWH ʾel-mōšeh ... lēʾmōr,* "Then the LORD instructed [spoke to] Moses ... saying." The geographical setting of the plains of Moab is provided for the third time in this cycle, here as an inset to the chapter introduction and for the fifth time in the Book of Numbers.[106] This repetition provides further emphasis on the fact that the material contained within is given in preparation for entry into the Promised Land. They were poised for entry and were in the process of getting final instructions for establishing a religious and social infrastructure for the nation. Added emphasis is provided with the imperative form *ṣaw* (command); Moses was instructed to direct the Israelites to carry out this plan of providing for the Levites throughout the tribal lands. That which followed was to provide guidance for the community of faith in their walk with the Lord. The Levites would provide a constant reminder to the Israelites of the need for faithfulness to Yahweh as the Levites themselves had demonstrated at Sinai in the incident of the golden calf. An inclusio is formed around terminology, and in a somewhat chiastic structure, for the Lord's provision of a special inheritance for the Levites among the cities of the various tribal territories in vv. 2 and 8, thus highlighting the central theme of this section.[107]

The Levites were to be provided by the various tribes designated cities in which to reside and prescribed lands around the cities for farming and pasturage. They would not own the cities and towns allocated for their usage, and neither would they be the sole residents of those towns, as Lev 25:32–34 implies.[108] They would not possess the cities as their own territorial inheritance but would have provision made from the inheritance of the other tribes. In fact, as Ashley has pointed out, "the terms inherit *(nāḥal),* inheritance *(naḥălâ),* and portion *(ḥēleq),* usually used of the tribes' landed property in Canaan, are avoided here."[109] Instead the Levites' inheritance was Yahweh himself; he was their "share and inheritance" (Num 18:20). Furthermore, they were supplied the tithes of the Israelites by the Lord as their

---

[106] Cf. Num 22:1; 26:63; 31:12; 33:48,50; 36:13.

[107] Cf. the Hb. text of v. 2, וְנָתְנוּ לַלְוִיִּם מִנַּחֲלַת אֲחֻזָּתָם עָרִים לָשָׁבֶת and that of v. 8, וְהֶעָרִים אֲשֶׁר תִּתְּנוּ מֵאֲחֻזַּת ... נַחֲלָתוֹ אֲשֶׁר יִנְחָלוּ יִתֵּן מֵעָרָיו לַלְוִיִּם

[108] The Levites could redeem their own houses in the Levitical cities, and during the Jubilee Year the houses were to be returned to them just as was done for other Israelites. Note v. 33 especially, "A house sold in any town they hold ... is to be returned in the Jubilee, because the houses in the towns of the Levites are their property among the Israelites" (Lev 25:33).

[109] Ashley, *Numbers,* 645.

inheritance (Num 18:21–24,30–32), and the Levite presence throughout the tribal territories would facilitate the rendering of the tithes by the individuals from the various tribes to the Lord. They in turn were to present to the Lord, via the Aaronic priesthood, a tithe of the very best of the tithes they had received from the Israelites (Num 18:25–29). The Israelite community was to function as a unity of tribal components, as the aggregate whole body as the people of God politically, socially, and religiously.

According to Joshua 21 each of the various clans of the Levites were granted cities among a given group of Israelite tribes. The Kohathites of Aaronic lineage received thirteen cities in Judah, Simeon, and Benjamin (v. 4), and the remaining Kohathites were provided ten cities in Ephraim, Dan, and one-half Manasseh (Cisjordan) (v. 5). The Gershonites were granted thirteen cities within the tribal territories of Issachar, Asher, Naphtali, and one-half Manasseh (Transjordan). The Merarites then received twelve towns from the territories of Reuben, Gad, and Zebulun. Most of these tribal allocations and their respective towns follow general geographical regions, moving from south to north, with the exception that the Merarite allotments were separated geographically, with several cities in the Upper Jezreel Valley (e.g., Jokneam) and then the remaining in Transjordan, separated by the tribal territory of Issachar in the southeastern Jezreel and Beth Shean Valley regions.[110]

**35:2b–5** In this section the focus is on the lands surrounding the cities that were to be contributed to the Levites for pasturage for their animals. These flocks and herds could be of their own animal husbandry activities or from those contributed among the tithes by the Israelites who lived in the region surrounding the given town. Joshua 21:11–12 distinguishes between the grazing lands, called *migrāšehā* (its pasturelands) that were given to the Aaronic Kohathites, and the botanical fields around the city of Hebron, called *śĕdēh hāʿîr* (the field of the city) and the surrounding villages granted to Caleb and his Judahite descendants via the Aaronic priesthood. The Levite land grants around the allotted cities were primarily for pasturage and not for botanical crop production.

Scholars have debated how the dimensions in vv. 4 and 5 should be interpreted. The Levitical pasturelands were to extend outward one thousand cubits (NIV "fifteen hundred feet") from the wall of the city (v. 4, *miqqîr hʿîr wāḥûṣâ ʾelep ʾammâ*, lit., "from the wall of the city and outwards one thousand cubits"), and the territory is described as two thousand cubits (NIV "three thousand feet") on each of the sides (v. 5, *maddōtem mihûṣ lāʿîr ʾet-pĕʾat qēdmâ ʾalpayim bāʾammâ*, lit., "you shall measure from the outside of the city on the eastern side 2,000 by the cubits"). The dimensions of the lat-

---

[110] For further discussion of the distribution of the Levitical cities see Howard, *Joshua*, 389–97.

ter are generally interpreted as meaning a square plot of land extending one thousand cubits outward from the city on each of the four sides. The incongruence noted by a number of scholars is based on the assumption that the total of two thousand cubits should be split into two parts of one thousand cubits and then that distance measured from the walls of the city. Whether the city was large or small, a measurement in the four directions of one thousand cubits from the city walls would yield an area larger than two thousand meters square (see fig. 1 below).

Milgrom cites the original work done by Ramban, who perceived that the two-thousand-cubit measurement was to be viewed from the outside of the city, simply being a measurement of the perimeter of the pastureland on each side. Verse 5 contains no reference to the walls of the city as in the preceding verse but instead cites the *pĕʾat* (side, border, edge) in the four primary compass directions. Thus the walled city, whatever its dimensions, functions as the epicenter point of the three-thousand-square-foot area.[111] A large Levitical city like Shechem or Gezer (Josh 21:21) would have less net pasturage acres than smaller towns like Debir or Jokneam (Josh 21:15,34). Similar to many earlier interpretations, Milgrom takes the analysis a step further by envisioning an expanding Levitical area extending out one thousand cubits from the wall of the city, where the total area for Levitical pasturage would measure two thousand plus $X$ by two thousand plus $Y$, where $X$ is the length along the east-west axis of the city and $Y$ is the length along the north-south axis of the city (see fig. 3 below).[112] Later in Jewish history this passage was used as the basis for determining the "Sabbath day's journey distance," which was generally measured at two thousand cubits from the gate of the city. Thus the territory would expand with the city as it grew and enlarged the perimeter of its fortification walls.

**35:6–8**    These verses provide a hinge linking vv. 1–5 to 9–34, in that some of the cities apportioned to Levites also would function as cities of refuge. Structurally the verses belong with the pericope of vv. 1–5, with the divine instruction formula introducing each section, in addition to the inclusio of vv. 2 and 8 mentioned in the discussion above.[113]

Forty-eight cities total would be provided by the various twelve tribes in accordance with the size of the tribe. Gray has pointed out on the basis of the second census in Numbers 26 that though the fulfillment of this instruction is recounted in Joshua 21, these cities were not apportioned precisely by the Israelites after they had arrived in Canaan. For example, Naphtali, with its military population of 45,400, contributed only three cities, whereas

---

[111] Milgrom, *Numbers*, "Excursus 74– The Levitical Town: An Exercise in Realistic Planning," 502–4.

[112] Ibid., 503.

[113] The NIV text thus mistakenly divides the chapter sections between vv. 5 and 6.

Ephraim, with a conscription of 32,500 and Gad with 40,500 each, contributed four. Issachar and Dan had much greater militias of 64,300 and 64,400 respectively, yet they contributed the same number of cities as the much smaller Ephraim. These observations, however, assume that the military conscription forces of Numbers 26 reflect the relative size of the total populations of each of the tribes, an assumption that may or may not have been congruent with the actual demographics of that day.

Further, if the suggestion of D. M. Fouts and C. J. Humphreys is followed that the censuses should be totaled in such manner that the term for "thousand" (ʾelep) be interpreted as "clan" or "military unit," then the alleged incongruences noted by Gray above would be lessened greatly.[114] Thus the three cities provided on the basis of Naphtali's conscription of forty-five units totaling four hundred men would be proportional to the four cities each provided by Ephraim and Gad based on their conscriptions of five hundred men. On the other hand, four cities each were provided for the Levites by Dan and Asher, though each had militias numbering four hundred men, the same as that of Naphtali. Still the relative sizes of the total population of each of the tribes are not necessarily to be implied from the relative sizes of each one's militia. Dan's four hundred men would be divided among sixty-four units or clans, with Asher's four hundred among fifty-three groups, perhaps implying a greater overall population than that of the tribe of Naphtali, which had only forty-five units or clans.

Six of the forty-eight Levitical cities were to be designated as cities of refuge, providing asylum and protection for someone who had committed manslaughter or other form of mortal injury to another individual. These cities provide the theme of vv. 9–34.

## (2) Cities of Refuge (35:9–34)

[9]Then the LORD said to Moses: [10]"Speak to the Israelites and say to them: 'When you cross the Jordan into Canaan, [11]select some towns to be your cities of refuge, to which a person who has killed someone accidentally may flee. [12]They will be places of refuge from the avenger, so that a person accused of murder may not die before he stands trial before the assembly. [13]These six towns you give will be your cities of refuge. [14]Give three on this side of the Jordan and three in Canaan as cities of refuge. [15]These six towns will be a place of refuge for Israelites, aliens and any other people living among them, so that anyone who has killed another accidentally can flee there.

[16]"'If a man strikes someone with an iron object so that he dies, he is a mur-

---

[114] D. M. Fouts, "The Use of Large Numbers in the Old Testament, With Particular Emphasis on the Use of *Elep*." (Th.D. diss., Dallas Theological Seminary, 1992); C. J. Humphreys, "The Number of People in the Exodus from Egypt: Decoding Mathematically the Very Large Numbers in Numbers I and XXVI," *VT* xlviii (1998): 196–213.

derer; the murderer shall be put to death. [17]Or if anyone has a stone in his hand that could kill, and he strikes someone so that he dies, he is a murderer; the murderer shall be put to death. [18]Or if anyone has a wooden object in his hand that could kill, and he hits someone so that he dies, he is a murderer; the murderer shall be put to death. [19]The avenger of blood shall put the murderer to death; when he meets him, he shall put him to death. [20]If anyone with malice aforethought shoves another or throws something at him intentionally so that he dies [21]or if in hostility he hits him with his fist so that he dies, that person shall be put to death; he is a murderer. The avenger of blood shall put the murderer to death when he meets him.

[22]"'But if without hostility someone suddenly shoves another or throws something at him unintentionally [23]or, without seeing him, drops a stone on him that could kill him, and he dies, then since he was not his enemy and he did not intend to harm him, [24]the assembly must judge between him and the avenger of blood according to these regulations. [25]The assembly must protect the one accused of murder from the avenger of blood and send him back to the city of refuge to which he fled. He must stay there until the death of the high priest, who was anointed with the holy oil.

[26]"'But if the accused ever goes outside the limits of the city of refuge to which he has fled [27]and the avenger of blood finds him outside the city, the avenger of blood may kill the accused without being guilty of murder. [28]The accused must stay in his city of refuge until the death of the high priest; only after the death of the high priest may he return to his own property.

[29]"'These are to be legal requirements for you throughout the generations to come, wherever you live.

[30]"'Anyone who kills a person is to be put to death as a murderer only on the testimony of witnesses. But no one is to be put to death on the testimony of only one witness.

[31]"'Do not accept a ransom for the life of a murderer, who deserves to die. He must surely be put to death.

[32]"'Do not accept a ransom for anyone who has fled to a city of refuge and so allow him to go back and live on his own land before the death of the high priest.

[33]"'Do not pollute the land where you are. Bloodshed pollutes the land, and atonement cannot be made for the land on which blood has been shed, except by the blood of the one who shed it. [34]Do not defile the land where you live and where I dwell, for I, the LORD, dwell among the Israelites.'"

Six of the Levitical cities, three on each side of the Jordan River, were to be designated as cities of refuge whereby a person who had committed manslaughter or caused some other form of unintentional death to an individual would be afforded asylum and protection from potential avenging by a member of the slain person's family. As both Israel and God's inheritance, the Levites resided in cities established throughout the land among each of the twelve tribes as living symbols of faithfulness and holiness to God. The entire land belonged to God, and he had granted it as an inheritance to his people. But although promise and inheritance were gracious gifts to the

nation, possession and prosperity were conditional based upon the faithfulness of the people to the covenant stipulations that defined the relationship
between God and humanity. Transgression of the stipulations of the covenant could lead to Israel's being dispossessed or driven out from their inheritance because their rebellion and rejection of God's sovereignty could bring
defilement to the land. Legislation in chap. 35 was designed to preserve the
wholeness, holiness, and purity of the Promised Land and is thus an extension of the Holiness Code of Leviticus.[115] These cities would be designated
after the conquest of the land west of the Jordan and the apportioning of the
land among the tribes (Josh 20:1–9). The structural outline of the pericope
is as follows:

Introduction: Divine Instruction Formula (v. 9)
   A  Instruction: Setting — When You Cross the Jordan (v. 10)
      a  Select some Towns as Cities of Refuge (v. 11)
      b  Places of Refuge from an Avenger (v. 12)
      a′ Six Towns for Cities of Refuge (v. 13)
   A′ Setting: Three Towns on Each Side of the Jordan River (v. 14)
      b′ Refuge for Israelites and Resident Aliens in Cases of
           Manslaughter (v. 15)
   B  Laws Governing Murder Cases (vv. 16–21)
   a  Iron   Stone   Wood (vv. 16 18)
   b  Blood Kinsman Executes (v. 19)
   a  Shove   Thrown Object   Fisticuffs (vv. 20–21a)
   b′ Blood Kinsman Executes (v. 21b)
   B′ Laws Governing Manslaughter Cases (vv. 22–28)
   $a^2$  Accidental Shove Thrown Object (v. 22)
   $a'^2$ Stone Dropped (v. 23)
      Community Judges Between Manslaughter and Murder (v. 24)
      Community Protects in Cases of Manslaughter (v. 25)
      Remain in Asylum until Death of the High Priest (v. 25b)
   A″ Case: Manslaughter Leaves Refuge City (v. 26)
   Blood Kinsman Executes w/o Guilt of Murder (v. 27)
   Remain in Asylum until Death of the High Priest (v. 28)
Recapitulation: Statutes and Judgments throughout Your Generations (v. 29)
   A  Whoever Murders Will Be Put to Death by Testimony of Two (+)
      Witnesses (v. 30)
   B  No Ransom for a Murderer—Put to Death (v. 31)
   B′ No Ransom for Manslayer—Remain in Refuge City (v. 32)

---

[115] Note that the parallel passage in Deut 19:1–13 emphasizes the division of the Cisjordan territory into three parts with each having a refuge city. It also further defines the premeditated aspect
that precipitated the murderous act, as well as several cases of accidental death.

A′ Execution of Murderer Atones for the Land (v. 33)
Summary Principle: Do Not Pollute or Defile the Land Where I Myself
  Dwell! (v. 34)

**35:9–15** The second pericope of the chapter commences with the standard formula for divine revelatory instruction used throughout the Book of Numbers, *wayĕdabbēr YHWH ʾel-mōšeh ... lēʾmōr,* "Then the LORD instructed [spoke to] Moses ... saying." The geographical setting of the plains of Moab (v. 2) is assumed in the temporal setting of the instructions, namely "When you cross the Jordan into Canaan." This repetition provides further emphasis on the fact that the material contained within is given in preparation for the entry into the Promised Land in faithful fulfillment of that which God had intended for his people to experience a generation before. This too parallels the introduction to Numbers 15, "When you enter the land that I am giving you," as they were poised for entry into the land and were in the process of getting final instructions for establishing a religious and social infrastructure for the nation under God.

Selected cities that would be determined later were to be set aside for providing refuge for a person who had somehow carried out an act that had led to the death of another. The manslayer had the responsibility of fleeing to the appointed city immediately after committing the crime so as to be afforded the opportunity for refuge from the potential kinsman avenger. Specifically, six cities were to be set aside for this purpose, three on each side of the Jordan River. In Josh 20:7–8 the Transjordan cities of refuge chosen were, from south to north, Bezer in the Reubenite territory, Ramoth Gilead in the central Gilead highlands belonging to the Gadites, and Golan in the Bashan region allotted to the Machirites of the tribe of Manasseh.[116] West of the Jordan were Kedesh in Upper Galilee from the territory of Naphtali, Shechem in the highlands of Samaria on the border between Ephraim and Manasseh, and Qiryat Arba or Hebron in the central hill country of Judah. On each side of the Jordan, the three cities were somewhat equidistant from each other and thus equally accessible to inhabitants of each side.

Ultimately the refuge city was provided for the safety and well-being of a person who had caused the accidental or unintentional death of another. The term translated "accidental" *(bišgāgâ)* in the NIV is the same as the word translated "unintentional" in Num 15:22–29, which addressed matters of atonement for inadvertent sins. Such sins by the community or an individual could have been committed out of ignorance of the law or accidental abrogation of its statutes. Such cases were not excusable but could be atoned for by offering the proper sacrifices. Thus forgiveness would be attained. Deliberate sins, however, in which a person defiantly rebels against God and

---

[116] See Num 32:33–42 for the broad geographical regions of the three tribes.

his law necessitated that the transgressor be cut off from the community.[117] The issue is first addressed in the Pentateuch in Exod 21:12–14, which states that a murderer is to be executed, but the unintentional manslayer should be afforded refuge in a place I [God] will designate." Prior to the establishment of the cities of refuge, sanctuary could be sought by laying hold of the horns of the altar of burnt offering in the tabernacle court.

The Hebrew terminology *gōʾēl* (avenger, kinsman) here and *gōʾēl haddam* (blood avenger, blood kinsman) in vv. 19,21,24,25,27 is the same term used of the kinsman redeemer in Ruth 2:20; 4:4,6 and is defined as one who "redeems" property or persons from another. In Lev 25:33 it denotes the redemption of property of the Levites that had been sold, and in Lev 25:47–54 the term is used several times related to the redemption by a kinsman of persons who had been sold into slavery. In the present context the "avenger of blood" was a kinsman who redeemed the lost life of the individual by exacting the life of the murderer.[118] On the one hand this form of meting out justice is an example of lex talionis, or the law of punishment in like compensation for the crime committed (e.g., "an eye for an eye"). Thus in the case of premeditated murder, in which there was malice aforethought and deliberate intent to do harm that resulted in the death of the victim, the crime was adjudicated by the execution of the murderer. The societal responsibility to carry out this judgment fell to the nearest surviving kinsman, beginning with the father, then followed by the eldest brother and on down the line. The permission to carry out this act was not an unrestrained right. Howard notes that "the 'avenger of blood' was not free to take private vengeance: the Bible clearly reserves vengeance to God alone (Deut 32:35; Isa 34:8; Rom 12:19)."[119] The city of refuge provided a safe haven for the manslayer until the community had opportunity to ascertain the nature of the crime and come to a conclusion as to whether murder or manslaughter had been committed.

**35:15** As previously noted in a number of statutory cases, the laws governing the cities of refuge were to be applied both to the resident Israelite and the sojourner or resident alien.[120] In the Book of Numbers several such cases are explicitly indicated as applying to residents and aliens; there were not to be two or more classes of people distinguished by the selective appli-

---

[117] For a detailed discussion of the punishment for the defiant "sins of a high hand," see Milgrom, *Numbers*, "Excursus 36: The Penalty of 'Karet,'" 405–8; also D. J. Wold, *The Biblical Penalty of Kareth* (Ann Arbor: University Microfilms, 1978).

[118] R. L. Harris, *TWOT*, "גָּאַל (gōʾēl)," 1:144; H. Ringgren, "גָּאַל, gāʾal." *TDOT*, 2:350–55; R. L. Hubbard, Jr., "The *Goʾel* in Ancient Israel: Theological Reflections on an Israelite Institution," *BBR* 1 (1991): 3–19.

[119] Howard, *Joshua*, 385.

[120] Cf. Ashley, *Numbers*, 651.

cation of halakhic legislation.[121] H. G. Stigers suggested that the *gēr* was "largely regarded as a proselyte," and D. Kellerman described the legal status of the *gēr* as parallel to the economic status of the *tôšāb* ("stranger who dwells"), though the latter did not enjoy all of the religious privileges of the *gēr*.[122] Israel was always to treat the sojourners and resident aliens well because they had experienced personally in Egypt all that being a sojourner entailed (Deut 10:19).

**35:16–21** Following the presentation of instructions for the establishment of the cities of refuge, the case laws governing murder and manslaughter are formulated in a structural pattern that G. Brin has called the "formula of option" utilizing the Hebrew sequence *ʾim* ... *ʾô* ("if ... or").[123] Two successive sequences of the pattern introduce first the laws governing murder and the avenging adjudication by the blood kinsman (vv. 16–21) and second the laws governing manslaughter and the responsibilities of the community in such cases (vv. 22–29).[124] Corresponding to the laws delineating the three means of committing murder with an instrument wielded by the hand of an individual is the thrice-mentioned adjudication, "the murderer shall [surely] be put to death," giving emphasis to the talionic code to be carried out. This penalty was initially set forth in Gen 9:5–6: "From each man I will demand an accounting for the life of his fellow man. 'Whoever sheds the blood of man, by man shall his blood be shed; / for in the image of God has God made man.'"[125]

The taking hold of certain potentially lethal objects with the hand(s), and then striking a person with that object, constituted murder if any form of malice was involved. The text delineates three such kinds of material objects that were considered lethal, specifically iron implements, whether farm tools or weapons, stone objects, such as grinding stones or stone-headed mallets, and wooden items, ranging from tree limbs to tool handles. To take any such

---

[121] In 9:14 the sojourner will keep the Passover in the same manner as the native Israelite. Likewise there was to be one law (equitable adjudication) for Israelites and sojourners governing sacrificial offerings (15:13–16), one law regarding atonement for unintentional sins (15:26–29), one law for exacting judgment against the intentional sinner who has defied the law (15:30), and one law for ritual purification of those who had come in contact with the dead (19:10). Parallel legislation is found in Exod 12:19,48,49; 20:10; 23:9–12; Lev 16:29; 17:8–15; 18:26; 19:33–34; 20:2; 22:18; 24:16,22; 25:6,23,35,45,47; Deut 1:16; 5:14; 10:19; 14:29; 16:11,14; 24:14–22; 2611–13; 27:19; 29:10; 31:12.

[122] H. G. Stigers, "*gēr*," *TWOT*, 1:154; D. Kellerman, "גּוּר *gûr*," *TDOT* 2:439–49.

[123] G. Brin, *Studies in Biblical Law: From Hebrew Bible to the Dead Sea Scrolls*, JSOTSup, 176 (Sheffield: JSOT Press, 1994), 90–101.

[124] For expanded discussion of the concept and function of the cities of refuge, see M. Greenberg, "The Biblical Conception of Asylum," *JBL* 78 (1959): 125–32; Milgrom, *Numbers*, "Excursus 75, 'Asylum Altars and Asylum Cities,'" 504–9.

[125] Cf. Exod 21:12–14; Lev 24:17; Deut 19:11–13.

kind of object in hand and strike another individual with malice aforethought constituted murder. Similarly to assault a person maliciously by
shoving him or by hurling a lethal object toward him such that he dies,
would constitute murder. Shoving deaths might occur when a person pushed
another off a precipice in the hill country or wilderness, or even onto a pile
of stones such that the blow to the head suffered by the fall caused the death
of the individual. One could cast stones by hand or by sling or throw an iron
object, thereby inflicting a moral wound, and be guilty of murder. In all such
cases the murderer was to be executed by the blood kinsman to avenge the
life and death of the victim, which was symbolized in the blood that was
shed in the process.

**35:22–29** The cases for determining manslaughter are presented in
reverse (chiastic) order of those cases of murder, first that pertaining to
shoving a person inadvertently or throwing an object that accidentally hits
and kills another individual (v. 22), followed by a single exemplar of the
three cases mentioned in vv. 16–18, namely the dropping of a stone on a person accidentally or unknowingly (*bĕlōʾ rĕʾôt*, "without seeing") by which a
mortal injury results. Deuteronomy 19:4–7 provides a few cases of accidental death, such as when a man is chopping down a tree and his axe-head flies
off the handle and strikes someone in the head causing death. Further quali-
fications are then added to adjudicating cases of manslaughter, first, that
there was no preexisting enmity (*wĕhûʾ lōʾ-ʾôyēb lô*, "and he was not an
enemy to him") between the two persons and, second, that the person causing harm to the other had not sought to harm the other (*wĕlōʾ mĕbaqqēš
rāʿātô*, "and he was not seeking his harm") such as might be the case if he
were "lying in wait."[126] These latter instances would constitute murder for
which there would be no refuge from the avenging relative of the victim.

The responsibility of discerning whether the cause of death of the victim
was accidental and/or inadvertent versus deliberate and/or intentional lay
upon the court of the congregation. The decision making by the community
leadership is phrased as "between the striker and the blood kinsman," or literally between the survival by limited incarceration of the manslayer and the
blood avenging execution by the kinsman of the victim. According to Josh
20:4, the one seeking asylum was to appear at the entrance to the gate of the
refuge city, often the location of the city's elders and judges who had been
given the responsibility to settle a variety of judicial cases, and there the
decision would be made. After determining a given case was accidental, the
congregation of this Levitical city would offer asylum and sanctuary for the
perpetrator of manslaughter. The mention that the person convicted of man-

---

[126] A more literal translation of בְּלֹא צְדִיָּה is noted here but as "unintentionally" in the NIV,
it would be a further indicator of the perpetrator's intent to do harm to the victim.

slaughter would be sent back to the city suggests that the trial would have taken place outside the city walls, whereby a person convicted of murder could be easily rendered to the blood kinsman for execution. One also assumes that the participation of the Levites whose lives were dedicated to the Lord would ensure fairness and justice in their decision making.

Once the person was convicted of manslaughter rather than murder, he was to remain in the sanctuary of his asylum until the death of the high priest. In effect the eventual death of the individual or that of the high priest ransomed the death of the victim. Noordzij suggests, however, that the death of the high priest "marks the end of an era," similar to the ancient as well as modern practice of a king, president, or governor granting amnesty or pardon to convicted felons.[127] The former view finds more contextual support since the text mentions that it was the death of the high priest[128] that enabled the release of the refugee from his imposed asylum, and not the length of the asylum nor the death of the one so confined. The Mishnah and Talmud concur with this interpretation, and as Ashley notes, "This view is also consistent with vv. 32–33, which do not allow any ransom to buy off the blood of the victim."[129] The mention of the anointing of the high priest highlights both the role of the priest as the one who carried out the atonement ceremonies for the sins of the nation throughout his days in office (Lev 16:1–34) and the role of the cities of refuge in maintaining the holiness of the land.

**35:29**  The preceding laws regarding the designation of refuge cities and the proper adjudication of cases related to their function are to be binding on the community throughout their generations, wherever the Israelites resided. Such would allow for the expansion of the number of cities of refuge as the nation expanded its borders or even the designation of such locales outside the national boundaries in the case of diaspora settlements of the Israelites in exile.

**35:30–34**  The final section addresses the issues of the number of witnesses necessary to bring a murder conviction, the prohibition of monetary compensation in lieu of paying the proper penalty for the crime, and the theological basis for maintaining justice in the land in capital cases. No one was to be executed on the basis of a single witness to a crime; a minimum of two witnesses were necessary to bring a conviction of murder in a capital crime.[130] Once the murder conviction had been gained, the blood kinsman

---

[127] Noordzij, *Numbers,* 301. Note also the discussion in Ashley, *Numbers,* 654.

[128] The rare phrase הַכֹּהֵן הַגָּדֹל is found only here and in Lev 21:10 in the Pentateuch. Elsewhere in the Hebrew Bible it occurs in Josh 20:6; 2 Kgs 12:10; 22:4,8; 23:4; 2 Chr 34:9; Neh 3:1,20; 13:28; Hag 1:1,12,14; 2:2,4; Zech 3:1,8; 6:11. As in v. 32, the high priest is often simply referred to as הַכֹּהֵן, "the priest."

[129] Ashley, *Numbers,* 654.

[130] Hb. plural form is used here לְפִי עֵדִים, "by word of witnesses."

was allowed to avenge the death of his relative. The minimum of two witnesses is consistent with cases delineated in Deuteronomy as well as ancient Near Eastern law codes, such as that of Hammurabi.[131]

Bribery, ransom, or other forms of compensation for the death of a human being were strictly prohibited, whether the death was deemed to be murder or manslaughter. Verses 31 and 32 are structured similarly, introduced by the statement "Do not accept a ransom [bribe]" *(lōʾ-tiqḥû– kōper)*. The Hebrew noun *kōper* is derived from the root *kāpar,* meaning to "atone for, ransom" or as Harris notes, "to atone for by offering a substitute."[132] Human life is a most precious commodity in the eyes of God. There was no monetary or sacrificial substitute for the taking of human life; only by the shedding of human blood could the death of another be atoned for, according to Pentateuchal law.

Hence the murderer must be executed by the blood kinsman, and the accidental manslayer must pay the penalty by remaining in asylum in the city of refuge until death or until the death of the high priest. In effect the eventual death of the individual or that of the high priest ransomed the death of the victim. The enactment of these laws would prevent bribery, whereby a person of means might buy his way out of paying the penalty for his crime.[133] In *Jubilees* 21:19 we likewise read that accepting a bribe for the shedding of human blood brought pollution to the land.

The concluding verses of this chapter emphasize the theological basis for the aforementioned laws governing adjudication in the case of the shedding of human blood. The two verses commence with the same structure, "Do not pollute [defile] the land where you are."[134] The shedding of the blood of innocent human beings was a pollution (*wĕlōʾ taḥnîpû,* "you shall not pollute/corrupt") and defilement (*wĕlōʾ tĕṭammê,* "you shall not defile") of the land. The term for pollution describes an uncleanness or corruption that results from an individual Israelite or the nation as a whole engaging in a variety of wrongful acts, including the transgression of the laws, statutes, and stipulations of the covenant (Isa 24:4–6), immorality and idolatry (Jer 3:1–10), or general godless acts of humanity (Job 8:13; 13:16; 17:8).[135] The term for defilement describes uncleanness or ritual impurity resulting from

---

[131] "The Law Code of Hammurabi," *ANET,* 2nd ed., 166 § 9–11,13. Cf. Deut 17:6; 19:15; Matt 18:16; John 8:17; 2 Cor 13:1; Heb 10:28.

[132] R. L. Harris, "כָּפַר (kāpar)," *TWOT* 1:453.

[133] Noordzij, *Numbers,* 301–2. Cf. Prov 13:8.

[134] Note the Hb. parallels in v. 33, וְלֹא־תַחֲנִיפוּ אֶת־הָאָרֶץ אֲשֶׁר אַתֶּם בָּהּ and v. 34, וְלֹא תְטַמֵּא אֶת־הָאָרֶץ אֲשֶׁר אַתֶּם יֹשְׁבִים בָּהּ, with the only variation being the additional יֹשְׁבִים, which is found in v. 33 in several manuscripts, including the Samaritan Pentateuch, LXX, Syriac, and Vg.

[135] L. Goldberg, "חנף," *TWOT,* 1:304.

diseases (Lev 13:1–14,57; Num 5:1–5), bodily emissions (Lev 15:1–33), contact with the dead (Num 9:6–11; 19:1–22), and breaking of the laws and statutes of the covenant. This defilement limited a person or group from participating in the full holiness of the community.

The Israelites were a people of the land, which was Yahweh's inheritance granted unto them. There in the Promised Land they were to be a light to the nations, revealing the holiness and righteousness of God. But since God cannot endure sin and iniquity, such as the shedding of innocent human blood, those causes of defilement must be exacted from the land. The prophets were clear in denouncing the leaders of Israel and Judah because of their unrighteous acts whereby the lives of the innocent were minimized and demeaned through bloodshed. Hence they would echo the words of this passage in calling for the just recompense of those abusive of the poor, the widows, the orphans, and others.[136] That recompense would be the extraction of the evil elements from the land they had defiled and polluted. Exile to the unclean lands of Assyria and Babylon and the destruction of the Temple in Jerusalem, which had been defiled by the sinfulness of the nation, would be the just atonement for the land. In fulfillment of the commitment of Num 33:55–56, God would eventually do to Israel what he intended for Israel to do to the original unrighteous inhabitants of the land.

### (6) Inheritance Laws: Zelophehad Clarifications (Laws and Land) (36:1–12)

[1]**The family heads of the clan of Gilead son of Makir, the son of Manasseh, who were from the clans of the descendants of Joseph, came and spoke before Moses and the leaders, the heads of the Israelite families.** [2]**They said, "When the LORD commanded my lord to give the land as an inheritance to the Israelites by lot, he ordered you to give the inheritance of our brother Zelophehad to his daughters.** [3]**Now suppose they marry men from other Israelite tribes; then their inheritance will be taken from our ancestral inheritance and added to that of the tribe they marry into. And so part of the inheritance allotted to us will be taken away.** [4]**When the Year of Jubilee for the Israelites comes, their inheritance will be added to that of the tribe into which they marry, and their property will be taken from the tribal inheritance of our forefathers."**

[5]**Then at the LORD's command Moses gave this order to the Israelites: "What the tribe of the descendants of Joseph is saying is right.** [6]**This is what the LORD commands for Zelophehad's daughters: They may marry anyone they please as long as they marry within the tribal clan of their father.** [7]**No inheritance in Israel is to pass from tribe to tribe, for every Israelite shall keep the tribal land inherited from his forefathers.** [8]**Every daughter who inherits land in any Israelite tribe must marry someone in her father's tribal clan, so that every Israelite will possess**

---

[136] See Isa 1:15–21; Jer 7:1–34; Ezek 9:3–10.

the inheritance of his fathers. ⁹No inheritance may pass from tribe to tribe, for each Israelite tribe is to keep the land it inherits."

¹⁰So Zelophehad's daughters did as the LORD commanded Moses. ¹¹Zelophehad's daughters—Mahlah, Tirzah, Hoglah, Milcah and Noah—married their cousins on their father's side. ¹²They married within the clans of the descendants of Manasseh son of Joseph, and their inheritance remained in their father's clan and tribe.

The concluding chapter of the Book of Numbers serves several purposes in the overall outline of the book and in the final cycle. First, the settlement of the problem of family inheritance through women's lineage completes the inclusio introduced in chap. 27, in which the issue of the inheritance of Zelophehad's daughters was adjudicated. Second, the general theme of land inheritance in the Book of Numbers finds specific application and culmination. Third, it expands the decision meted out in chap. 27, giving broader consideration and greater depth to the rights of women in Israelite society relative to land ownership and general matters of inheritance. A final verse concludes the book in the manner of those found in the Book of Leviticus, supplying a colophon that concludes the previous material and prepares for that which follows. Finally, this concluding chapter implicitly reflects the interest in the Pentateuch for genealogical reckoning, since as W. G. Plaut noted, "There are ten generations from Adam to Noah, ten generations from Noah to Terah, and ten generations from Abraham to the daughters of Zelophehad."[137] Genesis through Numbers thus evidence a literary unity.

The outline of the passage, which reflects the literary and thematic development of the continuing case of Zelophehad's daughters, is as follows.

Introduction: Gileadite Clans Appear Before Moses (v. 1)
A  Historical Precedent in the Case of Zelophehad's Daughters
      (Yahweh's Command) (v. 2)
  B  The Gileadite Case: The Integrity of Tribal Inheritance (vv. 3–4)
A'  Moses Presents the Case Adjudication (Yahweh's Command) (v. 5)
  B'  Zelophehad's Daughters May Marry Within the Tribal Clan (v. 6)
    C  No Inheritance Shall Pass from Tribe to Tribe (v. 7)
      D  General Principle: Female Heirs of Israel Marry Within the
          Tribal Clan (v. 8)
    C'  No Inheritance Shall Pass from Tribe to Tribe (v. 9)
  B"  Zelophehad's Daughters Comply With Yahweh's Command
        Through Moses (vv. 10–12)
A"  Conclusion to the Case and the Book of Numbers (v. 13)

---

[137] W. G. Plaut, *The Torah: Numbers* (New York: Union of American Hebrew Congregations, 1981), 307.

Note the chiastic structure of vv. 5–13 and repetitious elements that highlight the general principle derived from the adjudication of the case of the Gileadite clan. The case thus would become the precedent for future cases; Israelite women may become heirs to their father's territorial inheritance if he has no male heir, but they must marry within their father's tribe to maintain the territorial integrity of the original tribal allocation.

LEGAL PRECEDENT: HISTORICAL BACKGROUND OF THE REQUEST BY ZELOPHEHAD'S DAUGHTERS (36:1–2). **36:1–2** Resultant implications of the issue of female inheritance, as delineated by Moses in chap. 27, were raised by the family of Gilead ben Machir ben Manasseh of the sons of Joseph. The case is brought before the combined judicial council of Moses and the leaders of the families of Israel. The fourfold family lineage serves to distinguish the complainants as descendants of Joseph, specifically the Machirites who had chosen a territorial inheritance in the Transjordan area of the former kingdom of Sihon and Og in Gilead and Bashan (21:21–35). According to 1 Chr 5:23–26, the eastern Manassites expanded their territorial control through the Bashan-Golan Heights region, all the way to Mount Hermon. Later in their history they, along with the Gadites and Reubenites, were carried into captivity by Tiglath–pileser III to the Upper Euphrates region of Habor and the River Gozan at the end of his 733–32 B.C. campaigns.

The Machirites had acquired this territory by force from the Amorites in the region of Gilead because the land was desirable for the pasturage of their herds and flocks—not only by the Machirites but also by the entire tribes of Gad and Reuben (32:1–38). Assuming the Machirites had agreed to support the other tribes in the conquest of Canaan, as had the Gadites and Reubenites, Moses granted this clan the Gilead region because they defeated and dispossessed the Amorites who had been living in that region. As a geographical description Gilead referred to the hilly region of Transjordan extending northward from the Jabbok River to the Yarmuk River and from the Jordan River eastward to the arid lands of the Jordanian desert. The terminology used in 32:1 of the *běnê-gilʿād* ("sons/children of Gilead" or "Gileadites") also implies that Gilead was the name of one of the clans of the Machirites, which included Gilead's sons Iezer, Helek, Asriel, Shechem, Shemida, and Hepher (26:29–33). Hence Gileadite may refer to either the people living in the Gilead region or the subclans of the sons of Gilead ben Machir.

### The Lineage of Zelophehad's Daughters

| Num 26:29 | Num 27:1 | Num 36:1–12 | 1 Chr 2:23; 5:23–24; 7:14–19 |
|-----------|----------|-------------|------------------------------|
| Joseph | Joseph | Joseph | Joseph |
| Manasseh | Manasseh | Manasseh | Manasseh |
| Machir | Machir | Machir | Machir |

| Gilead | Gilead | Gilead | Gilead |
| Hepher | Hepher | | |
| Zelophehad | Zelophehad | Zelophehad | Zelophehad |
| 5 daughters | 5 daughters | 5 daughters | Daughters |

Hepher was the father of Machir, whose five daughters, Mahlah, Noah, Hoglah, Milcah, and Tirzah, had requested of Moses that their father's inheritance be passed on to them since there had been no sons in the family. The concern of the larger Gileadite clan was the possible loss of land to another Israelite tribe should the daughters of Zelophehad marry outside the tribe of Manasseh. They feared the integrity of their tribal allocation would be disintegrated. Under the Lord's direction Zelophehad's daughters were granted territorial inheritance rights in a decision that was meted out by Moses, thereby setting a legal precedent. This initial decision set forth that the land should remain within the family or tribe. The Gileadite leaders brought to the judicial proceedings the other legal precedent of the Lord's direction for the distribution of tribal territory by lot, and territorial sovereignty by tribe was to be maintained. That which was allocated to Manasseh from the beginning should remain within the tribal inheritance of Manasseh for the future generations.

## (7) The Case Presented by the Gileadite Clans (36:3–4)

³**Now suppose they marry men from other Israelite tribes; then their inheritance will be taken from our ancestral inheritance and added to that of the tribe they marry into. And so part of the inheritance allotted to us will be taken away. ⁴When the Year of Jubilee for the Israelites comes, their inheritance will be added to that of the tribe into which they marry, and their property will be taken from the tribal inheritance of our forefathers."**

**36:3–4** With these two precedents on the judicial table, the several clans of the Gileadites presented their case in two parts before Moses and the Israelite leadership for a legal decision. The closely parallel phraseology of vv. 3 and 4 suggests that these were the two component parts of the Gileadite claim. First was the question of one of the daughters of Zelophehad marrying[138] outside the Manassite tribe, in which case the property would accrue to the husband's tribe and thereby violate tribal territorial sovereignty. Part two related to the property laws that applied in the Year of Jubilee, every fiftieth year, during which property reverted to its original tribal or clan owner, and indentured slaves were emancipated (Lev 25:13–55). But the Jubilee statutes applied only to purchased property and not to property that had been

---

[138] The Hb. phraseology, וְהָיוּ לְאֶחָד מִבְּנֵי שִׁבְטֵי בְנֵי־יִשְׂרָאֵל לְנָשִׁים, lit. reads, "Now if anyone becomes the wife of the sons of the tribes of the Israelites."

inherited, such as that which accrued to the daughters of Zelophehad. Thus several scholars have considered the verse an editorial gloss because the inclusion seems tangential to the central issue.[139] As Budd and Sturdy note, however, the Jubilee statutes are herein rescinded in such a case, ensuring the preservation of the territorial boundaries of the tribes of Israel. The possible loophole in the Israelite property laws was closed.

The English term Jubilee is derived from the Hebrew *yōbēl* for the "ram's horn," which was blown to usher in that year of celebration and restoration. The Year of Jubilee was to be marked every fiftieth year after the conclusion of seven Sabbatical years.

### (8) Moses Presents the Case Adjudication at Yahweh's Command (36:5–12)

**5Then at the LORD's command Moses gave this order to the Israelites: "What the tribe of the descendants of Joseph is saying is right. 6This is what the LORD commands for Zelophehad's daughters: They may marry anyone they please as long as they marry within the tribal clan of their father. 7No inheritance in Israel is to pass from tribe to tribe, for every Israelite shall keep the tribal land inherited from his forefathers. 8Every daughter who inherits land in any Israelite tribe must marry someone in her father's tribal clan, so that every Israelite will possess the inheritance of his fathers. 9No inheritance may pass from tribe to tribe, for each Israelite tribe is to keep the land it inherits."**

**10So Zelophehad's daughters did as the LORD commanded Moses. 11Zelophehad's daughters—Mahlah, Tirzah, Hoglah, Milcah and Noah—married their cousins on their father's side. 12They married within the clans of the descendants of Manasseh son of Joseph, and their inheritance remained in their father's clan and tribe.**

**13These are the commands and regulations the LORD gave through Moses to the Israelites on the plains of Moab by the Jordan across from Jericho.**

As noted above in the chapter introduction, the presentation of Moses' response to the Gileadite clan's request is couched in a chiastic structure that highlights the general principle set forth in v. 8. Female heirs should marry within their tribe so that the divided inheritance of each of the tribes might be preserved with territorial sovereignty.

**36:5** The final didactic and halakhic section of the Book of Numbers begins with Moses faithfully commanding the Israelites on the basis of that which he had received from the Lord. We are not told explicitly of Moses' entering into the Tent of Meeting or standing at its entryway to receive instruction from Yahweh, as was his normal recourse, but that he did is implicit in the introductory statement that Moses "commanded the Israelites

---

[139] Noth, *Numbers,* 257–58; Davies, *Numbers,* 369.

according to the word of the Lord"[140] (*ʿal-pî YHWH,* lit. "from the mouth
of Yahweh"). That Moses and/or Israel faithfully followed the commandments of the Lord is one of the key themes of the Book of Numbers,[141] a
point that is repeated in the narrative in vv. 11 and 13. Faithful obedience of
God's people to his instructions is not only a major theme in Numbers but in
the entirety of Scripture. In the Pentateuch faithful obedience is one of the
requisites to blessing in the gift of the land, the fruitfulness of the land, the
unity of the community, and the general well-being *(shalom)* of the people.

**36:6**   So that there would be no reduction in the land apportioned to
each of the twelve tribes, no cross tribal land appropriations that would confuse property laws and rights were allowed. To maintain tribal territorial
sovereignty, the command received from the Lord was that Zelophehad's
daughters should marry the man of their choosing from among those of their
father's tribe, namely that of Manasseh. The statement that they "may marry
anyone they please" interprets the Hebrew phrase *laṭôb bĕʿênêhem tihyeynâ
lĕnāšîm* ("for the good in their eyes let them become wives"), about which
Harrison remarks: "The women were given a choice to marry appropriately.
The Hebrew expression "in the eyes of" refers to a person's cognitive facul-
ties of assessment or to intuitive spiritual discernment."[142] This phraseology
differentiates them from the later Israelites who in the days of the Judges
"did evil in the eyes of the LORD" (Judg 2:11) by doing "what was right in
their own eyes" (Judg 21:25).[143] In the chiastic structure this verse is paralleled in vv. 10–12, which present the faithful compliance of Zelophehad's
daughters with the stipulation.

**36:7,9**   In the chiastic structure of the chapter, these two verses are mir-
ror images of one another, nearly duplicating the principle of maintaining
tribal territorial sovereignty. No property inheritance of any tribe should
pass from that tribe to another. That definable portion had been allotted to
each of the tribes according to the stipulations set forth in Num 33:53–54
and 34:13–18. The law of the Jubilee Year also would be preserved, in that
any property acquired by a person or family of one tribe from another tribe
on the basis of debt payment or negotiated purchase would return to its original tribal ownership. The Transjordan tribes had already received their

---

[140] Author's translation here.

[141] Note the use of עַל־פִּי יְהוָה here and in Num 3:16,39,51; 4:37,41,45,49; 9:18,20,23;
10:13; 33:2,38 and the clause כַּאֲשֶׁר צִוָּה יְהוָה (or similar) here and in 1:19,54; 2:33,34;
3:16,42,51; 5:4; 8:3,22; 15:36; 16:40[Hb. 17:5]; 17:11[Hb. 17:26]; 20:9,27; 26:4; 27:11,22,23;
31:7,31,41,47; 36:10.

[142] Harrison, *Numbers,* 427.

[143] Cf. the Hb. phrase of Num 36:6, לַטּוֹב בְּעֵינֵיהֶם in the context of זֶה הַדָּבָר אֲשֶׁר־צִוָּה
יְהוָה in contrast to that of וַיַּעֲשׂוּ בְנֵי־יִשְׂרָאֵל אֶת־הָרַע בְּעֵינֵי יְהוָה in Jdg 2:11 and in Jdg 21:25
אִישׁ הַיָּשָׁר בְּעֵינָיו יַעֲשֶׂה.

allotments (chap. 32), and the other nine and one-half tribes would receive theirs upon entry and conquest of the land (Josh 14:1–21:45). The land ultimately belonged to God, who had given it as an inheritance to his people Israel. Whether the allotments were attained by special promised grant (Judah, Ephraim [including Joshua], and Manasseh) or by the casting of lots (Josh 18:10; for Benjamin, Simeon, Zebulun, Issachar, Asher, Naphtali, and Dan), this was accomplished according to the command and will of God.[144]

**36:8** At the focal point of the chiastic structure is the setting forth of the general principle derived from the adjudication of the case of the Gileadite clans and the daughters of Zelophehad. Female heiresses among any of the tribes of the Israelites were to marry within the clans of their own patriarchal tribes. That way the tribal territorial sovereignty would be maintained among the individual tribes. The text reads literally "so that the children of Israel might each possess the inheritance of his fathers." The combination of statutes regarding Sabbath and Jubilee years, along with this ruling regarding tribal sovereignty, would insure a healthy national structure of unity and egalitarian quality for the Israelites in their tribal structure for many generations to come.

**36:10–12** The outcome of the case of Zelophehad's daughters and the concerns of the Gileadite clans provides a fitting conclusion to the chapter, to the combined chaps. 26–36, and to the Book of Numbers as a whole. The daughters of Zelophehad faithfully complied with the instructions given by the Lord through Moses. As noted above on v. 5, faithful obedience to the Lord's commands is one of the key themes, if not the central theme, of the Book of Numbers. Note the parallel usage of the Hebrew ṣiwwâ (command) in the chiastic structure of vv. 5 and 6 with vv. 10 and 13:

36:5 Moses commanded the Israelites according to the word of Yahweh
   36:6 This is the word which Yahweh commanded for the daughters of Zelophehad
   36:10 According to that which Yahweh commanded Moses, thus the daughters of Zelophehad did
36:13 These are the commandments & statutes which Yahweh commanded by the hand of Moses for the Israelites

Harrison concludes that "these redoubtable women married into the tribe of their father, and in this way their inheritance remained in the holdings of Manasseh. It is gratifying that when the women presented an urgent petition to Moses about their rights of inheritance, they were provided for fully by a God who is concerned for the plight of the widows and orphans, and we are indebted to the šōṭĕrîm for recording a happy ending to the incident."[145]

---

[144] Cf. Josh 18:10; 19:51; 21:43–45.

## 8. Conclusion to the Case and to the Book of Numbers (36:13)

**¹³These are the commands and regulations the LORD gave through Moses to the Israelites on the plains of Moab by the Jordan across from Jericho.**

**36:13** The Book of Numbers concludes in a manner parallel to the beginning, with the faithful fulfillment of the commands of the Lord by his people. As Yahweh had said *(wayĕdabbēr YHWH)*, "The LORD spoke," 1:1), instructing the people to carry out the census of the Israelite men twenty years old or more, so Moses and the heads of the families dutifully completed the assigned task (1:19,54). The final verse also concludes the legislative section, in a manner similar to Lev 7:37-38; 26:46; 27:34; and Num 1:54; 2:34; 3:51; 5:4. Moses had communicated in faithful didactic fashion that which Yahweh had commanded, the manner for which he had been commended so often previously throughout the Books of Exodus, Leviticus, and Numbers.[146] The particular phraseology of the commandments coming via the hand of Moses recalls the use of similar expressions in Exod 35:29; 39:42–43; 40:33–38; and Lev 7:37–38; 27:34.

As the daughters of Zelophehad had been instructed—Moses commanded *(wayĕṣaw)* what Yahweh said *(lēʾmōr)*, to marry within their tribal clan to maintain the integrity of the tribal land allocations—these women demonstrated their loyalty to the covenant relationship to Yahweh. The emphasis in this concluding section is not to be placed upon the logistical limitations that confront the women concerning their potential marriage partners but upon the evidence of obedience to God's will and the illustration of faithfulness to the special and unique relationship God had fashioned with his people.

Furthermore, the conclusion serves to frame in a formulative manner the gender inclusiveness of the covenant relationship. The men had completed faithfully the charge given to them by God in the beginning, and in the conclusion (a kind of gender inclusio) the women likewise had carried out God's words in unwavering approbation.

---

[145] Harrison, *Numbers,* 427.

[146] Exod 29:35; 31:11; 34:34; 36:1; 39:1,7,21,31,32,42,43; 40:16,19,21,23,25,29,32; Lev 10:7; 16:34; 24:23; 27:34; Num 1:19,54; 2:33,34; 3:16; 4:37,41,45,49,49; 5:4; 8:20,22; 9:5,23; 10:13; 15:35; 17:11; 20:27; 26:4; 27:11,22,23; 29:30; 31:7,31; 33:2.

# Appendix: Literary Analysis of Numbers 22–24

GEOGRAPHICAL SETTING: Arabah of Moab (22:1)
Along the Jordan Across from Jericho

CYCLE I: FIRST MESSENGERS SENT TO BALAAM (22:2–14)
 A Balak Fears Israel: Sends First Messengers to Balaam (22:2–7)
 Introduction: Balak's Fear of Israel (22:2–4)
 a First Messengers Sent to Balaam (22:5a)
  b The Message: Curse the Mighty Israel (22:5b–6)
 a' Elders of Moab and Midian Journey to Meet Balaam (22:7)
 B Balaam's Response to the Messengers (22:8)
 I will bring back a word which Yahweh speaks to me
  C God's First Encounter with Balaam (22:9–12)
   a God Appears to Balaam (22:9)
    b Message of Envoy: Come Put a Curse on Israel (22:10–11)
   a God's Message: Do not go; Do not curse (22:12)
 B' Balaam Refuses to Go to Moab (22:13)
 A' Balak's Messengers Return Home to Moab (22:14)

CYCLE II: SECOND SET OF MESSENGERS SENT TO BALAAM (22:15–21)
 A Balak Sends More Messengers to Balaam (22:15–17)
 B Balaam's Response to New Messengers (22:18–19)
 "I would not be able to violate the word of Yahweh my God"
  C' God's Second Encounter with Balaam: Go and Speak (22:20)
 "Only the word which I speak to you, it shall you do."
 A' Balaam Departs with Messengers (22:21)

CYCLE III: GOD'S MESSENGER SENT TO BALAAM (22:22–40)
 A Angel of Yahweh Appears: Donkey Sees and Turns Away (22:22–23)
 B Angel of Yahweh Appears Second Time: Donkey Sees and Turns Away (22:24–25)
 C Angel of Yahweh Appears Third Time: Donkey Sees and Turns Away (22:26–27)
 D God's Third Encounter with Balaam (22:28–35)
 a Yahweh Opens Donkey's Mouth (22:28–30)
 b Yahweh Opens Balaam's Eyes (22:31–34)
  (a) Balaam Sees and Falls Prostrate
   (b) Behold I have come out as your adversary
    (c) The donkey saw me and turned away
   (b') So now I should kill you, and yet let her live.
  (a') Balaam Confesses His Sin
 c Yahweh's Message: Go and Speak (22:35)
  (a) "Go with the men;
   (b) but only the word I speak to you, you shall speak."
  (a') So Balaam goes with the princes of Balak
 E Balaam Meets with Balak (22:26–40)

(a) Balak Goes out to Meet Balaam (22:36)
   (b)  Balak speaks to Balaam: "Why did you not come?" (22:37)
   (-b) Then Balaam says to Balak, "Behold I have come to you." (22:38)
       "Now am I indeed able to speak anything?
       The word which God places in my mouth, that I will speak."
(a') Then Balaam went with Balak (22:39–40)

CYCLE IV:  THE FIRST ORACLE OF BALAAM (22:41–23:13)
  A  Balak Takes Balaam to Cultic Site (22:41)
  B  Balaam Prepares to Meet with Yahweh (23:1–3)
    "The word which he reveals to me I will tell you."
  C  Yahweh Meets with Balaam (23:4–6)
  D  Balaam's First Oracle (23:7–10)
    Introduction        (23:7a)
    a  Balak Summons Balaam to Curse Israel (23:7b)
    b  Balaam Cannot Curse what God (El) has not cursed. (23:8)
    c  Israel Incomparable among the Nations (23:9–10a)
    d  Balaam Longs to be like Israel (23:10b)
  E  Balak's Response to Balaam (23:11–13)
    a  Balak to Balaam: Why Blessing instead of Cursing? (23:11)
      b  Balaam: Yahweh Spoke Blessing (23:12)
        "Was it not what Yahweh put in my mouth,
        That which I must be careful to speak?"
    a'  Balak to Balaam: Alternative Site to Curse (23:13)
      (a) Where you may see them from there,
        (b)  But only its outer edge you will see,
        (-b') But all of it you will not see.
      (a') Curse him for me from there."

CYCLE V:  THE SECOND ORACLE OF BALAAM (23:14–26)
  A  Balak Takes Balaam to Another Cultic Site (23:14)
  B  Balaam Prepares to Meet with Yahweh (23:15)
  C  Yahweh Meets with Balaam (23:16–17)
    a  Yahweh puts a word in his mouth (cf. 23:4, "God") (23:16)
    b  Balaam Returns to Balak (23:17a)
    c  Balak said to him, "What did Yahweh speak? "(23:17b)
  D  Balaam's Second Oracle (23:18–24)
    Introduction (23:18)
    a  God Said Bless ... I Cannot Change It (23:19–20)
    b  God is with Israel (Yahweh his God is with him) (23:21)
    c  God (El) brought them from Egypt (23:22)
    d  There is no sorcery/divination against Jacob ... (23:23)
        And for Israel, What God (El) has done!
    e  Israel is like a lioness (23:24)
  E  Balak's Second Response to Balaam (23:25–26)
    a  Balak to Balaam: Do not Curse or Bless! (23:25)
    b  Balaam to Balak: "Everything Yahweh speaks I will do." (23:26)

CYCLE VI: THIRD ORACLE OF BALAAM (23:27–24:14)

A Balak Takes Balaam to a Third Cultic Site (23:27)

    a Balak to Balaam: "Come now, I will take you to another place. (23:27a)

        b Perhaps it will be pleasing in the eyes of (the) God, (23:27b)
For me to curse him from there."

    a' Balak takes Balaam to top of Peor overlooking Jeshimon (23:28)

B Balaam Prepares to Meet with Yahweh (23:29–30)

    a Balaam Said (23:29a)

        b "Build seven altars; prepare seven bulls and seven rams." (23:29b)

    a' Balak does what Balaam said (23:30a)

        b' Offered a bull and a ram on each altar (23:30b)

C Balaam's Third Oracle (24:1–9)

    a Introduction

        (a) Balaam saw that it was good in the eyes of Yahweh to bless Israel (24:1a)

        (b) And he did not go to practice divination (24:1b)

        (c) But he focused his face toward the wilderness (24:1c)
Balaam lifted up his eyes & saw Israel encamped by its tribes (24:2a)

        (d) And the Spirit of God came upon him. (24:2b)

        (e) Then Balaam took up his discourse and said, (24:3a)

    b Oracle of Balaam, Son of Beor (24:3b–4)

        (a) The oracle of the man whose eyes are focused. (24:3b)

            (b) The oracle of him who hears the words of God (El) (24:4)

            (b') Who beholds the vision of Shaddai,

        (a') Who falls but with uncovered eyes.

    c Blessing upon the Kingdom of Israel, Yahweh's Luxurious Plant (24:5–7)

    d Israel Whom God (El) Delivered from Egypt (24:8–9a)

    e He who blesses you is blessed (24:9b)
And he who curses you is accursed.

D Balak's Final Response to Balaam (24:10–14)

    a Balak to Balaam: Cursing to Blessing—Three Times! (24:10–11)

    b Leave without Honor: Yahweh has denied you

E Balaam's Final Response to Balaam (24:12–14)

    a Balaam to Balak: Didn't I Tell Your Messengers (24:12–13a)

        (a) I would not be able to disobey the word of Yahweh (24:13b)

            (b) By doing good or evil on my own. (24:13c)

        (a') "Only that which Yahweh speaks I will speak." (24:13d)

    b Balaam to Return Homeward: Advises Balak (24:14)
"Come I will advise you as to what this people will do to
your people in the latter days."

CYCLE VII: ORACLES FOUR THROUGH SEVEN OF BALAAM (24:15–24)

A Balaam's Fourth Oracle: Future Promise; vs. Edomites (24:15–19)

    a Introduction: Balaam the Seer (24:15–16)

(a) Oracle of Balaam, son of Beor, (24:15)
Oracle of the man whose eyes are focused.
   (b) The oracle of him who hears the words of God (El) (24:16a)
Who knows the knowledge of Elyon,
(a') Who beholds the vision of Shaddai, (24:16b)
Who falls but with uncovered eyes.
b The Vision of Balaam (24:17–19)
Introduction: Balaam Sees into the Future (24:17a)
   (a) A star from Jacob ... a scepter from Israel (24:17b)
      (b) Destruction of Moab / Sheth (24:17c)
      (b') Destruction of Edom / Seir (24:18a)
   (a') Israel Grows Strong (24:18b)
Summary: Ruler from Jacob To Destroy Survivors (24:19)
B Balaam's Fifth Oracle – Against the Amalekites (24:20)
a Introduction: Saw Amalekites (24:20a)
b Amalek First among the Nations – End in Destruction (24:20b)
C Balaam's Sixth Oracle – Against the Kenites (24:21–22)
Introduction: Saw Kenites (24:21a)
   A+ "Enduring is your dwelling place, (24:21b)
      B+ Placed in the rock is your nest (keneka). (24:21c)
      B- Nevertheless he shall be for burning – Kain (24:22a)
   A- Until Asshur takes you captive." (24:22b)
D Balaam's Seventh Oracle – Against Asshur and Eber (24:23–24)
Introduction: "Alas who shall live when God establishes it! (24:23a)
(a) Ships from the coast of Kittim, (24:24a)
   (b) They shall subdue Asshur, (24:24b)
   (b') The shall subdue Eber, (24:24c)
(a') So even he will be unto destruction." (24:24d)

CONCLUSION: BALAAM DEPARTS HOMEWARD (24:25)

# Selected Bibliography

Albright, W. F. "The Administrative Divisions of Israel and Judah." *JPOS* 5 (1925): 55–76.

———. "The Home of Balaam." *JAOS* 35 (1915): 386–90.

———. "The Oracles of Balaam." *JBL* 63 (1944): 207–33.

———. *Yahweh and the Gods of Canaan.* 1968. Winona Lake: Eisenbrauns, 1980.

Allen, R. B. "The Theology of the Balaam Oracles." In *Tradition and Testament: Essays in Honor of Charles Lee Feinberg.* Edited by J. S. Feinberg and P. D. Feinberg. Chicago: Moody Press, 1981.

———. "Numbers." *The New Expositors Commentary.* Grand Rapids: Zondervan, 1990.

———. "The Oracles of Balaam." Ph.D. Diss. Dallas Theological Seminary, 1974.

Alter, R. *The Art of Biblical Narrative.* New York: Basic, 1981.

Anderson, G. A. *Sacrifices and Offerings in Ancient Israel: Studies in Their Social and Political Importance.* Atlanta: Scholars Press, 1987.

Auld, A. G. "Cities of Refuge in Israelite Tradition." *JSOT* 10 (1978): 26–29.

———. *Joshua, Moses and the Land: Tetrateuch, Pentateuch, Hexateuch in a Generation Since 1938.* Edinburgh: T & T Clark, 1980.

Avi-Yonah, M., E. *Encyclopedia of Archaeological Excavations in the Holy Land.* 4 vols. Jerusalem: Israel Exploration Society, 1975.

Bamberger, B. J. "Revelations of Torah after Sinai." *HUCA* 16 (1941): 97–113.

Bartlett, J. R. "The Conquest of Sihon's Kingdom: A Literary Re-examination," *JBL* 97 (1978): 347–51.

———. *Edom and the Edomites.* Sheffield: JSOT Press, 1989.

———. "The Land of Seir and the Brotherhood of Edom." *JTS* 20 (1969): 1–20.

———. "The Moabites and Edomites." In *Peoples of Old Testament Times.* Edited by D. J. Wiseman. Oxford: University Press at Clarendon, 1973, 229–58.

———. "The Rise and Fall of the Kingdom of Edom." *PEQ* 104 (1972): 26–37.

———. "Sin and Og, Kings of the Amorites." *VT* 20 (1970): 257–77.

Ben-Barek, Z. "Inheritance by Daughters in the Ancient Near East." *JSS* 25 (1980): 22–33.

Beit-Arieh, I. "Edomites Advance into Judah: Israelite Defensive Fortresses Inadequate." *BAR* 22/6 (1996): 28–36.

Bienkowski, P., ed. *Early Edom and Moab.* Sheffield Archaeological Monographs, 7. Sheffield: JRS Collis, 1992.

Bimson, J. *Redating the Exodus.* Winona Lake: Eisenbrauns, 1980.

Binns, L. E. *The Book of Numbers: With Introduction and Notes.* Westminster Commentaries. London: Methuen, 1927.

Borowski, O. *Agriculture in Iron Age Israel.* Winona Lake: Eisenbrauns, 1987.

———. *Every Living Thing: Daily Use of Animals in Ancient Israel.* Walnut Creek: Alta Mira Press, 1998

Brenner, A. *Colour Terms in the Old Testament.* JSOTSup 21. Sheffield: JSOT Press, 1982.

Brichto, H. C. "Kin, Cult, Land and Afterlife: A Biblical Complex." *HUCA* 44 (1973): 1–54.

————. *The Problem of "Curse" in the Hebrew Bible.* Philadelphia: Society of Biblical Literature and Exegesis, 1962.

Brin, G. *Studies in Biblical Law: From the Hebrew Bible to the Dead Sea Scrolls.* JSOTSup 176. Translated by J. Chipman. Sheffield: JSOT Press, 1994.

Brisco, T. *Holman Bible Atlas.* Nashville: Broadman & Holman, 1998.

Brueggemann, W. *The Land: Place as Gift, Promise, and Challenge in Biblical Faith.* Overtures to Biblical Theology. Philadelphia: Fortress, 1977.

Budd, P. J. *Numbers.* WBC 5. Waco: Word, 1984.

Burden, T. L. *The Kerygma of the Wilderness Traditions in the Hebrew Bible.* American University Studies, VII. Theology and Religion, 163. New York: Peter Lang, 1994.

Burns, R. J. *Has the Lord Indeed Spoken Only Through Moses? A Study of the Biblical Portrait of Miriam.* SBLDS 84. Atlanta: Scholars Press, 1987.

Burrows, E. *The Oracles of Jacob and Balaam.* London: Burns, Oates and Washbourne, 1938.

Carpenter, E. E. and E. B. Smick, "Numbers." *ISBE*, 3:562.

Carroll, R. P. *When Prophecy Failed: Cognitive Dissonance and the Prophetic Traditions of the Old Testament.* London: SCM Press, 1979.

Clark, R. E. D. "The Large Numbers in the Old Testament." *Journal of the Transactions of the Victoria Institute* 87 (1955): 82–92.

Clines, D. J. A. *The Theme of the Pentateuch.* JSOTSup 10. Sheffield: JSOT Press, 1978.

Coats, G. W. "Balaam: Sinner or Saint?" *BR* 18 (1973): 21–29.

————. "An Exposition of the Wilderness Traditions." *VT* 22 (1972): 288–95.

————. *The Murmuring Motif in the Wilderness Traditions of the Old Testament: Rebellion in the Wilderness.* Nashville: Abingdon, 1968.

————. "The Way of Obedience: Traditio-historical and Hermeneutical Reflections on the Balaam Story." *Semeia* 24 (1982): 53–79.

————. "The Wilderness Itinerary." *CBQ* 34 (1972): 135–52.

Cody, A. *A History of the Old Testament Priesthood.* AnBib 35. Rome: Pontifical Biblical Institute, 1969.

Cook, F. C. *The Fourth Book of Moses Called Numbers.* London: Murray, 1871.

Craigie, P. C. *The Problem of War in the Old Testament.* Grand Rapids: Eerdmans, 1978.

————. "The Conquest and Early Hebrew Poetry." *TynBul* 20 (1969): 76–94.

Cross, F. M. *Canaanite Myth and Hebrew Epic.* Cambridge: Harvard University Press, 1973.

Davies, E. "Inheritance Rights and Hebrew Levirate Marriage." *VT* 31 (1981):138–44.

————. *Numbers.* NCB. Grand Rapids: Eerdmans, 1995.

Davies, G. I. *The Way of the Wilderness: A Geographical Study of the Wilderness Itineraries in the Old Testament.* SOTS Monograph Series, 5. Cambridge: Cambridge University Press, 1979.

————. "The Wilderness Itineraries: A Comparative Approach." *TynBul* 25 (1974): 46–81.

————. "The Wilderness Itineraries and the Composition of the Pentateuch." *VT* 33 (1983): 1–13.

Dearman, J. A. *Studies in the Mesha Inscription and Moab.* Atlanta: Scholars Press, 1989.

Dentan, R. D. "Book of Numbers." *IDB* 3:567–71. New York: Abingdon, 1962.

Douglas, M. *In The Wilderness: The Doctrine of Defilement in the Book of Numbers.* JSOTSup 158. Sheffield: JSOT Press, 1993.

———. *Purity and Danger: An Analysis of the Concepts of Pollution and Taboo.* London: Routledge and Kegan Paul, 1966.

Edelman, D. V., ed. *You Shall Not Abhor an Edomite for He Is Your Brother: Edom and Seir in History and Tradition.* Archaeology and Biblical Studies, 3. Atlanta: Scholars Press, 1995.

Engnell, I. "The Wilderness Wandering." In *A Rigid Scrutiny.* Nashville: Vanderbilt University Press, 1969, 207–14.

Fager, J. A. *Land Tenure and the Biblical Jubilee: Uncovering Hebrew Ethics through the Sociology of Knowledge.* JSOTSup155. Sheffield: JSOT Press, 1993.

Fisch, S. "The Book of Numbers." *The Soncino Chumash, The Five Books of Moses with Haphtaroth.* Edited by A. Cohen. Hindhead: The Soncino Press, 1947.

Fishbane, M. "The Accusations of Adultery: A Study of Law and Scribal Practice in Numbers 5:11–31." *HUCA* 45 (1974): 25–46.

Flanagan, J. W. "History, Religion and Ideology: The Caleb Tradition." *Horizon* 3 (1976): 175–85.

Ford, L. S. "The Divine Curse Understood in Terms of Persuasion." Semeia 24 (1982): 81–87.

Frick, F. S. *The City in Ancient Israel.* SBLDS. Missoula, MT: Scholars Press, 1977.

Fouts, D. M. "A Defense of the Hyperbolic Interpretation of Large Numbers in the Old Testament." *JETS* 40.3 (1997): 377–87.

———. *The Use of Large Numbers in the Old Testament.* Ann Arbor: University Microfilms, 1991.

Glueck, N. "The Boundaries of Edom." *HUCA* 11 (1936): 141–57.

———. "The Civilization of the Edomites." BA 10 (1947): 74–83.

———. *Explorations in Eastern Palestine,* II & III, *AASOR,* XV, XVIII–XIX. New Haven: ASOR, 1935, 1938–39.

———. The Other Side of the Jordan. New Haven: ASOR, 1940.

———. Rivers in the Desert. New York: W. W. Norton, 1968.

Gottwald, N. *The Tribes of Yahweh.* Maryknoll, New York: Orbis, 1979.

Grabbe, L. L. *Priests, Prophets, Diviners, Sages: A Socio-Historical Study of Religious Specialists in Ancient Israel.* Valley Forge, Penn.: Trinity Press International, 1995.

Gray, G. *A Critical and Exegetical Commentary on Numbers.* ICC. Edinburgh: T & T Clark, 1903.

———. *Sacrifice in the Old Testament.* Oxford: University Press Clarendon, 1925.

Greenberg, M. "The Biblical Concept of Asylum." *JBL* 78 (1959): 125–32.

Greenstone, J. H. *Numbers, with Commentary.* Philadelphia: Jewish Publication Society, 1948.

Hamilton, V. P. *Handbook on the Pentateuch.* Grand Rapids: Baker, 1982.

Haran, M. "Nature of the *'ohel mo'edh* in Pentateuchal Sources." *JSS* 5 (1960): 50–65.

———. "The Passover Sacrifice." In *Studies in the Religion of Ancient Israel.* VTSup 23. Leiden: Brill, 1972, 86–116.

———. "The Priestly Image of the Tabernacle." *HUCA* 36 (1965): 191–226.

———. "Studies in the Account of the Levitical Cities." *JBL* 80 (1961): 45–54.

———. *Temples and Temple Service in Ancient Israel.* Oxford: University Press Clarendon, 1978.

Harrelson, W. "Guidance in the Wilderness: The Theology of Numbers." *Int* 13 (1959): 24–36.

Harrison, R. K. *Numbers: An Exegetical Commentary.* Grand Rapids: Baker, 1992.

Hertz, J. H., ed. *The Pentateuch and Haftorahs,* 2nd ed. London: Soncino Press, 1978.

Hirsch, S. R. "Numbers." In *The Pentateuch: Translated and Explained.* Vol. IV. 2nd ed. London: Isaac Levy, 1964.

Hoffmeier, J. K. *Israel in Egypt: The Evidence for the Authenticity of the Exodus Tradition.* New York: Oxford University Press, 1996.

———. "The Structure of Joshua 1–11 and the Annals of Thutmose III." In *Faith, Tradition and History: Old Testament Historiography in Its Near Eastern Context.* Edited by A. R. Millard, J. K. Hoffmeier, D. W. Baker. Winona Lake: Eisenbrauns, 1994, 165–80.

Hort, G. "The Death of Qorah." *AusBR* 7 (1959): 2–26.

Howard, D. *Joshua.* NAC. Nashville: Broadman & Holman, 1998.

Hubbard, Jr., R. L. "The *Go'el* in Ancient Israel: Theological Reflections on an Israelite Institution." *BBR* 1 (1991): 3–19.

Humphreys, C. "The Number of People in the Exodus from Egypt: Decoding Mathematically the Very Large Numbers in Numbers I and XXVI. *VT* 47 (1998): 196–213.

James, E. O. *The Ancient Gods: The History of the Diffusion of Religion in the Ancient Near East and the Eastern Mediterranean.* London: Weidenfeld and Nicholson, 1958.

Jarvis, C. S. *Yesterday and Today in Sinai.* Edinburgh: Blackwood, 1931.

Jobling, D. "The Jordan a Boundary: A Reading of Numbers 32 and Joshua 22." In SBLSP, 1980. Edited by P. Achtemeier. Chico, Cal.: Scholars Press, 1980, 193–207.

Joines, K. R. "The Bronze Serpent in the Israelite Cult." *JBL* 87 (1968): 245–56.

Kaufmann, Y. *The Religion of Israel.* Chicago: University Press, 1960.

Keil, C. F. *The Book of Numbers.* Edinburgh: T & T Clark, 1869.

Kelm, G. L. *Escape to Conflict: A Biblical and Archaeological Approach to the Hebrew Exodus and Settlement in Canaan.* Fort Worth: IAR Publications, 1991.

———. "The Route of the Exodus" *Biblical Illustrator* 7 (1979): 11–32.

Kennedy, A. R. S. *Leviticus and Numbers.* New York: Oxford University Press, 1910.

Kennett, R. H. "The Origin of the Aaronic Priesthood." *JTS* 6 (1905): 161–86; 7 (1906): 620–24.

Kitchen, K. A. *New International Dictionary of Biblical Archaeology.* Grand Rapids: Zondervan, 1983.

———. "Some Egyptian Background to the Old Testament." *TynBul* 5–6 (1960): 7–13.

Labuschagne, C. J. *The Incomparability of Yahweh in the Old Testament.* Pretoria Oriental Series V. Leiden: Brill, 1966.

Lehmann, M. R. "Biblical Oaths." *ZAW* 81 (1969): 74–92.

Levertoff, P. *Midrash Sifre on Numbers.* London: Society for Promoting Christian Knowledge, 1926.

Levine, B. "The Balaam Inscription from Deir ᶜAlla: Historical Aspects." *Biblical Archaeology Today: Proceedings of the International Congress of Biblical Archaeology, April 1984.* Jerusalem: Israel Exploration Society, 1985.

———. "Book of Numbers." IDBSup. Edited by K. Crim, et al. Nashville: Abingdon, 1976.

————. *In the Presence of the Lord: A Study of Cult and Cultic Terms in Ancient Israel.* SJLA 5. Leiden: Brill, 1974.

————. *Numbers 1–20, A New Translation with Introduction and Commentary.* AB. New York: Doubleday, 1993.

Liver, J. "The Half-Shekel Offering in Biblical and Post-Biblical Literature." *HTR* 56 (1963): 173–98.

————. "Korah, Dathan, and Abiram." In *Studies in the Bible.* Edited by C. Rabin. Jerusalem: Magnes, 1961, 189–217.

Loewe, M. and C. Blacker. *Oracles and Divination.* Boulder: Shambhala Press, 1981.

Long, B. O. "The Effect of Divination upon Israelite Literature." *JBL* 92 (1973): 489–97.

————. "The Social Settings for Prophetic Miracle Stories." *Semeia* 3 (1975): 46–63.

Lucas, A. "The Number of Israelites at the Time of the Exodus." *PEQ* 76 (1944): 164–68.

McCarthy, D. J. "The Symbolism of Blood and Sacrifice," *JBL* 88 (1969): 166–76.

Macdonald, B. *Ammon, Moab, and Edom.* Amman, Jordan: Al–Kurba, 1994.

Malina, B. J. *The Palestinian Manna Tradition.* Leiden: Brill, 1968.

Mann, T. W. "Theological Reflections on the Denial of Moses." *JBL* 99 (1979): 481–94.

Margaliot, M. "The Connection of the Balaam Narrative with the Pentateuch." *Proceedings of the Sixth World Congress of Jewish Studies (1973).* Vol. 1:279–90. Edited by A. Shinan. Jerusalem: World Union of Jewish Studies, 1977.

Marsh, J. "Exegesis of the Book of Numbers." *IB* 2. New York: Abingdon, 1953.

Matthews, V. and D. Benjamin, *Old Testament Parallels.* 2nd ed. New York: Paulist Press, 1998.

Mauser, U. *Christ in the Wilderness: The Wilderness Theme in the Second Gospel and Its Basis in the Biblical Tradition.* Naperville, Ill.: Alec R. Allenson, 1963.

Mays, J. L. *The Book of Leviticus, The Book of Numbers.* LBC. Richmond: John Knox, 1963.

Mazar, B. "The Cities of the Priests and the Levites." *VTSup* 7. Leiden: Brill, 1960, 193–205.

Mendenhall, G. E. "The Census Lists of Numbers 1 and 26." *JBL* 77 (1958): 52–66.

————. "The Hebrew Conquest of Palestine." *BA* 25 (1962): 66–87.

————. *The Tenth Generation.* Baltimore: Johns Hopkins Press, 1973.

Meshel, Z. and C. Meyers. "The Name of God in the Wilderness of Zin," *BA* 39 (1976): 6–10, 148–51.

Meyers, E., ed. *OEANE,* 5 vols. New York: Oxford University Press, 1997.

Milgrom, J. *Cult and Conscience: The Asham and the Priestly Doctrine of Repentance.* Studies in Judaism in Late Antiquity, 18. Leiden: Brill, 1976.

————. *Numbers.* The JPS Torah Commentary. Philadelphia: Jewish Publication Society, 1990.

————. *Studies in Cultic Theology and Terminology.* Studies in Judaism in Late Antiquity, 36. Leiden: Brill, 1983.

————. *Studies in Levitical Terminology.* Vol 1. University of California Publications, Near Eastern Studies 14. Berkeley: University of California Press, 1970.

Miller, C. *The Representation of Speech in Biblical Hebrew Narrative: A Linguistic Analysis.* Harvard Semitic Museum Monographs, 55. Atlanta: Scholars Press, 1996.

Mitchell, C. W. *The Meaning of BRK 'To Bless' in the Old Testament.* SBLDS, 95.

Atlanta: Scholars Press, 1987.

Morgenstern, J. *The Ark, the Ephod, and the "Tent of Meeting."* Cincinnati: Hebrew Union College, 1945.

———. "Trial by Ordeal among Semites in Ancient Israel." *HUCA Jubilee Volume* (1925): 113–43.

Moriarty, F. L. "Numbers." *The Jerome Biblical Commentary.* Edited by R. Brown et al. Englewood Cliffs, New Jersey: Prentice-Hall, 1968.

Mullen, E. T. *The Assembly of the Gods: The Divine Coucil in Canaanite and Early Hebrew Literature.* HSM 24. Chico, Cal.: Scholars Press, 1980.

Nielsen, E. "The Levites in Ancient Israel." *ASTI* 3 (1964): 16–27.

Noordzij, A. *Numbers.* BSC. Grand Rapids: Zondervan, 1983.

North, C. R. *"Pentateuchal* Criticism." In *The Old Testament and Modern Study.* London: Oxford University Press, 1951.

Noth, M. *Numbers: A Commentary.* OTL. Philadelphia: Westminster Press, 1968.

Olson, D. T. *The Death of the Old and the Birth of the New: The Framework of the Book of Numbers and the Pentateuch.* BJS 71. Chico, Cal: Scholars Press, 1985.

———. *Numbers.* Interpretation. Louisville: John Knox Press, 1996.

Owens, J. J. "Numbers." *Leviticus–Ruth.* BBC 2. Nashville: Broadman, 1970.

Partain, J. G. "Numbers." In *Pentateuch / Torah.* Mercer Commentary on the Bible. Macon, Ga.: Mercer University Press, 1998, 145–84.

Patrick, D. *Old Testament Law.* Atlanta: John Knox Press, 1985.

———. *The Rhetoric of Revelation in the Hebrew Bible.* Overtures to Biblical Theology. Minneapolis: Augsburg Fortress, 1999.

Petrie, Sir Flinders. *Egypt and Israel.* New York: Macmillan, 1923.

———. *Researches in Sinai.* New York: E. P. Dutton, 1906.

Plaut, W. G. *The Torah: Numbers.* New York: Union of American Hebrew Congregations, 1981.

Polin, C. C. J. *Music of the Ancient Near East.* New York: Vantage, 1954.

Rainey, A. F. "The Order of Sacrifices in Old Testament Ritual Texts." *Bib* 51 (1970): 485–98.

Riggans, W. *Numbers.* DSB. Philadelphia: Westminster, 1983.

Rogers, C. "Moses: Meak or Miserable?" *JETS* 29/3 (1986): 257–63.

Rowley, H. H. *From Joseph to Joshua.* London: Oxford University Press, 1950.

Sadaqa, A. and R. *Jewish and Samaritan Version of the Pentateuch, With Particular Stress on the Difference between Both Texts.* (Hebrew) Tel Aviv: Tel Aviv University, 1965.

Sailhammer, J. H. *The Pentateuch as Narrative: A Biblical Theological Commentary.* Grand Rapids: Zondervan, 1992.

Sakenfield, K. D. *Numbers: Journeying with God.* ITC. Grand Rapids: Eerdmans, 1995.

Sasson, J. M. "A 'Genealogical Convention' in Biblical Chronography?" *ZAW* 90 (1978): 171–85.

Skehan, P. "The Biblical Scrolls from Qumran and the Text of the Old Testament." *BA* 28 (1965): 87–100.

Smick, E. B. "A Study of the Structure of the Third Balaam Oracle." *The Law and the Prophets: Festschrift for Oswald T. Allis.* Edited by John Skilton. Jackson: Presbyterian and Reformed, 1974.

Snaith, N. H. "Daughters of Zelophehad." *VT* 16 (1966): 124–27.

————. *Leviticus and Numbers*. The Century Bible. London: Thomas Nelson, 1967.

Speiser, E. A. "Census and Ritual Expiation in Mari and Israel." *Biblical and Oriental Studies*. Philadelphia: University of Pennsylvania Press, 1967.

Stanley, D. M. "Balaam's Ass, or a Problem of New Testament Hermeneutics." *CBQ* 20 (1958): 50–56.

Starr, I. *The Rituals of the Diviner*. Bibliotheca Mesopotamica 12. Malibu, Cal.: Undena Press, 1983.

Stern, E., et al., eds. *NEAEHL*. 4 vols. Jerusalem: Israel Exploration Society, 1992.

Sturdy, J. *Numbers*. CBSC. New York: Cambridge University Press, 1976.

Sumner, W. A. "Israel's Encounters with Edom, Moab, Ammon, Sihon and Og according to the Deuteronomist." *VT* 18 (1968): 216–28.

Thompson, J. A. "Numbers." *The New Bible Commentary, Revised*. Grand Rapids: Eerdmans, 1970.

Thompson, R. J. *Moses and the Law in a Century of Criticism Since Graf*. Leiden: Brill, 1970.

Tunyogi, A. C. *The Rebellions of Israel*. Richmond: John Knox Press, 1969.

Ulrich, E. *The Dead Sea Scrolls and the Origins of the Bible*. Studies in the Dead Sea Scrolls and Related Literature. Grand Rapids: Eerdmans, 1999.

van der Ploeg, J. "Studies in Hebrew Law." *CBQ* 12 (1950): 248–59, 416–27; *CBQ* 13 (1951): 28–43, 164–71, 296–307.

Vaux, R. de. *Ancient Israel: Its Life and Institutions*. 2 vols. New York: McGraw-Hill, 1961.

Walters, S. D. "Prophecy in Mari and Israel." *JBL* 89 (1970): 78–81.

Watts, J. W. *Reading Law: The Rhetorical Shaping of the Pentateuch*. The Biblical Seminar, 59. Sheffield: Academic Press, 1999.

Weinfeld, M. *Deuteronomy and the Deuteronomistic School*. Oxford: University Press Clarendon, 1978.

————. "Judge and Officer in Ancient Israel and in the Ancient Near East." *IOS* 8 (1977): 65–88.

Weippert, M. *The Settlement of the Israelite Tribes in Palestine*. Naperville, Ill.: Alec R. Allenson, 1971.

Weisman, Z. *Political Satire in the Bible*. Semeia Studies, 32. Atlanta: Scholars Press, 1998.

Wenham, G. J. *Numbers: An Introduction and Commentary*. Tyndale Old Testament Commentaries. Downers Grove: InterVarsity, 1981.

Wenham, J. W. "The Large Numbers in the Old Testament." *TynBul* 18 (1967): 19–53.

Wevers, J. W. *Notes on the Greek Text of Numbers*. SBL Septuagint and Cognate Studies Series, 46. Atlanta: Scholars Press, 1998.

Wharton, J. A. "Command to Bless: An Exposition of Numbers 22." *Int* 13 (1959): 37–48.

Whybray, R. N. *The Making of the Pentateuch: A Methodological Study*. JSOTSup 53. Sheffield: JSOT Press, 1985.

Wilson, R. R. *Genealogy and History in the Biblical World*. New Haven: Yale University Press, 1977.

Yadin, Y. *The Art of Warfare in Biblical Lands*. New York: McGraw-Hill, 1963.

# Selected Subject Index

# Person Index

# Selected Scripture Index